The Aviation Consumer Used Aircraft Guide

McGRAW-HILL SERIES IN AVIATION

David B. Thurston   Consulting Editor

The Aviation Consumer Used Aircraft Guide

Richard B. Weeghman, Editor

McGRAW-HILL BOOK COMPANY

New York   St. Louis   San Francisco   Auckland   Bogotá
Hamburg   Johannesburg   London   Madrid   Mexico
Montreal   New Delhi   Panama   Paris   São Paulo
Singapore   Sydney   Tokyo   Toronto

Library of Congress Cataloging in Publication Data

Main entry under title:

The Aviation Consumer Used Aircraft Guide.

    (McGraw-Hill series in aviation)
    Includes index.
    1. Used aircraft.   I. Weeghman, Richard B.
II. Aviation consumer. II. Series.
TL671.A93 629.133 0340422 80-22381
ISBN 0-07-002543-6

The authors of this book were Richard B. Weeghman, David B. Noland and David
A. Shugarts; with Bernard A. Lafferty preparing the section on the used aircraft as
an investment. Robert J. Petrilli was the managing editor, and the production
editor was Barbara Festa Hackett.

Contents

Twins

For further information about the editorial content of this publication or regular
subscriptions to *The Aviation Consumer* magazine for pilots and aircraft owners,
contact *The Aviation Consumer*, 1111 East Putnam Avenue, Riverside, CT 06878;
(203) 637-5900.

Introduction

Surrounded by layers of myth and hearsay, the used airplane presents the would-be buyer with a bewildering task of evaluation and selection. This volume, by the editors of *The Aviation Consumer*, is designed to separate fact from fiction and hangar talk, and to allow an accurate appraisal of aircraft models and makes from nearly the entire spectrum of general aviation.

It uses several unique approaches to provide in-depth information about the development history of entire model lines, their maintenance weaknesses and strengths, their value trend on the resale market and their safety records.

Each chapter provides invaluable comments and first-hand experiences of users themselves. This information brings to light the special qualities and hidden foibles of each aircraft and represents the candid input by pilots, operators, and owners. In addition, the history of each model is chronicled through the sometimes subtle and occasionally dramatic transitions and changes of an entire production run. To aid buyers in gauging a fair price, average retail costs are listed for all models and years.

To highlight the safety problems that might be related to the design of the aircraft, the editors of *The Aviation Consumer* have analyzed computer reports provided by the National Transportation Safety Board on specific makes and models. Supplementing these is a special chapter on comparative safety records of the most popular single- and twin-engine aircraft on the market.

To round out the picture, the editors have noted the availability of STCed modifications and alterations that might improve the value of an aircraft, critical Airworthiness Directives, and the names and addresses of aircraft associations that might help in evaluating or maintaining specific models.

Finally, we offer some tips for buyers using this book. A great deal of unhappiness can be avoided when buying a used plane by following this one simple rule: before laying out a large sum of cash for the aircraft, lay out a modest sum for a qualified mechanic to go over it with a fine-tooth comb. Discrepancies can then be used to confront the seller with a request for repair, or an equivalent cut in the sale price.

We cannot overstress the importance of an independent mechanic's blessing, even if the airplane has the proverbial "fresh annual."

The most widely used nationwide classified listing of used aircraft is *Trade-A-Plane*, Crossville, Tennessee. Other well-known publications devoted to used-aircraft listings are: *A/C Flyer*, Miami, Florida; *Aircraft Inventory Center*, Waco, Texas; *Aviation*, Brookfield, Connecticut; *Aviation Buyers Guide*, Paoli, Pennsylvania; *U.S. Aircraft Dealers Magazine*, Memphis, Tennessee.

Be aware that the prices listed in this publication are, for the most part, 1980 figures, and they may change with inflation. In the price tables, average retail costs will vary soonest for recent models because normally the price of an aircraft plunges sharply for the first few years before slowing down, and perhaps leveling off and rising.

The text of this book is reprinted from regular monthly issues of *The Aviation Consumer* and represents a cross section of aircraft of all classes and degrees of sophistication. Many are still in production; others are not. But all represent a treasure trove of good buys for the aircraft shopper who comes armed with the facts this book can provide.

Safety
Economics

Accident Rates by Aircraft Type

Are some aircraft inherently more dangerous (or safer) to fly than others?
Intriguing Safety Board figures single out some obvious winners and scary losers.

There's much debate about the relative safety of different types of aircraft. Are high-wings safer than low-wings? Are twins safer than singles? Does the centerline thrust of the Cessna Skymaster provide greater safety than conventional twins? Does the low stall speed of the Skylane make it safer than, say, a Mooney? Aircraft companies like to brag about safety features such as simplified fuel systems, stronger structures, fool-proof stall characteristics and so forth—and the aviation press (including *The Aviation Consumer*) is quick to praise those features that theoretically improve safety.

But the bottom line of all this debate is one simple statistic: How often does each type of airplane crash, and how likely are the pilot and passengers to get killed when it does? Theoretical safety is born in the minds of aircraft designers and engineers, FAA bureaucrats and aviation journalists. But real safety can be found only in cold, hard accident statistics for each type of aircraft.

The National Transportation Safety Board in 1979 released a massive study listing accident rates by aircraft types. The NTSB sorted out accident statistics for 48 different types of aircraft for each year from 1972 through 1976. Using FAA estimates of the number of hours flown by each type every year, the NTSB calculated the rates of total accidents and fatal accidents per 100,000 hours. And the numbers make it very clear: in terms of safety, not all aircraft are created equal.

Among competitive aircraft in the same general classification, it turns out, a pilot is at least twice as likely to get killed if he chooses the lowest-ranking model instead of the highest-ranking type. If you're looking for a two-place airplane, you're *four times* more likely to be killed if you make the wrong choice. Clearly, these statistics are of more than academic interest to aircraft owners.

In our master list of all 48 aircraft we have noted five items: total hours flown, total accidents, fatal accidents, total accident rate per 100,000 hours and fatal accident rate per 100,000 hours. The key figures are the last two, for they provide an equal basis of comparison for all types of airplanes.

Figuring the Exposure to Danger

It can be argued that faster airplanes deserve an adjustment in their rate because they can cover the same ground in less time. A 200-mph retractable with an accident rate similar to a 100-mph trainer on an hourly basis presumably would expose its occupants to only half the danger if both aircraft flew from A to B. This is certainly a valid way to look at it, but we have chosen not to do so because of the many complex assumptions necessary to figure a "speed adjustment index." Airplanes aren't always flown cross-country, particularly trainers. How do we account for the fact that a faster airplane would make more takeoffs and landings in a given number of hours than a slow plane flying the same routes? (Takeoffs and landings are generally more dangerous than cruising flight.) Faster planes are usually flown by better pilots, but they're also more likely to encounter severe weather that might contribute to an accident. Since it's impossible to account for all this in a quantitative way, we'll stick with the per-hour comparison.

How about the reliability of the numbers that go into calculating the accident rates? The listed number of fatal accidents can be considered quite accurate, since the NTSB keeps close tabs on them; it's unlikely that many fatal accidents have gone uncounted.

The figure for *total* accidents, on the other hand, probably has a certain amount of error built in. Some nonfatal accidents never get reported, we feel sure, and the line between an accident and an incident can be a shadowy one. The total accident figures, then, are probably accurate to no more than 10 percent.

Hours Flown—How Reliable?

The figures for hours flown are even more suspect. The FAA arrives at its numbers by querying a random sample of pilots; the figures are thus dependent not only on the accuracy of the sample, but also on the memory and/or motives of the aircraft owners. (Some business pilots, for example, may purposely inflate the hours flown to back up an exaggerated tax

Saints and Spinners

Comparative safety statistics for different brands of airplane are not widely publicized. (The manufacturers, understandably enough, don't like to talk about such things, particularly when their model has a worse safety record than a competitor.) The following list, compiled by *The Aviation Consumer* from NTSB figures, shows that all airplanes are not created equal.

Aircraft	Hours** Flown	Total Accidents	Total* Rate	Fatal Accidents	Fatal* Rate
Aero Commander 500, 520, 560	751.7	78	10.4	25	3.3
Aero Commander 560F, 680, E, F, FL, 700, 720	962.7	64	6.7	24	2.5
Aeronca 7 (Champ)	2,246.6	635	28.3	103	4.6
Beech 18	1,774.4	228	12.8	60	3.4
Beech 19, 23, 24	1,842.4	324	17.6	46	2.5
Beech 33, 35 H-V, 36 (post-1957 Bonanzas)	5,444.2	350	6.4	108	2.0
Beech 35 A-G (pre-1957)	1,767.0	251	14.2	68	3.8
Beech 55, 56, 58, 95 (Baron, Travel-air)	3,184.0	264	8.3	90	2.8
Beech 65/90	2,136.7	62	2.9	17	0.8
Beech 99/100	771.6	17	2.2	4	0.5
Bellanca 17, 14-19	669.3	143	21.4	38	5.7
Boeing 75 (Stearman)	1,069.7	350	32.7	41	3.8
Cessna 120/140	1,115.0	320	28.7	19	1.7
Cessna 150	20,531	2,111	10.3	276	1.3
Cessna 170	1,110.0	302	27.2	35	3.1
Cessna 172	15,142	1,373	9.1	222	1.5
Cessna 177 (Cardinal, RG)	1,921.6	288	15.0	42	2.2
Cessna 180	1,942.8	413	21.3	25	1.3
Cessna 182	7,755.6	878	11.3	157	2.0
Cessna 185	953.5	169	17.7	14	1.5
Cessna 188	1,472.4	327	22.2	26	1.8
Cessna 206	1,848.2	242	13.1	31	1.7
Cessna 210	2,682.8	408	15.2	83	3.1
Cessna 310	2,987.9	293	9.8	65	2.2

*Accidents per 100,000 hours flown

Aircraft	Hours** Flown	Total Accidents	Total* Rate	Fatal Accidents	Fatal* Rate
Cessna 337 (Skymaster)	1,046.1	109	10.4	32	3.1
Cessna 401, 402, 411, 414	1,979.0	109	5.5	28	1.4
Cessna 421	1,041.4	53	5.1	17	1.6
Cessna 500 (Citation)	311.2	4	1.3	0	0.0
Dassault Fanjet Falcon	700.3	8	1.1	1	0.1
Grumman 164 (Ag-Cat)	1,658.0	400	24.1	15	0.9
Gulfstream American (AA-1)	1,158.6	304	26.2	56	4.8
Gulfstream American (AA-5)	680.3	102	15.0	20	2.9
Lear 24, 25, 35, 36	695.2	20	2.9	6	0.9
Luscombe 8	553.9	253	45.7	28	5.1
Mitsubishi (MU-2)	547.3	24	4.4	10	1.8
Mooney M-20	3,243.3	367	11.3	79	2.4
Navion	552.3	89	16.1	21	3.8
Piper J-3 (Cub)	867.7	234	27.0	42	4.7
Piper PA-18 (Super Cub)	2,309.0	479	23.1	83	4.0
Piper PA-22 (Tri-Pacer)	2,028.1	434	21.4	66	3.3
Piper PA-23	4,001.5	302	7.5	104	2.5
Piper PA-24 (Comanche)	2,601.1	437	16.8	76	2.9
Piper PA-25 (Pawnee)	2,193.6	471	21.5	39	1.8
Piper PA-28 (Cherokees)	17,576	1,830	10.5	347	2.0
Piper PA-30, 39 (Twin Comanche)	1,463.1	172	11.8	28	1.9
Piper PA-31 (Navajo)	1,766.4	67	3.8	20	1.1
Piper PA-32 (Cherokee Six)	2,118.9	301	14.2	58	2.7
Piper PA-34 (Seneca)	844.1	84	10.0	13	1.5

**Hours flown x 1,000

deduction.) An example of the questionable accuracy of the FAA method is the fact that the 1978 estimate of hours flown by general aviation was actually *less* than 1977's—even though almost everyone agrees there were more planes flying more hours. So, the hours-flown figure shouldn't be considered accurate to within more than 10 percent, we believe.

This gives an overall accuracy to the final rates of plus or minus 20 percent for the *total* accident rate and 10 percent for the *fatal* accident rate. For this reason, we have not listed fatal accident rates to more than two significant digits, or the total rates to more than three. (The FAA and NTSB raw data in some cases allows the rates to be figured down the third or fourth decimal point, but such precision is mathematically unjustified.)

When comparing accident rates of different planes, keep in mind the estimated 10-20 percent possible error. If one aircraft has an accident rate of 2.3 and another rates 2.6, we see no reason to rush right out and trade in one for the other for the sake of the wife and kids. But we would consider a 50 percent difference in accident rates to be significant, and a 100 percent difference between the rates of comparable aircraft is no small reason for alarm, in our opinion.

Classifying Accident Rates

To minimize differences caused by pilot experience, type of usage and so forth, we have set up several categories of aircraft for comparison. In establishing an order of rank within each category, we have used only the fatal accident rate. However, we are also listing the total accident rate, which might indicate handling quirks on the runway or similar problems that will not usually kill anyone but might well injure people, pocketbooks and egos.

Two-Place Aircraft

Aircraft and Rank	Fatal Accident Rate*	Total Accident Rate*
1. Cessna 150	1.3	10.3
2. Cessna 120/140	1.7	28.7
3. Piper PA-18 (Super Cub)	4.0	23.1
4. Aeronca 7 (Champ, Citabria)	4.6	28.3
5. Grumman American AA-1 (Yankee, Trainer, TR-2)	4.8	26.2
6. Piper J-3 (Cub)	4.7	27.3
7. Luscombe 8	5.1	45.7

Accidents per 100,000 flight hours

The old post-war taildraggers that make up the majority of the list all seem to have roughly similar fatal accident rates—except for the Cessna 120/140, which is three times better in terms of fatal accident (but in the same ball park in total accidents). We haven't the slightest idea why this is so. The outrageously high total accident figure for the Luscombe (it has the highest total accident rate of any of the 48 airplanes) is almost certainly due to its very sensitive ground handling, which has apparently resulted in innumerable ground loops.

The only two modern aircraft on the list, the Cessna 150 and the Grumman American AA-1 Yankee/Trainer/TR-2 series, stand at the opposite ends of the scale. The Cessna 150's rate of 1.3 fatals per 100,000 hours ranks first among two-seaters—and in fact is unsurpassed by any single-engine aircraft or light twin. We think it's no coincidence that the safest lightplane is also the second most popular airplane in the world (after the Cessna 172). Who says safety doesn't sell? The 150 also has a total accident rate more than twice as good as any other two-seater—eloquent testimony to the safety factor of the nosewheel.

Grumman American's AA-1 series has a fatal accident rate *almost four times higher* than the 150, and a total accident rate nearly triple. These are sobering numbers indeed for anyone who flies the little Grummans. The AA-1's spin problems are well known (it has the highest stall/spin accident rate of any modern airplane), but apparently the aircraft's higher wing loading, high induced drag at low speeds and poor longitudinal stability contribute to a high overall accident rate.

Four-/Six-Place Fixed-Gear Aircraft

Aircraft and Rank	Fatal Accident Rate*	Total Accident Rate*
1. Cessna 180	1.3	21.3
2. Cessna 172	1.5	9.1
3. Cessna 206	1.7	13.1
4. Piper Cherokee	2.0	10.5
5. Cessna 182	2.0	11.3
6. Cessna Cardinal	2.2	15.0
7. Beech 19/23/24	2.5	17.6
8. Cherokee Six	2.7	14.2
9. Grumman AA-5 (Tiger/Cheetah)	2.9	15.0
10. Cessna 170	3.1	27.2
11. Piper Tri-Pacer	3.3	21.4

Accidents per 100,000 flight hours

The four-/six-place fixed-gear category shows some patterns remarkably similar to those of the two-place field. Among nosewheel aircraft, Cessna's bread-and-butter model again leads the pack with its good safety record. The 172's fatal accident rate of 1.5 is very nearly as low as the 150's—and the overall accident rate of 9.1 is even better.

And again, Grumman American's entry places last among modern aircraft in this category, with a poor 2.9 fatal rate—nearly double that of the Skyhawk. Overall accident rate of the AA-5 series, however, equals the Cessna Cardinal and beats the Beech Musketeer series.

There's also a third parallel to the two-place category. Another Cessna taildragger shows a surprisingly low fatal accident rate—in this case the 180. (Its overall rate, however, is quite high.) Oddly enough, the Cessna 170, also a taildragger, has a fatal accident rate of 3.1, more than twice as high as the

Grumman's Cheetah, *like its stablemate, had the poorest fatality record in its class. However, the Cheetah's overall accident rate is about average.*

Rockwell Commander *600s have double the fatality rate of the Navajo.*

180's. Again, we have no solid explanation for this state of affairs.

It's clear that among fixed-gear aircraft, Cessnas are by far the safest. Lumping the previous two categories together, Cessna aircraft sweep the first six positions. The aggregate fatal accident rate of the 150, 172, and 182 is an outstanding 1.6 per 100,000 hours. Such figures are convincing arguments for Cessna's approach to airplane design—an approach that includes high wings, very low stalling speeds, simplified fuel systems, and high elevator forces.

Piper's ubiquitous Cherokees also have a fine record, though not quite as good as the Cessnas. The NTSB has lumped all PA-28 models from the fixed-gear Cherokee 140 to the retractable Arrow into the same category; the aggregate fatal accident rate is a low 2.0 per 100,000 hours.

The only other direct Cessna-Piper matchup in this category is the big six-place utility aircraft: the Cessna 206 and Piper Cherokee Six. Again, the Cessna comes out on top, with a 1.7 fatal rate compared to 2.6 for the Cherokee Six. Total accident rates are about the same for both aircraft.

Single-Engine Retractables

Aircraft and Rank	Fatal Accident Rate*	Total Accident Rate*
1. Beech 33	1.0	4.6
2. Cessna Cardinal RG	1.6	8.2
3. Beech 36	1.7	4.7
4. Beech 35 (1964-76)	2.0	7.1
5. Mooney M-20	2.4	11.3
6. Piper Comanche	2.9	16.8
7. Cessna 210	3.1	15.0
8. Rockwell 112/114	3.1	14.0
9. Piper Arrow	3.2	11.3
10. Beech 35 (1947-63)	3.6	11.8
11. Ryan Navion	3.8	16.1
12. Beech 24 Sierra	4.0	15.2
13. Bellanca Viking	4.2	16.8
14. Bellanca 14-19	4.9	45.4
15. Piper Lance	5.9**	14.1**

*Accidents per 100,000 flight hours
**Insufficient hours flown for rates to be statistically reliable.

Among the single-engine retractables, the conventional-tailed Beech 33 Debonairs and Bonanzas show a significant safety advantage statistically over the entire class. The V-tailed late-vintage model 35 has a fatal accident rate twice as bad, however; and old 35 Bonanzas display a safety record that is significantly worse.

The old and new Bellancas—the Viking and the 14-19 Cruisemaster—have by far the worst record of any single-engine retractable that is amply documented.

The Piper Lance appears to have a more dismal record, but NTSB figures showed there were insufficient hours flown for the rates to be statistically reliable.

The Cessna 210 is ranked right in the middle of the pack, while the Cessna Cardinal RG, now out of production, came right next to the Beech 33 in fatal accidents, though its total accident rate seems disproportionately high—perhaps due to the high incidence of gear-up landings experienced by the aircraft.

Light Twins

Aircraft and Rank	Fatal Accident Rate*	Total Accident Rate
1. Piper PA-34 (Seneca)	1.5	10.0
2. Piper Twin Comanche	1.9	11.8
3. Cessna 310	2.2	9.8
4. Piper PA-23 (Apache/Aztec)	2.6	7.5
5. Beech 55/56/58/95 (Baron/Travel Air)	2.8	8.3
6. Cessna 337	3.1	10.4
7. Aero Commander 500, 520, 560A, E	3.3	10.4

*Accidents per 100,000 flight hours

Light twins have a worse fatal accident rate than single-engine aircraft, though the *total* accident rate is much lower. This suggests that twins are generally flown by better pilots who are less likely to have the minor groundloop and overshoot accidents that tend to balloon the total accident numbers for smaller aircraft. On the other hand, it appears that if you do have an accident in a twin, it's much more likely to be a fatal one. In single-engine aircraft, accidents are fatal about 10 to 20 percent of the time. Among light twins, the percentage ranges from 15 to 35 percent.

Piper leads the way in twin safety, with the Seneca and Twin Comanche in the top two spots. Only the Aero Com-

Old retractables *like the early Bonanzas, Bellancas and the Navion, shown here, have the worst record of the single-engine retractables.*

mander 500 series has a disproportionately high fatal accident record; all the others are bunched between the 2.2 and 3.0 levels. The Cessna Skymaster, which is sold as a safer, easier-to-fly alternative to conventional twins, actually ranks near the bottom with a 3.0 fatal rate.

Cabin Twins

Aircraft and Rank	Fatal Accident Rate*	Total Accident Rate*
1. Beech Queen Air, King Air	0.7	2.5
2. Piper PA-31 (Navajo)	1.1	3.8
3. Cessna 401, 402, 411, 414	1.4	5.5
4. Cessna 421	1.6	5.1
5. Aero Commander 560F, 680, 685, 690, 720	2.5	6.7

Accidents per 100,000 flight hours

Cabin twins have excellent safety records compared to all other groups in this analysis, almost certainly because this type of aircraft is flown by highly competent professional pilots. The only standout in the group is the Aero Commander 600 series, with an unusually high 2.5 fatal rate. The Commanders, in fact, are apparently more accident-prone than any other cabin-class twin in both fatal and total accidents.

Manufacturer Ratings

Out of sheer curiosity, we decided to compute grand total rates for Cessna, Piper and Beech. Accident rates were combined for all the airplanes on the chart in current production at each company (excluding cropdusters, turboprops and jets).

Here's how the Big Three stacked up in terms of overall safety records:

Manufacturer	Fatal Accident Rate	Total Accident Rate
1. Cessna	1.7	10.4
2. Piper	2.0	9.7
3. Beech	2.5	9.7

We have made no attempt to analyze these differences, only to present them in black and white, as they reflect what happened from 1972 to 1976.

Crash Survivability

The statistics also reveal some surprising numbers about the survivability of lightplane crashes. In general, light single-

Grumman American AA-1 *series has the poorest safety record of any modern tri-gear two-seater—three times worse than the Cessna 150.*

The Best & The Worst

Just for the record, here are the top six and the bottom five aircraft in the overall fatal accident list, not counting those normally flown only by professional pilots.

The Best
1. Beech 33 . . . . 1.0
2. Cessna 150 . . . . . . 1.3
3. Cessna 180 . . . . . . 1.3
4. Cessna 172 . . . . . . 1.5
5. Piper Seneca 1.5
6. Cessna Card RG . . 1.6

The Worst
1. Luscombe 8 . . . . . . 5.1
2. Bellanca 14-19 . . . . 4.9
3. Grum. Amer. AA-1 . 4.8
4. Piper J-3 Cub 4.7
5. Bellanca 7 . . . . 4.6

engine aircraft crashes are fatal about 10 to 20 percent of the time. For cropdusters, however, the figure is a startlingly low seven percent. The Cessna C-188, Grumman G-164 and Piper PA-25, the only cropdusters on the list, have an aggregate total accident rate of 22.0, which is more than twice as high as that of comparable nonagricultural airplanes. (This isn't surprising, considering the extraordinarily risky flying that most cropdusters must perform every day.) But for fatal accidents, the cropdusters averaged just 1.5—nearly as good as the Cessna 150. The three dusters on the list had fatal accidents only about seven percent of the time—two to three times better than comparable nonagricultural planes.

What that says to us is that designed-in crashworthiness can make a significant difference in the fatality rate of an aircraft. Cropdusters are the only aircraft designed to be crashworthy (they have roll cages, energy-absorbing material in front of and below the pilot and many other safety features).

Conclusions

Summing up, our little exercise in statistics has certainly shown that light aircraft safety is a complex matter. The question-marks are many; solid answers few. There are some conclusions that seem inescapable, however:

• The light single-engine Cessnas have the best safety records of any type of light airplane.

• The Grumman American single-engine airplanes and the Rockwell Commander twins have significantly poorer safety records than their rivals.

• Cabin-class twins are the safest type of light aircraft.

• The two-seat taildragger is the most dangerous type of airplane.

Beyond these conclusions we hesitate to tread. But at least some hard safety numbers will provide plenty of fodder for discussion and, we hope, some new awareness of safety on the part of aircraft owners and manufacturers alike.

The Aircraft as an Investment

How to turn the purchase of a used plane into a money-making proposition.
Don't buy without considering this often neglected formula, which
separates the winners from the losers via depreciation curves,
and tells the critical time to buy.

When it comes to buying an aircraft, there are as many considerations as there are pilots. When price is no object, especially if the aircraft will be earning its keep, a new airplane is a reasonable choice. But for many others, the used plane is a far more logical way to go.

In this case, the canny buyer will pay close attention to the resale curve of used planes in the market, since there are some golden investment finds that will not only provide good service at a much reduced purchase price, but will actually appreciate in resale value over the years.

The trick is to find which models stop depreciating, when they do so, and how fast they begin appreciating. The purpose of this article is to show how pilots can track the used-plane market and chart the resale performance of models they are interested in.

Imagine buying an airplane with the almost certain knowledge that you can sell it at a 30 to 50 percent profit in four to five years. (Consider the impact of this fact on a hesitant spouse.) This puts the airplane in a whole new light—as an investment with a return value that has few peers.

Since the upturn in value of used aircraft is related to the increase in new-plane prices, used-plane prices track inflation quite well. In fact, over the last six years, some airplanes have done as well as houses. The reason for this is that both homes and airplanes are labor intensive to manufacture, and in both cases the demand exceeds the supply.

But some aircraft are much poorer investments than others. In previous years, some airplanes in the five-to-ten-year-old category actually fell in value, whereas other models averaged a 12 percent-per-year appreciation. For the budget-minded potential purchaser, a judicious choice of airframe can protect the "nest egg" from being eroded by inflation. If he finances the purchase, the appreciation can pay the mortgage interest.

Protecting Your Investment

Security is another point the "airframe investor" should keep in mind. The insurance to protect the hull from all risks averages $1.70 per hundred dollars of value per year. This is for zero-deductible fire, theft, and vandalism; $50 deductible taxiing collision; and $250 deductible in-flight collision coverage. While this coverage may at first seem expensive, in terms of dollar value, it is cheaper than you could insure a coin collection, for example. If you add a rider to your home-owner's insurance to cover something like a coin collection, it costs you about $2.20 per hundred a year extra. So the hull insurance for an aircraft is far from exorbitant compared to other investment coverages.

Anticipating Appreciation

How can we predict the change in value of a given aircraft for the next, say, four years? It is not possible to predict what the economy will do with certainty, but double-digit inflation and interest apparently are here to stay. To predict the future, examine the past.

One method is to look at what a similar-model aircraft has done in previous years, and the most useful reference is a "bluebook" such as dealers use to guide them in buying and selling. One such reference is the *Aircraft Price Digest*; although it isn't offered to the general public, many a dealer will let you browse through his copy. You want to see both a current issue and one that is two to four years old.

Suppose it's 1980 and you're considering purchase of a 1976 Cessna 182. You picked the 1976 model because you know that most aircraft depreciate for about four years before the value levels and (if it's a "blue chip" investment) begins to climb. How much will it climb? Take a look at an older Skylane, such as a 1970 model. In the 1980 issue of *APD*, it lists at $21,500. In the 1978 issue of *APD*, it listed at $20,250. It has appreciated $1,250 in two years. For comparison with other aircraft, you probably want to convert to an annual rate. Take the amount of change and divide by the old price, multiply by 100 to obtain a percentage, then divide by the number of years between readings. In this case, $1,250 divided by $20,250 is 0.062, or a 6.2 percent appreciation. It occurred over two years, or about 3.1 percent a year, roughly. If you buy your 1976 Skylane and have made a good choice, it will probably appreciate about 3.1 percent yearly.

The more back issues of *APD* you can locate, the better your data will be; the best library would be a complete set going back 10 years.

Statistical Studies

When "bluebooks" are not available, the asking prices from classifieds such as *Trade-A-Plane* can serve as a good guide. If you total up the prices for a given model over a period of several issues, the average asking price will usually be within five percent of the "bluebook" price. You can basically ignore engine times and avionics, since these will tend to average out. The resultant price will be to the desired "mid-time engine, average-equipped" price.

For uncommon aircraft models the statistical sample for a given year may be too small to be accurate. To increase your data base on these models, determine the average price for *each* year the plane was made, from five years before the year you are interested in, up through the year of the publication. The more numbers you have, the more accurate the final average is.

Writing Your Own "Bluebook"

First, make a chart of all the years of production for the desired aircraft model (or at least for five years before the model year of intended purchase). Then, write down all of the asking prices for the given model under the proper year heading, as in the chart below. Use prices from two or three consecutive issues for smoother plotting. We have found that the lower prices asked for high-time airframes and run-out engines are balanced out by the pipe-dreamers who think their birds are gold-plated. Both extremes average out.

Next, average the prices for each year, as shown below. We have used the Piper Cherokee 180 as an example. Repeat the above process with an older issue of the same publication. It is best to have issues matching the same time of year, if possible. For example, spring prices tend to be higher than fall prices for most single-engine aircraft. When all of the old prices have been recorded, average each year and compare with the current prices. The year-by-year appreciation percentage can now be calculated.

Graphing the Prices

To further increase the accuracy of your statistics, it is a good idea to graph the change of price by the year for each of the two preceding sets of numbers. Mark off years as the horizontal coordinte, and value in thousands of dollars as the vertical coordinate in the graph at right. Mark off each yearly average for the current prices as an "X" on the graph.

When all values have been transferred to the graph, draw a smooth curve between the first and the last point on the graph. Pass the curve an equal distance above and below adjacent "Xs" that do not line up with the smooth curve. This is actually a form of averaging the adjacent years, and it helps to compensate for those aircraft models and/or years for which the statistical samples are small.

It is now possible to add the old-reference prices to this current-price graph. On the same sheet, put in the old prices as "Os," and draw a smooth curve between these data points. The two curves show at a glance what the price performance of the Cherokee 180 has been over the time span between the current and the old references (in this case, 27 months).

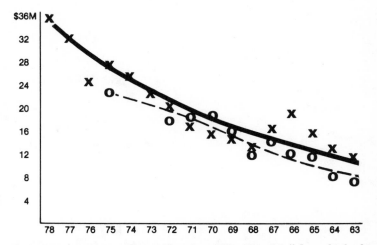

Charting prices for a Piper Cherokee 180. *The "Os" by which the lower line was plotted represent 1975 data points; the "Xs" for the upper line, 1978 data points. The shallow curves indicate a popular airplane that will be easy to sell.*

Interpreting the Graph

Note above, that both graph lies curve downward, since an older aircraft is always worth less than a newer version of the same model. The steeper the curve, the more the value changes from year to year. The point where the curve levels off is where depreciation stabilizes. *This is the best point at which to buy a used plane if investment value is the major goal. For most models, the "knee" or nadir of the curve is around four to five years.*

A shallow curve (nearly horizontal) for the older birds is the indication of a popular airplane. It indicates a high demand and/or a short supply. These planes are the easiest to sell when it eventually becomes time to upgrade. A continuing steep curve, on the other hand, indicates an unpopular aircraft, or one that has a larger supply available than the market can readily absorb. This is particularly true of the "trainer" aircraft. As flight schools surplus out their Cessna 150s, Cherokee 140s, and Arrows, the cut-rate prices and large supply causes steep drops in prices throughout the years. While the prices of these models will eventually start to go up, they will not track inflation as well as the "step-

Cherokee 180 Average Retail Prices

	'78	'77	'76	'75	'74	'73	'72	'71	'70	'69	'68	'67	'66	'65	'64	'63
Prices from March 1978 (in thousands of dollars)	$34.9	28.9	27	27.5	26	19.9	20.5	14.5		13	17	11	15.9	13.9	11.7	10.5
	37.8	32	23.9			23	18.5	16.2		15.4	14.5	14.4		11.5	12	10.3
	35	34.7	28			18.5	16.9			14.3	14	16.6		12.9	9.9	
	39.9					18.9	18.5				13.4	15.9		11.9		
	34.3					23.5					16.9			10.8		
March 1978 Averages	$35.9	31.9	26.3	27.5	26	20.8	18.6	15.4	—	14.2	15.2	14.5	15.9	12.2	11.2	10.4
Prices from December 1975				$23.2		16.5	15	15	14.9	15	11.5	10.9	9.5	8.5	10.3	
						16.9				12.9	12.5		12	10.7	7.9	
						14.5				11.8	13					
										12.9						
										13.8						
										12.9						
										13						
December 1975 Averages				$23.2		16.5	15.5	15	14.9	13.2	12.3	10.9	10.8		9.6	9.1

Depreciation Patterns

The pattern of depreciation for most airplanes is strikingly similar. The graphs here show how the bluebook retail values of 16 popular 1968 model aircraft changed over the years. With the exception of the Cessna Skymaster, the value of every one of the planes bottomed out when it was three or four years old, in 1971 or 1972. The lesson for the investor is clear—buy a three- or four-year-old airplane, and it is virtually guaranteed to appreciate.

Twins take the biggest nosedives in price, losing about half their value in four years. Only the Twin Comanche is worth anywhere near its original value. A 1968 Skymaster steadily declined in value for its first eight years.

Best investments are the retractable singles. The Bonanza, Comanche and 210 all rebounded strongly after three or four years and are now worth very near their original price. Only the 1968 Viking has failed to appreciate significantly since 1972.

Smaller fixed-gear aircraft have remained fairly steady, with very flat curves. This is due to the large turnover of flight school and rental aircraft, which gluts the used plane market.

Moral: the best investment in a used airplane these days is a four-year-old Bonanza, Cessna 210, Baron, or a 1971-72 Comanche.

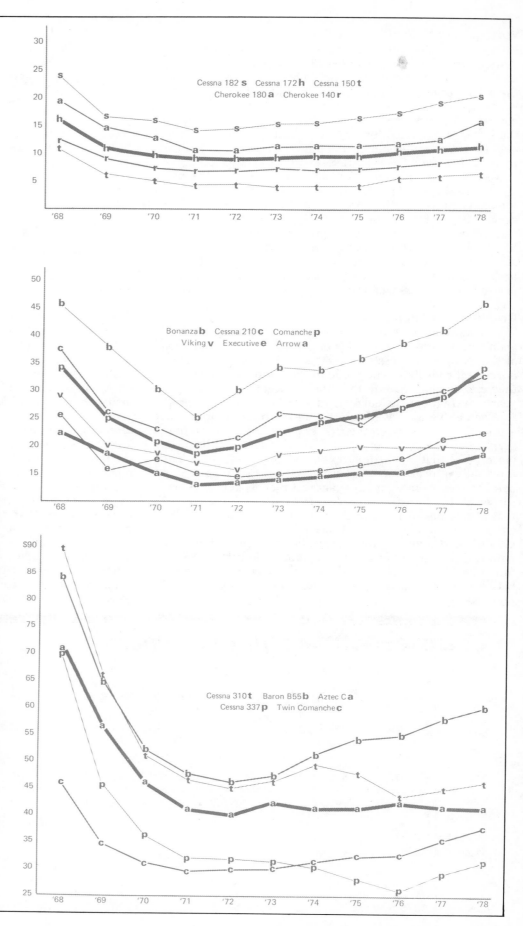

Cessna 182 **s**   Cessna 172 **h**   Cessna 150 **t**
Cherokee 180 **a**   Cherokee 140 **r**

Bonanza **b**   Cessna 210 **c**   Comanche **p**
Viking **v**   Executive **e**   Arrow **a**

Cessna 310 **t**   Baron B55 **b**   Aztec C **a**
Cessna 337 **p**   Twin Comanche **c**

1970 Model Aircraft Depreciation/Appreciation

	New Equipped List (winter '69-'70)	Used List (winter '73-'74)	Depreciation '70-'74 (first 4 years)	Used List (winter '77-'78)	Appreciation '74-'78 (next 4 years)
Grumman American					
AA1 Yankee Clipper	$10,495	$ 6,400	39%	$ 6,750	5.5%
Beech					
A36 Bonanza	$58,180	$41,050	29%	$52,000	27%
V35B Bonanza	$54,370	$39,600	27%	$47,500	20%
F33A Bonanza	$49,505	$35,700	28%	$42,000	18%
C23 Musketeer Custom	$19,990	$12,890	36%	$13,500	4.7%
Bellanca Viking 17-31 Super	$38,205	24,250	37%	$24,000	-1.0%
Cessna					
210K Centurion	43,590	$31,000	29%	$36,500	18%
A185E Skywagon	$29,575	$21,850	26%	$24,000	9.9%
182N Skylane	$26,410	$18,250	31%	$20,250	11%
177B Cardinal	$22,092	$13,800	38%	$19,500	12%
172K Skyhawk	$17,200	$10,800	37%	$12,500	16%
150K Commuter	$11,725	$ 6,100	48%	$ 6,250	2.5%
Champion 7GCBC Citabria	$11,430	$ 7,250	37%	$ 8,500	17%
Mooney Chapparal	$26,971	$16,250	40%	$22,250	37%
Piper					
PA-24 Comanche 260C	$40,555	$28,895	29%	$37,500	30%
PA-28R-200 Arrow B	$26,805	$19,850	26%	$21,750	9.6%
PA-28-235D Cherokee	$26,240	$19,100	27%	$20,000	4.7%
PA-28-180E Cherokee	$20,400	$14,100	31%	$16,500	17%
PA-28-140C Cherokee	$16,135	$ 8,990	44%	$ 9,500	5.7%

up" models—Cessna 182,s Cherokee 180s, etc.

Crossovers between old and new prices constitute another danger sign. The crossover means that the given model has depreciated between the old and the new references, in spite of inflationary pressures. When compared to other aircraft, these make a poor choice for investment quality. Note the crossover in the Arrow graph.

Mavericks

The above techniques capitalize upon the conservatism of the aircraft industry. The basic airframe models change very little from year to year (or even from decade to decade). There is no aircraft equivalent for Detroit's planned obsolescence and rust-out proclivities of automobiles. But some aircraft do not follow the rules, and these are harder to graph and interpret.

A prime example of such a maverick is the sleek retractable Mooney. The first blow to statistical standardization was the halt of manufacture in 1971. When a plane goes out of production, the entire fleet loses much of its glamour, and prices fall quickly. Apprehension over parts supply and service take a psychological toll. The lack of four-page color spreads in the aviation press cuts down the yearnings of potential purchasers.

In 1973, Republic Steel picked up the Mooney tooling and put the aircraft back into production. With the new planes back in the public eye, the used Mooneys of the 60's gained

back their depreciated value, and then some. Mid-1960's Mooney shot up 18 percent between 1976 and 1977, and appreciated at about 11 percent per year. But it was not to last.

In 1977, the new Mooney 201 was introduced to replace the Executive. The 201 is 20 knots faster than its predecessor, thanks to an extensive "clean-up" campaign. The result is a maverick of the second kind—model obsolescence. Because of the desirability of speed in the 201's category, the 1974-76 Mooney prices went way down. In 1978, a 1976 Mooney listed for $36,000, or two-thirds of what a brand-new 201 was selling for. This type of disturbance prevents the graph from being the smooth predictor of future price that it is for other makes and models. Nor does this imply that the mid-70's Mooneys are not good buys. At the depressed price, the reverse may be true. We are just pointing out the factors that limit the statistical approach to market prediction.

Picking the Best Investment

To view with the benefit of 20/20 hindsight, we hypothetically purchased a number of used single-engined aircraft in 1974. Each 1970-model aircraft was four years old and we paid full book list at the time. To see how we would fare in 1978, we assumed we could recover full list when we "sold" them all. (While it is difficult for an individual to get full list upon sale, it is also rare that he pays

"Blue Chip" Aircraft Investments

Year	Beech A36 Bonanza			Beech V35 Bonanza			Comanche 250/260			Cessna 210			Cessna 172			Cherokee Arrow* PA-28R-180/200		
	Buy '74	Sell '78	%	Buy '74	Sell '78	%	Buy '74	Sell '78	%	Buy '74	Sell '78	%	Buy '74	Sell '78	%	Buy '74	Sell '78	%
1960	—	—	—	17.4	26.5	52	13.1	17.8	36	11	19.3	40	5.8	8	38	—	—	—
1961	—	—	—	19.5	29	49	13.8	18.5	34	12	17.8	48	6.3	8.5	35	—	—	—
1962	—	—	—	22	30	36	14.5	19.5	35	13.9	19	37	6.8	9	32	—	—	—
1963	—	—	—	23	31	35	15.6	20.5	31	14.7	20.5	39	6.9	9.3	35	—	—	—
1964	—	—	—	27	38	40	15.6	21.5	38	17	24	41	7.5	9.8	31	—	—	—
1965	—	—	—	28	38	36	20.5	28.5	39	18.4	29.5	39	8.0	10	25	—	—	—
1966	—	—	—	30.9	40	29	23.4	30	28	20.3	27	33	8.4	10.8	29	—	—	—
1967	—	—	—	32.9	41.5	26	23.8	31.8	34	21.5	29.5	37	8.8	11.3	28	14.8	17.5	18.3
1968	37	47.5	28	34.1	44	29	25.4	33.5	32	24.1	31.5	31	9.4	11.5	11	15.3	18.3	19.6
1969	38.3	49	28	37.3	46	23	26.3	35.3	34	25.8	34	32	10.3	12	17	16	18.6	16.3
1970	41.1	52	26.5	39.6	47.5	20	28.9	37.5	30	31	36.5	18	11.4	12.5	9.6	16.9	19	12.4
1971	44.1	54	22.4	42	51	21.4	32.1	38.8	21	32.7	39	19	12.8	13.3	3.9	17.5	19.5	11.4
1972	50.4	59	15	45.5	54	18.7	36.8	40	8.7	37	40.5	9.4	13.3	14	5.3	25.1	24	-4.4
1973	69.2	61	-11.8	65.8	59	-10	—	—	—	48.9	42.5	-12	18.4	14.5	-21	36.7	26.5	-28

*The Piper Arrow is no blue chip, but it is included for comparison.

full list either.) The chart shows the wide difference between the various 1970 aircraft that we could have purchased in 1974. From among the fixed-pitch nonretractables, the Cherokee 180 was a star performer at 17 percent, followed closely by the 172 at 16 percent. For a light retractable, the Mooney was a star for the reasons mentioned above. The venerable Piper Comanche, at a whopping 30 percent, was the all-time value leader in the heavy singles class.

The Comanche may continue to climb in price, but we feel that the rate will taper off as the fleet becomes older. Maintenance becomes astronomical on older airframes as parts costs go up. The manufacturer presumably will be producing Comanche parts in smaller and smaller quantities as the years pass, so prices will increase geometrically.

Below is a partial list of losers and winners in the aircraft appreciation game:

Best Investments (1974-78)

Mooney Chapparal	Cessna 172 Skyhawk
Piper Comanche 260	Champion 7GCBC Citabria
Beech A36 Bonanza	Piper Cherokee 180
Cessna 210K Centurion	Beech V35, F33A Bonanza

Poor Investments (1974-78)

Bellanca Viking 300	Beech C23 Musketeer
Grumman AA1 Yankee	Piper Cherokee 140
Clipper	Piper Cherokee 235
Cessna 150 Commuter	Piper Cherokee Arrow

Extenuating Circumstances

When looking at any used plane, everyone wants recent paint, nice interior, new avionics, and a low-time engine. Add low-time airframe, all ADs complied, no damage history, and we have described the perfect aircraft. Any deficiency from the above is going to cost money to be set right. Any potential purchaser should be aware that the list price is based on all of the above items being in "average" condition. Any substandard item should have *half* the replacement cost deducted from the list price to determine the fair selling price. Likewise, add in half the cost if the item has been freshly replaced. Also, study the logs carefully.

In a recent quest for a replacement for our Cherokee 180, we found many times where we were looking at *three* planes at one time: the airplane as the salesman advertised it, a different plane as pictured by the logbooks, and yet a third plane as it appeared on the ramp. Most salesmen alluded to previus ownership by a "retired airline captain." This appears to be the plane huckster's equivalent to the used car salesman's "little old lady schoolteacher." But then the logs note the replacement of landing gear torque links on the port wing. And when you get around to crawling under the plane, you see some bent panels on the starboard wing that the log doesn't say anything about. It is much easier to keep looking until you find a plane where all three stories match—description, logs and airframe.

Don't be hasty in your aircraft purchase. It takes time to research the market and settle upon the plane you really want. Soon you'll be able to sort out the bad deals with no problem. Most planes are offered as fair deals, but some bargains are offered by people who want to sell *right now*, and are willing to give you a break. The used aircraft dealer's markup averages 15 percent for singles, so a "good deal" is defined as anything more than 10 percent off list for an average aircraft.

Conclusion

When the objective is to fly your own plane for the minimum number of dollars, the lowest-priced aircraft type is not always the best-dollar deal. The popularity of one type over another may well make the popular aircraft the better investment in the long run. In addition, it'll be easier to sell or swap the plane when your pocketbook dictates that it's time to move up.

Single-Engine Fixed-Gear

Cessna Skyhawk

Cessna's 172 Skyhawk is universally acclaimed as Everyman's airplane, a simple, safe, reliable craft that transports four people at the lowest possible cost. It is the world's most popular lightplane—more than 30,000 built—and has been in continuous production for 27 years with no design changes of consequence.

Cessna attempted to replace the Skyhawk with the sleek, modern Cardinal in 1968—it even shut down the Skyhawk production line altogether in anticipation—but the Cardinal flopped, was re-engined, and eventually discontinued, despite the fact that it was a fine airplane. In the Cardinal's place, Cessna put—you guessed it—a Skyhawk with a slightly bigger engine called the Hawk XP. Despite the fact that the Hawk XP wasn't as fast, roomy, quiet or economical as the Cardinal, it sold like hotcakes. There is truly something magical about the appeal of the Cessna 172.

History
The 172 was introduced in 1956, about the same time as the 150. It was basically a nosewheel version of the 170, Cessna's post-war standby. Both were offered that first year; when the 172 outsold the 170 by a ten-to-one margin, Cessna quickly dropped the taildragger. The first 172 had a straight tail, a "fastback" cabin and a 145-hp Continental. The 1960 "A" model got a swept-back tail; in 1963 the fastback gave way to Omni-Vision rear windows. There have been virtually no major airframe changes since. The 1964 172E got electric flaps (a step many pilots consider to be backwards).

In 1968, the Skyhawk got a new engine, the four-cylinder 150-hp Lycoming. This is perhaps the most important improvement ever made to the line. In 1969, a 52-gallon fuel tank option became available and in 1973 the leading edge of the wing was re-contoured which supposedly improved stall characteristics slightly. In 1974, goaded

by the surprising sales success of the speedy Grumman American Traveler, Cessna made some changes to the wheelpants and cooling airflow and picked up about seven mph cruise speed. The most recent change of consequence was the disastrous move to the 160-hp Lycoming O-320-H engine in 1977, a switch that Cessna no doubt sincerely regrets. (For details on the O-320-H fiasco, see the "Engines" section. At the same time, Cessna went to a 28-volt electrical system, which has created problems, particularly with landing lights and rotating beacons.

The superb reputation of the Skyhawk has been somewhat tarnished in the past couple of years, and it may take several years to polish it back to its former brilliance. Meanwhile, there are plenty of '68-'76 models around.

Used Skyhawk Marketplace
Because of the huge number of Skyhawks, the low price of the airplane and the huge turnover of flight school and rental airplanes, the used Skyhawk market is about as steady as they come. A recent issue of *Trade-A-Plane* counted 287 used 172s for sale. As a result, prices are well-established and don't vary much. You're unlikely to find a "steal" because the demand is so high; on the other hand, the supply is so abundant that nobody can get away with an asking price that's out of

line. Used-Skyhawk shoppers shouldn't waste a lot of time trying to save the last nickel; energy is better spent on careful selection and scrutiny of mechanical condition.

The resale value of the Skyhawk follows the classic curve; a fairly sharp drop after the first two years, with a "bottoming out" after four or five years and a very gradual rise in dollar value therafter. (The *real* value, of course, steadily declines because of the erosion of the dollar by inflation.)

Surprisingly, the *Aircraft Price Digest* shows no difference in value that could be attributed to the engine switch in 1968. In our opinion, however, the O-300-powered Skyhawks will not hold their value as well in the future, as replacement engines and parts become scarcer and more expensive. It's too early to tell how the engine problems of the 1977 and later models will affect future resale value, but smart, cautious buyers will certainly look with suspicion on them for some time to come.

Performance
The Skyhawk's performance is not exactly spectacular. Loaded up to gross weight, a 172 is lethargic, and we wouldn't want to try any hot-day high-field takeoffs in a heavy airplane. The 1977 and later models, with 160 hp, are noticeably more energetic, however,

The uninitiated may call it a "Piper Cub," *but this is the shape which millions around the world associate with general aviation.*

with a book-climb rate about 20 percent higher than the 145- and 150-hp versions. Cruise speed is a modest 120 to 130 mph under most conditions, with a fuel burn of about 8 gph. The post-73 models are faster by five mph or so because of better aerodynamics on those models. The 38-gallon standard usable fuel supply provides about four hours of flying with a small reserve, enough for a maximum range of about 500 miles if you really stretch it.

Optional 52-gallon tanks (48 usable) extend endurance to over five hours, enough for 600 miles or so. Payload is of course reduced when 52 gallons of fuel are aboard; count on three adults and no baggage at best.

Summing up, the Skyhawk provides the bare minimum of performance for four people. But it does carry four adults under most conditions, a feat which the 150-hp Piper Cherokee could not achieve until a Skyhawk-like wing was added to it in 1974.

Handling Characteristics

The Skyhawk is benign to the utmost, with rather heavy controls that inhibit fighter-pilot tendencies but make instrument work a pleasure. "Stable" is the word used again and again by Skyhawk pilots. Elevator forces are very heavy, which means that stalling is extremely difficult. The Skyhawk's handling characteristics are overwhelmingly average—partly because the airplane's universal popularity has helped establish the standards of normalcy. Almost by definition, the Skyhawk is the average airplane.

The Skyhawk does have outstanding characteristics in one respect: short-field performance. A skillful pilot can put a Skyhawk down in not much more runway than a so-called STOL specialty machine like a Rallye or a Maule. At light weights, takeoffs can be nearly as short. The Skyhawk's huge flaps allow it to come down very steeply, and we wouldn't hesitate to pit a Skyhawk against a Rallye or a Maul (both highly-touted as STOL airplanes) in a slow-flying contest.

Safety

Perhaps one of the reasons for the success of the Skyhawk is its superb safety record. The 172 has an overall accident rate of only 9.1 per 100,000 hours, better than any other four-place fixed-gear airplane. Fatal accident rate is 1.5, also excellent. (See the chart for a ranking of all aircraft in the four-place fixed-gear category.)

A look at specific categories of accidents shows the Skyhawk ranked high across the board. Out of the 32 most popular single-engine airplanes, the 172 ranks in the top ten in eight out of ten accident categories. It has the lowest rates of engine failure and in-flight airframe failure accidents of any lightplane. The categories in which the Skyhawk is only average are mid-air collisions (obviously a result of the 172's lousy visibility) and overshoot accidents.

The 172's good safety record is very likely due to a variety of factors, all shared by Cessna high-wing aircraft. High elevator forces and very low stalling speeds discourage stalls. The

Skyhawk's fuel system is a marvel of simplicity, with a well-placed selector that has only left, right, off and both positions. It is very hard to foul up the 172 fuel system, particularly if the pilot simply puts the selector on "both" and leaves it there, as most pilots do. In addition, the high-wing gravity-feed system requires no fuel pumps. And the Skyhawk's strut-braced wing may look old-fashioned, but there has never been a single fatal in-flight airframe failure in a Skyhawk in nearly 40 million hours of flying in the hands of sometimes-less-than-expert pilots.

Engines

The Skyhawk airframe has changed little over the years, but there have been some major engine changes. Which engine you get will play a big role in how happy you are with a used Skyhawk. Our advice can be summed up as follows: 1968-76 models, terrific; 1956-67 models, fair; 1977-80 models, awful.

For the first 12 years of its life, up through and including the 1967 172H, the Skyhawk was equipped with a six-cylinder 145-hp Continental O-300. This was basically an O-200 (used in the Cessna 150) with two more cylinders tacked on to the end. The O-300 has an adequate reliability record and an 1800-hour TBO, but it is quite expensive to repair and overhaul. "The problem is that you've got six of everything to replace instead of four," one overhauler told us. "An old engine like that can be a real can of worms." Overhaul prices for the O-300 run from $3,500 to $5,500

Model	Year Built	Number Built	Cruise Speed (mph)	Rate of Climb (fpm)	Useful Load (lbs)	Fuel Std/Opt (gals)	Engine	TBO (hrs)	Overhaul Cost	Average Retail Price
172	1956-59	4,022	124	660	940	37	Cont. O-300A	1,500	$5,000	$ 7,500
172A	1960	991	124	660	940	37	Cont. O-300C	1,800	$5,000	$ 8,250
172B	1961	987	131	730	875	42	Cont. O-300D	1,800	$5,000	$ 8,750
172C	1962	809	131	675	920	42	Cont. O-300D	1,800	$5,000	$ 9,250
172D	1963	1,027	131	645	970	42	Cont. O-300D	1,800	$5,000	$ 9,750
172E	1964	1,249	131	645	970	42	Cont. O-300D	1,800	$5,000	$10,000
172F	1965	1,569	131	645	970	42	Cont. O-300D	1,800	$5,000	$10,250
172G	1966	1,499	131	645	970	42	Cont. O-300D	1,800	$5,000	$10,750
172H	1967	1,619	131	645	970	42	Cont. O-300D	1,800	$5,000	$11,500
172I	1968	630	132	645	1,000	42	Lyc. O-320-E2D	2,000	$4,000	$12,250
172K	1969	1,684	132	645	985	42/52	Lyc. O-320-E2D	2,000	$4,000	$13,000
172K	1970	736	132	645	985	42/52	Lyc. O-320-E2D	2,000	$4,000	$13,500
172L	1971	679	132	645	985	42/52	Lyc. O-320-E2D	2,000	$4,000	$14,000
172L	1972	854	132	645	985	42/52	Lyc. O-320-E2D	2,000	$4,000	$14,500
172M	1973	1,139	132	645	965	42/52	Lyc. O-320-E2D	2,000	$4,000	$15,000
172M	1974	1,559	138	645	965	42/52	Lyc. O-320-E2D	2,000	$4,000	$15,750
172M	1975	2,225	138	645	965	42/52	Lyc. O-320-E2D	2,000	$4,000	$16,500
172M	1976	1,899	138	645	965	42/52	Lyc. O-320-E2D	2,000	$4,000	$17,000
172N	1977	1,724	140	770	876	43/54	Lyc. O-320-H2AD	2,000	$4,000	$19,000
172N	1978	1,724	140	770	876	43/54	Lyc. O-320-H2AD	2,000	$4,000	$22,000
172N	1979	1,849	140	770	876	43/54	Lyc. O-320-H2AD	2,000	$4,000	$27,000

or so. By comparison, the 150-hp Lycoming used in later 'Hawks cost several hundred to a thousand dollars less to overhaul.

Remanufactured O-300s are still supposedly available from Continental, but at a prohibitive price of $7,800. (That's more than the total value of a 1956 Skyhawk.) Parts for the O-300 are generally still available because many are interchangeable with the ubiquitous O-200, but they are expensive.

We've received many reports of cylinder problems from O-300 owners (just as with the O-200). "Would like to hear some suggestions on how to baby the Continental to avoid the cracked rings, jugs, etc. that are common to the engine," one 1967 Skyhawk ower asked us plaintively. Like the O-200, the O-300 does not handle 100 LL fuel very well; valve failure and plug fouling are commonplace in O-300s run on blue gas. As with the O-200, a "100-octane valve kit" is available for the O-300, which reportedly helps considerably. Careful leaning and the use of TCP anti-lead compound will also extend valve life.

The O-300 shares the carburetor icing problems of the O-200. Full, continuous use of carb heat is required in any reduced-power situation, and carb ice accumulation at cruise power is not unusual.

The good news under the Skyhawk cowling is the four-cylinder Lycoming O-320-E2D used from 1968 through 1976. It costs about $3,500 to $4,500 to overhaul, has a 2,000-hour TBO and a reputation for going well beyond that figure. Flight schools who put 100 hours a month on their airplanes and do careful maintenance regularly get 3,000 hours. "There's no better engine," one mechanic told us. The O-320 seems to handle 100 LL fuel with ease, although careful leaning is still recommended.

Partly as a result of the scarcity of 80 octane fuel and partly to cut costs, Cessna in 1977 ordered from Lycoming a redesigned version of the O-320 called the O-320-H2AD. This engine, of course, was a disaster and a major embarrassment to Cessna and Lycoming. Literally hundreds of 1977 Skyhawks suffered serious camshaft and valve train damage, at a cost of many thousands of dollars to their owners. In addition, there were a dozen or so abrupt engine failures caused by sheared oil pumps and accessory drive gears. In April 1978, Cessna recalled all 1977 and 1978 Skyhawks for major engine repairs.

Look closely at the panel *of any 1974-79 Skyhawk. If it has ARC avionics, check their service and repair history very carefully.*

Literally hundreds of 1977-80 Skyhawks suffered serious camshaft and valve train damage, at a cost of many thousands of dollars to their owners. In addition, there were a dozen or so abrupt engine failures in 1977-78 caused by sheared oil pumps and accessory drive gears. In April 1978, Cessna recalled all 1977 and 1978 Skyhawks for major engine repairs. The oil pump and drive gear problems were fixed, but the camshaft/tappet problems continued unsolved through the 1980 model. (Cessna finally gave up and changed to a different engine in 1981.) Lycoming tried three different camshaft/tappet modifications, but none of them worked, and the expensive problems continued unabated throughout the four years the O-320-H-powered Skyhawk was in production.

After Cessna switched engines, Lycoming belatedly came up with a fourth major modification it hopes will solve the problem once and for all. The modified engines will slowly work their way into the fleet by attrition, as original engines are replaced by the modified new and remanufactured ones. This most recent mod will be found on engines with serial numbers 7976 and above. We should point out that there is no assurance the latest mod will prove any better than the first three. "Lycoming hasn't convinced me yet on the O-320-H," one big engine overhauler told us. "I'm a hard man to convince."

We agree. We would not advise the purchase of a Skyhawk with engine serial number below 7976, except at an extremely low price that would account for the almost certain premature engine replacement. After 7976, the odds are better, but it's still far from a sure thing.

Because of the O-320-H problems, Cessna has a special 2,000-hour pro-rata warranty period. Thus, if you buy a Skyhawk with 900 hours and the engine fails after 100 hours, you'll get a new or remanufactured engine for half price.

Overhaul of the O-320-H is still something of an unknown factor, since few engines have accumulated 2,000 hours, and many overhaul shops are still rather gun-shy about it. A couple of big shops we talked to wouldn't even quote a price and hinted that they would prefer never to see the inside of an O-320-H.

Fortunately for Skyhawk shoppers, there are engine conversions available that will replace both the O-300 and the O-320-H. Ram Aircraft Modifications, Inc., Municipal Airport, Box 5219, Waco, Texas 76708 (817)752-8381, offers a 100-octane 160-hp O-320-D2G engine for all Skyhawks. Cost is rather high for pre-1968 Skyhawks, however: $9,000 installed. (That's nearly 70 percent of the total value of a 1967 airplane.) For 1977-80 models, the price is $6,600.

Owners of 1968-76 Hawks who are having 100 LL problems or merely want a little more horsepower may also convert to the Ram mod, for $5,800. Those owners also have the option of an overhaul with modified parts that raises compression to burn 100 octane fuel and increases horsepower to 160. This STC is owned by Pearce Aeronautics, Wichita, Kansas, (316)685-4552.

In addition, several companies offer conversions to the 180-hp Lycoming O-360 and constant-speed propeller. This makes a real performer out of the Skyhawk, but the price is high; more than $10,000. STCs for the 180-hp conversion are owned by Avcon Industries, 1006 W. 53rd North, P.O. Box 4248,

Wichita, Ks. 67204 (316)838-9375; Horton STOLcraft, Wellington Airport, Wellington, Ks. 67152 (316)326-2241; and Air-Con (formerly MASA) Route 2 Box 5, Belle Plaine, Ks. 67013 (316)488-3841.

If you're looking for a real rocket ship, a 220-hp Franklin can be installed by Seaplane Flying, Inc. P.O. BOX 2164, Vancouver, Wa. 98661, (206)694-6287.

Maintenance

The Skyhawk's strong suit has always been economy and low maintenance costs (low, at least, by aircraft standards). With a four-cylinder engine (1968 and later models) fixed-pitch prop, fixed gear and no cowl flaps, the average Skyhawk can get through an annual for $300 or so with no major problems.

Skyhawks do have their weak points in terms of maintenance, however. Late-model '77 and '78 Skyhawks with 28-volt electrical systems burn out landing lights at an incredible rate. One owner reports, "I've spent $323 for landing light bulbs in the last 212 hours of flight. That works out to $1.52 per hour ..." Cessna has offered a "landing light-improvement kit."

Older Skyhawks have problems with the nosewheel, particularly those flown by students and novice pilots who tend to land too fast. (Nosewheel problems can also reflect damage to the firewall where the strut joins it. This should be checked.) Mechanics tell us that Cessna wheels are notoriously chintzy and don't stand up well to punishment. Nose gear shimmy can also be a problem. Flap actuator jack screws have a troublesome history, and are subject to an AD in pre-1973 models.

Avionics

We normally don't talk about avionics in a used-plane article, but we'll make an exception in this case. The reason is the poor reliability record of the ARC avionics that are installed in virtually all Skyhawks since 1974. ARC has had serious management, production and quality control problems in the past five years, and the result has been a torrent of customer problems. 1977 and 1978 seemed to be particularly bad years.

If you're lucky enough to find a 1974 or later used Skyhawk with Collins, King or Narco equipment, you may save yourself future avionics headaches by buying it instead of an ARC-equipped airplane. If you have to buy an ARC-equipped airplane, ask for documentation of radio repairs and past problems. Check particularly the synthesizers in the 300 series navcoms. If the airplanes you're considering has a long history of avionics bugs, don't buy it. There are always plenty of Skyhawks around, and a buyer should do his utmost to find one with radios that have a good track record.

Modifications

In addition to the previously mentioned engine conversions, there is a wide variety of STCed Skyhawk mods. (The 172 population is so high that many small entrepreneurs with STCs are trying to get a piece of the Skyhawk market.) Among the more popular mods:

• Robertson STOL conversion includes a recontoured leading edge for older models and drooped ailerons. At a price of $4,500 for 1973-79 models and $6,000 for 1956-72 Skyhawks, the Robertson mod is hardly worth the money; the Skyhawk already has very good short-field landing performance, and the limited power means that takeoffs will never be spectacular, no matter what the wing is like.

• Horton STOLcraft also offers a STOL kit that is not as elaborate (or effective) as Robertson's. With a 180-hp engine and constant-speed prop installed (also offered by Horton), however, a STOL mod makes a bit more sense.

• Flint long-range fuel tanks add 24 gallons capacity at a cost of $1,540, plus about $750 installation. The tanks are mounted internally and do not change the contour or size of wing. Flint Aero, 336 Front St., El Cajon, Ca. 92020 (714)448-1551.

• B and M flap and aileron gap seals offer slight improvements in speed, climb and aileron response at a cost of about $400 installed. B&M Aviation, 2048 Airport Way, Bellingham, Wash. 98225. (206)676-1750.

Owner Society

The Cessna Skyhawk Association has 2,200 members and publishes a monthly newsletter. Although not in the evangelical mold of owner clubs like the Navion Society or Bonanza club, the CSA nevertheless is an active, going concern that fills a definite need. Cessna Skyhawk Society, Box 779, Delray Beach, Florida 33444; (305) 278-2116.

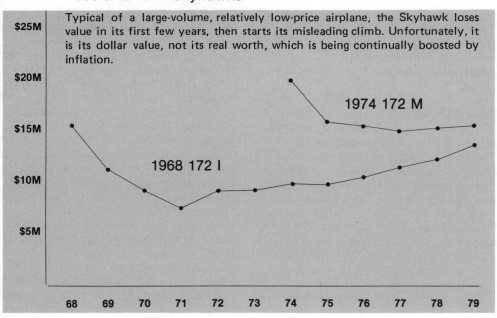

Investment Value Graph
—1968 and 1974 Skyhawks

Typical of a large-volume, relatively low-price airplane, the Skyhawk loses value in its first few years, then starts its misleading climb. Unfortunately, it is its dollar value, not its real worth, which is being continually boosted by inflation.

1974 172 M

1968 172 I

Owner Comments

"I am very satisfied with my Hawk and really enjoy flying it. The Lycoming O-320 engine is an absolute jewel. Oil consumption is only one quart in twenty hours and fuel consumption is 7.5 to 8 gph at 65 percent power. It handles very smartly and the flaps are very effective compared to a Piper Archer. The Archer's flaps seemed to have little effect at all. My Hawk is very stable for a light plane and when properly trimmed for climb, level flight or descent it flies hands-off very well. The seat is comfortable for extended flying.

"It is equipped with Cessna avionics and they have proven to be absolutely trouble free and reliable in spite of some adverse reports in your publication.

"The only serious drawback is visibility. It is ok straight ahead and straight down, but it is very poor to the rear and above. I would hesitate to fly into a busy terminal without a passenger to spot traffic for me."

"All in all I would say that the Skyhawk is the best thing going for the low-time pilot or the occasional pilot due to its economical, reliable nature and its easy flying characteristics. It makes an ideal stepping stone from a trainer.

"Three of us bought a cream puff, two-owner '67 Skyhawk the first of '78. Based on 188 hours flying time, our total expenses came to $27.56 per hour. Maintenance would have been minor if it hadn't been for a $1,200 annual. (We had to have two jugs rebuilt—not uncommon for the Continentals, we understand.) Other than the annual, we only spent $68.11 on maintenance and that was for a cracked engine mount we discovered while changing the oil.

"Other than for scheduled maintenance, we never missed a flight due to mechanical problems. Oh, we had to handprop her a time or two, but you can't beat that record for reliability.

"The purchase price was $12,600 which we knew was a grand or so high, but she was a two-owner, 1,200 TT with 170 hours on a zero-time overhauled engine, Also IFR, new interior and a new Imron paint job. We also got some creative financing: 100 percent loan, 12 years, $163.00 monthly payment.

"We would like to hear some suggestions on how to baby the Continental to avoid the cracked jugs, rings, etc., that are common to the engine."

"I own a 1978 C-172 on lease-back to a local FBO. The plane flies about 75 hours a month and is used mainly for instrument training and an occasional cross-country flight.

"In addition to the usual maintenance problems, I have had to constantly replace the landing lights and have so far been unable to secure the highly touted 'landing light improvement kit', which Cessna so prosaicly prescribes for 'owners experiencing unusually high bulb failure rates.' I'm sure I'll qualify since I've spent $323 for landing lights during the last 212 hours of flight. That works out to about $1.52 per hour.

"In addition to popping landing lights while on night approaches, I've had the exquisite thrill of aborting an instrument take-off when two push rods bent and the engine spilled oil and associated valve-train material all over the runway. My local FBO installed a valve train improvement kit (limited-travel lifters, etc.) but I'm still waiting for a rebate from Cessna.

"The cigarette lighter hasn't shorted out yet and burned up the electrical harness, but I'm sure that will happen soon.

"What do I like best about the plane? The Collins Radios! They're the only thing that works right."

"I own a 1965 172F with the Continental O-300C engine. I did not plan to buy a 172, and had been thinking of a 182-lane or a Cherokee 180. However, after a lot of thought, I realized that a "2½-place" airplane that goes 120 mph was appropriate for this 100-hour pilot, since most of my flying are short-hop (under 200 miles) solos.

"The airplane is very easy to fly. The controls are light and responsive, except for the rudder. Over the low-wing competition, I like the two doors and ease of entry. Also, the Cessna flaps are a big plus — I have never had to go around from a bad approach and they pretty well eliminate floating.

"I don't know how many hours it takes to age a Cessna airframe: by and large this airplane, with 3300 hours, does not show any age at all. It has a recent Imron paint job and fancy upholstery, and most people think it is a new airplane. Performance is pretty much by the book, with climb and airspeeds just about what the tables say, although fuel consumption is about .2 gph higher than book — mostly due to running it a little rich. Compared with a 1974 and a 1977 Skyhawk, which I have flown recently, the Continental "six-pack" is noiser on take-off and climb, and not significantly smoother, even with the two extra cylinders.

"I consider the power to be adequate. Most of my flying is at 1800-2000 lbs., and performance is perfectly good, but not stellar, at those weights. I would not want to fly at 2300 lbs. regularly."

"I consider the 172 the only realistic choice on the used airplane market for a four person family on a moderate income today.

"To me, the 1964 172E is the best possible combination of features available. It has manual flaps which provide optimum controllability on tight approaches and avoids an AD that applies to electric flaps only.

"172E also has a modern instrument panel with everything in what has come to be a conventional position, and plenty of room for all needed avionics. Mine has full IFR instrumentation."

Cause and effect. *This Skyhawk, on a ferry flight from the factory, suffered a failed accessory drive in its Lycoming O-320-H engine—hence the unusual parking spot.*

Piper Cherokee 180

Over the years, the Cherokee 180/181 has earned a niche as a kind of flying wheelbarrow, a dependable carryall powered by the most reliable engine in general aviation. Although the airplane has not distinguished itself in any one category like speed or looks, it has somehow managed to navigate between the AD and powerplant Scylla and Charybdis that have plagued other aviation standbys.

Owners in general regard them benignly since they are unlikely to malfunction grievously and soak up maintenance funds. Load-carrying ability is probably the 180's other forte, since it is edged out by both the Cessna Cardinal and Beech Sundowner in roominess. And in terms of speed, it chugs along in the propwash of GA's Tiger.

Nevertheless, with about a 1,100-pound useful load, the Cherokee 180 will lug a sizable slug of people, fuel and baggage with admirable economy.

History, Major Changes
The Cherokee 180 started out in 1963 with a 2,400-pound gross, a 1,200-hour TBO and a 30-foot wingspan. In '67 the TBO went up to 2,000 hours, thanks to new half-inch valves (up from 7/16). In 1968 it received a new instrument panel and a third window on each side of the cabin. Following the lead of the Arrow, the 180 gained an extra five inches of legroom in the rear seat in 1973 along with the larger cabin door and window, another 50 pounds in gross plus an extra two feet in wingspan. The new name: Challenger. Only one year later, it was to become the Archer.

The next significant modification came in 1976 with the tapered wing, a new 2,550-pound gross and the -181 designation.

Obviously, in searching for a used Cherokee 180, it makes sense to pick one with the longer cabin and to make sure when looking at pre-'67 models that the one-half-inch valves have been installed, to bring the TBO up another 800 hours. We have heard of at least one crash in a small-valve Cherokee 180 that was being flown well past the 1,200-hour recommended TBO and experienced

engine failure. And according to Lycoming, apparently a surprising number of owners have not bothered to update their engines.

Maintenance Record
The average cost for an annual inspection on the Cherokee 180 turned out to be $280, based on our 1977 subscriber survey. This is not only lower than for any other aircraft in the 180 class, but cheaper than figures we obtained for the lower category 150-hp Skyhawk and Traveler/Cheetah. Unfortunately, the unscheduled maintenance costs were not so low. These worked out to an average of $339 a year—$166 for airframe and $173 for engine. The Cessna Cardinal came out about $70 cheaper in this regard.

Owners reporting on the Cherokee 180's malfunction record singled out powerplant accessories, electrical system and panel instruments as the biggest headaches.

Most felt dealer/manufacturer backup support on this aircraft was fair to good.

Probably the most prominent problem

area in the early model pre-'68 180s was related to leaking fuel tanks, caused by poor sealant. Improved replacement sealants seemed to solve the problem satisfactorily, but FAA service difficulty reports show that the problem has reappeared. In the past four years, a total of 14 serious cases of fuel tank sealant deterioration has been reported in various Cherokee models, including the 180. A check of malfunction and defect reports shows other problems with cracked alternator and air conditioning brackets and leaking brake cylinders.

Airworthiness Directives
Although the Cherokee 180 has had probably more than its share of ADs through the years, they fortunately have been relatively minor ones and have cost little.

Among the prominent ones: a 1967 AD required inspection of fuel tanks for peeling of the sealant; in 1970 an AD called for inspection of exhaust mufflers for cracks and deterioration every 50 hours until an

In 1976, the Archer II 181 *introduced the higher-aspect ratio tapered wing, which pilots say offers a better climb and a less abrupt payoff in the landing flare.*

The 1975 Piper Archer, *the last Cherokee 180, with the so-called Hershey Bar, constant-chord wing.*

improved muffler was installed; in 1973 the piston pins had to be removed and inspected; in 1975 engines needed replacement of the oil pump shaft and impeller.

A 1978 AD requires inspection and replacement, if necessary, of the impulse coupling on various Bendix magnetos.

For a convenient rundown of all Cherokee 180 ADs in readable fashion, AeroTech Publications at P.O. Box 528, Old Bridge, N. J. 08857, provides an adList guide for $6.95.

Safety
Judging from the roster of accidents tallied by the National Transportation Safety Board for 1977, the Piper Cherokee 180 has no prominent safety weaknesses. Rather, the accidents that did occur tend to under-score the fact that no matter how intrin-sically safe an airplane is, pilots who work at it can go awry.

Hence, even in a supposedly unstallable airplane like the Cherokee 180, several pilots managed to stall and crash—one attempting to turn in a blind canyon, one in low-level buzzing and a couple of others in landing or takeoff situations at high density altitudes.

While the low wing and center of gravity and widely spaced main gear are supposed to provide as stable a ground platform as any airplane around, one pilot actually managed to groundloop or swerve in high winds and nose over, damaging the aircraft.

That old nemesis of so many pilots, fuel mismanagement, occurred in only a handful of Cherokee 180s during 1977. Half (two) crashed from poor flight planning and total fuel exhaustion, while the other two simply selected a low or empty tank and experi-enced engine stoppage. The Cherokee 180's fuel selector on the left cabin wall alongside the pilot's knee is not located ideally for visibility, but it is big and red and easy to switch. However, wrong-tank accidents apparently will be with us as long as there are tanks to be switched.

Although the 180 is no speed demon in a dive, two pilots apparently became spatially disoriented, according to the NTSB, and pulled the wings off in uncontrolled dives. Another flier experienced wing separation while attempting a low-level loop.

Resale Value
If you track the depreciation/appreciation chart for the Cherokee 180, you find the airplane represents a pretty good investment over the years. After the big initial dip in value from the date of purchase, the resale price levels off and begins to rise. The aver-age 1970 model was plotted as losing 31 percent in the first four years after purchase new, but in the next four years the sale price went back up by 17 percent.

Modifications
There are two major series of mods on the Cherokee 180 series, both designed to improve low-speed handling and add at least a modicum of STOL characteristics.

Horton Stol-Craft, Inc., Wellington Mu-nicipal Airport, Wellington, KS 67152, in-stalls wing leading edge cuffs, droop tips, dor-sal fin and vertical stabilizer vortex gen-erators.

Robertson Aircraft Corp. (15400 Sunset Highway, Bellevue, WA 98004) installs drooped leading edge, drooped ailerons, wing stall fences, drooped wing tips and ele-vator trim spring and fuselage flap.

Handling Characteristics
The Cherokee 180 is a fairly benign flying

Model	Year Built	Number Built	Cruise Speed (mph)	Rate of Climb (fpm)	Useful Load (lbs)	Fuel (gals)	Engine	TBO (hrs)	Average Overhaul Cost	Retail Price
PA-28-180-B	1963-64	1,090	143	750	1,170	50	180-hp Lycoming	1,200	$4,500	$11,500
PA-28-180-B	1965-66	1,975	143	750	1,170	50	180-hp Lycoming	1,200	$4,500	$13,000
PA-28-180-C	1967	642	143	750	1,170	50	180-hp Lycoming	2,000	$4,500	$14,500
PA-28-180-D	1968-69	1,233	143	750	1,250	50	180-hp Lycoming	2,000	$4,500	$16,750
PA-28-180-E, F	1970-71	493	143	750	1,250	50	180-hp Lycoming	2,000	$4,500	$17,750
PA-28-180-G	1972	318	143	750	1,250	50	180-hp Lycoming	2,000	$4,500	$19,000
Challenger	1973	601	141	725	1,035	50	180-hp Lycoming	2,000	$4,500	$20,500
Archer	1974-75	538	141	725	1,035	50	180-hp Lycoming	2,000	$4,500	$23,750
Archer II-181	1976	467	150	740	1,134	48	180-hp Lycoming	2,000	$4,500	$25,500
Archer II-181	1977	607	150	740	1,134	48	180-hp Lycoming	2,000	$4,500	$28,000
Archer II-181	1978	550	150	740	1,134	48	180-hp Lycoming	2,000	$4,500	$29,000
Archer II-181	1979	588	150	740	1,134	48	180-hp Lycoming	2,000	$4,500	$34,000

The Cargo bay *will hold a generous 200 pounds structurally. The louvers aft of the door indicate installation of an air conditioning unit—unique in aircraft of this class.*

about the older, short-wing models as paying out a bit soon for their taste, and not climbing out with sufficient alacrity.

Cockpit Design

The 180s have simple, effective controls like manual flaps, and a sensible handbrake that is probably the best parking brake in the industry. Beginning with the '76 models, Piper added a superb new door latching mechanism that locks the door like a bank vault by means of a massive lever.

Performance

The 180s can be expected to yield 135-140 mph in a top 75 percent cruise, burning about 10 to 11 gph; and 130-135 mph at 65 percent, burning about 8.5 gph. An Archer II *The Aviation Consumer* flew for an evaluation, equipped with full IFR avionics and air conditioning, was still able to carry full fuel, three adults and 104 pounds of baggage, which is pretty good on 180 horses.

Despite that, in retrospect, many owners who are thinking tradeup mention as the bird's biggest shortcoming its slow cruise speed—which is a good 16 mph slower than the 180-hp Tiger.

machine with few sneaky idiosyncrasies. The wide gear stance and low wing provide excellent ground handling, even in high wind situations. A Cherokee 180 is unlikely to sucker a pilot into an inadvertent stall even with the most calloused treatment.

A landing pilot who does not straighten out the rudder prior to landing in a crosswind may, however, get a swerve or ground-loop since the nosewheel is not automatically self centering. Otherwise, Cherokee 180s are a snap to land, though some pilots talk

Owner Comments

"We bought our Cherokee 180 when it was six years old, with 1,700 hours total time. The engine had its original half-inch valves. The salesman assured us that most of these engines would even exceed the 2,000-hour TBO number with no problems. We would find later, to our dismay, that it ain't necessarily so . . .

"The flight performance of the Cherokee 180 is quite good. We never have run out of rudder in crosswind landings. The "Hershey Bar Wing" of the Cherokee gives a couple of interesting flight characteristics—a high sink rate at low airspeeds, and an absence of ground effect when you flare. Power-off descents are quite steep, which is an advantage when you are a little high. An approach speed of 90 mph and 1,500 rpm seems best for us, and we always use full flaps for landing. A speed of 78 mph "across the fence" give the best landing. If you are three mph slower, she'll drop in like a brick; three mph faster, and you'll float an extra hundred yards.

"Rate of climb is marginal in the 180. At full gross you'll only get 600-700 fpm climb at 100 mph IAS at sea level, and you'll be down to 200 fpm at 7,000 feet. You have to keep assuring the controllers that you're still climbing if they've sent you high on an IFR flight.

"As per Lycoming's recommendation, we fly at peak EGT for all cruise flight. Our mechanics clean off the lead "BB's" and rotate our plugs every 50 hours. The plugs still look fine after 400 hours, so we

must be doing something right.

"One problem emerged when we began our instrument training—we discovered that low-wings are notoriously roll-unstable. If we peeked at our charts for more than

Aircraft Investment Value

The resale history of a 1971 Cherokee 180 shows a nearly level curve that gradually rises—the sign of a solid, but not spectacular used-plane investment.

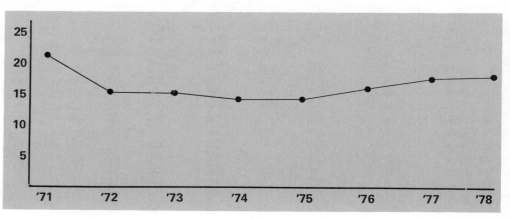

10 seconds (no exaggeration), we would look up at a 30-degree bank angle on the attitude indicator every time.

"We noticed some black powder when we drained our sumps on our first few flights. Then suddenly our left gauge read empty after just having been filled. The fuel float, which is a soft black porous plastic block, came floating to the top of the tank! The previous users had apparently routinely run the left tank dry. This allows the float to vibrate on the sender mounting rod, and to wear out the hole in the float. We have since avoided the problem by never running a tank dry. When we advised Piper of this problem, they thanked us, and sent us two new senders at no charge.

"The blade-type heated pitot tube of the Cherokee 180 doesn't get hot enough to melt off ice that forms in flight. We found we had to turn it on before takeoff to keep the pitot working on flights through snow. Also, we often had to use the alternate static source, due to the static hole in this blade-type device icing over when flying in snow. The pitot hole is also attacked by a mud-daubing bug in summer that plugs it solid at some New England airports.

"Our family really appreciates the large cargo area of the Cherokee 180. We often exceed the cargo capacity of our mother-in-law's Chevy trunk with our Cherokee baggage load. Interior room always seems ample, too. The only thing we don't like is the flimsy baggage door lock on our 1968 model. We have problems with broken keys, and with skin fracture around the lock. We understand that this has been improved on newer models, however.

"The service access for the Cherokee 180 is excellent. We appreciate being able to lift off the whole top cowling for preflight, especially during the bird nesting season. The lower cowling is also easily removed, after a bunch of screws are taken out. All engine components are thereby exposed quite easily for service. A velcro-sealed door in the rear bulkhead allows access to the tail cone. This hatch makes it easy to service the battery, ELT, and remote avionics.

"The large prop spinner caused an unsuspected problem one morning. When our runup revealed an unusual vibration, we taxied back for a closer look. It turned out that a puddle of ice had formed at the bottom of the spinner. We were able to knock it out with a screwdriver and then we continued on our trip. To prevent this, we have since left the prop stopped vertically to allow the water to run out in the winter.

"In four years and 800 hours of use, we had very few recurring problems. The main shock was when we swallowed an exhaust valve at 1,740 hours TT. It happened when we throttled back on approach to our home airport, so our landing was uneventful. After the engine was rebuilt, the Piper asbestos exhaust manifold gaskets blew out in about 20 hours. We installed some "blow-out-proof" ones we saw in *Trade-A-Plane* for 75 cents each. They have lasted over 700 hours so far.

"Annual flat rate for a Cherokee 180 at our local mechanics were $185 (but just went up to $205 in 1978. Our cheapest annual was $225; our worst was $425. The latter included three new tires and tubes, and new spark plugs (now more than $12 each!). We feel luckier than most.

This massive, no-nonsense lever *provides a good, secure door lock on 1976 and later models.*

"We noted the following Cherokee maintenance items:

"Nose strut: required rebuilding twice in four years. The thinly plated tube the seals bear against becomes pitted from sand picked up by the prop when taxiing. Peeling chrome abrades the O-ring seals. The prop clears the ground by only two inches or so when strut is low, so beware. No problems with main struts.

"Grimes beacon: the Grimes rotating tail beacon is a real headache, because of premature bulb failures. The G.E. type 1940 lamps are rated to last 40 hours; but our average is less than five. At $7.50 a bulb, this is nothing to sneeze at. Also, the bulbs are hard to find. Only one lamp ever lasted close to 40 hours. Apparently vibration of the vertical stabilizer causes the filaments to fatigue and break long before they burn out. Newer beacons use a bulb less prone to this problem, we understand. Because the beacon was inoperative such a large percentage of the time, we added a Hoskins belly strobe for supplemental lighting.

"Starter bearing: the starter Bendix in the Cherokee works against a large ring gear, just behind the propeller. This gear also carries the pulley for the alternator drive belt. This is a very nice arrangement, since failures of the alternator or starter cannot damage the engine. With direct-drive alternators, a bearing failure usually breaks gears and contaminates the crankcase with chips and pieces. And starters that engage accessory case drive gears often cause the same problems—a premature major overhaul due to pulverized gears.

"So we forgive the big disadvantage of the front-mounted starter: the Bendix is exposed to the weather, and it takes a beating. It gets water when it rains, plus dirt from the prop-wash. But in spite of this, we have had to tear it down for maintenance only once. The brass shim-stock bearing inside the drive pinion gear had worn out. Piper sells no individual parts for the $50 (!) Bendix. Rather, we paid a machinist $5 to make us a new bearing out of Oillite (oil-filled bronze). No further problems.

Archer panel height *is lower than a Cardinal, higher than a Tiger. The photo shows the visibility level during taxi.*

Traveler/Cheetah

In sheer weight of numbers sold, Gulf-stream American's economy four-placer may be regularly sandbagged by the unbelievable Cessna Skyhawk, and even trail the Piper Warrior by quite a bit, but it has a ferociously loyal band of followers. And they have quite a bit to brag about.

The Travelers and Cheetahs (as models built from 1976 on are called) will scoot past the Cessna and nip the Piper in a race, fly rings around both in terms of deft, light maneuverability and offer nearly unbeatable visibility. On top of that, they provide a distinct sporty alternative, with a roll-back canopy and fold-down rear seat plus zippy ground handling thanks to differential brake steering.

Pilots culling through the market for a 150- or 160-hp economy four-placer will find that the Travelers and Cheetahs match the used-plane prices of the Skyhawk and the Warrior almost dollar for dollar over the years since the line was introduced in 1972. So the choice will have to be based on something else.

Speed and Performance

If it's speed, the Cheetah/Traveler looks good. Although the company brochures tout cruise speeds of up to 146 mph, and users say this is obtainable, most owners report 75 percent power speeds between 135 and 140 mph are more realistic in day-to-day operations.

Thanks to a hike in power from 150 to 160 hp and some fancy new wheel fairings in 1977, Piper boosted the Warrior's cruise from a 10 mph deficit to within a hair of the Cheetah's, at least according to the book.

In range, the Cheetah, with an optional 51 gallons of usable fuel, is equal to or better than its competitors. The earlier Traveler models and standard Cheetahs, however, carry only 37 gallons usable, so they are at a considerable handicap against the Warrior and the Skyhawk.

In carrying ability, the Cheetah gives away only a few pounds of useful load to the Skyhawk, but trails the Warrior by about 86 pounds.

Handling

Traveler and Cheetah owners like to rave about the quick, light controls on their aircraft, and the airplanes get a gold star for ability to tackle potent crosswinds in a landing (NTSB figures suggest beginners have problems, though). But owners almost universally report the flaps are only modestly effective. One pilot went so far as to say they were "nearly useless" in providing a sufficiently steep approach angle to a landing, though they are quite helpful at least in adding drag at higher let-down speeds. According to the books, however, this doesn't seem to translate into longer landing distances over an obstacle. In fact, according to the charts, the Cheetah can get into a slightly shorter field than either the Skyhawk or the Warrior.

On the other hand, the Cheetah needs a longer distance to take off over an obstacle, by 1,500 feet or so. Owners report especially lackluster performance in high density altitude takeoff situations, also.

Ground handling in the Cheetah/Traveler is a joy, as owners tell it, since differential brake steering means a pilot can pivot the bird on a dime for parking in tight spaces. But all that extra braking apparently also eats up brake pads at a fairly high rate (one pilot said his lasted only 100-140 hours), and the free-castoring nosewheels have been known in the past for a tendency to shimmy on takeoff or landing. GA has made several fixes to inhibit this, however.

Naturally, some pilots weaned on conventional nosewheel steering may find the brake steering odd, or even a nuisance, especially when taxiing or taking off in a strong crosswind as the airplane tries to weathervane.

Owners also report the Cheetah/Traveler does not take gracefully to soft- or rough-field operations since the prop clearance is rather small, and a tendency of the airplane to pitch and bob on rough surfaces makes it easier to ding a prop. A shock absorber added in 1977 is designed to diminish this, and it's retrofitable.

The fiberglass main gear, however, is viewed as a low-maintenance item that tends to reduce the severity of botched landings.

Cabin Design

The sliding canopy is great fun in summer because you can taxi with your arm over the side like a convertible. And if you don't mind the great din and blast of air, you can fly with it open. But when it rains, everything gets wet, and people clambering in have to figure a way to do it without getting muddy feet all over the upholstery.

A nifty feature is a folding rear seat back that turns the rear of the cabin into a station wagon loading compartment suitable

The 1977 Cheetah *incorporated the most refinements to the basic model. Good speeds are related not only to good streamlining, but also to nearly rivet-free surfaces, because of bonded metal construction.*

for anything from golf clubs to 10-speed bicycles.

The far rear baggage compartment opening is, however, quite small and inconvenient, and big suitcases will have to be heaved in through the front of the cabin.

Naturally, with the sportiness of the sliding canopy come a few handicaps. Cabin speakers, for example, can't conveniently be mounted on the ceiling, so they are located under the windshield, which causes acoustical problems. Also, since there's no place for ADF sense antennas on top of the airplane, they must be placed underneath, where there is not sufficient fuselage length for good reception. The salvation of the aircraft in this sense was the introduction of ADF radios with combined sense and loop antennas like the King KR 86.

At least one owner also reported that his canopy leaked in the rain. However, we've heard so many complaints about leaking cabins, with high and low wings and doors, that we tend to think the problem is universal.

Human Engineering
Although the Travelers and Cheetahs don't have the Skyhawk's neat, simple fuel system in which both tanks feed automatically, the Gulfstream American aircraft have the next best thing. The fuel selector is right below the throttle pedestal in plain sight of both pilots, and it points to the gauge whose tank it is feeding from.

Also, the Traveler/Cheetah instrument panels have a lower than average profile that allows the pilot to get a superb view over the nose of the aircraft. Oddly, though, short pilots report they have difficulty getting the right combination of pillows to reach the rudder pedals. The front seat latching mechanism also has proved to be a nuisance to some, with one pilot saying the seat tracks had trouble standing up to normal wear and tear. And one of our *Aviation Consumer* pilots had the seat latch handle come off in his hand after repeated wrenches (in an older Traveler) failed to get the seat to track properly.

On older models the slip-ring parking brake was such a failure that some FBOs

As with any good station wagon, *the rear seating area becomes a loading compartment when the seat backs are folded forward.*

were placarding them telling pilots not to use them.

And while we've always liked the push-button starting on the Traveler/Cheetah compared with the sometimes awkward twist-and-push-till-your-fingers-ached method on most aircraft, one pilot reported a strange idiosyncrasy. While he was pushing the button for start, the button stuck in the collar ring, keeping the starter engaged after the engine caught—with disastrous results for the starter.

Model Changes and Improvements
The year 1976 marked the biggest changes in the line as the Traveler evolved into the Cheetah with a better-looking new cowling and a bigger horizontal tail to match that of the 180-hp Tiger, which was introduced the year before. In fact, from the firewall back, the Tiger and Cheetah are identical.

Aerodynamic improvements added about six mph to the airplane's cruise, boosting it from 140 to 146 mph with 75 percent power. The flap effectiveness was improved as well, by an increase in the allowable deflection.

Another host of changes was added in 1977. New soundproofing was incorporated,

with a doubling of all window thickness, making the windshield one-quarter of an inch thick. As a result of a series of wind tunnel tests instituted by Grumman, little cleanup touches were added. A rubber fairing even was placed on the rear edge of the nosegear strut to dampen out drag eddies.

In addition, the nose-strut shock absorber was incorporated, and the weather seal at the canopy-windshield juncture was improved.

In 1978 new more comfortable seating was installed, and so-called flight guard strips —U-joints—were placed on the trailing edges of flaps and elevators to reduce the chances of delamination.

Maintenance
Grumman American, then Gulfstream American, was quick on the uptake to catch those instances where debonding occurred on some models. Rivets were placed in flap corners as a protective measure, and owners report prompt, attentive response from the company on the problem.

An extensive problem also occurred involving deteriorating upholstery, and GA launched a widespread effort to make corrections at its expense.

Model	Year Built	Number Built	Cruise Speed (mph)	Rate of Climb (fpm)	Useful Load (lbs)	Std/Opt Fuel (gals)	Engine	TBO (hrs)	Overhaul Cost	Average Retail Price
AA5 Traveler	1972	154	140	660	929	37	150-hp Lycoming	2,000	$4,000	$13,000
AA5 Traveler	1973	250	140	660	929	37	150-hp Lycoming	2,000	$4,000	$13,500
AA5 Traveler	1974	234	140	660	929	37	150-hp Lycoming	2,000	$4,000	$14,000
AA5 Traveler	1975	193	147	660	929	37	150-hp Lycoming	2,000	$4,000	$15,500
AA5A Cheetah	1976	282	147	660	897	37/51	150-hp Lycoming	2,000	$4,000	$17,000
AA5A Cheetah	1977	240	147	660	897	37/51	150-hp Lycoming	2,000	$4,000	$18,000
AA5A Cheetah	1978	147	147	660	897	37/51	150-hp Lycoming	2,000	$4,000	$21,000
AA5A Cheetah	1979	147	147	660	897	37/51	150-hp Lycoming	2,000	$4,000	$23,000

Grumman American Traveler/Cheetah

On our Airframe and Powerplant Survey, owners report they spend an average of $357 for an annual inspection for their Travelers and Cheetahs. Unscheduled airframe maintenance averaged $263 each year and $97 a year for unscheduled maintenance to the powerplant and accessories.

Among the problems that recur in owner reports are: leaking fuel tanks, peeling paint, valve failure and high oil temperature, nose gear shimmy, bent nosegear forks and cracked nosewheel fairings.

In all, though, most owners seem to feel their airplanes experience lower maintenance problems and costs than other similar makes. Since Gulfstream American halted production, only time will tell whether the line will be continued by a new manufacturer, and how well GA will provide parts backup until then.

Airworthiness Directives
The Travelers and Cheetahs have been hit with about half a dozen ADs since the line came out in '72. The most notable was one in 1976 mandating a GA service bulletin calling for inspections for delamination along the trailing edges of wings, tail and control services, with the installation of "peel rivets" in the corners to prevent separation.

Prospective buyers should be aware of the fact that one particular production run of aircraft during 1974 and 1975 apparently was more severely affected by delamination problems. This is because for a while between April '74 and December '75 a different bonding material and primer combination were used, and these seem to have been more prone to deterioration with age.

Perhaps the most potentially costly to owners was an AD calling for the inspection and replacement of control cables and pulleys for wear, at a cost of up to $375, at the owner's expense.

Others required inspection/replacement of the rudder control bar and replacement of cowl hinge assemblies, and a pair of '77 ADs called for checking of the carburetor heat valve assembly for cracks and the alternate static source to prevent faulty gyro indications.

Modifications
The only STCs we are aware of, aside from those dealing with installation of accessories like autopilots and EGTs, is one by Van's Aircraft (of Forest Grove, Ore.) for fiberglass wheel fairings.

Owners' Association
We understand a Grumman American Aircraft Owners Club is being started up at P.O. Box 641, Gentry, Ark. 72734.

Safety
If any one kind of accident dominates the National Transportation Safety Board roster for Travelers and Cheetahs, it is the overshoot by inexperienced pilots. Time and again on the Safety Board breakdown from 1971 through 1976 Traveler/Cheetah pilots with only from three to 50 hours in the aircraft land long, go off the end of the runway and smash into fences and ditches.

This may reflect the difficulty of low-time pilots transitioning into an aircraft whose flaps provide less of a descent angle

Comparative Safety Record

Model	Fatal Rate*	Accident Rate*
1. Cessna 180	1.3	21.4
2. Cessna 172	1.5	9.0
3. Cessna 206	1.7	13.1
4. Cessna Cardinal	1.8	12.7
5. Piper Cherokee	1.9	10.4
6. Cessna 182	2.5	13.7
7. Beech 19/23/24	2.5	17.7
8. Cherokee Six	2.6	13.6
9. Cessna 170	3.1	27.1
10. Piper Tri-Pacer	3.2	21.3
11. Grumman AA-5 Tiger/Cheetah	3.9	20.2

*Accidents per 100,000 hours

than the average beginning trainer like the Cessna 150 or Cherokee 140.

Second most prominent type of accident is the hard landing, followed by a porpoise and perhaps a groundloop, sometimes with a gear collapse—again usually with pilots who have low time in the aircraft. The problem may be related to the distinctive ground handling characteristics of the airplane with differential brake steering, since loss of control, often during gusty crosswind landing situations, suggests transitioning pilots may still be adjusting to the atypical steering system on the aircraft.

Also evident on the NTSB list is a number of accidents caused when low-time-in-type pilots attempting to take off in high-density-altitude situations stalled or mushed and crashed. The takeoff charts should be carefully checked with this aircraft, as with all low-power four-placers in which the tendency is to fill up all the seats and go, no matter what the density altitude.

There was a handful of fuel exhaustion crashes, two related to what the NTSB said were erratic fuel gauges. The rest were attributed to inattention or poor planning, and in one case the pilot figured the range by the charts but neglected to lean the mixture to obtain the published figures.

As for an overall safety ranking with other aircraft in its class, the Traveler/Cheetah/Tiger line lumped together by the NTSB has a fair to poor accident history, and a very poor fatal accident record.

In figures provided by the Safety Board for the five years from 1972 through 1976, the Grumman American four-placers had an overall accident rate of 20.2 per 100,000 hours flown, which was exceeded only by the Piper Tri-Pacer (21.3), the Cessna 180 (21.4) and the Cessna 170 taildragger (27.1) in the four- to six-place fixed-gear category.

In fatal accidents, the GA aircraft had a figure of 3.9 per 100,000 hours—the worst of nine airplanes listed.

Combination fuel gauge and fuel selector *below throttle quadrant is a top feature. Owners report poor night lighting on some instruments, however.*

Owner Comments

"The cost per hour of operation of my '75 Traveler the past year has been $16.78 per hour. This includes two 100-hour inspections; all repairs including avionics, insurance, ELT battery, main battery, and all service including gas and oil. If $3 per hour is included for engine major escrow, the cost per hour rises to $19.78. If hangar and tie-down fees are included along with taxes, the total cost per hour is $25. I normally fly at 75 percent power which gives a conservative true airspeed of 135 mph. This is roughly 18 cents per mile, which, incidentally, compares with 26.5 cents per miles for my 1975 Olds 88 during the same year for approximately the same miles.

"I personally like the sliding canopy but must admit I do not deliberately fly in the rain—thus no wet problem getting in or out. The longest trip I have flown was when my wife and I let down back seats, put in two ten-speed bikes and flew to San Francisco by way of Wyoming, Montana, Washington and Oregon. It was great fun landing on small trips such as Sun River, Oregon, and enjoying the countryside on our bikes.

"The plane handles great and is very responsive. It has no bad habits and is comfortable enough to fly 3½ hours between fuel stops. I appreciate its styling and the visibility to the outside provided pilot and passengers. It is a neat airplane and for my kind of flying, the only thing I would consider trading it for would be a Grumman Tiger.

"Company back-up has been outstanding. I have experienced cowling hinge problems, control surface bonding separation on one flap and one elevator, and upholstery separation. The company provided the hinge, which was installed at my expense. The company sent a factory rep to examine the interior and control surface edges. Their response was to replace one flap, repair the elevator edge, and install U-channel cuffs on *all* control surface edges as per their 1978 aircraft and following. In addition they replaced the entire interior including all seats and side upholstery. The total cost to me was $50 for freight. Grumman paid for all parts and labor. Labor alone was 24.3 hours.

"One last thing. When I bought the plane it had a nose-wheel shimmy. This was corrected by installing a balanced tire and increasing the tension on the swivel mechanism of the nosewheel."

"In general, I have been very pleased with the Traveler, and I have never regretted selecting it over the other 150-hp choices I considered. The Traveler is faster, easier and more fun to fly, and cheaper to maintain than a Cherokee, Warrior, or Skyhawk.

"Since, however, noise level and fuel consumption seems to increase significantly if you insist on 75 percent power settings, I use 65 percent generally, say, 2400 rpm at 3,500 feet, and I can do around 125 mph—not bad at all for the quieter ride and reduced fuel burn.

"The handling is, very simply, outstanding—the controls are very light and responsive, with sort of a natural feel to them. Add the excellent visibility, and the result is a real fun airplane. Landings are easy, once you get used to the delicate control inputs necessary and learn to pin down approach speeds (it's a little on the slippery side). What's really nice is the landing gear, which is like nobody else's. The laminated fiberglass will absorb a really botched arrival—no thud, no bounce.

"On the other hand, landing on short and/or soft fields can be a little tricky. If a short field does have a genuine, high obstruction on the approach, there's no easy way to come down steeply short of slipping. Even an approach speed of 1.3 V_{SO} produces a relatively flat glide angle, since the flaps are useless. Soft fields are complicated by the very short prop clearance and springy nose gear. I'm leary of digging in the prop if there's any roughness at all on a turf runway.

"For IFR, the range on the 37-gallon Travelers is a little short. Also, the instrument panel has limited room for the fancy IFR stuff. Unless you like Narco avionics, which can effectively use the plentiful 3-1/8-inch holes, you'll be hanging the DME from the OAT gauge. On this subject, I highly recommend the King KR-86 ADF for these planes. Not only is it an excellent unit, it saves a three-inch hole, is tapered at the back of the box for installation at the very top of the radio stack, and optionally has a combined sense-loop antenna, the only thing that works well on these planes.

"The nose wheel tends to shimmy just before rotation and just after landing, and this seems to be due to the nut holding the entire assembly together losing its adjustment. The nose wheel is free-castering, but this seems to be a mixed blessing—park it anywhere you can drop it from a crane, but hell on brake pads, although these are cheap. More significantly, the steering-with-brakes routine is easy, except on ice.

"The newer parking brake arrangement is a definite improvement over the original slip ring device, which was inclined to hang up mechanically. The sunvisor arrangement on these aircraft tends to get broken. Unthinking renters open the canopy with the sunvisor improperly stowed and break it. The visibility in this aircraft is excellent. On the occasion when I fly another make aircraft I feel I have been inflicted with 'tunnel vision.'

"In the early models of the Cheetah were several cases of wheel pants cracking. The original fairing material for the landing gear deteriorated rapidly and would peel away in large pieces. I made two temporary repairs with gray duct tape on as many trips. These old style foam rubber fairings have apparently been improved as I have had no more repairs to make on renting newer models."

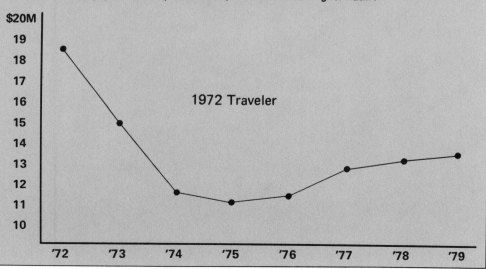

Aircraft Investment Value

The Traveler/Cheetah line shows a classic resale value curve, dropping rapidly, but bottoming out very quickly, in only three years (for the 1972 Traveler we plotted here). The steady climb after 1975 bodes well for used-plane buyers since the aircraft has appreciated in paper value by almost $2,500 since reaching its nadir.

1972 Traveler

Beech Sport/Sundowner

Beech's Models 19 and 23—popularly known as Musketeers, and later christened Sport and Sundowner by Beech—have always been the orphans of the blue-blooded Beechcraft family. While the Bonanza and Baron are sparkling performers that exude "class" and command high resale values, the Musketeers are frumpy-looking, slow and not much in demand by anybody. As a result, they can be purchased at very low prices. If you're looking for a big, roomy airplane at a very low initial cost, a used Musketeer, Sport or Sundowner may be a reasonable choice.

History

There are two basic series of Musketeers: the 19 and 23. Both are basically identical except for the engine; the 23 series has powerplants from 160-180 horsepower and is nominally a four-seater, while the Model 19 is equipped with a 150-hp Lycoming and is limited to two people under most conditions. (A retractable 200-hp version, the Model 24, is also available, but this report will deal only with the fixed-gear 19 and 23 models.)

The first Musketeer appeared in 1963, a straight Model 23 with a 160-hp Lycoming. (The first Cherokee, also 160-hp, had appeared two years before.) More than 500 Musketeers were sold that first year. In 1964, Beech inexplicably switched engines, a move it probably regrets now. The 1964 Musketeer, the first of the A23s, had an oddball 165-hp Continental engine called the IO-346-A. (It was basically an IO-520 with two cylinders chopped off.) As far as we know, the IO-346 has never been used on any other airplane, before or since. It was a "miserable engine," in the words of one overhauler we consulted, and tended to run hot in the Musketeer.

The A23 with the IO-346 was built until 1968, when the 180-hp Lycoming-powered B23 replaced it. The low esteem in which used-plane buyers hold

the Continental-powered A23 is reflected in the bluebook price of the 1968 A23: only $10,000, compared to $11,500 for the 1968 B23. What a difference an engine makes.

Meanwhile, in 1966, Beech had introduced a 150-hp trainer version called the Model 19 Sport, which was a two-seater with a gross weight of 2,200 pounds (150 pounds less than that of the A23).

In 1970, both models were given new designations: the C23 and B19. The C23 had a higher gross weight, 2,400 pounds, and the original gross weight of the B19 Sport was 2,250 pounds. But the FAA discovered that the 2,250-pound B19 could not meet the minimum certification requirements for climb performance—much less its optimistic book figures—at that weight. So it issued AD 73-25-4, which limited gross weight of all B19s built up to that time (serial numbers MB-481 through -616) to 2,000 pounds. If a special Beech kit was installed, gross could be raised back up to 2,150. (All Sports built after 1973 incorporated the

mods and had gross weights of 2,150 pounds.) If you're shopping for a 1970-73 model, be sure the Beech kit has been installed. Also, owners of '66-'69 models would be wise to limit their gross weight to 2,150, although it's not required.

The C23 and B19 have continued in production largely unchanged since 1970. The B19, which had been Beech's primary trainer, was discontinued in 1979, however, to make way for the Skipper.

Performance

In a word, miserable. *Aviation Consumer* readers report true airspeeds in the 115-125 mph range for the 180-hp models and perhaps 105-110 for the 150-hp Sports. Considering that a 180-hp Grumman Tiger can reach 160 mph, those are pretty dismal numbers.

Perhaps an even more serious performance shortcoming is rate of climb. The Sport, in particular, borders on the dangerous in hot weather. One Sport pilot reports, "Hot weather causes the rate of climb to fall to as low as 400

As a trainer, *the Sport has two main handicaps: relatively high rental cost and something it shares with the Sundowner, a terrible NTSB record of hard landings and overshoots.*

fpm, even out of low-lying fields such as Teterboro." Another writes, "I have noticed at or near gross weight, my Musketeer falls off in performance in hot weather much more than the book shows." One Beech dealer at an airport with a short runway was forced to halt training operations in the summer because the takeoff margins over the trees were simply too close for comfort.

Payload and Range
Both the 19 and 23 models have huge 57-gallon fuel supplies (some models of the Sport have only 52). With engines that burn 8-10 gph, it's obvious that the Musketeers will stay in the air longer than most people care to ride in little airplanes. Since the planes are so slow, however, actual range is not as outstanding, although still very good for planes of this category. The 180-hp models should fly up to 600 miles with reserve; the 150-hp Sport will cover about the same distance, but take longer to do it.

Unfortunately, fuel capacity is usually limited by weight considerations. The 23 models generally have a useful load (equipped) of around 900 pounds; thus four adults and 100 pounds of luggage will leave enough for only 20 gallons of fuel. To use all 57 gallons, it's usually necessary to limit cabin load to about 550 pounds—three good-sized adults.

The Sport's equipped useful load generally runs around 600-650 pounds, or two people and full fuel. But some

Sport operators have found that even this modest load is often too much for reasonable climb performance in the summer.

Handling Characteristics
By all reports, the Musketeer is a nice-flying airplane. Typical owner comments: "Very good handling and stable. . .big-plane feel, excellent handling. . .solid feel, good control response." The Musketeers have surprisingly light ailerons and well-coordinated rudders. There are no major trim changes with gear or flap extension, although we've recieved reports that the longitudinal trim stability is not good in some airplanes, perhaps because of the stabilator.

The stall characteristics of the airplane are rather abrupt, and there is little stall warning. "When she quits flying, she really quits," one reader wrote.

The Musketeers do have one rather nasty characteristic on landing. They have a pronounced "porpoising" tendency, particularly with flaps down, and many a student has performed rather stupendous multiple-bounce acts before gasping spectators. This characteristic, combined with the abrupt and emphatic stall, makes the Musketeers the all-time champions in the hard-landing league. (See the "Safety" section for details.) Not surprisingly, there have been several ADs on the landing gear and a major one on the wing attach fitting. Obviously, the

Unique landing gear design *is never seen with wheel pants, despite the needed boost in speed they might offer.*

landing gear should be meticulously checked before purchase.

Creature Comforts
Here is where the Musketeers shine. The cabin is huge, particularly the rear seats, and owners rave about comfort and quality of the interior. Unfortunately, the Sport usually won't carry enough weight to put people in the back seats, but the front cockpit is also much roomier than comparable two-seaters, particularly the Cessna 152. The penalty paid for the big cabin, of course, is extra weight and frontal area, which no doubt play a large role in the airplane's poor performance.

Model	Year Built	Number Built	Cruise Speed (mph)	Rate of Climb (fpm)	Useful Load (lbs)	Fuel (gals)	Engine	TBO (hrs)	Overhaul Cost	Average Retail Price
19	1966-67	288	131	680	736	52	150-hp Lycoming	2,000	$4,000	$ 7,500
A19	1968-69	192	131	680	736	52	150-hp Lycoming	2,000	$4,000	$ 8,000
B19	1970-72	76	131	680	900	52	150-hp Lycoming	2,000	$4,000	$ 9,000
B19	1973	63	131	680	900	52	150-hp Lycoming	2,000	$4,000	$ 9,750
B19	1974	108	131	680	900	52	150-hp Lycoming	2,000	$4,000	$10,500
B19	1975	47	131	680	900	57	150-hp Lycoming	2,000	$4,000	$12,000
B19	1976	37	131	680	900	57	150-hp Lycoming	2,000	$4,000	$13,000
B19	1977	48	131	680	900	57	150-hp Lycoming	2,000	$4,000	$15,000
B19	1978	37	131	720	1,000	60	150-hp Lycoming	2,000	$4,000	$16,000
23	1963	554	128	880	1,025	60	160-hp Lycoming	1,500	$5,000	$ 8,000
A23II	1964-65	345	138	880	1,025	60	165-hp Continental	1,500	$5,000	$ 8,500
A23-AII	1966	93	178	880	1,025	60	165-hp Continental	1,500	$5,000	$ 9,500
A23-AIII	1968	25	138	880	1,025	60	165-hp Continental	1,500	$5,000	$10,000
Custom III	1967	73	138	880	1,025	60	180-hp Lycoming	2,000	$4,500	$ 9,500
B23 Custom	1968-69	178	138	880	1,025	60	180-hp Lycoming	2,000	$4,500	$11,500
C23 Custom	1970-71	176	138	792	1,025	52	180-hp Lycoming	2,000	$4,500	$13,750
C23 Sundowner	1972-73	72	143	792	1,025	52	180-hp Lycoming	2,000	$4,500	$14,750
Sundowner	1974	108	143	792	1,025	52	180-hp Lycoming	2,000	$4,500	$17,500
Sundowner	1975	147	143	792	1,025	52	180-hp Lycoming	2,000	$4,500	$19,500
Sundowner	1977	104	143	792	1,025	57	180-hp Lycoming	2,000	$4,500	$23,000
Sundowner	1978	113	143	792	1,025	57	180-hp Lycoming	2,000	$4,500	$27,500
Sundowner	1979	142	143	792	1,025	57	180-hp Lycoming	2,000	$4,500	$36,500

Beech Sport/Sundowner

Safety

The Musketeer has a rather mediocre safety record—significantly poorer than similar aircraft such as the Cessna Skyhawk and Piper Cherokee. The fatal accident rate of the 19, 23 and 24 series combined during the period 1972-76 was 2.5 per 100,000 flight hours. The comparable figure for the Skyhawk was just 1.5, and the Cherokee came in with a 2.0 fatal accident rate. The Musketeer series also fares poorly in terms of all accidents, with a rate of 17.6 per 100,000 hours. The Skyhawk's overall rate is just 9.1; the Cherokee's 10.4.

Close examination of NTSB accident records reveals that the Musketeer's weak point is landings. It ranks worst of all 33 aircraft for which the NTSB gathered statistics in the "hard landing" category, with a 3.50 rate, nearly five times higher than both the Skyhawk and Cherokee. (Thus, nearly 20 percent of all Musketeer accidents are hard-landing mishaps.)

The Musketeer series rates very poor in overshoots and groundloop accidents. It has a groundloop rate higher than any other nosewheel aircraft now in production, and an overshoot rate second only to the Grumman AA-5 series. Obviously, if you plan to buy one of the little Beechcrafts, you'd better be sharp on your landings.

Resale Value

The Musketeer, Sundowner and Sport are notorious for their poor resale value. New aircraft decline rapidly in value, and the market for older models, particularly the Continental-powered airplanes, is sluggish. Several used-plane dealers have told us that the *Aircraft Price Digest* "bluebook" figures for the Musketeers are too high; but even the APD numbers are not encouraging.

For example, a 1975 180-hp Model 23 Sundowner cost $31,000 new and four years later was worth $21,000 in the bluebook, 68 percent of its original value. By comparison, a 1975 Piper Archer (also 180 hp) cost $28,100 new and was worth $25,750—fully 92 percent of its original value. As another example, a 1970 Sport and a 1970 Skyhawk both sold new for about $17,000. In 1979 the Skyhawk was worth $13,500; the Sport only $10,000. (These are all "Bluebook" figures, remember; the actual market value of the Beechcrafts is reportedly even less.)

Three of a kind: *Sport, Sundowner and Sierra all have basically the same cabin and wings and progressively more windows. These were the '76 Bicentennial models.*

One reader writes that he purchased a slightly used 1976 Sundowner in late 1976 for $28,000. Eighteen months later, he decided to sell it, hoping to get the bluebook *wholesale* price of $20,000. After getting no interest at all from anybody in his area, he called Beech headquarters and asked for a list of Beech dealers. He called every Beech dealer east of the Mississippi, and the best offer he got was $14,500. After asking his bank for help, he was finally able to unload it for $16,500 after six months of effort. "Bluebook" retail value was supposedly $24,000. One Wisconsin aircraft broker sums it up, "Resale value of the airplane is horrible."

One reason for the sluggish Musketeer market is the fact that virtually all new airplanes are sold to captive Beech Aero Clubs, which are required to buy them and must replace them every three years. Thus, there is a constant forced flow of used Sports and Sundowners into the used-plane market, and not many people who want to buy them. Beech dealers certainly don't want to buy used ones; they have enough trouble getting rid of their own three-year old aircraft.

Modifications

We're aware of no major STCed airframe or engine modifications available for the 19 and 23 series—not even a set of wheel pants to boost the anemic speeds. (That's because of the knuckle-action trailing-beam linkage.) Nor is there an owner's club, such as that for the Bonanza. The population of Musketeers is low compared to that of Skyhawks and Cherokees, and Musketeer owners don't tend to be the rich, enthusiastic types who own Bonanzas. As a result, there probably aren't enough potential customers to entice many budding STC modifiers to come up with Musketeer mods.

Summing up

The plusses of the airplane are room, handling, sturdy construction and good quality; the negatives are dismal performance and a poor safety record, particularly landing accidents. Apparently most people believe the negatives outweigh the positives; resale value is very low. But this, of course, works to the advantage of the pilot who doesn't care much about performance and safety, or who wants a large cabin at any sacrifice.

Owner Comments

"I flew a 165-hp Musketeer for 250 hours. It lacked climb performance at gross on warm days, but delivered block speeds of 120 mph at less than nine gph, and with 60 gallons of fuel, had more range than I did.

"Although slow for the horsepower, it is superbly comfortable, and has a solid feel and good control response. Crosswind performance is excellent. Go-arounds may be initiated with full flaps with little loss of climb performance. Landings are easy, but tend to be long if speed is not controlled."

"The Musketeer is a rugged aircraft. The dimensions of its parts (wheels, spars, frame, etc.) inspire a feeling of security in both the pilot and passengers. The quality of its construction is apparent to even the lay observer.

"There are several minor areas of criticism. The door latch is poor, and there is no safety latch to insure secure closure. I have had the door pop open on two occasions during takeoff before I learned to double check it. The fuel management system is complicated, since the left tank pumps directly into the engine while the right tank pumps both into the engine and into the left tank. Even though I have always found parts available, I have found them to be extremely expensive."

"My partner and I own a 1965 Beech Musketeer A-23 with the 165 hp fuel-injected Continental. We have had the plane one year.

"*Performance:* Slow. For flight planning, I use 100 knots.

"*Handling:* Big-plane feel and fairly stable. When she wants to quit flying, she quits; on landings I keep airspeed up to 80 mph without flaps. Landings with flaps, it wants to balloon and is very light on gear; brakes will just slide till flaps dumped.

"*Maintenance:* Total 1978 expenses, including annual, were $1,368 for 150 hours tach time. We have a few problems that still need taking care of, such as a new door hinge.

"*Comfort:* Reason I bought the plane over 172 or Piper is size of cabin. A little noisy, but all planes this vintage are noisy.

"*Parts availability:* A joke. Beech thinks they are gold-plated and waits until they get an order for at least 50 of an item to ask someone if they want to build the parts.

"*Backup:* The local Beech dealer won't talk to you unless you have a new Bonanza or King Air."

"My Musketeer was a 1963 Model with the 160-hp Lycoming engine. It was a very good-handling, stable airplane. However, I bought it mainly for its longer range than an older 172 I owned. It would carry 60 gallons of fuel.

"Shortly after I purchased it, I lost the left main gear while landing. Since then (1977) an A.D. has been issued on those models, having the gear inspected for possible cracks. I flew it for approximately two years after that incident and had very few maintenance problems.

"The Musketeer was never known as a speedy airplane, but I feel it is roomier and more comfortable than any other aircraft in its class. The visibility from the cockpit is excellent. It is also very capable in cross-wind landings because of its extremely wide gear."

"I have a 1975 Beechcraft Sundowner with 635 hours on it. I have been basically very satisfied with this aircraft, and particularly with the attention to quality and detail that Beechcraft is well known for. The handling characteristics are that of a heavier and more stable aircraft and are most satisfactory for fairly long-distance, cross-country flights. The performance is somewhat less than comparable to other 180-horsepower airplanes, but I feel that the degree of comfort, headroom, excellent ventilation and visibility, plus the access of two doors, is worth the slight decrease in speed.

"I find that at 65 to 70 percent power, at all altitudes up to and around 9,000 feet, I consistently operate on nine gallons per hour with a true airspeed of about 122 to 125 mph.

"Maintenance has not been much of a problem at all, and the average cost of an annual inspection runs about $290. The only major complaint I have had is that this past winter, large areas of paint came off the airframe. After corresponding with Beechcraft, they agreed to pay half the cost of a new paint job, though the plane was well out of warranty. I thought this was a good representation of Beechcraft's concern for the quality of their products."

"In 1976 I purchased an IFR '76 Sundowner with 500 hours on the engine for $28,000. In 1½ years I put 600 hours on the aircraft with no more than the normal mechanical problems. Spring of 1978 I decided to sell and called several dealers. For months the aircraft was left at various dealers to be sold on consignment.

"Bluebook price was $19,500—$24,000, and I would have settled for anything close to the bottom end. Towards the end of the summer of 1978 I began to worry and called Ronson Beechcraft (Trenton), Beechcraft East and Suburban Beech. All showed little interest. When I visited Surburban Beech, he refused to bid on my aircraft, saying that he already had more than enough Sundowners in inventory.

"It was now late August, with not even one offer for the airplane. I then called the Beech factory in Kansas for their ideas. They promptly sent me a list of Beech Dealers. I called every Beech dealer from Atlanta to Maine to offer my airplane. Maine Beechcraft offered me $14,500. (By the way, they still had not sold their 1976 Bicentennial Sundowner, which they had been trying to sell for over a year.)

"After several further calls to Beech, they finally agreed that the Sundowner was not the most marketable aircraft around. They said that I could get a fair price if I traded up on a new Beech product.

"In final desperation, I contacted the bank where the airplane was financed. Explaining the situation to them, I asked if they could use their influence to get the aircraft sold to one of the dealers whose inventory they finance. After several months, the aircraft was finally sold to a dealer for $16,500. I had to pay the bank an additional $3,500 on my loan.

"The bank was surprised with what they found in trying to sell the Sundowner, and stated that they would hesitate to finance any Sundowners or Sports in the future."

Double-door entrance *convenience leading to a superb, roomy cabin are chief virtues of the Sundowner, according to most pilots.*

Cessna 180

Although usually thought of as a bushplane, the Cessna 180 has the kind of versatility that makes it anything but an anachronism, despite its tail-gear configuration.

It might be classified as a Skylane without a tricycle gear, since the Cessna 180 Skywagon has the same engine and nearly equal weight and performance. Most buyers select this airplane, which is still in production, and has been since 1953, because they have a specialized use in mind, such as skydiving, or flying from floats or skis or wheels out of short, rough fields.

A total of 5,762 have been built through 1976. Though production of the model has never again reached the highs of the early 1950s, when 600 to 800 were built each year, the line seems to be making a slow comeback from the 1971 low of 56 aircraft. In 1979, 116 were built.

Value

It would appear that this aircraft holds its value fairly well over the years. The original '53 models are reported going for an average price of $15,000 equipped, which is only about $1,000 less than they went for new from the factory, equipped.

In fact, the 180 traditionally is worth more than its sibling 182 for same-year models. Example: although you can probably find a used 1965 model Skylane for about $18,000, a comparable 180 would most likely go for $19,000, even though they have the same powerplant.

Although the taildragger does not handle quite as well as the Skylane from paved runways, it is, in general, considered a fairly benign example of the species, not given to great treachery or unusual ground-looping tendencies. However, it can be a bit of a handful in a strong gusty crosswind. An optional crosswind landing gear was offered in 1967.

The strut-braced four-placer is powered either by a 225-hp Continental O-470-A in its earliest configuration, or a 230-hp O-470-K, -L, -R or -U engine in later models. All but the -U version use 80 octane, incidentally, consuming this at a rate of about 11 gph when the throttle is set to 65 percent power.

History

There have been no dramatic changes in the Cessna 180 model since its introduction in 1953. The gross weight went up twice, however; it went up 100 pounds with the 180A in 1957 and went up another 150 pounds in the 1964 G model as an optional six-seat configuration was offered along with an extra side window. Then with the 1973 J model a cambered leading edge was added to the wing, which improved low-speed handling characteristics. The '74 model introduced optional skylights and lower door windows.

Standard fuel capacity for the 180 was 55 gallons to begin with: then this was raised to 65 in 1964 along with the upped gross weight. At the same time, optional fuel of 84 gallons was offered. The 180 models have simple, easy-to-manage fuel systems with "left," "right" and "both" tank selection positions.

Bush Operations

The main justification for the 180 naturally centers around its ability to operate in rough or unfinished fields. Like most Cessna singles, it has a sturdy set of "spring" gear struts that can take a lot of abuse. The tailwheel configuration also creates less drag in high grass or sand or snow for takeoff, and in the three-point attitude the prop arc is given a bit more ground clearance.

Just about the only competitors to the 180 of a fairly contemporary design are the Helio Courier and the Maule. The Helio is the most "exotic" STOL aircraft of the bunch, with its special low-speed control devices. The Maule, of course, is fabric covered.

While the Cessna 180 is no slouch in getting in and out of rough fields, it offers "STOL" performance only a mite better than its sister ship, the tricycle-gear Skylane. Though it would appear the tail-dragger would have a bit of an edge in other performance categories since it has one less drag-producing gear strut hanging out in the breeze, the Skylane enjoys a small margin in cruise speed and in useful load.

Cabin Capacity

Since loading flexibility is supposed to be the Cessna 180's forte, it has easily removable seats and yard-wide doors on either side of the cabin, though it lacks the extra convenience of a double rear-door arrangement like the Cessna Stationair. There is also an extended rear compartment, added in 1967. It is big enough to hold the center passenger seats when folded up, along with the rear passenger seats—or 50 pounds of cargo, provided the weight and balance limits haven't been overreached.

Like its stablemate, the Skylane, the Model 180, later called the Skywagon, is a good load carrier. With full standard fuel, it can be counted on to haul four 170-pounders and still have enough useful load left over to take on 100 pounds or more of baggage,

A flying truck, *the 180 comes without wheel pants, Omnivision or stylishly swept tail.*

depending on the amount of accessory equipment on board.

It will then offer a range of about 470 nm, including taxi, takeoff and a 45-minute reserve.

Airworthiness Directives

The Model 180 has had a fairly peaceful AD career through the years. Only a handful were issued, and none of these was a real bummer. Probably the most energetic one was issued in 1973 and affected several braced-wing Cessna models. It required replacement of defective wing-spar attachment fittings, and the full cost was borne by the company.

By the same token, there have been no major problems with the powerplant. At most, an AD in 1963 required valve replacement at overhaul time.

Safety

Despite the presumably higher exposure to mischief that any taildragger used for bush operations might have, the Cessna 180 has an excellent safety record. In fact, it was credited with the best (lowest) fatal accident rate of 33 different makes and models of aircraft in a special accident study conducted by the NTSB. It ranked about in the middle in terms of its overall accident rate, fatal and nonfatal.

When compared with the other 32 aircraft in the one area where it might be expected to have a problem—ground loops —the Cessna 180 was ranked eighth worst. It also showed up better than half the other aircraft in the hard-landing category. And despite the natural tendency of pilots to try to get 180s in and out of short fields, the aircraft was rated among the two least likely to be involved in an undershoot accident, and among a handful least likely to crack up in an overshoot.

Modifications

The most extensive upgrading mod available for the Cessna 180 is probably the Robertson STOL package. There are three main alterations involved: installation of a cambered leading edge to the wing, placing a stall fence on top of the wing between the flaps and ailerons and incorporation of a "drooping" aileron system that works in conjunction with the flaps.

These changes drop the takeoff distance over a 50-foot obstacle from 1,205 feet to 710 feet and the landing distance over 50 feet from 1,355 feet to 688 feet. They also lower the approach speed from 70 to 47 mph and cut the stall to about 37 mph.

The price is $3,820 for 180J 1973 and later models, which already have a Cessna-installed cambered leading edge, and $5,170 for earlier models.

Robertson Aircraft Corporation, 839 West Perimeter Road, Renton, Wash. 98055.

Another modification designed to get a little more efficiency out of the Cessna 180 wing is offered by B&M Aviation in the form of aileron and flap well gap seal kits. The kit price is $140. Installation usually takes about 12 hours of labor.

B&M Aviation, 2048 Airport Way, Bellingham, Wash. 98225.

Optional cubbyhole *in the rear can be used to store the seats when cargo is hauled.*

Owner Comments

"Some of the early ones had solid tailwheels, which were just wretched. They were real vibrating horrors. When I flew them down in Mexico we had a wonderful brake modification. Our mechanic would cut pucks out of old truck brake shoes, and believe me, GMC made a far better brake puck than Goodyear did.

"On short-field landings, the best technique is to come in real tail-low, touch it down, dump the flaps and stand on the brakes and shove the yoke full forward. You sort of hop, skip and jump for about 200 feet, the tail comes down with a resounding bang, and there you are. You couldn't possibly take off in the same distance, even with a JATO bottle.

"We regularly fly way over gross. Forty-eight gallons of fuel, 200 pounds for me, plus five Mexicans at 150 each, plus 100 kilos of other stuff. The tires looked underinflated and the gear was bowed, but it always got off all right, even at our field elevation of 6,000 feet. But the takeoff was definitely a prolonged and dream-like affair.

"You want to check them closely for ground-loop damage. All the old ones have been around once or twice. Look for loose rivets where the gear goes into the fuselage. You may have a gear that's been improperly replaced and is out of line. That's quite common.

"Anybody who consistently tries to three-point a 180 is either a fool or a genius. People who try that usually end up riding bucking horses. It skips and hops and bounces all over the place.

"A 180 spins beautifully, loops nicely and rolls reasonably well.

"Never had any fuel cell trouble, never had any engine trouble or prop problems, either Hartzell or McCauley

"If the plane is getting reasonable use, and there's nothing major wrong with it, an annual costs about $350 to $400."

"Mine was a 1953 model. The A models, '53 through '55, had big problems with the oil coolers. The temperature gauges went right up to the red line after takeoff and just sat there. A mechanic told me that Continental's fix was a blast tube out of the temperature bulb. In the old ones with the oil cooler that lies on its side, you had to be damn careful about long

Model	Year	Number Built	Average Retail Price	Cruise Speed (mph)	Rate of Climb (fpm)	Useful Load (lbs)	Fuel Std/Opt (gals)	Engine	TBO (hrs)	Overhaul Cost
180	1953-58	N/A	$16,000	157	1,110	1,010	55	225/230-hp Continental	1,500	$4,800
180	1959-61	1,085	$18,000	160	1,130	1,175	65/84	230-hp Continental	1,500	$4,800
180	1965-70	729	$20,500	162	1,090	1,105	65/84	230-hp Continental	1,500	$4,800
180	1973-74	208	$26,000	162	1,100	1,152	65/84	230-hp Continental	1,500	$4,800
180	1975	235	$28,000	162	1,100	1,152	61/80	230-hp Continental	1,500	$4,800
180	1976-77	283	$32,500	162	1,100	1,152	61/80	230-hp Continental	1,500	$4,800
180	1978	93	$36,000	162	1,100	1,152	61/80	230-hp Continental	1,500	$4,800
180	1979	115	$40,000	162	1,100	1,152	61/80	230-hp Continental	1,500	$4,800

hot climbouts because you got severe oil temperature problems, which could lead to shortened overhaul life and catastrophic failures, although nothing ever happened to me.

"I have quite a few hours with the 225, and it's a good engine. It's definitely more economical than the 230. In normal cruise you can run it at 11 or 11½ gallons per hour. I could have run it even leaner, but there was that cooling problem.

"When we got 'em really clean, with normal loads—say two or three people—and full tanks—I flight-planned at 145 mph. Anybody who claims they cruise around at 160 is full of it. The 230s don't go any faster, and they burn 12½ to 13."

"The 180 has cowl flaps and they were forever breaking, coming off, and cracking. There's no such thing as a Cessna cowl flap that works reliably for a long period of time. They just vibrate too much, and then the linkage tears out. Overall, though, they were very low maintenance airplanes. I had no complaints at all.

"The old 225 engine had a different timing than the 230, and sometimes we'd get one timed wrong at an annual, and it would run rough as hell. It's a fairly common mistake that mechanics make in the older models.

"It's very demanding to land. I consider it harder to land than my Staggerwing. For one thing, it has lousy ailerons, especially at low speeds. With the 180 in a gusty crosswind, I get the feeling I'm about three twists of the wheel behind the airplane. I don't like that at all in a tailwheel airplane.

"They are definitely rugged. A friend of mine hit a tree on takeoff once, bent one gear back and broke the main spar on the right side. He was 100 miles from the nearest mechanic, so he spliced the spar with a coconut log, lashed a piece

of corrugated tin roofing over the broken leading edge, tied the gear on with bailing wire and flew home."

"I had a '64 model, and a lot of those airplanes were pretty doggy around the engine compartment. Things were very tight in there, and the exhaust system, being very complicated, gave us a lot of headaches. The single exhaust systems were apparently a lot better. My mechanic charges me a flat rate of 16 hours labor for an annual, plus discrepancies.

"Watch out you don't get one that's been used for hauling parachute jumpers. So many are used that way, and they tend to break a lot of cylinders because of the constant full-power climbing followed by power-off glides. Those jump pilots really beat hell out of the airplanes."

"The original Goodyear brakes were terrible. Anybody who had any brains put Clevelands on them.

"I thought the '56 and '57 models were the best that I flew. (Latest one I've flown is a '64.) They were lighter and seemed to climb better."

"If you're looking to buy one, you have to watch out for the worm gear arrangement in the horizontal stabilizer trim. It was always working loose. One of the first things to do on any used 180 is give the stabilizer a hefty shake. It was a pretty expensive job to tighten it up.

Since the 180 is an immensely popular floatplane, we have contacted owners of float-equipped 180s and included the following comments:
"One thing to look for is corrosion or damage to the floats. If they need bottoms on them, it's real easy to spend $5,000 to $7,000. That's normal for

The 180's milieu: *turf, grass, unprepared fields.*

rebuilding a set of floats.

"Corroded fuselage skins are another big problem. Look around the rivets and the seams.

"One thing you should be very careful about buying a used 180 floatplane: when it comes out of the factory, it has a special factory corrosion-proofing package, but some people will take a standard 180 and put it on floats, and they're not corrosion-proofed. They don't have the stainless steel cables, zinc-chromated interiors and so forth. You should be very sure it's a factory seaplane. There's really no satisfactory way of corrosion-proofing except to do it at the factory."

"Be careful about previous submersion. If it's been submerged and restored correctly, then you're okay, but not more than one out of ten is done right. And very often there's no record of submersion. A guy will flip it over, hose it off and try to sell it real quick. We've run into that problem a lot down in Louisiana. Inspect for silt up inside the headliner, behind the panel and places like that, since those places are hard to wash out quickly.

"There will sometimes be wrinkles in the skin around the firewall if the airplane has been landed hard.

"You can count on a float-equipped 180 for about 120 miles per hour. The newer ones are a little faster, and some people will pull more power, but for a normal 65 percent cruise, 120 is the best you'll get with a float-equipped airplane. Fuel flow at that speed runs right around 12 gallons per hour."

PERFORMANCE SPECIFICATIONS FLOAT-EQUIPPED CESSNA 180

Gross Weight	2,950 lbs.
Standard Empty Weight	1,850 lbs. (Amphibious floats 2,110 lbs.)
Standard Useful Load	1,100 lbs. (Amphibious floats 840 lbs.)
Cruising Speed	147 mph
Service ceiling	16,000 feet
Rate of climb	990 fpm
Takeoff run	1,280 feet
Landing run	735 feet

Buyers of used 180 floatplanes *should check for factory corrosion proofing and a history free of submersion.*

Thanks to Belford D. Maule, authentic aircraft bargains still do exist, in the form of the M-4 and M-5 series of high-wing taildraggers. With the price of new aircraft shooting out of sight, and the cost of used planes steadily rising with the tide of inflation, the Maules represent a relatively inexpensive alternative.

Since many of the older Maules are powered by Franklin engines, a shadow had been cast on the future maintainability of the aircraft after Franklin went out of business in this country and was bought by the Polish company, Pezetel. However, moves by Pezetel to resume the supply of engines and parts to the United States throw a new light on the marketability of old Maules.

And for anyone willing to accept the design rationale of the Maules, including a fabric-covered tubular steel fuselage and tailwheel configuration, some rather impressive savings of around 40 percent can be registered over comparably powered Cessnas and Pipers.

History

The first M-4 saw the light of day in the 1950s in Jackson, Mich., as a one-of-a-kind designed by B. D. Maule, who at the time was better known for other aircraft products like tailwheels. He certificated the aircraft in 1961, calling it the BEE-DEE M-4, but later christened it the Jetasen. The company then moved to Spence Field at Moultrie, Ga.

The first M-4 had the same 145-hp Continental engine as the Cessna 172. In 1965 that was dropped in favor of the bigger 210-hp Cont. IO-360, which in one form or another has been available, on and off, up to the present in various Maules. In 1967, however, a 220-hp Franklin engine was introduced, with a 180-hp Franklin offered in 1970 as an alternate powerplant. Only a handful of the 180-hp models were built, however, in 1970 and '71; and in 1975 the last 220 Franklin

bowed out as Franklin went overseas.

In its place in 1977 the Lycoming O-540 with 235 hp was made available. Then in 1979 the universally popular 180-hp Lyc. O-360 made its debut in the Maules, followed in 1980 by a turbocharged Lycoming IO-360 with 210 hp.

Aside from a continuing series of engine switches, the only significant change in the Maule design took place in 1974 when the M-5 appeared, with an enlarged vertical and horizontal tail along with greater-span flaps—both designed to enhance slow-flight and short-field capability. In addition, the fuel capacity was raised from 42 gallons to 65 gallons.

Powerplant Dilemma

The prospective Maule buyer might well throw up his hands at the prospect of selecting the best engine-airframe combination from the bewildering array available. Until recently, the dilemma was heightened because the most highly regarded engines in the older Maules—the Franklins—were out of production, and the supply of parts left over from the inventory auction in 1975 had an unpleasantly finite future.

Two main parts suppliers for Franklins have been serving the market: the Carl Baker Co. in Van Nuys, Calif. (213-786-3120) and George J. Heinley in Lake Placid, Fla. (813-465-4324). Baker had bought up the lion's share of the inventory at the '75 auction; Heinley is an old Franklin hand who's been a company distributor for some 25 years. But even with both of these organizations, the supply of some items like cylinders and dampers became really tight.

In 1980, however, Pezetel, through Melex USA in Raleigh Durham, N.C. (919-828-7645) and Seaplanes, Inc. in Vancouver, Wash. (206-694-6287) has resumed engine parts delivery for the 220-hp Franklin and some others, with prospects for complete engine deliveries in the future, now that Poland has received certification on the engines.

How does the Franklin 220 compare with the Continental 210? People intimately familiar with both tell us the Franklin is a smoother-running powerplant that is easier to maintain and more fuel economical. And of course the Lycoming 235 and 180 added to the line in 1979 are perennial

Standard Maule demo takeoff, *lightly loaded. Flaps are two-position; pilots report ailerons lack sufficient authority at low speeds.*

Safety Record

Despite the Maule's reputation as an "easy to fly" taildragger, a National Transportation Safety Board runout of accident briefs for the five years 1974-78 shows a disproportionate number of groundloops and swerves in the aircraft. We tallied 38 of these, one of them fatal.

Common problems were loss of directional control and improper compensation for wind conditions—often by pilots with little time in Maules or taildraggers.

The nature of the Maule as a bush machine also placed the aircraft in quite a few hazard situations, with pilots presumably tackling rougher fields and less suitable off-airport landing sites more often than normal. As a result there was a significant number of hard obstacles on bad terrain, sometimes with gear collapse. We counted 21 of these.

Next highest accident cause was engine failure with 16 listed. The largest single subgroup: carburetor ice, with four accidents. One fatal engine failure caused a fire in the cabin. The FAA as a result proposed additional sheet metal be placed between the engine compartment and the cabin.

Next highest accident cause: stalls, with 12 of these—five of them fatal. Two of the fatals resulted from low passes (one during moose spotting), two others from over-gross weights and loading aft of the center of gravity envelope.

Weather problems claimed nine accidents—four of them fatal, while there were only five fuel mismanagement accidents, none fatal.

Two instances of airframe failure were listed—both fatal. One occurred in snowy weather, and in the other a horizontal stabilizer failed because of a fatigue fracture during normal cruise.

favorites known for reliability and good service. Since the turbocharged Lycoming is basically the same as the powerplant installed in the ill-fated Rockwell 112TC, which was dropped from production, potential buyers might wish to exercise caution: this powerplant was not held in universally high esteem.

Performance

The degree to which the various dramatically named Maules (Rocket, Lunar Rocket, Strata and Astra Rocket) yielded equally dramatic performance has been a matter of controversy for some time. The aircraft has always been promoted by the factory as a true STOL (short takeoff and landing) vehicle that could outrace almost anything of equal horsepower in the skies.

The speed bubble was pricked to a large extent when it was disclosed that improper placement of static ports in early models had generated erroneously high airspeed readings that actually were as much as 13 mph off the target.

When the static ports were correctly positioned, *Aviation Consumer* reporters logged speeds as high as 167 mph true with 75 percent cruise in the 235-hp Maule, but many owners claim no better than 155 mph or so in real life on the average with their 220-hp and 235-hp models. In a flyoff conducted by *The Aviation Consumer* with a Piper Dakota about equally loaded, the Piper walked away from the Maule with an eventual speed advantage of at least five mph when both machines were firewalled to eliminate tach error.

The 235-hp Dakota also climbed better.

Short-field Work

Where the Maule is supposed to shine is in getting in and out of little fields. While some of the Maule promotional material touts takeoff and landing distances over 50-foot obstacles of 600 feet or better, the dangerously skimpy handbook that goes with the airplane doesn't hint at performance figures in this area. And while some Maule owners rave about the STOL qualities of their bird, others say it's a far cry from what's advertised.

The Maules achieve some pretty impressive takeoffs and landings when lightly loaded, but they owe their performance less to great aerodynamic sophistication than to a low power and

wing loading.

While the spanwise enlargement of the flaps may have improved the descent profile, it apparently resulted in diminished lateral control at low approach speeds because the ailerons were shortened. And users complain that aileron control in gusty conditions is too slow for comfort. On top of that, the big vertical tail makes control difficult in just mildly strong crosswind landing situations.

Pilot Engineering

Pilots are universally flattering when it comes to describing the Maule's tailwheel configuration. Most say it is the easiest taildragger of all to manage in takeoff and landing. Part of this comes from the surprisingly gentle deck angle of the aircraft on the ground. Transitions are quite easy for tricycle-gear pilots.

The control reaction on the Maules is quite pleasant in flight also (with the exception of aileron control at slow speed, as mentioned before), and thanks to a clever coupling of aileron and rudder tab, adverse yaw is compensated for almost automatically.

Cockpit design is austere and primitive. Control knobs are almost indistinguishable from one another. The two-way fuel selector is of antique vintage with soft detents. The fuel system incorporating auxiliary wingtip tanks is described by pilots as a great nuisance, since fuel in the tips must be transferred to the mains by electric fuel pump.

Seats are commonly described as flimsy; visibility as poor. The rear seat has one seatbelt for both riders. No

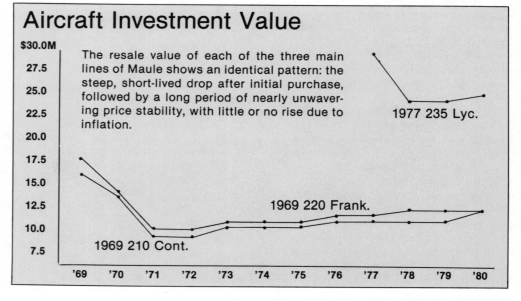

Aircraft Investment Value

The resale value of each of the three main lines of Maule shows an identical pattern: the steep, short-lived drop after initial purchase, followed by a long period of nearly unwavering price stability, with little or no rise due to inflation.

1977 235 Lyc.

1969 220 Frank.

1969 210 Cont.

$30.0M / 27.5 / 25.0 / 22.5 / 20.0 / 17.5 / 15.0 / 12.5 / 10.0 / 7.5

'69 '70 '71 '72 '73 '74 '75 '76 '77 '78 '79 '80

shoulder harnesses are available for rear-seat passengers. Front-seat shoulder harnesses were added only by FAA mandate, in 1979; they are retro-fittable, however, to older models.

If anyone should wish to augment the older 42-gallon fuel system with the auxiliary wingtip tanks, this, too, is available for $995 worth of hardware, including welded aluminum fuel tanks.

Maule pilots advise wearing earplugs or headsets insulated against the tremendous din that intrudes upon the cockpit from prop and engine noise.

Maintenance & Support
Maule operators are almost universally flattering about both maintenance demands and factory support. The airplane is so basically simple that there is little to go wrong; and when it does, it's easy to fix. One troublesome component, however, is the tailwheel. This is ironic since tailwheels were among the company's first products. Nevertheless, many owners say they prefer to switch to Scott tailwheels for greater strength and diminished shimmy problems. Other owners report problems with vent lines spewing fuel overboard, but Maule says this has been fixed with check valves.

One aspect of the family-operated Maule business—Belford and June Maule literally run the show—is what Maule operators describe as fairly quick, pleasant service. There are no overlapping bureaus and management nets; problems appear to get direct attention and a caring reaction.

Airworthiness Directives
The Maule series has had a rather quiet history of AD problems with only 10 called against the company since 1965.

Guts of the Maule *is this welded tubular structure with a fiberglass cocoon covering. The battery is under the cabin floor.*

The most recent one, in 1979, modifies the tail-to-fuselage front attach tube to prevent cracking and failure. Maule is supplying parts free, according to customers. As Belford once told *The Aviation Consumer* when asked what happened when the short 90-day warranty expired: "If it's our fault, we fix it."

Three other ADs in the last decade centered on problems with fuel line leakage and interruption of flow to the engine.

Resale Value
One area where the Maule does not shine is as an investment that will be worth lots more as the years go by and inflation pushes everything up. The Maules take the usual plunge in resale worth after initial purchase, but instead of appreciating like most aircraft worth their salt, simply hold onto about the same paper value, year after year. A Maule represents nowhere near the investment value of a Cessna 180, for example.

Where there is an advantage, however, is for the used-plane purchaser who simply wants to get a piece of flying machinery that won't break the bank in the first place.

For the pilot who can forego the luxury of all-metal construction and maybe a tricycle gear, the Maule has to be one of the greatest bargains going. Shopping for, say, a 10-year-old airplane, the buyer would have to lay out about $22,000 for a Cessna 180 (230-hp powerplant, taildragger, too)—or 43 percent more than the price of a 10-year-old Maule with a 220-hp Franklin—$12,500, according to the *Aircraft Price Digest*. To get a Piper Cherokee 235 of equivalent vintage, he'd have to pay $20,000 or 38 percent more; a Cessna 182, $21,500. Even a plain-vanilla Cherokee 180 would cost a healthy $16,500, or 24 percent more than the Maule.

Naturally, the cost of a new Razor-back covering for the fuselage and empennage (that's fiberglass cloth, dope impregnated) might add another $3,500 or so, and buyers should keep this in mind. However, the wings are all metal—and this includes spar, ribs and covering.

Model	Year	No. Built	Average Retail Price	Cruise Speed (mph)	Rate of Climb (fpm)	Useful Load (lbs)	Fuel (gals)	Engine	TBO (hrs)	Overhaul Cost
M-4	1962-64	81	$ 7,600	150	700	1,000	42	145-hp Cont.	1,800	$5,000
M-4-C	1965-67	10	$ 8,250	150	700	1,000	42	145-hp Cont.	1,800	$5,000
M-4-210C	1965-66	67	$11,600	165	1,280	850	42	210-hp Cont.	1,200	$5,900
M-4-210C	1967-69	47	$12,250	165	1,250	850	42	210-hp Cont.	1,500	$5,900
M-4-220C	1967-69	37	$11,800	175	1,250	1,020	42	220-hp Frank.	1,500	$5,500
M-4-180C	1970-71	5	$10,800	155	1,000	1,050	42	180-hp Frank.	2,000	$5,000
M-4-220C	1970-73	153	$14,000	175	1,250	1,020	42	220-hp Frank.	1,500	$5,500
M-4-210C	1973	16	$16,000	165	1,250	850	42	210-hp Cont.	1,500	$5,900
M-5-210C	1974-76	291	$18,500	158	1,250	950	65	210-hp Cont.	1,500	$5,900
M-5-220C	1974-75	58	$17,500	173	1,250	1,000	65	220-hp Frank.	1,500	$5,500
M-5-210C	1977	14	$21,000	158	1,250	950	65	210-hp Cont.	1,500	$5,900
M-5-235C	1977	198	$25,000	172	1,350	900	65	235-hp Lyc.	2,000	$6,500
M-5-235C	1978	41	$27,500	172	1,350	900	65	235-hp Lyc.	2,000	$6,500
M-5-235C	1979	55	$30,000	172	1,350	900	65	235-hp Lyc.	2,000	$6,500
M-5-180C	1979	8	$27,500	155	1,000	1,000	65	180-hp Lyc.	2,000	$4,500

Owner Comments

"As the previous owner of two different Maules, first a 1972 220 M4 and then a 1976 235 M5, I find the 235 M5 to be far more stable and have a better cruise speed. The 235 was a real pleasure to fly, although very noisy. Maintenance and upkeep are where the Maule shines. The front seats are large enough, but the back is a little crowded.

"There is one thing that needs changing: the fuel system. They should enlarge the main fuel tanks and do away with the tip tanks and all the transfer pumps, lines, switches, wires, etc. That is a nightmare!

"Although the Maule has a very good short-field performance, it will not cruise as fast or land and take off as short as B.D. claims. I find it very comparable to a Cessna 180 in this respect. Although it won't lift nearly the load as the 180, I found it to be a good, honest 150-mph airplane. However, at this speed, figure on at least 14 gallon-per-hour fuel.

"The factory is excellent for parts and service."

"I have been flying a 1972 M-4 (220 Franklin) for three years. The plane is used for towing gliders, carrying jumpers, and some back-country work. The aircraft is phenomenal. We start out at 5000 feet MSL, and go up from there.

"Repair charges have been minimal so far. The AD on the horizontal stab which came out last year—the factory had shipped the parts, free, before I made the call.

"I can count on 140-145 mph cruise at 20 inches and 2400, 9500-12500 MSL, at 9.6-10 gph.

"The worst problems are noise and lead fouling of the plugs. There is not much to do for the noise, and no amount of leaning or TCP seems to help the fouling. We don't have 100LL here.

"All things considered, I think the aircraft is spectacular. I have put it down on dirt tracks on desert, rough dirt strips, and handling is fine. Could use more powerful brakes, however.

"By the way, the cylinder head temps run cold, and the oil runs hot! Maybe some of your readers have a solution for that.

"Love that airplane."

"Generally speaking my M-5 has been easy to maintain and not overly expensive. The few factory replacement parts I have required were supplied in a minimum of time.

"The aileron roll rate could be a little better at slow speeds, and there is a tendency to run out of elevator when landing if there is no weight in the back seat or baggage area (M-5-235).

"Cruise speeds fall a little short of factory figures; however, overall performance is quite good.

"The noise level is a little high, but not unbearable.

The M-5 Maules *have a two-piece molded fiberglass cowl. Some pilots complain that this makes a thorough pre-flight impossible.*

"The Maule has very good ground manners for a taildragger and is easy to land with a little practice.

"All things considered, I am quite pleased with Maule."

"A few comments on a 1964 Maule:

"Points for the airplane: Good ground visibility for a taildragger. Fair cruising speed for 145 hp, but well below the book figures. Good entrance and egress for crew and passengers. Good stall characteristics. Good slow-flight performance. Adequate brakes. Effective flaps.

"Points against the airplane: Very noisy cabin. Air and water leaks in all doors. Flimsy front seat structure. Pilot's seat back broke during a landing flare-out. Should have gussets or braces between seat and back frame tubing. Poorly designed fuel sump drain. Tightening a loose drain fitting, twisted and cracked fuel line causing a fuel leak under the pilot's seat. Could not climb within 3,000 feet of published service ceiling on a nearly standard day with one passenger and a 400-hour engine. I would not consider this an STOL airplane at gross weight with the 145-hp engine. No doubt the 200+ hp engine improves this considerably. The original Maule tailwheel could not be shimmy dampened adequately. A Cleveland tailwheel was installed and this problem eliminated.

"I feel it is a reasonably good airplane, but sold it in favor of the roomier cabin and better altitude performance of a Skyhawk."

"I bought a Maule in the belief that there was a high degree of correlation between performance charts and actual airplane performance. I operated the airplane for some 200 hours while becoming convinced that, for the Maule, what the book says and what the airplane does are light years apart. Operation from a good gravel strip 800 feet long was just barely possible with little or no safety margin, salesman's guarantees and performance chart figures to the contrary.

In the Maule cockpit, *dual controls are standard, as is this no-frills panel. Fuel transfer pump buttons are above the right control wheel; old-fashioned fuel selector valve on the left lower fuselage wall.*

The Aviation Consumer Used Aircraft Guide

Piper Tri-Pacer

As a precursor of the fixed-tricycle-gear fleet, the Piper Tri-Pacer was a smashing success back in the American Graffiti days of the 1950s and sold in the thousands. But as the final off-shoot of the fabric and welded steel tube taildragging Pacer, it had worked its way out onto the end of the evolutionary line. As a result, it went defunct after 1960, and the world was inherited by the slightly bigger, roomier, all-metal Cessna 172, which seems destined to be built forever.

The Tri-Pacer did, however, endow the flying world with at least one airplane less than three decades old that would carry four and could be bought for about the price of a new Chevy—$5,000 to $8,000.

Although the Tri-Pacer has the age to call upon the charisma that often surrounds other elderly aircraft, it somehow falls flat in this department, and your girl (or guy) is not likely to swoon on first meeting. The Tri-Pacer is stubby (short-coupled), hard to climb into, dark and cramped once you're inside and held together with a small forest of wing, tail and landing gear struts.

Its Strong Suit: Economy
It has one great, endearing quality, though, according to users: It's dirt cheap to own and operate. It will chug along on seven to nine gph (depending on the powerplant), cost around $15 an hour (excluding insurance, for 100 hours a year) and will slip through an annual inspection for as low as $200, according to some owners.

The Tri-Pacer was built with four consecutive Lycoming powerplants of 125, 135, 150 and 160 hp. Models with the two larger engines also had optional fuel that raised the tankage to 44 from the standard 36 gallons.

Performance and Handling
With a useful load of less than 800 pounds for the smaller-engined models to less than 900 with the larger ones, the Tri-Pacers generally can heft three adults and maybe some baggage along with full fuel at book speeds of from 119 mph to 134 mph. Owners report these figures are in the ballpark.

As old as it is, the Tri-Pacer has interconnected ailersons and rudders, in an effort to simplify pilot coordination in turns. Although the airplane is elevator limited and extremely difficult to pull into a real stall break, the Tri-Pacer has a well-founded reputation for being a sinker. Pilots report they can generate a rate of descent with power off of up to 1,500 fpm. The aircraft has two-position flaps that will yield 15 and 40 degrees.

If you believe in being able to control each wheel brake separately, you'll find the Tri-Pacer primitive in the sense that it has only a single hand lever. The probability is that this is a contributing factor in serious ground handling problems, especially among low-time-in-type pilots, whenever there are gusty winds or crosswinds.

Parts availability from both the factory and various supply houses like Univair and Wag-Aero is reported pretty good by owners.

The A.D. Situation
Among the Airworthiness Directives leveled against the aircraft through the years, perhaps three deserve continued special attention. One of these warns against scratched or cracking tail brace wires and requires a check every 100 hours to prevent the possibility of a "catastrophic" in-flight failure. Another requires the fuel selector valve to be checked for a positive detent and accurate markings for the pilot so there is no doubt as to when the lever is on which tank. This also must be checked every 100 hours. The third requires that the right fuel tank be placarded to warn against any but straight and level flight when that tank is less than a third full (with six gallons), to guard against engine stoppage on takeoff and climbout.

Improvements
As for modifications and improvements, some Tri-Pacers have received the ultimate compliment of being preserved in metal, with the fabric skin discarded. The STC for that was held by Albert Snyder of Skycraft Corp. in Yardley, Pa., but he hasn't done that kind of work for some time.

Another STC allows owners to restore some of the airplane's lost charisma by converting the tricycle gear back to conventional gear. This is done by Redwood Aviation Enterprises at Metropolitan Airport in Santa Rosa, Calif.

A beneficial forestalling of the normal 1,200-hour TBO on the 150- and 160-hp engines to 2,000 hours is obtained by the installation of one-half inch exhaust valves.

Safety
Perched on its milking stool tripod landing gear, the Tri-Pacer doesn't look like the

The first PA-22 Piper Tri-Pacer, *a 1951 model with a 125-hp engine.*

sturdiest of vehicles for ground operations. And judging from the National Transportation Safety Board's rundown of Tri-Pacer accidents over 1975 and 1976, it isn't.

A large portion of the accidents involved nosing over, groundlooping or swerving with gear collapse. Many of these resulted from landing and attempting to taxi in high, gusty winds that caused the pilot to lose direction control or simply blew the airplane over.

A lot of gear collapsing resulted from hard landings, and undershooting, with frequent mention of high sink rates on final approach. Most of these problems involved low-time-in-type pilots who obviously hadn't gotten the hang of controlling the notorious Tri-Pacer sink rate on final with judicious use of power. Quite a few occurred with an instructor in the right seat during practice landings.

A number of accidents occurred when pilots mushed or stalled on takeoff with four riders aboard and the aircraft couldn't gain sufficient altitude to avoid obstacles, or encountered turbulence.

Obviously, pilots should be wary of considering the Tri-Pacer a four-place aircraft,

A truncated right front door, *plus a left rear one, make for interesting entry and egress techniques.*

especially in high density altitude situations. Several takeoff crashes resulted when heavily loaded Tri-Pacers tried to get off from turf fields or soft runways, but we infer from user comments that many owners frequently use the aircraft at airports without hard-surface runways, and that they consider it a good short-field bird.

The other noteworthy trend brought out by the NTSB report was fuel mismanagement, which is a common one for many aircraft. Many Tri-Pacer pilots either selected the wrong (empty) tank or just ran out of fuel. In one fatal case the pilot positioned the fuel selector valve between tanks, experienced engine stoppage, stalling and crashing, presumably with his head down in the cockpit trying to find out what the problem was.

Although there was a bunch of engine failures from mechanical problems, we found only one from carburetor ice.

In a special NTSB study of single-engine aircraft accidents, the Tri-Pacer was listed as the fifth worst out of 32 aircraft in overshoot accidents.

Owner Comments

"The 150-hp Tri-Pacer is only a marginal four-place airplane with a current 1,248-pound empty weight (according to the book). With four average individuals this would leave only 12 gallons of fuel, not a significant amount, since it burns eight gallons per hour. Three adults form a more reasonable number of passengers. With 18 gallons of fuel in each wing and eight in the auxiliary tank under the rear seat, which refuels the right wing tank while the engine feeds from the left, I have about five hours of flying. Standard procedure is to take off on the left tank, at altitude switch to the right tank for 90 minutes, then back to the left tank while pumping the additional eight gallons into the right.

"There is a right-side door for the front-seat passengers, and a left-side door for the rear. It's great fun if your passengers are long-legged girls in mini-skirts. Entry and egress are disasters if you plan to give your Aunt Millie a ride.

"The most recent annual was accomplished for less than $80. Typical annual costs for the last decade have not exceeded $150 yearly. Even tied down through 10 New York State winters, there has been no great transfusion of money to keep the aircraft flying.

"For a number of years, though, I had to replace the brake shoes at each annual, until one repair facility, which is noted for its nit-picking, decided to turn the brake drums. This ended the annual replacement of shoes. Once I did have a brake diaphragm rupture, leaving me without brakes. (This is not an expensive part, and it would be wise to carry a spare on cross-country trips.)

"Shock chords are a continuing maintenance item for the Tri-Pacer. Finally a mechanic who owns a pristine 1957 Tri-Pacer suggested that instead of using two light cords or one heavy one, use one light and one heavy in combination. This pro-

duced landings which were a bit stiffer, but the shocks lasted several years.

"As an experienced pilot, I'd say that the Tri-Pacer is a good, safe aircraft which is extremely stable in windy conditions. I physically could not stall it during a commercial check ride. The examiner tried, and failed as well. It will, however, exhibit a 2,000 fpm rate of descent in a nose-up attitude.

"The fuses for the master switch are located in a box under the pilot's seat, and are inaccessible in flight, and reached only with great difficulty on the ground. The master has a two-position feature which allows you to select the spare fuse. It is recommended that a circuit breaker be installed. The battery is equally hard to get at. Checking the battery requires the removal of the right seat. The installation of a ground service plug makes good sense.

"The Tri-Pacer is built for people who are either small, or who are intent on becoming good friends. Spacious appointments are not the Tri-Pacer's virtue.

"Noise is a big factor in the plane. Even though I'm accustomed to it after several hundred hours, passengers are bothered by

Model	Year	Number Built	Cruise Speed (mph)	Useful Load (lbs)	Fuel Std/Opt (gals)	Rate of Climb (fpm)	Engine	TBO (hrs)	Overhaul Cost	Average Retail Price
PA-22-125	1951-52	533	119	795	36	550	125-hp Lycoming	2,000	$3,700	$4,750
PA-22-135	1953-54	1,890	123	790	36	620	135-hp Lycoming	1,500	$4,000	$5,500
PA-22-150	1955-57	3,177	130	790	36/44	750	150-hp Lycoming	2,000	$4,000	$6,500
PA-22-150	1958-60	2,027	130	790	36/44	750	150-hp Lycoming	2,000	$4,000	$6,500
PA-22-160	1958-60	N/A	134	890	36/44	800	160-hp Lycoming	2,000	$4,100	$8,500

The closely spaced landing gear, *equipped with bungee cord shock absorbers, has failed many a new Tri-Pacer pilot attempting to cope with high surface winds and hard landings. One alternative is modification back to the Pacer's conventional gear.*

the racket, even while wearing ear protection.

"A Tri-Pacer may be the best all around four-place airplane on the used market. My experience with a 1953 135-hp model showed it to be a fast, inexpensive and thoroughly forgiving family airplane.

"The 135 model cruises at 120-125 mph true, will carry four people, burning seven gph or less. It is a surprisingly good short-field airplane, even with 135 hp. If you happen to be over six feet and more than 200 pounds, it is crowded, but for an average-size person it is just great. It is a terrific three-place-and-baggage airplane. It will not stall in the true sense, just gets really slow and sinks at 1,500 fpm. Keep the speed at 80, and it is just like any other airplane. The interconnected controls make it a good feet-flat-on-the-floor or rudders-only airplane.

"A good inspection will include looking at the aft tubing for rust, condition of the motor mount rubber bushings, the exhaust system and the landing gear bungees. If it is covered with Ceconite or Razorback, chances are that it will outlast you. Realistic prices for the 135 seems to be in the $5,000-$6,000 range and that seems fair for an aircraft that will out-perform the older 172."

"I am based on a 5,240-foot MSL strip in Albuquerque, and my 160-hp Tri-Pacer has lifted 625 pounds of people with full tanks and still climbed at 300 fpm.

"By letting the speed literally build up to 85 on the ground, jerking one notch of flaps, she literally jumps into the air. At a climb speed of 85 mph the VSI says 900 fpm. At 7,500 feet and 2400 rpm she indicates 125 mph. I burn seven and three quarters gph and one quart of oil every eight hours.

"With power off, she has a sink rate of

close to 1,000 fpm, so be ready with the throttle. She also has a glide ratio like a streamlined crow bar.

"I guess what I like most is that I don't have an arm and a leg invested, yet I have an airplane that out-performs a lot of the more modern ones.

"In the spring and early summer we get some snappy winds here, and she is a mite squirrelly. But that only tends to remind you that you are flying—keep your head out of the cockpit.

"I've had no problem so far with parts. We have a couple of mechanics here who grew up with the Tri-Pacer, and I'm sure there are lots more around the country."

"For the money, you can't beat a Tri-Pacer's performance. I have the 150-hp model. More than 20 years later you can spend $20,000 more than a Tri-Pacer cost new and only gain five or six mph in cruise or topspeed. You might even lose on fuel flow, payload and high-altitude performance. At 4,500 MSL I true 128 mph—five mph more than the handbook calls for.

"One rumor I keep hearing is that the Tri-Pacer has the gliding angle of a brick and is very unforgiving during the landing phase. This is a bunch of baloney. I have no trouble making my approach at 65 IAS, landing smoothly and turning off in less than 300 feet. Maybe some pilots need a bit of extra training?

"I find my airplane very easy to fly. It responds quickly and easily to all control forces and has no bad habits. From shortly after takeoff to landing flare it can be flown with just two fingers and a bit of trim.

"As I have discovered during my re-building project, the Tri-Pacer is a very simple, rugged airplane. Anyone with basic mechanical ability should have little trou-

ble accomplishing oil changes, brake shoe replacement and other preventive maintenance items. The only items you have to watch are exhaust stud nuts, which have a habit of loosening and vibrating off (I double-nut mine to prevent this), and holes or cracks in the muffler assembly.

"The ubiquitous Piper right-hand cockpit door leads to some gyrations for people attempting to mount up, but can be mastered with a little practice. Once inside, there is enough room for four adults, but nothing to spare. In other words, it's a bit snug, especially if you're overgrossed around the midsection. Leg and head room up front are no problem for me (5'11", 175 lbs.), while leg room in the rear depends on how the front seat occupants adjust their seats. Ventilation is good from three window-mounted vents and one good-sized cockpit vent. The heater is simple and effective, although we don't get to use it much here in Southern California.

"You can't blame the Tri-Pacer, but parts ordered directly from Piper or its dealers can get pretty hairy. A new snubber for my nose gear, for example, cost me nearly $20, a set of hardware for my wheel fairings more than $112. It appears that every time the 'cost of living' goes up five percent Piper and everyone else in the business raises prices 20 percent. You can avoid most of this aggravation, however, by buying used parts from numerous suppliers, or by making your own.

"Based on 100 hours per year, I estimate hourly operating costs to be slightly less than $15. That includes fuel, oil changes every 25 hours, tiedown fees and annual maintenance requirements. Insurance is not included because individual requirements vary too much. Direct operating costs, fuel and oil, are less than $12 per hour. Compared to current local flying club costs of $22 wet for a Cessna 150 two-placer, this is just short of stealing money for the low budget pilot-owner.

"The flaps only have two positions, 15 and 40 degrees. Neither is particularly effective, but then you don't need them much, either. The brakes are operated with a single hand-lever and are adequate, but not spectacular. They can be improved by changing from drum to disc types. There is no differential braking, in any event. The master switch is hidden under the pilot's seat, along with the starter button and fuel selector. It's unusual, but it may come in handy some day if anyone should try to steal your bird. He'd go nuts trying to find the button unless he was familiar with Tri-Pacers.

"All in all, I think the Tri-Pacer is the finest airplane for the money available anywhere. Even without the cost factor, it's a fun machine that is safe and easy to fly, while delivering very respectable performance under a very wide range of conditions."

Cessna Skylane

Cessna's 182 Skylane is only the third most popular lightplane in the history of the world. (The first and second, of course, are the 172 and 150.) It is the keystone of Cessna's step-up marketing strategy, perched strategically in a sales niche between the low-profit "starter" airplanes like the 150 and 172 and the high-profit, high-performance 210 and twin-engine line. The 182 is *the* basic high-performance aircraft, the cheapest airplane available that can haul four people and their baggage a long way, comfortably, and at a reasonable speed.

The Skylane was introduced in 1956 (the same year as the 172) and the two aircraft signaled the dawn of Cessna's two-decade dominance of the single-engine field. There have been remarkably few changes in the years since. The engine has remained basically the same, the 230-hp Continental O-470. In 1960, in keeping with the styling tastes of the times, the Skylane got a swept tail; in 1962 a rear window and electric flaps. Gross weight has grown steadily over the years, from the original 2,550 to 2,650 pounds in 1957, 2,800 in 1962 to 2,950 in 1970. (Empty weight has climbed, too, so useful load of the late models isn't that much better than the old ones.) Overall, there have been remarkably few changes.

Performance

Book cruise speeds have run consistently over the years between 160 and 165 mph (140-145 knots), with evolutionary aerodynamic refinements making up for the speed penalty of higher gross weights. Most owners report they achieve these speeds without much trouble, although many prefer to cruise at lower power settings to save fuel, and 130 knots is a speed mentioned by many owners. For 230 hp, that's not very fast—the retractable Mooney 201, for example, flies 30 knots faster on less horsepower. Speed is not the airplane's strong point. Climb is excellent, however, with 1,000 fpm easily obtainable at heavy weights and up to 1,500 fpm at lighter weights (both at sea level, of course).

Handling

Stability is the key word that describes the Skylane in the air; pilots praise it as an IFR platform and a reasonably comfortable ship in turbulence. Stability is a two-edged sword, however, and with it the pilot must usually accept heavy control surfaces. The Skylane is no exception; it handles ponderously, especially in pitch. In fact, with full flaps and two people in the front seat, flaring to land takes an inordinate amount of muscle and maximum back trim. Regular Skylane pilots will quickly develop healthy biceps. This also is one penalty of having a wide center of gravity.

The airplane is quite gentle at low speeds, and the huge elevator forces make it virtually impossible to stall by accident. Slow-speed maneuvering in a Skylane inspires great confidence; one doesn't have the feeling of flying right on the edge. Aileron control at low speeds is relatively clumsy, however, and gusty crosswinds can present a problem upon landing.

Loading

Loading up a 182 is a delight; it's one of the few airplanes in which you can usually fill all the seats, all the tanks and the baggage compartment and still be legal (and safe).

On a well-equipped airplane with long-range tanks, however, even the Skylane demands a bit of fuel/passenger juggling. But generally speaking, Skylane pilots don't bother much with weight and balance. If it fits, it's probably legal.

Center of gravity balance is another thing that doesn't concern Skylane owners too often. One owner reports he can put himself in the front, two 200-pounders in the back and fill the baggage compartment to its maximum and still be within c.g. limits.

Passenger Comfort

The Skylane is a big, roomy, four-seater, and treats its rear-seat passengers especially kindly. However, the airplane is quite noisy, and this factor can make long flights fatiguing without a good pair of expanding foam earplugs. The Skylane has two wide doors, which makes entry and exit a simple affair.

Safety

The Skylane is generally regarded as a safe airplane. In 1977, for example, there were only 30 fatal accidents in Skylanes, a rather low number considering the fact that there are more than 8,000 Skylanes now flying. Most fatal accidents involved bad weather.

The Skylane has among the best stall/spin accident rates of any aircraft. In 1977, not

With room for four and plenty of fuel and baggage, *the Cessna Skylane has dominated the high-performance scene for almost two decades.*

a single Skylane accident was attributed to a stall or spin by the NTSB, and only a tiny handful were labeled "failed to obtain/maintain flying speed," normally a very common cause of accidents. A recent study of NTSB accident data, in fact, showed that the Skylane has the lowest rate of fatal stall/spin accidents of any light aircraft.

The Skylane also shines in the area of fuel management, another major factor in design-induced accident causes. In 1977 there was not a single case of fuel starvation in a Skylane—clearly the result of the high-wing, gravity-feed system and the stone-simple left-right-both fuel selector. There was also not a single case of an in-flight structural failure; partly due to the very heavy pitch forces, which make it virtually impossible to pull hard enough to overstress the airplane. The high-drag fuselage and fixed gear also limit speed buildup in an unintentional dive. Cessnas with wing strut braces also have an excellent record of holding together when highly stressed.

Several clear patterns emerge from a study of the Skylane's minor nonfatal accidents, in our NTSB printout. A disturbing number of carburetor ice accidents showed up in 1977, and although the 182 isn't as prone to carb ice as the 150 (which happens to have the worst carb ice accident record of any airplane), it is still up there among the leaders. Anybody who flies a Skylane regularly in heavy weather should invest in a carb ice detector.

There is also a surprising number of accidents caused by water in the fuel, suggesting that the Skylane's quick drains or fuel caps might stand some improvement.

Of special interest to shoppers for used Skylanes is the airplane's rather high incidence of hard landings and gear-bending overshoots. In fact, the bent firewall is perhaps the major thing to look for in any used Skylane, always the result of a hard or nose-low landing. The extreme nose-heaviness of the airplane is also hard on nosewheels, and

Buyers of used 182s *should check for damaged firewalls and leaking fuel cells—the two biggest repair costs on a Skylane.*

there were several cases of severe shimmies and buckling nosewheels that resulted in accidents in 1977.

The Skylane also appears to be involved in a high frequency of accidents in which density altitude is a factor. This is probably the result of the pilot's overconfidence in the airplane's performance. The Skylane climbs so well under normal circumstances that pilots don't hesitate to take them into extreme high-altitude conditions. At least a half-dozen density altitude accidents were recorded in 1977.

Overall, however, the Skylane's safety record is superb. Lots of power, a big wing, heavy pitch forces and a simple fuel system are clearly the keys to a safe airplane.

Maintenance
Here is another of the Skylane's strong points. The airplane is relatively simple and robust, without retractable gear, and the payoff there is lower maintenance costs. Owners report annuals cost as little as $200, with the average about $250-$300 with no major discrepancies.

There are two major ADs to look out for: the Hartzell and McCauley propeller ADs (which have also affected virtually all airplanes with constant-speed propellers) and the Goodyear rubber bladder directive. The

Skylane has little history of propeller troubles, but leaky fuel tanks are perhaps the major maintenance problem of the airplane. Experience has shown that the older rubber bladder cells have a lifetime of about six to eight years, and if you're shopping for a 182 any older than that, you should count on replacing them soon after you buy—at a cost of about $600 apiece plus labor.

The Continental O-470 engine has a good record, although it doesn't seem to be as reliable as the four-cylinder carbureted Lycomings. TBO is 1,500 hours, and a well-maintained engine should meet or exceed this figure without too much trouble. It's not uncommon, however, for an O-470 to need a top overhaul after 800-1,000 hours, usually due to excessive valve guide wear. We're told that occasionally the alloy from which the guides are made is substandard.

Some 1975 and 1976 Skylanes had special engine problems that a used-aircraft buyer should be aware of, however. These models had the O-470-S engine, which had a new ring design. (The O-470-R had been used since 1962.) Some O-470-S engines had break-in problems and used excessive amounts of oil—as much as a quart per hour in some cases. Continental never really figured out the problem and switched to the high-compression O-470-U in 1977. Most of

Model	Year Built	Number Built	Cruise Speed (mph)	Rate of Climb (fpm)	Useful Load (lbs)	Fuel Std/Opt (gals)	Engine	TBO (hrs)	Overhaul Cost	Average Retail price
182-A	1956-57	1,753	155	1,210	1,010	55	230-hp Cont. O-470-L	1,500	$4,800	$12,000
182-A&B	1958-59	1,648	159	1,030	1,090	55	Continental O-470-L	1,500	$4,800	$13,000
182-C&D	1960-61	1,239	162	1,030	1,090	65/84	Continental O-470-L	1,500	$4,800	$14,750
182-E&F	1962-63	1,459	162	980	1,190	65/84	Continental O-470-R	1,500	$4,800	$16,000
182-G&H	1964-65	1,175	162	980	1,190	65/84	Continental O-470-R	1,500	$4,800	$17,250
182-J&K	1966-67	1,820	162	980	1,175	65/84	Continental O-470-R	1,500	$4,800	$18,250
182-L&M	1968-69	1,549	162	980	1,175	65/84	Continental O-470-R	1,500	$4,800	$20,000
182-N	1970-71	769	160	850	1,310	65/84	Continental O-470-R	1,500	$4,800	$22,000
182-P	1972-74	1,009	166	1,010	1,169	61/80	Continental O-470-R	1,500	$4,800	$24,000
182-P II	1975-76	1,699	166	1,010	1,169	61/80	Continental O-470-S	1,500	$4,800	$29,000
182-Q II	1977	811	160	1,010	1,169	61/80	Continental O-470-S	1,500	$4,800	$33,000
182-Q II	1978	624	160	1,010	1,169	61/80	Continental O-470-U	1,500	$4,800	$34,000
182-Q II	1979	710	160	1,010	1,169	61/80	Continental O-470-U	1,500	$4,800	$41,000

the oil-burner O-470-S engines have been replaced by now, and it seems that once the engine is successfully broken in, there's no problem. Some engines, however, just never broke in.

Another maintenance problem of the Skylane is the cowl flaps. They simply fall off with great regularity, making an alarming bang in the cockpit if the failure occurs in flight. The culprit is the hinge and hinge pin; check them closely on any used Skylane.

The Skylane seems to have suffered less from 100 LL problems than other 80-octane airplanes. Nevertheless, careful leaning, plug rotation and 50-hour oil changes are recommended, along with the use of TCP if lead fouling is indeed a problem. We have one report of an engine failure caused by lead fouling in a Skylane.

One other maintenance item to look for: standard Skylanes have paper air filter elements that can swell up in heavy rain and restrict airflow. Permanent foam filter elements are better.

Summing up, the two major items that any shopper for a used Skylane should check closely are the firewall alignments and the condition of the rubber bladder fuel cells.

Modifications

The basic Skylane engine/airframe combination has been so successful that there have been relatively few STC'd modifications. Chief among them are STOL mods. Robertson Aircraft offers the most effective and expensive STOL mod; less elaborate systems featuring new leading edge cuffs, sealed ailerons and stall fences (but without the drooped ailerons of the Robertson mod) are offered by Horton and MASA, both in Wichita.

In addition, Flight Bonus, Inc., P.O. Box 665, Hurst, TX 76053, has STCed a series of drag reduction mods that are supposed to boost cruise speed by an astonishing 23 mph. They are achieved by new gear strut and wheel fairings, aileron gap seals and engine baffling. Flight Bonus, Inc. estimates improvements can be made incrementally to a Skylane at a cost of about $200 for each extra mph in speed gained. For the full 23 mph, of course, that would come to $4,600.

Skylane Club

There is a Skylane owners' organization, the Cessna Skylane Society, P.O. Box 779, Del Ray Beach, Florida 33444; 305-278-2116. Unlike some other clubs, the Skylane Society is a privately owned for-profit organization. It is run by an ex-airline pilot named Paul Morton. Membership is $12/yr., which includes a monthly newsletter. There is also an annual convention.

Owner Comments

"For 230 hp the Skylane is not very fast or economical on fuel. But for short- and high-field work it is super. It is also great to have a service ceiling that will push nearly 20,000 feet, and I find it will perform to handbook specs.

"Maintenance is one of the Skylane's strong points. I have never had an annual run over $150. This is because I keep on top of everything during the year, doing as much as legal myself. There is no retractable gear to check, the design is very sound and the record of the O-470 speaks for itself. Even though I put more money into gas per mile, I feel the low annual and maintenance costs balance in my favor, making the overall operation very economical for a high-performance single.

"On the earlier models the leaf-spring landing gear makes it very easy to bounce a landing. On the opposite side of that coin, it is very easy to sink it in without punching the gear through the airframe on a short-field touchdown. The old Goodyear brakes would chatter when taxiing, making passengers nervous. Cleveland conversions can solve this problem, and improve the braking, without costing an arm and a leg.

"Other than being a very economical cross-country plane, the Skylane's strongest point is its power-to-weight ratio that performs super at my high altitude (4,250 feet) home airport and takes me securely across the western mountains."

"The C-182 is, in my opinion, the finest compromise I can imagine in a four-place light aircraft. Our aircraft, based in California, has been all over this continent, and never missed a beat. We now have over 4,000 hours on the airframe with no signs of undue wear. The most expensive main-

tenance by far is on the Narco avionics, which cannot fairly be included with the airframe.

"We like the capability to take four heavy adults and baggage anywhere in this simple, uncomplicated aircraft. The airspeed is reasonable, usually 130 knots, and I don't have to pay retractable insurance rates. I find that a little foresight in entering a destination airport traffic pattern more than makes up for the few knots of extra airspeed my friends' retractables have.

"In five years and 2,000 hours we have had no major maintenance except an engine overhaul and a new interior. We couldn't be more pleased.

"The only operational problems are a slight tendency to accumulate carb ice if visible moisture is present, and plug fouling on 100 LL fuel. The carb air temperature gauge gives ample ice warning and in all cases the carb heat control proved to be adequate. My practice now is to apply enough carb heat to keep the gauge at a comfortable indication and then lean to the desired EGT."

"I can only compare the 182 against our previously owned 172. Both performed and handled well, and we had no abnormal maintenance with either. From a comfort standpoint, however, there is no comparison. The 182 is much roomier and far smoother in rough weather. By the same token, the cost of operating a 182 is higher since the additional 80 horses up front require more hay. The manual's speed performances are optimistic as our airplane is approximately eight mph slower. Fuel consumption varies from 11 gph to a maximum of 14. Oil consumption

Aileron control at low speeds *is less than dramatically crisp. Crosswind landings can be counted on to give the pilot a workout.*

Plenty of power, *big wing, simple fuel system, and heavy pitch forces are the keys to building a relatively safe aircraft.*

is approximately one quart per hour.

"One thing I don't understand is why Cessna uses a cheap fiber material for the instrument panel. Also, several of the airplane's original instruments were not backlighted, which necessitated the use of a flashlight for night flying—even with the overhead lights on. We corrected this by the installation of two adjustable red post lights."

"Since my purchase of a new 182 demonstrator I've flown 200 hours. I am quite happy with the airplane, which is more than I can say for how I feel about the manufacturer.

"My first experience with Cessna came when I requested installation data for the Cessna 300 autopilot. Cessna absolutely refused to provide any information or documentation to aid installation. I ended up designing my own installation; fortunately I was a flight controls engineer for 14 years.

"At approximately 300 hours the vacuum pump failed, and it was not covered by the warranty. The Cessna dealer in Reno who replaced the pump at a cost of $246, indicated that the pump failure at 300 hours is normal and can be expected, a fact which has since been verified by several other Cessna mechanics. A vacuum pump with a 300-hour mean time between failures is somewhat less than comforting during IFR flights.

"Also the electrical system, in my opinion, is totally unacceptable for an airplane that is certified for IFR flight. Many pilots are today in the cemetery because of electrical failures which could be easily avoided with a back-up battery, a couple of switches, and some systems monitoring components totaling less than $150. That is, 'easily avoided' if you are an engineer. Cessna provides no information or equipment, standard or optional for a back-up electrical system. I think it is high time that we get on an airplane like the 182 a little more than a $60 belt-driven alternator. Bad vacuum pumps and electrical systems have killed a lot of pilots.

"Definitely on the bright side is the 100-octane low rpm version of the old, reliable Continental O-470-U. The cabin noise level is low enough to make pilot conversation with the rear-seat passenger possible. Even an eight-hour flight is not fatiguing. The fuel consumption is also startling—average consumption was 9.35 gallons per hour.

"About the only thing that would keep me from buying another 182 is the manufacturer's downright unfriendly, uncaring attitude towards its customers."

"In my experience with the 182 sterling qualities always come to mind. The first is the machine's slow-flight capability, which is really an unsung virtue. There are no surprises in slow flight and no cooling problems either. The airplane just hangs in there. The second item is cold starting down around zero temperatures. If the engine is equipped with the direct-injection priming system, a knowledgeable pilot is halfway there. The other half is to give it six shots of prime, pull the prop through six blades and repeat at least once and preferably twice. The rest of the procedure is by the book, including two rapid shots on the throttle just prior to starter engagement. Thus prepared, the engine will start instantly with no chance of an induction system fire.

"The Skylane requires a pronounced effort to maintain a nose-up altitude at touchdown. The airplane wants to lower its nose rapidly after touchdown, and nose gear loads can damage the firewall, if the pilot's not careful."

"I bought my 182 from a student pilot who realized that it was not a trainer after he did some expensive damage to the nosewheel on landing.

"The airplane has been very reliable. I had to put about $2,500 into it shortly after I bought it, in items like the engine mount, exhaust gaskets, and avionics. Annuals run about $300, and routine maintenance about another $300 during the year. The engine shows every sign of

going happily to TBO, and the rest of the airframe is in fine shape.

"A Cessna 150 it's not, and it doesn't fly or handle like one. It's a heavy airplane, and aileron response is deliberate. A gusty approach can be a lot of work and sweat, and its usual nose-heaviness makes a touchdown with full back elevator mandatory, especially with flaps (or expensive nosewheel damage can easily result). But that same heaviness yields a marvelous hands-off stability for extended flight, augmented in our case by a wing-leveler. I can't think of an airplane I'd rather spend five hours in, and I've done it several times in this one."

"When we purchased the airplane, a 1965 model, we did a thorough inspection and discovered the classic 182 problem of the buckled firewall. The initial evidence was an unevenly worn nosewheel, and closer inspection of the belly immediately aft of the firewall showed a slight inward buckling. Pulling the cowl showed the deformation of the firewall itself, which bows out in the vicinity of the casting that holds the nosewheel strut. A new firewall was installed by the dealer, who 'ate' about $1,500 on the deal.

"The firewall repair is difficult to do well and should be done by one experienced in the exercise. New firewalls are evident by their beefier construction, including two steel straps that run diagonally across the firewall toward the nose wheel mounting point, and which are partially covered with aluminum ribbing structure.

"I have been advised that the new firewall is a real benefit compared with the factory original, and a well-done installation is worth a few extra bucks at purchase time as insurance against the time you find a gopher hole with your name on it. A firewall job poorly done could cause grief, however, because the whole airplane has to be rerigged (everything seems to bolt to the firewall) and a poor rigging job would cause the airplane to fly out of trim.

"Shortly after purchase, the left fuel tank developed a seepage leak at the rear fuel port. Tightening the hose fitting made the problem worse, so we dumped 30 gallons of fuel, removed the tank, and had it patched. The tanks have a poor reputation in these planes, and must now be replaced by order of a new AD, but at that time we decided to take our chances and get the tank repaired ($88 instead of $350+ for a new tank). The vendor who fixed the tank would not warranty his work because of the poor history of repairs with these tanks, but two years later things seem to be hanging together. Also keep in mind that the rubber interconnect hoses behind the headliner are probably junk after several years, and these will have to be replaced as well. Ours looked so bad on the right that we dumped the fuel out of that tank as well just to replace the rubber hoses."

Cessna 150

Cessna 150s abound like lemmings to provide a truly mass market in fairly "modern" configuration aircraft at prices that range from modest to dirt cheap. Although most begin life as trainers, they can provide fairly inexpensive personal transportation and good sport flying for any whose financial and performance aspirations are not too high.

The 150 line is an all-metal, tricycle-gear derivation of the venerable Cessna 120 and 140 tailwheel models. It first showed up in 1959, and in the years to follow it established itself as the world's premier trainer, multiplied in staggering numbers and continued right up to today (as the 152) in what has become a dynasty of no small proprtions.

The line has undergone a bewildering number of modifications and "improvements" over the years, but the basic qualities have remained immutable:

Durability—The aircraft are built to take it. Otherwise they never could survive the incessant pounding and man-handling of bumbling students, the rigor of bone-rattling beginners' landings, the buffeting of stalls, the wrenching of practice spins and the dynamic and thermnal wear and tear on the engine of simulated emergency landings, slow flight and touch-and-goes. The Cessna 150 has few secrets. It has few elements and components that haven't been tested and tried to a faretheewell.

Capacity—The 150s, especially the post-1965 models, have a baggage space of monumental proportions, but all have a cockpit of straightjacket dimensions. Cessna engineers through the years have bowed the doors out, lowered the floor pans, pared away the center pedestal and even lowered the seats in an attempt to provide more millimeters of cabin room. But they still haven't made the cabin structure basically any wider. Hence, any two adults of more than medieval stature who fly together in a Cessna 150 are destined to develop a close relationship for the duration of the flight.

Speed—When the original, bulky-fuselaged 150 showed up on the aviation scene in 1959 powered by a peanut-sized 100-hp Continental O-200, it would cruise at 121 mph at 75 percent power. The 1980 model, after a raft of changes like redesigned cabin, swept tail, modified wheel fairings, better streamlined cowling and bigger engine—today cruises at 123 mph at the same power setting.

Visibility—Nothing to brag about, despite rear-window "omni-vision."

The Cessna 150 Aerobat would seem to have the makings of an ideal aerobatic trainer, since it allows students to transition right into an airplane they feel comfortable with. There's a nicely illustrated instructional manual and a well-planned curriculum to whet a student's appetite.

Experienced aeobatic pilots give it good marks in such maneuvers as spins and aileron rolls. But it has serious shortcomings when it comes to anything much more sophisticated. Since it has a control wheel rather than a stick, for example, pilots say that while doing point rolls, the "other rider" can expect to be pummeled by the pilot's elbows as he whips the wheel back and forth in the cramped cockpit.

The Aerobat also is not designed for negative maneuvers, and this not only excludes a whole repertoire, but means the engine will not operate upside down for any length of time.

Instructors also report that one marginal characteristic of the airplane is its tendency to get moving too fast when coming down from an inverted position, as in a split-S or perhaps even on top of a roll. Also, the prop pitch seems set so "fine" that it's too easy to overspeed the engine in descending maneuvers.

But the airplane probably suffices at least to give students a taste of something other than straight-and-level, as an appetite-whetter to advance to better aerobatic aircraft, or to allow him to get out of awkward situations he may never have encountered before.

Societies—There are none for the

The classic 150: *more than 20,000 built during a 18-year production run.*

Cowling on the 152 is a big improvement over the 150 cowl, which, to be opened, required removal of the prop.

Cessna 150, that we know of, excepting that sizable fraternity of pilots who earned their wings in the bird.

Handling—Forgiving and always recoverable but sharp-edged enough to demand the precision that lots of instructors prefer. The bird has a dandy set of "para-lift" flaps which will allow awesome approach angles, but until a diminution of full flap angles from 40 to 30 degrees on the 152, the bird was known as an anvil in a balked-landing go-around with full flaps. In general, though, the 150 is a delightful airplane to fly.

Powerplant—The introduction of 100 LL initially gave the Continental O-200 powerplant in the Cessna 150 a dose of lead-fouling problems, but users have learned to live with low-lead fuel by increased care to leaning, changing sparkplugs and oil more often, and by use of TCP additive. Deterioration of valve seat heads has been reduced by substitution of new ones made of a different material. Buyers should check to see if the newer valve seats have been installed.

The Cessna 152 comes with a 110-hp Lycoming O-325 engine that copes with low-lead fuel more gracefully. Reports of unexplained reduction of

static rpm or uneven operation in this engine led to a Lycoming service letter listing several possible causes. One of these was possible excessive wear or looseness on the ball end of the push rods, and shortening of the rods.

Flexibility—There is a patroller version with long-range fuel tanks and a plexiglass door and a seaplane version that never quite caught on because of what old salts regard as too long a takeoff run with floats. There is also an aerobatic version that is an oddity with a wheel rather than a stick control and performs aerobatics like an old maid aunt compared with the likes of the Pitts Specials, Great Lakes and CAP 21 and even the Bellanca Decathlon.

Comparative qualities—Stacked up alongside the newer production two-place trainers like the Beech Skipper and Piper Tomahawk, the Cessna 152 shows up surprisingly well in nearly every performance category. Only in styling and visibility is the basic old Cessna airframe eclipsed by the newer birds—which doesn't say much for "modern" lightplane technology.

The first Cessna 150s had poor visibility to the rear, thanks to the full-enclosed cabin, were placarded against spins and had a not unattractive, stubby, vertical tail. They had manual flaps that were a delight to operate, with a lever between the seats. Baggage space, though, was quite limited. The airplane also had a disquieting idiosyncrasy which would manifest itself at odd times, as after a flight, when the pilot had just taxied up to the fuel pump and shut down the engine. The airplane might then slowly and majestically raise its nose up to the sky and squat—*clank*—on its tail.

But in the 1961 model 150, this trait was corrected by relocating the main landing gear struts two inches aft on the cabin. Also, rearward visibility was improved a mite by the enlargement of the two little aft windows by about 15 percent.

In 1964 the most dramatic change in the history of the line was instituted: the fuselage was chopped down behind the wing and a neat, little wraparound window placed in the rear. This was

The 150 panel is a familiar sight to hundreds of thousands of pilots.

Model	Year	Number Built	Average Retail Price	Cruise Speed (mph)	Rate of Climb (fpm)	Useful Load (lbs)	Fuel Std/Opt (gals)	Engine	TBO (hrs)	Overhaul Cost
150	1959-62	N/A	$ 4,500	121	740	630	26/35	100-hp Continental	1,800	$3,400
150	1963-66	1,831	$ 5,300	121	740	535	26/38	100-hp Continental	1,800	$3,400
150	1967-71	8,095	$ 6,750	122	670	535	26/38	100-hp Continental	1,800	$3,400
150	1972-75	4,376	$ 8,000	122	670	535	26/38	100-hp Continental	1,800	$3,400
150	1976-77	2,399	$ 9,750	122	670	535	26/38	100-hp Continental	1,800	$3,400
152	1978	1,193	$11,000	121	715	550	26/39	110-hp Lycoming	2,000	$3,500
152	1979	1,262	$14,000	121	715	550	26/39	110-hp Lycoming	2,000	$3,500
150 Aerobat	1970-72	342	$ 7,500	122	670	496	26/38	100-hp Continental	1,800	$3,400
150 Aerobat	1973-75	180	$ 9,000	122	670	496	26/38	100-hp Continental	1,800	$3,400
150 Aerobat	1976-77	124	$11,250	122	670	496	26/38	100-hp Continental	1,800	$3,400
152 Aerobat	1978	73	$13,800	121	715	550	26/39	110-hp Lycoming	2,000	$3,500

the birth of "omni vision." At the same time, a generous-sized baggage space was opened up under the little rear greenhouse window. Perhaps to accommodate the extra baggage, the 150 received its first jump in gross weight, 100 pounds, from 1,500 pounds up to 1,600 pounds. The C-152's gross went up another 70 pounds to 1,670.

In 1966 Cessna felt impelled to cut the price of the 150 by a stunning 10 percent from $7,825 to $6,995. Adding a bit of flair (though negligible aerodynamic improvement) Cessna went to the modish swept vertical tail on the 150.

In addition, 50 percent more baggage space was added as they moved the cabin wall aft by one bay. On top of that, the electric stall warning horn was given the boot in favor of the wailing, sighing symphony of a pneumatic reed stall warning which could not be disconnected by the failure of an electrical circuit.

In another rather radical change the same year, Cessna did away with the quick, sure manual flaps and introduced the very modern and very languid electric flaps.

The 1967 models marked the first attempt to give cramped 150 pilots a bit more elbow room—by bowing out the doors slightly for an alleged three-inch increase in cabin diameter. Also, the floorboard just aft of the rudder pedals was lowered slightly. Other little touches: the seven-inch nosewheel strut extension was shortened to four inches and an alternator replaced the traditional generator for better power output at lower rpms.

This was the year the seaplane version was introduced—a delightful-handling machine that failed to make it in the big time, ostensibly because it took just too long to become unstuck and away on takeoff in the lake country where every cattail length of lake run had to count.

In the 1968 model, Cessna provided yet another smidgen of knee room by paring a couple of inches off the width of the center console separating the pilot and copilot knees. A revised flap system was offered to allow "hands-off" flap retraction.

The 1970 model gained one esthetic distinction: cambered wingtips.

A year later in 1971 the 150 inherited the nice tubular landing gear struts of the Cardinal, for smoother touchdown and taxi, along with a 16 percent wider track width. To quiet the

drumming of the prop air against the cowling and windshield slightly, the propeller was extended out front a bit. Also the landing light was moved from the wing, where it never seemed to illuminate the correct portion of the runway, to the nose inlet.

The 1975 models were marked by newly styled speed fairings and cowling that generated an alleged five-mph higher cruise speed. In addition, both fin and rudder area were increased to provide more rudder power in crosswind landings.

The year 1976 saw the introduction of vertically adjustable pilot seats, and 1977 was the year of a pre-select flap control (again like the Cardinal's) along with a new vernier mixture to replace the traditional push-pull plunger.

The 1978 Cessna 152 introduced the new 110-hp Lycoming engine, a (troublesome) 28-volt electrical system, a one-piece cowling and redesigned fuel tanks that reduced the unusable fuel to 1.5 gallons. Flap extension was limited to 30 degrees to give better performance during a balked landing. And the new Lycoming engine gave an extra 200 hours of TBO over the Continental—2,000 hours.

Modifications

The Cessna 150 can be given half as much horsepower and turned into a pint-sized STOL machine, thanks to a brace of alterations offered by several companies.

Firms providing the engine switch are MASA (Mid-America STOL Aircraft, Inc., Wichita, KS) and Avcon

Industries, Inc. (also of Wichita). Those offering STOL alterations are Robertson Aircraft corp., Renton, Wash. and Horton, Inc. at Wellington, KS.

MASA and Avcon install 150-hp Lycoming engines in place of the normal 100-hp Continental. This makes for a big jump (up to about 950 fpm) in climb performance, a fairly healthy increase in cruise speed (up to 145-150 mph) and a small loss in useful load (about 30 pounds).

Avcon also notes that some extensive juggling of weight is necessary to accommodate the bigger engine, mostly involving shifting the battery from the engine compartment to the tail section.

Robertson provides what appears to be the most elaborate STOL treatment to Cessna 150s. This includes a sophisticated flap-aileron interconnect system with drooping ailerons that work at different angles to match flap angles. Also part of the mod are recontoured leading edges, stall fences, conical cambered wingtips and, if needed, aileron gap seals.

For less money Horton installs a leading-edge alteration, along with a new landing light lens for wing-mounted models, stall fences on top of the wing, aileron fences plus "drooped" wingtips.

The purpose of both STOL installations is to lower stall speeds and provide more controllability near and in the stall regime.

For pilots who prefer taildraggers, Custom Aircraft Conversions, Inc. in San Antonio, Texas, can supply landing gear kits.

The first 150 was this 1959 model. *It was basically a ten-year-old 140A with a nosewheel.*

The Aviation Consumer Used Aircraft Guide

Owner Comments

One flight school operator was so pleased with the 150 as a trainer that he likened it to the J-3 Cub as one of the all-time low-maintenance classics:

"It's been an amazing airplane. I'd parallel that with the J-3 almost." Problems? "You have the usual matter of guys pulling out the starter cable. As for reports that the nosewheel shimmies, if you land real fast on it, it'll shimmy, as it might on any airplane. But that's the usual thing with a training airplane. I wouldn't say that the maintenance is high on it. For the beating that they take, they're excellent."

"The only problem with the Cessna 150 as a cross-country machine is the way it reacts to turbulence—you really feel the bumps. You get jolted around, compared with a larger four-place airplane. Nevertheless, it's mainly a lot of fun, and maneuverable to fly.

"Aside from a cracked crankcase, the only other maintenance problem I've had is with the nose strut, which I had to have overhauled. I bought it from an FBO where it had been used as a training plane, but it really held up to the wear and tear pretty well. Aside from the time in the logbooks, you couldn't tell how much it had been flown, and how hard. It had 2,850 hours on it when I bought it."

"One problem with the airplane is the way the fuel system feeds unevenly, even with the tank selector on *both*. One wing gets heavy, so you have to compensate with aileron. And with my airplane it's usually the right tank that feeds first, so if you're flying from the left seat, you have to compensate for your weight and the fuel in the left tank."

"It spins okay, but winds up pretty fast; it really whips around compared with other planes I've spun in training."

"Cabin size is very limited for two full-sized people. You're elbow to elbow. Visibility is all right, but if they'd put a 172 type windshield in, it would be much better; and, of course, top visibility isn't that good."

"In all, it's fun to fly, to go up and toy around with, and it's not that expensive fuelwise."

"We had the Horton STOL conversion on our 150, and it worked out beautifully. It just makes a good, complete all-around plane, though my husband and I probably will go to a larger four-place next time. We don't really need the STOL for short fields; we just feel it makes the airplane safer.

"The only mechanical problem we've had with it was once on a long trip the alternator went out and we lost all our electronic equipment, got lost in a midwestern dust storm and had to make an expediency landing. But I think Cessna makes a good airplane."

"What I like about it is that the maintenance is relatively inexpensive—this is the fourth airplane I've owned, and the newest one. The one thing I don't like about it is that to me it is a very boring airplane. Also, I don't like the fact that every time you pull up to a gas pump people ask you if you are a student on a cross-country. And, you know, when you're paying money for an airplane, you like to have people say it looks nice when you pull in to the pump. It's an ego thing.

"I think the handling is fairly good, but I'd prefer lighter ailerons. My old Swift had lighter ones, for example. I like the way it spins for training. It's very predictable; it goes into a spin the same way every time. To avoid problems on a balked landing, I teach my students to use just 20 degrees of flaps, and about the only time I teach them to use 40 degrees is if they get real high on the approach. My instructor taught me that, looking on 40 degrees as just an extra drag device. Electric flaps, especially on a balked landing, are a real problem since you don't have any climb capability with full flaps.

"The noise level, as in most light airplanes, is unbearable, and I think that's an area where improvement could be made. I have a 1967 model.

"I use it quite a bit for cross-country in addition to training, and it works out pretty well. It's got pretty good range. You can figure it is a three-hour airplane, and then you have 45 minutes' reserve.

"I would like to have a little more top speed on the airplane for cross-country

The Aerobat, *although certified for loops, rolls and spins, is a rather poor aerobatic trainer.*

cruising. I had considered buying a Grumman American Trainer, but the initial cost is a little higher. And when I bought the airplane, I wanted to do some flight training on my own, and the Grumman was supposedly more of a pilot's airplane, and I was working with low-time students.

"The nosewheel is a constant problem —that's one of the weak links in the airplane. I've had nosewheel shimmy ever since I bought the airplane, and though the shimmy damper was rebuilt and rebushed, it never helped. I've had no real problem with the strut, except that it deflates about every two months, but that seems to be normal."

"The airplane has a really outstanding fuel system, with just one lever for both tanks. But the uneven feeding of the tanks is disconcerting. On a long trip, one tank will be on empty, and the other on half, and you sit there hoping the other one will start feeding pretty soon and they'll even themselves out. They always do, eventually.

"In terms of maintenance, when something goes wrong with the old pull starter solenoid system, that's a $70 replacement. When they went to the key starter system, that meant the replacement cost went up to about $250."

This Cessna photo *makes the 150 interior look roomy, but it's actually very narrow and cramped, as any 200-pound instructor will testify.*

Yankee/AA-1

If any modern airplane deserves the hackneyed label "sports car of the air," it's the AA-1, the little two-seater built from 1969 until 1978 by American Aviation and its successor company, Grumman American. Originally called the Yankee, the AA-1 series was later sold under a confusing array of names like Trainer, Tr-2, Lynx and T-Cat. Most people call the AA-1s Yankees, however, and we shall do the same in this article for the sake of simplicity.

Only about 1,500 Yankees are now flying, and the used-plane market is not particularly active. However, the AA-1 is becoming a "cult" airplane, which keeps prices fairly high. Although the Aircraft Price Digest lists retail prices as low as $6,000, Yankee buffs report that only the real dogs sell for less than $8,500 or so.

The AA-1's snappy handling qualities and fighter-like canopy are its big selling points, along with low operating costs. However, the Yankee has a very poor safety record, and any potential buyer—particularly a low-time Cessna-trained pilot—should search his soul before deciding to tackle one of general aviation's most challenging airplanes.

Genealogy
The airplane started life as the BD-1, Jim Bede's vision of a cheap, simple airplane for the common man. Bede ran out of money before the BD-1 was was certificated and a new company, American Aviation, was formed to complete certification and start production of the airplane. It first appeared in 1969 as the AA-1 Yankee Clipper. The stall characteristics of the original Yankee were rather abrupt, and it had a severe tendency to "get behind the power curve," so the leading edge of the wing was modified in 1971. This model was the AA-1A "Trainer." Both the Yankee Clipper and the Trainer were built in 1971, but production of the "hot-wing" Clipper was halted in 1972 after a total of 459

had been built. The AA-1B was introduced in 1973 with a 60-pound gross weight increase (up from 1,500 to 1,560 pounds) but no major design changes. The AA-1B was offered in two basic models: a rather Spartan version called the "Trainer" and a dolled-up model called the Tr-2. The Trainer had a climb prop for pattern work, while the Tr-2 had a cruise prop that gave it poorer climb but better cruise speed.

In 1977 the AA-1C model was introduced, with a larger horizontal stabilizer to improve longitudinal stability and spin recovery, and a gross weight boosted to 1,600 pounds. The dual-path marketing continued under new names; the T-Cat was the flight school airplane with climb prop, while the Lynx was the "personal" sportplane with a cruise prop.

Production was halted in 1978, mostly because of production start-up problems after the factory was moved from Cleveland to Savannah, Ga. It's also possible that the airplane's poor safety record—and the resultant high rate of product liability lawsuits—played a role in the decision to suspend production.

Handling and Performance
To pilots accustomed to the heavy controls of a Cessna, the Yankee is full of surprises. They start while you're taxiing out for takeoff; there is no nosewheel steering. One guides the airplane by differential braking only; the nosewheel is free castoring. The rudder is very sensitive on the ground, and plenty of student pilots have ended up in the weeds when the wind blows.

Pitch and roll control are also very, very quick. It's very easy to overrotate a Yankee on takeoff, and fingertip pressure is all that's needed for most pitch changes. The short wings and big ailerons produce lightning-quick roll response, a trait that has given birth to fighter pilot fantasies in thousands of pilots, we imagine. For all its agility, however, the Yankee is not approved for aerobatics. Loops, rolls and spins are forbidden. We imagine that plenty of pilots have done rolls and loops in the Yankee anyway, but we can't emphasize enough that the airplane should never be spun intentionally. If a company pilot flying an AA-1A with a spin chute can't recover from a spin (it happened), it's unlikely that Joe Average

AA-1B was introduced in 1973. *The only major change from the AA-1A was an increase in gross weight from 1,500 to 1,560 pounds.*

AA-1s appeal *to sporty hot-rod types.*

will.

Performance of the Yankee is good at higher speeds, but poor at the low end. Cruise speeds range from 115 to 130 mph or so, depending on whether a climb or cruise prop is installed. These speeds are 10 to 20 mph faster than other popular two-seaters such as the 150, and even the new Tomahawk and Skipper trainers.

At sea level on mild days, the Yankee has a reasonable climb rate—from 660 to 760 fpm, depending on the model. But in hot weather at high field elevations the climb rate falls off drastically, to the point that some pilots hesitate to take along a passenger when the density altitude climbs above 6,000 or 7,000 feet unless the runway is very long and the terrain flat.

Range is rather limited because of the small 22-gallon fuel supply (four gallons less than the Cessna 150). Like most trainers, the Yankee can't quite manage to legally carry full fuel and two large people when reasonably equipped. A typical useful load is around 450-500 pounds, which leaves 320-370 pounds for people and baggage. Unfortunately, because of its rapid drag buildup at high angles of attack, the Yankee doesn't handle overload situations as well as, say, the 150. This is one airplane in which gross weight limits should be respected.

Safety
No doubt about it, the AA-1 has a terrible safety record by comparison with other modern aircraft. According to NTSB statistics for the period 1972-76, the Yankee's fatal accident rate was 4.8 per 100,000 flight hours—nearly triple that of the Cessna 150, and much higher than any single-engine airplane then in production. NTSB records show the Yankee has abnormally high rates of stall, spin, and engine-failure accidents, in addition to ground loops, hard landings and undershoots.

The safety record of the AA-1 and the design features that contribute to it were outlined in detail in the November 1, 1979 issue of *The Aviation Consumer,* so we will summarize here only briefly: the Yankee has a combination of high induced drag and low longitudinal stability at takeoff and landing speeds. In short, it sinks like a brick and is very twitchy on the controls. The root of the induced-drag problem is the short wings and boxy fuselage, which build up drag quickly at low speeds. The poor stability is basically the result of the small tail size and short fuselage.

The Yankee also tends to go flat in a spin; if this occurs, the airplane is unrecoverable. Unlike all the trainers currently on the market, the Yankee is not certified for spinning, and has not been tested by the FAA beyond one turn.

On the plus side of the safety ledger, the AA-1 is, by most reports, more crashworthy than most aircraft. It is a stoutly built little airplane, with rigid bonded honeycomb skin surrounding the cabin area. Because the honeycomb cannot be easily tapered in thickness,

Model	Year	Average Retail Price	Number Built	Useful Load (lbs)	Cruise Speed (mph)	Rate of Climb (fpm)	Fuel Capacity (gals)	Engine	TBO (hrs)	Overhaul Cost
AA-1 Yankee	1969	$6,000	174	493	134	710	22	108-hp Lycoming	2,000	$3,500
AA-1 Yankee	1970	$6,300	257	493	134	710	22	108-hp Lycoming	2,000	$3,500
AA-1 Yankee	1971	$6,500	26	493	134	710	22	108-hp Lycoming	2,000	$3,500
AA-1A Trainer	1971	$6,800	245	493	125	765	22	108-hp Lycoming	2,000	$3,500
AA-1A Trainer	1972	$7,000	234	493	125	765	22	108-hp Lycoming	2,000	$3,500
AA-1A Tr-2	1972	$8,000	Incl.	493	125	765	22	108-hp Lycoming	2,000	$3,500
AA-1B Trainer	1973	$7,250	237	585	124	705	22	108-hp Lycoming	2,000	$3,500
AA-1B TR-2	1973	$8,700	Incl.	585	133	660	22	108-hp Lycoming	2,000	$3,500
AA-1B Trainer	1974	$8,000	207	585	142	705	22	108-hp Lycoming	2,000	$3,500
AA-1B Tr-2	1974	$8,750	Incl.	585	133	660	22	108-hp Lycoming	2,000	$3,500
AA-1B Trainer	1975	$8,500	103	585	124	705	22	108-hp Lycoming	2,000	$3,500
AA-1B Tr-2	1975	$9,000	Incl.	585	133	660	22	108-hp Lycoming	2,000	$3,500
AA-1B Trainer	1976	$9,000	N/A	585	124	705	22	108-hp Lycoming	2,000	$3,500
AA-1B Tr-2	1976	$9,500	N/A	585	133	660	22	108-hp Lycoming	2,000	$3,500
AA-1C T-Cat	1977	$10,750	122	598	129	750	22	115-hp Lycoming	2,000	$3,500
AA-1C Lynx	1977	$10,750	Incl.	598	135	700	22	115-hp Lycoming	2,000	$3,500
AA-1C T-Cat	1978	$12,500	88	598	129	750	22	115-hp Lycoming	2,000	$3,500
AA-1C Lynx	1978	$12,500	Incl.	598	135	700	22	115-hp Lycoming	2,000	$3,500

Grumman American Yankee/Trainer

the AA-1's skin is a lot thicker than it has to be in many places. Likewise, the tubular spar has a constant thickness all the way out to the tip, again because it's too expensive to taper it. These production economies add unnecessary structure and weight, which hurts performance—but they do make the plane stronger in a crash. One flight school reports that in four low-altitude stall accidents it experienced, there were no major injuries.

Maintenance

Readers and mechanics tell us that the AA-1 is a good, simple, reliable machine in most cases. Annual costs as low as $150 are reported. As with most aircraft, however, there are some things to watch for if you're shopping for a used AA-1.

The biggest potential maintenance headache is delamination of the bonded skin, in pre-1976 models. Starting in the early '70s, there were a few isolated cases of de-bonding, mostly at the trailing edges of the ailerons, flaps and tail surfaces. By 1975, delamination became more widespread, however, and an Airworthiness Directive was issued in 1976 that required "peel rivets" to be installed at strategic points. The problem was especially serious in airplanes built from April 1974 to December 1975. During this time, Grumman American switched from the Whittaker bonding sealant it had used for years to a new American Cyanimide glue known as "purple passion" among production workers. "Purple passion" was strong, but it deteriorated

rapidly. Grumman American won't tell us the precise serial numbers of airplanes built with the defective sealant, but we estimate that 1974, '75 and '76 AA-1B models with serial numbers from approximately 400 to 600 are affected.

Used-plane buyers considering an AA-1 from this era should give bondlines close scrutiny—particularly aircraft in warm, humid coastal regions such as Florida, where the problem appears to be the worst.

Other maintenance checkpoints: Pre-1976 AA-1 models tend to run hot during the summer, and the AA-1s seem to have had more than their share of cylinder problems. Check compression carefully, particularly the rear cylinders. AA-1s didn't have oil coolers until 1977 (a retrofit kit is available from Grumman American), and the hot oil—combined with an unusual "upside down" oil ring—contributes to many cases of glazed cylinder walls and high oil consumption, with top overhauls often necessary around the 700-800-hour mark. One big AA-1 operator reports that the oil cooler kit and reversal of the oil ring (technically illegal, by the way) help significantly. We've also received reports that the AA-1C, which uses a high-compression 100-octane version of the O-235 Lycoming, has lead-fouling problems when run on hi-lead 100-octane green gas. One flight school reports several partial engine failures and precautionary landings because of lead fouling.

Overall, the little Lycoming has a

good record, and the 2,000-hour TBO seems realistic.

If you're considering an airplane with damage history—and the AA-1's high accident rate means that a lot of used Yankees will have had major repairs—check the quality of the repairs carefully. The honeycomb sandwich skin is a mystery to most mechanics, and a botched repair job is a real possibility. If you do buy an AA-1, keep in mind that not every mechanic will want to work on it.

Another minor maintenance checkpoint: the nosewheel. If it hasn't been greased regularly, or adjusted correctly, severe nosewheel shimmy can result.

Because of the Yankee's pitch sensitivity and porpoising tendencies—and the high probability of training duty—many have damaged nosewheel mounts. Check this area carefully, and make sure the repair has been done according to an approved procedure.

The country's Yankee maintenance guru seems to be Kenny Blackman at Western Air Sales in Everett, Wash. Blackman volunteered to offer advice to any *Aviation Consumer* reader looking for a used Yankee, and we strongly suggest that he be consulted. Phone is toll-free: 800-426-1690.

Modifications

Several engine mods are available for Yankees. Jimmy Collins, Rte. 4, Box 810, Jefferson, TX, offers STC paperwork for 150-hp and 160-hp Lycoming engine installations. Useful load is reduced by 50 or 60 pounds, however, and the higher fuel consumption limits range severely. Collins is reportedly working on a gross weight increase, but as far as we know, he has not yet obtained it.

The aforementioned Kenny Blackman at Western Air Sales has an STC for a high-compression version of the O-235 that puts out 125 horsepower and reportedly solves the lead-fouling problems of the 115-hp engine in the AA-1C models. Blackman is also working on a host of aerodynamic, gross weight and fuel capacity improvements, but these are not yet approved. Blackman also says he has modified the horizontal stabilizer on one airplane, which dramatically decreased stall speed and improved longitudinal stability. Blackman and his Yankee-loving pals also have formed the American Yankee Association, 12503 25th Ave., SE, Everett, Washington 98204.

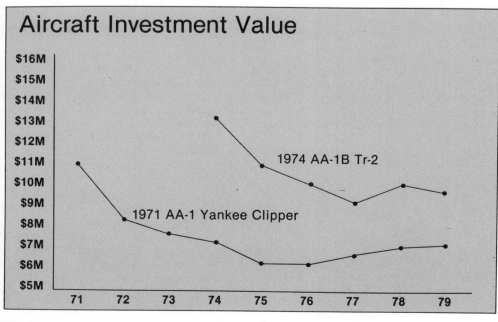

Aircraft Investment Value

1974 AA-1B Tr-2

1971 AA-1 Yankee Clipper

Owner Comments

"With a climb prop here in Albuquerque (5,300-foot elevation, with density altitude over 9,000 feet on summer afternoons), my T-Cat gets a consistent 123-125 mph, with 128 in winter at 7,500-8,500 altitude. With a cruise prop—on a Lynx that I flew for about 10 hours—I got a consistent 134-135 mph.

"With a climb prop, full fuel, and only one person aboard in summer at 90 degrees, I have a takeoff roll about 2,500 feet, and climb about 400-500 fpm.

"However, for runways under 5,000 feet, with density altitude over 5,000 or 6,000 feet, I do *not* recommend full gross weight. The short wings, low power, and 17-to-1 wing loading mean a very long takeoff roll (I've often seen 3,500-4,000 feet at or just below gross on 85-90-degree day at the 5,300 elevation we have here). With obstacles at the end of the runway, or rising terrain just off the runway, or simply a short runway—like the Coronado Airport 4,200-foot runway—it becomes unnecessarily thrilling on takeoff at anything near gross weight when the temperature is over 75 degrees, even with the climb prop. With a cruise prop ... I'm not about to try it.

"It is a great plane for single-pilot operation, and I would recommend it heartily for good, competent pilots who stay ahead of a plane, are used to fairly high approach speeds (70-75 KIAS) and fast sink rate. The visibility is excellent. It is much better in turbulence than a Cessna 150 or 172 because of that high wing loading. But where this plane shines—besides its very high speed for a 115-hp engine—is handling. It is truly a sports car. It has the typical and exquisite Grumman inputs. Comparing it to Cessnas and Pipers, it is a Porsche or Alfa Romeo compared to a station wagon. The 'light' handling is not a boon in severe turbulence, though.

"On the ground, its handling is also excellent—incredibly sharp turns are routine. With its short wings, it fits almost anywhere, and gets in and out of really tight places. However, in strong crosswinds, it has a tendency to "weathercock"—like the Cheetah and Tiger and taildraggers—and there is noticeable use of the rudder/brake on the side opposite the wind.

"Landings are excellent—if you know what you are doing. I really like them, compared to most other planes. The approach is fast (70 knots with flaps, 75 without, and 65 knots *with* power), and the sink rate is high (about 1,200 fpm or more in the few short glances I've made), but it is like a lot of twins and heavy singles. In fact, training in it means a 150 or Tomahawk will be a cinch, but more importantly, transition to heavier planes or twins will not be as difficult or hazardous.

"I do recommend it as a training aircraft with a conscientious and good flight instructor who insists on perfection in students. However, for a lax instructor, or student or pilot who is used to 'forgiving' aircraft like a 150 or 172, a pilot can get himself into real trouble if he is not careful—especially if his rudder and aileron coordination is poor on base and final. A skid in this short-wing speedster can result in a quick spin. (My instructor was superb, insisting not only on very high standards, but spin training—in *other* aircraft.)

"It is terrible on a soft-field takeoff because it takes such high airspeed to lift off. Combine it with a short field, and you have real problems, even well under gross weight. A grass field at 5,000 elevation at 85-90 degrees is going to require at least 4,000 feet to get off even 100 pounds below gross. It is *superb* at a short-field landing with its high sink rate/high descent angle and low float (especially 65 KIAS with power). And it has incredibly strong landing gear. I once 'blew' a landing and hit the ground so hard my glasses almost came off, and the plane sprang back in the air and immediately hit solidly again—not even a crack on those strong landing gear.

"Indeed, I've seen a Lynx that crashed (pilot leveled it just as it hit the ground): it hit so hard that the wheel pounded into the bottom of the wing and left a dent, and the leg (reinforced fiberglass) was severely damaged, with splinters everywhere, but the leg did not break off. In that same crash, the ground tore the metal off the last two feet of the wing like a sardine can, and the spar—which houses the fuel tank—dragged in the dirt, but the fuel did not leak, and later measurement of the spar showed no deformity. The Lynx and T-Cat are built very strong, especially that landing gear—and if a pilot gets behind the plane, he'll need that super landing gear.

"Maintenance is very low: change of tires, plugs and oil, and that's about it. The 100-hour inspections are rarely over $130 even now. The engine is super reliable. Another T-Cat with over 900 hours, however, had low compression in the cylinders and fouled plugs. Good leaning technique helps, but I'm sure the training use of these planes puts a lot of strain on their engine.

"The in-flight noise is loud. There is no insulation in the roof and the din is high. Some twins make as much noise, but I haven't found many single-engine planes that make this much. I recommend earplugs; I strongly recommend headphones.

"The fuel quantity and range is low: 24 gallons, only 22 usable, and about 250 nm (once I went 300 nm, but adrenalin content was high, and I had only four gallons left when I landed)."

Boxy fuselage *is cheap to build but aerodynamically inefficient.*

Piper Super Cub

The Piper PA-18 Super Cub is the original bushplane, and plenty of pilots still swear it's the best STOL (Short Take Off and Landing) aircraft flying today. Super Cubs abound in Alaska, where the loads are heavy and the landing strips are short and rough, but they are also a favorite of sport pilots who want a cheap, strong-flying craft just for fun. More than 10,000 of the fabric-covered anachronisms have been built over the years, and the Super Cub is now entering its 31st year of production at Piper's Lock Haven plant, which turns out a couple of hundred a year, regular as clockwork.

History

The Super Cub is, of course, a direct descendant of the hallowed Piper J-3 Cub, which first appeared back in 1940. The J-3 was spruced up into the PA-11 in 1948, and the first PA-18 Super Cub, which appeared in 1950, was very similar to the PA-11. Called the Super Cub PA-18-95, it had a 90-hp engine, no flaps and the old Cub-style elevator. That first year, a 115-hp Lycoming-powered version (the PA-18-105) was also available, and it had the flaps, counter-balanced elevator and other features that were to distinguish Super Cubs from their forebears. (In fact, some purists don't really consider the 90-hp version to be a "real" Super Cub, even though it was produced in small numbers until 1961.)

In 1951, power of the Lycoming version was boosted to 125, then to 135 the next year, and finally to 150 in 1955. The Super Cub has remained virtually unchanged since 1955, probably the longest career of any airplane without major modifications. (Speaking of longevity records, much has been made recently of the Bonanza's 33-year career, supposedly the longest of any airplane. But the Super Cub beats that; starting with the J-3 in 1945, the Cub series has been in production for 35 consecutive years. To those who argue that the J-3 and PA-18 are not the same

model type, we would point out that the changes from the J-3 to PA-18 are certainly no greater than the metamorphosis of the Bonanza from a 165-hp airplane into the current 285-hp version.)

Performance

Quite simply, for heavy loads and short fields, the Super Cub has no peer. Only the big, expensive Helio Courier can approach the Super Cub's STOL performance, and some Super Cub users insist it will outperform the Helio when both are heavily loaded. One Alaskan operator reports, "I've been full circle from PA-12s to 170s, 180s, 185s and a Helio Courier, and when you get right down to the dirty work, the Super Cub fits our needs better than anything built." Another Alaskan says, "Up here, the Super Cub is pretty much considered the ultimate airplane for bush flying and performance."

According to the book, a Super Cub's takeoff ground roll is 200 feet at max gross weight. Pilots tell us of 300-foot takeoff rolls under heavy overload con-

ditions. One Super Cub owner wrote to tell us the results of a short takeoff contest he witnessed. With a 20-mph wind down the runway, a PA-18 got off the ground in exactly 19 feet. The Super Cub has won the annual takeoff competition every year it's been held.

Standard useful load is about 800 pounds, but overloads are common, particularly with the float-equipped version, which has more room to lash on excess cargo. We've heard of Super Cubs carrying five people with aplomb (pilot, one passenger sitting on another's lap in the back seat, and one hanging on each float). One bush pilot reports hauling a whole dressed-out moose, plus the hunter, in a Super Cub.

The Super Cub's performance formula is simple: a big, high-lift wing and a monster engine. The Cessna Skyhawk uses the same basic engine, but has a gross weight 550 pounds higher, and a smaller wing. It's easy to see why huge overloads are almost the rule with the Super Cub, and why gross-weight performance is so spec-

The Super Cub is virtually unchanged since 1955, *except for the paint job. This means older models hold their value well, since the new ones don't make them outdated.*

tacular. "With just the pilot and a little bit of gas, the climbout angle approaches vertical," reports one owner.

Unfortunately, the Super Cub's horizontal performance is not so spectacular. In fact, it's downright awful. Max cruise is only 115 mph. Drag is so high that it's almost pointless to use max cruise power, so many operators choose to fly at very low power settings at perhaps 90-100 mph.

Fuel capacity of the Super Cub is 36 gallons in all versions except the 90-hp model, which had only one 18-gallon tank in the left wing. (The others have another tank in the right wing.) The 36-gallon supply provides perhaps four hours of endurance, for a maximum range of a shade over 400 miles. It's definitely not a cross-country airplane, although it can match most of the two-seat trainers in that regard—at a much higher fuel consumption.

Because of its odd mix of performance capabilities, the Super Cub is primarily a working airplane, occasionally a "fun" STOL sportplane or trainer and virtually never a practical family transportation machine. For that sort of duty, a Cessna 150, Cherokee 140 or other two-seater will fill the bill just as well for far less money.

The Super Cub is approved for limited aerobatics. It loops and spins nicely, but rolls are a real chore because of the ponderous aileron response.

Safety
Like most of the old taildragger aircraft, the Super Cub has a poor safety record. In fact, it has the highest accident rate (overall and fatal) of any aircraft still in production, according to NTSB statistics for the period 1972-76. The Super Cub's fatality rate is three times higher than that of the Cessna 150, for example.

This may be partly due to the type of flying Super Cubs do. Bush flying, fish-spotting, coyote hunting and such are rather dangerous activities for which the Super Cub is widely used.

The Super Cub rates particularly poorly in stall accidents, "uncontrolled collisions with the ground" (as the NTSB calls them) and mid-air collisions. A study of stall/spin accidents covering the years 1965-73 shows the Super Cub with a fatal stall/spin rate of 2.36 per 100,000 hours, poorest of any current production airplane except for the Bellanca Citabria. (The

Bluebook Prices

Model	No. Built	Retail Price*	Model	No. Built	Retail Price*
90-hp			1963	173	$13,750
1950-55	4,617	$ 7,000	1964	153	$13,750
	(incl. 125-135-hp)		1965	138	$14,000
1956-61	2,914	$ 7,500	1966	125	$14,000
	(incl. 150-hp)		1967	136	$14,250
115-hp			1968	170	$14,500
1950	522	$ 7,250	1969	106	$14,750
125-hp			1970	64	$15,000
1951-52	1,420	$11,000	1971	54	$15,500
135-hp			1972	47	$16,000
1952-54	2,565	$12,000	1973	9	$16,500
150-hp			1974	124	$17,250
1955-57	2,334	$12,750	1975	142	$18,000
1958-60	1,404	$13,000	1976	156	$19,000
1961	225	$13,500	1977	198	$20,000
1962	124	$13,500	1978	188	$21,000
			1979	200	$24,000

*For 1950-60 airplanes, price includes com radio. For 1961-79 airplanes, price includes nav-com, full panel, vacuum system, lights, electric starter. In all cases, price assumes mid-time engine, good fabric and paint, no major damage history. Dealer wholesale prices are about 30 percent below retail.

Citabria's statistics include its Aeronca predecessors, now out of production.) By comparison, the Cessna 150 has a rate of 0.55 and the top-rated Cessna 182, 0.17—nearly 15 times better than the Super Cub. The NTSB's "collision with ground" category is too vague a category upon which to draw conclusions, but the Super Cub's poor showing in the mid-air collision category is probably the result of its poor visibility and use in low-level maneuvering activities such as fish-spotting, etc.

On the other side of the coin, the Super Cub has a very low rate of engine failure accidents, hard landings and overshoots.

Creature "Comforts"
By modern standards, the Super Cub is a cramped airplane. Although a bit roomier than the old J-3, the PA-18 is still far from comfortable. The fuselage dimensions of the J-3 and PA-18 are actually identical, but the Super Cub wing spar does not protrude into the cabin, allowing the seats to be raised and moved back a bit, which gives a roomier feeling and eases the contortions the pilot must endure. With two people aboard, baggage space is severely limited; the Super Cub is a reasonable cargo hauler only with the rear seat removed.

The PA-18 can safely be flown solo from either front or rear seat. Although the Super Cub is more nose-heavy than the J-3, the Super is generally soloed from the front, while the J-3 is soloed only from the rear. These restrictions

are the result of differing regulations only; both aircraft have an extremely wide c.g. tolerance.

As in most high-wing airplanes, visibility is very poor, particularly in the landing pattern. The Super Cub has a skylight-type window in the top of the cabin, but this provides little relief. (There are a few 135-hp L-21 military observation versions of the Super Cub still around; they have much better visibility down and to the rear through greenhouse-type rear windows.) Like most taildraggers, the Super Cub has poor visibility over the nose during taxi, and a back-and-forth weaving is necessary for safe taxiing.

Owners report the airplane to be fearsomely noisy. One *Aviation Consumer* staffer recalls that his ears rang for three days after a 1,000-mile trip in a 1952 Super Cub.

Handling Qualities
The Super Cub flies like a ... well, like a Cub. It's stable, not very responsive, and generally tolerant of less-than-expert piloting technique in the air—although it will stall with a sharp break, a trait that may surprise Cherokee-trained pilots.

The Super Cub is a taildragger, of course, and has all the handling liabilities of that breed: inherent instability on the ground, terrible visibility during landing and takeoff, and severe bouncing tendencies upon landing. Within the framework of taildraggers, however, the Super Cub is relatively easy to handle, with none of the crow-hopping tendencies of the Cessna 180 or ground-loop love of the Luscombe. The standard model, however, comes with heel brakes, which are an abomination for anyone used to conventional toe brakes. For pilots not clever at toe-and-heel shifting, these can provide a hasty introduction to a groundloop in gusty, crosswind conditions.

Resale Value

The Super Cub holds its value well, particularly the later models. This is not surprising, since there have been so few changes to the line. A well-cared-for 1975 model with 400 hours on it has more intrinsic value than a 1978 model with 1,000 hours, and could probably be bought for the same price. Late-model Super Cubs, in fact, don't seem to follow the standard aircraft depreciation pattern, which is a decline of about four years, followed by a leveling off or (in the case of a sought-after aircraft like the Bonanza) steady appreciation. A 1975 Super Cub, for example, sold new for $19,700, but dropped in value only to $16,500 the next year (about 15 percent depreciation, compared to the usual 20 percent first-year loss of value for the average aircraft). After just two years, the value of a 1975 Super Cub climbed up to $17,250, and has remained steady at that level since. Thus the airplane has never been worth less than 85 percent of its original paper value (not counting inflation). A 1974 Super Cub is today worth what it cost new—and not even the blue-chip Bonanza can match that claim. Like-

Horizontal performance is lackluster, vertical performance awesome.

wise, a 1969 Super Cub is today worth 10 percent *more* than its original price, an astonishing display of value.

It's not likely that current production Super Cubs will do as well, however; the current price of $30,000-plus is highly inflated, and it's doubtful that a 1980 Super Cub purchased today will ever fetch $30,000 again (assuming reasonable inflation rates). On the other hand, surging prices for new Super Cubs help keep the value of used ones high.

Shopping Checklist

Even though the Super Cub has remained virtually unchanged over its lifetime, there are a few optional features that any used-plane shopper should look for. Among the appraisal points of the Super Cub:

• Metallization. Some Super Cubs have been "metallized," which means the steel tubing in the fuselage and tail feathers has been coated with zinc (aluminum in the early models). This is a very desirable feature, for corrosion of the metal tubing is a common problem in older Super Cubs. The airplane's paperwork should indicate if it has been metallized, and there is also a stamp on the firewall attesting to it. You should also visually inspect the tubing, of course.

• Metal belly skin. This is another big plus, although in some cases the blessing may be mixed. The metal skin is obviously more resistant to damage and aging than fabric, and the mod includes extra beefy tubes in the rear fuselage. Unfortunately, the metal belly also may be a signal that the aircraft was once a cropduster, and therefore subject to the ravages of chemical corrosion, in addition to having the hell flown out of it. The agplane version with metal belly was available from 1952 through 1960. Since then, the metal belly skin has been an option on non-duster Super Cubs, so check this out carefully.

• Fabric. The 1971 and later model Super Cubs have Ceconite Dacron covering, a fairly long-lived fabric. The 1970 and earlier models were covered with Grade A cotton, which has a lifespan of three to 10 years, depending on care and conditions. (Some cold-weather operators prefer the cotton because it doesn't shrink as much as Ceconite in frigid temperatures, but most people prefer the synthetic fabric.) If the bird you're looking at has cotton, count on replacement at a cost of $3,000 to $4,000 within a few years.

• Cleveland brakes. These were fit-

Investment Value

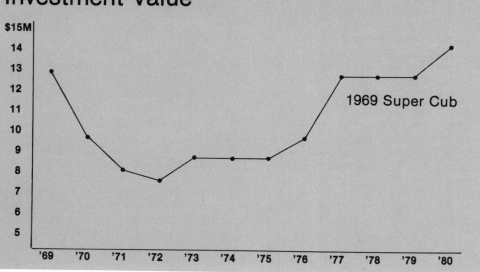

1969 Super Cub

ted to the 1978 and later models, and can be retrofitted to older aircraft. They are a desirable feature.

- Tailwheel. Several different tailwheels have been available over the years; the eight-inch double-fork Scott is the best.
- Strobe light. A tail-mounted strobe was made an option on 1973 and later models.
- Fuel gauges. Electric gauges replaced the old visual gauges in the 1976 and later models. Although neater looking, they are less accurate, and many pilots prefer the old-style gauges.
- Alternator. A 60-amp Alcor alternator kit was made standard equipment in 1977. A standard generator was used from 1950-76, but the Alcor kit is retrofittable to older models, and is a desirable feature if the airplane is equipped with radios, strobe lights or landing light.
- Vacuum pump. A wet-type vacuum pump was available on 1954-62 models, and a dry pump on 1963-80 versions. The wet pumps, although more expensive and messier (they tend to vent a fine spray of oil overboard), are more reliable, have a longer lifespan and may be overhauled fairly inexpensively. (Dry pumps can only be replaced.)
- Wing corrosion-proofing. About 1965 (even Piper couldn't tell us exactly) zinc chromate corrosion-proofing was applied to all wing parts. If the aircraft you're looking at is of mid-60s vintage, remove an inspection panel and check for yourself. (Greenish yellow is good; silver is bad). At about the same time, more hard 4130 steel and heli-arc welding were incorporated in Super Cub fuselages.
- Flaps and ailerons. After 1977, flaps and ailerons were covered with metal instead of fabric, mostly for ease of construction. They are retrofittable to older aircraft. Although cheaper to

Piper PA-18 Super Cub

Engine	Cruise Speed (mph)	Rate of Climb (fpm)	Std. Useful Load (lbs)	Fuel Capacity (gals)	TBO (hrs)	Overhaul Cost
150-hp Lycoming O-320-A2A	115	960	804	36	2,000*	$4,000
135-hp Lycoming O-290-D2	109	870	872	36	1,500	$3,600
125-hp Lycoming O-290-D	112	940	655	36	2,000	$3,600
90-hp Continental C-90-F	100	710	700	18	1,800	$3,000

*Pre-1968 models may be equipped with 7/16-inch valves. In that case, TBO is 1,200 hours.

build, they are not repairable if damaged, a disadvantage for remote operators.

More important than all the niggling mechanical changes over the years is the individual history of the aircraft you are buying. Try to avoid aircraft used for glider or banner-towing, crop-dusting or heavy bush work. Pipeline patrol aircraft, on the other hand, are usually desirable despite the high airframe times, because they are flown long distances at low power settings, which puts very little strain on the engine, landing gear and structure. As with any used aircraft, have a knowledgeable mechanic go over the airplane with a fine-tooth comb. This is critical for the aircraft such as the Super Cub, which are more likely to have suffered abuse or damage sometime in their history.

Maintenance Checks
Have your mechanic check these common Super Cub trouble spots with special care:

- Fatigue cracks in wing strut threaded clevis bolts.
- Worn out landing gear hinge and shock strut bolts and bushings.
- Corrosion in fuselage steel tubing, particularly in lower rear.

- Internal rusting of wing struts. This is not widespread, but has occurred on some aircraft and is the subject of an AD.
- Top rudder hinge bushing, especially on those aircraft equipped with rudder-mounted Grimes beacon.
- Loose or worn out elevator trim jackscrew, particularly in aircraft used for glider or banner towing.

Generally, the Super Cub is a rugged and robust aircraft that is extremely easy to fix in the field. The only trouble spot may be the fabric covering and steel tube structure, which are unfamiliar to many mechanics accustomed to all-metal aircraft. The engine is very reliable, and has a 2,000-hour TBO.

Naturally, compliance with all ADs should be checked. Actually, the Super Cub has been subject to relatively few ADs; a 1964 model, for example, has just eight directives, about half the number of a Cherokee of similar vintage.

Parts and Customer Supprt
Since the airplane is still in production, the parts situation is excellent, even for very old aircraft. Piper still supplies virtually any part of any Super Cub. Only problem is that Piper parts are rather expensive. A better alternative may be Univair Aircraft Corp., Rte 3, Box 59, Aurora, CO 80011. Univair also supplies virtually any Super Cub part—at prices often far less than Piper's. For example, the threaded lift strut bolt, which has been the subject of a recent AD, costs $53 from Piper and $19.50 from Univair. The company also publishes a complete parts catalog for the PA-18 series.

Some Super Cub parts are also available from Wag-Aero, Inc., in Lyons, Wisc.

From a distance, *it's hard to tell a 1959 Super Cub from a 1979 model. There have been practically no changes to the airplane in the past 20 years.*

Owner Comments

"I have owned a 1952 '125' Super Cub, a 1963 '150' Super Cub, and a 1960 '95' Super Cub. The 125 was a good airplane; however, I consistently had problems with engine temperature. The oil temperature would get so hot sometimes, the engine smelled like it was burning. I had it approximately eight months and had this problem on and off the whole time. The Piper distributor never could find the trouble. (I might add that I purchased this airplane used.) When the engine would get hot, the only solution was to close the throttle and dive the airplane, which would cool the engine down. Usually, the problem didn't recur on that particular flight.

"Takeoff roll was in the neighborhood of 200-300 feet with flaps. Cruise was in the 90- to 95-mph range with standard metal prop, and fuel consumption at cruise six to seven gph. Other than engine overheating, the airplane gave me no problems.

"The 150 was my favorite. This airplane would do anything you asked of it. The 150 Lycoming always purred along with absolutely no problems whatsoever. Takeoff, with light fuel and solo, was almost vertical. My technique for shortest possible takeoff was stick full back, add full throttle, reach down and pull full flaps, and you were immediately airborne. Immediately upon breaking ground, forward stick was applied to keep from getting a stall as you got out of ground effect. Takeoff roll at gross *plus* probably averaged in the 200- to 300-foot range. I equipped this airplane with Alaskan "tundra" tires. With these, I flew off sand beaches along south Louisiana, where I would go fishing. The brakes, although adequate with standard 800x4 tires, were useless with the big tires. They carried only four psi pressure, and when you taxied across dry sand, they made a track on the sand that looked like you had rolled a ball on it.

"When I purchased this aircraft from a fish-spotting outfit, the airframe had approximately 4,300 hours on it, and the engine had about 700 hours since new. The fuselage had been metallized, and I had no rust problems while I owned it. When I bought it, it had a 61-inch pitch prop on it and it would give a good, honest 120 IAS with this prop. When I changed to the standard 56-inch prop, the IAS dropped to about 105 to 110 IAS at 2,000 feet.

"You could see the look of surprise on Cessna 172 drivers as I would pass them in level flight with the 61 prop that was on the airplane when I first bought it. I really don't think that takeoff performance suffered much with this prop and the loads I normally carried.

"Fuel consumption I thought was high, probably averaging nine to 10 gph at the low altitudes, full rich. Leaned out it would burn eight to 8½ gph at 5,000 feet. Stalls were always gentle, with the airspeed indicator reading around 40-45 mph.

"This airplane would haul anything you could put in it, and it still is the only airplane I have ever flown that I felt had more than enough power to do anything I wanted to do.

"The 95 is another story. I purchased it

Trim, mag and carb heat controls are on the left cockpit wall.

used, also. It had the 'plane booster' wing tips on it and all these did was add weight and block visibility to the sides. I had flown a 95 previously without these tips, and it was a sweet-flying airplane. My airplane performed about like a 65-horse J-3 or 7AC, with a cruise of 80-85 mph at about 5½ gph. I flew it out of a 1,100-foot strip, and on a warm day with a heavy load, it was close. I really feel the booster tips hurt this particular airplane more than they helped and would never put them on any airplane I owned."

"I picked up my 1976 Super Cub at the factory in Lock Haven and have since amassed 210 hours on the plane. I bought it with the metal belly pan, because I feel it is a necessity for the type of in-and-out flying I do—into nurseries for the commercial purchasing of plants and shrubs for our business.

"I installed 8.50x6 tires for better flotation on rough, furrowed fields. They're a heck of a lot cheaper than the tundra tires, which go for something like $800 apiece, I'm told. It also seems to brake better with the Cleveland system installed. It's definitely a tail raiser, almost a nose-tipper.

"The stainless steel control cables were prematurely replaced at 200 hours, apparently wearing flat where they pass through the eyelets on the struts. Vibration of the engine has necessitated repeated welding of the muffler cover, and has loosened paint on the wheel strut cover. Nothing big, though.

"I have had a definite problem with a recurring mold or fungus, a black film that forms on the painted surfaces throughout the plane. A good scrubbing will eliminate for a while, but it always comes back. The airplane has always been hangared."

Parts availability *is still reported to be very good.*

Taylorcraft

Anyone looking for absolutely the cheapest possible airworthy certified airplane might consider the Taylorcraft. This fabric-covered two-seat taildragger can be bought for as little as $3,000—although the one you get for that price will be right on the ragged edge of airworthiness.

Even a good, solid airplane that will fly for several years without major work can be had for $5,000 or so—less than the price of a cheap little compact car. With Piper Cubs approaching $10,000, the T-Craft may just be the cheapest airplane on the used market, with the possible exception of an occasional Ercoupe or Luscombe.

History

The Taylorcraft was designed by C.G. Taylor, the man who designed the Piper Cub. In the early '30s, Taylor and William T. Piper joined forces, with Piper supplying the money and Taylor providing the engineering for the Taylor Cub, as it was originally known. But Piper and Taylor had a falling out and Taylor went off on his own to build the Taylorcraft. The Model A in 1937 soon evolved to the Model B, the basic series with which this article deals. The new T-Craft was quite different from the Cub; it had side-by-side seating, wheels instead of sticks and a completely different wing.

The first Taylorcrafts to appear in any number, in 1939 and 1940, were the BL-65, BC-65 and BF-65, powered by Lycoming, Continental and Franklin 65-hp engines, respectively. (Almost all the Lycoming and Franklin engines have since been replaced with the Continental.) The BC-12 model was introduced in 1941, with a few minor modifications and, most importantly, a better grade of steel in the fuselage tubing. Production was suspended during the war, and then resumed in 1946 with the BC-12D, which had a new tail. Thousands of T-Crafts were built that year, the first of the expected post-war aviation boom, and the majority of used T-Crafts on the

market today are 1946 BC-12D models. The company went bankrupt in late 1946, but was reorganized and continued production of the BC-12 series with both 65-hp and 85-hp engines. The Model 19, an improved version, was introduced in the late 40s, and a couple of hundred were sold before the company went bankrupt for the last time in 1957. The Model 19 had the 85-hp engine, a gross weight up 300 pounds to 1,500, a 24-gallon fuel system to replace the 12-and 18-gallon tanks in previous models, an overhead skylight, improved brakes, a bigger baggage compartment, and other improvements.

Amazingly, the airplane was resurrected again in 1973 by a former Taylorcraft dealer named Charles Feris. Feris spent years tracking down parts and tooling from the final bankruptcy sale, got the FAA to approve a Continental 100-hp installation, and began building the Model F-19. About 150 have been built since 1973, and the F-19 continues in production in Alliance, Ohio, the hand-crafted product of a small group of dedicated old-timers, many of whom built airplanes for C.G. Taylor himself

35 years ago.

The Taylorcraft has recently undergone still another transformation. The Alliance plant is now producing the F-21 model, which has the 118-hp Lycoming engine in place of the Continental, along with improved cabin heat.

Accommodation

Like most of the old post-war two-seat taildraggers, the Taylorcraft is hopelessly cramped for anyone of reasonable stature. (Apparently, people were shorter back in those days.) Two adults sit tightly shoulder-to-shoulder, and anybody over six feet will find his knees clanking against the instrument panel. (The seats are not adjustable.) Headroom is also at a premium.

Owners tell us the old Taylorcrafts are terribly noisy, and our own flights in the newer F-19 model confirm that things haven't changed much. It's terribly noisy, too. And the cabin heat doesn't work very well.

Overall, the Taylorcraft is Spartan at best, but bearable for two medium-sized people and a bit of luggage.

Slim, **tapered fuselage** gave the Taylorcraft 20 mph over the Cub with the same engine.

Instrument panel is simple, to say the least. *Taylorcraft is one of the few post-war two-seater taildragger to have yokes instead of sticks. Very early models had auto-type steering wheels.*

Flying Qualities

The Taylorcraft is not particularly pleasant in the air. Aileron control is terribly sluggish, and adverse yaw is pronounced. The airplane is widely known as a "floater;" this is primarily because of the very low wing loading, barely more than six pounds per square foot—less than some gliders. The Cessna 150, by comparison, has a wing loading of 10.0 pounds per sq. ft.

As a result of its low wing loading, the Taylorcraft has a very low landing speed, and pilots tend to bring it in way too fast and float forever. Proper approach speed is an astoundingly low 50-55 mph. The Taylorcraft is a relatively clean airplane (compared to the Cub, at least) and it has no flaps. This creates a very flat glide angle, which contributes to the floating problem. On the other hand, it can be slipped very well, which gives a good rate of sink.

Gusty crosswinds are the Taylorcraft pilot's mortal enemy, again because of the low wing loading. Like any other taildragger, the Taylorcraft is unstable on the ground and will not settle firmly onto the runway after a hard touchdown above the stall speed, instead rebounding and ballooning. Naturally, any taildragger might be a real handful in the beginning for a pilot who has no tailwheel experience. Tricycle gear pilots are urged to get a thorough checkout and not be frightened off after the first few wild bounces and swerves. Most folks learn eventually.

In turbulence, the Taylorcraft does better than most airplanes with low wing loadings. The 23012 airfoil provides excellent pitch stability, although the ride is bumpy.

Performance

The Taylorcraft's strong point is performance. C.G. Taylor designed the aircraft as a sort of "high-performance" Cub, and it is much faster than the J-3—up to 20 mph faster. This puts the speed at about 95 mph with the 65-hp engine, and over 100 mph with 85 hp. The later F-19 models with the 100-hp Continental will hit 115-120 mph, and the later 118-hp Lycoming F-21 is expected to cruise near the redline.

Rate of climb is also good, in one sense—from 500 fpm to 800 fpm or so, depending on power and loading. That may not sound like much, but it comes at a very low 55-60 mph, so climb angle is not bad at all.

Range is inadequate by modern standards, but compared with that of other old taildraggers, it is quite good. With a 12-gallon tank, figure on 200 miles; some later BC-12D models have 18-gallon tanks which extend range to 350 miles or so. The 19 and F-19 versions have 24 gallons, which brings range up to that of "modern" two-seaters such as the Cessna 152.

In terms of efficiency, the 65-hp Taylorcraft gets better mileage than any other nonexperimental airplane we can think of short of a powered glider. A speed of 95 mph on 4.0 gph works out to about 24 mpg—better even than the vaunted Mooney 201.

Safety

According to National Transportation Safety Board statistics, the Taylorcraft has a fairly good safety record compared to that of other aircraft of similar type and vintage. Like all old taildraggers, the overall accident rate is high: 24.8 per 100,000 flight hours. (That compares to just 10.3 for the Cessna 150.) Many of the old taildragger accidents are minor landing mishaps, however, and do no major damage or injury. In terms of *fatal* accidents, the Taylorcraft ranks better than most of its contemporaries: 2.6 per 100,000 hours. The J-3 Cub, Luscombe, Aeronca Champ and Ercoupe all have fatal rates of 3.9 or better. Among vintage two-seaters, only the Cessna 120, at 1.70, has a lower fatal accident rate. The 150, at 1.35, has

Model	Year	Average Retail Price	Number Built	Cruise Speed (mph)	Rate of Climb (fpm)	Fuel Capacity (gals)	Engine	TBO (hrs)	Overhaul Cost
BC	1939-40	$5,000	NA	90	500	12	65-hp Cont.	1,800	$2,750
BL	1939-40	$5,000	NA	90	450	12	65-hp Lyc.	NA	$2,750
BF	1939-40	$5,000	NA	90	450	12	65-hp Franklin	1,500	$2,500
BC-12	1940-41	$5,000	NA	95	500	12	65-hp Cont.	2,000	$2,750
BC-12D	1946-50	$5,000	NA	95	500	12/18	65-hp cont.	2,000	$2,750
BC-12D-4-85	1947-50	$6,000	NA	110	600	18	85-hp Cont.	2,000	$3,000
Model 19	1950-57	$8,000	NA	110	600	18/24	85-hp Cont.	2,000	$3,000
F-19	1974	$9,250	25	115	775	24	100-hp Cont.	1,800	$3,400
F-19	1975	$9,500	25	115	775	24	100-hp Cont.	1,800	$3,400
F-19	1976	$9,750	29	115	775	24	100-hp Cont.	1,800	$3,400
F-19	1977	$10,250	30	115	775	24	100-hp Cont.	1,800	$3,400
F-19	1978	$12,000	28	115	775	24	100-hp Cont.	1,800	$3,400
F-19	1979	$13,750	16	115	775	24	100-hp Cont.	1,800	$3,400

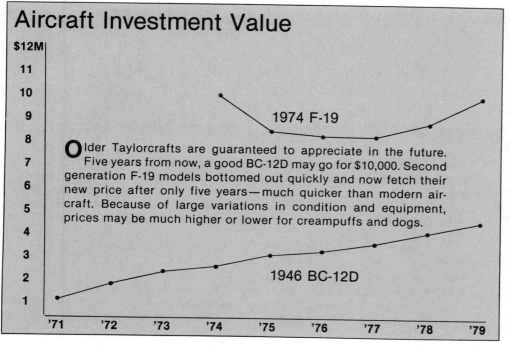

Aircraft Investment Value

Older Taylorcrafts are guaranteed to appreciate in the future. Five years from now, a good BC-12D may go for $10,000. Second generation F-19 models bottomed out quickly and now fetch their new price after only five years—much quicker than modern aircraft. Because of large variations in condition and equipment, prices may be much higher or lower for creampuffs and dogs.

1974 F-19

1946 BC-12D

one of the lowest fatal rates of any single-engine airplane, according to the NTSB. (All figures are based on the period 1972-76.)

The Taylorcraft ranks very poorly in stall accidents, with only the Aeronca Champ and Sedan having a higher stall accident rate. A more detailed study of stall/spin accidents, covering the years 1965-73, verifies the NTSB figures. It shows the Taylorcraft ranked 30th of the 31 aircraft in the study—above only the four-seat Aeronca in having a poor record. On the other hand, no Taylorcraft was involved in a mid-air collision during the period of the NTSB study—a surprising fact, considering the notoriously poor visibility of the airplane.

Appraisal Points

In a 35-year-old airplane there is high potential for deterioration and hidden structural problems. We strongly recommend that potential purchasers hire a mechanic familiar with Taylorcrafts to carefully inspect the airplane. One of the first places to check is the steel tubing in the lower rear fuselage. This is where all the water usually ends up, and it is a traditional trouble spot in Taylorcrafts, just as it is in other old taildraggers. Carefully check that all drain holes are clear, particularly those in the lower landing gear tube. If water collects there, it can freeze and distort the tubes.

The condition of the fabric is the most

important thing to consider—even more important than the engine. After all, a complete recover job will cost $3,000 to $4,000, while a major overhaul on the 65-hp Continental goes for a comparatively paltry $2,700 or so. All older Taylorcrafts originally had Grade A cotton covering, but most have since been replaced with Dacron (Ceconite), fiberglass or other synthetic fabric. When properly applied, these fabrics will last up to 20 years.

The current production F-19 has been covered with Dacron from 1976 on. The 1973-75 models used either Dacron or cotton. The Dacron fabric should be good for another decade, but cotton installed in the early '70s should be due for replacement any day now.

Prices and Investment

As we stated before, the rock-bottom $3,000 tag for a Taylorcraft is probably as low as anything with wings. The average BC-12D will fetch from $5,000 to $6,000, depending on fabric and engine condition. The 85-hp post-war Model 19s command a surprising $7,500-$12,000, with only a real dog going for $7,000. The late-model F-19s are currently worth $9,000 to $13,000. Age alone plays only a minor role in the price of any Taylorcraft; the difference between 30 and 40 years is largely academic.

A Taylorcraft makes a reasonably good investment. Although not imbued with the blue-chip appeal of the J-3 Cub,

a Taylorcraft well maintained can do nothing but appreciate. You could have bought a very nice Taylorcraft BC-12D for $1,200 ten years ago; the investment would now be worth about $5,000—a nice return of about 16 percent per year. At that rate, a Taylorcraft will bring $20,000 in 1990. Don't be surprised.

Parts, STCs, Organizations

The parts situation is excellent for Taylorcrafts. The factory in Alliance instantly can supply virtually all airframe parts, and fun-flying oriented outfits like Wag-Aero and Univair also sell them. We're told that Dan Smith, Box 636, W. Helena, Ark., also sells a good selection of Taylorcraft parts.

Numerous STCs and modifications are available, including a popular one for replacing the 65-hp engine with an 85-hp powerplant. There are even several versions of aerobatic Taylorcrafts with clipped wings and larger engines—up to 180 hp. A clip-wing T-Craft with a big engine makes an excellent aerobatic machine because of the nearly symmetrical airfoil, which enables the airplane to fly negative-G maneuvers with ease. Airshow pilot Duane Cole puts on a remarkable demonstration in such a plane.

As in the case of most old airplanes, there is an enthusiastic owners organization, populated by T-Craft fanatics who know every bit of arcane history and maintenance procedures for the airplane. We strongly urge any prospective purchaser to get in touch with the president of the Taylorcraft Owners Club, Bruce Bixler, 12809 Greenbauer, Alliance, OH 44601; 216-823-9748.

Fully enclosed engine *contributed to the Taylorcraft's high speed.*

Ercoupe

The Ercoupe (also known as Aircoupe, Forney, Alon and Cadet) may be one of the most significant light aircraft ever built. Designed 40 years ago by Fred Weick, it was the first lightplane to have a nosewheel, the first to be certified as nonspinnable and the first to be built on an automobile-style production line. As important as all that may be, one fact makes the Ercoupe worth looking at today: it is still a rather good value on the used-plane market, a cute little metal two-seater that can fly cross-country at 110 mph at a price as low as $5,000. For many people who like to fly but can't afford it, the Ercoupe is one of only a handful of aircraft that can still be bought for the price of a small car. In these days of $8,000 Piper Cubs and $25,000 Cessna 152s, the $5,000 Ercoupe deserves a close look.

The Ercoupe, of course, has always had its loyal followers and sneering doubters. It was introduced when every other light training aircraft had a fabric fuselage, high wing, a tailwheel and a scary record of stall/spin accidents. The Ercoupe, as it was originally called, was designed from the beginning as a safe, easy-to-fly airplane that would appeal to the hordes of non-pilots expected to buy aircraft after World War II. In fact, the Ercoupe was designed to feel as much like a car as possible. It had a foot brake like a car. On the ground you steered with the wheel, just like a car. And there were no rudder pedals. (The rudders were automatically coordinated with the ailerons, so that as the pilot banked into a turn, the motion of the wheel also activated the appropriate rudder.)

The Ercoupe's big claim to fame, however, was the fact that it was "stall-proof." Elevator travel was limited so that the pilot did not have enough pitch authority to bring the aircraft to the stall angle of attack. And if the Ercoupe was incapable of both a proper stall and uncoordinated flight, there was no way in the world it was going to spin.

If there are no rudder pedals, one is tempted to ask, how does the pilot counteract torque effect on takeoff and climb? Answer: the airplane does most of the counteracting all by itself. The twin tails are cleverly located just out of the prop blast, which reduces "torque effect" considerably. Secondly, the engine is canted down and to the right, so that the engine also helps pull the nose back to the right during climb. We're told that several Ercoupe owners, questing after more speed, have at great expense remounted their engines perfectly straight only to discover that the airplane was slower than before. No one knows why.

Because it was so unconventional and easy to fly, and obviously aimed at the unwashed masses, many elitist pilots disdained the Ercoupe. "I'd never fly an airplane without rudder pedals," was a typical attitude at the time, one that has carried over into the '70s. For a time, this disdain among certain pilots depressed the prices of used Ercoupes to extremely low levels. But an equally devoted band of Ercoupe lovers has now restored prices to the point that it is no longer the cheapest aircraft on the used market. (That honor is currently held by the Taylorcraft.)

There was perhaps another reason that some flight schools and instructors didn't like the Ercoupe when it was first introduced: it was so easy to fly that people didn't need much instruction. It was quite common for students to solo Ercoupes in less than five hours, and we know of one gentleman who made his first solo flight after slightly more than one hour of dual instruction in an Ercoupe.

Chronology

The history of the Ercoupe line is a tortuous one. Production first began in 1939. Engineering Research Corporation built 113 65-hp Ercoupes between 1939 and 1941. (The "Er" in Ercoupe are the initials of the company.) In 1946, however, things really began to roll, and over 4,000 Ercoupe model 415C models were built in just nine months —a rate of production matched only by the Piper Cub and approached by no aircraft since then. Engineering Research continued production until 1950 of 415D, E and G models, turning out a total of 5,000 airplanes. The C and D models had 75-hp Continentals; the E and G were equipped with 85-hp engines. In 1950, the rights to the Ercoupe were sold to Universal Aircraft, which continued to make parts, but never went into production. In 1958, a company called Forney took over the line, and went back into the production with a spruced-up model called the Fornair F-1 Aircoupe. It had a 90-hp·Continental and

This 1949 model *has been repainted and refurbished, as have many Ercoupes.*

modified interior and instrument panel. Forney built a couple hundred airplanes before halting production in 1960. The rights to the Aircoupe bounced around for a few years before being purchased by Alon, Inc., which built another couple hundred airplanes between 1965 and 1967. It was then sold to Mooney Aircraft, which built 59 single-tail, three-control versions called the Mooney Cadet. In 1973, rights were sold to Univair—the same company that bought it in 1950—which now manufactures parts. There is no chance that the airplane will ever be revived again, so the Ercoupe will never match the Cub and the Bonanza for longevity.

Design Changes

For an aircraft whose career spanned nearly 30 years, the Ercoupe underwent surprisingly few design changes. Besides the engine power increases, the only major design change in the original Ercoupe was the addition of rudder pedals as an option on the 415G model in 1949. The option was made available mostly because so many potential customers said, "Sure I'd buy one, but only if it had rudder pedals." Ercoupe boosters insist that the rudder pedals were only a psychological crutch, and that the airplane didn't fly much differently. The Forney Aircoupe had minor interior changes and metal-covered wings in place of fabric. (All fuselages were metal from the beginning.) Alon's major contribution to the Ercoupe was a new sliding canopy in place of the original airplane's fixed canopy with a sliding panel. Mooney wrought the most visible changes on the Ercoupe. The Mooney model, known as the Cadet, was, in fact, so modified that it was hardly an Ercoupe at all.

In an attempt to obliterate what it con-sidered to be the Ercoupe's bad image, Mooney not only scrapped the twin tail, but also restored full control movement and added stall strips to the wing to *make* the Ercoupe stall. We're not sure what the logic behind this move was, but it was successful, for the Cadet is reported to stall quite sharply and spin readily.

Most of these modifications, plus countless others, have been retrofitted to older models. Most Ercoupes, in fact, have been modified to some degree, and a totally original Engineering Research-built Ercoupe is something of a rarity, and will probably have some extra value because of it. (Ercoupe owners, like the owners of Swifts, Navions and other vintage aircraft, are modification nuts who will cheerfully tack on any performance- or convenience-boosting gizmo they can get their hands on.)

Another popular modification is a strengthened dual-fork nosegear. Early Ercoupe nosegears took a real beating in the hands of five-hour student pilots and other pilots who hadn't mastered the crab-it-on crosswind landing technique.

Flying Qualities

Is the Ercoupe really stall-proof and spin-proof? To the best of our knowledge, no Ercoupe has ever been spun, and the airplane's type certificate states that it is characteristically incapable of spinning. Whether the Ercoupe stalls, however, is subject to some debate. The stall-limiting device on the Ercoupe is nothing fancy, simply a stop on the control column that prevents the pilot from pulling back too far on the wheel. Under most circumstances, this simple expedient does not allow a pilot to stall. (It would seem that some sort of whip stall in an exaggerated climb attitude would be possible, although recovery would be im-

Without speed fairings, *the trailing beam landing gear can be seen.*

mediate.)

If it can't truly stall, the Ercoupe certainly can descend at an extremely high rate with the power off and the wheel pulled all the way back. It's likely that a pilot could walk away from such an impact—something not many pilots of fully stalled airplanes have done.

Surprisingly, the National Transportation Safety Board accident reports show a substantial number of Ercoupe crashes caused by what the NTSB labels "stall," or "stall/spin." In fact, a 1975 study of NTSB accidents, show a rate higher than many supposedly "hot" airplanes like the Piper Comanche and Bellanca Viking. According to the report, the Cessna 182 has a stall/spin accident rate half that of the Ercoupe's.

We're not quite sure how to explain this discrepancy. Perhaps the NTSB's definition of a stall is a liberal one; the Board's computers require *something* to be entered in the slot labeled "type of accident" and it's likely that many Ercoupe "stall/spin" crashes don't involve true aerodynamic stalls, but perhaps be more properly labeled "stall/mush."

Model ERCOUPE	Year	Number Built	Average Retail Price	Engine	TBO (hrs)	Overhaul Cost	Cruise Speed
415 A-B	1939-41	112	$4,500	Continental C-65	1,800	$2,800	100
415 C	1946	4,309	$5,000	Continental C-75	1,800	$2,800	105
415 D	1947	445	$5,000	Continental C-75	1,800	$2,800	105
415 E	1948	142	$5,300	Continental C-85	1,800	$3,000	110
415 G	1949	35	$5,300	Continental C-85	1,800	$3,000	110
FORNEY							
Fornair F-1	1958-60	138	$5,500	Continental C-90	1,800	$3,000	120
ALON							
A-2	1965	85	$6,000	Continental C-90	1,800	$3,000	124
A-2	1966	136	$6,300	Continental C-90	1,800	$3,000	124
A-2A	1967	20	$6,500	Continental C-90	1,800	$3,000	124
MOONEY							
A-2A	1968	46	$8,000	Continental C-90	1,800	$3,000	124
M-10 Cadet	1969	8	$8,500	Continental C-90	1,800	$3,000	110
M-10 Cadet	1970	50	$9,000	Continental C-90	1,800	$3,000	110

Ercoupe

In any case, it's damn hard to get an Ercoupe to fall out of the sky hard enough to kill the pilot.

Ercoupes handle nicely in the air; the ailerons are pleasantly quick and the visibility superb. Unlike other 1946-vintage two-seaters such as the Cub, Taylorcraft and Luscomb, the Ercoupe has a fairly healthy rate of descent when the power is pulled back. The inevitable corollary to this trait is a rather unremarkable rate of climb. In fact, *Aviation Consumer* pilots have flown 75-hp Ercoupes whose rates of climb were virtually nonexistent above 4,000 feet on a warm day. The 90-hp Forney and Alon versions are preferable if you plan to do mostly two-people flying.

The Ercoupe's biggest flying quirk is the rather unorthodox crosswind landing technique. Since there are no rudders in the original Ercoupes, the pilot must crab into the wind all the way to touchdown. Although most pilots shudder at the thought of touching down in a 30-degree crab, the Ercoupe has trailing beam landing gear expressly designed for this sort of thing, and once the mains touch, the airplane instantly straightens out. (A favorite bit of Ercoupe lore describes how Boeing used the Ercoupe to train its pilots to make crosswind landings in the 707. Because of its low-hanging engine pods, the 707, like the Ercoupe, can't lower a wing into the wind in a conventional manner.) Ercoupes have demonstrated safe landings in 40-knot crosswinds, something unthinkable in any of its tail-dragger contemporaries and most modern tricycle gear aircraft.

Ercoupes equipped with rudder pedals—and a lot of them have been converted, to the dismay of Ercoupe purists—may be slipped to a landing in the conventional manner, but Ercoupe pilots tell us the old crab-it-on method works better even with the modified aircraft. If you do plan to make conventional crosswind landings, make sure the airplane you buy has an optional nosewheel-to-rudder linkage. Otherwise, you'll blow a lot of nosewheel tires.

Safety

The Ercoupe's record of stall/spin accidents isn't perfect, as we previously noted, but it is anywhere from two to 10 times better than other aircraft in this class. Crashworthiness is also markedly superior to that of most aircraft. (Ercoupe designer Fred Weick later designed the Ag-1, the first really crashworthy lightplane and the forerunner of all modern agricultural aircraft, which have crashworthiness light-years ahead of standard business and personal light aircraft.) "The Ercoupe is an amazing aircraft in terms of safety design and engineering," according to Ed Slattery of the National Transportation Safety Board. "The I-beam under the seat is twice as rugged as the one in a Bonanza. The whole airplane is designed to collapse sequentially right down to the cabin." (Slattery flew certification tests on the Ercoupe for the FAA and owned one for years.) NTSB statistics seem to back him up. Less than a quarter of all Ercoupe stall/spin accidents were fatal—a lower percentage than any other aircraft listed in the stall/spin study.

Two areas where Ercoupes have a bad accident record are: in-flight airframe failures and engine failures. Ercoupes were rated third worst among 32 singles in these categories by an NTSB study in 1979.

Maintenance

Early Ercoupes had a staggering parade of Airworthiness Directives. The 1946 and 1947 415C and D models drew a total of 26 AD notes, the largest number of any airplane in our used aircraft series so far. (And that was back in the days when ADs weren't issued as freely as they are today.) However, the picture improved rapidly with later models. The 1949 415G had only seven ADs, and the later Forney and Alon models had only a handful. The Alon Aircoupes, built from 1965-67, in fact, have only one AD note,

against the Bendix magneto in the C-90 engine.

If you're shopping for a '46 or '47 model, have a knowledgeable Ercoupe mechanic carefully go over the aircraft's paperwork to ensure AD compliance. Of particular importance is AD 59-5-4, which requires beefup of the rear wing spar.

Ercoupe experts tell us there are two maintenance items to check closely when shopping for a used Ercoupe. The first is corrosion, which of course can creep into any 30-year-old all-metal airplane. The second is the nosewheel, which may have been subject to all sorts of pounding by student pilots in the aircraft's earlier life. (Most Ercoupes have modified nosegears.) The nosegear problem, we're told, isn't nearly as bad as it used to be, since most Ercoupes are now in the hands of loving owners, who fly them carefully.

Even those airplanes with the double-fork nosewheel are susceptible to nosewheel shimmy if the ball joints in the nosewheel-to-control-wheel-to-aileron linkage are loose. Tightening up the nosewheel steering linkage can run well over $100; check it closely.

Although the Ercoupe doesn't really stall, it can of course develop high sink rates, and plenty of student pilots have made plenty of hard landings in plenty of Ercoupes. If the seat or seat support looks broken or bent, call in an experienced Ercoupe mechanic to check the wing spars and the landing gear for damage or deformation.

Although the metallized wings are, of course, easier to maintain, they weigh anywhere from 30 to 40 pounds more than the original fabric wings—a significant weight penalty that amounts to at least 10 percent of the Ercoupe's cabin load, and that 40 pounds makes a noticeable difference in climb rate of the 75- and 85-hp models. A ragwing covered with a "lifetime" fabric-like Ceconite may be the best buy, and an airplane so fitted will probably cost less in the bargain.

For a 30-year-old aircraft built by a company that went out of business years ago, the Ercoupe's parts availability is remarkably good—probably better than for Cessna or Piper aircraft of the same vintage. Univair, Inc. (Route 3, Box 59, Aurora, Colo. 80011; 303-364-7661) still makes Ercoupe parts, and most are available for immediate shipment. Wag-Aero in Lyons, Wisc. (414-763-9588) also sells some Ercoupe parts, and there are several smaller parts outlets specializing in Ercoupes.

Performance

Although the Ercoupe's claim to fame is safety, its performance is not bad at all. Owners report real-world cruising speeds of

"Steering wheels" *guide the Ercoupe on the ground and draw the scorn of some pilots.*

The Aviation Consumer Used Aircraft Guide

110 mph with the 90-hp engine on a fuel consumption of about five gallons per hour. The 75- and 85-hp versions are good for perhaps 100 mph. Fuel capacity is 24 gallons (two wing tanks of nine gallons each and one fuselage tank of six gallons), good for a range of 450 miles or so with a small reserve. Standard useful load is about 500 pounds for most models, which limits legal load to full fuel and two 170-pounders—with nothing left over for baggage. Add a few instruments, and the useful load declines still further.

Prices

Ercoupe price tags range from a low of about $4,000 for a really doggy 75-hp 415C to upwards of $8,000 for a shiny Mooney Cadet or a showpiece Alon. Average price for a reasonable Ercoupe seems to be in the $5,000 range, with the later Alon models worth about a thousand more. As with any vintage aircraft that is prized by its owners, Ercoupes are often lavishly rebuilt with leather interiors, exotic instrument panels and polyurethane paint jobs. Prices for these showpieces, of course, will often be outrageous.

Organizations

Ercoupe owners are blessed not with just one, but *two* owner organizations. The Ercoupe Owners Club is the larger; it sponsors fly-ins, offers cut-rate insurance and publishes a magazine called *Coupe Capers.* (Address: P.O. Box 15058, Durham, N.C. 27704) A smaller group, the International Ercoupe Association, limits itself to publishing a monthly newsletter of technical advice and letters from members. Its address is Route 1, Box 151, Stilwell, Kans. 66085. The President is Kelly Viets; 913-681-2622. We strongly advise any prospective Ercoupe buyer to contact one or both of these organizations for advice.

Service

Like other odd old airplanes, the Ercoupe requires a knowledgeable mechanic. "Most A&Ps really clobber Ercoupes," one owner told us. There apparently is no single well-known Valhalla of Ercoupe maintenance, but the Ercoupe Owners' Club did recommend Willman Air Service in New Smyrna Beach, Florida.

If you're not willing to fly that far, write one of the clubs for the name of an Ercoupe mechanic in your area. One of the benefits of owning an Ercoupe is that you are surrounded by hundreds of fanatical Ercoupe owners anxious to help you out.

Cockpit is tight, *but passengers under the age of ten don't seem to care.*

"I bought a 415C several years ago. It was very clean and had a low-time engine. I got a real bargain for $2,500. It has a climb prop with an 85-hp engine, and I can get about 105 to 108 cruise at about 5.5 gallons per hour. It's a good little cross-country airplane; I've flown it to Florida on three occasions. It's quite comfortable and the visibility is excellent. But if you put two people and some baggage in it, you really know you're carrying a load. It loves the ground. They claim 500 feet a minute climb for the first five minutes, but mine never does that well. I don't see how some of those early 65-hp models even flew.

"One problem is that the 85-hp engine is rated at 2550 rpm. But there's no way you can turn 2550 on that engine with the props that are available, unless you go to a flat pitch, about 46 inches. With a cruise prop the takeoff roll went up a little, but the cruise went up to 114, and the engine seemed happier because it had a load on it. But the Continental O-200 makes a real airplane on it."

"I bought a new Alon in 1967 for about $7,500. I wasn't planning to buy an airplane at all, but I went out to the airport with a buddy, and was so enamored with the looks of it—the bucket seats and the big-time operator instrument panel that I practically bought it on the spot. I can remember no maintenance or mechanical problems in the two years and 500 hours I owned it, except for the fading seat covers.

"By luck I fell into the best possible plane for the type of pilot I was at the time—a courageous 50-hour neophyte. I assiduously tried to spin it one day, and found out later that if I had managed to do it, I probably wouldn't have had enough control authority to recover. I used to do things in the Ercoupe that I've never done since, like flying over Westchester County Airport and shutting the engine off. It was such a kindly, gentle airplane, and so easy to land in a crosswind—the crabbed crosswind landings worked beautifully—it would just squeak on and straighten right out.

"It was extremely cozy and uncomfortable, though. The Ercoupe was a perfect example of why nobody flies a two-seat aircraft once they get their license.

"Performance was okay. It was one of those airplanes that had wonderful book figures, but didn't come anywhere near them. They claimed 120; it would do about 100. It seemed to climb all right with the 90-hp engine; I went in and out of some pretty short fields. The classic thing they warned me about was the high rate of sink you could get on final. If you got it too slow, it would mush down at a tremendous rate. I never found it to be a problem, though."

Piper J-3 Cub

A used Piper J-3 Cub just may be a better financial investment than gold bars, tax-free municipal bonds or real estate investment trusts. The standard Cub in its heyday had a list price of $1,595, and a few years ago a pretty good Cub could be had for $3,000. But today, the market seems to be going right out of sight.

A 1980 issue of *Trade-A-Plane* carried ads for more than a dozen J-3s, with asking prices ranging from $6,000 to $10,500. We recently heard of a mint-condition all-original Cub that sold for $12,000. Not bad for a 30-year-old airplane with 65 horsepower and a cruising speed of 70 mph. At the other extreme, a rather high-time J-3 used as a trainer for the past 30 years reportedly sold for $3,500 in 1977. The logbook showed a total airframe time of 80,000 hours, we're told.

J-3s typically command $3,000-$4,000 more than Champs, Luscombes and Taylorcrafts of comparable vintage and performance.

Another example of the Cub's special appeal: in the same issue of *Trade-A-Plane* there were several four-place 150-hp Piper Tri-Pacers advertised. Most were 10 years newer than the typical Cub, and carried twice as many people 50 mph faster. Some were going for under $5,000; none was higher than $7,000. The Cub, it appears, has a visceral appeal that can only drive prices higher in the future. By 1990, it'll probably take $20,000 to buy a half-decent J-3. The Cub is widely heralded as a fun-flying machine, but it's an even better inflation hedge.

History

The E-2 Cub first appeared in the early '30s, powered by a tiny Salmson radial engine. The J-3 model, with which we are concerned here, first went on the market in late 1937. The '37 model J-3 had a 37-hp Continental A-40 and nine-gallon fuel tank. The next year, a 50-hp Continental was available as an option. In 1939, the Cub was spruced up a bit with the addition of a steerable tailwheel and a 12-gallon tank. A 50-hp Lycoming and a 50-hp Franklin were also made available as options that year, and over 1,300 were sold.

In 1940, the Cub attained the classic form in which most J-3s survive today. The 65-hp Continental A-65 became the standard powerplant, with Lycoming 65 and Franklin 60-hp engines available. (The Continental was the most popular by far, and the vast majority of surviving Cubs have the Continental.) Production tapered off drastically in 1942 because of the war and halted altogether the next year, but 5,000 L-4 military models were built from 1942-45. The L-4 was identical to the standard J-3 except for color (olive drab, of course) and the inclusion of military options like a gas heater and an electrical system.

After the war, civilian production started up again in late 1945. The banner year for Cubs was 1946. In those twelve months, an incredible 6,320 J-3s rolled out of the Piper factory—surely a record for the most civilian aircraft of any type manufactured in one year. At one point, Cub production reached 50 per day, or one every 10 minutes. Piper old-timer Walter Jamouneau told us, "If the weather was bad for a couple of days, we were in real trouble. We couldn't find enough rope to tie 'em all down with."

The bubble burst quickly, though, and only 720 Cubs were built in 1947. In 1948, the J-3 was replaced by the PA-11, which had a bigger cockpit and a fully cowled engine. In all, 19,978 J-3s were built. The year-by-year production breakdown looks like this:

1937.......25	1942......296
1938......647	1945......938
1939....1,347	1946.....6,320
1940....1,977	1947......720
1941....1,855	

Performance

By all objective standards, the Cub is a pretty lousy airplane. Cruising speed is usually around 70 mph; maximum range about 175 miles with a 15-minute reserve. A typical useful load is about 400 pounds, enough for two adults and a full load of fuel (12 gallons in a fuselage tank just behind the engine). Passenger accommodations are cramped and Spartan, especially in the front seat. Even compared with its 65-hp con-

Photo by Rocky Weldon

This is a fairly ratty 1946 model. *With a mid-time engine and lifetime fabric, it's worth about $5,000—more, if it weren't painted white.*

temporaries like the Champ, Taylorcraft and Luscombe, the Cub is very slow and cramped.

Its strength, however, is short-field performance and docile handling. Owners report takeoff rolls of around 200 feet. In a stiff breeze, the Cub can take off virtually in its own length and land across most runways.

For speedy, convenient transportation, then, the Cub is the worst possible choice. For the $8,000 price tag of a good J-3, one could buy a 1975 Cessna 150, which is all metal, flies 110 mph and is, by comparison, quiet, roomy and easy to fly.

But of course nobody buys a Cub for speed and convenience. The usual reason is reverse snob appeal. Cub owners are proud of their airplane's slow speed, lack of electrical system, non-existent cabin heat, cork-and-wire fuel gauge, etc. The typical Cub owner is like the owner of a vintage MG-TC—immensely proud of his obsolete, impractical and uncomfortable vehicle. But the J-3, like the TC, is a classic. A buyer in search of a Cub will settle for nothing else, and that's one reason prices are so high.

Prices
Average price of a standard yellow Cub in pretty good shape, with Ceconite or Polyfiber fabric and a mid-time engine (400-600 hours), is about $7,000-$7,500. (Year of manufacture seems to be irrelevant. The older planes, if anything, may command slightly higher prices for their antique value.) A barely flyable airplane with a run-out engine and/or bad fabric might go for as little as $5,000. Many Cubs, however, have been painstakingly restored by doting owners and are in literally better-than-new condition. With fresh engines, these airplanes will probably sell for $10,000 or more.

Appraisal Points
The two big appraisal points are the engine and fabric. The Continental 65 has a rated TBO of 1,800 hours, but if the plane is

flown regularly, it's not unusual for one to go 3,000 hours before needing overhaul. Many Cubs, however, have sat ignored for years, and this disuse can drastically shorten engine life. It's almost as important to check for regular usage as it is to check total engine time. A 1,000-hour engine that has been run regularly may give you more service than a 500-hour engine that's been sitting for three years.

The other critical appraisal point is the fabric. Unless you are a fanatic about authenticity, the traditional Grade A cotton should be avoided at all costs, for its lifetime is short—perhaps five to eight years if stored inside, and less if it's parked out in the weather—and the cost is astronomical. The so-called "lifetime" fabrics like Ceconite and Polyfiber will last as long as you're likely to own the airplane.

Fabric condition can be checked by use of a punch-tester, a tool most mechanics should have. Don't forget the control surfaces. A Cub advertised as "wings and fuselage Ceconite" may still have cotton-covered control surfaces—which will need recovering in a few years, at a cost of $700 or so. Cost of a complete recover job can run from $3,000-$4,000, depending on how

particular you are. You might run into difficulties, however, just finding someone to do the fabric job. The vast majority of mechanics these days won't even touch fabric, and many of those who will work on the stuff don't really know what they're doing.

Our advice: buy an airplane with recently installed Ceconite or Polyfiber, and then you can forget about the fabric until the year 2000 or so.

Next thing to look at when buying a Cub is the steel tubing in the rear fuselage, back by the tailwheel. The drain holes in this area are usually inadequate, and the 4130 steel tubing made in those days was nowhere near as good as the 1020 chrome-moly steel used today. Rusty lower longerons are the almost inevitable result. It's the standard problem with Cubs.

Another typical Cub trouble area is the fuel tank. The original tanks were made of lead-coated steel, and they rust out regularly at the bottom, where the fuel line goes in. Be especially wary of tanks in the 1940-45 models, when the factory was skimping on the lead coating.

Virtually all Cub cowlings are laced with cracks; don't worry much about them. The "eyebrow" cooling vanes over the cylinders also crack regularly—again, no great cause for alarm.

Also, check the wing struts for rust. They're made out of the same mild steel as the fuselage tubs, and some may be rusty on the inside by now. A recent Airworthiness Directive requires inspection of the struts for rust; make sure the AD is done before you buy the airplane.

The brakes can also be a problem. Even when the brakes are good, they're lousy, but when they're bad . . . Expander tubes cost about $100 to replace; if the brakes are bad, ask the seller to knock off $200 for a new pair.

Check the tires. A brand new set of tires should last virtually forever if you land on grass, but 8.00 x 4 tires are not easy

The panel is, *to say the least, simple. This aircraft has non-original instruments, which detract from its resale value.*

While the right hand *grasps the control stick, the left works the throttle, fuel on-off switch and pitch crank, in descending order on the left sidewall.*

to find these days and the list price just went up to about $100—each.

Engines

Many Cubs have been re-engined over the years. You'll find them often with 75-hp, 85-hp and 90-hp Continentals. Unless the aircraft is operating out of a high-altitude airport, however, these larger engines do little but add to fuel consumption and noise. (Rate of climb is better, but the 65-hp engine is adequate.) The airframe is so dirty that even a 150-hp engine will barely put a Cub over the 100-mph mark. We consider the 65-hp Continental engine to be the perfect Cub engine. However, the bigger engines usually add about $500 to the value of the plane, unless you're talking about a perfectly restored ultra-original J-3—in which case the non-standard engine will detract from its value as a genuine antique.

The Lycoming 65, although rated at 65 hp, does not have the oomph that the Continental does, but it uses noticeably less fuel—about 3½-4 gallons per hour (the Continental uses about 4-4½ gph). The Franklin engine is exceedingly rare these days, and we wouldn't recommend one because it's so hard to get parts. (The Polish firm Pezetel may one day be back in production with the Franklin 125, and some of those parts fit the old 60, we're told.) A Lycoming-powered Cub will bring $600-$800 less than a Continental-powered one; the Franklin will cost $1,000-$1,200 less.

Parts

Surprisingly, the Cub parts situation is excellent. Piper stocks only a few parts at outrageously high prices, but an outfit in Wisconsin called Wag-Aero makes virtually any spare part at non-antique prices. (Example: An aluminum fuel tank from Wag-Aero is $140. Piper charges $400 for a heavier, rust-prone steel tank.) Frankly, there's no reason Piper should be ignoring the Cub parts market, since there are as many Cubs still flying as there are Aztecs (about 4,000 of each).

Wag-Aero stocks such a complete inventory of Cub parts that you could build a complete airplane from Wag-Aero parts. (They call the kit the Cuby.) Wag-Aero, Box 181, North Road, Lyons, Wisconsin 53148; (414) 763-9588. Another source of Cub parts is Univair in Aurora, Colorado; (303) 364-7661.

Maintenance and Operating Costs

At first glance, you'd expect the operating costs of a stone-simple airplane (no electrical system, vacuum system, etc.) that burns four gallons of fuel per hour to be very low. For an airplane that's well maintained by a mechanic who knows Cubs, that can be the case. But it's an unfortunate fact that few mechanics know anything at all about Cubs, and many owners will find themselves financing the learning curve of the local A&P. This is especially true in the case of fabric work. An inexperienced mechanic can spend 20 hours fiddling around with a little dope and fabric, and there's $500 shot.

Fabric work aside, there's very little to go badly wrong. An engine overhaul is under $2,000 (a pittance compared to a Cherokee), and liability insurance is around $200 per year. We wouldn't recommend hull insurance; the cost of major repairs is so high in proportion to the total value of the airplane that some insurance companies charge outrageous prices for hull insurance—in the five-

Cabin door swings down, *but climbing in still requires contortions. Door can be opened in flight for occupant cooling.*

to seven percent range.

In general, direct operating costs for a Cub amount to about $8 per hour, with the total running about $10 to $12 per hour, assuming no major fabric work has to be done.

Flight Characteristics

The Cub is known as the most docile and forgiving airplane of its peers (Champ, T-Craft, Luscombe, etc.). The stall is gentle, although there is a definite break, unlike some of the bob-weighted and elevator-limited aircraft of today. Spins are legal in a Cub, and it will recover hands-off after any number of turns. Rotation is fairly slow, and rate of descent during spins is moderate.

Big problem in flying a Cub is the extremely light wing loading. By comparison, a 150 is heavy. (If you want numbers, we got numbers: J-3, 7.0 lb./sq. ft.; Cessna 150, 10.0 lb./sq. ft.). Consequently, the J-3 is very rough-riding in turbulence and very susceptible to gusty crosswinds. Pilots used to heavier airplanes must also remember not to leave the airplane without tying it down. A 30-knot gust can literally carry the airplane away. In fact, we'd guess that most airframe damage to Cubs occurs when the plane is sitting on the ground, tied down improperly or not at all.

By normal aircraft standards, the Cub is exceedingly difficult to land or take off. This is due, of course, to the tailwheel configuration. Tailwheel aircraft are inherently unstable on the ground and therefore prone to swerving ground loops, which can damage wingtips and landing gear. In addition, a tailwheel aircraft is susceptible to huge ballooning bounces on landings. The combination of bouncing and swerving has humbled more than a few transitioning pilots.

It should be pointed out that J-3s are hideously noisy. Our figures showed 99 dBA, significantly louder than any aircraft we've ever tested. At low frequencies, it registered an ear-splitting 112 dB. Ear plugs are an absolute must, and forget about trying to talk to your passenger.

Propping

Starting an airplane without an electrical system is a dangerous, nerve-wracking business. Fanatical caution is the only safe approach. We personally feel that it's dangerous to hand-prop any airplane not tied down. Fortunately, the 65-hp Continental usually starts easily. (We know one owner who hasn't missed starting on the first pull in six months.) Nevertheless, any buyer new to the art of propping should get a thorough checkout and approach the propeller as something that is waiting to chop your head off—which it is.

Color

Believe it or not, color can make a big difference in the selling price of a J-3. Most came from the factory painted yellow, and this color has become closely associated with the airplane. A real Cub must be yellow, just as a real MG-TC must be British racing green. An unyellow Cub suffers an immediate loss of value estimated at $1,200-$1,400 by one Cub connoisseur. (Conversely, if you're selling an unyellow Cub, it would probably pay to have it painted.)

For Joiners

There is a Cub owners club, and although it doesn't seem as active as, say, the Navion or Bonanza owner groups, it could certainly provide some information. President is John T. Geoghegan of Ojai, Calif.; (805) 526-6238. Another good source of information is the Experimental Aircraft Association, Hales Corners, Wisconsin 53130; (414) 425-4860.

Shock absorbers are bungee cords—*in effect, glorified rubber bands just like the ones you once used to lash your Pet Rock to the back of your ten-speed.*

Owner Comments

"I owned a '46 Cub and instructed in others. Mine had a C-90 conversion and I flew it regularly from a 600-foot farm strip. If I bought another, I'd get the stock 65-hp Continental because the noise is deafening with the C-90 or C-85, and cruise increase over the 65 is negligible.

"As in most old airplanes, the tubing can corrode. Check the tubing in the tail by removing the inspection plate under the stabilizer.

"The Cub is a responsive plane to fly that takes off in a hurry, but it's a compromise in some respects. It's slower than 7 AC Champ, Taylorcraft BC-12D, and Luscombe 8A, it is flown solo from the back seat, and is more cramped than the other 65-hp relics. It's nicer to land than the Champ, which has a soft gear, but visibility around a front seat passenger is horrible.

"I loved my Cub, but I'd probably choose a T-Craft (I owned a BC-12D once) over a Cub. The T-Craft has side-by-side seating, a wheel control, gets off just as fast as a Cub, is much faster, and sells for much less."

"It has two abilities. The first is training. Although when I train students, the majority of time is spent on communications, navigation, use of the other auxiliary systems, primary flying is a necessity which is often glossed over. Since buying my 1941 Continental-powered J-3, I have consciously compared Cessna 150s and Piper 140s to the Cub. My conclusion: too many elements interfere in the learning process when using the newer planes. The Cub has low horsepower, no flaps, poor instrument placement (in the front cockpit) but terrific visibility. The person who solos a J-3 must have a grasp of attitude flying, and he cannot hide poor approaches with use of flaps.

"The second ability is for pleasure. The J-3 maneuvers on a dime. My plane has taught me more about formation flying, short field landings, and off-airport landings than I had ever known before. Since I occasionally take aerial photographs, the open door and window provides excellent field of view. These must motivate most buyers to pay the inflated prices.

"My last comments deal with perfor-

Photo by Rocky Weldon

mance. Here you may get the most disagreement. Some pilots are able to get 300-foot takeoffs and landings, and 500 feet per minute climbs. I've noticed approximately 65 mph cruise (door open), and about 5 mph more with it closed. I felt that the Cub was slightly slower than a Champ in side-by-side flying."

"I presently own a J-3 Cub with a wooden spar, I purchased it in June of 1975 with an A-65 Continental engine. I replaced the A-65 with a C-85 engine.

Original Cost: $3,750
To Cherry Condition: $4,000
Total Investment: $7,700
Wollem Floats: $1,500
Total: $9,200

"I have not seen a good J-3 on the market for less than $6,000. I would put mine on the market for $7,200 plus $1,500 for the floats.

"Maintenance costs (April 1976-April 1977): $3.60 per hour including insurance; mechanic did work at N/C for free use of the airplane.

"Reliability: Need I say much here? I flew 200 hours last year with no problems; low and slow—who has more fun than a J-3 owner? The A-65 and C-85 engine (Continental) will accumulate carburetor ice very readily. All FBOs should have one J-3 Cub in their fleet; students would make better pilots.

"Performance: Exceptional—stalls, spins, loops (not too many with a wooden spar), very forgiving; I entered a J-3 contest last summer at an antique aircraft air show and took the short-field takeoff in 163 feet, landed in 150—200 feet.

"Handling quirks: None to speak of. I fly solo from both front and rear seats, placarded for rear seat only, solo. The L-4 has excellent visibility, no blind spots, no slop in the controls; crosswind landings can be a problem though, because of the large high-lift wing and the low gross weight. Empty weight: 828 pounds. Gross weight: 1,220 pounds.

"Bad models: I have flown four different J-3s and they all handle very well. I don't think there are any bad models.

"For the man who desires a fun-performance plane, you cannot beat this plane. It would appear that owners are hanging on to these little jewels."

"I purchased the airplane in 1976 for $4,000. The engine at the time of purchase had 234 hours since major; the airframe had the same time since complete sandblasting, painting of frame, and cover in Ceconite.

"My annual insurance costs $230 for all the coverage I can get.

"I just repainted the entire airplane with dope—total cost was less than $200.

"I fly over mountains and I cruise honestly at 77 mph, and climb at approximately 400 fpm with two on board. The engine starts on the first pull no matter how long it sits without use.

"I can consistently beat a 75-hp Cub off the ground and to altitude. I attribute this to an excellent engine and clean wing.

"I burn almost exactly 4 gph and, in fact, use my gallons burned to figure my flight time. I've checked the fuel consumption time and again and it always averages 4 gph. So far 100 octane hasn't caused me any problems.

"I change oil (high detergent) every 25 hours and check my plugs at this time also. I have checked my cylinders and valves with a borescope—they look excellent.

"So by burning 4 gph (at 70 cents per gallon), flying 150 hours per year, figuring six oil changes, $230/yr. for insurance, $60 for an annual, and $90 per year for nonessentials, I fly for $5.25 per hour. That's flying about as cheap as it can be."

"I am the owner of a 1946 J-3 Cub with C-85, and I love it. It is fun to fly and very cheap, burning an average of four gph with the 85-hp engine.

When I bought the plane a year ago I did not yet have my private ticket. Everyone said I was crazy to pay $6,500 for it, but now I think it is worth more. It was perfectly restored with a low-time engine when I bought it. During this year I have put 270 hours on it and this week will take the check ride for my commercial license. There are not many planes in which one can build time so cheaply.

"This plane has many faults by the standards of Cessna and the rest. It is terrible to land in a crosswind, cold as the devil in the winter, and you might as well drive if you are in even a moderate rush.

"It was very easy to start even during this cold winter. The coldest day I flew was 14 degrees, but with the dual impulse coupling it kicked over immediately every time.

"You definitely cannot do power-off landings in cold weather. The engine will ice up and stop. The carburetor heat is just not enough. My mechanic set the idle up from 600 to about 850 to help this problem and I learned to make all my approaches at about 1400 rpm in cold weather.

"My plane has a very low-pitch prop, so it leaps off the ground but seldom cruises faster than 65 mph.

"I always fly low and slow on numerous short trips; never over 150 miles, and 600 feet is the perfect J-3 altitude.

"The airplane is pure enjoyment—all the pleasures of flight wrapped in a beautiful yellow package."

J-3 Cub photo by Robert E. Drew

Cessna 120/140

Cessna's Model 120 and 140 were part of the crowd of post-war two-seat taildraggers. More than 7,000 120s and 140s were built during their six-year production run, and thousands are still flying today. Although perhaps lacking the classic appeal of the J-3 Cub or the funky uniqueness of the Ercoupe, the 120 and 140, with side-by-side seating, all-metal fuselage (and in some cases metal wings), and relatively good ground handling, may be the best choice among the post-war two-seaters from a purely practical point of view.

History

The 120/140 genealogy is short and fairly simple. Both airplanes were introduced in early 1946. The 140 was the "luxury" airplane and had flaps, a standard electrical system, fancy upholstery and a rear side window. The 120, aimed primarily at the flight school market, had no flaps, no rear window, plain upholstery and no standard electrical system. (An electrical system was optional, however, and many were sold that way.) In 1949, Cessna dropped the 120 and spruced up the 140 into the 140A. Changes included a new all-metal tapered wing with a single strut (the precursor of Cessna wings for the next 30 years), and the option of a 90-hp Continental engine in place of the 85-hp powerplant in the 120 and 140 models. Only about 500 of the 140As were built, however, before the line was discontinued in 1951. Nearly a decade was to pass before Cessna resurrected the basic 140A design, put a nosewheel and a 100-hp Continental on it and called it the 150.

Resale Market

A recent issue of *Trade-A-Plane* listed 140s for sale at asking prices ranging from $4,900 to $9,000, with most clustered around the $5,500 to $6,500 range. Since *Trade-A-Plane* asking prices are generally higher than the eventual selling price, we can conclude

that the average 140, in good (but not showpiece) condition with a mid-time engine, can be bought for $5,000 to $6,000. The *Aircraft Price Digest* lists "retail" prices of $5,000 for the 120, $5,500 for the 140 and $6,000 for the 140A. The 120 and 140 owners we consulted for this article confirmed current selling prices in this range.

As with most older aircraft, year of manufacture has virtually no effect on asking price. Condition and equipment are what count. A well-maintained 1946 model with a low-time engine would command a better price than a neglected 1948. Price range can be rather extreme in these old clunkers; a run-down old 120 in need of a wing cover job might be had for $2,500, while many 120/140s have been lovingly restored by doting owners and come equipped with fancy radio packages, polyurethane paint, wood-grain instrument panels and sheepskin seats. You probably couldn't touch one of those showpieces for much under $10,000. Incidentally, geography seems to play a part in the pricing structure. The same aircraft will command up to $1,000 more on the West Coast, we're told.

Because the 120/140 is mostly metal and fairly common, and very similar in basic design to the ubiquitous Cessna 150 and 152, it has less "antique appeal" than aircraft like the Cub,

Champ or Luscombe. For this reason, the value of the airplane is pretty well determined by its capabilities: a 100-mph two-place airplane that's real noisy and kind of hard to land. Nevertheless, the 120/140 does have antique value. The Cessna 150, for example, is basically a nosewheel 140, offering virtually identical performance, accommodation and operating costs. Yet a run-of-the-mill 1960 C-150 is worth only about $4,600—a thousand or so less than a comparable 1946 model 140.

This fact bodes well for 140 owners; the antique factor is likely to drive prices up in the future, while the price of old 150s is likely to remain at the $4,500 level, where it has been for the past several years.

On the other hand, if you are shopping purely for cheap aerial transportation, and have no interest in antique appeal or taildragger chauvinism, it makes little sense to spend the extra thousand or two on a 140. The 150 is the equal of the 140 in nearly all practical matters, and has the advantages of a nosewheel and those big barn-door flaps. But, as one loyal 140 owner put it, "Who can swagger away from a 150?"

Performance

The 120 and 140 clip along at a pretty good rate. Owners report true airspeeds

The 140 had fabric-covered wings and double struts. *The spiffed up 140A, of which only 500 were built, had an all-metal wing and a single strut.*

of between 95 and 105 mph on a fuel burn of about five gallons per hour. This is quite comparable to the Cessna 150, which flies a little bit faster on about six gph. Climb rate is nothing spectacular, of course. One owner reports, "When I'm fully loaded, I know we'll get to altitude eventually, it's just a matter of when." The same owner reports a maximum altitude of about 11,500 feet with two people and half fuel. (Lighter, altitudes of 14,000 feet are reportedly attainable.) Some 140 pilots cheerfully fly over 9,500-foot mountain ranges, though we're not sure we'd be so bold.

The 120/140 has excellent range for this class of aircraft. The 25-gallon tank gives a no-reserve endurance of about five hours. Thus, 400-mile legs are quite practical with a reasonable reserve. Other post-war two-seaters have fuel capacities in the 10-15-gallon range, making them impractical for cross-country travel.

Accommodation
The 120/140 cockpit is cramped, at best. The seats are the fixed-bench type, so very tall pilots will find their knees tangling in the control wheel and short ones may need a pillow to reach the pedals. The cabin is also very narrow, a trait which the 150 unfortunately inherited. The feeling of confinement is heightened by the poor visibility through the small rear windows. (The 120, remember, has no rear windows at all.) By contrast, modern trainers like the Tomahawk and Skipper, with their wide cabins and superb visibility, are a quantum leap ahead of the 120/140 (and most other two-seaters of that era).

One trait that is especially oppressive in the 120/140: cabin noise. Virtually every owner who wrote to us mentioned the unbearable cabin din, which is apparently worse than in even its post-war contemporaries. The only solution is a good set of ear plugs (we find the E-A-R foam-expansion plugs to be by far the best—and cheapest).

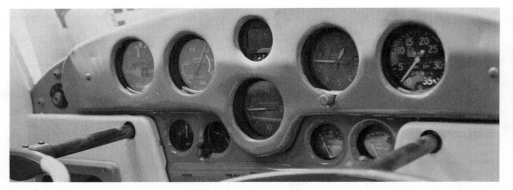

Panel has the ambiance *of a 1949 Hudson Hornet—and a side window to match.*

Handling
Most 120/140 pilots praise the airplane's handling qualities, particularly the light, crisp aileron control. "Compared to the comparable fat-wing planes of the same period (T-Craft, V Cub, Champ) the roll control is a dream," gushes one owner. Adverse yaw is also reportedly less than in those similar aircraft. "The flaps are a joke," says one 140 owner, "but it's pleasant arm exercise."

On the ground, the 120/140 has the typical tailwheel instability problems: a strong tendency to get sideways and spin out during the takeoff and landing rolls, and a propensity for huge ballooning bounces if the plane touches down too firmly at too high a speed. These traits are of course considered "normal" by taildragger pilots and can usually be adjusted to, in some degree at least. "You never make a good landing by accident," reports one owner. Along the spectrum of taildraggers, the 120/140 is considered about average in ground handling: not as forgiving as the Cub, but easier to keep straight than the Luscombe. Ground controlability is aided greatly by the toe brakes, a vast improvement over the heel brakes in some old taildraggers.

One bad habit of the 120/140 breed is a tendency to nose over; it's pretty likely that any 140 on the used market has at least one noseover somewhere in its history. The problem is so common that many 140s have "wheel

extenders," which are spacer blocks on the landing gear legs which move the wheels a few inches forward. This of course reduces the noseover tendency. If you buy one without the wheel extenders, you should consider adding them.

Safety
The 120/140 has an excellent safety record, according to NTSB crash statistics. The aircraft has a fatal accident rate of only 1.5 per 100,000 hours, second only to the Cessna 150's 1.3 among two-seaters. (These figures apply to the period 1972-76.) Total accident rate is very high, however: 27.5 This is nearly triple the rate of the 150, but about on par with comparable two-seat taildraggers. Apparently, most 120/140 accidents are minor landing and takeoff accidents (typical of taildraggers) that don't kill people.

In stall/spin accidents, the 120/140 rates poorly, although better than its two-seat taildragger contemporaries. Its fatal stall/spin rate is 1.08 per 100,000 hours, more than five times higher than the Cessna 182, the leader in stall/spin accident avoidance. But comparable aircraft like the Cub, Champ and Luscombe have fatal stall/spin rates ranging from 2.3 to 4.7, more than quadruple the 140's rate. Still, it appears that more than two-thirds of 120/140 fatal accidents are stall/spin crashes.

Model	Year	Number Built	Average Retail Price	Cruise Speed (mph)	Rate of Climb (fpm)	Useful Load (lbs)	Fuel Capacity (gals)	Engine	TBO	Overhaul Cost
Cessna 120	1946-49	2,172	$5,000	105	640	715	25	85-hp C-85 Continental	2,000	$3,000
Cessna 140	1946-49	4,904	$5,500	105	640	610	25	85-hp C-85 Continental	2,000	$3,000
Cessna 140A	1949-51	525	$6,000	110	640	600	25	85- or 90-hp Continental	2,000	$3,000

According to NTSB statistics, the 120/140 has a rather high rate of groundloop accidents, second only to the Luscombe among two-seat airplanes. According to the numbers, the 140 groundloops about four times as often as the J-3 Cub.

Maintenance

The cost of maintaining these old small aircraft is usually quite low. The 85-hp and 90-hp Continental engines are reliable, and the airframes are so simple that there's little to go wrong, as long as the owner pays attention and doesn't let things go to seed. The one major expense could be the fabric covering on the wing, which will need replacing at intervals ranging from five to 20 years, depending on the type of fabric and whether the airplane is hangared. Even this expense can be avoided by replacing the fabric with metal, or by buying a 140 already so equipped. Metal wings are 30 to 40 pounds heavier than the fabric, but most people consider the weight penalty worth its price.

The 120 and 140, like all aircraft, have their weak spots in terms of maintenance. Here are some items to carefully check before purchasing any 120 or 140:

• Look for damage in the lower door posts, near the wing strut attach point. This critical structural member may be damaged by rough-field operation, groundloops or corrosion.

• Corrosion in carry-through spar. The top skylight window is notoriously leaky, and water often drips down onto the wing spar carry-through structure in the top of the cabin. The water col-

lects in the channeling and can cause corrosion.

• Cracks in the tail structure and rear fuselage. A 120/140 expert tells us, "The tail is the weakest part of the airplane," and is subject to cracks in that area, particularly around the tailwheel attach point.

• Broken or bent gear boxes. The gear box—the support structure for the attachment of the landing gear to the fuselage—may have taken a real beating from student pilots 35 years ago and neophyte taildragger pilots since then. The box can be inspected from the outside by removing the landing gear fairing and from the inside by removing an inspection plate in the cabin floor.

• Broken tailsprings. Check to ensure the steel leaf-type tailwheel spring is still springy, but not saggy. A broken spring will cause complete loss of control on landing and could do major damage to the airplane, particularly the elevators.

• The drag wires and anti-drag wires in the "ragwing" 120s and 140s often are loose or broken. Check them.

Modifications

Like most vintage aircraft, 120s and 140s are highly modified by doting owners. Most of the 120/140 mods are of the minor cosmetic variety, however, and there is nothing like the mod mania that afflicts owners of Navions, Swifts and old Bonanzas, for example. Here is a list of some of the more popular 120/140 mods:

• Continental O-200 engine. As the supply of the C-85 and C-90 engines shrinks inexorably, some 120/140 owners have turned to the 100-hp Continental, the same engine used in the C-150. It's literally a bolt-on conversion, with no modifications required to the engine mount or cowling. Both speed and fuel consumption are slightly higher.

• Since the O-200 is now also out of production, some pilots have installed the O-235 Lycoming (108-115 hp). This does require some major rework under the cowl. Performance should be better yet, although one proud owner of a standard 140A swears that he can keep up with a friend's Lycoming-powered 140 in cruise and nearly so in climb.

• Metal wings. A popular mod, with good reason. Aluminum wing skins turn the 120 and 140 into an all-metal airplane, with no worries about fabric replacement ever.

• Airtex interior. An original interior in a 120/140 is pretty rare (the headliners usually rot out first). Airtex is located at 259 Lower Morrisville Road, Fallsington, PA 19054; 215-295-4115.

• Wheel extensions. As previously mentioned, these move the wheels forward slightly on the landing gear legs, reducing the noseover tendency.

• Cessna 150 seats. These can easily be fitted and allow fore-and-aft adjustment.

• Cleveland brakes. The original Goodyear brakes were rather touchy and demanded constant careful attention; otherwise they could lock up, causing a ground loop and possible major damage. Cleveland brakes are more powerful and more reliable. (Be careful with the extra stopping power, however; too much will put you on your nose.) Parts for the Clevelands are also cheaper and more readily available.

• Mixture control. There is much confusion about mixture control in the C-85 and C-90 engines. Many 120s and 140s have none; it was either removed at some point in the airplane's history (perhaps by flight schools nervous about fumble-fingered students) or never installed at all. (Mixture controls were considered optional luxuries in those days.) Many people believe the old Stromberg carburetors in these engines cannot be leaned safely in flight, but veteran 140 owners assure us it can be done. However, they point out two factors: The carburetor must be in absolutely perfect shape, or the mixture control may just kill the engine; and the mixture control travel is very short, only about an inch. Thus the control is very sensitive, and pilots accustomed to longer control travel on other aircraft may kill the engine by pulling too far, too fast. Leaning reportedly lowers fuel consumption by about one-half gallon per hour at high altitudes. It has no effect at all below 5,000 feet, however.

Owner Organizations

Owners of 120s and 140s are blessed with two organizations. The West Coast 120/140 Club may be the most active; they publish a monthly newsletter and organize fly-ins. Address is 2055 Sterling, Menlo Park, CA 94025. The Cessna 120/140 Association is located at Box 92, Richardson, TX 75080. We're told there is a big rivalry between the two clubs.

Unless you're a petite brunette, climbing in or out of a 140 is an exercise in gymnastics. This bit of 1946 Cennsa PR cheesecake was probably designed to distract the viewer from the small doors and cramped cockpit.

Owner Comments

"I bought my 1946 Cessna 120 about a year and a half ago for $6,500, a premium price. The engine had about 700 hours on it.

"My bird has metallized wings, poly paint, an electrical system (which was optional on the 120), right-side toe brakes, and a 720-channel navcom. It has no mixture control (optional on the 120).

"The performance is consistent with its 85 horsepower—slow but thrifty. Cruise speed runs from a little over 90 mph at economy settings to just about 100 mph at max cruise. Fuel consumption tends to be about 5 gph; more like 4 gph for touch-and-go operations. Although the plane needs only a reasonable amount of runway, operation at high density altitude does require planning because of low climb rates. Rate of climb seems to be around 500 fpm at sea level, dropping off to 100 fpm at 7,000 or 8,000 feet. A mixture control may affect the climb at higher altitudes.

"Handling is very nice. On the ground, I can just see over the nose, so that taxiing is not so snake-like. The toe brakes are effective and easy to hit. I think that the toe brakes help make the plane so difficult to groundloop. More than once I've gotten into a fine swerve and thought that a groundloop was inevitable, but regained control with full rudder and some braking.

"Handling in flight is quite good. The ailerons and rudder have a lot of authority. This is particularly useful in the flapless 120, as the plane can be put into quite a slip. Makes it come right down. Stalls are not particularly exciting, although there is little warning (my metal wings rattle softly for just an instant).

"Number one on the maintenance trouble list has been chronic brake trouble. I still have the original Goodyear brakes. These do a fine job of stopping the airplane, but their reputation as maintenance hogs seems to be well deserved. In the first year that I owned the plane, I spent more on fixing up the Goodyear brakes than it would have cost me to convert to Clevelands.

"The most expensive repair to date has been replacement of the propeller. The old one suffered premature curling of the tips. Don't know why they can't make props that can cut through asphalt without being damaged!

"Comfort is not exactly the adjective one would use to describe the experience of riding in a 120. 'Cozy,' perhaps. Or maybe 'loud.' Seating is definitely shoulder-to-shoulder. I even feel cramped when flying solo if I'm wearing my win-

ter jacket. The noise level should encourage everyone to wear earplugs. Winter flying brings to one's attention the numerous drafts, and the heater barely compensates. The heater is, in fact, nearly worthless.

"I have had no problem obtaining parts, but then I haven't needed much in the way of specialized parts. Operating costs for the past year totaled $4,400 for 200 hours, a $22-per-hour average.

"An idiosyncrasy that can cause trouble: the fuel tank selector handle points left for left tank, forward for right tank, and right for off. When the previous owner took me up for a test flight, he switched it to off instead of right tank (before run-up, fortunately)."

"The only slightly bad points are somewhat limited rear visibility for those used to 'omnivision' and a higher noise level than is common in trainers today. The first is handled by looking around and up through the skylights (standard equipment on all 120/140s, although some have been modified to remove the top windows—a bad idea, in my opinion) and the second by earplugs, intercoms and additional soundproofing that would amaze Cessna if they knew about it.

"We have found Cessna to be very cooperative and helpful, with some exceptions which seem to involve individual dealers rather than company policy. Often the local dealers will out-of-hand say, 'Oh, parts for that old thing are all custom ordered, takes six weeks, $200 at least,' when in fact the factory can supply the part from stock for $50 (actual instance—nosebowl for 1946). Some parts are, in fact, out of stock at the factory and must be made by hand; others seem priced way out of line—like $60 for a cowl latch; yet I bought a complete, brand-new bottom cowl with four latches from a local dealer for $100 last year. The parts situation is helped a great deal by the fact that many 150 parts are direct replacements—notably most engine parts, and some of the sheetmetal from early 150s. Finding an airworthy part is usually very easy; finding an airshow-winning, super clean part is sometimes difficult and/or expensive.

"One of the better things Cessna does is supply a wide range of documentation on the airplane. A parts manual and a service letters summary is available from dealers, and these will answer most questions if studied carefully.

"For some reason, good, clean rudders are very difficult to find. Elevators are no problem. Front doorposts are very rare also (or expensive), and gearboxes,

the welded steel things to which the rest of the airplane bolts, are rare/expensive. These last two items exist, I think, because of the classic taildragger accident: running off the runway into a ditch and hooking one wheel, which tears out the gearbox and bends the doorpost. Both items are, however, obtainable—just not usually as cheap as you would think.

"Corrosion can be a problem in airplanes parked near the ocean, and should be thoroughly investigated by a buyer; parked outside, the skylights leak and water runs down inside the roof and runs into the rear spar. Collecting there, it causes corrosion which is nearly invisible from the outside, but weakens the carry-through significantly. Any loose rivets or signs of flaking of this member is a sign the wings should be pulled off and a thorough inspection made."

"My '46 C-120 has a rebuilt C-85-12 which now has over 200 hours on it. I cruise between 90 and 100 mph at a power setting of 2300 to 2450 rpm. At those speeds I average 5 gph fuel consumption.

"My altitude and altitude performance is limited because of the Stromberg carburetor, which has very limited leaning capabilities. I rarely run the engine at higher rpms (other than full throttle on takeoff and climb) because of the noise level. The only negative aspects to the plane, in my opinion, are the noise level and cramped cabin.

"However, the sensation of flying, sensitivity to controls, stability, and doing what an airplane is supposed to do far outweigh the negatives. Without flaps, one must become proficient in slipping to lose speed or altitude. Properly trimmed, hands-off flying is easy. On landing, one must take care to control the airplane until rollout is finished because the tailwheel becomes free-wheeling if allowed to turn more than 15 degrees right or left. The airplane is sensitive to turbulence and over-controlling; hence, holding a heading or altitude takes considerable skill and a light touch. All this serves the pilot well, I believe, because more modern, high-performance singles become easy to manage due to the 'honed' skills developed in this venerable taildragger.

"Maintenance costs are minimal. Parts do not seem to be a problem. The West Coast Cessna 120/140 Club, Inc. keeps its members informed of who has what, etc., as well as much other pertinent information for those who fly these planes."

Aerobatic Aircraft

Aerobatic aircraft have been growing dramatically in popularity since the early '70s as more and more pilots discover the fun of flying loops, spins and rolls. And more than a few pilots have taken aerobatic instruction just because they feel it will prepare them for unusual-attitude emergencies and sharpen their airmanship. New aerobatic aircraft are quite expensive, but there is a good selection of used aerobatic aircraft on the market.

If you're shopping for a factory-built aircraft, the selection is rather limited. The most popular aerobat on the market is the Bellanca Citabria, closely followed by its higher-performance stablemate, the Decathlon. Cessna sells a few dozen aerobatic 150s and 152s every year. At the higher end of the cost scale are the Great Lakes open biplane, and the king of the aerobatic world, the Pitts Special. In addition to these factory-built types, there is a plethora of homebuilt and antique aerobatic aircraft, but they are too varied for the scope of this article.

Shopping for a used aerobatic aircraft requires some extra diligence on the part of the buyer. Aerobatics imposes far greater strain on an aircraft than normal flying, and a few hundred hours of four-G pullups and redline-speed recoveries take their toll in the structural integrity of the airplane. Control cables stretch from constant full-deflection movement, engines work harder because of incessant power and airspeed changes, high-rpm dives and full-power climbs. Heavy G-forces put extra stress on not only the wing structure, but also every instrument, bracket and fitting in the airplane. Airplanes that have been used for aerobatic instruction may also have been accidently pushed beyond their limits by inexperienced students.

In short, a microscopically thorough structural examination is absolutely essential for the purchase of any used aerobatic airplane. Find the best man available to do the inspection and pay him what he's worth.

Champion/Bellanca Citabria
More than 4,000 Citabrias have been built since the airplane's debut in 1964. It is a

direct outgrowth of the old Aeronca 7AC Champ, which was introduced in 1946 to compete with the Piper Cub. The very first 7ECA Citabria had a 100-hp Continental O-200, but it was shortly replaced by a 115-hp Lycoming when the need for more power became evident. The 115-hp 7ECA model has continued in production since then without major changes.

In 1967, a higher-powered 150-hp version was introduced called the 7GCAA. This was so successful that in 1968 Champion introduced two more 150-hp versions: the 7GCBC, with a longer wing and flaps; and the 7KCAB, with inverted fuel and oil systems that allowed limited negative-G "outside" maneuvers. The inverted-system model was discontinued in 1978, but the other two 150-hp models have remained in continuous production along with the 115-hp Citabria.

Prices range from about $6,000 for a doggy old 100-hp or 115-hp version to $20,000 for a pristine, low-time '78 GCBC. A quite respectable five-year-old 150-hp GCAA can be had for $12,000 or so.

Performance of the Citabrias ranges from marginal to fairly adequate, depending on the engine. Pilots of the 115-hp model will find it necessary to dive steeply to achieve entry speed for virtually all maneuvers, and a good part of your "aerobatic" time will be spent climbing laboriously back to altitude.

Control response is far from snappy, just barely adequate for the basic roll, loop and spin maneuvers. Control forces are extremely high; small, weak persons may have trouble achieving maximum roll rate.

All in all, the Citabria has become general aviation's primary aerobatic trainer mostly because it's the cheapest airplane around that's certified for aerobatics. A 1964 vintage 7ECA also happens to be the cheapest used aerobatic airplane available.

Shopping for old tube-and-fabric airplanes requires a bit of extra care. All Citabrias are covered at the factory with Dacron, which supposedly has a life expectancy of up to 20 years with proper care. (However, we've seen cases where Bellanca fabric has worn out in as little as two years.) Older Citabrias are fast approaching the time where worn-out fabric is a real possibility, so make sure you check it carefully. (And be sure to check every surface. The wings may be fine while the tailfeathers are rotting off.) Another check point: Citabrias built between July '67 and March '68 had short-lived cotton fabric instead of Dacron. Also check closely for rusty tubing, particularly in the area around the tailwheel.

There has been a definite improvement in the past two years, but quality control and workmanship should be checked closely on older models. Specific problems have been

Bellanca Citabria *is world's most common—and cheapest—aerobatic aircraft. Performance is minimal, however, and control response sluggish.*

cracking fairings, leaky fuel tanks and loose side windows. (One owner of a 1966 model reports he blew out three side windows doing slow rolls.) Also check the wing ribs very carefully in the early models. (The same owner with the popping windows reports that a few months after he sold it, every rib in the airplane had to be replaced.)

When buying any aerobatic airplane—and older Citabrias in particular—it's absolutely necessary to inspect the airplane's structure minutely for signs of overstressing. A well-worn Citabria has probably performed literally thousands of loops in the hands of beginning aerobatic students, so there's no telling what sort of punishment it's been subjected to. We would advise hiring a Bellanca mechanic to thoroughly check over any used Citabria for structural problems before buying.

A recent AD underlines the need for careful structural inspection. AD 77-22-5 requires replacement of the front wing struts with beefier versions. Compliance with this AD is an absolute must; aerobatics are prohibited without it.

Another critical AD applies to the front seat. We know one case in which the seat failed while the aircraft was in a 60-degree nose-up attitude entering a loop. The student in the front seat toppled back into the instructor's lap, pinning the stick full back. After some heroic contortions, the instructor managed to recover the airplane. We

Bellanca Decathlon *is designed for inverted "outside" maneuvers. Quality control problems plague older models.*

don't want to dwell on horror stories, but they do underline the importance of carefully checking any aerobatic airplane. Aerobatics impose a whole different set of strains on an airplane, and the results of a structural problem can be fatal.

Bellanca Decathlon

The Decathlon was introduced in 1971 as a higher-performance "big brother" to the Citabria. The primary difference between the 150-hp Citabria and the Decathlon was the wing, which had a nearly symmetrical airfoil which gave good performance in "outside" negative-G maneuvers. Redline airspeed is 185 mph (compared to the Ci-

tabria's 165), and it is approved for all aerobatic maneuvers except the lomcevak (an end-over-end tumbling snap roll) and the tailslide. Aileron response is somewhat better than the Citabria's. (The aileron system was redesigned in 1977 and aileron control improved even more.) The Decathlon is also available with a constant-speed prop, which gives better vertical performance and eliminates the possibility of engine and prop overspeeding. The Decathlon has the Bellanca-STCed inverted oil and fuel system of the Citabria 7KCAB. With the 1975 model, Bellanca switched to the highly regarded Christen inverted system. The Decathlon is generally regarded as an excellent aero-

Cessna A150

Model	Year	No. Built	Retail Price
A150K	1970	226	$ 7,000
A150L	1971	49	$ 7,200
	1972	65	$ 7,500
	1973	86	$ 8,000
	1974	93	$ 8,500
A150M	1975	85	$ 9,000
	1976	74	$10,500
	1977	49	$11,500
A152	1978	73	$14,000
A152	1979	70	$26,000

150-hp Citabria (7KCAB)

Year	No. Built	Retail Price
1969	28	$10,000
1970	50	$10,500
1971	7	$10,750
1972	43	$11,500
1973	48	$12,000
1974	81	$12,500
1975	63	$13,000
1976	46	$14,000
1977	19	$15,000

Pitts S-1S

Year	No. Built	Retail Price
1971-74	30	$14-$16,000
1975	6	$15,000
1976	10	$19,000
1977	6	$21,000
1978	3	$23,500
1979	1	$24,000

Pitts S-2A

Year	No. Built	Retail Price
1972	40	$24,000
1973	26	$24,500
1974	23	$25,000
1975	23	$26,000
1976	19	$28,000
1977	24	$30,000
1978	15	$31,000
1979	30	$32,500

Great Lakes 2T-1A2

Year	No. Built*	Retail Price
1974		$25,000
1975		$26,000
1976	*Total of 145 aircraft built	$28,000
1977		$30,000
1978		$32,000

115-hp Citabria (7ECA)

Year	No. Built	Retail Price
1964	63	$ 7,000
1965	374	$ 7,200
1966	58	$ 7,300
1967	89	$ 7,400
1968	68	$ 7,500
1969	57	$ 7,750
1970	62	$ 8,000
1971	26	$ 8,250
1972	73	$ 8,500
1973	95	$ 9,000
1974	75	$ 9,250
1975	65	$ 9,750
1976	54	$11,000
1977	43	$12,500
1978	53	$13,750
1979	53	$15,000

Bellanca Decathlon (8KCAB)

Year	No. Built	Retail Price
1971	3	$11,000
1972	48	$12,000
1973	65	$13,000
1974	41	$13,700
1975	59	$14,500
1976	58	$15,500
1977	82	$17,000
1978	82	$19,000
1979	33	$22,500

batic trainer. The Citabria can be characterized as an airplane that happens to be certified for aerobatics, but the Decathlon deserves its label of a real aerobatic machine. We feel it still falls well short of aircraft designed from the ground up for aerobatics (like the Pitts), however. But we've gotten quite a bit of static on this score from some pilots.

In 1978, Bellanca introduced the Super Decathlon, which has a 180-hp engine for better vertical performance. However, very few of these are on the used-plane market. Unfortunately, the Decathlon shares the quality-control problems of the Citabria. In past *Aviation Consumer* surveys, owners of 1975 and older Decathlons report instances of peeling paint, loose fairings, rattling exhaust systems and other glitches. In addition, the Decathlon was hit with an expensive AD on the wing nose ribs. (Decathlons used extensively in outside maneuvers—the prime design use of the airplane —in many cases had formed severe cracks in the ribs.) It is critical to assure that any pre-1975 Decathlon has had this AD-required repair or replacement taken care of in a very professional manner. We would also advise careful checking of the elevator stop bolt; although there's no AD on it, we know of at least one case in which the elevators jammed in the full down position because of a worn bolt. We've also had reports of jammed ailerons in 1972-74 models. Again, the lesson: have the airplane checked closely by an experienced Bellanca mechanic before buying.

The Decathlon, like the Citabria, does not depreciate much. A 1974 model, for example, after an initial sharp drop from its new list price of $21,000 to $15,100, has held nearly steady in value since 1975, and is now selling for $14,500.

Cessna Aerobat

If the thought of a fabric-covered tail-dragger doesn't appeal to you, consider the Cessna Aerobat, a beefed-up checker-winged version of the ubiquitous Cessna 150/152. Although the Aerobat is usually considered the least able aerobatic aircraft on the market, it has the durable attributes of the 150/152—reliability, economy and familiarity.

Like the 115-hp Citabria, the Aerobat is approved for only positive-G maneuvers such as the loop, barrel roll and spin. Control forces are much lighter than the truck-like Citabria's, but the Aerobat has less aileron power and is therefore somewhat sloppy. Aerobatic instructors tell us that a four-point roll in an Aerobat is a challenge of the highest order because of the imprecise aileron control. The Aerobat also has poorly harmonized controls; there is lots of elevator power but not enough rudder. Another problem is its tendency to overspeed the engine and propeller during recovery from spins and loops. For this reason, check out the engine of any Aerobat carefully.

The Aerobat is unique among the aircraft listed here for its side-by-side seating and control wheel. Aerobatic purists like to be on the centerline of the airplane for better visual references, and a control stick is superior to the standard wheel for aerobatic maneuvering. On the other hand, the side-by-side seating makes for better student-to-instructor or pilot-to-passenger communication—an important and often overlooked consideration. (Just try listening to the fine points of a slow roll over a scratchy intercom with the wind whipping around.)

On the other hand, the side-by-side seating of the Aerobat is notoriously cramped, and energetic aerobatic rolling maneuvers usually result in a flurry of flying

Cessna Aerobat *provides aerobatic flying in a familiar airplane. This 1973 model sells for about $300 more than the standard 150.*

elbows that can pummel the unsuspecting passenger.

The Aerobat should be inspected carefully for fatigue cracks. Steel and wood won't fatigue as easily as aluminum will, and the Aerobat is the only aircraft listed here that is all aluminum. Otherwise, the Aerobat has all the familiar checkpoints of the 150: nose gear and firewall, main gear boxes and valve problems due to use of 100 LL fuel.

Cessna introduced the first Aerobat in 1970; prices start at about $7,200 for that model—about $500 more than the standard 1970 model 150. Original price was about $12,500 equipped; the Aerobat depreciates more rapidly than the Citabria. (A 1970 115-hp Citabria sold originally for $3,000 less and is worth $1,000 more today.)

Pitts S-1 and S-2

The Pitts Special biplane has long been regarded as probably the best aerobatic airplane in the world. Originally designed as a homebuilt in the late '40s, the Pitts has dominated competition aerobatics for more than a decade, and the design is still the most popular homebuilt airplane design in history. (More than 400 homebuilt Pitts are now flying.)

In 1971, the airplane was certified and put into production. (We will deal only with factory-built aircraft in this report. Although the workmanship on a homebuilt is often far superior to that of any production planes, it is sometimes a lot worse, and we would have severe doubts about pulling six G's in an amateur-built airplane, unless we knew the builder and his reputation rather well. In any case, buying a homebuilt is a high art that may be the subject of an entire article.)

There are two basic models of production Pitts: the single-place 180-hp S-1S and the two-place 200-hp S-2A. More than 200 airplanes have been produced, mostly the two-

Great Lakes *biplane was resurrected from 1929—and died out in 1978 after a five-year production run. As of mid-1980, there were plans to resume production again, however.*

placer, which is used extensively by commercial operators for advanced aerobatic instruction. (Homebuilts are not legal for commercial use, so flight schools must use a factory-built model.)

The Pitts excels because it is immensely overpowered (the power-to-weight ratio of the S-1S is double that of the Bonanza, and climb rate is a staggering 2,600 fpm at gross weight), extremely responsive in all axes, and has lots of drag, which prevents it from building up speed too quickly when pointed straight down. The Pitts does every aerobatic maneuver known to mankind, and does most of them better than any other airplane. If you are interested in unlimited aerobatics, there is simply no other production airplane worth considering.

But the Pitts definitely has some big drawbacks. It is extremely difficult to land because of its atrocious over-the-nose visibility, twitchy traits on the ground and very high approach speeds. Cabin environment is lousy; the airplane is cramped, noisy, windy and cold. Most Pitts' are equipped with canopies, which partially solve the latter two problems. Without a canopy, of course, wintertime operations are virtually impossible. (Incidentally, the standard Pitts canopy rails are notoriously deficient, and many are fitted with "outlaw" homebuilt-type rails.)

For an airplane as refined as the Pitts was before it started production, it has had a surprising number of airframe ADs, and one owner reports that "quality control is not as good as it could be." There have been modifications of the tail struts, wing attach fittings and interplane struts. Battery boxes are reportedly substandard, resulting in possible damage from acid leakage. The first 10 or 15 airplanes off the line had serious problems with peeling paint and bad primer on the steel tubing.

The two-hole S-2A has also suffered more than its share of problems in the powerplant department, with early models suffering from familiar ADs on the piston pins and oil pump, along with the ubiquitous Hartzell prop AD.

Resale value of the Pitts is quite good—not surprising considering the fact that the production backlog at times has been over a year. A 1974 S-2A that sold new for $28,000 is still worth $28,000 today. (Not even the Bonanza can match that resale record.) The Pitts doesn't even take the usual first-year plunge in value; that same $28,000 1975 S-2A dropped only to $26,000 after one year and appreciated slowly ever since. Any used Pitts is virtually guaranteed to appreciate. (We're not counting declines in value due to using up engine overhaul time, of course).

Pitts S-2A *is the ultimate aerobatic trainer. This particular aircraft has front cockpit covered. Note symmetrical airfoil for better inverted performance.*

Great Lakes

For those who want a slightly more civilized aerobatic biplane, there is the Great Lakes 2T-1A-2. First designed in 1929, the Lakes was recertified with up-to-date systems and a 180-hp Lycoming and put into production in 1974. When production stopped in 1978, a total of 138 "new" Lakes had been built. (Sales were still excellent, but dramatic price increases in vendor equipment like engines and props, plus skyrocketing labor rates in Wichita, put the projected price of the 1979 model so high that the company figured nobody would buy one.)

In 1980, however, it was announced that production will resume under new ownership.

The Great Lakes is a two-seater and somewhat larger than the Pitts, so its vertical performance is less spectacular. Control response is also less whippet-like, although still quite good. (Pilots tell us the roll response is about like that of the Decathlon.) The Lakes has full inverted systems and can perform the full complement of outside maneuvers.

On the plus side, the Lakes is very easy to handle on the ground and has a much slower landing speed than the Pitts. As a result, any taildragger pilot should be able to solo it after a few trips around the pattern, and even nosewheel pilots should be able to solo after a few hours of practice.

There is only one major service problem to watch out for: leaky fuel tanks in the '74-'77 models. Check very closely for fuel stains. The only airframe AD requires an inspection for cracks in the heater muff every 25 hours when the heater is in use. (Since the airplane has an open cockpit, we wouldn't worry too much about being overcome by carbon monoxide fumes, but apparently the FAA believes otherwise.) Also check carefully for battery leaks. If a battery cap is left loose, a few seconds of negative-G maneuvering will spray acid into the innards of the instrument panel. (This is a common problem of most aerobatic

aircraft.)

The Lakes is unusual because of its grade-A cotton fabric. (Most modern fabric-covered aircraft use Dacron, fiberglass or other synthetic fabric.) When hangared and cared for properly, grade-A can last as long as 10 years, but it should be checked very carefully before purchase. In any event, a used Great Lakes buyer should be prepared for a complete recover job every 10 years or so. If you're considering a five-year-old airplane, that means your recover job will be due in another five years or so.

The Great Lakes has an excellent reputation for quality. The aircraft are virtually hand-built, and we know company president Doug Champlin was firmly committed to top-notch quality control. As an example, all Lakes have 12 coats of primer paint; as a result the airplane has had none of the paint and fabric problems that have plagued the Bellancas and early production Pitts.

Other Choices

There is a handful of other production aerobatic aircraft on the market which we'll mention briefly. Beech made a couple of dozen aerobatic straight-tail Bonanzas in the late '60s; if you can find one, the price will be between $40,000 and $50,000. Some Musketeer, Sport and Sundowner models in the late '60s and early '70s were sold with optional aerobatic kits (make sure the ventral fin has been added; there was an AD after some spin problems). Prices should be in the $10,000-$15,000 range.

Perhaps the very best aerobatic trainer available is a French import called the CAP-10. Less than a dozen are flying in this country, but the sleek all-wood low-winger has almost Pitts-like performance with the comfort of an enclosed cockpit, gentle landing characteristics and superb visibility from a bubble canopy. Prices of used CAP-10s are hard to pin down, but new ones are selling for a phenomenal $40,000-plus.

Helio Courier

After nearly 20 years of production as a short-takeoff-and-land aircraft par excellence, the Helio Courier has at least temporarily been consigned to limbo and production halted. Used-plane buyers, at least, should be reassured to know that the factory is still producing parts and is reported to have a good inventory at hand.

Forming the backbone of the Helio line before the cutoff in the late 1974 were two basic models, one powered by a 295-hp engine, the other a 250-hp powerplant. Both are six-cylinder Lycomings.

The main offshoots from this lineage were a twin-engine version with a pair of 250s mounted on the high wing, and a turboprop Stallion powered by a 680-shp PT6. Only one twin was built, and of the 21 or so Stallions produced, 19 of them are reported to have gone to Cambodia. One Stallion was sold for civilian use.

Most of the landplane versions of the Helio Courier have conventional gear with a tailwheel. Late in the production cycle a tricycle-gear Courier was offered, and about 19 of these were built. In all, some 550 Couriers were built.

Design Features
The Helio Courier's main claim to STOL stardom is a marvelous wing that will provide vigorous lateral control at nearly any speed in or out of a stall, and allow the aircraft to be slowed up to a point beyond which most other aircraft have long since given up flying.

The design features that endow the wing with these unusual flying characteristics are full-span automatic Handley Page leading-edge slats in front and electrically operated slotted flaps over 74 percent of the span in the rear, plus Frise ailerons acting in conjunction with arc-type spoilers, which project from the upper surface of each wing.

History
The basic concept of the aircraft was the brainchild of a pair of Bostonian academics from MIT and Harvard—Prof. Otto Koppen and Dr. Lynn Bollinger. This evolved from an airplane-in-every-garage vision to a four-seat Model H-391B certificated in 1954.

This was followed by a four-to-five-seat Model H-395 in 1958 and the Model H-395A in 1959, and so on, as detailed in the accompanying charts.

The Helio Aircraft Corporation founded by Bollinger and Koppen in 1969 became a division of General Aircraft Corporation and was named a company instead of a corporation. Presently the assets are owned by Helio Aircraft, Ltd., and arrangements are being devised with an eye to restoring the Helio line to production. The plant is located in Pittsburgh, Kansas.

One good source of reconditioned Helios and training for the aircraft is Larry Montgomery at Larmont Aviation in Spartanburg, S.C.; 803-576-9036.

Naturally, the STOL attributes of the Helio Couriers suit them ideally for use as a bushplane, floatplane and counterinsurgency military craft. Over 150 were sold to the U.S. Air Force. As an extra safeguard against the hazards of operating in this manner, the airplane was endowed with unusual structural strength, designed to protect the occupants in a crash. Therefore, the cabin section has a massive welded steel framework. Egress from the six-seat cabin is provided in an unusual arrangement by a port-side pilot door and a starboard door alongside the center pair of seats.

Although the Helio Courier most logically is a specialty aircraft adept at getting in and out of unprepared fields, it is regarded as an ultra-safe utility airplane by some pilots, who fly it in a less demanding fashion. In this manner, the main benefits are the unusually slow landing speeds and the controllability with which to get out of almost any tight spot. The drawbacks are the speed limits imposed by a landing gear that won't retract, and, for all but the handful of tri-gear models, all the handling qualities that go with tailwheel aircraft.

Furthermore, the bigger engine is geared and therefore prey to extra maintenance considerations.

STOL Handling
Pilots attracted by the safety features of the aircraft also should be aware of the fact that a good bit of seasoning is required to become accustomed to getting the most out of the Helio in its true STOL mode. The average apprentice tends to discover that in a good, steep STOL approach, a Helio can develop an astonishing rate of descent that allows the unwary pilot to get behind the power curve, as in any conventional plane.

A fine touch is required to master the

Courier was a favorite aircraft *of the military and the Central Intelligence Agency during the Vietnam war. CIA agents, in fact, posed as Helio salesmen to gain entry into many nations around the world, a contributing cause to the company's eventual demise.*

Helio Courier

Helio in a maximum-performance approach, where some of the characteristics of a lifting body come to light.

Nevertheless, the adept pilot can expect to be rewarded with sterling short-field performance that delivers a takeoff run over 50 feet of only 610 feet and a landing over a 50-foot obstacle of just 520 feet (in the 295-hp model, at gross).

Slow flight, power on, is credited with being 26 knots/30 mph.

Despite the massive, condor-like wings, the aircraft will surprise the novice with its facile controllability and a smooth kind of "ball-bearing" aileron response. Paradoxically, in cruise the ship is so stable it feels as though a hidden autopilot were keeping it on track.

Stories are legion about ways in which the unique STOL qualities of the Helios, and their ability to turn on a dime at low speeds, have averted disaster. Pilots like the Rev. Bob Bryan like to point out how the airplane allows the luxury of an abrupt change in direction or a go-around in the

Huge vertical fin *provides good stability at low speeds, but also catches every gust of wind. As a result, Courier is among the most difficult of all aircraft to land in windy conditions.*

last seconds of the flare where other airplanes would normally be committed. Bryan has taken advantage of the seaplane Helio's unusual qualities to land *across* rivers blasted

by super-strong crosswinds and, to get off extremely short, sheltered sections of water before venturing into rough open sea that would have swamped the aircraft.

The Helio's slower-than-average takeoff and landing speeds add extra longevity to floats by diminishing the battering they must take at higher speeds.

Powerplants
The big 295-hp Lycoming GO-480-G1D6 engines are smooth-running but come burdened with a mere 1,400-hour TBO. And expect to part with some $11,000 for an overhaul.

Modifications
To our knowledge, there are none. The tricycle-gear configuration originally stemmed from the STC held by an outside company, but this was acquired by Helio. Naturally, this is one airplane Robertson doesn't need to provide with a STOL kit.

Options
Rajay turbocharging is available for the 295-hp engine, but not the 250-hp version. Naturally, floats and skis are adapted to the Helios. And optional fuel tanks can raise the normal fuel capacity from 60 gallons

Courier shows the source of its claim to fame: *the beslatted wing, with nearly full-span flaps. On top, out of sight, are spoilers for roll control at low speeds.*

Model	Year	Average Retail Price	Cruise Speed (mph)	Rate of Climb (fpm)	Useful Load (lbs)	Fuel Std/Opt (gals)	Engine	TBO (hrs)	Overhaul Cost
H-395	1956-58	$28,000	162	1,250	1,100	60	260-hp Lycoming	1,200	$10,000
H-395A	1959-64	$32,000	162	1,250	1,100	60	260-hp Lycoming	1,200	$10,000
H-500 Twin	1965	$100,000	170	1,830	1,465	160	250-hp Lycoming	1,200	$6,500
H-295	1965-68	$55-65,000	165	1,150	1,320	60/120	295-hp Lycoming	1,400	$11,000
H-250	1965-68	$35-40,000	152	1,050	1,440	60/120	250-hp Lycoming	1,200	$6,500
H-295	1969-73	$60-70,000	165	1,150	1,320	60/120	295-hp Lycoming	1,400	$11,000
HST-550	1970-72	$250-300,000	217	2,200	2,275	120/224	680-shp P&W	3,500	$40,000
H-295	1974	$75,000	165	1,150	1,320	60/120	295-hp Lycoming	1,400	$11,000

to 120 gallons. Range without the optional tanks at 75 percent power is a short-legged 572 nm/660 sm.

One operator familiar with both the normally aspirated and Rajay-turbocharged powerplants said he was able to get the full 1,400-hour TBO with the Rajay versions, though it usually seemed to require a top overhaul somewhere along the way before then.

Airworthiness Directives

The biggest AD on the Helio Couriers, issued in 1971, required inspection of the wing center section steel carry-through fitting on the lower main wing spar for cracks or corrosion. It required X-ray inspections of the fittings and modification of the carry-through assembly and fittings if problems were discovered, or installation of reinforcing straps. Later production models incorporated "improvements" designed to correct the alleged problem.

It is generally felt in Helio circles that the correction was really unnecessary and had been triggered by a bizarre set of circumstances involving an airplane that had been rammed into a dock, incorrectly repaired, and then later crashed in a thunderstorm.

Other ADs called for inspections to guard against cracks in the vertical fin front spar, aileron-interceptor actuator bell-cranks, fin upper hinge attachments, and horizontal front spar splice plates.

Operators regard these problems as peculiar only to the early model Helio Couriers.

Maintenance

The airplane seems to be regarded as a rather straightforward one to maintain, requiring no unique expertise or abnormal expenses. A particularly seasoned Helio maintenance expert located in the northeast is T. M. Mack Close of Gardner, Mass. This A&P maintains a stable of some 30 Helios for various owners and operators.

Jungle Aviation and Radio Service, Inc. in Waxhaw, North Carolina, has an STC that permits removal of the port-size rear door post and installation of a second door alongside. This permits a double-door arrangement that allows loading of stretchers and other wide cargo items.

Load Carrying

Most Helio Courier operators feel the airplane is unnecessarily load limited and that the aircraft is structurally and aerodynamically able to carry more. There is hope that the necessary paperwork will be done to raise the gross to more realistic levels permitted both by the military and other nations.

The airplane has a six-place cabin configuration, but as with many bush-utility aircraft, the tendency is (wisely or not) to throw in anything the sizable cabin can hold.

Ground Handling

The airplane is regarded by many as something of a bear in a crosswind situation, since that big vertical tail—so useful for slow-speed stability—is a fine target for a crosswind to send weathervaning. One solution to the problem is the crosswind landing gear provided by Goodyear.

The Competition

The Maules and Robertson mod STOL aircraft are generally regarded as the biggest competition to the Helios. Indeed, operators of both the Helios and Robertson Cessnas say the Cessnas can be depended upon to get in and out of fields of just about the same puny dimensions as the Helios.

But the difference is that the Helio will maintain lateral controllability right to the ragged edge with somewhat greater sureness, according to the people we talked to.

On the other hand, some Cessnas like the 206 can carry a bigger load, though the nosewheel configuration jeopardizes their ability to operate out of unprepared fields.

Associations

There presently are no Helio Courier societies or associations, though there is some feeling that one should be formed, according to Dr. James Zuckerman of Concord, Mass.

Owner Comments

"My first Helio was a one-year-old 250-hp model. After eight years and 1,500 hours we traded it for a 295-hp tri-gear model and have logged about 420 hours on that.

"The first plane had had pretty hard use on the engine in demonstrations, and I didn't help any at first practicing my slow flight and impressing my friends, all of which gave me some soft cylinders at about 700 hours on the engine. At the high angle of attack in flying at 40 mph, the front cylinders didn't seem to get enough cooling, even with the cowl flaps open. (At least that was my theory.)

"Having gotten some of that nonsense out of my system, I am flying the new plane much more conservatively, climbing out at reasonable airspeeds and demonstrating slow flight at reduced power only, allowing a little sink, rather than trying to impress folks by holding altitude at high power settings. The amazing thing is the control at the slow speeds, which is just as surprising when gliding power off. As a matter of fact, I would occasionally shut down the engine on the 250 and soar when my glider club friends didn't show up!

"Some of the factors that influenced my decision to fly Helios can be summarized as follows:

"Safety: As a physician (eye surgeon) trained in physics, etc., with an engineer graduate for a father, the relationship of speed and crash forces has long been obvious. Ignored by many, it is a fact that doubling the speed of any vehicle increases the energy by four times! Related to flying, this means simply that your head hits the dashboard with four times the force at 80 mph as it does at 40 mph. Having mopped up a lot of foreheads in

Helio Courier H-295 seats six. *Massive tubular framework is hidden beneath compartment liners.*

Courier panel is big and utilitarian. *Note airspeed indicator that reads down to 40 mph.*

my business, to me this makes sense. Consider what happens if you stub your toe while landing your bird at 60 mph and hit the ditch. I will be two times safer in a similar incident touching down at 40 in my Helio.

"The same applies, if the need arises, settling into the ocean waves or into a forest. Of course, no one really expects to do that, and as people accept the idea of always selecting a nice, long pavement to land on, they quit worrying about the ever-increasing landing speeds of our aircraft.

"Maintenance will be somewhat higher, with the wing-slat system, etc. The engine takes a high-cost overhaul due to the gearing, etc., and I dread to think about it, to the point of trying to fly a little more carefully with regard to engine management.

"Another source of complaint might be the low wing loading and bumpiness in turbulence, though we seem to be used to that, and strong crosswinds may be a problem in ground handling and landing. Of course, the trick in a 30-knot crosswind is to land across the runway, and a few hundred feet would be plenty. Unfortunately, sometimes you have a hard time at controlled fields getting them to let you do it. We had no problems with the conventional gear after we changed to crosswind wheels, and have had no problems with the tri-gear, though it is very tall and the vertical tail catches a lot of wind.

"In conclusion, I don't believe we have ever regretted our choice of plane.

L. L. Hyde, M.D.
Kansas City, Mo.

Perhaps the biggest single user of Helio Couriers, outside of the military, is JAARS, Jungle Aviation and Radio Service, Inc., which flies on missionary work in some of the most remote areas of the world. They own 19 Helios, and by virtue of their status in serving indigenous foreign peoples have been eligible for aid in getting the use of military surplus Helio equipment. JAARS subjects its Helios to the most punishing kind of work, and two of its representatives volunteered these comments:

"Our founder, William Tounsend, was driving by in Kansas one day and saw this airplane 'hovering' up there above the trees and decided 'that's the airplane we need for our work in the jungles,' so he found the factory, got a demonstration, and it was only a few months later that our pilot, Bob Griffin, picked up our first Helio and flew it to Ecuador in 1955.

"The Helio Couriers are fantastic airplanes. They do take some maintenance, but they provide a great deal of reliability. And the tubular steel framework around the cabin combined with the low impact speed in case of an engine failure have brought us a tremendous safety factor. We have never had a fatality in operating the aircraft from 1955 to the present day. And though we've had numerous crashes, the Helio has been capable of bringing people through in fairly good shape without serious injuries.

"To use the airplane in a true STOL mode does take a capable pilot, however, and I wouldn't encourage people to invest the money they cost unless they really needed an STOL-type airplane. They're too slow in cruise, and actually, for the cost, they're too limited in payload. But for our situation, where it's almost impossible to get a strip longer than 250 meters, it is still the aircraft that lets us operate in those very marginal conditions.

"As for the payload situation, we are presently working with the Helio Corp. to get them to take a little more realistic look at the payload capability. What we're interested in now is getting Helio to put in the paperwork to increase the gross weight. "The aircraft we use mostly is the H-295. The airplane is very rugged and gives very good service, indeed. Our highest time aircraft now has over 5,000 hours on it, and they are very simple. The 100-hour inspections seem to be routine. The GO-480 has a 1,400-hour TBO, but we believe it should be higher. We overhaul our own engines, and we find them to be in good condition when we tear them down.

"The gearing does not require extra work between overhauls, but at the overhaul it becomes a bit expensive.

"Although the wing is complicated with the 'tomahawks' (spoilers) and slats, it really does not require much extra care and attention. You can go through many hundred-hour inspections without finding any problem in the wing."

Roy Minor
Stuart Shepard
Jungle Aviation and
Radio Services, Inc.

"I learned to fly completely in the Helio, with the crosswind gear. I have one of the last Helios built, a '74 model. I'm a physician, (an obstetrician) and had a clinic at Hanscom AFB (where they marketed the Helio Couriers). And as I watched the Helios fly there, I thought to myself, it looks as though they are stopping in mid-air and flying backwards. So I became interested in the Helios.

"I purchased one, and now fly at least once a week to Nantucket, where I am a consultant to a hospital. I don't use it for its true (STOL) purpose. And I think it's fair to say there are four kinds of people who own Helios. The first require what the Helio can do, and virtually no other airplane will work in and out of a 400-500-foot strip. The second group consists of those people who need a tail-dragger with short-field capability. The third group of people are those who fly the airplane because it's simply the safest plane in the air, and that's the main reason I fly it. It's an incredibly safe aircraft. And the fourth group of people are those who I think it would be fair to call 'Helio nuts,' and there are a lot of them. And once you learn to taxi it in the exaggerated attitude on the ground, you just think it's unnatural to fly anything else.

"There's one tricky thing about landing a Helio that you must accept. And that is when you get going very slowly, particularly in a headwind situation where your track across the ground is almost nil. You're right down around 30 knots at 10 feet off the ground and you can get into a position where, if you add more power, the torque of the airplane will carry you right off the side of the runway. So what most of us do in the Helio is come in a little faster—instead of 30, come in at 40 or so. If you find yourself in the aforementioned position, accept the fact that you are going to have a hard landing and put it down. As soon as you cut power, the plane will land wherever it is."

Dr. James Zuckerman
Concord, Mass.

The Aviation Consumer Used Aircraft Guide

The 206 is Cessna's ranch wagon and utility carryall: six seats under a parasol-like wing, and double cargo doors that will swallow anything up to 44 inches wide. One of the real haulers, it will lug about as much useful load as anything else in the skies with fixed gear and one piston engine.

With few significant changes, it has trundled down through the years under one name or another as Cessna's high-wing answer to the Piper Cherokee Six.

Model History

It started out in 1964 as the Skywagon 206, and in '71 transitioned into the Stationair 206. In 1980 it became the Stationair 6. The only change of any consequence has been the small boost in horsepower in '68 from 285 to 300 in the normally aspirated 206 and in 1977 from 285 to 310 in the turbo model.

Early models had engines with a 1,200-hour TBO, or 1,500 hours if equipped with nickel or nimonic exhaust valves. The turbo model, introduced in 1966, has always had a 1,400-hour TBO. From 1970 on, all normally aspirated models came with 1,500-hour TBOs.

With the Stationair 206 designation in 1973 came a slight change to the wing airfoil thanks to the addition of a cuffed leading edge. This didn't affect stall speeds or takeoff and landing distances, but added a bit of extra stability and controllability at lower speeds.

In 1975 new wheel fairings gave the aircraft a six-mph boost in cruise speed.

The only significance of the U (for utility) prefix to the various 206 models is that the aircraft comes out of the factory with only the pilot's seat. Several cargo kits are available for mortuary, photographic, portable stretcher, agricultural spray and skydiving pursuits. An underbelly fiberglass cargo pod adds 300 pounds to the aircraft's load-carrying ability—within the original useful load limits, of course.

Also, the Stationairs can be fitted with floats or skis, unlike their competitor, the Piper Cherokee Six.

Cherokee Six Competition

Since the aircraft beg for comparison, it should be noted that although through the years the two aircraft have had very similar load-carrying capability, the Piper has significantly better figures for takeoff and landing over a 50-foot obstacle, and it can carry slightly more fuel.

Also, the Cherokee Six Lycoming powerplant enjoys a 500-hour edge in TBO over the Continental IO-520 in the Cessna. To our knowledge, however, this version of the -520 has not suffered from the cracking crankcase problem that hit Bonanzas and Barons quite seriously.

High-altitude operators should note also that until the 1980 Turbo Saratoga came along, Piper did not offer a turbo version of the Cherokee Six.

Performance

The Stationairs can be counted on to carry a phenomenal payload of 900 to 1,050 pounds; figure on six 170-pounders and maybe 50 pounds of baggage on top of a full 80 gallons of fuel (optional tankage; standard tanks hold 63 gallons). And that's calculated on the basis of 100 pounds of optional equipment, avionics, etc.

Look for top cruise speeds (at 75 percent power) of from 164 to 170 mph in the normally aspirated models, with 13 to 15 gph fuel consumption.

Handling

Pilots report the aircraft is stable in rough weather. But it is a big, heavy bird and flies accordingly and not with great sprightliness. One pilot, a CFI who had lots of Cessna Skylane time, said it took him about 50 hours to feel comfortable flying the Stationair. Pilots also report it develops a "surprising" rate of sink on final with full flaps. And as with many aircraft with a long center of gravity envelope, it is extremely difficult to flare on landing without hitting nosewheel first unless there's weight in the rear.

As for little idiosyncrasies, one pilot who regularly flies long distances over water noted that ditching in an emergency, with flaps down, poses an exit problem for rear-compartment passengers since the rear doors won't open if the flaps are lowered.

Except for the paint scheme, *the '77 Stationair is nearly indistinguishable from all its forebears and followers. This model, however, had the small cleanup and wheel fairings that allowed a six-mph boost in cruise.*

Cabin Accommodation

The greatest thing about the Stationair's cabin is access through double doors on the starboard side, with a floor height that makes for easy loading and no stooping. For certain cargos the flat floor (with the exception of small concavities scooped out for the rear-seat passengers' feet) is touted as an advantage over the Cherokee 6's, which has a wing spar hump in the center section. Unlike the Piper, however, the Cessna's fuselage becomes narrower and lower toward the rear, which means less comfort for people in the third tier of seats. With the 1978 models, club seating is available as an option, and the permissible baggage load in the rear compartment goes up by 60 pounds to 180. The Stationair has no front baggage compartment like the Cherokee 6, though, of course, it can be fitted out with a cargo pod.

Maintenance

Operators report several maintenance problem areas with the Stationair 206 series. Leaking fuel tanks is one of the most common. In 1978 Cessna put out service instructions for inspection of Goodyear bladder tanks since there were frequent reports of deterioration. With the 1979 models Cessna introduced as standard 92-gallon wet-wing tanks.

Exhaust stack cracking came in for additional criticism by owners, as did various problems with the AiResearch turbochargers. Cessna has issued service letters on both matters.

In 1972 Airworthiness Directives

Typical seating arrangement, *with tapering rear cabin—this in a '72 Stationair.*

were issued to correct two other problems involving the 206 models: inadvertent retraction of wing flaps and cracking or bolt looseness in fin and rudder attachments.

And in 1977 Teledyne Continental issued instructions to check for signs of possible "distress" of the engine's main bearing and transfer collar. In general, owners report maintenance costs are "sobering" and "not cheap."

Operational Problems

Fuel flow fluctuations were reported by Model 206 operators at level-off after long climbouts, and these appear to reflect a continuing pattern of vapor lock problems in 200 series Cessnas. An AD has been issued to bolster Cessna's service data on the matter.

One operator reported that he had special difficulties starting the engine in hot climates (100 degrees F) because of vapor lock, and often simply had to wait 20 or 30 minutes after engine

shutdown to get a start.

Safety

The Stationair 206 has an exemplary safety record. Its fatal accident rate places it among the top (best) three aircraft in its class (four-/six-place fixed-gear aircraft). In an NTSB ranking with 32 other single-engine aircraft of all classes, the 206 was fifth best in fatal accident rate and seventh best in total accident rate.

Other rankings by accident type in the NTSB's special study show the model 206 betrays no major safety weaknesses—except it is about in the middle of the pack in hard landings. This might be expected of a utility aircraft that is often flown heavily loaded and that exhibits, according to pilots, a high sink rate on final if not monitored closely with power.

The aircraft exhibits a fairly good record in all these other categories, however: undershoots, overshoots,

Model	Year	Number Built	Average Retail Price	Cruise Speed (mph)	Rate of Climb (fpm)	Useful Load (lbs)	Engine	TBO (hrs)	Overhaul Cost
206	1964-65	437	$22,250	163	1,075	1,540	285-hp Cont.	1,200	$6,750
206 A/B	1966-67	476	$24,000	164	920	1,815	300-hp Cont.	1,200	$6,750
T206 A/B	1966-67	Incl. above	$25,500	200	1,030	1,845	285-hp Cont.	1,400	$8,000
206 C/D	1968-69	534	$26,500	164	920	1,880	300-hp Cont.	1,200	$6,750
T206 C/D	1968-69	Incl. above	$28,000	200	1,030	1,845	285-hp Cont.	1,400	$8,000
206 E	1970-71	254	$29,250	164	920	1,880	300-hp Cont.	1,500	$6,750
T206 E	1970-71	Incl. above	$31,250	200	1,030	1,620	285-hp Cont.	1,400	$8,000
206 F	1972	173	$30,500	164	920	1,620	300-hp Cont.	1,500	$6,750
T206 F	1972	Incl. above	$33,000	200	1,030	1,905	285-hp Cont.	1,400	$8,000
Stationair	1973-74	704	$33,500	164	920	1,520	300-hp Cont.	1,500	$6,750
T-Stationair	1973-74	Incl. above	$35,000	200	1,030	1,905	285-hp Cont.	1,400	$8,000
Stationair	1975-76	941	$40,000	169	920	1,620	300-hp Cont.	1,500	$6,750
T-Stationair	1975-76	Incl. above	$42,000	200	1,030	1,556	285-hp Cont.	1,400	$8,000
Stationair	1977	502	$46,000	169	920	1,620	300-hp Cont.	1,500	$6,750
T-Stationair	1977	Incl. above	$48,500	200	1,030	1,555	310-hp Cont.	1,400	$8,000
Stationair	1978	426	$48,500	169	920	1,520	300-hp Cont.	1,500	$6,750
T-Stationair	1978	Incl. above	$52,000	200	1,030	1,556	310-hp Cont.	1,400	$8,000
Stationair	1979	NA	$50,000	169	920	1,620	300-hp Cont.	1,500	$6,750
T-Stationair	1979	NA	$56,000	200	1,010	1,556	310-hp Cont.	1,400	$8,000

ground loops, in-flight airframe failures, engine failures, midair collisions, stalls and collisions with obstacles, or ground and water.

Investment Value

As an investment, the 206 models show a very quick recovery from the initial drop in value, but their climb in resale value from then on is extremely modest. They're obviously not collector's items like Bonanzas.

A comparison with the Piper Cherokee Six shows a very similar curve, however, suggesting neither is highly valued over the other.

Modifications

Numerous modest changes have been made to the 206 line via the Supplemental Type Certificate route. STOL kits are offered by Robertson, Horton and Martin Machining. As usual, Robertson's appears to be the most extensive, incorporating a flap-

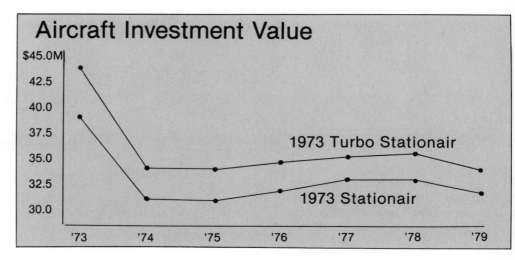

actuated aileron droop system along with a recontoured leading edge and flap-actuated elevator trim.

Flint Aero in Santee, Calif., offers longer wingtips with increased fuel capacity, and FloAir, Inc. in Wichita,

Kan., provides a 26-gallon aux fuel tank in the baggage compartment.

Others supply various blister windows and camera ports, and RAM Aircraft in Waco, Tex., will install the Continental TSIO-520-M engine.

Owner Comments

"I was the American Consul at Merida, Yucatan, Mexico, for three years, and for the last two I covered my Consular District with a Cessna 206. I flew some 550 hours in those two years throughout Mexico.

"I have nothing but praise for my 1976 model Stationair II. When I bought the aircraft it had 300 hours, and up to the time I sold it at 900 hours-plus, I never experienced any engine problems whatsoever. With full IFR equipment I still could put 1,050 pounds in the cabin plus a full load of gas.

"Once, when a member of the President's family came to see the Mayan ruins, I flew three hefty Secret Service agents and two even more hefty Mexican agents on a 300-mile round robin of sites to be visited. With a full load of fuel I must have been 300 pounds over gross when I took off from Merida at 8 a.m. with the temperature at 80 degrees. I selected the longest runway (about 7,000 feet), since there was no wind, and I was amazed that at the midway intersection we were 300 feet in the air and climbing at a respectable 450 fpm.

"Tips on flying a 206: Lean it out—even when you taxi. Keep it leaned on descent to max possible. Make long gradual descents with cowl flaps closed, as much throttle as possible, keeping the furnace hot, and unwind the prop. Do *not* let the cylinder head temperature fall off rapidly. Sharp pullbacks on the throttle should be avoided! On takeoff, reduce

power as soon as it is safe. Unless you are loaded for bear, a gradual reduction in power can be made immediately after liftoff. With a bit of this TLC, the Teledyne-Continental IO-520-F-9 engine will literally last forever. Further, with clever leaning and good descents, I would average 13 gph for short hops, and 11.5 gph for longer ones. Even at full bore, properly leaned, I never used the 15 gph stated in the Cessna publications. I once flew from Merida to Miami International Airport, a distance of approximately 600 nm, in four hours and 15 minutes on 52 gallons of fuel! Of course my progress was expedited by the arrival of two MiGs out of Havana who molested me for 20 minutes or so some 55 miles north of that island! The 206 performed wonderfully even when they pulled in front of me and hit the afterburners!

"Of course, not all was peaches and cream with this aircraft. I was flying in a very tropical climate, to put it mildly. So, I would land at Chichen Itza at 9 a.m. to show off the Mayan ruins to a visiting VIP and an hour later the engine was completely "vapor locked" as the temperature on the field exceeded 100 degrees F. At these extreme temperatures, the procedure for "purging" vapor locks on this fuel injected engine simply did not work. If there was any wind, I would park the plane facing into it, keep the cowl flaps open and open the oil check door on the top of the engine cowling to let the heat escape. Many times,

however, I simply had to wait 20 or 30 minutes after engine shut-down before I could get a start. However, these were under very unusual and extreme temperature conditions.

"Full-stall landings are fun; it carries a half ton in the cabin 650 nm at 140 knots with an hour reserve. What twin can match this? It may be slow but I found it got me there 'fustust with the mostes.'

"In 550 hours' operation, under the most difficult operational conditions, I spent less than $1,000 in maintenance costs plus about $700 in annual inspections. Most of the $1,000 was on ARC avionics.

"Ditching procedures are not fully explained in the operator's manual. If one uses flaps to make a nice easy landing on the ocean, one must also get the flaps up in a hurry. It's impossible to open the cargo doors with the flaps extended. Nowhere did I see this explained in the emergency procedures for my 1976 model.

"Advice: If you are looking at a recent model Cessna 206, make sure the Continental IO-520 engine has been thoroughly checked—it doesn't take abuse too kindly. Make sure it has been inspected and modifications made for crankcase cracks under AD 77-13-22. Check for oil consumption. An engine in good condition should not use more than one quart every five hours. This engine is a honey if it has not been abused. Unfortunately, the 206 is an aircraft that many pilots will fly hard and long without giving it the care it deserves—simply because it performs so well without complaint for so long."

Piper's PA-32 Cherokee Six is an old standby, an immensely practical load hauler that's been in production for over 15 years now, and will doubtless continue for 15 more years. It is one of only two six-passenger fixed-gear airplanes available (the other is the Cessna 206) and is a favorite of air taxi and freight haulers. It is the mainstay of the funeral directing business, since a coffin won't easily fit into any other single-engine aircraft. (Recent Piper ads show a Cherokee Six swallowing a piano.)

Older Cherokee Sixes are available for as little as $20,000; it's doubtful many airplanes can deliver more payload per dollar than a 1965 Six. For the private owner, the airplane's attraction is its six full-size seats, plus a seventh kid seat as an option, and the relative simplicity of a fixed-gear airplane. (For the ultimate in simplicity and low maintenance, a 260-hp version with fixed-pitch prop would be unbeatable.) The Six is pretty slow, however—about 150 mph, on the average—and its high fuel consumption makes it less and less attractive as the price of fuel keeps rising dramatically. Nevertheless, the Cherokee Six is a good airplane for the niche it fills, and will certainly continue to be in demand.

History
The first Cherokee Six hit the market in 1965. Only the 260-hp model was available that first year, but the 300-hp option was added in 1966. There have been very few major changes over the years. Gross weight has remained at 3,400 pounds, and the engine has never been changed. The wing wasn't touched until 1980, when the tapered outer wing panel that had been added to the entire Cherokee series finally reached the PA-32.

Among the minor changes: 1968 260-hp models got larger exhaust valves which extended engine TBO from 1,200 to 2,000 hours. (Virtually all 1965-67 260s have since been updated with the better valves.) In 1970, the Six got a new panel and power quadrant with twin-style control levers instead of standard plungers. In 1974, an extra window was added, mostly for styling reasons. The fin was stretched six inches in 1975.

Obviously, there is little to choose from among the various Cherokee Six models. Model year should play little role in choosing an airplane, except in terms of depreciation patterns. A 1974 airplane with 800 hours and good paint and interior may be "newer" than a much used and abused 1977 model—even though it could cost $10,000 less.

Used Plane Market
The Cherokee Six market is very strong these days. As major airlines retreat from smaller cities, the air taxi market is growing rapidly, and the Six is an almost perfect airplane for an air taxi operator. It will carry six people and their luggage (although not always with full fuel), and may be quickly converted to a freighter by removing the seats. As a result, prices and demand for used Sixes are high. The "best buy" airplanes—the 300-hp 1975-76 models which have reached the bottom of their depreciation curves and will only rise in value in the future—are particularly hard to find at reasonable prices. Airplanes without cargo doors are easier to come by, because an air taxi operator wouldn't consider a Six without one.

The market for older Cherokee Sixes in the $25,000-$30,000 price range is somewhat softer, although still good. Commercial operators generally don't want airplanes this old, and they tend to be bought more by private owners.

Used Cherokee Sixes hold their value well. Pre-1970 models now sell for very near their original list price, and no used Six is worth less than about 80 percent of the original price—even the 1975 and '76 airplanes that have reached the bottom of their depreciation curves.

Performance and Loading
The Cherokee Six is a powerful brute. People buy it for carrying capacity, not speed. And even a well-equipped IFR Six can carry a whopping useful load of 1,500 pounds or so. That's enough for six people and full tanks, although

Contributing to the length of the snout *just aft of the engine (in this 1978 Six-300) is an eight cubic foot, 100-pound baggage compartment.*

well-equipped airplanes may not be able to take on additional luggage. We're told that the Six handles overloads with aplomb, and we imagine that air taxi operators sometimes **exceed gross weight limits when five passengers with luggage appear at the ticket counter.** According to the book, the 300-hp Six will lift its maximum legal load at better than 1,000 fpm, a healthy rate of climb indeed.

There is one fly in the Cherokee Six's loading ointment, however. It is one of the few single-engine aircraft to have a zero-fuel weight limit. The total weight of the airplane, passengers and baggage may not exceed 3,112 pounds, even in reduced fuel situations. This would limit cabin load to about 1,300 pounds in all cases.

Speed is not the Six's strong point. Speeds as high as 174 mph are claimed, but owners tell us that 150-155 mph (about 130-135 knots) is more like it, at least at power settings that don't drink up the fuel at an alarming rate. And as **avgas passes $1.50 per gallon, the Cherokee Six's poor fuel economy** becomes very alarming indeed. At about 16 gph for the 300 and 14-15 gph for the 260, fuel mileage is about nine mpg, a rather dismal figure. (The Mooney 201 does almost twice as well.) But if you want to carry six people and bags in an airplane that costs less than $30,000, there's not much choice.

Range is reasonable, if not stellar. With 84 gallons of fuel, you wouldn't want to fly more than five hours at most. That would be good for perhaps 700 miles at the outside. With IFR reserves, 600 miles is about the limit.

Loading balance is no problem. Any reasonable loading will keep the airplane within its c.g. envelope. A front baggage compartment helps in this regard.

260 or 300?

About 75 percent of the Cherokee Sixes now flying are 300-hp fuel-injected models; the remainder have 260-hp carbureted versions of the same basic six-cylinder Lycoming O-540 engine. There has been a small but steady demand for the 260 engine over the years, but it was finally discontinued in 1979 after only eight were sold in 1978.

The price difference between the 260 and 300 ranges from $1,000 in the 1966 airplanes to $5,000 in the 1978 models.

There is little real performance difference between the two models. The 300 is listed as up to 17 mph faster

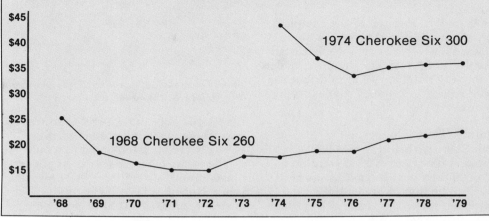

Aircraft Investment Value

The graph shows that the Cherokee Six retains its value very well. The 1968 model "bottomed out" on its depreciation curve after the usual three-to-four years and has increased in value by almost 50 percent since then. You would have been very smart to buy a used '68 model back in 1972. The 1974 Six 300 bottoms out in only two years, a strong testimony to the airplane's basic value.

than the 260, but owners tell us the difference is less—more like five mph, barely enough to be noticeable. Rate of climb and service ceiling are somewhat less with the 260 (850 vs. 1,050 fpm and 14,500 vs. 16,250 feet for a 1971 model). However, gross weights of the 260 and 300 are the same in all model years, and the lighter empty weight of the 260 Six means that it actually has a larger useful load than the 300. Fuel consumption of the 260 is also less, of course (by about two gallons per hour), **and that means an additional 40-50-pound payload bonus over a long trip.** With equal payloads, the climb rate and service ceiling of the 260 would be a lot closer to those of the 300 than the book figures (which are for gross weight, of course) suggest.

The 260 is generally a more reliable engine than the 300, although both have reasonably good reputations. "The 260 is a fine engine, the 300 not as fine," one big used-plane dealer told us. "You usually end up replacing a cylinder or two in a 300 before you get to overhaul." Both engines, however, are rated at a 2,000-hour TBO.

There is a big difference in the overhaul cost of the 260 and 300—as much as $2,500. One shop quoted us $6,150 and $8,250, and Lycoming's **remanufactured engine prices are $10,207 and $14,503. That** amounts to well over a dollar per hour savings for the 260.

On the other hand, the 300's fuel-injection system makes it more resistant to induction icing, an important safety factor.

Overall, however, there is much to be said for the 260-hp engine for the private owner who won't constantly be toting maximum loads through ice storms. Over 2,000 hours of flying, the 260 would cost up to $10,000 less to keep in the air (counting initial purchase price, overhaul costs and fuel savings).

Appraisal Points

There have been so few major changes in the Cherokee Six that there's surprisingly little difference between a 1967 and 1979 model. There are certain options to look for when selecting an airplane, however. Among them:

• Cargo door. Most Sixes have one, but older 260s may not. Unless you plan to use it mostly as a four-seater with little baggage, we'd recommend choosing a Six with a cargo door.

• Club Seating. Available on 1977 and later models, the face-to-face rear seating gives a fancy cabin-class feel.

• Air Conditioning. Although heavy, air conditioning may be worth its weight in chronically hot areas of the country. Add about $500 to $1,000 to the price for the luxury of a cool cabin.

• Seventh Seat. If you have five or six kids, it may come in handy, but it is not practical for a seventh adult.

• Fixed-pitch props. Some early 260s had fixed-pitch props. We wouldn't recommend one; climb and cruise speed both suffer. A constant-speed propeller may be retrofitted, however.

•Auxiliary fuel tanks. Virtually all Sixes have four-tank 84-gallon systems, but a few were ordered with only the 50-gallon standard main tanks. This limits practical range to well under three hours and less than 400 miles; we wouldn't recommend going without the aux tanks.

•Autopilot. Because of the complex fuel system, it's hard to keep a Six in balance laterally, so an autopilot is advisable. The "Autoflite" in older models is not very reliable, we're told, but the more recent "Altimatics" have a good record.

Maintenance

The Cherokee Six is an $80,000 airplane new, and even if you buy a $20,000 used one, the maintenance is going to be that of an $80,000 airplane. "Over the years, the airplane was fairly expensive to maintain," one long-time Six owner wrote us. "There were a number of ADs." According to *Aviation Consumer's* '78 Airframe and Powerplant Survey, annuals cost about $500, with additional unscheduled maintenance amounting to another $500 or so per year, on the average. Both figures are better than those of

This 1973 model, *which is currently worth about $32,000, has only three windows on each side. A fourth was added the next year.*

the Cessna 206. But Piper's factory support, parts availability and warranty service were all rated "poor" by owners.

The entire Cherokee series has been plagued with a number of ADs over the years. None has been catastrophic, however, and several have been only niggling.

The fuel system has been the target of several repeat ADs. The fuel selector was targeted in 1967, 1970, and 1976. In 1977 the NTSB recommended a fourth AD to combat rusty check valve actuators in the selector, but no AD was issued. Have a mechanic carefully disassemble the fuel selector before you

buy.

Another nagging fuel problem that won't go away is the well-known fuel sealant syndrome of all Cherokees. The sealant eventually breaks down, causing slow leaks. Worse, the sealant can break loose and clog the fuel system, particularly the Six 300's injectors. That spells possible engine failure and big repair bills. A 1967 AD requires careful inspection of the fuel system every 200 hours on 1965-67 models, but Piper supposedly "fixed" the problem in '68 and later models with a new sealant. A 1978 NTSB recommendation, however, stated, "Continuing dif-

Year	Model	Average Retail Price	Number Built	Useful Load (lbs)	Fuel Std/Opt (gals)	Cruise Speed (mph)	Engine	TBO (hrs)	Overhaul Cost
1965	PA-32-260	$19,000	317	1700	50/84	158	260-hp Lyc. O-540-E4B5	2000	$6,000
1966	PA-32-260	$20,000	533	1700	50/84	158	260-hp Lyc.	2,000	$6,000
1966	PA-32-300	$23,000	135	1600	50/84	168	300-hp Lyc. IO-540-K1A5	2,000	$8,000
1967	PA-32-260	$21,500	156	1700	50/84	158	260-hp Lyc.	2,000	$6.000
1967	PA-32-300	$23,750	294	1600	50/84	168	300-hp Lyc.	2,000	$8,000
1968	PA-32-260	$22,500	98	1700	50/84	158	260-hp Lyc.	2,000	$6,000
1968	PA-32-300	$24,000	135	1600	50/84	168	300-hp Lyc.	2,000	$8,000
1969	PA-32-260B	$24,250	139	1700	50/84	158	260-hp Lyc.	2,000	$6,000
1969	PA-32-300C	$25,500	284	1600	50/84	168	300-hp Lyc.	2,000	$8,000
1970	PA-32-260B	$25,000	46	1700	50/84	158	260-hp Lyc.	2,000	$6,000
1970	PA-32-300C	$26,500	168	1600	50/84	168	300-hp Lyc.	2,000	$8,000
1971	PA-32-260D	$26,000	23	1700	50/84	158	260-hp Lyc.	2,000	$6,000
1971	PA-32-300D	$28,000	78	1600	50/84	168	300-hp Lyc,	2,000	$8,000
1972	PA-32-260E	$28,000	45	1700	50/84	158	260-hp Lyc.	2,000	$6,000
1972	PA-32-300E	$30,000	137	1600	50/84	168	300-hp Lyc.	2,000	$8,000
1973	PA-32-260	$30,000	65	1700	50/84	158	260-hp Lyc.	2,000	$6,000
1973	PA-32-300	$32,000	191	1600	50/84	168	300-hp Lyc.	2,000	$8,000
1974	PA-32-260	$32,000	51	1600	84	157	260-hp Lyc.	2,000	$6,000
1974	PA-32-300	$35,250	170	1550	84	174	300-hp Lyc.	2,000	$8,000
1975	PA-32-260	$34,000	43	1600	84	157	260-hp Lyc.	2,000	$6,000
1975	PA-32-300	$38,500	188	1550	84	174	300-hp Lyc.	2,000	$8,000
1976	PA-32-260	$39,000	24	1600	84	157	260-hp Lyc.	2,000	$6,000
1976	PA-32-300	$43,000	130	1550	84	174	300-hp Lyc.	2,000	$8,000
1977	PA-32-260	$41,000	23	1600	84	157	260-hp Lyc.	2,000	$6,000
1977	PA-32-300	$46,500	113	1550	84	174	300-hp Lyc. IO-540-K1G5	2,000	$8,000
1978	PA-32-260	$47,000	8	1600	84	157	260-hp Lyc.	2,000	$6,000
1978	PA-32-300	$53,000	202	1550	84	174	300-hp Lyc.	2,000	$8,000

ficulties have indicated otherwise." The Board cited 14 cases of sealant glopping up the fuel systems of Cherokees in recent years. No AD was issued, however, and the problem apparently remains unresolved. (At least one company, Skycraft Corp. in Yardley, Pa., does a booming business repairing and resealing Cherokee fuel tanks.) Have a mechanic carefully inspect the tanks and fuel system of any Cherokee Six before purchase. Allow about $500-$600 for removal and reseal, if necessary.

Both the 260 and 300 engines are reasonably reliable, although cylinder work is more likely in the 300 because of the higher compression. Make sure the ADs on the piston pin (pre-1974) and oil pump (pre-1973) have been complied with, and if you're buying an old 260, assure that it has half-inch valves.

The brakes and electrical systems are mentioned by owners as constant high-maintenance areas; other trouble spots mentioned are the throttle cables and exhaust systems. Also, we have gotten repeated reports of poor sealing around the doors, particularly in older models.

Both FAA airworthiness alerts and our own reader feedback mention cracked upper wing skins in older Cherokee Sixes. One Alert states, "There have been many small cracks found in the upper wing skins about eight inches forward of the trailing edge. The cracks are located near rib station 9, 10 and 12 on each wing. The cracks seem to be in an area where there is only a single layer of skin." Considering the Six's relatively high rate of in-flight airframe failure, this area should be closely checked on older aircraft. Piper did devise a fix for the cracking wing skin. But no AD was ever issued, and some Sixes may not have had the fix, which involves the installation of reinforcing gussets. Check the aircraft logbook to see if this fix has been made, particularly in 1965-67 airplanes.

Safety

Overall, the Cherokee Six has an average safety record. During the period 1972-76, according to NTSB statistics, it had a total accident rate of 13.7 accidents per 100,000 flight hours. Fatal accident rate was 2.6. Both these numbers fall about in the middle of the four-/six-place fixed-gear group. (See chart.)

In some categories of accident , the

Through this gaping rear cargo door *have passed pianos, coffins, even people.*

Six had a good record; in others, not so good. The rate of stall accidents was among the lowest of any airplane. (Not surprising, considering the Cherokee wing's well-known resistance to stalls.)

On the other hand, a surprisingly large number of Cherokee Six accidents were the result of "engine failure"—a category that includes fuel starvation, not just mechanical engine failures. A CAB study of engine failure accidents from 1965-69 lists a total of 53 Six engine failure accidents during that period, for a rate of 7.6 per 100,000 hours. That contrasts with the average of 4.6 for all single-engine aircraft. Statistically, the CAB said the Cherokee Six had a "very high" rate of engine failures.

The Six's record of engine failures seems to be improving, however. An *Aviation Consumer* study of accidents from 1973-77 shows an engine failure rate of 3.9 per 100,000 hours—nearly twice as good as the 1965-69 record. This improvement may be the result of the many ADs on the airplane's fuel system. (See the "Maintenance" section for details.)

Fuel mismanagement has been a continuing problem, however. According the the CAB report, fuel mismanagement accounts for 32 percent of all Cherokee Six engine-failure accidents—twice the average proportion among single-engine planes. The Six has a four-position fuel selector that requires much switching.

In 1979 the fuel system was modified to a "left-right-off" system with a capacity of 96 gallons. This is a major improvement, but unfortunately, the vast majority of used Sixes in the field still have the old system.

As for purely mechanical engine failures, the CAB study shows a rate of 2.6 per 100,000 hours for the years 1965-69—more than triple the 0.8 average for the single-engine planes as

a group. *Aviation Consumer* figures for the 1973-77 period show an improved rate of approximately 1.3 mechanical engine failures. That's still a lot higher than the NTSB's average for single-engine aircraft in general, however.

The Six also shows up poorly in airframe failure accidents. In fact, the PA-32 had the highest rate of FIFAFAs (Fatal In-Flight Airframe Failure Accidents) of any current production fixed-gear airplane, according to an *Aviation Consumer* study for the years 1964-77. To put things in perspective, that's only nine FIFAFAs in five years and two million hours of flying. Still, that's nine more than the Cessna 172 had during the same period in 15 million hours.

But overall, the Six has a reasonably good safety record. A Six owner could probably improve his chances by paying close attention to the fuel system, which has historically been a major source of trouble.

Mods and Clubs

There is not a plethora of mods available for the Cherokee Six. The only major one of which we are aware is the excellent Robertson STOL mod, which drapes full-span flaps along the wing trailing edge and uses spoilers for roll control. We have not flown the Robertson Six, but similar systems on the Piper Seneca and Beech Bonanza offer excellent short-field performance and remarkably crisp aileron control at slow approach speeds.

We know of no owners' club or association for the Cherokee Six, probably because the airplane is a working machine without a lot of emotional appeal. Owners rarely dote and fuss over their Sixes; they just fly the hell out of them. However, a consumer-oriented clearinghouse for technical and maintenance information would be a good idea, in our opinion.

Owner Comments

"I owned a 1967 Piper PA-32-300, N4131W, from January, 1968 until February, 1979. I purchased the airplane from a distributor when it was about six months old, had about 150 hours, and it had over 2,200 total time when I traded it.

"Over the years I found the airplane to be a dependable performer, able to match the performance tables in the owner's manual. It had a useful load of more than 1,500 pounds, even after all the stuff I hung on it.

"It was a real load hauler, handling six adults with no problem, and having capacity for full fuel and a generous amount of baggage.

"A word about the seventh seat: its use is practical only for a child. The interior is much more livable without the seventh seat in place.

"Over the years the airplane was fairly expensive to maintain. There were a number of ADs. Some I recall related to the stabilator balance weight, control wheels, vertical fin attach bracket, landing gear torque links, fuel selector valves (two or three), fuel tank vents, fuel tank caps, and front baggage compartment door.

"There were ADs on the propeller requiring new blades and, two or three years later, modification of those blades. I went through several fiberglass spinners until Piper replaced the fiberglass with metal.

"I had continuing problems with air leaks around the front and rear doors. New rubber stripping would help for a while.

"The nosewheel fairing cracked a few times, but I suspect the major cause was lineboys.

"After some years the main tanks began leaking, and I had them removed, disassembled, cleaned, resealed and repainted.

"When the plane was three years old, I discovered rivets working and cracks developing in the top of the wings. After several months Piper devised and paid for the fix under warranty. Every 1967 or earlier Cherokee Six I have ever looked at

had the same trouble.

"The small turn-and-bank indicator failed about every 400 hours and required overhaul or exchange.

"Perhaps because of the long routing, the propeller and mixture control cables failed. Brake maintenance was required regularly, but I had no specific problems or failures.

"The Autocontrol III autopilot, with heading hold (no couplers), was the most satisfactory piece of equipment on the airplane. In 11 years and 2,200 hours it did not even require adjustment, and it was in use regularly.

"The electric trim was next to useless. It was very slow, and in cold weather the lubricant on the trim system congealed and the electric trim would not work.

"One of the better features of the airplane was the manual flaps.

"The electrical system was a continuing source of trouble and mistrust. I must have replaced the alternator five or six times, at least. The electrical system always surged, and the maintenance people were never able to correct it. I had one vacuum pump failure in flight at about 900 hours. The alternator failures were always inflight.

"The rotating beacon never worked for very long at a time. After I had the strobes installed, I quit using the rotating beacon.

"Fuel management required the pilot's attention, with four tanks to look after.

"The main fuel injection unit required overhaul at 400 hours, and again at 1,800 hours. The last time, the airplane was grounded for more than six weeks. There was also an AD on the fuel flow divider.

"The engine developed two weak cylinders at 1,100 hours and, from an abundance of caution, I elected to have it majored, with Chrome Plate cylinder assemblies. In retrospect this was probably a mistake. Of the six Chrome Plate cylinders, one had to be replaced within 100 hours, and that and another one within 200 more hours.

"I would recommend the PA-32-300 for anyone who needs the load carrying

Front baggage compartment, *behind 300- or 260-hp Lycoming, helps balance heavy loads.*

capability. But the owner must expect the fuel and maintenance costs which accompany it."

"We bought a 1973 model used with about 1,500 hours on it and ran it to 2,000 hours with no engine work and absolutely no problems. The airplane was a comfortable, pleasant, unexciting "plain gray" workhorse that did everything asked of it and did it safely.

"The disadvantages of the 1973 model were that it was noisy (boy, was it noisy!); it was slow (135 kts), and it had the worst fuel system I ever saw. You were guaranteed to be flying with one wing low or holding some opposite aileron because of fuel imbalances. The last two disadvantages (fuel imbalance and noise) caused us to buy a 1976 Skylane (new). Though the Cessna flew just fine and certainly was quiet and didn't have the fuel imbalance, it was always perceived by non-pilots as "the little plane" because of the size of the cabin and the high wing. It was clear within a few hundred hours that this was not the airplane for our company's flight department as long as there were non-pilot passengers.

"A marvelous airplane, sturdy and reasonably fast. Its performance has been greatly enhanced, moreover, by the installation of the Robertson STOL package, including spoilers. Stall speed is lowered significantly by the new leading edge cuffs and full span flaps, and there is full roll control effectiveness to and through the stall.

"We currently operate into a 1,200-foot gravel strip in Vermont with no problem whatsoever. The Robertson STOL kit makes a great airplane even greater."

Doors front and rear, left and right, *enhance ease of access for all six riders.*

Single-Engine Retractables

Beech Bonanza

The word "legend" is tossed around rather freely when people talk about airplanes, but the Beechcraft Bonanza probably has a better claim to legendary status than any other modern lightplane. The Bonanza was the first high-performance post-war design (it was introduced in 1947). It has been in continuous production since then, and is still considered by many to be the best single-engine airplane flying.

The Bonanza's astonishing success is the result of excellent performance, sleek good looks, responsive handling and a "Mercedes of the air" image. The loading limitations, high parts prices and cracking crankcases are not part of that legend, however.

The used Bonanza market is unique. Because of the high demand for used Bonanzas and the incredible price escalation of new ones, it is routine for a decade-old Bonanza to be worth more than it cost new. Many owners report paying top dollar for a used Bonanza, then selling it a couple of years later at a profit. Like the Piper Cub and certain other classic airplanes, the Bonanza is a good inflation hedge as well as a flying status symbol.

A prospective Bonanza buyer should carefully examine his motivation for buying. On a coldly rational cost-effective basis, a used Cessna 210 or Piper Comanche will generally provide more airplane per dollar. But pilots seem to be more impressed by macho appeal, plush interiors and the "feel" of the airplane. In this realm the Bonanza is supreme. We wonder how many used-aircraft buyers choose to buy Bonanzas after objective comparisons with other makes. Most, we suspect, simply decide to buy a Bonanza and don't even look seriously at other types. For those buyers, the question is merely which used Bonanza is the best buy?

Models

There is a bewildering variety of Bonanza models. There are three basic types: the Model 35, the classic V-tail form of the aircraft that has been in continuous production since 1947, with power ranging from 185 to 285 hp; the Model 33, introduced in 1960, with a conventional tail and engines ranging from 225 to 285 hp; and the Model 36, a "stretched" six-seat conventional-tail version introduced in 1968 with a 285-hp engine. (Adding to the confusion is the fact that the 33 model was called the Debonair for seven years.)

Engines

Early Bonanzas up through the G35 in 1956 had Continental "E" series engines. Although the powerplants are reasonably reliable, the supply of parts and knowledgeable mechanics for these engines is rapidly dwindling. Continental no longer makes remanufactured E series engines, and there are no more crankcases or crankshafts being made. Other parts are generally available, but rapidly becoming more expensive as production dwindles. Cost of an overhaul for an old Bonanza is about $4,000-$5,000, a hefty fee considering that the airplane itself may be worth only $15,000, even with a fresh overhaul.

Later Bonanzas have either the IO-470 or IO-520 Continental engines. Prior to 1970, both these engines were rated at 1,200 hours TBO. In 1970, the valves were improved, and TBO went up to 1,500 hours. Older engines overhauled with the better valves also have the 1,500-hour TBO. This should be a major checkpoint for buyers.

Cracking Cases

Literally thousands of Bonanza owners have suffered the "Curse of the Cracking Crankcases," either directly or indirectly because of overhaul considerations.

IO-520-B and -BA engines built prior to mid-1976 have a severe problem with crankcase cracks. The overhauling of those engines has virtually ceased because no reputable overhauler will sign one off without a new post-1976 "heavy" case. The cost of case replacement added to normal overhaul cost is about the same as the cost of a remanufactured engine from the factory, which now includes the heavy case. The result has been a bonanza (sic) of reman IO-520 business for Continental, and the elimination of the option of a lower-cost standard overhaul. The factory does offer some credit for cracked cases on trade-ins for remanufactured engines, but in most cases, "light case" Bonanza buyers will find themselves paying a couple of thousand dollars more than the usual overhaul cost when their engines are due for rebuilding.

The lineup: 36 (left rear), 35 (foreground), 33 (right) series of the Bonanza. The 36 series was stretched ten inches ahead of the wing, and therefore doesn't have rear c.g. problems.

Incidentally, beware of the phrase "heavy case" in advertisements for used Bonanzas. There have been at least three "heavy" case versions designed to combat the cracking problem. The first two didn't work. Only those engines manufactured or remanufactured after July 1976 have the true "heavy" case which, it appears, has finally solved the cracking problem.

We simply do not recommend the purchase of an IO-520-powered Bonanza without the heavy case, unless the buyer plans to install a remanufactured engine shortly afterwards.

Maintenance Problems
The other two major Bonanza maintenance checkpoints are shared with various other aircraft: the Hartzell prop AD and the leaking Goodyear rubber fuel tanks. The prop AD—which applies only to IO-520-powered Bonanzas—generally costs $500-$700.

The fuel tank AD is not as expensive in most cases, since only an inspection is required. However, if a leak is discovered, replacement can be costly. There is no consistent pattern, but most Bonanzas built between 1961 and 1975 are subject to the Goodyear AD. All Bonanzas have rubber bladder tanks of some sort, and their life expectancy is six to eight years. Replacement cost can run between $1,000 and $2,000, depending on the model.

Several *Aviation Consumer* readers mentioned vacuum pump failures, and the Airborne pumps used in many Bonanzas have a poor record. Failure of the vacuum pump in IFR conditions, of course, can be fatal.

Safety
The Bonanza's safety record is generally good—with a couple of important exceptions. According to *Aviation Consumer* studies of NTSB and FAA statistics for the period 1972-76, the 33 and 36 models have excellent records (see the list of single-engine retractable accident rates at the beginning of the book). The 33, in fact, has the lowest fatal accident rate of any single-engine airplane, and the 36 is not far behind.

The V-tail 35 model is another story. Newer V-tails, including the 1964 S model and later models, all with 285-hp engines, have a reasonably good fatal accident rate, but the older models rank very poorly, with a fatal accident rate nearly twice as high as the later V-tails and nearly quadruple that of the 33 series.

In-Flight Breakups
A major reason for the poor fatal accident rate of the older V-tails is the relatively very high rate of fatal in-flight airframe failures in those models. Over the years, there have been more than 200 Bonanza in-flight breakups, in which we estimate some 500 people

Bonanza 35 Fatal Inflight Airframe Failure Accidents

Model	Number FIFAFAs	Number Produced	Percent FIFAFA*
35	71	1500	4.8
35R	0	13	0.0
A35	17	701	2.4
B35	11	480	2.3
C35	20	719	2.8
D35	14	298	4.7
E35	10	301	3.3
F35	6	392	1.5
G35	7	476	1.5
H35	2	426	0.4
J35	5	396	1.3
K35	4	436	0.9
M35	10	400	2.5
N35	4	280	1.4
P35	7	467	1.5
S35	7	667	1.1
V35	5	622	0.8
V35A	5	470	1.1
V35B	3	n.a.	n.a.
Total	208		

have died. We have reprinted above a chart of the in-flight breakup rates of the various Bonanza models. As you can see, the old ones are the worst, with the 1947-48 "straight 35" having an especially high breakup rate. (The lower percentages for late-model V-tails are a bit misleading, however, since they haven't had enough time to

Model	Year Built	Number Built	Cruise Speed (mph)	Rate of Climb (fpm)	Useful Load (lbs)	Fuel Std/Opt (gals)	Engine	TBO (hrs)	Overhaul Cost	Average Retail Price
Bonanza 35	1947-48	1,500	172	950	1,092	39/60	185-hp Continental	1,500	$5,000	$ 13,000
A35	1949	699	170	890	1,075	39/60	185-hp Continental	1,500	$5,000	$ 14,750
B35	1950	479	170	890	1,075	39/60	196-hp Continental	1,500	$5,000	$ 16,000
C35	1951-52	719	175	1,100	1,050	39/60	205-hp Continental	1,500	$5,000	$ 17,000
D35	1953	297	175	1,100	1,050	39/60	205-hp Continental	1,500	$5,000	$ 18,000
E35	1954	705	184	1,300	953	39/60	225-hp Continental	1,500	$5,500	$ 19,000
F35	1955	392	184	1,300	978	39/60	225-hp Continental	1,500	$5,500	$ 20,000
G35	1956	489	184	1,300	1,003	39/60	225-hp Continental	1,500	$5,500	$ 20,000
H35	1957	464	190	1,225	1,080	39/60	240-hp Continental	1,500	$6,000	$ 24,000
J35	1958	663	200	1,250	1,080	39/60	250-hp Continental	1,500	$7,000	$ 26,000
K35	1959	435	195	1,170	1,118	49/70	250-hp Continental	1,500	$7,000	$ 27,000
M35	1960	399	195	1,170	1,118	49/70	250-hp Continental	1,500	$7,000	$ 28,500
N35	1961	279	195	1,150	1,270	50/80	260-hp Continental	1,500	$7,000	$ 30,750
P35	1962-63	467	195	1,150	1,270	50/80	260-hp Continental	1,200	$7,000	$ 32,500
S35	1964-65	665	205	1,200	1,385	50/80	285-hp Continental	1,200	$7,500	$ 40,000
V35	1966-67	625	205	1,136	1,485	50/120	285-hp Continental	1,200	$7,500	$ 43,250
V35TC	1966-67	555	224	1,225	1,450	50/120	285-hp Continental	1,400	$8,500	$ 47,500
V35A	1968-69	468	203	1,136	1,440	44/74	285-hp Continental	1,200	$7,500	$ 46,500
V35A-TC	1968-69	252	230	1,225	1,373	50/120	285-hp Continental	1,400	$8,500	$ 51,500
V35B	1970	142	198	1,167	1,313	44/74	285-hp Continental	1,500	$57500	$ 49,500
V35B-TC	1970	110	230	1,225	1,373	50/120	285-hp Continental	1,400	$8,500	$ 54,000
V35B	1971-72	185	198	1,167	1,313	44/74	285-hp Continental	1,500	$7,500	$ 55,000
V35B	1973-74	295	198	1,167	1,313	44/74	285-hp Continental	1,500	$7,500	$ 61,000
V35B	1975	128	198	1,167	1,313	44/74	285-hp Continental	1,500	$7,500	$ 77,000
V35B	1976	131	198	1,167	1,313	44/74	285-hp Continental	1,500	$7,500	$ 70,000
V35B	1977	120	198	1,167	1,313	44/74	285-hp Continental	1,500	$7,500	$ 75,500
V35B	1978	109	198	1,167	1,313	44/74	285-hp Continental	1,500	$7,500	$ 81,500
V35B	1979	123	198	1,167	1,313	44/74	285-hp Continental	1,500	$7,500	$ 95,000

Model	Year Built	Number Built	Cruise Speed (mph)	Rate of Climb (fpm)	Useful Load (lbs)	Fuel Std/Opt (gals)	Engine	TBO (hrs)	Overhaul Cost	Average Retail Price
Bonanza E33	1968	80	185	930	1,188	50/80	225-hp Continental	1,200	$6,000	$ 36,000
E33A	1968	68	200	1,200	1,385	50/80	285-hp Continental	1,200	$7,500	$ 44,000
E33C	1968	13	200	1,200	1,382	50/80	285-hp Continental	1,200	$7,500	$ 41,000
E33	1969	34	185	930	1,188	50/80	225-hp Continental	1,500	$6,000	$ 37,250
E33A	1969	40	200	1,200	1,385	50/80	285-hp Continental	1,200	$7,500	$ 45,250
E33C	1969	11	200	1,200	1,382	50/80	285-hp Continental	1,200	$7,500	$ 44,250
F33	1970	19	185	930	1,188	50/80	225-hp Continental	1,500	$6,000	$ 39,000
F33A	1970	26	198	1,167	1,288	44/74	285-hp Continental	1,500	$7,500	$ 48,500
F33C	1970	4	200	1,200	1,382	50/80	285-hp Continental	1,500	$7,500	$ 47,500
F33A	1971	33	198	1,167	1,288	44/74	285-hp Continental	1,500	$7,500	$ 51,500
G33	1972-73	49	193	1,060	1,365	50/80	260-hp Continental	1,500	$7,500	$ 51,500
F33A	1972	51	198	1,167	1,288	44/74	285-hp Continental	1,500	$7,500	$ 55,000
F33A	1973	62	198	1,167	1,288	44/74	285-hp Continental	1,500	$7,500	$ 58,000
F33A	1974-75	146	198	1,167	1,288	44/74	285-hp Continental	1,500	$7,500	$ 63,500
F33A	1976-77	131	198	1,167	1,288	44/74	285-hp Continental	1,500	$7,500	$ 70,500
F33A	1978	81	198	1,167	1,288	44/74	285-hp Continental	1,500	$7,500	$ 75,500
F33A	1979	NA	198	1,167	1,288	44/74	285-hp Continental	1,500	$7,500	$ 92,000

build up a high number of accidents.)

The typical scenario of a V-tail breakup is this: the pilot gets into bad weather and/or heavy turbulence, the airplane gets away from him, and comes apart in the ensuing high-speed dive and/or pullout, which exceeds the structural limits of the plane. The reasons for the high breakup rates of V-tail Bonanzas are not crystal clear, but we believe the problem has two major facts: structural weak points and handling qualities.

Structural problems most likely to play a big role in the high break-up rate of the 1947-48 model 35. Those years, the Bonanza had unusually thin wing skins and no shear web in the leading edge of the wing—structural shortcuts designed to save weight. Although the breakup problem abated somewhat after Beech beefed up the wings in 1949, it did not go away, particularly in the A through E models. The problem seemed to move back to the tail; while the majority of "straight 35" breakups involved wing failures, the majority of failures in later models occurred in the tail. Some critics have faulted Beech for not installing nose ribs in the stabilizers, particularly after the "overhang" in front of the spar was increased with the C model. Accident investigators report a pattern of tail failures in which the stabilizer skin fails and folds over the spar.

Any airplane will fall apart in the air if pushed far enough past its airspeed or g-load limits, and Bonanzas don't break up unless pushed past their limits. The question is, why do the pilots of older V-tails allow their craft to exceed speed and load limits so much more often than pilots of other airplanes?

The answer, we believe, may lie in the handling qualities of the V-tail Bonanzas.

The V-tail airplane has very light ailerons and low lateral stability, what the test pilots call high spiral divergence. Once a wing

drops a little, it tends to keep going. In instrument weather and turbulence, this low rolling stability can put the pilot into the "graveyard spiral" quickly.

The V-tail airplane is also very light on the controls in the pitch axis. This low longitudinal stability means turbulence or pilot inattention will cause larger, quicker airspeed and altitude excursions. The light controls also mean that just a moderate pull on the wheel results in a sharp pullup and high g-forces.

The V-tail Bonanza's low longitudinal stability is exacerbated by the rather narrow center-of-gravity envelope. (Some models even have 30 pounds of lead in the nose to counter the balance problem.) With any passengers in the back seat, a Bonanza can be very close to its aft c.g. limit, and it's not uncommon for V-tails to be flown illegally beyond their aft limit. An aft c.g. further reduces the V-tail's already low longitudinal stability, making the airplane even more sensitive in pitch and making wheel forces even lighter.

The low stability in the roll and pitch axes can team up against the pilot. A typical scenario: pilot looks down at chart while gust drops right wing. Airplane begins rolling to the right, simultaneously dropping the nose and picking up speed. Pilot looks up from chart, notes very high airspeed, and pulls back on the wheel abruptly. Airplane pulls six g's and breaks off the wings or tail.

The famous "Bonanza waggle" may also play a role. The V-tail has very poor Dutch roll (yaw) characteristics in turbulence. In extreme cases, severe turbulence may yaw the plane to such high angles that the tail could literally be blown off, particularly at high speeds, according to some engineers.

Ironically, the poor stability in all three axes is due mainly to the design of the V-tail itself. The straight-tail 33 and 36 Bonan-

zas have much better stability, and an almost perfect record of in-flight breakups (only two that we're aware of).

Another factor may be the sensitivity of the V-tail ruddervators to flutter. The V-tail Bonanza's margin of flutter is fairly small, and tests have shown that as little as two ounces at the trailing edge of the ruddervator—a piece of ice, or even a repaint job—can cause flutter under some conditions.

Stall/Spin

Older Bonanzas also show up poorly in stall/spin and fuel mismanagement accidents. According to NTSB accident statistics for the period 1965-73, the Bonanza had a fatal stall/spin accident rate of 0.68 (per 100,000 flight hours)—second only to the Beech 23 series (Sierra, Sundowner, etc.) among modern aircraft still in production. By comparison, the Cessna 210 had a fatal stall/spin rate of only 0.24—only about a third as high.

The Bonanza does have a sharp stall, often accompanied by a wing drop. There is little aerodynamic buffeting as warning of an impending stall. Some pilots have reported severe wing drops, even to the point of ending up on their backs in certain situations. We asked a former Beech engineer about the Bonanza's stall, and he said that no two Bonanzas stall alike. "Even at the factory, some of them were very straightforward in the stall, while others dropped off rather abruptly."

Another major cause of design-induced accidents is fuel mismanagement. Again, the Bonanzas are older near the top of the list in fuel mismanagement accidents. According to a 1964 CAB report on fuel mismanagement, the Bonanza ranked second (to the Piper Tri-Pacer) in fuel mismanagement accidents that year. An NTSB study for the years 1965-69 ranks the Bonanza as having the highest incidence of fuel starvation accidents of any

The 1957 Bonanza *incorporated a major series of wing and tail strengthening features.*

light aircraft. And a study of fuel starvation accidents during 1970-72 puts the Bonanza in the "higher than average" group along with three other aircraft.

The reason for the Bonanza's high incidence of fuel mismanagement accidents is presumably due to the placement of the fuel selector and the rather odd fuel pump operation in older models. The selector valve is on the floor under the pilot's left leg, which forces the pilot to crane his neck and divert his attention from the windshield and instrument panel to change tanks. Consequently, Bonanza pilots may switch tanks by feel, a riskier procedure. Also, the selector detents are poorly defined in some models, and it's possible to hang up the selector between tanks, which shuts off the fuel. If an engine does quit from fuel starvation, the Bonanza pilot faces a dilemma: turn on the boost pump or not? If he doesn't, according to a CAB study, the engine may take as long as 35 seconds to restart. If he does, he may flood the engine if the pump is left on too long. The owner's manual of one model Bonanza instructs the pilot to turn on the boost pump "momentarily" when switching from a dry tank. The pilot must tread a narrow line between a fuel-starved engine on one hand and a flooded-out engine on the other hand. Not a happy choice.

And then, of course, there is the notorious "fuel unporting" syndrome that has resulted in numerous Bonanza accidents and lawsuits against Beech. In extended slipping or skidding maneuvers or in fast turning type takeoffs in pre-1970 models, fuel would slosh away from the fuel pickup

if the tank was less than half full. Beech issued a service letter as far back as 1961 on the fuel unporting phenomenon. It warned that fuel unporting was a possibility after a turning takeoff, and stated that in such a case the air bubble in the fuel line would "reach the engine at about the same time the airplane becomes airborne and could cause momentary power interruption." The letter went on to say, "This does not create a hazard . . ." We think a lot of people would argue with that statement.

In any case, the FAA had identified 16 accidents caused by fuel unporting by 1971, when an AD was finally issued. The AD required no modification of the fuel system, merely a yellow arc on the fuel gauge and an admonition not to take off or slip or skid excessively if the fuel was in the arc. Beech did modify the tanks in 1970, and offered a retrofit kit for older Bonanzas, but only a handful of the retrofit kits were sold. Thousands of pre-1970 Bonanzas still have the unmodified tanks and are susceptible to fuel unporting. We would strongly urge any buyer to check whether the baffle kit has been installed, and to install it himself if it has not been done.

Summing up, while the straight-tail 33 and 36 models and the more recent 285-hp V-tail airplanes have good to excellent safety records, the older V-tails rank poorly. These older less-than-$30,000 Bonanzas are an attractive buy, but they are not for the overconfident or underqualified. More than 30 percent of the fatal accidents in older V-tails are in-flight breakups, and the stall/spin and fuel mismanagement accident rates are

also quite high. Clearly, the older Bonanzas demand the pilot's full attention and adequate skills.

Loading

Early 185- and 225-hp Bonanzas have useful loads of about 900 pounds with normal equipment, and equipped useful load has grown over the years as horsepower increased to about 1,200 pounds in later 285-hp models. (The all-time Bonanza lifting champ is the 1968-69 straight 36 model, which had a standard useful load of 1,620 or about 1,400 with normal equipment.) Although 1,200 pounds is a fairly creditable figure, it is well short of the later Cessna 210s. Standard useful load of the 35 model took a big jump in 1961 with the N35 and another in 1964 with the S35, paralleling horsepower increases to 260 and 285. Generally speaking, Bonanzas are not full-seats-and-full-fuel airplanes with baggage, even the 285-hp four-placers.

However, most owners find that their loading is limited by c.g. restrictions before gross weight restrictions. The 35 models have especially narrow c.g. envelopes and it is very easy to load them aft of the limit, even with the 30-pound lead weights that some Bonanzas have in the nose for ballast. In many cases, it simply isn't possible to put two adults and significant baggage in the rear of a Bonanza, no matter how much fuel is off-loaded. In fact, c.g. problems become more pronounced with less fuel because the Bonanza's leading edge fuel tanks are ahead of the c.g. As a result, c.g. moves aft as fuel is burned off. This can be quite tricky for the pilot, who may be entirely legal when he takes off, but could find himself well out of the c.g. envelope to the rear as he approaches his destination after a long flight.

One of the results of a too-far-aft c.g., of course, is decreased pitch stability and lightened stick forces. Considering the Bonanza's already light pitch control forces and its tendency to build up speed quickly, an out-of-c.g. Bonanza can really take a pilot by surprise. If you plan to buy a Bonanza for four-person weekend outings, be sure to do some sample weight-and-balance computations for each particular airframe you look at.

Model	Year Built	Number Built	Cruise Speed (mph)	Rate of Climb (fpm)	Useful Load (lbs)	Fuel Std/Opt (gals)	Engine	TBO (hrs)	Overhaul Cost	Average Retail Price
Bonanza 36	1968-69	184	195	1,015	1,620	50/80	285-hp Continental	1,200	$7,500	$51,000
A36	1970-73	291	193	1,030	1,443	44/74	285-hp Continental	1,500	$7,500	$65,000
A36	1974-75	288	193	1,030	1,443	44/74	285-hp Continental	1,500	$7,500	$69,000
A36	1976-77	385	193	1,030	1,443	44/74	285-hp Continental	1,500	$7,500	$85,000
A36	1978	228	193	1,030	1,443	44/74	285-hp Continental	1,500	$7,500	$110,000
A36TC	1979	222	193	1,030	1,443	44/74	285-hp Continental	1,500	$7,500	$130,000

Performance

Here is where the Bonanzas shine. The first ones totally outclassed all the competition in performance, and there's still no single-engine airplane in production today that will catch a good clean V35B. All Bonanzas deliver excellent speed for their horsepower and therefore good fuel economy. Book speeds range from 170 mph for the old A and B models to 205 mph for the V35 (and a snorting 230 at altitude for the turbocharged V35 TC). Real-world speeds may be somewhat lower than the book (and sometimes the airspeed indicators) say, but owners nevertheless report good speeds: 190 to 200 mph for the 250, 260 and 285-hp models, and 175 to 185 mph for the Bonanzas with the 225- to 240-hp engines. Fuel consumption runs from a high of about 16 gph with the 285-hp models to 10 gph with the E-185.

Rate of climb is also energetic, with only the very oldest Bonanzas climbing less than 1,000 fpm at gross weight (by the book, at least). Bonanzas are excellent short-field aircraft, partly because of their good performance, partly because of the rugged landing gear. The gear, incidentally, is so beefy that virtually the same gear is used for the Baron, which weighs a ton more.

Creature Comforts

Again, the Bonanza is strong in this respect. The cabin is quite large, especially in terms of headroom. (In fact, most pilots look like midgets while flying Bonanzas because of the high roof and window line.) Backseaters aren't quite as well off because of the fuselage taper, but room is still adequate. Excellent visibility from broad windows accentuates the feeling of roominess of the airplane.

Interior appointments are traditionally excellent in Bonanzas. Beech apparently believes that a man who pays five or ten times the price of a Cadillac expects to have a quality interior—a philosophy apparently shared by few other manufacturers. Interior plushness is an important part of the Bonanza mystique.

Rear passengers in V-tail Bonanzas are usually miserable in turbulence, however. The V-tail looks neat and is the shining symbol of the Bonanza line, but it does a lousy job as a tail. In turbulence, the V-tail models fishtail excessively, usually requiring several oscillations to recover from a good jolt. (See the "Modifications" section for a report on the Airskeg yaw damper, which apparently works quite well.)

The 36 and A36 Bonanzas have a "club car" seating arrangement, with two pairs of rear seats facing each other. With three or four people aboard, this is a wonderfully roomy compartment, but a fifth and sixth person make things chummy indeed. Virtually no one ever flies six full-sized people in an A36 (till the '79 models) because there is no room at all—literally none—for baggage. A small baggage compartment was added in 1979.

Many models of the 33 and 35 Bonanzas are called five- or six-seaters, but this is an optimistic delusion. A fifth or sixth seat, if installed, fits in the luggage compartment and is suitable only for very young children. In most cases, c.g. and/or baggage loading considerations make it impossible to use the rear seats, even given a supply of willing children with cast-iron stomachs.

Handling

The Bonanza has a uniquely fortuitous blend of aerodynamics and ergonomics that results in marvelous flying characteristics. Pilots praise it for well-harmonized and responsive controls, and many owners have told *The Aviation Consumer* that the Bonanza is the easiest of all planes to land. (Our own personal experience tallies with those opinions.) The "feel" of the Bonanza is another major element of the airplane's legend.

Modifications

There is a welter of airframe modifications available for Bonanzas, and many owners have modified their older aircraft to the point that they're virtually indistinguishable from brand-new '78 models. Among the more popular Bonanza mods:

- Airskeg aerodynamic yaw damper, which supposedly improves V-tail wagging in turbulence. (Walker Engineering Co., Los Angeles, Calif., 213-272-1248)
- Cosmetic mods include one-piece windshields, late-model side windows, baggage doors, pointed spinners and a host of other interior and exterior touch-ups. Biggest of the specialists in this field is Beryl D'Shannon Aviation Specialties, Inc. in Jordan, Minn., 612-492-2611.
- A brand-new modification now on the market is the Smith Speed Conversion, a wide-ranging aerodynamic cleanup program that, it's claimed, boosts max speed of the 285-hp models to about 220 mph. Cost is about $8,000, and if you don't get your full 220, you don't pay your full $8,000. Smith Speed Conversions, Johnson, Kansas, 316-492-6224.
- Numerous engine conversions are available to upgrade older Bonanzas to 240-, 250-, 260- or 285-hp engines. Also, a recent STC allows conversion to a 300-hp Lycoming, which has the uncracking crankcase and a 2,000-hour TBO. Con-

Here's a quick rundown of the "milestone" Bonanza models with which major changes occurred:

35	Original airplane, 185-hp engine, 2,550-pound gross weight.
A35	Thicker wing skin, heavier spar carry-through.
C35	205 hp, 2,700-pound gross weight, larger tail with wider-angle V.
E35	225 hp.
F35	Third side window, stronger tail.
H35	First of "second generation" Bonanzas with O-series engine. 240 hp, gross weight 2,900 pounds, major structural beef-up.
J35	Fuel injection, 250 hp.
N35	260 hp, third side window enlarged, fuel capacity increased to 74 gallons.
P35	New instrument panel.
S35	First of "third generation" Bonanzas, 285 hp, extended cabin. Very close to current configuration.
V35TC	Turbocharged model, 132 built 1966-70.
V35B	Current production model.
33	First straight-tail model, 225 hp, named "Debonair."
C33A	285 hp.
E33	Renamed Bonanza.
E33C	Aerobatic model.
36	Straight tail, lengthened fuselage, cargo door, 3,600-pound gross weight.

tinental conversions are done by D'Shannon (address above); Lycoming mod is by Machen, Inc., Spokane, Washington, 509-838-5326.

For other available mods, we suggest the American Bonanza Society Newsletter's "Aviation Mart" advertising section.

American Bonanza Society

Perhaps the best of all the owner groups is the American Bonanza Society. Membership is nearly 7,000, and accounts for more than half of all Bonanza owners. The Society's newsletter is relatively sober and technically oriented, without so much of the gushy effusiveness of other aircraft owner association newsletters. In fact, for the past several months, members have been treated to a blow-by-blow account of the club president's hassles with Continental over a cracked crankcase. Anybody shopping for a used Bonanza should get in touch with the American Bonanza Society at 215-372-6967.

Owner Comments

"The Bonanza is excellent for cross-country flight in smooth air. In turbulence, you quickly find that yaw stability leaves much to be desired. Rear-seat passengers find the well-known Bonanza tail wag to be particularly objectionable.

"Weight-carrying capability of the Bonanza is good, but it is nearly impossible to load it to gross weight without exceeding the aft c.g. limit. Even with careful arrangement of the load, our weight and balance computations generally run out of aft c.g. before reaching gross weight.

"The Bonanza is fun to fly. It handles nicely and offers ample performance. All of us had previous experience in high-performance singles, and little trouble was encountered in learning to fly and land the Bonanza smoothly. Some undesirable characteristics deserve mention, though. Low-speed aileron control becomes sluggish, making for interesting encounters with gusts on short final. Stalls call for an alert pilot, since the plane tends to drop its left wing abruptly at the break. In this circumstance the pilot finds himself looking for more rudder control, as he does during landings in strong crosswinds. Also, in the transition from landing approach to go-around, the pilot finds himself straining to keep the nose down while he takes out the high degree of nose-up trim used in the approach. The bungee interconnect in the controls gets criticized from time to time, particularly after crosswind landing and other maneuvers performed using cross-controlling.

"Hot starts of the fuel-injected Continental engine can be exasperating. When cold, it generally starts after the first few blades.

"Parts are extremely expensive. A simple oil drain duct costs $12. The Beech dual control yoke costs $990. A simple machined part for the seat back costs $21.29. The new fuel cell costs $494, but by the time it was installed we were out $842.85. We found this out after discovering that one cell leaked and could not be repaired. The cell was replaced, but the replacement also leaked and it was, in turn, replaced. The FBO applied for reimbursement credit from Beech, and was finally applied four months later. The reimbursement covered the parts and installation but did not cover some $40 in freight charges. The FBO said we were fortunate since Beech generally does not make reimbursements that complete. We did not consider ourselves fortunate at all.

"After the fuel cell, the second most expensive of these maintenance items was replacement of the vacuum pump. This makes the fifth vacuum pump on the plane since new, indicating a history of problems in the pressure system. We recently replaced the pressure regulator as well."

"As with most older aircraft, performance is somewhat less than published figures after antennas, rigging and engine age impose their penalties. Our F model (225 hp) trued out at 163 mph while our M model (250 hp) gives an honest 182 mph. Twenty-five additional horsepower gives 19 more miles per hour. We have often wondered whether Beech did more than just increase power. The additional power, speed and perhaps a bit of redesign also provided a firmer IFR platform."

"Takeoffs and landings require no special effort or techniques. Good landings are relatively simple to achieve. Short-field takeoffs and landings equal, or even better, what we have been able to get from a Cessna 182.

"The well-known yaw is there occasionally, in certain air conditions. Riding the pedals eliminates most. The Airskeg is also an aid toward reducing yaw.

"When modifying a Bonanza, don't expect to get all of your money back. Windows, panels, cabin interiors, wing lights, and paint can be changed but you will still be flying an older Bonanza that looks pretty with essentially the same performance as before. If you do modify, our recommendation is to use only Beech parts. When turning a plane over to a modifier, insist on a written completion time. We had our F-35 tied up for four months on one occasion and seven weeks on another. My number one recommendation is to save the money you would put into major modification and trade up.

"In order to more fully understand the cost, performance and specification differences between the various models we made an analysis of true value based on weighted age, speed, range, useful load, and cost.

The results were fascinating: In the $20,000-$30,000 bracket the K and M models were outstanding. The J model was dragged down by range limitations.

"Why own a Bonanza? The answer is simple. For $30,000, a 19-year-old aircraft will outperform the new Skylane RG and Rockwell 114 costing twice the Bonanza investment. The performance differences are even greater when compared to the Skylane or Dakota costing approximately one and one-half times more. Justifying an aforementioned new aircraft with its high initial depreciation is difficult in the face of Bonanza performance, dependability, resale value, and flexibility for modification."

We asked Bill Guinther, current president of the Bonanza Society, to offer a few tips for buyers of used Bonanzas. Keeping in mind that Bill is both very knowledgeable about these airplanes and at the same time a professional Bonanza booster, we offer his comments:

"When Beech engineers started to make plans for a civilian single-engine high-performance airplane after World War II, they asked military pilots what should be included in a civilian airplane. The answer that came back was 'very light control forces.' Most of the fighter pilots cited the Spitfire's balanced controls as most desirable, stating that the newer P-51 Mustang, with its bigger engine, had very heavy stick forces. Therefore, the engineers at Beech decided that the airplane they planned would have balanced surfaces with very little force changes through the whole range of airspeed.

"The 1947 'straight' 35 is still one of the finest-flying, best-feeling airplanes ever designed. Of course, in those days most of the pilots had military background flying high-performance airplanes, so the light control pressures were not a detriment.

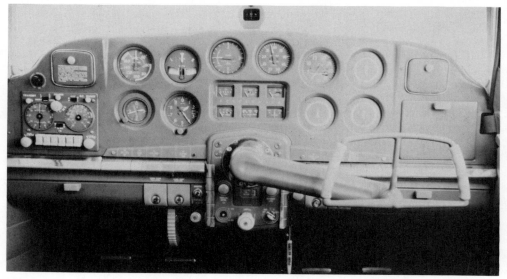

Original instrument panel *had familiar throw-over yoke and under-panel trim wheel. Virtually everything else has changed since then. Biggest panel revamping occurred in the 1962 P35.*

How well will the 1975 V35B hold its value? *You can buy it today for $77,000, and if the trend of the last 25 years continues, you'll be able to fly it until the year 2000 and then sell it for $88,000. By then, a brand new 2000 V35B will cost about $350,000.*

The first Bonanza, having a gross weight of 2,550 pounds, had a very low stall speed (46 mph) which meant it had outstanding short-field performance. Today's Bonanza, with an increase of more than 100 hp and 1,000 pounds gross weight, requires more takeoff and more landing space.

"The soundproofing in the early Bonanzas was almost nil. The normal cruise in the early Bonanzas required only 2050 rpm or less, and it was not unusual to cruise at 1900 rpm, keeping the engine and prop noise to a minimum. A large number of these early Bonanzas are still flying, and although new parts from Beech are sometimes hard to come by, a few very successful used parts dealers stock virtually everything required to build the early Bonanza. Aircraft and Engine Enterprises in Moore, Oklahoma, and Alex Rich in Oxnard, California have always been able to supply any hard-to-get part.

"New E series engines are no longer available from Continental. Any good engine overhaul shop can overhaul the E, and there are shops like Lou Stalling's in Tulsa, Oklahoma, that specialize in engine overhaul for Bonanzas for $3,600.

"The very early Bonanzas had an AD issued on the center section of the spar which required regular x-ray inspections. There are modifications on the center section which strengthen it enough to eliminate the need for this inspection. The AD on the tail casting, however, is much more important. One of the improvements in the newer Bonanzas is that the tail casting which required inspection was replaced by a constructed bulkhead. There are many old wive's tales about tail flutter as a result of cracked castings. Flutter cannot be introduced in the tail of the Bonanza without having elevator surfaces out of balance. If the tail surfaces are out of balance, the flutter can be induced between 140-160 mph indicated. It is extremely important, therefore, to check any Bonanza, especially newly painted Bonanzas, to be sure that the elevator has been balanced.

The Bonanza is extremely trim-stable in pitch and you can go from full power to zero power and have less than a five-mph airspeed change. Probably the most difficult part of flying the Bonanza would be getting used to the zero roll stability; i.e., if a wing is dropping, however slowly, it will continue to drop at the same rate. When I was selling Bonanzas, I would insist on at least a wing-leveler autopilot."

"The first engine on our 1968 V35A went to 1,750 hours and was showing good compression. Oil had been changed every 25 hours since new, but we got nervous about paying the core charge if the crankshaft or case went bad. The engines have needed a cylinder or two topped because of valve guide and exhaust valve wear, but we count on 1,600 per engine.

"An S or V model Bonanza is an excellent buy because the style hasn't changed in 12 years—the performance stays the same and they can be updated to look like new."

"In terms of performance, my 1973 F33A delivers book or above speeds and climb rate; that is to say, 175-177 knots true at 75 percent power and 172-174 knots true at 65 percent. Timed rates of climb average 900 fpm at altitudes below 3,000 feet. The quality and workmanship are second to none and suggest an attention to detail that is simply not available in any similar aircraft.

"As in every airplane, there are areas for improvement. Of primary importance to me are the Continental crankcase AD, the Hartzell prop AD, and the fuel cell AD. (My fuel cells turned out to be Uniroyal, so I'm okay for now.) The engine burned or spilled an inordinate amount of oil, but the installation of a Walker Airsep has cured that. My pet peeves are two: the price of parts is astronomical; i.e., $116 for a voltage regulator and $134 for an ammeter.

"Beech loves to issue service letters. I have received no less than 10 in the year I have owned the airplane. While I admire their concern for safety, the cost of the various retrofits and inspections has amounted to a considerable sum.

"Having flown both models, I feel the F33A is more stable in yaw response in turbulence than the V-tail, but still displays some fishtailing.

"Overall, other expenses have been reasonable, with annuals going for about $400. While a Bonanza is a more expensive aircraft to own in terms of initial cost and parts, it offers superior performance and a quality of construction second to none. It is a rugged, dependable machine which holds its value very well."

"The performance of the S35 Bonanza is excellent, but not quite as advertised. Although my partner and I are used to cruising at 75 percent power on Lycoming-engined aircraft we have owned before, we have chosen to fly our Bonanza at 65 percent power for greater engine smoothness and reduced noise level. This consistently produces block-to-block speed to 160 knots, and the altitude chosen seldom changes this.

"The Bonanza handles more smoothly than any Piper or Cessna product I have flown. I find no other characteristics to be unusual except for the tail-waggle in turbulence. The Bonanza is the easiest airplane to land smoothly consistently of any aircraft I have flown. This feature alone is probably reason enough to buy the airplane.

"Maintenance for us has been no big problem since we have owned the airplane only 600 hours and many problems have yet to arise. The big maintenance problems are the two recent AD notes out on engine crankcase cracking and Goodyear fuel tank bladders. Our aircraft did have one crack problem, but in several hundred hours since the crankcase was replaced we have had no additional problems. Any pilot contemplating purchase of a Bonanza absolutely must insure that the engine has the new heavier crankcase, and has had new fuel bladders installed. The only maintenance problem which has not been resolved is the large amount of oil thrown off by the wet vacuum pump. The pump works adequately, although vacuum is almost always on the low side, but there is always oil along the firewall and belly of the airplane. So far, we have not been willing to bear the expense of converting to a dry-type vacuum pump. It has had no effect upon the operation of the aircraft, but it is bothersome.

"In slightly over 15 months of operation, including one annual inspection, and insurance (coverage which must include a private pilot without an instrument rating) has averaged between $41 and $42.

"We found that the best insurance coverage was available through Don Flower and Assoc. in their group insurance policy available for members of the American Bonanza Society. They indicated to us that time in type was more important than obtaining an instrument rating in order to reduce premiums. But how do you accumulate 25 hours of Bonanza time when none are available for rent?

Cessna 210

They laughed at Cessna's fetish for high-winged airplanes way back in 1959 when the company took a Cessna 180 airframe and, in a most unconventional manner, retracted the landing gear into the fuselage. Today, the evolution of that airplane, the Cessna 210 Centurion, has become the world's best-selling large single, by far.

History

Though not able to trace its ancestry back as far as the Beech Bonanza of the post-World War II epoch, the 210 has a 21-year history that encompasses three different engines and cabins and two different wings plus a host of other systems modifications.

Since the first model appeared in 1959, the gross weight has risen nearly half a ton from a modest 2,900 pounds to a hefty 3,800 pounds, making the airplane the heaviest single in production for general use. The horsepower has risen from 260 hp to 300 hp and the cruise speed peaked out just under 200 mph/174 knots.

A turbocharged model introduced in 1965 has gone on to outsell its normally aspirated sibling by nearly a two-to-one ratio. At the end of 1977 no less than 5,796 Cessna 210s had been delivered with production at an all-time high of over 700 a year to meet the burgeoning demand.

Major Evolutionary Changes

In 1962 the cabin was enlarged slightly and given rear windows. But basically the airplane remained a four-placer. Then in 1964 a major engine change was made, going up from 260 hp to 285 hp. The first turbo model appeared in 1966. In 1967 another significant change involved replacing the strut-braced wing with a cantilever one, while boosting fuel capacity from 65 gallons to 90. The airplane cabin still could not be considered a six-placer, however; it was, at best, a four plus two (kids).

Then in 1970 a major cabin modification provided six adult seats with extra baggage space in the rear, and the gross weight was raised by 400 pounds to its current 3,800 pounds. Next, in 1971 takeoff horsepower was raised to 300. And in 1972 the old

engine-driven hydraulic system was replaced with an electro-hydraulic system. The pressurized P-210, introduced in 1979, is the pinnacle of single-engine performance.

Naturally, 1970 and later models are desirable for the extra cabin space and extra load-carrying ability, and '67 and later models for the extra 25-gallon fuel capacity.

Performance and Handling

Speed, useful load and range are the 210's strong suits. With a top cruising speed of 196 mph/171 knots, the later model 210s yield a range with reserve of nearly 1,000 sm—greater than any other single aside from the Mooney 201, to our knowledge.

With an IFR-equipped, fully fueled payload of about 970 pounds, the late-model Cessna 210 can haul the astonishing load of five adults and about 22 pounds of baggage for each rider. No other single comes close except the Piper Lance, which is still about 70 pounds shy. To accommodate all this weight, an unusually broad center of gravity envelope tolerates loading

extremes that would cause aerodynamic havoc in other airplanes.

Of course, the rear two seats are a bit cramped for long flights, and they pose entry and exit problems—but they are available if needed. Furthermore, there is a separate baggage compartment in the rear.

Left and right front-seat cabin doors provide extra flexibility for the forward four seats.

In terms of handling, as the heaviest airplane in its class at gross, the 210 must be treated with respect—something quite a few pilots neglect to do, judging from the accident reports provided later on showing overshoots, undershoots and hard landings. For so large an airplane, however, the airplane should not be faulted on its aerodynamic agility, since it has very quick, light ailerons. The airplane is heavy in pitch control, however, and with its limited elevator is difficult to maneuver into a full-stall break, but naturally, it will mush with the best of them at low-power, low-speed situations.

Despite windows all-around, visibility is

The strutless, cantilever wing *made its debut in the 1967 model, with fuel capacity up to 90 gallons.*

limited by the high wing inside a turn; and the instrument panel is so high that when the average pilot has cranked his seat high enough to see over it, he can't see out to the left without ducking his head under the window jamb.

Cabin Comfort, Finish
A fairly common complaint among 210 owners is that the general quality of the cabin interior is not commensurate with the caliber of the airplane as a prestige top-of-the-line product. Though the Royalite material on the instrument panel is light and conveniently removable, it in particular often comes in for criticism as looking "cheap."

A number of owners also complain that their 210s are not weatherproof, that they leak rainwater through the cabin, passenger doors and baggage doors. We are unable to tell whether, on this score, the 210 is any worse or better than other airplanes, since aircraft door sealing and weatherstripping has always been an occult art, with mixed success on many models.

Cabin width (44 inches in the middle) and height (47 inches) makes for sufficient passenger and pilot comfort in the front four seats, and in the cantilever-wing models the wing carry-through beams are located behind the front-seat passengers where they are out of the way.

Comparison
Stacked up against the Piper Lance and the Beech A-36 Bonanza, the late model 210 is a speck faster than the A-36 and about 15 knots faster than the Lance. The 210 carries a useful load about 130 pounds over that of the A-36, but about 13 pounds shy of the Lance. The 210's cabin is two inches wider than the A-36 at the widest, but again comes out second best to the Lance by about four inches. The 210 comes out second to the Lance in baggage space and baggage structural capacity.

Maintenance
The biggest problem reported by owners is the landing gear system, especially in the pre-1972 models with the engine-driven hydraulic system, as opposed to the later electro-hydraulic one. The task of maintaining these older ones, with accumulator, power pack, filter and hydraulic pump, was described by one mechanic as "a pain in the ass."

Owners reported long delays in getting gear system parts for the older models, too, when the gear saddle A.D. triggered a rash of repairs, though this may have eased off somewhat lately. An independent IA mechanic we often consult with (John Dennis

of Poughkeepsie, N.Y.) characterized the landing gear system on recent models as relatively robust and simple and requiring comparatively little maintenance.

Though some owners complained about the high cost of parts, Dennis said he felt Cessna's (and Piper's) were not high compared with other manufacturers like Beech and Rockwell.

He warned prospective purchasers of pre-64 model 210s to have a mechanic make a thorough inspection or face the possibility of spending "big bucks" to make extensive corrections, especially in the gear system.

In general, owners can expect to pay $500 to $600 for an annual inspection on a "perfect" airplane, but $1,000 or more for the average ship with a few small discrepancies. Like all large, sophisticated airplanes, the 210 takes care and money to keep operating properly.

A.D. History
The one dark shadow looming over the purchaser of a used 210 is the notorious landing gear saddle problem, which affects all 210s built from 1960 to 1969. Fatigue cracks began showing up in alarming numbers in the early seventies, usually after the airplane had accumulated 1,000-1,200 hours. FAA records show 181 cracked saddles from 1970-75, and there were possibly hundreds of other unreported cracks.

Typically, the cracks would be found during annual inspections. If they weren't, the saddles would eventually break altogether. The pilot then would discover his problem when one landing gear leg would hang up in the half-way position. Ten messy, expensive gear-up landings by 210s with

The first three Cessna 210 prototypes *appeared in 1956, '57 and '58.*

broken saddles were reported in one 30-month period.

An AD was finally issued in 1976. Immediate saddle replacement was required for 1960 and 1961 models, but the replacement saddles themselves must be replaced every 1,000 hours—the replacement saddle is just as defective as the original. Cost of replacement is about $1,000-$1,500, so any purchaser of a 1960 or 1961 model should count on at least $1 per hour for saddle replacement. And be sure to check how soon the replacement is due — the owner may be trying to sell the plane just before his saddle replacement is due, and you could be stuck with the bill a few hours later. In all cases, inspect the saddle closely to insure that it hasn't cracked already.

The 1962-67 models had the same original defective saddles as the '60 and '61s, but differences in the retraction system allow an improved saddle to be fitted as a replacement. But there's a kicker. The "improved" saddles, it turns out, aren't much better than the originals, and we have reports of replacement saddles breaking in as few as 300 hours. According to an FAA report, "The so-called 'improved' saddles have served only to extend the life of the part, rather than

eliminate the cracking/breaking problem . . . the problem has persisted and now includes airplanes with the improved saddles." The AD still requires a dye-penetrant inspection annually once the replacement saddle has accumulated 1,200 hours.

Nineteen sixty-eight and 1969 models had the "improved" saddles as original equipment, and they must be inspected at 1,200 hours and annually thereafter. Expect them to break eventually. In all cases, the saddles should be closely inspected.

In 1970, the landing gear system underwent a major redesign, and there has been no recurrence of the problem that we know of.

Potential buyers of 1960-64 210s should also be on the lookout for other gear problems. Another 1976 AD requires replacement of the hydraulic landing gear actuators on those models—a $2,000 job. Make sure that AD has been accomplished. There have been no reports of recurring actuator problems, so an airplane with modified actuators should be all right.

Safety Record

If you fly a Cessna 210, statistically your greatest potential for an accident is from an engine stoppage. But only about half of

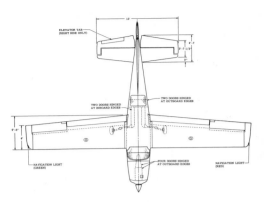

these accidents will be caused by an actual engine malfunction; the rest will be the result of fuel mismanagement, including simply running out of fuel. Several stoppages will occur because of water or other contamination in the fuel.

These are among the salient facts disclosed by a study of all the Cessna 210 accidents reported by the NTSB for the two years, 1975 and 1976.

Out of 181 accidents reported, fully 32 percent, or 58, were related to engine stoppages. Other large tolls were related to gear-up landings (22 or 12 percent), im-

Model	Year Built	Number Built	Cruise Speed (mph)	Useful Load (lbs)	Rate of Climb (fpm)	Fuel Std/Opt (gals)	Engine	TBO (hrs)	Overhaul Cost	Average Retail Price
210	1960	610	190	1,160	1,300	65	260-hp Continental	1,200	$5,750	$16,500
210A	1961	171	190	1,160	1,300	68	260-hp Continental	1,200	$5,750	$18,000
210B	1962	281	184	1,220	1,270	65/84	260-hp Continental	1,200	$5,750	$20,000
210C	1963	156	184	1,220	1,270	65/84	260-hp Continental	1,200	$5,750	$21,000
210D	1964	283	191	1,260	1,210	65/84	285-hp Continental	1,200	$6,750	$24,000
210E	1965	224	191	1,260	1,210	65/84	285-hp Continental	1,200	$6,750	$26,000
210F	1966	101	190	1,435	1,115	65/84	285-hp Continental	1,200	$6,750	$27,500
T210	1966	147	220	1,335	1,280	65/84	285-hp Continental	1,400	$8,000	$30,000
210G	1967	122	192	1,440	1,000	90	285-hp Continental	1,200	$6,750	$29,500
T-210G	1967	104	223	1,350	1,115	89	285-hp continental	1,400	$8,000	$32,500
210H	1968	125	192	1,440	1,000	90	285-hp Continental	1,200	$6,750	$31,000
T-210H	1968	65	223	1,350	1,115	89	285-hp Continental	1,400	$8,000	$34,500
210J	1969	136	192	1,440	1,000	90	285-hp Continental	1,500	$6,750	$32,500
T-210J	1969	45	223	1,350	1,115	89	285-hp Continental	1,400	$8,000	$37,500
210K	1970	181	188	1,552	800	90	285-hp Continental	1,500	$6,750	$36,000
T-210K	1970		219	1,620	930	90	285-hp Continental	1,400	$8,000	$39,000
210-KII	1971	171	188	1,552	860	90	300-hp Continental	1,500	$6,750	$38,000
T-210K	1971		219	1,620	930	90	285-hp Continental	1,400	$8,000	$41,000
210LII	1972	220	188	1,552	860	90	300-hp Continental	1,500	$6,750	$40,000
T-210L	1972		223	1,476	1,030	90	285-hp Continental	1,400	$8,000	$42,500
210LII	1973	351	188	1,552	860	90	300-hp Continental	1,500	$6,750	$42,500
T-210LII	1973		223	1,476	1,030	90	285-hp Continental	1,400	$8,000	$45,000
210LII	1974	474	188	1,552	860	90	300-hp Continental	1,500	$6,750	$44,500
T-210L	1974		223	1,476	1,030	90	285-hp Continental	1,400	$8,000	$48,000
Centurion II	1975	531	188	1,552	860	90	300-hp Continental	1,500	$6,750	$48,000
T-210II	1975		223	1,476	1,030	90	285-hp Continental	1,400	$8,000	$54,000
Centurion II	1976	520	197	1,552	860	90	300-hp Continental	1,500	$6,750	$51,500
T-210II	1976		227	1,476	1,030	90	285-hp Continental	1,400	$8,000	$57,500
Centurion II	1977	719	197	1,552	860	90	300-hp Continental	1,500	$6,750	$55,000
T-210II	1977		227	1,476	1,030	90	310-hp Continental	1,400	$8,000	$65,000
Centurion II	1978	680	197	1,552	860	90	300-hp Continental	1,500	$6,750	$61,250
T-210	1978		227	1,476	1,030	90	310-hp Continental	1,400	$8,000	$72,500
Centurion II	1979	685	197	1,552	860	90	300-hp Continental	1,500	$6,750	$75,000
T-210	1979		227	1,476	1,030	90	310-hp Continental	1,400	$8,000	$84,000

proper IFR operations (20 or 11 percent) and all-around poor pilot judgment (30 or 17 percent).

Since 28 engine stoppages (or 15 percent) were caused by a malfunction of some sort, pilots might give some attention to the causes reported in the NTSB listings.

The greatest number of failures—four—was caused by engine crankshaft failures. Three stoppages were caused by failure of the throttle control in some fashion (throttle control shaft broke at rod end; throttle link failed because of throttle control rod end pin; uniball rod end allowed bearing to slip off ball over washer).

Two more stoppages resulted from mixture control failures (mixture control bolt missing, lock nut found in nacelle; mixture control assembly broke—FAA advisory circular 20-7N).

And another pair occurred when the oil quick drain opened during flight, causing the engine to lose all its oil.

Seven engine stoppages were for undetermined reasons.

Gear-up Landings

Of the 22 gear-up landings, a little over half occurred because pilots were distracted or simply forgot to lower the gear; however, in three of these instances pilots had some excuse in that the gear warning horn was not working.

There seemed to be no obvious pattern in the gear-up malfunctions, except that in two cases the gear actuator or actuating cylinder failed.

Fuel Mismanagement

The large number of fuel mismanagement problems might come as a surprise to anyone familiar with the typical "infallible" high-wing Cessna fuel system that normally allows the pilot to dispense with tank switching. However, in the 210 the "both" tanks position is not available, and pilots must switch from left to right tank in the conventional manner.

According to the NTSB accident reports, two engine stoppages resulted when the pilot inadvertently allowed the one tank to run dry, and then was unable to restart the engine, despite the fact there was sufficient fuel in the other tank.

In one of the instances the Safety Board said the pilot, who had low time in the 210, did not turn on the electric fuel pump when switching from the dry left tank to the right tank. Evidently, the gravity feed is not sufficient to do the job, though fuel injection engines are usually difficult to restart when starved of fuel.

What is surprising is that most pilots tagged with fuel mismanagement simply used every drop of available fuel and were obliged to make forced landings. Since there is a generous 89 usable gallons of fuel available—enough for five to six hours at high cruise speeds—it's mystifying why so many pilots apparently wanted more.

One possible contributing factor might be the poor location of the fuel gauge on the right side of the instrument panel rather far away from the pilot for easy viewing. Only

in the brand-new '78 Model 210s has this situation been altered by locating the fuel gauges down on the lower throttle pedestal directly above the fuel tank selector switch.

Though this makes for a logical pairing of gauges and switches, it remains to be seen whether this location, way below the pilot's normal scan, diminishes the number of fuel exhaustion cases. A prominent low-fuel warning light would seem to be a logical addition to this airplane, and all others, for that matter, along with a way to measure the final gallon or two with extreme precision.

Pilots are warned in the operating handbook to avoid prolonged slips with fuel tanks less than one-quarter full. Since one pilot actually "flamed out" in this condition while slipping for a crosswind landing approach, the warning should be heeded.

It also behooves 210 pilots (and all others, of course) to drain the fuel tanks for water and sediment—a fairly simply exercise on the high-wing Cessna. Six of the Cessna 210 engine stoppages resulted from water or contaminents in the fuel.

Although 20 crashes (all but one fatal) occurred when pilots got in over their heads in IFR weather, only two cases were reported of severe structural damage from overstressing the airplane. In one of these the airplane tumbled out of a thunderstorm in pieces; in the other the pilot brought the airplane back to base with bent wings after approaching within five miles of a thunderstorm. The 210 has a much better record than the Bonanza in this respect.

Although prop clearance (with a three-bladed prop) is a better-than-average 10.89 inches, 210 pilots caution that the geometry of the airplane seems to make for a greater-than-average danger of striking a prop when taxiing over uneven surfaces, as from sod to ramp.

Most of the other problems in the 210 reported in the two-year NTSB rundown involved undershooting and overshooting or hard landings or groundlooping, all of which suggests poor pilot judgment and inability to properly handle a big, heavy, high-performance airplane. In two cases, the airplane actually was blown over onto its nose from high winds while taxiing.

Societies

The National 210 Owners Assoc. was organized in 1976 and reports it has about 500 members so far. Yearly membership fee: $25. There is a quarterly newsletter. Although there are regional directors, the main address is 7726 Gloria Ave., Van Nuys, Calif. 91406. Tel.: 213-994-2323 or 213-782-4313.

Instrument panel for a '75 turbo 210, *with fuel gauges at the right of the radio stack.*

Owner Comments

"The performance and handling of the aircraft are very good. The only thing that has to be watched is to plan your descent since the aircraft is aerodynamically clean and needs time to descend from IFR cruising altitudes without reducing the power too much. Comfort in the cabin is very good. There is enough room to sit upright as opposed to feeling like you are sitting on the floor, and the cabin is well heated and ventilated.

"Maintenance costs have been high. We averaged $17.74 an hour in 1977. One problem has been the cylinders, and five of the six had to be replaced for low compression. One for a stuck ring which wore the cylinder, and the other four for leaking exhaust valves. Other high maintenance items are the Cessna 300 series avionics. Parts availability from Cessna has been adequate, but a number of times Cessna has failed to get a part out as promised, leaving the aircraft stranded on the ground. Parts availability from Van Duesen has been good, when they stock the item.

"The most prominent idiosyncrasy is water leakage around the baggage door. Regardless of the maintenance hours devoted to this problem, the door still leaks in heavy rain. Cold weather starting is nearly impossible below 10 degrees F unless the sun has been on the airplane during the day."

"We purchased a new Cessna 1975 Turbo 210 II, which was fully equipped with Cessna 400 avionics.

"When we picked up the aircraft at Wichita, the paint was literally falling off. Flying from Cessna's field to Wichita Int'l, the autopilot 'ran wild' when switched to approach couple mode, the DME was inoperative, the number two navcom was erratic, the pilot's door and baggage door leaked, the ADF was inoperative, and approach control did not receive our transponder. We could not arrange for repairs at the Cessna factory, so decided to return to Oregon for warranty work. Unknowingly, we decided these were routine 'new car' problems.

"In the ensuing 18 months and 450 hours, everything that could go wrong proceeded to do so. By then the aircraft had been painted three times; had two KN65 DMEs installed, but *never* had one operative (remember, DME is required at or above 18,000 feet and this was a turbo); had two encoding altimeters; two altimeters; two vacuum pumps; two top overhauls (including replacing two cylinders due to manufacturing defects); two baggage doors; totally new wing root seals; door seals; window seals; and a complete return trip through the factory to solve the water problem. In all the time we owned it, it leaked.

"Water ran through the top shoulder harness attachments, down the shoulder harness, onto the carpet and wicked throughout the plane. At any time, you could remove the floorboards and find standing water.

"While the avionics and instruments continued to deteriorate, we continued to pay. Cessna refused to pay for top overhaul number one but did pay part of number two. Most avionics repairs were paid for by us, but regardless of who paid, we *never* had a DME. The airplane was used 90 percent for business, but by the end of our first year we figured that our 200-mile average commute would have been twice as fast by car if we counted the number of missed days due to downtime.

"Finally we sold the plane. Our only bright note is that some sucker paid us $1,000 less than our original cost. We will never buy another new Cessna aircraft."

"Perhaps my best reaction to ownership of a 210 is the fact that I am trading my 1969 model plus $35,000 for a new 1978 model. I feel that this is the finest single manufactured. It is the only true six-placer.

"Characteristics are: good speed, fantastic payloads, and the best instrument platform around. No weight and balance problem as with the Bonanzas.

"But there are some shortcomings: the typical Cessna ten-cent-store plastic panel, noise, and less than desirable visibility.

"Maintenance costs have been good. I spend more on my King Avionics than the airplane. I replaced first engine with factory reman at 1,250 hours; never had a gear or engine case crack. But I would strongly recommend three-blade prop in lieu of two-blade on older models due to noise problem."

"I purchased a used 1961 Cessna 210A in 1975 and was advised to replace the main gear actuator shaft and gear assembly (approx. $340 per side), and the main gear saddles. No other problems were apparent with the aircraft, from log book studies and a current inspection.

"With the exception of replacement of the gear actuators and saddles, the first year's annual inspection cost $1,074.

"The second year's annual, with the exception of a fuel cell which leaked in cold weather, cost $866.

"In terms of performance, I am delighted with the airplane. I frequently fly with one or two passengers at 2350/2400 rpm. Consistently, true airspeed checks out at 194/196 mph—eight to 10 miles above the speeds shown in the book. Numerous ground checks, combined with winds aloft, verify the accuracy of that speed.

"At approximately 6,000 msl, fuel consumption is 12 to 12.5 gph. At 12,000 msl fuel consumption approximates 10 to 10.25 gpm.

"The gear has been totally reliable for extension and landing, although on occasion, either on landing or after takeoff, the gear doors have failed to close because of a problem with a switch in the gear console. This switch has been adjusted once ($30) and replaced twince in 350 hours of use.

"Rate of climb is excellent with one or two on board—1,500 feet per minute near sea level in moderate weather is normal at full throttle. Rate of climb of 1,000 fpm is standard throughout most of the year, at an airspeed of approximately 130 IAS.

The first production model *in 1960, complete with cowling "darts."*

"We consistently flight plan 160 knots, and usually find we are closer to 165 in actual practice on IFR work.

"The only objection is that shoulder room in the front seat is a little less than desirable with two 200-pound men up front. Other than that, it's an ideal one-to-four person airplane, a remarkably economic plane for its speed and range."

"I own a 1974 210 and after 500 hours, I can say that handling is great and loading with six adults and baggage is no problem. It seems to fly the same with four or six people aboard. I feel the cost of operation is no more than a Skylane. (I owned a 1973 model previously.) I usually get fuel down to 13.5-14 gallons per hour, and with a 160-165-knot cruise it is cheaper to run than Skylane.

"However, I am disappointed with the engine. At the present time I am topping all six cylinders because of burnt exhaust valves and worn rings. I change oil and filters regularly at 50 hours and usually cruise 60 to 65 percent power.

"After owning two 210s (I had a 1967 Turbo also), I would own nothing else. I think that it is the greatest single around." air."

"Both 210s we've owned (a '68 and a '73 model) consistently performed at and above book specs in all categories, particularly speed. Gas consumption of the later model was a constant problem, with the engine burning 16 gph at 66 percent, with the book calling for 14.5. Two Cessna dealers were unable to correct the problem.

"The 210 is not a responsive aircraft on the controls, but can be relied upon to provide very few surprises in most flight regimes. Ground nosewheel steering is stiff, sluggish and difficult, with brakes always being needed.

"Our '68 model was good. The '73 was another story. The aircraft was assembled poorly, with obviously poor workmanship and components. On one flight, I had the turn and bank fail, the vacuum pump go out, and, upon landing, the starter motor went bad. Our annual inspection was over $1,800, with very little AD work. Maintenance bills were high, even though usage was less than 250 hours per year operating

Landing gear saddle *is a source of expensive perennial problems on older 210s.*

Last major cabin change *came in 1970 with six seats and a 3,800-pound gross.*

two- to four-hour flights at 66 percent power. We seldom had a flight where some cheap little part didn't fail."

"The landing gear on the 210 is not cheap to maintain. For a system as complex as it is, however, the gear is remarkably reliable.

"Our 1971 model does not have a saddle problem, but it does have an engine-driven hydraulic pump which has given us some grief.

"Proper rigging of the gear is very important, and this takes a lot of maintenance time. If your mechanic does not already service 210s or similar aircraft, he will have to shell out about $1,000 for a set of jacks.

"On the other hand, the gear works beautifully most of the time and (so far) can always be pumped down if the main pump fails. But make sure all the microswitch wires are intact, or funny things can happen. For example, if the uplock microswitches don't close, neither will the doors.

"One other gear item not specifically mentioned by Cessna: If you lose your electrical system (or turn off the master switch), the landing gear doors will open and you will lose about 20 mph—worth remembering for long overwater flights. This is not true in those newer aircraft with electrically driven hydraulic pumps. An electrical failure in a newer model means pumping the gear down by hand.

"We have had good support from Cessna on our gear problems except for one instance: We had some seals changed on the left main gear actuator by Reading Aviation (during an engine change) and thereafter, that gear did not always lock down the first time. Sometimes it took five or six tries! Our mechanics (Fitchburg-Colonial Aviation in Fitchburg, Mass. who, incidentally, have done very well by us) found that they could make the gear work right by reindexing the gear one tooth.

"Unfortunately, this was not approved by the Cessna manual. So we had an aircraft that worked right when put together 'wrong,' or worked wrong when put together 'right.' It took some time and many

phone calls before Cessna would admit in writing that reindexing the gear was acceptable. We never recovered any money from Reading or Cessna for this, although it cost us well over $400 to straighten the mess out.

"The nosegear is more than two feet behind the prop. If you park on the grass, fire up, and taxi toward the pavement, make sure you have an extra $1,000 in your pocket. The prop clearance is quite small (even with a three-bladed prop). At some point the prop will be over the pavement and the nosewheel will be in the grass. If there is a small dip there, and/or if you apply brakes and compress the nose strut, the prop will hit.

"The nosegear oleo strut is also a bit underdesigned and needs constant maintenance—the engine is just too heavy for it.

"The 210 has a capacitive fuel gauge system that is quite accurate. Its one problem is that occasionally one side or the other will start reading zero intermittently. You have two choices here. You can pay your mechanic a lot of money to figure out the solution; or you can open the zipper on the right side of the headliner and pull out and reinsert the two detector plugs on the fuel gauge control box a few times to clean the contacts. This works very well and the price is right.

"Our 210 came with a full complement of Cessna radios. In the seven months or so that we struggled with that setup, we had an IFR-qualified aircraft for about one day! I wrote to Cessna complaining about this, but did not get an answer for over a year, by which time we had replaced the system with a TSO'd King system. We have been very happy with that system—in fact, we have the same system in all our aircraft now.

"I would have to say that the 210 is the best-flying aircraft I have ever flown. It is a remarkable instrument platform with practically no tail-wag.

"The weight-carrying ability of the plane is superb. I have done many weight-and-balance calculations and have found very few realistic situations which would put the aircraft out of balance."

Bellanca Viking

Loaded with charisma and personality, if slightly short on spec numbers, the Bellanca Viking may represent a good dark-horse but for a pilot who yearns to own and operate a fairly potent single at a modest price. The builder's 1980 bankruptcy may adversely affect backup, though.

Loyal Bellanca owners may writhe at the mention, once again, that the Viking incurs a rather greater than average drop in resale value than its peers over the years, but this very fact might enhance the aircraft's value as a used-plane purchase. In fact, a typical Viking will cost some $13,000 less than a Piper Comanche of the same vintage.

The disadvantages to longevity commonly cited are, of course, the aircraft's wooden wing and Ceconite fabric covering over a tubular frame. As we've mentioned before, if checked and maintained, there's no reason the sitka spruce and mahogany wing won't stand the ravages of time as well as a metal wing. (If a wooden spar can decay, a metal one can corrode.)

The fabric covering naturally will need replacement some day—maybe not for 10 to 15 years, maybe in six or so, depending on whether the aircraft is hangared or left out in the elements. This will effect a cost penalty at that point of about $4,500. (This was a rough quote from Minuteman Airways in Middletown, Pa., one of the large eastern Viking dealers.) A specially fine finish with extra coats of dope and hand rubbing naturally will add to the price.

Any prospective Viking purchaser obviously would be wise to enlist the services of a mechanic familiar with this type of aircraft and its wooden structure before consummating a deal.

As for upkeep maintenance, if we are to believe the considerable owner comment we received on the Viking, it is unusually low for an aircraft of this size and engine class. Several owners reported much lower expenses for annual inspections and 100-hour checks on Vikings than they encountered with similar all-metal aircraft of the Cessna 210/Bonanza type.

Quality and Performance
Probably because the Viking is so distinctive.

and not your run-of-the-mill mass-production aircraft, Bellanca owners seem to develop everything from unabashed affection to defensive pride in their airplanes. A Viking owner worth his salt will gush interminably about the quality of workmanship, exquisite finish and handsome interior furnishings.

Indeed, the outsider can expect to find on a well-kept Viking a superb smooth finish unmatched by any of the aluminum, rivet and overlap-metal-mongery common in most of general aviation. And for some years the Bellanca factory has turned out some of the most elaborate interior upholstery of any lightplane we know of.

How much do the sleek exterior cocoon and uniquely curved, tapered wooden wing contribute to performance? Most Bellanca owners are modest and slightly apologetic on this score. They admit they don't get the 200-mph plus speeds of the Cessna 210 and Bonanza (at least on nonturbo models), and they confess to a rather lower useful load and fuel capacity than they'd like if they had their druthers. Owners tell us they can count on a top cruise speed of around 165 knots/190 mph, while burning around 15 gph in normally aspirated models. The speeds go up to 190 knots/218 mph with the turbos at 20,000 feet.

Standard fuel capacity is 60 gallons, with three metal tanks in each wing. The three in

each wing have a single filler cap and feed into each other. An optional 15-gallon rear fuselage fuel tank is also available. Obviously, at 15 gph, this means three to four hours' cruise with reserve, and a rather modest range for this class of aircraft.

As for useful load, the Viking's is roughly on a par with the 200-hp retractables like the Mooney 201 and Cardinal; it is several hundred pounds below that of any of the big 300-hp retractables like the Centurion, Bonanza or Lance.

Handling
If Viking owners are mildly self-deprecating about performance, they tend to get euphoric over handling characteristics. Indeed, the aircraft has extremely pleasant, light ailerons, and though it's not rated for aerobatics, it's often been taken on dramatic aerobatic exhibition tours as part of the promotional effort.

Harmony of controls is somewhat lacking, though, since the Viking has rather heavy pitch forces.

The one flight characteristic that requires a bit of special attention from the neophyte is the aircraft's ability to develop a surprisingly high rate of descent on final approach, which must be controlled with judicious use of power. Some feel the use of a vernier throttle complicates this process.

Vikings offer a choice of engines: *Continental or Lycoming. The unturboed Lycoming has an extra 500 hours of TBO (2,000 hours vs. 1,500 for the Continental), but is a bit heavier.*

Bellanca family picture. *Vikings and Citabrias both have wooden wing spars, welded tubular fuselages and fabric covering.*

Touchdown in a crosswind can provide a surprise, also, if the nosewheel is not straightened out with the rudder pedals, since it tends to cock to the side with the rudder, in the Cherokee fashion. One pilot lost control and ran off the runway in this kind of situation, according to the most recent five-year NTSB listing of accidents.

The rather sensitive nosegear steering also leads to a tendency to overcontrol among newcomers making a transition into the aircraft. Conversely, while taxiing, the pilot will note the turn radius is rather wide.

Cabin and Cockpit
Most owners rate the cabin a bit cozy. Also, older Vikings had short-backed bucket seats that compromised comfort over the long haul; later models have more pleasant reclining seatbacks. Rear-seat riders also can expect rather modest footroom, since the carry-through wing spar impinges on space.

As for control placement, the Viking has an old-fashioned overhead pitch trim crank similar to the Piper Aztec's. Since 1973, Vikings have had a single fuel selector switch between the pilot and copilot. Before that, there was a separate one for main tanks and another for the aux tanks, and there were conventional cluster fuel gauges. This setup may have contributed to the surprisingly large number of fuel mismanagement accidents reported in the NTSB files—especially in the older 17-30 Vikings. Post-73 models have an exceptionally prominent vertical fuel gauge just to the left of the control wheel.

Up until May of 1968, Vikings also had an unusual combination flap and gear actuator system that worked off the engine-driven hydraulic system and was positioned between the pilot/copilot seats. In 1968 electric flaps were incorporated, and the control levers mounted on the front panel in the conventional fashion.

Viking Accident Statistics
Examination of the National Transportation Safety Board accident briefs for the 17-30 and 17-31 Vikings from 1972 through 1976 shows that by far the largest problem related to engine failure from poor pilot fuel management, followed by a forced landing.

We counted 21 such cases where pilots simply exhausted all the fuel, or switched to an empty tank and couldn't get the engine restarted. Some of these pilots had only a few hours in the Viking, but others had over a hundred.

In nine other instances the Bellanca fliers lost directional control of the aircraft after touchdown and either swerved off the runway or groundlooped, which may bear testimony to the sensitivity of the nosewheel steering. Five of these pilots were fairly inexperienced in the aircraft—with from 15 to 56 hours, but the other three pilots had 330 to over 1,000 hours in the bird.

In seven cases pilots damaged the aircraft with hard landings, overshoots or undershoots, a figure perhaps not unexpected in powerful, fairly heavy single-engine aircraft. Half of these pilots were fairly inexperienced in the aircraft, with six to 87 hours; the others had from 340 to 6,000 hours in Vikings.

There were seven cases of airframe failure logged by the NTSB in the five-year listing. Three of them resulted when pilots flew into thunderstorms or bad weather; in another case a section of the plywood skin on the right wing separated because of turbulence below the clouds, but the aircraft landed safely. Another pilot was caught in the vortex of a heavy air transport, and the wing skin ruptured, with longitudinal cracks in

Model	Year Built	Number Built	Cruise Speed (mph)	Useful Load (lbs)	Rate of Climb (fpm)	Fuel Std/Opt (gals)	Engine	TBO (hrs)	Overhaul Cost	Average Retail Price
Viking 17-30	1967-70	290	188	1,300	1,840	58/92	300-hp Continental	1,200	$6,750	$19,000-$22,500
Viking 17-30A	1971-74	419	188	1,108	1,085	60/75	300-hp Continental	1,500	$6,750	$24,000-$32,000
Viking 17-30A	1975-77	129	188	1,108	1,085	60/75	300-hp Continental	1,500	$6,750	$35,000-$46,000
Viking 17-30A	1978-79	106	188	1,108	1,085	60/75	300-hp Continental	1,500	$6,750	$52,000-$60,000
Super Viking 17-31A	1969-70	34	190	1,375	1,800	60/75	290-hp Lycoming	1,400	$7,350	$21,000-$23,000
Super Viking 17-31A	1971-74	104	190	1,190	1,800	60/75	300-hp Lycoming	2,000	$8,350	$24,500-$33,000
Super Viking 17-31A	1975-77	23	190	1,100	1,170	60/75	300-hp Lycoming	2,000	$8,350	$36,500-$47,500
Super Turbo Vik. 17-31ATC	1969-70	11	235	1,305	1,800	72/92	290-hp Lycoming	1,400	$6,750	$24,000
Super Turbo Vik. 17-31ATC	1971-72	23	235	1,190	1,800	72/92	300-hp Lycoming	2,000	$8,350	$28,000-$31,000
Turbo Viking 17-31ATC	1973-75	75	222	1,053	1,170	60/75	300-hp Lycoming	2,000	$8,350	$35,000-$41,000
Turbo Viking 17-31ATC	1967-77	17	222	1,053	1,170	60/75	300-hp Lycoming	2,000	$8,350	$46,000-$52,500
Turbo Viking 17-31ATC	1978-79	16	222	1,053	1,170	60/75	300-hp Lycoming	2,000	$8,350	$60,000-$68,500

both wings, but he landed safely. The cause of another separation was unknown; and in one, deteriorated wing spars caused the separation.

Anyone on the lookout for a used Viking should check with Miller Flying Service in Plainview, Texas (806-293-4121). The Miller organization has been a longtime hub of Bellanca activities. As we mentioned before, Minuteman Airways in Middletown, Pa. is one of the bigger eastern dealers. They report they have a good trade in used Vikings.

There were only some 13 to 15 active Bellanca Viking dealers around the country when the factory was still in business. This naturally was a handicap in getting good service from people intimately familiar with the aircraft. Now that the company has shut down and filed for bankruptcy, the future prospects for parts is clouded, to say the least.

As for Bellanca owner associations, as far as we know, there is none presently active for the Vikings.

Also, there are no special modifications or STCs that we know of for the Viking. Doors for the main landing gear were added as an option in late 1967 for the 17-30 model. They add 8-12 mph to cruise speeds and cost $878. There is no door to cover the nose-gear, which simply projects down below the engine nacelle. One was built in 1975, but not adopted as a permanent feature.

Airworthiness Directives

The most prominent and expensive A.D. was the one in 1976 requiring inspection of the wooden wing to detect deterioration, after one Viking experienced airframe failure and the aircraft was found to have structural decay.

The factory has picked up the cost of repairs and replacement for this A.D. during a one-year period that ended in 1977. However, owners had to pay inspection costs and installation costs that could add up to $700. Bellanca reports only six or seven aircraft needed major repairs.

The 1980 bankruptcy of Bellanca has thrown the future of the Viking line (and the outlook for parts supplies for older aircraft) into serious doubt. At this writing, negotiations were going on for the sale of the company.

A vigorous and flourishing Bellanca company can be regarded as a much-needed cornerstone to an industry that needs that extra element of variety and customer choice, which a few dominant big companies cannot alone provide.

In the beginning . . . *there was the 1959 model 14-19-3 with the famous triple tail. Actually, the 14 series goes back to 1937.*

Owner Comments

"In the last three years I have owned two Super Vikings and used them almost entirely for my business. The first was a used 1972 Super Viking with a Continental engine. I accumulated 900 hours on this aircraft before trading to a used 1976 Turbo Bellanca on which I now have over 300 hours.

"Operation: All systems have operated quite well and always been very reliable. The earlier Super Vikings, up to the 1973 models, had a tendency toward leaky gas tanks. It is usually the main tanks that leak. To correct this problem costs approximately $500 per gas tank, due to the fact that the top of the wing must be cut out (it is wood, you know), tank removed, welded, and then reinstalled with lots of hand finishing and painting.

"Also, some early models up to 1973 had steel piston rods in the landing gear hydraulic retract cylinders. These tended to corrode and cut the O-rings, causing hydraulic fluid leakage and loss of pressure. Replacement of these rods to the stainless steel rods cost approximately $125 per main landing gear.

"Caution: Don't let the shop just polish out the rough spots on the rod: they will charge over $100, and the problem will recur within 50 hours. Check all hydraulics for leaks before purchase, especially the retract cylinders. If the rods look rough, don't let the shop just replace the O-rings as they will only last about 10 hours.

"The Continental engine never gave me a problem, and I had it remanufactured at 1,500 hours. I had turbos overhauled at 250 hours due to a faulty controller spring that was causing power surges above 7,000 feet MSL. This caused a little difficulty even though the overhaul work was being done by Rajay, the manufacturer of the turbos; I learned that Bellanca does make modifications, but neither Bellanca nor Rajay could seem to get together to

quickly fix the problem. After a week or so all was resolved, and there has been no further problem.

"A nice Bellanca feature is that the turbos are completely automatic, but you can turn them off via a little switch on the panel. Your engine will then behave as though normally aspirated. It is the only aircraft with automatic turbos that I know of with this feature.

"To avoid possible fuel mismanagement, especially with models before 1973, I learned to switch tanks strictly by time and do not rely on the fuel gauges.

"Service: Living in Southern California, I have found nearby Air Repair in Santa Paula, California to be convenient. Service in other parts of the country may not be as good, I have heard, but I have no personal experience. Air Repair is your best bet on the West Coast. Bellanca, as far as I am concerned, is a good company. Whenever special parts not in local stock have been required, the factory has always come through, even if it took overtime. Undue criticism of the smaller aircraft manufacturers of this country does nothing but promote the big three.

"Radios: King radios work well, *except* transponders (KT76s) in both aircraft give trouble. Some say they can't be grounded to a fabric-covered plane.

"Performance: Superb! Takeoff, climb (1,000 to 1,100 fpm at 120 IAS), cruise, landing—a complete delight. I can't say enough. A little cramped for four inside; however, wife, child and I (a six-footer) fit fine.

"In the 1972 Continental-powered airplane, I cruised consistently at 155 knots at 13.5 gph. The gas tanks are a little small (72 gallons), only enough for three hours plus reserves. A little noisy inside, especially during fast descents and at low altitude below 4,500 feet MSL operation.

"In the 1976 Turbo model, rate of

climb is a little slower (800 to 900 fpm at 120 IAS) due to a heavier nose. Cruise is usually at 165 knots at 15.5 gph below 12,000 feet. Above that it really shines; at 20,000 feet 190 knots at 16 gph. Noise much better than 1972 Continental model.

"Conclusions: The Turbo is definitely the only way to go. There is something about taxiing to the ramp in a custom-made aircraft that attracts attention. The interiors are gorgeous (wives especially like them), and the outside finish always looks new and always receives compliments.

"Bellanca Vikings are not the metal prefab type and must be treated accordingly. A hangar is almost always essential unless you live in the dry desert climate. I have had my share of mechanical problems (usually with limited downtime), but then I use the aircraft a great deal. I expect wear and tear and do not expect the factory to replace at no charge a part that I have worn out, or that has become obsolete because of new developments. There may be bigger six-place all-metal singles, but the Bellanca Viking, in my opinion, is definitely the tops for private and personal transportation. A few compromises have to be made to own and operate a Viking, but isn't that what we all do when we accept private air transportation?"

"We purchased our third Bellanca last year. We're presently owners of a 1976 model Super Viking, having bought it used with only 259 hours on the Lycoming engine. Sine then we have flown it over 125 hours, and to date have had no malfunctions with the airframe, engine, accessories, Century III autopilot or the all-King radios. The only problem really was the air noise coming from leaky door seals; I corrected that myself by adding a little self-sticking foam tape at the leaking areas.

"Our first Bellanca was a Bellanca 260B. In 1970 we traded for a used 1969 model Super Viking 300. Although I was very satisfied with the performance and reliability of this craft, I felt I needed more seats and payload; so in 1973 I switched to a Skymaster 337P, followed by a Centurion in 1975.

"The 1973 Skymaster 337P almost broke me. Downtime was over six months each year, with all kinds of serious ADs, engine and accessory problems, structural cracks and gear malfunctions. Fed up, I switched to a 1975 Centurion. Although far more reliable than the Skymaster, the Centurion was costing me two to three times more to keep running than the Bellancas.

"The Viking does have its weak points, such as less payload, small cabin, a relatively high stall speed, fewer dealerships, etc., but its strengths far outweigh its weakness.

"When nonowners think of the Viking, they think of speed and performance, but Bellanca 'nuts' take pride in its superb handling and its showpiece interior appointments, both of which are by far the *best* in the single-engine field.

"Let's consider first, though, the Viking's performance, which has often been bad-mouthed by the aircraft press, ever since the speedy Mooney 201 came on the scene. The Bellanca is speedy, and book speeds are easily surpassed by most pilots even in multi-antennaed, fully-equipped Vikings. Side-by-side speed runs with a Bellanca and my former Centurion showed no surprise when the Bellanca easily outran the 210. What did surprise us, though, was that the Centurion indicated five mph more *while being passed!* My own Bellanca on other speed comparisons has indicated eight mph less than a Mooney 201 and proved over 10 mph faster than the Mooney and a tad faster than the straight-tailed Bonanza. It is unsurpassed

Unusual in general aviation *is a rear fuselage aux tank, holding 15 gallons or about an hour's cruise flight.*

in its get-up-and-go even when at gross, and it climbs to altitude 300-500 fpm faster than either the Skymaster or Centurion. I generally flight plan for 165 knots and expect to consume about 15 gph on the average at 75 percent.

"Bellanca controls are beautiful! A joy to fly gracefully or to whip around. Light, precise, and unsurpassed in the air, the Viking, however, tends to be a bit heavy on the ground. Its steering radius is quite wide, and the pedals require a heavy foot to steer. Also, when using rudder in a cross-wind landing, you have to remember to let go of the rudder pedals before the nose-wheel touches since the nosewheel is always connected to the rudder pedal. But once in the air, the Bellanca makes up for all its little ground-handling quirks. Fast, slow, climb, descend, flaps, wheels up or down, the Viking shows no dirty tricks, no noticeable pitching up or down; it's a most stable platform, even in the most turbulent IFR conditions. Approach speed is 90 mph, and consistently smooth landings are easy to master; the landing gear is very forgiving.

"Viking interiors are not only the most beautiful in the industry; they are also durable. I've recently examined ten 20-year-old Bellancas, and their original interiors all look a lot newer than the already peeling and cracked six-month-old Cessna interiors. Even the Centurion's interior looked ratty after two years' use.

"In my experience, maintenance of the Bellanca has been far less than any other high-performance craft I've owned. Only three times in my eight years with Bellanca has my craft been laid up between annuals: first in 1968 with a blown jug in the 260B; second in 1972 with a burned out generator; and third in 1973 with a busted vacuum pump. The structure itself has provided virtually no trouble at all. An AD on the wing has been a nuisance, but if the plane has been hangared and maintained, there is no problem."

Viking instrument panel, *with vertical engine gauges to the left of the throttle quadrant.*

Meyers/Rockwell 200

An airplane designer who set out to beat all competitors in speed, strength, quality and maintainability would do well to study the story of the Meyers (Aero Commander) 200. The aircraft achieved all these goals at its debut back in 1958 and even today has few peers in those respects. But range, payload and comfort were severely limited, and it failed in the one aspect that matters under the American free enterprise system: it could never turn a profit for its builders.

Accounts vary, but about 133 of these airplanes were built before production ended in 1967, and a recent check of the U.S. registry showed only about 68 still in license (with a couple dozen still flying overseas, or about 90 all told).

Those who own a Meyers 200 today have a 200-mph airplane that is supposed to rank among the strongest singles ever built (some say overbuilt) and incorporates features like semi-Fowler flaps that lower the stall speed to 54 mph, and shoulder harnesses as standard equipment in the front seats—forced on other manufacturers now by regulation, but incorporated by Meyers more than two decades ago by choice.

The great bulk of Meyers owners have never seen an Airworthiness Directive on the airframe, which may be a tribute to the integrity of the product or to the small size of the fleet and resulting low profile to FAA attention. Meyers owners have suffered ADs on the props, engines (including the cracking-crankcase Continental IO-520) and some appliances, but only the prop ADs have caused much vexation, judging from owners' comments. Likewise, maintenance costs reported by owners are extremely low for a complex airplane, and direct costs are eased by the high-speed cruise performance, which puts the airplane in the neighborhood of 14 miles per gallon in fuel economy.

One trouble with the Meyers 200 is the seats: there are only four of them

and it's cozy in back. This is merely a symptom of another problem that neither Meyers nor Aero Commander ever got around to addressing: the low 3,000-pound maximum gross weight and consequent lack of useful load, which runs around 900 pounds after the avionics are accounted for. When the Meyers took to the airways in the early 1960s, this was on a par with other airplanes in its class, such as the Beech Bonanza and Debonair, Cessna 210 and Piper Comanche. But all of these later added another row of seats, inched up the gross weight and offered the flexibility to haul five or six people a short distance or four people a long distance. The Meyers was doomed to remain a four-placer that can legally haul only two people plus baggage when the 80-gallon (74 usable) tanks are full.

However, the owners are fond of pointing out that all the paperwork for a gross weight raise to 3,300 pounds

was completed years ago and may still—someday—gain FAA approval; so in the meantime, some fly as if this were the legal limit.

History
The Meyers 200 was the last finished design of Al Meyers, who gained fame for the OTW ("Out To Win") biplane trainer of wartime years. Establishing a corps of engineers and craftsmen at Tecumseh, Michigan, Meyers also performed extensive work on a light twin that never saw production, and in postwar years turned his attention to a strongly built, speedy two-placer, the Meyers 145. Though certificated, this was practically a custom airplane, and few were ever built. The design did spawn the model 200, however, which has been described as "a 145 cut lengthwise and widened." It flew in 1953 but took until 1958 to be certified. It went into production and the first copies issued forth in 1959, but in

A generally slick aerodynamic package, despite the blunt nose, affords the Meyers its speed. Owners like to boast that the nosewheel is so well engineered it doesn't need a shimmy damper. Hidden beneath the smooth curves is a massive tubular framework that comprises the fuselage and cabin and the wing out to the landing gear.

the next five years Meyers built and sold only about 40 of them, before falling onto financial straits.

Along came Aero Commander, which was just then embarking on what became a career of trying to prove to itself that it can't build a single-engine airplane economically. Aero Commander's misapprehension was that the only problem in Tecumseh was high labor costs, which could be cured in a trice if the Meyers were built in Albany, Georgia. Aero Commander did turn out 95 of the Meyers 200s there from 1965 to 1967, but spent a lot of money in the effort, and a sharply escalating price tag couldn't save the Meyers from the fate of the Lark and the Darter (not to mention the 112 and 114 of later years). Aero Commander is rumored to have spent $4 million building airplanes whose total (list) value was $3 million, apparently using as its guideline the old saw about making a small fortune out of a big one.

During the Aero Commander years, the horsepower went from 260 to 285, to create the model 200D, but this was a change overseen by Meyers. Most other differences between the Meyers design and the Aero Commander execution are cosmetic, although speed was enhanced a bit by flush-riveting the wings on top. Since most Meyers aircraft in license today are of the Aero Commander ilk anyway, it adds a little snob appeal if one has a Meyers-built Meyers.

There is a distinction to be made if one has the original 200A and has a yen for more horsepower: this model needs some structural beef-ups, whereas the 200B and C will accept the 285-hp as almost a plug-in replacement. The holder of FAA approval to do the re-engining is Beaumont "Pard" Diver of Tecumseh Aircraft (Al Meyers Airport, Tecumseh, Mich. 49286;

Instrument panel is plain, flat, and utilitarian, *but manifold pressure and tachometer and fuel flow are relegated to the right in front of the copilot.*

phone 313-447-3752). Diver is the last active member of the old Meyers Aircraft crew and is known among owners for his ability to make just about any part necessary to keep the plane flying.

In 1968, Aero Commander sold the tools and certificates for the Meyers to Interceptor Corp., which set about to revolutionize general aviation (yet again) with a pressurized turboprop version, the Interceptor 400. The fabled 400 showed the slick airframe could be driven to cruise at about 275 mph behind a Garrett TPE 331 and could be pressurized to a legal 22,000 feet, provoking aviation writers of the time to call it a "dream come true." Unfortunately, only two were built and only one survives. Undercapitalization and the morass of FAA regulations left the company bankrupt, and it had only a dozen solid orders, when the machine was certificated in 1971. The company was reformed as Interceptor Co. and later went under the holding company, Prop Jets, Inc. (Box 1882, Boulder, CO 80306), whose head, Peter Paul Luce, holds onto all the type certificates and

a glimmer of hope that the 400—or maybe even the 200—may still return to production. In 1977, Luce licensed Carl Branson (Branson Aircraft, Unit B, 4275 Broadway, Denver, CO 80216; phone 303-825-3530) to put the 200 into production, but this fell through. Branson's company is still important to Meyers owners, however, because he retained the country's largest collection of spare parts for the airplane.

Performance

While some may look upon the 200-mph-plus cruise speed as the airplane's most enticing attraction, it is not the sole allure of the Meyers. Certainly, owners are happy to report cruise speeds in the neighborhood of 205 mph at 75 percent power, burning about 16 gallons an hour, and are equally pleased with moping along at "only" 195 mph burning 13.5 gph.

But the speed should be viewed with other performance features, like the low stall speed with full flaps, and the high gear-extension speed. The gear can be dropped at 170 mph (or even

Model	Year	Number Built	Average Retail Price	Cruise Speed (mph)	Rate of Climb (fpm)	Useful Load (lbs)	Fuel Std/Opt (gals)	Engine	TBO* (hrs)	Overhaul Cost
200A	1959	5	$26,750	195	1,150	1,130	42/80	260-hp Continental	1,200	$5,800
200A	1960	6	$26,750	195	1,150	1,130	42/80	260-hp Continental	1,200	$5,800
200B	1960	7	$28,000	195	1,245	1,025	42/80	260-hp Continental	1,200	$5,800
200B	1962	10	$28,000	195	1,245	1,025	42/80	260-hp Continental	1,200	$5,800
200C	1963	3	$29,500	195	1,245	1,025	42/80	260-hp Continental	1,200	$5,800
200C	1964	6	$29,500	195	1,245	1,025	42/80	260-hp Continental	1,200	$5.800
200D	1965	6	$33,000	210	1,450	1,015	42/80	285-hp Continental	1,200	$6,800
200D	1966	69	$34,000	210	1,450	1,015	42/80	285-hp Continental	1,200	$6,800
200D	1967	20	$36,000	210	1,450	1,015	42/80	285-hp Continental	1,200	$6,800

*Up to 1,500 hours TBO with improved valves.

210 mph in an emergency), a valuable tool for slowing up to enter the airport pattern. In addition, little or no trim change is required for flap or gear extension, which obviates extra pre-landing fiddling.

Push-pull tubes drive the ailerons and elevator, giving a direct-drive feel to the controls in comparison with cable-driven aircraft. Some pilots report a "heavy" feel to the controls, possibly created by the small radius of the yoke, but most of our surveyed owners consider this a virtue, making the Meyers a "good instrument platform." One owner went against the grain and declared it to be "very unstable in the roll axis," however. Takeoff and climb require a healthy amount of right rudder.

There is some disagreement among Meyers owners about landing the airplane. Most maintain that it develops a sharp sink rate that must be arrested by a large dose of power; cut the power too abruptly in an attempt to stop floating, and you get the hard landing you were trying to avoid.

Others say there is still ample elevator left in the flare (if flared low enough) not only to achieve a fine landing, but to cut the rollout to a bare minimum. Book figures call for a 1,150-foot landing over a 50-foot obstacle.

Why Buy It?

Undoubtedly, the lack of useful load costs the Meyers a lot on the used plane market. A 1967 Meyers 200D listed in that year for $35,365 and still draws $35,000 to $40,000 today, which is great tribute to an old airplane. But when this is matched against a 1967 V35 Bonanza, which listed then for $43,875 and now runs about $44,000, the comparison for some favors the Beech, with its five seats. Likewise, a 1967 Cessna Centurion sold then for $40,107 and now for about $33,500, also approaches the Meyers speed, and it has six seats. And both the Beech and Cessna are currently in production.

Further, if the Meyers suffered any comparison against four-seaters, it would have to include, say, a 1977 Mooney 201 selling for about $46,000, offering nearly the same speed on a lot less engine, and having the advantage of current production and support. Likewise with a 1977 Piper Turbo Arrow, now selling at around $45,250.

Still, Meyers owners are a little cultish and aren't interested only in utilitarian concerns. Rather, they are very proud of being able to walk away from other retractables by a knot or two at firewall speeds, and they prize the rugged construction. In both respects, they particularly like to fly or park alongside a Bonanza, and love it when somebody notices how much thicker the sheet metal is all over the Meyers, compared to the skins on the V-tail of the Beech. It should be mentioned, however, that the reputed extra strength of the Meyers is not documented in tangible terms like utility category (as the Bonanza is).

Safety Record

While it is unfair to make much of an accident record that could be greatly changed by the addition or subtraction of just one accident due to the small fleet size, we did query NTSB and obtain reports on Meyers accidents from 1974 through 1978 and have performed the arithmetic for the sake of information.

The airplanes suffered a total of 11 accidents in the period, one of them fatal and two others causing serious injuries. Posing 68 aircraft in the domestic fleet and assuming flight time of 100 hours a year (which is almost precisely what the Meyers owners reported to us), this would result in a total accident rate of 32.4 per 100,000 hours and a fatal accident rate of 2.9. For reference, earlier studies show the major single-engine retractables with

Fuel management *calls for switching to four separate tanks with the lever at the left of the pilot's leg. Fuel gauge shows only the fuel in the tank selected.*

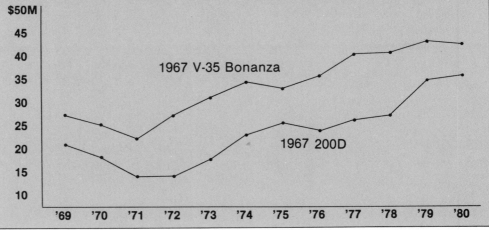

Investment Value

The last (1967) production model of the Aero Commander 200D shows a phenomenal increase in value through the last decade amounting to 240 percent from its low point in 1971. This exceeds even that of the Beech Bonanza V-35 during the same period—a rise of 187 percent.

1967 V-35 Bonanza

1967 200D

'69 '70 '71 '72 '73 '74 '75 '76 '77 '78 '79 '80

The aircraft has the luxury of both aileron and pitch trim. *The unorthodox pitch trim is the knurled vernier knob above the mike; aileron trim is located at the left of the white-tipped throttle control. Mixture is below and between throttle and prop.*

total accident rates ranging from 6.4 to 16.8 per 100,000 hours, and fatal accident rates from 2.0 to 3.8. Thus, the Meyers would appear to be about twice as bad as the worst single-engine retractable overall, but about in the middle as far as fatal accidents. Again, we find the Meyers numbers too small to use for meaningful comparison: one fatal accident less and it would have been best in its class.

Among causes for the 11 accidents, fuel system problems and fuel mismanagement top the list. In one case, a hose fitting came loose, and in another the lining of the metal-braided fuel hose sprang an unseen leak and sucked air. The grapevine of Meyers owners has spread the word, and many have replaced these metal-braided lines with ones that more readily reveal the leaks. In two other accidents, pilots ran out of fuel or ran tanks dry and killed the engine. The fuel system does require some attention, since there are four 20-gallon (18.5 usable) tanks, with a selector and a single gauge located on the left subpanel alongside the pilot's leg. On any fairly long trip, there will be two or three changes of tanks, and the only way to read the gauge for a tank is to switch to it.

The rest of the accidents were assorted. One resulted from a propeller failure, where the propeller had not been properly repaired according to an AD issued three years earlier. There was an accident involving engine failure for unknown reasons and another where the pilot over-leaned the mixture attempting to cope with high density altitude on takeoff. Two other accidents were runway mishaps—a hard landing and a skid into a snowbank. One pilot flew into the ground because of diverted attention (he survived) and another flew into a hill in IFR weather (he and his

passenger died).

Every Meyers owner we talked to was thoroughly indoctrinated with the safety features of the aircraft, and many tell of accidents they know about where the airplane took a terrible bludgeoning but the pilot walked away, because of the 4130 steel tubing that comprises the major structure of the fuselage and center section. Our small group of accident reports did not confirm or refute this. We do note the absence of any stall-spin accidents in the sample (the Meyers is reputed to maintain aileron control throughout the stall) and the absence of inadvertent gear-up landings. The detented gear lever is situated to the left of the throttle and is crowned by a massive wheel-shaped metal knob, easily distinguished from the flap-shaped flap lever of more discreet dimensions situated on the right of the throttle. An oddity is a vernier-type elevator trim control located where one would normally expect the mixture handle to be. However, we cannot think of a way

this quirk might contribute to design-induced error.

An engine-driven oil pump does double duty in operating the gear and extending the flaps. A wobble pump near the pilot's left knee serves as the backup for this system, so only a hydraulic leak could put the whole affair out of commission. Even then, there is a free-fall procedure for the landing gear, although a no-flaps landing would be necessary.

One of the subtle Meyers touches is the boarding step, which extends hydraulically when the gear are extended, and tucks itself away behind a cover when the airplane is cleaned up.

Maintenance

While a lot of the airplane is assembled from off-the-shelf fittings, Meyers owners report better success in certain areas, like fuel and hydraulic system maintenance, if the mechanic who works on the plane has been "educated" about it through experience. One owner said a mechanic caused the engine to cut out intermittently by installing a fuel fitting backwards, for instance.

We queried the entire registry of Meyers owners about maintenance costs and got responses from 23—a third of the fleet. Averaging their reports, an annual for the Meyers will be flat-rated at $287 and will actually cost $585 when the work is done. They report an average of $278 worth of unscheduled airframe maintenance a year, and $224 worth of unscheduled engine work, the airplane being out of service an average of nine days a year. All of these

Sports car interior *means fancy molded seats and "togetherness" in the rear. Note shoulder harnesses for the front seats.*

numbers are quite good in comparison with other aircraft (even those a couple of years old).

A Meyers with original brakes (Goodrich or Goodyear) is said to be miserable, both in performance and in the need for replacement brake pads at frequent intervals. A change to Cleveland brakes costs about $1,000 and converts the brake rating to "excellent," according to owners.

The Continental IO-470 and IO-520 engines started out with 1,200-hour TBOs, and many of the planes available on the used market will have original engines. Later powerplants got 1,500-hour TBOs. The IO-520 is notorious for cracking crankcases and drew ADs on the subject, but none of the Meyers owners reported any such problem. Their main AD annoyance is the propeller—either Hartzell (one AD) or McCauley (three ADs over the years).

Slick Electro magnetos came with the airplane, but apparently haven't irked the owners by malfunctioning frequently. The Airborne dry vacuum pump suffered an AD, and some owners have replaced several.

Two owners complained about not being able to get the door to seal well, creating excessive cabin noise. A major aggravation is the back-seat bench, a vacuum-formed plastic affair which breaks down with age. Vinson Vanderford (5852 Bogue Road, Yuba City, CA 95991; phone 916-673-2724) is a Meyers Association stalwart who copied the mold and had fiberglass replacements built for the many owners who have redone the interiors of the Meyers.

Conversions

Vanderford and 17 other Meyers Association members have banded together in a company (Mycom Development) seeking to gain a supplemental type certificate on a turbocharged Meyers, using a 310-hp TSIO-520R with a Garrett blower and a Hartzell three-bladed Q-tip propeller. It has flown and can hit 244 mph, they say. Their efforts also include drag reduction work: burying the landing lights in the wings and getting rid of the huge rotating beacon atop the tail, which tuft tests showed was one of the greatest sources of airflow separation on the otherwise extremely clean airframe. They also intend to seek a separate STC for Hoerner-type wingtips to improve roll rate, applicable to any Meyers model.

Daniel G. Skaggs (1155 A Ave. West, Seymour, IN 47274) told us he is working on a 400-hp installation of a Lycoming IO-720 on one of his 200Ds and expects to have it flying in about a year.

An owner with a run-out IO-470 engine who wishes to step up the 200D's IO-520 should contact the aforementioned Pard Diver at Tecumseh Aircraft, who has retained FAA approval for the mod.

Anybody thinking about buying a used Meyers should get in touch with a fellow named Gid Miller, in Frenchtown, N.J.; 201-996-2730. Miller is perhaps the country's reigning Meyers dealer. He usually has at least a couple in stock and probably knows the price and location of any others on the market.

Owners Association

The Meyer 200 Owners Association is a small but active group which stages an annual fly-in and issues a newsletter about four times a year. President is Chuck Haines, 1806 Hummingbird Drive, Costa Mesa, CA 92626.

Owner Comments

"The Meyers 200D has got to be the greatest plane ever built. Performance is tops and true IAS of 225 is not uncommon.

"The landing gear gave us some problems. A loose fitting on the hydraulic system caused many headaches. Once the problem was corrected the plane was flawless.

"The Meyers is the Ferrari of the sky. All high-performance airplanes should be modeled after this thoroughbred."

"With the steel cabin and wing center section, I feel safer in the Meyers than any other aircraft."

"Huge semi-fowler flaps require a great deal of power to handle approaches. It flies heavy, much like a military trainers on the approach, but is excellent for short-field landings."

"The McCauley prop has had, if memory serves, three ADs. The oil-filled mod was just done.

"The fuel lines with metal braid on outside are bad leakers. All were replaced with Aeroquip.

"Brakes (Goodyear) were never very good. They were replaced with Clevelands in April this year. They are excellent!

"Body integrity is good but the door is a nonfixable problem. It closes fine on ground but deforms in flight to create air leak and uncomfortable slipstream noise to right seat passenger."

"This is most trouble-free aircraft I have owned. My maintenance costs have been practically nil. I have flown this aircraft over 700 hours. This cost reflects parts

Semi-Fowler flaps *crank down 40 degrees and reduce the stalling speed to an astonishing 54 miles per hour.*

only as I am an A&P mechanic. However, the dependability I have experienced is fantastic.

"Having flown most high performance singles, I chose the 200D over others because of its outstanding performance, strength, and looks. The 'hangar tale' that it does not climb well is untrue. It will climb 1,000-1,400 feet fpm at 130-140 indicated."

"At initiation of cruise, the bird has a very definite 'step,' and it will fall off that step if anything more than very light turbulence is encountered. The step cruise is 10 to 15 mph higher than a turbulent cruise condition will permit.

"It is a good instrument platform except for one bad trait: it is very unstable in the roll axis, but a good wing leveler takes care of that.

"The landing gear rigging and maintenance must be done by a competent mechanic with a thorough knowledge of the bird."

"My purchasing decision rested among three airplanes: Bonanza, Centurion, and the Meyers. Evaluation of the Bonanza and Centurion proved those two airplanes were poorly constructed, over advertised, and over priced. The Meyers was hand-built, super strong, extremely fast, and fuel efficient.

"Best cruising altitude for the Meyers is between 8,000 to 12,000 feet. Single pilot, one person, 80 gallons of fuel, averages 13 gph at 195 mph true.

"It rides much like a Baron through turbulence and is very stable.

"Descending from cruising altitude to terminal speeds in major TCAs normally

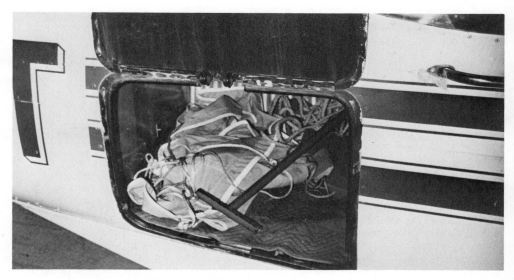
Baggage compartment *holds a respectable 200 pounds structurally.*

placed me in with heavy jets with no problem. The 240 mph red line enables the airplane to stay at jet approach speeds and land at major terminals with no fuss.

"Landing speed of 75 mph makes the aircraft extremely good in tight spaces. Operating the airplane at 350 hours a year averaged $10,000 for fixed and variable cost.

"If a product has to be carried, the three passenger seats can be removed in 40 seconds, giving a considerable amount of space. Any competent mechanic can work on this airplane, as all the systems are straightforward and require only a basic knowledge to figure out the most complex parts of the airplane."

"I am generally very pleased with this Meyers 200D manufactured by Aero Commander. Understandably, since manufacture was discontinued, parts availability presents a potential problem. However, the integrity of the airframe and a powerplant similar to the Bonanza (IO-520C) have not presented any major problems for me.

"Since I purchased the aircraft two years ago, the only major problem was in the hydraulic system for gear and flap operation. This has been corrected and no further problems in over a year.

"Flight characteristics are superb. Excellent speed, climb and slow flight with low stall speed and ability to operate economically at 10.5 gph.

"Range is satisfactory, but I regret that the aircraft was not certified for a higher gross weight.

"I recommend this as a fine aircraft, although I would be happier to know that parts and service were more readily available."

"There is no finer single-engine aircraft. The airframe and systems have never had an AD. It has a wider flight envelope, higher gear-down speed and better specs than any other single. All claims made in the manual are true. I have owned my aircraft for 12 years and my maintenance costs are less than $300 a year, total.

"The aircraft handles so well that my wife transitioned from a 150 to it and felt that the Meyers handled better the first time she flew it.

"As the aircraft gets older, some problems have arisen. The fuel hoses must be replaced. We have warm, dry weather, but some metal lines need checking for corrosion. The Meyers Association has a full list.

"I have never purchased any piece of machinery that has performed as well or been as reliable as this aircraft."

Massive bar alongside the door *eases entry and typifies what operators characterize as a quality of being "overbuilt."*

Old Mooneys are among the most popular used aircraft. Better than 4,000 of the M20 series (four-place, 180- and 200-hp) were built between 1955 and 1971, and they are beloved for their performance and efficiency,

General Characteristics of the M-20 Series:

Speed—Although Mooneys are fast, cruise speeds and climb rates claimed in the owner's manuals are usually quite optimistic (some cruise figures go as high as 187 mph), and we understand that up until recently they were calculated on aircraft weights way below gross. Nevertheless, the airplanes are still faster than other aircraft of similar power, sometimes by as much as 10 or even 15 mph. The other side of the coin is the fact that slowing down can be a real problem in Mooneys, thanks to the clean design and absurdly low gear-lowering speeds.

Handling—Stiff ailerons, with a short-travel control wheel and torque tubes instead of cables. A feature called Positive Control (PC) was made standard equipment on all Mooneys built between 1961 and 1975. PC is basically a wing-leveler autopilot that can't be turned off. For maneuvering, the PC can be cut out for short periods by pressing a button on the yoke. Some pilots praise it as an IFR lifesaver; others detest it and go to great lengths to short-circuit the system.

Visibility—Lousy. Tiny two-piece windshields and small side windows give a definite claustrophobic feeling in the older models.

Cabin room—You don't get something for nothing, and the price of high speed generally is a cramped cabin. The small windows on the older models add to the closed-in feeling of Mooney passengers, especially the back-seaters.

Gear and flaps—Until 1968, Mooneys had quick, simple manual gear and flap systems. The gear usually was justified by owners by its low maintenance, but it could be a thumb smasher, and it took up valuable floor space needed for manuals, etc. The flaps were lowered by positioning a lever and then pumping away on a small handle under the panel. In 1969, gear and flaps went electric.

Landings—Pilots often report having difficulty landing Mooneys with finesse consistently. Old hands blame this on a tendency of fliers to come in too hot, and floating excessively in ground effect during the flare. Nevertheless, the problem is exacerbated by mediocre flaps and difficulty getting an adequately steep approach without picking up excessive speed.

There is a bewildering variety of Mooney models and designations. We will group them into five categories.

1. Old M20s with wooden
   wings and tails   (M20, M20A)
2. Small-cabin 180-hp (M20B, M20C)
3. Small-cabin 200-hp   (M20E)
4. Large-cabin 200-hp   (M20F)
5. Large-cabin 180-hp   (M20G)

We do not include the later Mooney M20J 201 or M20 K 231 in this report.

Performance figures should be taken with a grain of salt. Note that in 1968, claimed speed and climb numbers changed singificantly. This was not the result of any change in the airplane, but apparently a new set of conditions for flight testing.

Price figures are for aircraft equipped with a 360-channel navcom, ADF, VOR, full panel, long-range fuel tanks and, when available, the PC wing-leveler. Price assumes 600 hours on the engine, with good paint and interior. Prices should be adjusted according to the equipment and condition of the individual aircraft.

Mark 21 and the Ranger.

The small-cabin 180-hp Mooney M20C series comprises among the most efficient and economical of all lightplanes. Real-world cruise speeds are in the 160-mph range with the 180-hp engine. While the 180-hp Arrow was considered underpowered and replaced with the 200-hp version, the Mooney has reasonable performance even with 180 hp. Rear seat room is minimal, however, and the M20C series offers marginal living space for long trips with adults in the rear seats.

The carbureted 180-hp Lycoming

A 60's vintage M20C Mooney. *The entire tail section pivots fore and aft for pitch trim.*

O-360 is very reliable, probably one of the best aircraft engines ever built. The O-360s built before 1968 had small exhaust valves and a short 1,200-hour TBO. The 1968 and later engines had half-inch valves and 2,000-hour TBOs. Early engines can be upgraded to a 2,000-hour TBO by installing half-inch valves, and potential buyers should check for this.

Wooden-wing, Wooden-tailed M20.
These can be bought dirt-cheap, for good reason. Airworthiness Directive 69 5-3 requires an inspection of the wing and tail every six months, at an average cost of $500 per inspection. Many M20s have had metal tails installed, which still leaves an annual wing inspection bill of about $200. If you happen to be a A&P mechanic and can do the wing work yourself, the Mark 20 would be a very good bargain; otherwise, we wouldn't recommend one.

M20E Super 21 or Chaparral.
This is the hot-rod of the Mooney line with a listed 75 percent cruise speed of up to 187 mph, although 170-175 is a more reasonable figure for a run-of-the-mill used plane. Climb rate is listed at 1,400 fpm for some models, much better than a new Bonanza.

Drawbacks are the tight rear seat shared with the M20C, and the Lycoming IO-360 200-hp engine. IO-360s built before 1971 have a short 1,200-hour TBO and a poor record of reliability. If overhauled with an up-

Extra fuselage stretch *and greater window area in the executive models helps overcome traditional Mooney cabin coziness.*

dated camshaft and dowel pins, however, TBO may be increased to 1,600 hours. Early IO-360s had weak connecting rods; make sure that stronger rods have been installed. Engine logs should be checked very carefully.

M20F Series
Popularly known as the executive, it was introduced in 1960 to quiet the cries of long-suffering Mooney back-seat passengers.

The fuselage is stretched 10 inches, and useful load and fuel capacity are increased. Some speed is sacrificed, of course, but the extra room and load quickly made the Executive the best seller of all the Mooney models. It remains the best all-around compromise among the used Mooneys.

The only fly in the ointment is the troublesome IO-360 engine, whose problems the Executive shares with the Chaparral. Again, check engine AD compliance carefully and try to get an engine that is updated with the new cam and dowel pins.

M20G Statesman
This combined the stretched fuselage of the Executive and the economical, reliable 180-hp Lycoming of the Ranger. (All Statesmen have half-inch valves and 2,000-hour TBOs.) However, the airplane proved to be somewhat underpowered, didn't sell very well and was taken off the market in 1970. But for pilots who don't need to haul heavy loads, the Statesman may be the best bargain of all the Mooneys, with its larger cabin and good engine.

Model	Year	Number Built	Average Retail Price	Cruise Speed (mph)	Rate of Climb (fpm)	Useful Load (lbs)	Fuel Std/Opt (gals)	Engine	TBO (hrs)	Overhaul Cost
M20	1955-57	197	$ 9,000	165	900	1,035	35	150-hp Lycoming	2,000	$ 4,000
M20A	1958-60	497	$12,000	180	1,150	1,010	35/52	180-hp Lycoming	2,000	$ 4,500
M20B	1961	221	$15,000	182	800	925	52	180-hp Lycoming	2,000	$ 4,500
M20C	1962-65	1,244	$17,000	182	1,150	1,050	52	180-hp Lycoming	2,000	$ 4,500
M20C	1966-67	430	$18,750	182	1,150	1,050	52	180-hp Lycoming	2,000	$ 4,500
M20C	1968-69	295	$21,000	172	1,000	1,050	52	180-hp Lycoming	2,000	$ 4,500
M20C	1970-71	99	$23,000	172	1,000	1,050	52	180-hp Lycoming	2,000	$ 4,500
M20C	1974-75	84	$27,500	172	1,000	1,050	52	180-hp Lycoming	2,000	$ 4,500
M20C	1974-75	84	$33,000	172	1,000	1,050	52	180-hp Lycoming	2,000	$ 4,500
M20C	1978-79	N/A	$50,000	172	1,000	1,050	52	180-hp Lycoming	2,000	$ 4,500
M20E	1964-65	690	$19,000	187	1,110	1,000	52	200-hp Lycoming	1,600	$ 6,000
M20E	1966-69	538	$20,750	187	1,110	1,000	52	200-hp Lycoming	1,600	$ 6,000
M20E	1969-71	155	$24,000	182	1,400	975	52	200-hp Lycoming	1,600	$ 6,000
M20E	1974-75	45	$30,000	182	1,400	975	52	200-hp Lycoming	1,600	$ 6,000
M20F	1967-69	837	$25,000	179	1,330	1,100	64	200-hp Lycoming	1,600	$ 6,000
M20F	1970-71	75	$27,500	179	1,330	1,100	64	200-hp Lycoming	1,600	$ 6,000
M20F	1975	71	$33,000	179	1,330	1,100	64	200-hp Lycoming	1,600	$ 6,000
M20F	1976-77	132	$35,000	179	1,330	1,110	64	200-hp LYcoming	1,600	$ 6,000
M20J (201)	1977	377	$43,750	195	1,030	1,100	64	200-hp Lycoming	1,600	$ 6,000
M20J (201)	1978	395	$51,500	195	1,030	1,100	64	200-hp Lycoming	1,600	$ 6,000
M20J (201)	1979	135	$56,000	195	1,030	1,100	64	200-hp Lycoming	1,600	$ 6,000
M20K (231)	1979	247	$61,000	210	1,080	1,100	73	210-hp Continental	1,800	$ 7,250

Fixed-gear Masters

From 1963 to 1965, Mooney built about 160 of these M20Ds, fixed-gear versions of the 180-hp mark 21. The vast majority of Masters have been converted to retractable gear, so check carefully that a so-called Mark 21 is not really a converted Master.

Good Years and Bad

Mooney connoisseurs tell us the best Mooneys ever built were the 1964 and 1965 Mark 21s—the 180-hp models with manual gear and flaps. If they've been updated with half-inch valves, so much the better.

However, early 200-hp Super 21s (1963-64) had some serious engine troubles, and should be avoided—or at least bought with caution at lower-than-book prices.

Check Points

Look over the nose gear very closely. Mooneys are susceptible to damage from mishandling by lineboys during ground towing operations.

Check trim tab. The 1961-64 M20Cs had problems with trim tabs that tended to get bound up.

Where To Go

A poll of Mooney owners taken by the International Mooney Society once ranked the top four Mooney dealers in the country for service and selection of used aircraft. The runaway winner was McCauley Aviation in Pine Bluff, Arkansas. The rest of the best:

2. Willmar Air Service, Willmar, Minn.

3. Dugosh Aviation, Kerrville, Texas (best place for wooden wing and tail work).

4. Ft. Dodge Aviation, Ft. Dodge, Iowa.

Modifications

Surprisingly, there is only one major modification widely available for the Mooneys—a Rajay turbocharger. New price installed is about $8,000, and a used Rajayed Mooney will command from $3,000-$5,000 more than a standard airplane, depending on how old it is. Before a sale is finalized, a buyer of a used Rajay Mooney should check that it can pull sea level power (28-29 inches) at 17,000 feet and 75 percent power at 20,000 feet and a max altitude of 30,000 feet. Rajay Industries, 2602 E. Wardlow Road, Long Beach Airport, Long Beach, CA 90801.

Owner Comments

Maintenance and Operations

"My biggest complaint is the lack of service personnel with a background in Mooneys. My last annual inspection cost $625, of which $225 was for the propeller AD. I had some serious airframe problems. On the landing roll the nose had a tendency to dart sharply either left or right. The IA said the steering and nose-gear linkage had been checked, and nothing was worn or loose. Later I wrote the Mooney factory asking their assistance. I'm still waiting to hear from them—seven months later.

"Recently I contacted Mooney dealer Reliant Aviation in Albany, Oregon, and asked them about the problem. They suggested several possible causes, and as a result we were able to determine that a nose-gear steering horn bushing kit ($14.95) was needed. Three days later the kit arrived, and the problem was solved. I highly recommend Reliant Aviation for Mooney owners in the Pacific Northwest.

"I've also had excellent success dealing with Charles Mosier of Arkansas Instruments in Little Rock, Ark. His company overhauls Mooney instrument clusters, and their service is exceptionally fast."

"Repair of gas tank leaks and replacement of landing gear rubber biscuits cost $1,200. Fuel was leaking in the wheel wells and off the wing roots into the cabin area. They found the shaft through the nose-gear rubber biscuits rusted one-third of the way through from water collection. Nose-gear adjustment: $150.

"If the nose gear rubber is replaced, be sure the mechanic lines up the nose gear and rudder. Mine didn't. As a result, the airplane, a '65 Super 21, swerved disconcertingly when taking off and transitioning from nose-gear steering to rudder control. The same thing happened on landing. A friend had the same problem with his Mooney."

"Mechanics frequently complain about tight work space and difficulty in removing cowlings and inspection plates. Ohio's Wittenbrook has a good Mooney following, but it's a 'one-horse' outfit. Mooney deserves more."

"I used to think the Mooney required a lot of maintenance, but after lengthy discussion with the partner responsible for maintenance, I would say it's only a tad higher than average in cost if all work is done by shop people. You can quickly bring the cost down by unbuttoning and closing it up yourself, and doing a few other time-consuming but undemanding chores that mechanics must charge for.

"With the exception of the engine, durability is outstanding. We've changed tires, of course, and a few other minor things like nose-wheel shims, etc.; but as a whole, the plane, at age 12, is as good as new. The engine is another story. We elected to have it majored upon compliance with that disastrous AD a couple of years ago. The engine at that time was a T. W. Smith major, so this represented the second overhaul. After about 60-70 hours, the whole thing had to be done again.

"Then about six months ago we discovered a hairline crack in the engine case. We could have fixed it (for under $1,000), or traded, or put in another overhauled or remanufactured engine. But—and I think this spells out our feelings about the Mooney very clearly—we elected to have a virgin engine installed, right off Lycoming's assembly line. We even let Lycoming install it; if any problems developed, we didn't want to get into a hassle between manufacturer and installer. The price tag was high (about $8,000), but we think it was a better bargain than the alternatives."

Executive panel *has multi-type throttle quadrant, unusual placement of the gear lever high up on the left side of the panel.*

High-level hatch *takes shoulder muscles for loading heavy baggage.*

Handling

Our club's '67 Executive handles well throughout its performance range—stall to 200 mph. But the controls, even with P.C. punched in, make for a handful because of the stiff, solid feel. This built-in stability is swell 95 percent of the time, but to really maneuver, you'll end up with a tired thumb and arms."

"Handling is also a joy. Once you become accustomed to the short-coupled, rod-connected controls, the analogy to a sports car is very appropriate. Crisp responses and predictable handling make it an excellent IFR airplane, although precise altitude-holding requires a little more attention than in some other planes. And recovery from an accidental spin (intentional ones are prohibited) is breathtaking until the control surfaces decide to bite in, usually 1½ to 3 turns after application."

"Pitch changes are excessive when full flaps are retracted on go-arounds. The ailerons are stiff at cruise speeds, but this poses few problems. Even with full flaps, short, steep approaches are impossible. The aircraft is difficult to get down from altitude with the rpm limits imposed, and it floats badly on landings."

"An operational inconvenience is the relatively low gear-down speed (104 knots). This is aggravated by the need to use power where descending to avoid over-cooling, and the extremely clean design that takes the airspeed up to 140 knots with little encouragement."

"I like the manual gear very much. Once

you get the knack, it doesn't take a lot of muscle and is actually quicker than the electric."

"Stability and panel layout on my 180-hp M20C made the aircraft extremely suitable for IFR work without the need for an autopilot, although the cramped quarters required care in the stowing of charts.

"In operating the aircraft I had to be on top of the following items:

"Carburetor air temperature—engine was very prone to carb ice. Top of cowl and windshield must be kept properly sealed to prevent rain from entering and destroying radios. The manual landing gear must be lubed every 50 hours. In freezing weather, care must be taken to see that the flaps are not frozen in up position; otherwise the hydraulic actuating mechanism can be damaged. Airframe icing—aircraft would carry some ice but would lose all climb capability with any accumulation whatsoever. I never solved the problem of fuel siphoning overboard through the fuel caps in a climb with full tanks. New fuel caps did not help, and I noted that the 1964 models had a different type of cap."

Performance

"Economical performance has got to be the Mooney's strongest suit. Even after seven years, I'm continually amazed at four- to six-hour trips averaging nine gph and 160+ mph in our '64 Super 21 at modest (60%-65%) power settings, and with adequate reserves. We have a well-equipped panel, but still have about 620 pounds of payload with full tanks."

"In a fly-off with a '55 Bonanza with the standard 225 Continental the results were as follows: Climb from 1,000 to 6,000 feet resulted in the Mooney's winning by 10 seconds. There was no discernible difference at full cruise power at 4,000 feet. I use a cruise climb of 120 mph, and this nets me approximately 800 fpm to about 5,000 feet; then about 500 fpm up to 8,000 feet, then 300-400 fpm up to 11,000 feet. This is with my standard load of two adults, one child and a full load of luggage and utilizing the ram-air above 5,000 feet."

"Cost of operation is very low for the performance. In 1977, DOC was $13.50/hr. including gas, oil, 100-hour inspections, parts and $2/hr. engine reserve. This is at power settings of 55-70 percent power and true airspeeds of 120-130 knots. (*No way will it make the advertised cruise speeds,* at least not with 1,000 hours on the engine. In an air race, at low altitudes, full power, and running light, it averaged *165 mph* over a 400-mile closed course.) Fuel consumption is about 7.9 gals./hr."

"At 10.5 gph the aircraft would give me 165 mph at 7,000 feet although that

dropped to 145 mph at 2,500 feet. With careful leaning I could often get the same speeds at less than 10 gph."

Comfort

"Cabin comfort is adequate in the front seats, with the possible exception of space to shift my size 15s around when they get tired of resting on the pedals. Much has been written about the Mooney's cramped cabin, but I'm 6'3", weigh in at 250 pounds and, except for the entry-exit procedure (which takes a little practice), am perfectly comfortable on long flights."

"As for cabin comfort, study your way in and out, but once inside, it has all the room you need, even with four aboard. The cabin is noisy, and the door has an air whistle because it doesn't fit well, and the interior plastic has begun cracking."

"As is often stated, you wear a Mooney like a pair of jeans. They are always tight, but comfortable. The front seats are narrow, to allow for the manual gear handle, and the nosewheel compartment awkward but after some conditioning it works out. By the way, I am 6'1" and weigh 175 pounds. Noise levels, especially the prop beating on the windscreen, are high but in the final analysis about average for older airplanes. Luggage room is ample and it will hold as much as the trunk of my Oldsmobile Cutlass. Visibility is fair to good with the nose sitting up quite high. Rear seat room is quite adequate for all but the taller people. As in all low-wing single-door aircraft, entry and exit should be an Olympic event."

General Impression

"I found the *quality of the workmanship* which went into the airframe to be *excellent.* With over 2,000 hours on the aircraft it was very tight, and the panels, with the exception of some minor hangar rash, looked like they had just been made."

"*Quality of workmanship,* design and attention to detail on my '66 M20C is *remarkable.* For example, note the covers on the aileron hinges, the seals on the control surface joints, flush rivets and torque tube control rods."

"Our club fliers love the Mooney and will upgrade Mooney for top economy and speed in its price range."

"The Mooney is one of the best cross-country aircraft I have seen. However, I feel that this is not the airplane for a beginner due to the poor IFR panel layout, the difficulty in descending from altitudes, the excessive float on landing and the manual gear system."

"The aircraft is currently *appreciating* at about the general inflation rate. Thus its real value is nearly constant."

Piper Arrow

When future aviation historians look back on the current era, Piper's Cherokee series may well stand out as an achievement rivaling, if not surpassing, such monuments as the Bonanza or the Cessna 172.

The original design was a lineal descendant of a two-place homebuilt, John Thorp's "Sky Skooter." At Piper, Karl Bergey and Fred Weick (the latter was the designer of the Ercoupe) breathed upon the design to make a more salable four-placer, and the Cherokee was born.

What's remarkable about this basic design isn't so much the basic, original Cherokee as the fact that it has been successfully developed into a multitude of growth versions. These include various fixed-gear versions, some with the original "mattress" wing, some with the newer tapered version, with power ranging from 150 to 300 hp and seating ranging from two to seven; and retractables including the four-place Arrow, the six-seven-place Lance and Saratoga, and the twin-engine Seneca—basically still a Twin Cherokee.

In this instance, we'll take a look at one of the most popular members of the Cherokee tribe, the basic four-place retractable, the Arrow. Whoever at Piper had the bright idea of putting fold-up wheels on the Cherokee deserves more than just the key to the executive washroom; since its introduction in 1967 the Arrow has been the best-selling "light retractable."

Actually, the Arrow's introduction in 1967 was something of a milestone in the industry, since it represented the first real entry by one of the Big Three into the field of light retractables, an area hitherto totally dominated by Mooney. True, Piper *had* offered a 180-hp version of the Comanche, but the price differential between that model and the Comanche 250 was small enough so that the majority of buyers opted for the bigger engine.

Of course, there was more to the Arrow than just its light retractable character. Piper also used the Arrow to introduce a new instrument panel arrangement, with the flight instruments in the "sacred six" arrangement rather than the earlier random

scatter, and the power instruments moved to the bottom-of-the-panel position they've occupied ever since. The power controls were changed from the traditional plunger type to a multiengine-style "Sports Power Console," which has since not only remained standard in the various Cherokees but has also been adopted by many other manufacturers.

No Belly Flops

Most important, though, was the Arrow's automatic landing-gear actuation system, designed to prevent both belly flops and premature retraction. Not only did the system work as advertised; it contributed heavily to both sales and rentals of Arrows, allowing a whole new segment of the flying public to enjoy the benefits and satisfaction of retractable flight, since insurance companies were considerably more sanguine about allowing low-time pilots with little retractable experience to fly the Arrow than they would have been for ships without the auto-gear feature.

The gear system has remained basically unchanged throughout the history of the model, and is a very simple one: impact air is taken from a probe on the left side of the fuselage, which is subject to airflow from the propeller blast as well as the aircraft's forward speed. This pressure is conducted

to a chamber where it acts on a fairly large diaphragm; as long as the pressure exceeds a certain value (corresponding to about 105 mph power off or 85 mph with full power), the diaphragm holds a hydraulic valve closed against spring pressure. Should the air pressure decrease, the valve opens and the gear free-falls into the down-and-locked position just as it would in an emergency gear extension — in fact, it's the same valve. At the same time it moves the valve, the diaphragm trips a microswitch to sound a horn and light a light to warn the pilot that, although the gear has lowered, the gear handle is still in the "up" position.

Override

Emergency gear lowering—in the event the electrically driven hydraulic system has failed—is done by pressing a small lever between the seats. This manually opens the valve in the automatic unit, regardless of airspeed; moving this lever the other way overrides the auto unit to keep the gear up at any airspeed. In earlier Arrows, the handle was spring-loaded and had to be held to keep the gear from extending when practicing stalls or slow flight. Later versions incorporate a latch, as well as a flashing amber "auto ext. off" light to remind the pilot the auto feature had been locked out. This, incidentally, can be a safety feature in the

1975 model has a bluebook *retail value of $29,000. Dealer wholesale is about $24,500, and some hard bargaining should get the price down near $26,000. This price applies to an average IFR airplane with a mid-time engine.*

event of an engine failure. In earlier models, the gear would come down at best glide speed, reducing an already underwhelming glide, unless the pilot could spare a hand to hang on to the overrride lever while still flying the plane and trying to restart the engine.

The Arrow stacks up pretty much in the middle of the other light retractables, in terms of performance. It's not as fast as the Mooney, of course, and even gives away a few knots to the Cessna Cardinal RG; but then, it's considerably roomier than the Mooney. It is, of course, both cheaper and better-performing than the Beech Sierra; on the other hand, one can ask, "What price retractables?" since the Arrow's performance is not much better than that of the Gulfstream American Tiger—which has a fixed-pitch prop, the cheaper to operate and maintain 180-hp engine, and a virtually foolproof system to prevent gear-up landings: fixed gear.

Owners generally report Arrow speeds in the 160-165 mph range, at about 10-12 gph, depending on leaning procedures. This provides a reasonable speed without the high fuel consumption of the bigger retractables.

Piper held the original price through 1967 and 1968; in 1969 base price rose to $17,500 for the basic 180-hp Arrow, while at the same time the 200-hp version was introduced for only $500 more. Obviously, most purchasers opted for the bigger mill, even though its TBO was only 1,200 hours vs. 2,000 hours for the 180. Of course, not all the engines went all the way to TBO. Even so, the 180-hp version of the Arrow hung on until 1971, by which time the price differential between the two models had risen to $1,250.

The Stretch

In 1972 came a significant change to the line: the introduction of the Arrow II. The modifications included a five-inch fuselage stretch between the front and rear seats, for better leg room in back and a wider door, and a 26-inch wingspan increase which allowed a 50-pound boost in gross weight. Stabilator span was also increased, and this

was the year the locking auto-gear override appeared.

TBO had gone to 1,400 hours in 1971 with the introduction of larger bearing dowels; with a redesigned camshaft, appearing on all the Arrows by 1973, TBO went to 1,600 hours. Buyers of used pre-73 Arrows that have been through an overhaul should have a good look at the engine logs to see whether the big dowels and/or new camshaft were installed at the overhaul; otherwise they're still stuck with the 1,200-hour TBO.

Since 1972, relatively few significant changes appeared in the design until 1977, when the Arrow III was announced with the semi-tapered wing already in use on the Warrior and Archer series; pluses for the new wing are slightly better performance and improved handling, as well as a considerably flatter glide. Also introduced in 1977 was the Turbo Arrow III, which mates the basic Arrow III airframe with a turbocharged six-cylinder Continental similar to that used in the Seneca II, with a new and rather exotic-looking fiberglass cowling. TBO on the turbo engine went back down to 1,400 hours.

For a retractable, the Arrow has fared relatively well in the Airworthiness Directive arena; there are 14 extant on the oldest (1967) model, but many are relatively minor, dealing with such things as replacement of an induction hose, tightening the fuel strainer drain, and fixing the electric trim switch. The major ones include replacement of gear retraction fittings—this is a 1968 AD which should have been complied with in almost all airplanes by now—and a more recent nosegear trunnion replacement called for in a 1976 AD. The 1975 AD calling for adjustment and possible replacement of quick-disconnect rear seats in almost all Pipers applies to the Arrow, but few seats have had to be replaced outright.

The 1972 and later models are somewhat more desirable, since the five-inch stretch did a lot for rear cabin leg room; the increased span and higher aspect ratio improved both climb and cruise a bit despite

Pitot mast below pilot's window *senses airspeed and automatically lowers the landing gear below 105 mph, power off. Because of this feature, insurance companies often will insure pilots with a minimum amount of retractable time.*

the 50-pound gross weight increase. Things to look out for include a history of engine problems—some IO-360s were, frankly, lemons—and perhaps a history of erratic gear operation, which could require replacement of the auto-gear actuator or the electro-hydraulic power pack.

Parts and Service

Parts and service are, for once, no particular problem; the aircraft continues in production, and parts commonality with earlier Arrows and with other Cherokees is excellent, so any Piper dealer should have, or be able to get, whatever is necessary. The airplane is a relatively easy one to work on; even the gear system is fairly accessible, and the average mechanic—whether at a Piper dealer or an independent—will probably have encountered enough Arrows to have developed some modicum of expertise.

Model	Year	Number Built	Average Retail Price	Cruise Speed (mph)	Rate of Climb (fpm)	Useful Load (lbs)	Fuel Std/Opt (gals)	Engine	TBO (hrs)	Overhaul Cost
PA-28R-180	1967-69	1,247	$17,000	162	875	1,120	48	180-hp Lycoming	2,000	$5,500
PA-28R-180	1970-71	33	$19,500	162	875	1,120	48	180-hp Lycoming	2,000	$5,500
PA-28R-200	1971	230	$20,000	166	910	1,140	48	200-hp Lycoming	1,600	$5,800
Arrow II	1972-73	786	$25,000	165	900	1,130	48	200-hp Lycoming	1,600	$5,800
Arrow II	1974-75	703	$28,000	165	900	1,130	48	200-hp Lycoming	1,600	$5,800
Arrow III	1976-77	N/A	$31,000	165	900	1,130	48	200-hp Lycoming	1,600	$5,800
Arrow III	1978	317	$40,000	165	900	1,130	48	200-hp Lycoming	1,600	$5,800
Turbo III	1977	427	$41,500	192	940	1,362	72	200-hp Continental	1,800	$7,250
Turbo III	1978	373	$45,000	192	940	1,362	72	200-hp Continental	1,800	$7,250
Arrow IV	1979	N/A	$53,000	165	831	1,149	72	200-hp Lycoming	1,600	$5,800
Turbo IV	1979	N/A	$58,000	192	940	1,362	72	200-hp Continental	1,800	$7,250

Piper Arrow

Owner Comments

"As for comfort, performance and handling, I think an Arrow offers about everything you would want in a four-place airplane. And it is a legitimate four-place airplane; you can carry four people with baggage, and get book performance from it.

"What I especially like about the Arrow is that it is a good cross-country airplane. You can cover 600 miles non-stop in about 3.7 hours. As for fuel consumption, 9.5 gallons an hour at cruise (2400 rpm at 23 inches) is consistent.

"I have had no difficulty getting parts—they seem to be readily available.

"The Arrow has a reputation for having a rather rapid sink rate once the power is cut. There is some truth in this, but it isn't as bad as some non-Arrow pilots believe. However, an Arrow does land more smoothly with a little power.

"I would also point out that the Arrow's cockpit is rather spacious. Although I'm tall (six feet, two inches, 230 pounds), I do not feel cramped in it.

"The Arrow is a stable airplane that handles with ease. Trim it up, and it nearly flies itself. This reduces pilot fatigue on long cross-country flights.

"As for maintenance, the Arrow costs a little more for an annual because of its retractable gear. The price in this area as of 1976 for an annual was about $265 plus parts."

"The Arrow is a very comfortable two-place airplane, but marginal for our family of four—crowded in back, and hard on passengers for long trips.

"Most of our flying is in the West and we get only marginal performance climbing out of high-altitude fields. You need to be alert and extremely aware of density altitude. We plan early morning departures and only partially full tanks, which of course limits the effective range. Again, with only two people, no problems.

"The finish on the plane has held up exceptionally well, as has the interior. Resale value seems good according to what I see in the advertisements.

"No surprises in flying the Arrow, with very straightforward systems. It's helpful to make approaches at 85-90 mph with a little power—nose gear tends to drop heavily after landing rollout, but if one is alert to this, it can be prevented.

"The Arrow is a good used plane in the $17,000 to $20,000 range, that won't be used exclusively at high density altitudes. It's economical to operate, parts and service readily available and no surprises for the pilot transitioning to retractable gear and constant-speed propeller.

"The cost of our annual inspections ran from $234 to $350. Maintenance items have included: starter motor replaced, $100; landing gear hydraulic pack, $250; AD on Hartzell prop, $350; vacuum pump, $170. The cost of one major annual cost us $1,200 when we replaced oil lines, heater muffs, rebushed the gear, replaced nose strut housing, brakes and rebuilt the mags. (All these prices are from about 1976; adjust accordingly.)

"Every 50 hours I change the oil, filter, inspect and rotate sparkplugs and check the compression. This runs about $30. I add one quart of oil every 9-10 hours (the engine has 1,600-plus hours now.) The compression remains unchanged during all these years. We cruise at 155 mph, average 9.5-10 gph. I feel the Arrow 180 is economical, and a good buy; I'm generally very pleased."

"I've operated a 1971 Arrow on a lease-back operation for about a year. In that time, it's flown 150 hours or so, and we're satisfied with the airplane. From a flight school's point of view, it's an attractive airplane because it's so easy for Chero-kee 140 and 180 pilots to transition into. The automatic landing gear system is excellent. I've never even heard of an Arrow ever being landed gear up. If anything goes wrong, the wheels simply come down. It's also a simple gear system from the maintenance point of view.

"Our airplane has 2,200 hours total time, and 600 hours on a major overhaul. According to the logbook, the first engine went 1,600 hours, which is 200 hours more than the TBO at that time, which was 1,400. (They raised it to 1,600 hours in 1973 when the better dowel pins were introduced.) All in all, we've found it to be one of the more economical retractables, because the Cherokee line is so familiar to most mechanics, and therefore relatively easy to work on.

"We've had no major problems with the engine, although I've heard other people have. (I know one pilot around here who broke a rod in a brand new 1973 Beech Sierra.)

"We get about 160-65 mph on 11 gph, which isn't bad. Interior room is adequate, at least in the front seat. However, the back seats are lacking in knee room—a situation Piper corrected in 1972. It's still better than an older Mooney, though. (I'm a large person, and I can take the "sports car feel" only so long.)

"We figure on $400 to $500 for a 100-hour inspection, and the last annual cost $1,000, even with no major problem. (We might have gotten stung a bit by the local mechanic, however. He insisted on replacing the fuel pump because the fuel pressure gauge vibrated like crazy. I've flown half a dozen Arrows, and they all do that.) Our airplane has a couple of other annoying quirks like a manifold pressure gauge that lags and sticks, but overall, most of our problems with the airplane have involved the radios (Narco Mark 12s and Mark 16s, incidentally). It's a good airplane maintenance-wise because it's simple, and doesn't shake itself to pieces.

"Before we started renting out this aircraft, we did a thorough study of total operating costs, including depreciation, overhaul reserve—the whole nine yards. Based on a purchase price of $22,000 for the used airplane, we arrived at $23 per hour, which is rather low for a retractable airplane."

"We'd advise anyone buying a used Arrow to do a retraction test and a detailed inspection of the landing gear. For reasons I won't go into here, we bought the airplane without having a mechanic look it over, and had to spend $1,000 putting in torque links and some other stuff. (Ours was a 1968 model.) We then gave it a major overhaul, and almost immediately had to put in a new cylinder. Overall, we're not very pleased with the amount of maintenance it's needed."

Baggage access is good, but like all Cherokees, the Arrow has but one door.

Cessna Cardinal RG

The Cessna Cardinal RG involuntarily followed the tenet, "Live it up, die young and leave a beautiful corpse." Considered by many to be one of the handsomest lightplanes to roll off a production line, the Cardinal RG enjoyed an all-too-brief eight-year manufacturing span before being terminated.

The line was discontinued in 1978; naturally, this cast some doubt on parts availability in the future. Termination of production also usually has a depressing effect on resale values, probably for the reason just mentioned.

Cardinal RG owners, however, tend to be extremely proud of their aircraft and characterize them as well above normal in good looks, cabin room and comfort, and visibility, not to mention handling. The Cardinal RG, though, seems to have been troubled over the years with more than its fair share of nettlesome problems with accessories and peripheral components.

Competitors
Its main competitor in the used-plane arena is probably the Piper Arrow series, though of course the Mooneys and Beech Sierras also share the 200-hp retractable market slot. The Cardinal RG is a clear winner over all the others except the Sierra in cabin room and comfort, and can leave all but the Mooneys in its wake when it comes to cruise speed. On top of that, it has probably the best load-carrying capacity in its crowd, by a small margin.

General Appraisal
Although the brochures describe the Cardinal RG as a 148-knot/170-mph cruiser, most owners report real-life cruise speeds more in the neighborhood of 140-145 knots/161-167 mph. This still puts it a few knots slower than the Mooneys, especially the 201s. Pilots regard their Cardinal RGs as fairly frugal aircraft for the speed, though, and report fuel consumption of from nine to 10 gph.

They say the birds ride well in tur-

bulence, have nice-handling controls, provide a stable "instrument platform" and behave admirably in slow flight. To go with the gorgeous, roomy cabin, they report it is "almost impossible" to load the aircraft out of the center of gravity envelope.

Baggage loading is a bit awkward, though, since suitcases that fit through the horizontally mounted baggage door then must be finessed into one of two vertical slots on either side of the wheel well hump. This unfortunately sits right in the middle of the baggage compartment.

Everybody raves about access to the cabin through the pair of four-foot-wide doors. On the other hand, nearly everybody complains about how difficult it is to get the doors to seal properly. Since they catch every passing breeze like sails, they are easily stressed out of rig. The result all too often: a lot of needless cockpit din from air whistling through the seals, and the danger of an in-flight shower bath when rain is encountered.

In this respect, the Cardinal RGs share the aquatic fate of other Cessnas, if we are to believe owner reports, since many simply leak in the rain—not just from door seals, but windshield joints as well.

One owner noted ruefully, "Once,

while flying through heavy rain, we nearly drowned a right-seat passenger, and have on occasion dampened the pilot."

Pilots also report poor heating for rear-seat passengers.

History of Model Changes
Since the Cardinal RG's introduction in 1971 the aircraft has undergone only a few modest changes through the years. The '72 model picked up a few knots in cruise speed and a slightly better climb rate, thanks mainly to a new prop. This model also did away with the fixed cabin steps and instead placed foot pads on the landing gear struts.

The '73 model came out with a slightly redesigned nose cowl and upped the usable fuel from 50 to 60 gallons. In addition, it changed the fuel selector system from one limited to "off" and "both," to one that also provided "left" and "right" tank selections.

In 1976 a larger instrument panel was installed, along with simplified landing gear hydraulics and a stronger nose gear trunion.

In 1977 the fuel selector was standardized with those of the rest of the Cessna single-engine fleet.

And in 1978 the aircraft was given a 28-volt electrical system and an improved gear retraction power pack.

Super good looks and aerodynamic styling *go together in the Cardinal RG to produce the best cruise speeds in its class—except for the Mooneys.*

Resale Value

The Cardinal RG shows a fairly standard resale value curve, dropping in price the first few years, and leveling off nicely. However, only time will tell how the line's discontinuance will affect these curves. Tracking the first '71 model, we found it shed about $11,000 in the first three years and then began to recoup by another $4,000 or so on the average in the next four to five years. The '75 model Cardinal RG bottomed even earlier, in just two years, after losing only $8,000, and then held fairly steady for the next three years.

Safety Record

The Cardinal RG appears to have a better than average accident rate among single-engine retractables. Based on NTSB data from 1973-1977, it has about 1.4 fatal accidents per 100,000 flying hours and nine total accidents per 100,000 hours.

The largest proportion of accidents—about one-third—in the Cardinal RG was attributed to engine failures, though these were seldom fatal.

Stall/spin/mush accidents in this type aircraft were fairly infrequent; and quite a few pilots landed gear up because they forgot to lower it.

Out of the 78 accidents reported in the NTSB records for the five-year period there were two in-flight airframe failures. One which occurred in weather was fatal; in the second case the pilot overstressed the aircraft and bent the wings, but actually managed to land safely.

A total of 12 of the 78 accidents, or about 15 percent, were fatal.

All the Cardinals have a "both tanks" selector system, which usually tends to greatly diminish fuel mismanagement problems.

After engine failures and wheels-up landings, the third greatest cause of Cardinal RG accidents involved ground loop/swerve problems.

Powerplant Failures

To check whether there was some pattern to the engine failures, we scrutinized the Safety Board listings for the '76-'78 period and found that the largest number—five—was related to magneto defects. Furthermore, all the problems were associated with engine accessories, not with the basic core of the Lycoming IO-360, which, of course, had its share of problems some

A perfectly normal touchdown—only with the nosegear jammed in the up position. The pilot, who shut down the engine on a quarter-mile final to lessen damage, said his glider training came in handy.

years ago.

However, one group of Cardinal RG co-owners reported a disturbing problem with the Lycoming IO-360. It quit three times on final approach. The first two times the engine stoppage was not discovered until safely on the runway, when the pilots found the powerplant windmilling when they tried to add power to taxi off the active. Mechanics attributed the stoppage to lead-fouled plugs.

The third stoppage occurred during a prolonged descent to an airport with power reduced during a 20-mile final. The aircraft was set down on the face of a gully and severely damaged, as was the pilot.

Other problem accessories included: engine fuel pump, fuel line fasteners, oil pump, prop governor and fuel injection diaphragm.

Of the 58 accidents logged during the last period examined, only three were attributed to undershoots and overshoots—a much lower frequency than is usually associated with the heavier singles like the Cessna 210 and Bellanca Viking.

Maintenance Problems

Cardinal RG owners reported a lengthy list of apparently chronic maintenance problems, most of them related to accessories. As one owner put it: "If it were in my power, I would give a medal to the man who developed the Cardinal design, and I would throw in jail the man choosing the equipment sources."

Below are the nine problem areas most frequently reported by owners who responded to our reader feedback request:

• Repeated alternator failures.
• Bendix magneto breakdowns, big repair bills.

• Cracking exhaust pipes, needing welding.
• Malfunctioning fuel quantity gauges.
• Alternate air induction doors breaking.
• Vented fuel caps allowing water in fuel tanks.
• Engine running hot.
• Malfunctioning landing gear mechanism, especially hung-up nosegear.
• Landing gear horn malfunctioning.

Owners attempting to cope with these problems rated dealer and manufacturer support fair to poor. In our December 1, 1978 airframe and powerplant survey of subscribers, the Cardinal RG had the highest frequency of malfunctions and next-to-worst record of dealer/manufacturer support in the 200-hp light retractable category.

The average cost of an annual inspection in '78, based on our survey results, was $482. Later reports suggest this has naturally risen with inflation, and several owners reported paying approximately $1,200 for the annual.

Landing Gear Headaches

Among the most pernicious problems, according to owner reports, are those involving the landing gear. These center on several aspects of the mechanism and the nose gear doors (the main gear folds into open wheel wells with no doors). Looking through Cessna's service information summaries, we found a recurring theme involving ways to deal with landing gear problems by new rigging methods and new kits and component improvements. The potential Cardinal RG buyer would do well to determine whether these have been complied with. However, judging from an equally long list of Airworthiness Alerts issued through the years by the FAA, dwelling on landing gear problems, it would seem the fixes may not guarantee a troublefree service life with the Cardinal RG.

Following are some of the gear problems isolated by subscribers:

"The landing gear was a constant headache (in a '73 RG). Sometimes the gear would not retract, other times it would not extend and would require manual pumping to extend the gear. On more than one occasion the gear would not completely retract, and would cycle in and out of the gear wells. A misrouted hydraulic line rubbing against the gear mechanism during retraction and extension caused a gear-up landing."

"A week after the warranty expired (on a '76 RG) the aircraft had to be landed with the nose gear up, and an unsafe indication. The FAA GADO determined the cause was internal failure of the selector valve. The valve was returned to Cessna, which bench checked it okay. Since then, numerous letters to the manufacturer rendered no assistance unless I was willing to fly the aircraft to Wichita for a landing gear overhaul at my expense. Further troubles developed in the electrical landing gear indication system. After five incidents of unsafe gear indications it was found to involve the magnets in the down-lock pressure switches. New magnets and switches solved the problem."

"Gear warning horn was always a problem—apparently a very cheap, sloppy design."

"I experienced repeated problems with landing gear retraction and extension, until the heavy-duty solenoid kit was installed."

"We have experienced emergency gear pumpdowns when the hydraulics died and false gear up/down warning light when gear was down. The FBO finally replaced the hydraulic pump assembly after several attempts to replace brushes, etc., at our expense, naturally. The gear warning still occurs occasionally, but resolves itself within a minute or so."

"In the course of two years, I have had to repair the landing gear warning system at least five times (on a '76 RG). The first three times I had to replace the metal arm-with-a-roller that activates a microswitch via the throttle linkage beneath the engine. Fortunately, I met someone who informed me that I needed to replace the small cam that activated the arm. Indeed, the cam proved to be grooved. The arm-with-the-roller has not failed since. However, connecting wires have come loose two or three times. Lycoming IO-360s shake a lot; the vibration causes many maintenance problems."

"The biggest maintenance problem has been the retractable gear. I landed nose gear up once, and had a great deal of difficulty lowering it on six other occasions. The problem was finally diagnosed as the uplock fork on the nose gear. Many hours and dollars were spent adjusting the mechanism and retraction tests. The factory was called direct many times trying to find the answer. I have kept the old "bent" fork as evidence.

"To get the nose gear down—the emergency pump won't do it—enter a very nose-high power-off stall. Recover smartly, and at the same time lower the gear handle. The nose gear will pop out."

"A particular weakness cropped up on the hinges of the forward gear door and the hinge on the cowl for the door. The teflon bearings, pins and hinge were worn badly."

One California pilot who sent us photos of his Cardinal RG landing with the nose gear stuck in the up position is still trying to figure out what the trouble was. He was quite rueful because his insurance company refused to renew his aircraft policy after the incident (though it later relented after he wrote a long letter explaining his case).

At last word he suspects that "the squat switch that prevents gear retraction unless the nose gear strut is fully extended may be the culprit."

This same pilot was able to finesse himself out of a complete gear-up landing only 10 hours after it was returned to service following the nose gear failure. After all attempts at getting the gear down failed, the pilot put the aircraft on autopilot, traded his seat with a non-pilot, rear-seat passenger and crawled over the back seat into the empennage with a screwdriver and a flashlight.

His account: "Unbelievable as it may seem, the hydraulic reservoir was empty. I poured a quart of engine oil into the system and got a complete and successful landing gear extension.

"A simple, five-cent 'O' ring failure was the cause of the hydraulic leak that left the reservoir empty. The 'O' ring failed while airborne, and it is believed the inner diameter surface of the ring was damaged in some threads in a fitting."

The FAA's Airworthiness Alerts also mention several reports of the nose gear

Year	No. Built	Average Retail Price	Cruise Speed (mph)	Rate of Climb (fpm)	Useful Load (lbs)	Usable Fuel (gals)	Engine	TBO (hrs)	Overhaul Cost
1971	212	$22,500	166	860	1,170	50	200-hp Lycoming IO-360	1,400	$6,000
1972	70	$23,500	171	925	1,035	60	200-hp Lycoming IO-360	1,600	$6,000
1973	150	$24,000	171	925	1,035	60	200-hp Lycoming IO-360	1,600	$6,000
1974	160	$26,500	171	925	1,035	60	200-hp Lycoming IO-360	1,600	$6.000
1975	195	$27,000	171	925	1,035	60	200-hp Lycoming IO-360	1,600	$6,000
1976	264	$29,000	171	925	1,035	60	200-hp Lycoming IO-360	1,600	$6,000
1977	215	$32,500	171	925	1,035	60	200-hp Lycoming IO-360	1,600	$6,000
1978	97	$37,000	171	925	1,035	60	200-hp Lycoming IO-360	1,600	$6,000

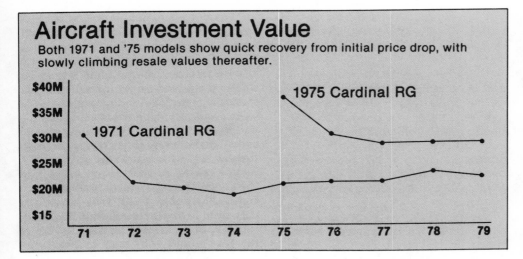

Aircraft Investment Value

Both 1971 and '75 models show quick recovery from initial price drop, with slowly climbing resale values thereafter.

1975 Cardinal RG

1971 Cardinal RG

remained full. Venting problems were usually blamed, often involving the fuel caps themselves.

As for ARC avionics operation, pro and con reports were about evenly divided in number.

Maintenance Costs

Averaging the maintenance costs of airframe, powerplant and ARC avionics for several owners who kept meticulous records yielded an hourly cost of about $9, not counting reserve for overhaul.

Conversions

The only STC we found recorded was one for addition of wing leading edge cuffs and vortex generators on the vertical stabilizer, by Horton STOL Craft at Wellington, KS 67152.

To our knowledge, there is no association of Cardinal RG owners.

In summary, then, the Cardinal RG presents a frustrating combination of attributes and shortcomings that might challenge the wisdom of a potential buyer. Without a trustworthy, knowledgeable mechanic to lean upon, the owner might find the aircraft could nickle-and-dime him or her to death (to use a pre-inflation expression) thanks to accessory breakdowns.

Offering nice pilot handling, great looks and good performance, the airplane still represents something of a mechanical enigma and never really evolved as far as its potential suggested.

uplock being inadvertently moved to the gear up position while maintenance work or inspections were being performed. This led to binding during subsequent retraction and prevented a reliable extension. "A nose gear-up landing is the usual result when this condition occurs."

Other Airworthiness Alerts singled out problems with the main gear actuator, involving such items as loose or broken support assembly attach bolts, cracked or broken support tubes, pins and nuts. Several cases of nose gear actuator rod end failure triggered a Cessna introduction of an improved type of rod end.

In summary, Cardinal RG landing gear problems appear legion and chronic—buyers be wary.

Fuel System Problems

The fuel system is the cause of other troubles reported by owners. The early models had no left-right switching capability, which bothered some pilots, and there is no retrofit of the later RG selector system. Said one owner: "We learned the hard way that if the fuel lever was left on "both" and the plane parked even one degree tilted, up to nine gallons would siphon out of the high wing. Left on "L" or "R," the problem vanished. After the plane was sold, we were informed one of the gas caps had not been vented since it left the factory."

Pilots with the older both/off system reported unequal feeding of wing tanks in flight to the extent where one tank would feed till empty while the other

Owner Comments

"The 200 horsepower Lycoming is a hungry brute, and has ingested, with no damage to itself, two alternate air door springs and pins, which seem to give up the ghost every several hundred hours. The absence of a fuel quick-drain forward of the fuel filter and gascolator is surprising and, in my case, was costly since the prior owner, through carelessness, allowed water contamination of fuel to develop with resulting damage to the fuel pump and servo unit. The modest cost of installing the quick-drain, accessible at the oil dip stick hatch, has given me much peace of mind.

"I also installed quick-drains for the wing tanks. In my estimation, these are items for which a prospective buyer should look, because Cessna did not put them into the bird, unless the purchaser asked and paid for them. Also, the exhaust system, sans the mod kit, is susceptible to repeated cracking, as is the fiberglass cowling.

"On the subject of aircraft handling, I am pleased with the stability in slow flight at normal cruising altitudes and approaches, as well as at cruise speed and configuration at altitudes near the service ceiling. The aircraft never feels squirrelly.

"Should a prospective buyer be looking

at an RG with a towel bar antenna installed on the vertical fin, be advised that unfailing performance of the glideslope may require a separate glideslope antenna to be installed just behind the top of the wind screen, as the contour of the cabin seems to block out the glideslope signal from reaching the towel bar antenna on the vertical fin.

"In six years nearly every part I have needed was not available on the East Coast. Invariably I found myself producing

Pilots rave about the spacious, airy cabin. *However, dromedary hump of the gear well impinges on baggage room.*

Instrument panel on a 1972 RG. *The '76 panels were enlarged on the right. Pilots complain of poor lighting on the gauge cluster at the bottom of the panel.*

dividends for Bell Telephone shareholders—long distance to Wichita, with unexplainable delays, even when I requested shipment AOG.

"On one occasion, I wrote to the company to inquire about removal of the cabin access steps, which could raise even more havoc in the event of a WUL (wheels up landing). After considerable delay and follow-up, I finally received a curt reply, 'Cessna does not authorize this modification.' The step was deleted, however, on more recent models.

"As for flight performance, I paced my RG against a same vintage Piper Arrow, each engine having approximately the same number of hours on it, and utilizing similar power settings. The RG lost no time in showing its tail feathers to the low-winger."

"The first problem to hit me was overheating. Cylinder head and oil temperatures would redline when climbing at or below 80 knots, even with full rich mixture and open cowl flaps. Everyone, including my mechanic, dismissed the problem as inherent in the airplane's design. However, I noticed that the engine's top rear baffling (a 1½-inch strip of neoprene rubber) was so inadequate that the air had bent it backwards. I reinforced it with thicker material, and that ended the overheating-during-climb problems.

"The RG has an automatic alternate induction air system. It is composed of an aluminum box in front of the engine (below the alternator) with a small door held closed by a spring in its attaching hinge."

"I would like to offer this advice to those planning to buy a Cardinal RG: Most important, get one with the Bendix mags replaced after September (79). The ADs on

this mag are legion—too numerous to keep track of. And, in September, the AD proved that over 95 percent of the mags had to be replaced outright, a $300 to $500 expense.

"The fuel tanks can carry a lot of water or sludge behind the baffles if they become plugged. Rocking the wings back and forth usually can bring more water to the drains. The only way to clean them is to drain them completely and clean the holes in the bottom of the baffles.

"However, I consider this plane a step above the rest of the Cessna line below the turbos. I like its room (and doors), its performance and handling."

"The Cardinal RG will do everything the book says it will, and sometimes better. People who get less don't know how to use the aerodynamics of the plane to offset the moderate horsepower. The cabin is roomy and comfortable with plenty of leg room front and rear, and with headrests and recliner seats in all positions my people find it great for sleeping enroute. Incidentally, I am 6'4" tall, close to 200 pounds and I feel just as comfortable in the back seat. The interior design is a marvel for such a streamlined fuselage. With four and a half hours fuel on board, we carry four men and overnight bags safe and legal. With five and a half hours fuel we carry three of the same.

"I do not recommend RGs for back country work—you'll get her in all right, but you will have to taxi out, providing those little wheels are still in the right places.

"So far I have replaced or overhauled: gear motor, one flap motor, starter motor, alternator, vacuum pump, scores of landing lights, attitude indicator, turn coordinator, fuel gauges, oil pressure gauge, oil pressure sensor, cyl. head

temp. gauge, localizer needle movement (jammed dead center on IFR approach), manifold pressure gauge, strobe sender, several oil quick drains, and prop spinner ($150 installed).

"Believe it or not my radio gear has done well even though it is Cessna. My present attitude indicator is spooky, though. While taking an FAA IFR checkride, the AI rolled over on its side 90 degrees during our liftoff as we departed on an IFR flight plan. I noticed the FAA man get wide-eyed and told him to relax because partial panel was about the only way I knew how to fly IFR, anyway, with all the equipment failures I had been through. I went ahead with my act, and he passed me. For that handy ability I shall always be indebted to Cessna."

"On hot or warm days the CHT will redline unless cowl flaps are full open, mixture enriched, high angles of attack avoided for extended periods. The engine runs hot.

"Because of narrow wings, the fuel gauges are nearly useless. Also, lineboys will tend to underfill, sometimes by 15 gallons, because wing tanks are long and narrow. I always refuel myself.

"A couple of windscreen leaks near the door posts have never been adequately repaired.

"The plane has been on stilts three times in the past year. Once for a broken O-ring in the brake system, once for a seal in the main gear actuator, once for a discontinuity in the gear hydraulics (which automatically dropped the gear over the Nevada high desert on a hot day, and which necessitated manually pumping the gear into lock-down).

"The plane is a joy to fly. Aileron response is crisp. Visibility is good.

"The ARC avionics (knock on wood) have been superb."

"My brother owns a 182, so I can compare these aircraft. The 182 carries more, can land and take off significantly shorter. The RG handles much more crisply, burns two gph less, is prettier, about two knots faster when the cowl flaps can be closed."

"The bad news is relatively minor—the usual Cessna glitches. The oil pressure gauge worked about a third of the time, and the right gas gauge worked perhaps a quarter of the time. Both gauges were cheerfully replaced several times under warranty by a dealer who couldn't have cared less; the problem lasted the life of the plane.

"The avionics gave somewhat less trouble than we expected. The 300A autopilot in particular was a joy; didn't misfunction and light years over our previous 200A."

Rockwell 112

One of the most interesting and attractive aircraft to make a debut in the last decade, the Rockwell 112 faces an uncertain future as a used-plane buy. This is because the model has been discontinued, and the giant parent company has bailed out of the single-engine business.

This might make potential 112 used-plane customers wary, since they have little reason to be confident there will be a continuing supply of parts and factory backup as the years roll by.

On top of that, the severing of a line usually has a depressant effect on the resale value of the models out in the field—unless they reach that magic "classic airplane" status.

Owner Ambivalence

The combination of an attractive design, occasional healthy discounts and lackluster performance tends to induce among owners a poignant ambivalence toward the 112 line, according to the comments we received from out in the field. The magnificent styling of the airplane, the cavernous cabin and great pilot visibility are the factors that most often charm the pilot into submission.

Rarely, though, will he be completely blinded to the not inconsiderable list of shortcomings on the Rockwell 112. As with a spouse, the pilot often makes his choice and lives with it.

"On balance, I am pleased with my purchase," explained an Illinois owner. "I am happy when I look at it, I am relaxed and comfortable flying it, and I have come to accept its inconveniences."

Inconveniences

These are (to recite from owner experience): inferior speed and load carrying ability, too few dealers, too many expensive service letters and bulletins, and poor parts availability. (Frankly, we don't know how much significance to attach to this complaint, since it seems to be a universal one for all aircraft, according to the results of our airframe and powerplant survey.)

Most owners talk about getting no more than about 130 knots/149 mph out of their aircraft, which can be eclipsed by a fixed-gear Gulfstream American Tiger, not to mention the Piper Arrow, Cardinal RG and Mooney 201.

Depending on the model, 112s generally have 30 to 150 pounds less useful load than the other 200-hp retractables. The margin diminishes with the newer A and B models, which had their gross weights raised.

Advantages

Aside from great looks and a beamy cabin, nice handling qualities are most often touted by owners. Control response is light and pleasant, yet pilots say they enjoy the good stability they want in an "instrument platform." The trailing beam landing gear comes in for more than its share of praise, and any pilot who has found his most botched touchdown salvaged by this forgiving feature in the Rockwell 112 will wonder why the entire industry hasn't adopted it. A handicap in crosswind landings, however, is what owners describe as inadequate rudder authority.

On the 112 and 112A, before the wings were extended on the 112B model, a truly

awesome descent angle could be achieved on final approach thanks to extraordinarily efficient flaps. Overshooting in one of these airplanes could be managed only by the grossest negligence on the part of the pilot planning final approach.

The wing extension on the B model diminished the plummet index somewhat, along with the roll rate, but it did add a healthy dose of gross weight to finally bring the aircraft up to a truly competitive position in the 200-hp retractable class.

Model Transition

The A model, which was introduced in 1974, upped the gross from a severely deficient 2,550 pounds to 2,650, gaining about 77 pounds of useful load in the process, to 962 pounds.

Since the 112s had been having problems in getting a tight door fit because of warping, Rockwell introduced a kit to replace the fiberglass doors with aluminum ones. Presumably all the 112s in the field received this update.

The fuel quantity remained the same—48 gallons usable standard, 68 gallons optional. There is one unusual aspect to the fuel capacity, however. There is the same size wing

A superb aesthetic package, *the Rockwell 112, with its "half-a-T-tail," may have paved the way for the full T-tail rage of the late 70's.*

tank in both aircraft, but for the standard fuel load the fuel filler cap is located inboard; for the optional load it is positioned outboard, and the wing dihedral allows more fuel to be poured in.

Used-112 buyers might keep this in mind when looking over the field, since it makes sense to get the larger capacity. New caps can be cut outboard, with the inner ones sealed up, but why go to the bother and expense?

The B model, introduced in 1977, picked up the 16-inch extension on each wing that was introduced the year before when the 112TC turbocharged model made its appearance. This permitted a higher gross weight of 2,800 pounds, which in turn brought the useful load to a respectable 1,027 pounds.

The turbocharged TC model was flight tested by *The Aviation Consumer*. It disclosed rather poor climb and cruise performance. The TC-A and Alpine models simply incorporated another 37 pounds of soundproofing, which lowered the decibel level.

Without the extra soundproofing, the 112s in general are characterized by owners as quite noisy.

The convenient, but unusual location of the front-seat shoulder harness *in the seat back was questioned by a 112 owner. Would it hold up in a crash impact? According to Rockwell engineers, the seat back and harness arrangement is designed to take the same nine-G forward load required of all light aircraft under the FARs. The back itself is locked, even in reclining positions, to handle the load, says Rockwell.*

Maintenance

Perhaps the greatest millstone the 112 owner has to bear, aside from speed and climb and load deficiencies, is the cost of keeping the airplane maintained, and keeping up with what owners describe as an incessant run of expensive modifications. They are quick to praise Rockwell's willingness to pay for new parts, but note that as a rule this doesn't include a willingness to shoulder the cost of labor expense, which usually is greater by a large factor.

Some owners report the service letter/bulletin flow seems to have diminished recently, and that may be a sign that Rockwell has finally uncovered and fixed all the bugs. But potential used-112 buyers would be wise to check over not only the ADs, but the service letter and bulletin compliance on any model they are considering buying.

The fact that Rockwell 112 dealers and experienced 112 mechanics are harder to find than for other brands seems to compound the maintenance problem. On top of that, some Rockwell 112 parts are not common ones, one owner reports, and this makes replacement more of a chore. Even the nosewheel tow hook isn't matched by ramp tows on some airports, one pilot said.

Recurring problems are reported with the left door windows and fuel selectors, along with cracking interior plastic panels. Apparently many pilots tend to slam the door on their side by grabbing the small vent window, and after a while the windows begin to crack.

Surprisingly, through all of this, the general tenor of the user comments was that the parent company, Rockwell International, had an exceptionally helpful attitude and would in general bend over backward to help the owner, often chipping in for extra costs not covered by warranty or agreements.

The picture that emerges is one of a manufacturer keenly interested in doing the best job it can, but handicapped by a small dealer network and an aircraft design that never reached its true potential.

Airworthiness Directives

There have been only a half dozen or so ADs on the 112 line, and most of the cost for these was picked up by the company. Among them were replacement of cracked spinner domes, replacement of oil pressure hose assemblies, inspection and/or replacement of aileron and elevator trim tab hinges, and modification of front seats and belt attachments. There also were several ADs on the Lycoming IO-360 engine.

Model	Year Built	Number Built	Cruise Speed (mph)	Useful Load (lbs)	Rate of Climb (fpm)	Fuel (gals)	Engine	TBO (hrs)	Overhaul Cost	Average Retail Price
112	1972	26	165	1,020	1,000	60	200-hp Lycoming	1,400	$4,000	$23,500
112	1973	97	165	1,020	1,000	60	200-hp Lycoming	1,400	$4,000	$24,500
112A	1974	103	161	959	1,020	48/68	200-hp Lycoming	1,600	$4,000	$25,500
112A	1975	150	161	959	1,020	48/68	200-hp Lycoming	1,600	$4,000	$26,500
112A	1976	88	161	959	1,020	48/68	200-hp Lycoming	1,600	$4,000	$28,500
112-TC-A	1976	107	187	1,070	914	48/68	210-hp Lycoming	1,200	$4,750	$35,000
112-B	1977	44	163	1,027	950	48/68	200-hp Lycoming	1,600	$4,000	$32,500
112-TC-A	1977	45	187	1,070	914	48/68	210-hp Lycoming	1,200	$4,750	$40,000
112-TC-A	1978	26	187	1,070	914	48/68	210-hp Lycoming	1,200	$7,000	$52,500
Alpine	1979	20	187	1,070	914	48/68	210-hp Lycoming	1,200	$7,000	$70,000

Rockwell 112

The cockpit of a 112 *can be depended upon to have as standard equipment a wing-leveler that's normally an option in most aircraft. An unusual alarm bell alerts the pilot against landing gear up.*

Modification

The most important mod to the 112 is the Machen Inc. substitution of a whopping 300-hp Lycoming IO-540 engine and three-bladed prop. The resulting so-called Machen Magnum is supposed to give a 30-mph boost in speed (to about 165 knots/190 mph cruise at 6,500 feet) and 45 percent boost in climb, to 1,330 fpm. Useful load jumps up 250 pounds over that of the 112A, along with the new 3,000-pound gross weight.

Cost for the mod is about $32,000, with credit of probably $4,500 to $8,000 subtracted for an exchange engine.

Trailing-beam landing gear: *a pilot's friend*

Service Difficulties

Malfunction and defect reports on the 112 over a five-year span show a high frequency of fuel selector valve problems, often leaking fuel into the cockpit. The fuel selector doubles as a quick drain. (More on that later.)

Safety

Inspection of National Transportation Safety Board accident briefs over a seven-year span from 1972 through 1978 shows that the highest frequency of accidents resulted from engine failure. There was no single trend in powerplant malfunctions, which ranged from material failure to water in the fuel and fuel mismanagement.

The several cases of fuel exhaustion reported could not be attributed necessarily to failure to switch tanks. The 112 has a fuel selector system rare among low-wing singles, since it permits the pilot to select both tanks or use the conventional left and right positions. The tendency of the system to feed heavily with one tank before the other begins feeding (as in the Cessna 150) may, however, induce pilots to rely on single-tank switching to maintain better wing balance, and this would take away the safety factor.

The selector also doubles as a fuel drain switch when the pilot pulls up on the lever. This apparently led to one engine stoppage, since the NTSB report noted the quick drain valve had not properly seated, and air entered the system. The pilot made a forced landing.

Despite the aircraft's forgiving landing gear system, there were half a dozen or more instances of hard landings and resultant damage or gear collapse. Two of these were attributed to improper compensation for wind conditions, which may or may not reflect on the 112's rudder authority.

There also was a handful of accidents related to stalls and spins. In two instances aircraft were damaged or crashed while pilots were practicing stall recoveries.

There was only one case of airframe failure. The aircraft evidently tangled with bad weather, with thunderstorms in the vicinity, according to the NTSB.

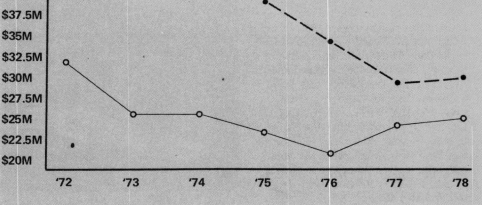

Aircraft Investment Value

The Rockwell 112s show a fairly auspicious pattern in resale value, declining for the first four or so years, then starting back up. The sudden dip in the '72 model plotted in the solid line in 1976 may have been related to the introduction that year of the turbocharged model. The '75 112A is plotted with a dashed line.

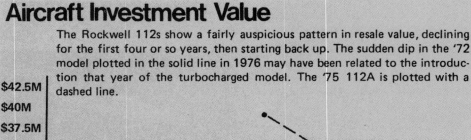

The Aviation Consumer Used Aircraft Guide

Owner Comments

"I bought this model deliberately despite my belief that the Cessna Cardinal RG is the best all-around airplane in the class. The Rockwell is deficient in cruise speed, superior in interior comfort and equal in range. The big difference, however, is that the 112 appears to sell at a discount of 15-20 percent compared with Cardinals and Arrows. For me, that was the determining factor.

"It lands simply, cruises at 130 knots, flies easily with a minimum of surprises, is unreasonably restricted in gross weight, and gives a guaranteed seven hours at 65 percent.

"Non-fliers like to ride in the 112. I travel with business associates often, and they comment on the interior room and comfort, the pleasing lines of the aircraft, the ease of entrance through two large doors. A comfortable passenger is a very desirable goal for me, both as a pilot and as a businessman.

"The plastic interior panels and battery access are a horror story. The plastic is always cracking in a new location, and battery removal is time-consuming and irritating, particularly at -10 degrees F. A rear cabin bulkhead panel should be manufactured as a "mod kit" with an easy opening door to the aft fuselage.

"Parts availability and cost and service bulletin compliance are the big drawbacks to Rockwell ownership. Mufflers, for example, cost $400 and take two weeks to get. Further, the factory seems incapable of packing a kit of more than three components without shortage. This detracts from an owner's appreciation of the Rockwell free service bulletin parts program. My aircraft spent six weeks AOG in a nine-month period because of incomplete kits. I needed two fuel selectors in less than a year. Not only was the kit incomplete, but one of the installation drawings was pictured in "mirror image."

"Also, a potential Rockwell owner must reconcile himself to traveling farther and waiting longer for mechanical service. He should find an experienced Rockwell mechanic and remain with him.

"On balance, I am pleased with my purchase. I am happy when I look at it, I am relaxed and comfortable flying it and I have come to accept its inconveniences."

"While my '75 112A is roomy, easy flying and comfortable, it is noisy and somewhat underpowered. Maintenance costs have been disastrously high. It has gone through many starters, ring gears and alternators as well as the hydraulic pack, fuel pump, vacuum pump and many other hydraulic and electrical components. Electrical failures have been numerous with total loss of electrical power in one case.

"Many modifications of the fuel system, seats, control system and landing gear have been required, most of which was done at my expense.

"At only 1,100 hours the Lycoming engine developed a bad piston, which led to a top overhaul, then a cracked crankcase requiring a major overhaul at less than 1,200 hours total time.

"Maintenance costs have been several times higher than the Rockwell estimates—about $15 per hour not including fuel, insurance or other fixed charges.

"Factory support has been poor, and initial training of my dealer was inadequate. Although this area [California] is supposedly one of Rockwell's major markets, they removed their factory tech rep almost two years ago. Parts availability is poor to fair, particularly on parts peculiar to the 112A.

"When the aircraft is running well it is a pleasure to fly but this has been an infrequent experience."

"The performance of my Machen conversion with the IO-540 Lycoming is fair. My impression is that a Turbo Arrow can outperform my plane, with the larger engine. The range is poor—three hours; squeeze hard for four hours.

"There is no Rockwell dealer in Spokane Wash., and for the first few months there were five service bulletins—aileron hinges, wing beefup, seat belt and seat attachments, fuel selector and rib in vertical tail stabilizer. Parts were free, but labor costly—nearly $2,000."

"Since purchasing our '75 112A new, it has been back to the factory twice for modifications and once to southern California for various repairs. The cooperation of the Rockwell people has been very good.

"The factory has paid for most modifications, which in my case was probably in the area of $20,000. They furnished parts at no cost to my mechanic whenever the problem was theirs. I cannot say enough about the warranty on this aircraft. Rockwell even reimbursed us to bring it to them for certain modifications.

"After the first couple of years, the annual has cost me about $350.

"By comparison with other 200-hp retractables, my plane is slow. However, there is not a more comfortable single-engine retractable that I have ever flown in. It lacks speed, but makes it up by comfort.

"The airplane is a fine machine to fly. It does have a tendency to become overgross rather quickly, if the 72-gallon fuel tanks are filled. I would strongly recommend this aircraft to anyone."

"We have been generally quite satisfied overall with our '75 112A.

"As for weak points, useful load equipped is 888 pounds. This requires careful attention to loading, and on most cross-countries we fly with tanks filled to 48 gallons, which is indicated at a tab in the filler opening. Speed is an honest 130 knots, with an extra five knots at lighter weights.

"The aircraft is noisy.

"The shoulder harness is attached to an inertia reel at the base of the seat and threaded upward through the back of the seat. I don't believe this would hold in even a mild collision."

Access is superb through a pair of wide doors. *Early fiberglass ones were hard to close snugly, so Rockwell replaced them with metal ones.*

Lake Amphibian

The Lake amphibian is just about your only choice if you're looking for a reasonably priced land-or-water aircraft of fairly recent vintage. A hulking Cessna 185 on amphibious floats offers comparable speed, payload and land/water capability, but the minimum price for an amphib 185 runs about twice that of a Lake LA-4. The Lake is not a bushplane, but for personal and sport flying on the water, it is the most logical alternative to the older Seabees and Rivieras.

History
The Lake first appeared in 1956 as the Colonial C-1 Skimmer, a 150-hp three-place machine. Power was increased to 180 hp, and seating capacity was upped to four in 1958. In 1960, the Skimmer got a new name—the Lake LA-4—along with a stretched bow and other improvements. Production halted in 1962, however, then started up again in 1963 under a new marketing arrangement. In 1970, the 180-hp Lycoming was replaced with a 200-hp engine (both models were produced simultaneously for a few months, but the 180 was soon dropped altogether). There was one straight seaplane version of the LA-4 built (no wheels) and a couple of dozen turbocharged versions of both the 180- and 200-hp models are now flying.

Performance
Performance of the Lake is not as good as that of a 200-hp landplane, but it can match the performance of a 300-hp 185 on amphibious floats. Speeds as high as 150 mph are advertised, but we feel that these are fantasies of overzealous Lake marketing. Most owners report speeds in the 125-135 mph range for the 200-hp model. The airplane has a large wing, so load-carrying and takeoff performance are quite good, especially on the 200-hp models. (Owners report that the 180-hp airplane is rather sluggish with three or four people, but fine with two.) In fact, the 200-hp Lake could almost be called a STOL airplane. Owners report ground rolls of under 400 feet on land, and the normal approach speed is a low 65 mph.

Useful loads average about 800 pounds for a VFR 180-hp airplane and about 950 pounds for the 200-hp models—quite comparable to 180-hp and 200-hp landplanes. Fuel capacity is 40 gallons, with 14-gallon float-tanks available as an option on later models. Range with standard tanks is somewhat limited—about 350-400 miles with a small reserve.

Capacity
Inside room is adequate in the front seats, but rear seat room is fairly tight. The baggage must be loaded into the front compartment through the two gull-wing front doors, which, as one owner told us, is a "Class A pain in the butt."

Systems
New Lake owners will also have to adjust to the overhead engine controls and the airplane's reverse trim response to power: power on, nose down; power off, nose up. This characteristic is often criticized, but we feel the criticism is exaggerated—the trim changes are minor and can be adjusted to easily.

Also check out the heater situation closely. Because of the engine location, engine heat is not used to warm the cabin, so a separate heater must be installed. (It runs on aviation fuel, but consumption is too low to be noticed, in most cases.) The heater can be a maintenance headache, so check it carefully. And don't forget to subtract the heater's weight from your useful load.

The Janitrol heaters installed in 1971-75 Buccaneers have been faulted for lack of capacity, but one mechanic told us this was the fault of the thermostat, not the heater. The Janitrol usually requires less maintenance than the Southwind heater installed before 1971 and after 1975.

Maintenance
The Lake is a rather complicated airplane with more than the usual number of systems. Gear, flaps and trim, for example, are all hydraulic. When the great bugaboo of all seaplanes or amphibians—corrosion—enters the picture, the possibility arises for truly horrendous maintenance problems in old or poorly maintained aircraft, especially those flown in salt water. Many used Lakes will be advertised as "never flown in salt water," but they should nevertheless be carefully inspected for corrosion by a knowledgeable

Low profile in the water *makes the Lake much more stable than float planes. The Lake is also much more efficient—it will haul as big a load just as fast as a 300-hp Cessna 185 on amphibious floats, costing twice the price.*

Lake mechanic.

One mechanic described a $7,000 repair job due to corrosion in a 1969 LA-4 that had been flown in salt water. He also reported continuing problems with the landing gear and hydraulic systems, both aggravated by corrosion.

Water operations can also be hard on the hull structure. Because of the vagaries of winds, waves and submerged objects, the possibility of a hard landing in any seaplane is high, and the internal structure should be carefully examined for possible impact damage.

As in other fairly rare, specialized aircraft, it is absolutely critical that a Lake be maintained by an experienced Lake mechanic, even if you have to fly half way across the country to find one. Three FBOs in the East with excellent reputations and long experience with Lakes are: Berkshire Aviation, Great Barrington, Mass.; Lake New England, Laconia, N. H.; Northern Airways, Burlington, Vermont.

There are other Lake specialists scattered around the country. Lake Aircraft itself would not give us a list of preferred maintenance shops, saying that any mechanic can work on one with no problem. Letters from readers and conversations with mechanics indicate otherwise.

Powerplant
The 180-hp engine has a better service record than the 200-hp IO-360. The 1960-66 180-hp Lakes had engines with TBOs of 1,200 hours; 1967-70 models have a 2,000-hour TBO. (TBO of the earlier engines is raised to 2,000 hours if the larger half-inch valves have been retrofitted.) TBO of the early 200-hp engines was only 1,200 hours, raised to 1,400 in 1972 and 1,600 in 1974. Earlier engines may have the 1,600-hour TBO if retrofitted with new camshafts and piston pins.

In general, though, the IO-360 seems to run better in the Lake than in any other installation. This is due to the exposed pylon mounting of the engine, which gives better airflow around the engine. Lycoming tests

Clamshell door entry *is reminiscent of Mercedes 300SL. Both sides can open, but not at the same time.*

showed that the Lake installation ran very cool.

One persistent maintenance problem with Lakes: cracks in the engine cowl. Mounted high on its pylon, the engine is apparently more susceptible to vibration.

Support
We get reports of uneven factory support. One owner told us it was excellent, another described a four-month wait for a flap. Another mechanic said, "Some days its good, some days its bad; you never can tell." Many Lake "dealerships" are individuals who work out of their homes and sell only two or three airplanes a year.

Insurance
Amphibian owners usually pay a steep insurance penalty for water operations. Where a 200-hp retractable-gear landplane with a hull value of $25,000 can be insured for about 2¼ percent or $500 to $700, for a standard floatplane, the rate can be as high as 7 to 8 percent or $2,000. The Lake falls

about halfway in between. One broker quoted us a premium of six percent of hull value per year for a Lake valued at $25,000. That comes to $1,500. Liability insurance is also somewhat higher than for standard land aircraft. A $1 million policy with a $100,000-per-passenger limit would cost about $400 in a Lake, compared with about $250 for a standard 200-hp retractable.

A policy with no passenger limit would be difficult to find for a Lake—especially with a transitioning pilot. According to one broker we talked to, the cost could be as high as $1,600.

A Texas broker, John Nichols, has specialized in Lake coverage for the past eight years (713-354-2148). According to Nichols, a buyer of a used Lake can get insurance more easily and cheaply by having a 10-hour checkout from a Lake-approved instructor. Lake Aircraft gives a 10-hour course free to anyone who buys a new aircraft, but says it can't check out owners of used aircraft. For a list of approved check-pilots, get in touch with Lake Aircraft, Division of Consolidated

Model	Year	Number Built	Average Retail Price	Cruise Speed (mph)	Rate of Climb (fpm)	Useful Load (lbs)	Fuel Std/Opt (gals)	Engine	TBO (hrs)	Overhaul Cost
C-1	1957	23	$10,250	112	700	790	30/39	150-hp Lycoming	2,000	$4,000
C-2 IV	1958-59	128	$13,750	135	800	830	30/39	180-hp Lycoming	2,000	$4,500
LA-4	1960-65	82	$15,000	131	800	850	40	180-hp Lycoming	2,000	$4,500
LA-4	1966-69	102	$18,000	131	800	850	40	180-hp Lycoming	2,000	$4,500
LA-4	1970-71	26	$20,500	131	800	850	40	180-hp Lycoming	2,000	$4,500
LA-4-200	1970-71	53	$25,500	150	1,200	1,065	40/55	200-hp Lycoming	1,600	$6,000
LA-4-200	1972-75	N/A	$29,500	150	1,200	1,065	40/55	200-hp Lycoming	1,600	$6,000
LA-4-200	1976-77	N/A	$34,000	150	1,200	1,135	40/54	200-hp Lycoming	1,600	$6,000
LA-4-200	1978	N/A	$40,000	150	1,200	1,135	40/54	200-hp Lycoming	1,600	$6,000
LA-4-200	1979	N/A	$47,000	150	1,200	1,135	40/54	200-hp Lycoming	1,600	$6,000

Aeronautics, Inc., at Laconia Airport, Laconia, N.H. 03246; 603-524-5868, or Box 399, David Wayne Hooks Memorial Airport, Tomball, TX 77375.

Safety

NTSB records checked by *The Aviation Consumer* listed 22 Lake Amphibian accidents in 1974 and 1975, two of them fatal. Total Lake population then was about 600; that puts the Lake fatality rate at one per 600 airplanes per year. This is twice as good as the overall general aviation figure of one fatal accident per 275 airplanes. For total accidents, the Lake also rates slightly better than the average: one accident for every 55 Lakes each year, compared with one accident for every 38 airplanes per year for the total aircraft population. (About half of the Lake accidents in 1974 and 1975 happened during water operations.) All this makes us wonder why the Lake has higher insurance rates than the average aircraft.

The secret to flying the Lake safely is to get a thorough checkout (five hours at an absolute minimum; ten hours is better) from an experienced Lake instructor. One insurance broker told us that an amazingly high percentage of Lake accidents occurs in the hands of new owners of used Lakes in their first few hours of water flying. A good checkout is important when purchasing any used airplane, but in the Lake it is critical.

Here, then, are buying guides for the various Lake models:

The Skimmer first appeared in 1956 as a 3-place airplane powered by a 150-hp Lycoming. The bow was two feet shorter than the later Lakes, and wingspan was four feet shorter. Consequently, the Skimmers tended to porpoise somewhat, and climb performance was something less than spectacular. There probably aren't more than a dozen C-1 Skimmers still flying, and if one comes up for sale it could cost anywhere from $8,000 for a real dog to $13,000 for a refurbished airplane with a fresh overhaul and lots of radios. In 1958 the Skimmer got a

Panel *is somewhat Spartan, but visibility is superb.*

180-hp engine, which helped cruise and climb somewhat, in addition to making it a four-place airplane (barely). A handful of C-2s are still flying, but rarely does one come up for sale. They are usually prized by their owners as rare classics.

A few dozen Lakes (both 180s and 200s) were built with Rajay turbochargers. The 180 turbo model is generally unsatisfactory. With the extra 40 pounds of the turbo installation, plus the heavy-duty heater needed for high altitudes, the useful load declined to the point that an IFR turbo 180 is a two-passenger airplane. The 200 turbo is somewhat better, but the turbo's utility is limited because of the airplane's small fuel supply—made even smaller by the appetite of the heater working full blast in the high-altitude chill. We wouldn't recommend a turbo Lake except for regular operation from high-altitude airports or water. The airplane is basically a low-altitude fun machine, and not even turbocharging turns it into a good cross-country airplane.

A used LA-4-180 can be a very good bargain. There is simply no cheaper way to carry

four people around in an amphibian, although performance was rather marginal with four full-size adults. There are probably at least 100 LA-4-180s flying, but they are rather hard to find—most have been through two or three owners by now, and they tend to be firmly ensconced in happy homes.

One important thing to look for: Lake 180s built from 1965 to 1970 did *not* have zinc chromate treatment. Any airplane of this vintage that has even been *near* salt water should be avoided. Our choice as the best year: a 1971 model, which has the zinc chromate treatment and the 2,000-hour engine. Second choice: a 1960-64 model with the new valves retrofitted to bring TBO up to 2,000 hours.

The Buccaneer, introduced in 1970, turned the Lake into a true four-place airplane, and it is a major improvement over the 180 in terms of performance. Climb rate is quite good, and a 200-hp LA-4 will indicate about 125-128 mph. The Buccaneer also had optional seven-gallon float-tanks on each side, which extended endurance from a marginal three hours to four-plus hours. This is a desirable option; look for it. But don't fill the tanks except when you really need the extra fuel. The full floats lack the buoyancy of empty ones, and can make crosswind water operations difficult. The floats are also very susceptible to bending or kinking; inspect them closely.

Unfortunately, the early 1970s were a bad time for the Buccaneer's IO-360 Lycoming. Check closely to see that all engine ADs have been complied with and try to find one updated to a 1,600-hour TBO.

Our choice: a 1975 model, which has the 1,600-hour engine and improved landing gear grease fittings, which solved the gear hangup problems of earlier models that weren't perfectly maintained.

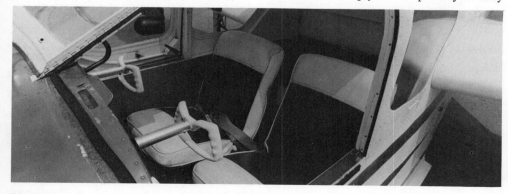

Interior *has good room in front, fair in back. Upholstery appears to be early Nash Rambler.*

Owner Comments

"We have a 200-hp Lake of '73 vintage with low time on the engine and airframe. The engine performs satisfactorily, although for its size it does not deliver anywhere near the cruise airspeed of comparable landplanes. If the Lake indicates 110, it is doing well. As such, it is a poor cross-country aircraft unless you don't mind flying all day to get to your out-of-the-way paradise.

"Engine and airframe maintenance has been good. The seals around the clamshell-type hatch used on the Lake are extremely poor in that they continuously leak and spray water whenever it rains or the plane is landed in the water. There are several hull and wing float drains that must be opened prior to flight to drain water from the various hull compartments. These take forever to open and close, and it seems that a quicker way could be devised to do it. By the time you preflight the Lake, the sun is setting and it's time to go home again. The Lake is also extremely noisy, and I would think it could be made much quieter.

"There is another area where the Lake stands out from other modern aircraft. Its ground handling ability is lousy and should most surely be improved. The nosewheel can only be moved by constant pressure on the brakes and a somewhat higher than normal taxi speed, which I consider hazardous to safe ground operations. It will quickly, and without warning, swerve to either side and become a monster to get straight again without great gobs of power and brake stabbing. There is a technique to solve this; however, I consider it dangerous for the novice, and since there are no brakes on the copilot side of most Lakes I've been in, this makes things most interesting for an instructor checking out the new guy.

"There is no reason for a modern-day aircraft to have such a poor setup for ground steering. I wonder how many aircraft have been wiped out by Lake pilots trying to get straight on the taxiway again.

"To summarize, I like the Lake except for the areas mentioned above. It is a fun airplane, but one that has to be respected for both its shortcomings and its inherent danger areas as well. We've punched a few holes in the hull, but have not found them difficult or expensive to repair. The insurance is, of course, high since it's a seaplane. For instruction and rental purposes it is over $2,000 per year. It can be easily damaged if you are not extremely careful."

"I purchased a 1976 Buccaneer last year and have 280 hours to date.

"The airspeed indicates between 128-130 at 75 percent power, 123-125 at 65 percent. The airplane seems to go faster as the load is increased. As advertised, true airspeeds of 150 mph can be obtained at altitude.

"The 200-hp fuel-injected Lycoming gives an average of 10 gph. This can be reduced to 9-9.5 gph at cruise or increased to 11-12 gph if several water landings and takeoffs are performed.

"The two front seats are adjustable fore and aft. I am 6-2, 200 pounds and have more than adequate space. The rear compartment is smaller, but adequate. The rear seat is a bench type and fine for two adults or three children.

"Advertised useful load is 1,135 pounds. With avionics, etc., I have a useful load of 1,025 pounds. That allows 250 pounds for full fuel and oil and 680 pounds for passengers and baggage (four 170-pound passengers and 95 pounds of baggage). Practically speaking, carrying me (200 pounds), my brother (240 pounds), our two wives (285 pounds) and full fuel, it will leave the water nicely. People keep telling me that this is a three-passenger airplane off the water, but I think they are talking about the 180.

"Handling is a strong point. The Lake has a very positive feel and response, probably as a result of using push rods instead of cables.

"The cabin is long enough to sleep two when the back seat is removed—a bit tight, but adequate for those fishing trips into the Allagash where there is no shore to drive up on. We throw out the anchor and sleep in our houseboat.

"Visibility is unequaled. The wing is behind the cabin and so is the engine. This allows a full panoramic view.

"The slow stall speed (45 mph), strong hull, ability to land almost anywhere, and cruise speed near the maneuvering speed make for a very safe machine. The Lake is a fun airplane. The exhilaration of making a smooth water landing on the step or rising out of a pond is unparalleled."

"Before I bought a used Lake, I hired two mechanics to check it out. Here's what they missed, as I found out later, to my chagrin: two leaking hydraulic lines ($200); miserable original equipment brakes—repaired and replaced with Clevelands ($1,200); more than $2,000 worth of internal structural damage. In other words, an average mechanic may not be too capable when it comes to evaluating a Lake.

"Other problems: I had a high-speed turning left skid occur, due to some sort of nosewheel problem. The repair was $11,000; $2,000 of this went to correct previous hull damage.

"The interesting thing was that the right flap was destroyed. It took four months to get a new one. Why? Because nobody, I repeat nobody, had one. We called all over the country. We were told that left flaps were available, but that only right flaps had takers.

"Do you know why only *right* flaps are in demand? It took Lake four months (all summer) to provide one. And even the mechanics who fixed it were embarrassed by the enormous costs of parts."

"All in all, the Lake has done everything I have asked of it, and a little bit more. Now if they would come up with a little more horsepower, I'd sign the order tomorrow."

Try this *in your $360,000 pressurized Baron. This scene sums it all up for many Lake owners.*

Piper Comanche

The Piper Comanche has gained the reputation of a classic among used high-performance retractables. Its performance is slightly more modest than that of a Bonanza of the same vintage, but then Comanche prices are generally about 20-30 percent lower. Comanches were built for 14 years (1958 to 1972) in 180-, 250-, 260-, Turbo 260- and 400-hp models before the recession, the Arrow and the great flood wiped out the line for good. All models had four seats except for the 260-hp line, which seated up to six.

The Comanche's performance is still up-to-date. *The Aviation Consumer* flew a then brand-new 1976 Rockwell 114 side-by-side with a 1972 Comanche C. Using an identical engine, the Comanche flew faster and climbed better by a noticeable margin—and it had more seats, fuel capacity and useful load to boot.

The Comanche line does have some drawbacks, however. The airplane is notoriously difficult to land smoothly because of a tendency to float during the flare. "People tend to approach at 85 or 90, and that's too fast," one Comanche fan told us. "Eighty is just right."

Some Comanche owners also report a tendency to wheelbarrow on a crosswind takeoff where the pilot holds a bit of pressure on the nosewheel to prevent premature liftoff. One pilot reports that he even pumped up his main gear oleos higher than normal, and this tail-high attitude required a more positive pull-off, countering the wheelbarrowing.

Takeoff roll is fairly long; this fact combined with the low ground clearance of the main gear make the Comanche a poor short- and rough-field bird.

The airplane has a good reputation for its handling in the air, with light ailerons, a docile stall and moderate sink rates at normal approach speeds. Visibility is poor, though. Comanche cabins are reasonably roomy, but the instrument panel tends to be old-fashioned looking and confused in layout. The Comanche series has suffered a rash

of Airworthiness Directives (ADs) in the past few years—six in 1974 and 1975 alone. Older models have had as many as 32 ADs. Potential owners should assure that all have been compiled with before purchase. Also, check the aileron spars for cracks. It's a common problem, but no AD has been issued.

One operating quirk to watch for: when the Comanche landing gear is raised, the emergency gear handle between the seats pivots from a vertical position to horizontal on the floor. If a Jepp case or other object gets in the way, the gear will jam, the circuit breaker will blow, and serious gear problems may arise later. The Comanche gear needs regular expert maintenance from a shop that knows the bird intimately. (Most long-time Piper dealers know their Comanches well.) Newer dealers without much Comanche experience should be quizzed carefully.

The Comanche 180 is highly regarded for its economy, but it is certainly no hauler of great loads. Owners report speeds of 160-165 mph on eight to ten gallons per hour. Rate of climb is 700 to 900 fpm at gross weight. The 180 came with a hand brake until 1960; after that, most were built with optional toe brakes. The optional 90-gallon fuel tanks became available in 1961. A full load of gas

gives a phenomenal nine-hour endurance, but limits payload to two people and baggage. Electric flaps were introduced in 1962, but many people consider this a step backward. The 1960 and 1961 models are best for eventual conversion to the 250-hp engine.

Our choice of 180s: a 1961 model with 90-gal. fuel, toe brakes, manual flaps and half-inch valves (approximate cost: $16,000-$18,000).

The 250, built from 1958 to 1964, is the classic Comanche, perhaps the best plane available today for under $20,000. (A 1963 250-hp Comanche costs about the same as a 1958 250-hp Bonanza.) All 250-hp Comanches have four seats, and with their healthy useful loads, it is practically impossible to overload them when they have standard fuel tanks. Preferable models are 1961 and later, which had a higher gross weight and useful load, plus optional 90-gallon fuel tanks. Owners report cruise speeds in the 180-185 mph area on 13-15 gph; one claims 190-plus with a new-rebuilt engine. Climb rate is strong: about 1,000 fpm, according to owners.

The carbureted 250-hp Lycoming engine is a good one, as long as it has half-inch valves. TBO is then 2,000 hours, and readers report engine times up to 2,300 hours.

Comanche B. *Introduced in 1966, the B featured six seats, more windows and a fuel-injected 260-hp engine.*

The 260-hp model was introduced in 1965, but the big change didn't occur until 1966. The '65 model is thus unique—the only four-seat carbureted 260-hp model. (The '65 model, because of its smaller gross weight, has the highest book rate of climb of any Comanche except the 400—a robust 1,500 fpm.) In 1966, the fuselage was stretched slightly to allow two extra seats and more windows, fuel injection was added, and gross weight was upped 200 pounds to 3,100 pounds. Because of the extra gross weight, book speed is only slightly higher than the older 250s, but with the same load, the Comanche B is about five mph faster than the 250, according to reader reports. The B is also a bit quieter than the 250 because of its thicker windshield and side glass. The slightly longer fuselage gives the 260 better longitudinal stability than the 250—an advantage for IFR flight.

The C model, the ultimate refinement of the breed, was introduced in 1969. Recognizable by its "shark-nose" cowl, the Comanche C had another 100 pounds gross, which raised standard useful load to a whopping 1,427 pounds. In order to avoid aft c.g. problems, however, the prop was moved forward several inches, resulting in the shark-nose effect. The C model also introduced cowl flaps and an aileron-rudder interconnect to the Comanche line. The 1971 may be the best buy of the C models; its engine had half-inch valves and a 2,000-hour TBO, and it can be bought for $2,000-$3,000 less than a '72 model, which is not appreciably different. The 1970, '71 and '72 models are not plentiful, however. Only 128 were built during those three years (including the turbo models), so it is doubtful that more than a couple of dozen '71 standard Comanche C models are still flying today.

The Turbo Comanche C was introduced in 1970 and was built for three years until the Comanche line expired in 1972. The "second throttle" dual Rajay turbo system boosted high-altitude (25,000 feet) cruise speeds to 228 mph at 75 percent and 209 mph at 55 percent. At more reasonable altitudes of 12-15,000 feet, the Turbo Comanche will true about 200-210 mph on about 16 gph.

The Turbo's modified exhaust system results in a noticeably quieter cabin, especially at altitude. The engine itself is beefed up to take the higher manifold pressures (normal turbo cruise is 27 inches, and continuous operation at 29 inches is allowable).

A shop that specializes in Comanches reports no unusual maintenance costs on the turbo, and says that turbo models seem to have engine lives just as long as the standard Comanches'. For the Comanche buyer looking for 200-mph speeds, the Turbo C appears to be a much better choice than the 400. Although the purchase price of the Turbo C is about $7,000 higher than the 400's, the buyer may recoup the difference in gas and overhaul costs.

The Comanche 400 appeared in 1964 and disappeared after only one year on the market, for some good reasons. A total of 145 were built, and they have become something of a collector's item. The 400 has the basic four-seat Comanche airframe, but the engine is a monstrous 400-hp eight-cylinder Lycoming IO-720.

The engine and airframe marriage was not a happy one, however, for the Comanche 400 is a nose-heavy gas guzzler whose performance is only a little better than the Comanche 260's. Cruise speed is listed at 213 mph, and owners report an honest 210-220 mph at 75 percent cruise—but at an excessive fuel flow of about 20-22 gallons per hour. At 10,000 feet and 65 percent power, speed drops below 200 mph and fuel consumption is about 18 gph, according to owner reports.

Compared to a 1966-68 Comanche B (260 hp), which sells for about the same price ($30,000-$33,000), the 400 rates poorly indeed. Gross weight is 500 pounds higher than the 260's, but since the 400 weighs 337 pounds more empty, the useful load advantage is only 163 pounds. Because of the 400's voracious appetite for fuel, the cabin payload is actually less than the 260's for any flight of more than about 300 miles. With the optional 130-gallon tanks full, in fact, an IFR Comanche 400, for all its brute power, is a three-passenger airplane.

The original Comanche 400 gained a

Later Comanches *offered optional fifth and sixth seats. Check your weight and balance before loading up this much luggage.*

reputation for being notoriously hard to start, especially when hot. The problem was the Bendix 700 magneto used on early versions of the IO-720 (it tended to slip out of proper timing). Lycoming solved the problem on later engines by going to 1200 magnetoes, but all Comanche 400s originally had the troublesome 700 mags. Most have been converted to the 1200 series, and we wouldn't advise buying one without the conversion.

Other points to bear in mind: an average IO-720 overhaul will cost about $12,000, compared to about $7,000 for the 260-hp model. Also, check carefully for leaks in the bladder-type rubber fuel cells, which tend to start rotting after 10 or 15 years.

Getting parts also appears to be a problem. One owner writes, "Anyone who has flown a 400 Comanche very long has had his airplane down on the ground and unable to find parts for it."

Despite its astronomical operating costs, the 400 has a loyal cadre of owners, most of whom see the plane as a classic collector's item. The plane is a delightfully stable IFR platform, exceptionally smooth, and its rate of climb is unmatched by any conventional single-engine airplane. For the pilot with plenty of money to invest in a unique attention-getter, the Comanche 400 may be a good choice. For anybody else, a slightly newer 260 at the same price is a far better deal.

Model	Year	Number Built	Average Retail Price	Cruise Speed (mph)	Rate of Climb (fpm)	Useful Load (lbs)	Fuel (gals)	Engine	TBO (hrs)	Overhaul Cost
PA-24-400	1964-65	148	$36,000	213	1,600	1,550	100	400-hp Lycoming	1,800	$11,500
PA-24-260	1965-67	791	$30,000	185	1,320	1,427	60	260-hp Lycoming	2,000	$ 7,000
PA-24-260	1968-69	148	$35,000	185	1,320	1,427	60	260-hp Lycoming	2,000	$ 7,000
PA-24-260	1970-72	N/A	$42,000	185	1,320	1,427	60	260-hp Lycoming	2,000	$ 7,000
PA-24-Turbo 260	1970-72	N/A	$43,000	182	1,370	1,372	60	260-hp Lycoming	2,000	$ 7,000
PA-24-250	1958-61	N/A	$18,500	181	1,350	1,110	60	250-hp Lycoming	2,000	$ 6,500
PA-24-250	1962-64	N/A	$22,000	181	1,350	1,110	60	250-hp Lycoming	2,000	$ 6,500
PA-24-180	1958-61	N/A	$16,000	167	910	1,010	60	180-hp Lycoming	2,000	$ 4,500
PA-24-180	1962-64	N/A	$19,000	167	910	1,020	60	180-hp Lycoming	2,000	$ 4,500

Societies

The International Comanche Society is located at 1359 McClean Blvd., Wichita, KS 67203. Anyone considering the purchase of a used Comanche should get in touch. The Society puts out a monthly newsletter called the *Comanche Flyer* that is useful for anybody who owns or contemplates owning a Comanche.

Modifications

Airplanes that are out of production and cherished by their owners tend to have lots of mods, and the Comanche is no exception, although it hasn't been rejuvenated to the degree that, say, the Navion has. Robertson STOL kits are popular among Comanche owners, with reportedly good results. (Sink rates can get frightening, however, during a careless approach.) Several 180 Comanches have been converted to 250-hp configuration with a minimum of paperwork and modification. Carbureted 250 and 260 engines may be converted to fuel injection, another relatively easy conversion. An accessory one-piece windshield is also a popular mod. Rajay turbocharger kits are available for 1966 and later Comanche 260s (or 1965 models converted to fuel injection) and 400s.

The ultimate Comanche, if it exists, would be a Robertson STOL turbo 400. Such a beast could cruise at 260 mph, climb to 35,000 feet or so and presumably take off and land in a cow pasture.

Service

According to the International Comanche Society, the best Comanche mechanic in the country is John Dean of Midwest Piper in Wichita. Dean has owned several Comanches, flown them all, and writes a monthly column of maintenance advice in the *Comanche Flyer*. Midwest Piper's phone is: 316-682-5551.

One expensive maintenance item: An AD on the Comanche 250's Hartzell prop will cost $400-$600 every 1,000 hours.

Owner Comments

Comanche 180

"Speed: an honest 160, and another five mph in cold weather. Handling: excellent. It is harder to make good landings than in airplanes like the Cherokee or 172, but much easier than in Mooneys. In the 1959 model there are no brakes, just the single brake lever. This makes tight turns with differential braking impossible.

"Instruments: there is a very illogical panel on these old models, and no center stack for the radios.

"Comfort: much larger and more comfortable than the Cherokee, even though it gives the same performance as the Arrow. Must be the higher aspect ratio wing. This airplane is *roomy* for 180 hp. Heater and ventilation very deficient in 1959.

"Maintenance: I had gear problems. A tip to any buyer: if the plane has over 1,200 hours and has not had the gear bushings replaced, count on $1,000 to get it done. That cost me $800 in 1972.

"The 180 has two fuel tanks, which hold 25 gallons each when filled to the bottom of the filler neck, and 30 gallons each right to the top of the tank. It states in the owner's manual that to put the last five gallons in each tank, the airplane should be absolutely level, fore and aft and side to side.

"My experience is that you can get only about three additional gallons in each tank by this procedure, milking in the last bit.

"Using an EGT, I get less than 10 gph at 75% power and 7.4 gph at 55%, so the fuel supply is very adequate, even considering my personal policy of being on the ground with an hour's fuel supply remaining.

"There has been much comment about the Comanche being difficult to land, especially because of the tendency to float. It does, but most of this can be eliminated with very careful attention to airspeed on approach. It has excellent handling qualities in a crosswind.

"I had been used to the trim tab on the right of the pilot's seat, and at first wasn't too sold on the ceiling-mounted trim crank in the Comanche, but it doesn't bother me now—I'm used to it.

"I do not have one drill hole anywhere in the plane to stop metal cracking. I feel that is outstanding, considering the 2,100 hours and about 18 years on the airframe.

"Cockpit room is excellent and comfortable, and this kind of handling, economy and speed are hard to come by otherwise.

"The cockpit lighting for night flying leaves much to be desired.

"I think people often mistakenly characterize the 180 Comanche as "underpowered." This all depends on what the individual wants or needs. The 180 does a good job for me at a good airspeed, and generally my load-carrying requirements are 300 to 500 pounds under gross."

"The airplane does have some drawbacks. The cabin is very noisy, and the panel layout isn't very good. However, it is a very stable airplane, and it has a gentle stall. I usually fly at 6,500 to 8,500 feet and with 20.5 to 21.4 inches and 2300 rpm it trues out at 160 mph. After leaning I burn anywhere from 8.5 to 9.5 gph. Where else can you get this kind of performance?

"I also find these airplanes can get very uncomfortable in summer because they are not well vented in the cabin.

"In winter cold, it can be very difficult to get the prop turning over fast enough to get a good start, perhaps because of the distant location of the battery from the starter motor.

"It is my personal opinion that the Comanche was the best plane ever built, and Piper sure lost a jewel when they removed it from their line."

"I bought my 180-hp Comanche in 1969, and for the first few years was sure I made a mistake because of constant maintenance requirements and an ever-increasing list of problems that seemed to have no solution.

Comanche instrument panel *is old-fashioned looking and rather disorganized. Accessory one-piece windshield eliminates center post, makes cockpit quieter.*

"I then heard about and decided to try Dan Claycomb, Service Manager, at Penn Air, Inc., Blair County Airport, Martinsburg, Pa., who is supposed to be a Comanche expert. Needless to say, the first 100-hour inspection from them was expensive (around $1,200), most of which involved correcting problems that had accumulated over the years on my gripe list.

"In the years since using Penn Air for service, I can think of only one instance where maintenance was required in between 100-hour inspections.

"However, I think the fuel drain system stinks. The drain is performed from the inside of the cabin and drains near the center of the fuselage about halfway along the wing cord. To inspect the drained fuel, you need two people and a very long handled glass, or must crawl under the airplane to a most inaccessible place, particularly if you are dressed in a business suit."

"Despite its age, the quality of workmanship cannot be duplicated today. This aircraft was way ahead of its time. What other aircraft had complete internal corrosion coating and all stainless steel control cables 16 years ago?

"Performance is outstanding and puts many of today's small retractables to shame. We continually outrun 200-hp Arrows and Sierras and strangely enough many of the local Mooneys.

"At altitude we true out at 154-160 mph at 70 percent power. Recent extensive cruises gave us fuel consumption of 8.6 gph average, leaned at altitude. Miles per gallon run from 16 to 18.

"This is an excellent instrument aircraft, even with an archaic "autopilot" and somewhat scattered panel.

"Adversely, the ADs tend to drive one up the wall, but have to be expected on older aircraft. If kept up to date, they are not a prohibitive burden, and in most cases inspection indicates remedial work is not warranted.

"One fault with the four-cylinder O-360 model is the vibration on start-up and shutdown. This has caused a series of exhaust stack cracks and heater jacket fractures. The cross-over exhaust system is probably a contributor. A good maintenance program on the gear and aircraft, along with occasional equipment mods should keep these aircraft around a long time."

Comanche 250/260

"It's a super aircraft. I have over 600 hours in two of them. But I haven't made a good landing in two years—and never with passengers along. It doesn't make any difference what technique I use; nothing works well.

"I cruise at 9,000 and 10,000 feet with about 20-21 inches mph at 2300 rpm. This gives me a true airspeed of 174 mph at the start with full fuel. Then the speed climbs

Rare Bird. *This 1965 Comanche 260 is the only four-place 260-hp model built.*

slowly to about 178-179 mph with the aux tanks burned off and one hour from each main.

"The airplane is very hard to start in winter if it's been out all night. I end up running the battery out, and now I'm installing an external power plug to make this less of a hassle.

"For taxiing I have both toe brakes and a center handbrake. Ground maneuverability is excellent. However, I have been unable to eliminate a problem with the parking brake. Sometimes it locks in the "on" position; therefore I simply never use it, since I don't trust it.

"As for climb performance, I don't seem to be able to get the advertised 1,400 fpm; 1,000 fpm is more like it, and that only at low altitudes. It takes me about 15 minutes to get to 9,000 feet.

"I file 150 knots IFR and cruise at 23 inches or full throttle above 6,000 feet, with 2200 rpm. This reduces wear and noise. I get about 14 gph at 65-70 percent power with about a quart of oil added every three hours or so.

"The landing gear is suspect. I have it inspected every 50 hours, including a retraction test, since the Comanche seems to have a history of wheels folding up from time to time.

"The fuel cells have to be inspected every 100 hours. The fuel gauges are totally unreliable. The fuel caps vent fuel on climb with full tanks. Tightening these works for a while, but not for long. The central draining system (on the floor) makes it impossible to check what you have drained for water or sediment. You also must check to make sure that the drainer has stopped after you release the lever, and you need an outside observer for that unless you want to climb outside again.

"I believe, overall, that my Comanche is one of the finest high-performance singles around. It is fast and comfortable. Too bad they stopped making them."

Comanche 400

"Performance is better than that of any single you can buy today, and better than that of a lot of twins. Honest cruise speed at 75 percent power between 8,000 feet and 12,000 feet is in the 210-220-mph range. Quite a few 400 pilots say that they get 220 TAS up there, although some get less.

"This airplane carries 130 gallons of fuel, for over six hours at normal cruise, so 1,200 miles is a reasonable (not maximum) range. By slowing down, you can stretch the range to 1,500 miles.

"The 400 will get into and out of small fields. In fact, mine is based on a field with 2,900 feet of runway, and I seldom use more than half of it. (I now have Robertson STOL, but the figures I just gave are based on performance before that).

"Rate of climb is solid at 1,000 fpm, right on up to cruising altitude.

"Fuel consumption at normal cruise is about 20 gph.

"Handling is great. The 400 handles very much as my 250 did. I find that I need a bit less right rudder on takeoff, probably because of the balanced rudder on the 400. Stalls are gentle, but Comanches have a tendency to sink unexpectedly on final approach. I haven't figured that one out, maybe it's piloting technique.

"A lot of 400s went for years without tender loving care. Mine was one of those, and I spent a lot of time, money and energy getting the airframe in good condition. Since I did get it in shape, the maintenance has been reasonable. By that I mean I spend what one would expect to have to spend on a complex airplane.

"One problem that has recurred is with the flaps. They hang up at times. This results in a slightly uneven extension, or blowing the circuit breaker, and I have had to replace the motor. I still cannot figure out why Piper went to electric flaps, when the manual ones worked so well."

Navion

The Navion is one of aviation's old-timers, a big roomy turtle of an airplane that was first introduced in 1946. Along with the Bonanza, it formed the vanguard of modern civilian aircraft. Unfortunately, the Navion fell far short of the Bonanza in performance, and it lasted in its original form only about six years (the Bonanza, of course, is still going strong). For all its performance shortcomings, however, the Navion has always had a loyal band of followers; some 1,600 Navions are still flying, and there have been a half dozen reincarnations (most of them flops) over the years. The last attempt to revive the Navion, in the form of the Rangemaster, was in 1976. The airplane's survival as a production airplane and as a reasonable used airplane is due largely to the American Navion Society, perhaps the most enthusiastic of any aircraft owner's club.

The Navion holds the distinction of being the least expensive retractable on the market today. A mere $12,000 will get you into a good older Navion, and for $15,000 you can pick up a late '50s D or E model. Maintenance costs can be high, however. If you buy a Navion solely because it's cheap, beware of the trap that afflicts many used plane buyers: you may be buying a $12,000 airplane, but you'll be maintaining the equivalent of a $75,000 one, for the Navion is every bit as complex as a Bonanza or 210, since it has retractable gear, constant-speed prop, cowl flaps and so forth—plus the "bonus" of a hydraulic system.

A large percentage of Navions now flying are kept in pristine shape by doting owners, and many have been modified and rebuilt to an astonishing degree. An unmodified Navion, in fact, is something of a rarity.

History
The first Navion appeared in 1946, the first year of the post-war lightplane boom. It was built by North American as that company's entry into the civilian market, and was pro-moted as a general aviation P-51 (so was the Rockwell 112 almost three decades later, and it didn't last long either). The 1946 and '47 models had Continental 185-hp engines, with a takeoff rating of 205 hp. North American built over 1,100 airplanes in those two years, and then sold the rights in 1948 to Ryan in San Diego, which built 1,200 more before halting production in 1951. Ryan called their version the A model, and installed a 225 Continental in the later years. The 1951 B model, which had a 260-hp geared Lycoming GO-435 engine, was the last model of the original genuine Navion.

The Navion remained dormant until 1955, when Ryan sold the rights to a Texas company which rebuilt and updated old Navions with Continental IO-470 engines of 240, 250 and 260 hp. (These models are known as the D, E and F.) In 1960, new production of the Navion resumed in Texas, with a door in place of the original canopy, greatly increased fuel capacity and the 260-hp Continental. About 50 of the so-called Rangemaster G models were sold before Hurricane Carla wiped out the factory. A group of American Navion Society people bought the rights and built a handful of Rangemaster Hs with 285-hp Continental IO-520s, but the company folded again. The Rangemaster H had two abortive rebirths in the mid-70s, but only a half-dozen or so were built.

Performance
You'll rarely find a Navion owner who talks about performance. There's a good reason—it's pretty bad by modern standards. The early 205-hp models in stock form can usually cruise at about 140 mph on 11 gph. The 225-hp versions will do about five mph faster while using a gallon per hour more fuel. (Compare the 225 Navions 145-mph cruise to the 175-180 mph speeds of a 225-hp Bonanza.) The 240-, 250- and 260-hp second-generation D, E and F Navions will do about 155 mph or so. The 1951 B model with the geared 260-hp Lycoming has the most inefficient of all the Navion engines—according to Navion Society figures, it can manage only about 153 mph while burning 13.1 gph. Other low-priced used retractables like the Comanche 180 and the early Mooneys fly faster on much less fuel.

Many Navions are somewhat faster than the speeds we've listed because of careful aerodynamic modifications performed by the owners. Flush windows, modified tails and a host of fairings can add five to seven mph to those speeds. We've flown one highly modified 225-hp Navion whose owner claims 155 mph. (He's been honing and modifying it for 15 years.)

It's a bit difficult to state the range of a "typical" Navion, since the fuel capacity varies widely from model to model. The basic fuel system has 40 gallons, but many

The Navion: *slow, sturdy and much modified by doting owners.*

Original Navions *had the horizontal stabilizer set at a high negative incidence, which caused considerable drag. Most Navions have the "Palo Alto Tail" conversion, which reduces the incidence and adds about three mph to cruise speed.*

Navions have an extra 20-gallon tank under the rear seat or in the baggage compartment, and there are several different types of tip tanks available. The later Rangemasters had fuel capacities of up to 108 gallons, though of course that much could be carried only if cabin load were limited. Generally speaking, the older Navions with 60-gallon tanks can fly about 600 miles or so with a decent reserve. Heavy cabin loads will reduce this somewhat.

Loading

The average Navion weighs 1,900-2,000 pounds and has a gross weight of either 2,750 or 2,850, for a useful load of around 800 pounds. That is not particularly good. Four people and 100 pounds of bags leaves virtually nothing left over for fuel. The 260-hp model B is even worse. Its useful load is little better than the A model's, but it burns 20 percent more fuel, so load would be even more limited for the same trip.

The re-engined D, E and F models had increased gross weights that made the airplanes somewhat more practical for long trips. Useful load of the typical 260-hp Rangemaster is about 1,200 pounds, which allows a decent range even with four passengers and 100 pounds of luggage.

Passenger Comfort

A good part of the time a Navion owner spends *not* talking about performance is used to brag about passenger comfort. The Navion

is a *big* airplane, hulking high on its gear, and the passenger almost feels as if he's mounting an airliner as he climbs up onto the wing and into the cockpit. Although not as roomy as an airliner, the Navion is certainly roomier than the aforementioned Mooney and Comanche 180. The rear seat is a broad bench-type seat into which three people can wedge themselves without excessive torture, but we wouldn't recommend a long trip sitting like that. (With five people aboard, the Navion can't carry enough fuel to fly very far, so that problem should not arise.)

The seats are high and erect, much in the manner of the autos of the late '40s (not surprising). Navion riders feel a certain stateliness lacking in modern aircraft, whose passengers are wrapped somewhat more efficiently but less comfortably.

Unfortunately, nobody much cared about soundproofing in those days, and the cabin noise level in most Navions is high. The bad effects of cabin noise on passengers (and pilots) is universally underrated, but we think it is almost as important as cabin size and seat to the long-term comfort passenger comfort on a long trip. Many owners have done their own soundproofing jobs, however.

Handling

On the ground, the Navion is heavy and solid, rolling over ruts and cracks without undue clanking. The beefy construction and heavy landing gear are the result of North American's intent to sell military versions of the Navion (about 250 L-17s were eventually built) so the gear was built extra strong to meet military specs. In the air, the airplane is also very stable, in both roll and pitch, and makes a fine instrument platform.

The Navion's big selling point is its short-field capability. According to company brochures, the A model had a takeoff ground run of only 560 feet, and the later Rangemasters supposedly got off the ground in only 425 feet. Both of those figures are doubtless wildly inflated, but the Navion is in fact an excellent short-field machine. It has a moderate wing loading and a high-lift airfoil that combine to levitate the airplane off the runway with little effort. Starting in 1948, a three-position flap switch allowed takeoffs at half flaps, which shortened the roll considerably. The 1946 and '47 models had only two positions—up and do—and takeoffs had to be made with flaps up, but many of these earlier Navions have been modified with updated flaps.

For landing, full flaps and idled throttle will produce an astounding sink rate of 2,500 fpm at about 75 mph, which results in very steep approach angles and short landing rollouts.

Maintenance

Here's where a buyer in search of cheap transportation could get burned if he's not careful. The Navion has a staggering number of ADs. Have your mechanic check compliance carefully. Navion owners staunchly refute the airplane's reputation as a maintenance hog, and while a well-maintained and constantly flown Navion may not be too expensive to keep up, not all Navions will be either well used or well maintained. In fact, used Navions seemed to be divided into two general types: the neglected old dog that hardly ever flies and the pampered showpiece, with not much in between. Needless to say, the neglected dogs should be avoided at all costs, unless the buyer is

Avoid Navions like this one—*a tired, doggy 260B with the inefficient, expensive-to-run geared Lycoming engine.*

searching for a refurbishing project and is willing to sink prodigious amounts of time and money into restoration, just for the fun of it. Practically speaking, it would be much cheaper and quicker to simply buy a cream-puff in the first place.

Here is a brief rundown of potential trouble spots in used Navions:

• Landing gear. The Navion's hydraulic gear is notoriously unreliable. Retract links have been a problem in the past, and should have been replaced according to AD 61-12-4. The gear is hydraulically actuated, which complicates things further. Some owners have purposely limited hydraulic pressure to reduce strain on the system, with the result that retraction time can be as long as 15 or 20 seconds in some airplanes. The hydraulic system also means one more thing to remember during takeoff and landing, since the hydraulic system must be turned on and off for each retraction and extension cycle.

Some North American Navions may still have the original single-piston pumps, which were very troublesome. Most have been replaced with better pumps; if you buy one with the old pump, it should be replaced as soon as possible.

Also check the main gear for loose trunnions, a common problem. If they are loose or worn out, the gear won't stay up. Another common problem is nose-gear shimmy, usually caused by a hard landing or rolling over ruts. (Most Navions have a tail modification that increases speed but decreases pitch authority, so it's fairly easy to land on the nosewheel occasionally. More on the tail mod later.)

• Propeller. Original Navions had the Hartzell diaphragm-type variable-pitch propeller. The diaphragms always leak after a while, and must be replaced and adjusted fairly regularly.

• Corrosion. North American-built airplanes were completely zinc-chromated inside, and have generally resisted corrosion well. However, Ryan cut back on the corrosion-proofing to save money, so a Ryan-

Navion instrument panel *reflects the state of the art in the late '40s, but many owners have updated their panels.*

built A or B model should be closely checked for corrosion. Early Ryan models may be partly chromated, since they were built from parts bought from North American.

• Cooling. All the early Navions had updraft cooling, which was very inefficient. Many have been converted to downdraft cooling, which is a big improvement, and any Navion of 225-hp or more should definitely have downdraft cooling. The B model with the 260-hp Lycoming had oil temperature problems, but this can be cured with a larger aluminum oil cooler.

Parts
For many old aircraft—the Swift or Lus-

combe, for example—parts can be a problem. In most cases, however, Navion spares are still plentiful. When the military bought the L-17 version in the late '40s, it also ordered enough spares to last for the next century, and those parts have since found their way into civilian hands and are available to Navion owners. Best source is the Navion Society.

Certain parts are hard to come by, however. Because of the high frequency of gear-up landings, inboard flap hinges, certain nose gear parts and lower engine mount parts are in short supply.

Parts problems are also developing with the 205- and 225-hp Continentals in the early Navions. Continental no longer makes

Model	Year Built	Number Built	Cruise Speed (mph)	Rate of Climb (fpm)	Useful Load (lbs)	Fuel Std/Opt (gals)	Engine	TBO (hrs)	Overhaul Cost	Average Retail Price
Navion	1946-47	1,109	155	1,050	900	40/60	185-hp Continental	1,500	$ 5,000	$10,000
A	1948-50	946	155	1,050	900	40/60	205-hp Continental	1,500	$ 5,000	$11,000
B	1951	319	155	1,110	968	40/60	260-hp geared Lyc.	1,200	$11,000	$12,250
D	1958	15	165	1,200	1,000	108	240-hp Continental	1,506	$ 5,500	$12,500
E	1959	3	170	1,250	1,000	108	250-hp Continental	1,500	$ 6,500	$13,000
F	1960	12	175	1,300	1,000	108	260-hp Continental	1,200	$ 6,000	$14,500
Rangemaster G	1961	17	179	1,150	1,290	108	260-hp Continental	1,200	$ 6,000	$20,000
Rangemaster G-1	1962-64	131	179	1,250	1,390	108	260-hp Continental	1,200	$ 6,000	$22,500
Rangemaster H	1967-70	52	191	1,300	1,315	108/40	285-hp Continental	1,200	$ 7,500	$25-$30,000
Rangemaster H	1975-76	5	191	1,375	1,315	108/40	285-hp Continental	1,500	$ 7,500	$42-$45,000

Price is for basic stock aircraft with nav/com, ADF, aux tanks, 600 hours on the engine, with good paint and interior, and no major damage history. Many Navions have been highly modified, however, and will command higher prices, depending upon how extensively they have been rebuilt.

Performance is for stock aircraft. Most have been modified to some degree and will perform slightly better than these figures.

The hydraulic landing gear *on the Navion is notoriously unreliable. Hydraulic system must be turned on and off for each extension and retraction cycle.*

remans for these models, and has stopped production of critical parts like the crankshaft and crankcase. However, it's quite simple to convert any Navion to an IO-470 or even an IO-520.

Safety

By far the most common Navion accident is the gear-up landing, partly because the gear doesn't work all the time and partly because Navion owners tend to be low-time retractable pilots who forget to put the wheels down. Although expensive, the gear-ups rarely hurt anybody.

Fuel exhaustion or starvation accidents do hurt people, however, and the Navion has more than its share. An NTSB study from the '60s places the Navion right up with the Tri-Pacer and Bonanza as the aircraft most susceptible to fuel mismanagement. The original unmodified Navion fuel system was very straightforward. Two 20-gallon wing tanks were interconnected through a small sump tank in the fuselage, and the pilot could select only on or off. However, most Navions have been modified with fuselage tanks, baggage compartment tanks or tip tanks, and the plumbing and valving can get a bit tricky. Many Navions have only one fuel gauge, so in addition to carefully switching tanks, the pilot must also remember to reset the gauge selector to make sure that he's reading the same tank that's feeding the engine.

Another NTSB study ranks the Navion as the fifth worst among 32 singles in engine failure accident rate and in-flight airframe failure.

If you do crash a Navion, you're probably better off than you would be in most modern aircraft. It's built like a tank, to military

standards, and the cabin section is particularly beefy.

Modifications

Speed-crazed Navion owners have raised the practice of souping up airplanes to an art form. (That's not surprising, considering what there is to start with.) There is virtually no such thing as a stock airplane anymore, and some are hardly recognizable as the lumbering old North American bird. Here's a partial list of the mods available:

• Engines. Navions are regularly converted to 240-, 250- or 285-hp Continentals, and there is even a turbocharged 285-hp model flying.

• Canopies and windows. The original Navion had windows sealed with big strips of rubber molding that stuck way out into the slipstream and played havoc with the airflow. In addition, the two-piece windshield gave it the frumpy look of a 1948 Plymouth. Many owners have added flush-mounted one piece windshields and larger side windows, which add about three mph and spruce up the appearance.

• "Palo Alto Tail." The Navion's tail was inexplicably set at a rather high negative incidence, which requires excessive forward trim. Properly trimmed at cruise, the stabilizer, elevator and trim tab were all cockeyed to the breeze, not a particularly efficient state of affairs. The "Palo Alto Tail" mod resets the tail incidence, and the drop in trim drag increases speed by about three mph. (Some owners have accomplished the same thing by changing the incidence of the wing.) According to the Navion Society, virtually every Navion now flying has the tail mod.

• Wing root fillets. Not much speed increase, but Navioneers say it looks better.

• Toe Brakes. Most Navions have the original hand brake, which takes lots of muscle and makes tight turns difficult. Some have been modified with toe brakes to make them behave more normally on the ground.

• Fuel tanks. Two different kinds of fuselage auxiliary tanks and three different types of tip tanks are available. For Navions above 240 hp, the tips can hold as much as 34 gallons each, for a total of 108 gallons.

• Wingtip extensions. Sometimes called "zip tips," Navion wingtip extensions increase the airplane's modest rate of climb slightly. Obviously, you can't have both zip tips and tip tanks.

This is only a partial list; the parade of panel, interior and cosmetic mods available to Navion owners is almost endless.

Navion Society

Certainly the most enthusiastic owners club in the country, the American Navion Society is a must for anyone thinking of buying the airplane. ANS members are blindly and totally loyal to the Navion—they call themselves Navioneers and Navionettes, and worship the Navion as "perhaps the finest light aircraft ever built." In its newsletter, the Society modestly takes credit for "catapaulting the NAVION (they always reverently capitalize the name) from the world's most maligned to the world's most admired and desired plane." Hmmmmm.

Despite the occasional pretentious puffery, the Navion Society does an excellent job of providing technical advice and parts, in addition to sponsoring several Navion fly-ins a year. Of the 1,600 or so Navions still flying, 1,200 are owned by Navion Society members, a percentage unmatched by any other owners' organization. American Navion Society, Box 1175, Municipal Airport, Banning, California 92220. Tel.: 714-849-2213.

Summing Up

If you're looking for cheap, efficient transportation, forget the Navion. An old Skylane will haul a bigger load; an old Mooney or Comanche will go a lot faster on less fuel and will probably cost less in maintenance. But for antique appeal and a feeling of brotherly love, the Navion is a good choice. And if you absolutely must have the cheapest possible retractable, there isn't much choice.

The later Rangemasters provide decent performance and a roomy interior for a low initial price.

In any case, we wouldn't recommend the B model with the geared GO-435 Lycoming unless you plan to upgrade to the IO-470 engine soon after purchase. It has less performance and higher operating and maintenance costs than even the 225-hp models.

Owner Comments

"Navion is a comfortable-riding, roomy and docile plane. The feeling is similar to an old Packard. They were the luxury vehicle of their day, retain all of those good features, and have added a few more over the years. A Navion is very stable in rough air, and turbulence to others is just mild chop to us. The original windows were big, but the replacement single side windows are huge, and this contributes to rear-seat passenger comfort because the view is so little restricted, and you do not get the feeling that you are sitting in a bucket.

"In general it is a sturdy old bird. There are few if any cracks in the skins, the big wheels make them easy to move around on rough ground. The brakes are reliable and positive. (Our 1948 Ryan has the original brakes, and a panic stop might put you into the windshield.) The canopy latch is designed so that when it is locked, the handle turns around freely, and this makes it impossible to force the handle. When a whole line of planes at our airport was broken into, the Navion had damage to the canopy edge where the would-be thieves tried to pry in with a screwdriver, but they could not do it.

"The fact that the Navion sits very high makes it easy to taxi at night on a big airport where lower planes sit down in a sea of blue lights and cannot distinguish the pattern of taxiways. Of course, it also means that very high jacks are needed for an annual, but they are simple to make and quite a number of owners have their own, and will lend them.

"The Navion's c.g. is in a good position, and fuel use does not adversely affect it. If you load the baggage compartment too heavily, you cannot taxi, because the nosewheel will not come down onto the ground. This keeps you from taking off with the c.g. too far aft.

"The American Navion Society is based in California, and this could lead to very big phone bills for us on the East Coast. However, there are regional chapters, and anyone can call for advice much nearer home. The more local the advisor is, the more likely he is to know where to buy parts or who has one to swap. There are a few shops which specialize only in Navions and keep necessities in stock. They are spread around the country so wherever you may be, help is somewhere nearby.

"There are a number of perfectly legal engine options, and you can go faster than your friends. All it takes is money (to get the bigger engine, have it installed, buy a new prop, get more insurance, and buy that much more gas) and some time for the work.

"The famous hydraulics problem does not seem to exist. A properly maintained Navion takes gear and flaps up and down without incident. Other less-than-perfect aspects do exist, however. The plane is not very easy to get into. Or at least, it cannot be done very gracefully. Very few of them (mostly B models) have baggage doors, so luggage is hard to load. No new baggage doors are available, so only old ones from salvage can be installed—and they are scarce. Other scarce parts are: inboard flap hangers, and canopy locks. In many cases ventilation is poor in the cabin, but that is curable. Unless toe brakes have been installed, the turning radius on the ground is pretty wide."

"I sold my first Navion, N91532, in the summer of 1975 for the (then) unheard price of $14,500 without any radios. The reason for the high price was because it had been converted to a 225-hp down-draft cooled version of the original E-series engine. Was the airplane worth it? You bet it was. I decided to spend the money improving it because two previous owners had spent over $25,000 in improvements to the original airplane.

"Strangely the Navion has survived in spite of the fact that it has never had the benefit of a 2,000-hour engine. I have never seen a Continental of any type go more than 800 hours before requiring major surgery. Stuck rings, burned valves, worn out oil pumps and cracked cylinder heads are all I ever see. Although Continental cannot be blamed for poor installations and poor cooling baffling such as we see on all the high-performance engines, other aircraft equipped with these engines seem to have similar longevity and service problems.

"Of the Navions I have owned, I am convinced that the E-series 225-hp engine probably has the best service life. One Navion had approximately 450 hours when I bought it and I flew it 150 hours and sold it. The engine had its last major overhaul in 1965. The new owner is still flying it (three years later) and it hums along nicely at about 160 mph on less than 11 gph. Based upon my accumulated experience, I believe the primary reason this particular engine does so well is because it has the very well baffled, down-draft cooling system developed and still available from Sy Symons of Torrance, Calif. Sy has been turning out the conversion kits for over 20 years. Sy Symons, 213-534-2161 or through Blues Flying Service, 213-534-4471.

"Incidentally, the hydraulic system stories seem to come from misinformed or jealous competitors or underfinanced owners who insist on 'sole ownership' of an airplane, and who cannot afford any outlay for maintenance. They buy and struggle with maintenance and never catch up. Typically I have found the single-unit control valve assemblies normally go for 20 years without service. We replaced a 'New York' hydraulic pump recently. It had been installed originally with the 240-hp engine in 1959. The hydraulic actuating cylinders typically go the same 20 years if they are flown often enough (five to 10 hours per month at least)."

"I purchased a 1950 B-model in December, 1977. In my opinion this is the best model Navion ever built. The only problem is with the GO-435-C2 260-hp engine. This is an older type geared prop and not as reliable as the newer engines.

"In 1961 I also had a B-model with the same engine, and this was my chief complaint then. I replaced it with an IO-470-H Continental, flew it for a satisfactory 200 hours and then sold it.

"I am replacing the engine of my present aircraft with an IO-520-BA Continental, with a three-bladed prop. The cost of this replacement is just over $15,000, by using a factory remanufactured engine."

The Navion stands tall on its gear, *so boarding is a bit more adventurous than usual. Sliding canopy adds to the fun.*

Few airplanes have gone so far on looks and charisma as the Globe and Temco Swift series. In production for only half a decade, used Swifts have been the focus of such intense interest that a myriad of modifications has been devised for everything from powerplants to tailwheels. Far from being in the "defunct and unavailable" category, Swift parts are readily available and often of new manufacture.

The Globe Aircraft Co. dropped a 1941 pre-World War II steel tube, fabric-covered wooden-wing design to build Beech twin trainers; then in 1945 it certificated a re-designed version with all-metal construction and retractable gear—the GC-1A. This had an 85-hp Continental and a Beech-Roby controllable-pitch prop.

In a matter of months, the 85-hp version was dropped in favor of a 125-hp Continental, and the GC-1B was born, using an Aeromatic prop. In the face of financial difficulties, Globe subcontracted everything to the Texas Engineering and Manufacturing Co. (Temco) and then went bankrupt in 1947, whereupon Temco took over until the line was terminated in 1951. Temco also built about 17 tandem modifications called the T-35 Buckaroo for a military competition, but lost to the tricycle-gear Beech T-34 Mentor. In all, about 375 of the 85-hp and 1178 of the 125-hp models were built. Some 640 Swifts of all powerplant persuasions are believed to survive.

Later all rights to the Swift were sold to what is now known as the Univair Aircraft Corp. near Denver, Colorado. And this company remains the main source of replacement parts and equipment for the line.

Flying Qualities
Despite its name and delightful lines that suggest great styling finesse, the airplane in its original configuration must be considered draggy and not very fast. Consider that even with 125 horses, the retractable-gear Swift can be given a good run for the money by a fixed-gear Grumman American Trainer with only 108 hp. In its original cowling,

even the muscular 220-hp Franklin-powered modification at 180 mph full cruise will be eaten alive by the 200-hp four-place Mooney 201. Granted, that's an extreme example that represents a few decades of engineering thinking, but on the other hand, with a cruise of 125 to 130 mph, a 125-hp Swift is not terribly faster than a 100-hp Cessna 150, which can register 120 mph if pushed at altitude.

Perhaps the most pleasant aspect of flying a Swift is the feather touch of the controls. The airplane looks nimble, and it is—in spades. Thanks to construction under the old Part 4 certification requirements, the airplane not only handles like an aerobatic airplane, it is, stressed to 7.2 Gs positive and 4.4 Gs negative.

Oddly, however, the airplane is placarded against intentional spins, reportedly because of a tendency to tighten up and flatten out as the turns build up.

Landing the airplane has given lots of pilots fits, and the short-coupled bird has a long record of groundlooping with slow-footed pilots, especially in gusty crosswinds.

The 220-hp Franklin *just fits inside the stock cowl.*

The preferred method of landing is to touch down on the main wheels, which takes an extra bit of finesse. The takeoff phase has taken its toll also, mostly because the 85-hp version is a bit underpowered, and on a warm day the 125 is no rocketship, and pilots tend to sail off into the trees or abort too late to avoid careening off the runway.

Living up to its reputation as a hot little ship in one way, at least, the Swift is suited to a fairly fast final approach of about 90 mph, according to many Swift pilots, although the stall is straightforward and quite tame.

In terms of human engineering, Swifts have fantastic visibility, cramped quarters

Now for the interesting part: *a 125-hp Swift ready for the flare.*

Slotted leading edge *is supposed to improve the stall.*

Franklin engines, outer wing panel fuel cells, gear motors, retractable tailwheel kit and many others.

Swift Alturair, 1405 N. Johnson, El Cajon, Calif. 92020. Molded fiberglass speedcowlings, down-draft engine baffles, Buckaroo wingtips, auxiliary fuel tank kits, instrument panel glare shields, rudder tip fairings, engine mounts and battery relocation kits.

Univair Aircraft Corp., Rt. 3, Box 59, Aurora, Colo. 80010, holds the type certificate on the Swift and can provide nearly every conceivable part and component needed for the aircraft.

Several modifications are almost universally considered worthwhile on the Swift series. One of these provides a more secure

for two adults in nonadjustable seats, an absurdly located trim crank alongside the pilot's ear, a noisy cockpit, and over-the-gunwhale entry and exit. Strangely, the flap lever is shaped like a wheel and the gear like a flap.

Aircraft Systems
The airplane has hydraulic gear and flaps, with a small electric hydraulic pump. It has two 13.8-gallon wingtanks that pilots feel makes the aircraft too short-legged when larger engines are added.

The early tailwheels were either fully swiveling and devilish, or steerable, and mounted with small shock absorbers.

Load Carrying Ability
The 125-hp models have a useful load of 585 pounds, which would allow for two adults, full fuel and about 64 pounds of baggage in the small rear compartment (which is supposed to be able to take 100 pounds structurally). This is located directly behind the seats, and access is gained by tipping the seatbacks forward.

Modifications
There is a raft of these, most prominent of which are the engines. As far as we know, STCs have been obtained for 11 powerplants in addition to the original 85-hp and 125-hp Continentals. Among these are the Continental C-90, O-200, C-145 and IO-360; Lycoming 125-, 150-, 160-, 180- and 200-hp engines; and Franklin 165-, 220- and 250-hp turbo engines.

However, only the following are around in any numbers: 145-hp, 150-hp, 180-hp, 210-hp and 220-hp.

Major STC holders and the modifications they can supply are:

Hugh Evans of Machen, Inc., S. 3608 Davison Blvd., Spokane, Wash. Conversions to 210-hp Continental and 220-hp

Model	Price Range	Approximate Cruise Speed	Comments
GC-1A (85 hp)	$5,000-$8,000	110-120 mph	Only about 20 still are in existence. Most have been re-engined.
GC-1B (125 hp)	$6,000-$12,000 basket case: $3,500	125-130 mph	Most common stock model.
Re-engined models:			
145-hp Continental	$6,500-$12,500	130-135 mph	Common conversion, easily done. No modification of cowl, baffling or exhaust system required.
150-hp Lycoming	$10,000-$15,000	135-140 mph	Constant-speed prop improves takeoff and and climb greatly over 145 hp.
180-hp Lycoming	$16,000-$18,000	160-165 mph	
210-hp Continental	$18,000-$22,000	165-170 mph	Climb rate: approximately 1,800 fpm
220-hp Franklin	$20,000-$25,000	170-175 mph	Much more efficient than Continental, especially at altitude.

Total number built: 1,550, 90 percent of them in 1946; about 400 85-hp models; 1,150 125-hp models.

Note: Many Swifts have been painstakingly modified by owners and may be capable of slightly higher speeds than listed. Some higher-horsepower Swifts are lavishly equipped with avionics and may therefore command higher prices than listed.

type of canopy hatch fastening than the single central latch on the original models. It seems that the old hatch, which hinges from the front, tends to open a bit in flight at the rear corners, causing a lot of wind noise. The mods generally devise a way to hold the corners of the hatch more securely.

Another useful modification is an electric boost pump to replace the hand wobble pump on the original models. With the wobble pump, losing an engine shortly after takeoff from fuel starvation because the engine-driven pump had gone out would require a distracting amount of pumping by the pilot to get the engine going again. With the electric pump, the pilot merely switches it on for takeoff and landing in the conventional way.

The Swift Association has the rights to this pump, and for $10 to cover paperwork will permit installation by Swift owners, who normally purchase the pump from a commercial supplier.

For a little extra comfort, pilots can install Cessna 150 seats, which are lighter than the original ones, and can be fitted on tracks so they are adjustable.

Owners who are willing to sacrifice the classic original cowl can gain quite a bit of efficiency by installing fiberglass cowls and special engine baffles designed to reduce cooling drag.

Since the original 12-volt motor that drove the hydraulic pump was a bit on the weak side, many owners have switched to motors of greater output.

And in the past, as the brake clips became loose on the old Goodyear brakes, resulting in locked brakes and groundloops, owners normally installed Cleveland wheels and brakes as a cheaper alternative to fixing the old ones.

Typical Swift cockpit: *strange-looking wheels, plastic panel trim.*

Among the mods that are regarded with mixed feelings is one that adds a dorsal fin to the airplane to smooth out tail-wagging in turbulence. An undesirable side effect is the increased tendency of the airplane to weathervane on crosswind landings because of the extra vertical surface.

Also, there are several different canopy designs, one-piece windshields and different wingtips for any who are interested. But it must be mentioned that there seems to be a growing trend back toward the original classic configurations. A new interest even has developed in the little 85-hp model.

Safety

Prospective Swift owners should be aware of the fact that the aircraft has a devastating safety record. Among 15 aircraft no longer in production compared in an accident study by the NTSB, the Swift had the worst fatal accident rate, by a considerable margin.

Adding on 18 other current production aircraft to the roster still left the Swift with the worst record of all.

Among all 33 aircraft, the Swift had the highest engine failure accident rate and the second highest accident rate for in-flight airframe failure.

Association

There is no more dedicated fraternity than Swift fliers, who have their own International Swift Assn., Box 644, Athens, Tenn. 37303. They regularly have massive fly-ins of gorgeous Swifts of every configuration. They also publish a newsletter that goes back over a decade.

Swift Rationale

Charlie Nelson of the Swift Association has a few sage bits of advice for any pilots who might be considering ownership of a Swift. He suggests it is not the pedestrian type of airplane you buy merely for transportation and then lock in the hangar and forget between trips. It is for the connoisseur who loves performance and appreciates that the aircraft has evolved into a classic. It takes an extra bit of finesse to handle, says Mr. Nelson, and all too often John Q. Pilot who has flown Musketeers and Cherokees all his life will be biting off more than he can chew unless he's willing to undergo thorough transition training by an experienced, current Swift pilot—not just any old instructor familiar with taildraggers in general.

If this sounds a bit chauvinistic, Nelson can cite all too many examples where insufficient experience with the bird resulted in the loss of airplane and/or pilots. A typical example: a botched takeoff, a climbout behind the power curve, terminated by a spin into the ground.

James W. Young's classic: *raw aluminum polished till it gleams.*

Owner Comments

"When a Swift owner tells you how fast his Swift is, you must first take into account his 30-year-old airspeed indicator. Then look at his static system. That has proven to be a major factor in "fast" Swifts. Some Swifts I have flown give accurate true airspeeds like this for cruise: 125 Continental: 125 to 130 mph, 145 Continental: 135 to 140 mph, 150 Lycoming: 145 to 150 mph, 180 Lycoming: 160 to 165 mph, 210 Continental: 170 to 175 mph. The constant-speed propeller is the major factor in climb.

"The Swift is especially susceptible to corrosion if it is near salt air. Wing, horizontal, and vertical ribs are good candidates to look at. The forward horizontal stabilizer spar is a must to inspect, especially outboard of the tail fairings. A mirror, flashlight and screwdriver will be needed to see this area. Intergranular corrosion is becoming a problem in unprotected Swifts there.

"The forward horizontal spar and the bulkhead it attaches to are fatigue areas if many snap rolls have been performed. Also check the rear horizontal spar attach bracket for loose rivets.

"The hydraulic system is actually very simple and can be worked on quickly and cheaply. I have rebuilt both left and right actuators in the wheel wells, counting removal and replacement, in three hours.

"The major problem with the hydraulic system is the electric motor which runs it. The motor is adequate if maintained. However, for people who don't want to spend time once a year to clean the armature, several high-power replacements are available. I have one from Joe Zito that has been working for five years and retracts the gear very quickly.

"Although there are multitudes of avionics and modifications that have been legally installed on Swifts, there are certain mods that are worth mentioning: Cleveland wheels and brakes, Scott steerable tailwheel, wingtip strobe lights, Temco turnover structure, trim wheel relocation, flat instrument panel, bubble windshield, almost any canopy conversion, most engine conversions, any auxiliary fuel installations, downdraft cooling systems (generally requires a special cowling), battery relocation, shoulder harnesses, wingtips are optional depending on personal preference, long gear doors, electric fuel boost pump, and large capacity gear motor.

"The so-called heavy and light landing gears are really a fallacy. The only real difference in the ELI and ADEL landing gears is the shock strut operation, not their weight-on strength.

"The stock Continental 85- and 125-hp Swifts are becoming rare birds. The updraft cooling is not adequate for hot summer days. Oil temps and cylinder head temps generally go over the redline on climbout in the summer. The C-125 also has a non-counterbalanced crankshaft that has a tendency to vibrate and break bearing journals.

"The heavy-case C-125-2 came out to remedy the problem but was not really adequate until the C-145 balanced crankshaft was introduced. For these reasons many 125 Swifts have very low time. C-85-powered Swifts also are found to be low-time aircraft. There are many Swifts flying with less than 1,000 hours total time. However, low time on a Swift may mean considerable damage, corrosion, and wrinkles. The best Swifts are the ones that have been flown and cared for.

"Manuals and parts are available from the holder of the type certificate: Univair Aircraft Corp., Route 3, Box 59, Aurora, Colorado 80011."

Chuck Lischer, Jr.
9905 Via Francis
Santee, Calif. 92071

Lischer is on the Board of Directors of the Swift Association and has several STCs on Swifts and does airshows in his Swift. He also helps a small company which holds STCs for Swifts named Swift Alturair, 1405 N. Johnson, El Cajon, Calif. 92020. —Ed.

"From May 1972 until August 1976 I owned a Model GCIB 125-hp Globe Swift S/N1106 N80913, manufactured August 1946.

"During this period, the total accumulated time was 305 hours and a recorded 760 takeoffs and landings. The total Swift expenses were $5,268.54, or $17.27 per tach hour. This included gas, oil, maintenance, liability insurance (no hull), tiedown, annual inspection, aircraft improvement, city, state and Federal taxes, registration and radio license. The actual total cost is even $21 less because I bought the Swift for $3,700 and sold it for $5,800. The breakdown of these expenses is as follows:

"Extraordinary items included under maintenance are two rebuilt cylinders (No. 3 and 5) in 1976; conversion from Goodyear brakes to new Clevelands in 1975; a transponder installed in 1974; a No. 1 cylinder head in 1973 under warranty.

"Some of the good points include outstanding aileron response during aileron rolls; it is very easy to make wheel landings—keep her at 80 mph on final and then give just a touch of power with the vernier at touchdown—a perfect wheels landing every time; it makes beautiful 2-G tight turns; it is hard to forget to put down the gear—a horn is tied into throttle position, plus there are visual wires on the gear, and gear lights. This is an attractive, very responsive aircraft that is truly a delight to fly.

"Some points to be careful about:

"The clips on the Goodyear brake discs pop out on takeoff and then lock up the wheel, unknown to you. On landing, the lock-up causes disintegration of about one-third of the inner section of the wheel hub. This happened three times in one year, which prompted my switch to Clevelands, which work beautifully. The hub disintegration never caused a tire to come off, but there is no way to taxi without a brake, so you must tow it in.

"The hydraulic flap and landing gear circuit always seem to leak a little, so you absolutely must check the hydraulic reservoir weekly. This is really not a difficult task, and I must say I never had a landing-gear retraction failure. Quite often when the hydraulic fluid is low the flaps will not retract on initial start-up.

"The C125-2 Continental engine sparkplugs are very prone to lead fouling with 100-octane low lead. The plugs would completely fill up with lead balls every 15-20 hours.

"During my first demonstration of rolls with an instructor the rudder bar spring broke. This was no problem, though, as the left-side rudder was still okay.

"The Swift does not have brakes on the right side, so this makes things a little hairy during the first hours of transition for the poor instructor."

Auxiliary fuel tanks *like this one fit outboard of the original tanks.*

Beech Debonair

History has smiled on Beech's "dowdy" old Debonair. With old age it has climbed in prestige from the status of also-ran to one of the most sought-after queens of the used-plane fleet. Once considered a ho-hum performer, as engine power and cabin sizes in other aircraft were growing by leaps and bounds, the 225-hp Beech has won a niche in a fuel-hungry world as a sensible, economy aircraft.

With its more powerful and glamorous V-tailed cousins smarting from a history of in-flight structural breakup problems, the prosaic conventional tailplane arrangement of the Debonairs looks better than ever. On top of that, it shares with its straight-tail Bonanza kin the most outstanding safety record of any single-engine aircraft.

History

The Beech 33 Debonairs were in production for one fortuitous decade, between 1960 and 1970. The line went through five model changes in the process—the most significant of which marked the introduction of a large, tapered third window at the rear of the cabin.

The 225-hp Continental IO-470 remained throughout, with only one small accessory change. The Debonair name was dropped by Beech with the 1968 model for the "Bonanza" moniker in favor of a stronger identification with the then-more prestigious butterfly-tailed birds.

To chronicle specific significant changes, the A33 model in 1961 added a small rear window to the aft portion of the cabin, raised the maneuvering speed from 142 to 147 mph, upped the gross weight by 100 pounds and provided a hatshelf.

The B33 model in 1962 made a significant change to the fuel system. Earlier models had been burdened with four separate wing tanks—two 25-gallon mains and two 10-gallon aux tanks, as an option. This gave a stan-

dard usable capacity of 44 gallons, or 63 gallons with the optional aux cells.

Since excess fuel from the fuel injection system is routed from the aux tanks to the left main cell only, pilots must remember to use the left main cell till it is about half full before switching to the aux tanks.

A further inconvenience, and possibly a safety hazard, is the fact that the fuel gauge on the 33 and A33 models reads only the tank selected, not total fuel on board.

With the B33 model, Beech eliminated the separate aux cells, incorporating the standard Bonanza two-tank system with a left and a right main. This brought optional fuel up to 80 gallons (74 usable) and provided a full-time display of fuel in both tanks simultaneously, no matter where the fuel selector was positioned.

At the same time the picturesque, but rather haphazard grouping of flight instruments and controls in the Debonair was replaced with a more sensible panel configuration. And the line of the vertical tail was changed slightly with addition of a small fillet at the fuselage juncture.

With the C33 in 1965 the big third

window came on line, and the dorsal fin reached its full flowering. The rear bench seats of earlier models were abandoned in the C model for individual rear seats. And the gross weight made another small jog by 50 pounds up to a total of 3,050.

Other little touches to the C model included a new ram's horn control wheel, a larger hat shelf and better heater.

The E model in 1968 and the F model in 1970 brought no significant improvements or changes.

Investment Value

As an investment, the 33s must be ranked with the rest of the gold-plated Beech Bonanza line. They bottomed out quickly years ago, and then began a steady climb through the years, pushed by inflation and the rising price of new models. We tracked a 1962 B33 and a 1969 E33 to follow the price curve, and found the older model had climbed right back up to within about $2,000 of its original (paper) value ($29,300). The later model displayed an equally strong growth curve, appreciating in (paper) value from a low point of $24,000 to $36,000 in 1980.

When does a Debonair stop being a Debonair? *With the 1968-70 E33 and F33 models, when they were called Bonanzas. The last evolution of the line had the steeply swept windshield, big rear windows and dorsal fin with air intake.*

Handling

To the pilot's touch, the 225-hp Debonairs share with their fellow Bonanzas a felicitous blend of efficient aerodynamics and delightful handling qualities. The machines are endowed with just the right aileron and elevator response—strong, smooth and effective. Owners point out, though, that the other side of the controllability coin is an enlarged workload in instrument conditions, because a wing drop left unattended may keep right on rolling.

As with most of the Bonanza genre, the Debonairs exhibit crisp stall behavior with a modest amount of prewarning buffet—with a clean break and maybe a wing drop. The Debonair is no Cherokee or Skylane in this category; it will not bobble up and down interminably with the control wheel held full back.

Unlike its contemporary, the Piper Comanche, the Beech Debonair is a cinch to land gracefully nearly every time, though one pilot said the interconnected aileron and rudder on his aircraft made gusty crosswind landings a bit of a challenge, and rather more work than he'd like.

Performance

Though the Debonair will climb with surprising smartness in a short-field situation, it is no Redstone rocket on the way to cruise altitude. Pilots count on no more than 500 to maybe 600 fpm on a typical cross-country climb. This is rather typical even of bigger-engined Bonanzas, however.

But such is the price of economy, apparently, since leveled out in cruise, the 33 Debonairs yield a tidy 170 to 175 mph (148 to 152 knots), burning 11.5 to 12 gph. Naturally, some Debonair fliers claim true airspeeds up near 180, and higher, but we are inclined to think this is a bit out of the ordinary.

The modest 225-hp powerplant also

gives rise to a fairly common complaint among Debonair pilots that high density altitude situations demand quite a bit of caution.

As with all Bonanzas and Barons, the Debonair offers a fine gear-lowering speed of 165 mph/143 kts on B33 and later models (though the earlier ones were limited to 140 mph/122 kts). Naturally, the higher limits mean greater facility in mixing with fast traffic at high-density airports.

Cabin Design

Pilots and passengers who climb into even the old B33 model with the tiny truncated rear windows cannot help but be impressed with the feeling of breadth and airiness in the Debonair. Naturally, the enlarged windows of the C and later models enhance this quality even more. On the B33 and older models, the rear bench seat is something of an anachronism today, but is surprisingly wide and comfortable.

Baggage compartment structural capacity is a generous 270 pounds, though owners caution that exceeding the aft limits of the weight-and-balance

envelope is a matter for close computation, if not quite the concern merited in the V-tail models.

Cockpit Engineering

Like all the Bonanzas, the Debonairs have the single throwover wheel as standard equipment. And they share the reversed and often painful (to the pocketbook and pride, mostly) arrangement of the gear and flap levers. The NTSB recently called on the FAA to require a conversion on new production Bonanzas, and guard shields on gear levers to prevent inadvertent gear retraction on the ground for aircraft already configured in the reverse way.

Our check of NTSB accidents for Debonairs in the five years from 1974 to 1978 showed the greatest single cause of nonfatal accidents was inadvertent gear retraction on the runway. There were three of these in a total of 16 nonfatal accidents.

Pilots used to the conventional power control arrangement of (left to right) throttle, prop and mixture, might also find the location of the mixture control below the throttle a bit confusing.

The fuel selector is discretely posi-

The instrument panel *is one of the major variables in the Debonair. This one has dual control wheels instead of the standard throwover wheel.*

Model	Year	Number Built	Average Retail Price	Cruise Speed (mph)	Rate of Climb (fpm)	Useful Load (lbs)	Fuel Std/Opt (gals)	Engine	TBO (hrs)	Overhaul Cost
33	1960	233	$25,000	180	1,010	1,170	50	225-hp Continental	1,500	$5,600
A33	1961	152	$26,000	180	960	1,255	50/70	225-hp Continental	1,500	$5,600
B33	1962	200	$27,000	185	960	1,225	50/80	225-hp Continental	1,500	$5,600
B33	1963	137	$28,000	185	960	1,225	50/80	225-hp Continental	1,500	$5,600
B33	1964	89	$29,000	185	960	1,225	50/80	225-hp Continental	1,500	$5,600
C33	1965	157	$32,000	185	980	1,196	50/80	225-hp Continental	1,500	$5,600
C33	1966	86	$34,000	185	980	1,196	50/80	225-hp Continental	1,500	$5,600
C33	1967	62	$36,000	185	980	1,196	50/80	225-hp Continental	1,500	$5,600
E33	1968	81	$35,000	185	930	1,188	50/80	225-hp Continental	1,500	$5,600
E33	1969	34	$36,000	185	930	1,188	50/80	225-hp Continental	1,500	$5,600
F33	1970	20	$38,000	185	930	1,188	50/80	225-hp Continental	1,500	$5,600

tioned on the floor below the pilot's left knee. However, we noted no accidents caused by fuel starvation or exhaustion in the five-year period studied. And that's rare.

New Debonair pilots must also learn not to turn on the electric fuel boost pump routinely during landing or take-off, since the engine will be flooded. One accident was credited in the Safety Board listing to pilot use of the boost pump on final approach, resulting in an engine stoppage.

Safety

As we mentioned before, the Debonairs share with all the straight-tail Bonanzas an excellent all-around safety record when compared with other single-engine retractables. The fatal accident rate per 100,000 flight hours for the Beech 33 as a group (that includes the more powerful straight-tail 33 Bonanzas and Debonairs, too) was 1.0 compared with 2.9 for an old rival, the Piper Comanche, and 4.0 for a sister ship, the Beech 24 Sierra. The total accident rate for 33s also was the lowest among the 13 aircraft studied by *The Aviation Consumer* in a special NTSB runout of accident statistics.

The greatest single cause of fatal accidents among the 11 reported in the five-year runout among Debonairs was VFR pilots getting caught in IFR conditions they couldn't handle. Another flew into a thunderstorm. There were no in-flight structural failures, however. And only one fatal was related to a mechanical failure—this one blamed on an errant fuel pump.

Along with accidental gear retractions, the greatest cause of nonfatal accidents among the Debonairs was engine failure—one because of a faulty magneto, another because the mixture was set too lean; the third, unknown.

There were no other clear accident trends, just a scattering of isolated problems: a groundloop, a stall, an overshoot in gusty conditions ...

Owners may have shoulder harnesses retrofitted, but at the stinging price of around $900, according to one pilot.

Owners also should ask for the updated GAMA format Pilot's Operating Handbook. It is much more informative than the original.

Maintenance

Owners who replied to our request for feedback on the Debonairs said the air-

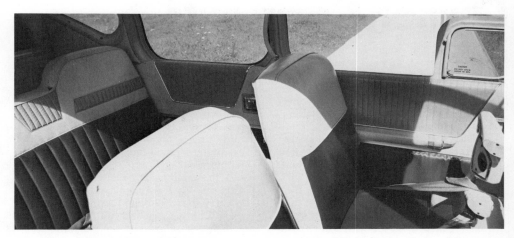

The B33 Model Debonair, *like this 1963 edition, have the small rear windows, bench seat in the rear and two-piece windshield. Baggage capacity is a healthy 270 pounds structurally.*

craft offers an average maintenance load, compounded by what they characterized as the high—"outrageously high," one said—cost of parts. However, they reported satisfaction in general with service on the airplane and good backup from the factory, with reasonable parts availability—something that speaks well for Beech after a decade and more of a gap in production.

The most expensive single event—and a not uncommon one, at that—that gives trouble on the Debonair is a set of Goodyear fuel cells that have begun to deteriorate. Naturally, this problem is shared with other aircraft as well. Debonair owners report parting with $2,000 for replacement of the two wing cells. Prospective buyers would do well to determine whether the original tanks are still in the airplane—and then negotiate a reduced price or expect to shoulder a massive repair bill in the near future. Buyers should also look more favorably on Debonairs with Uniroyal cells, since they last longer.

Another chronic problem with Debonairs involves the Goodyear brakes. Pilots report that replacing them with Clevelands ends a raft of troubles. Owners of 33 and A33 models note that the old-style instrument panel is a special bear for maintenance. The powerplant's greatest shortcoming is probably its modest 1,500-hour TBO. Operators report frequent high oil consumption and plugs loading up when 100LL is used in place of the 80 octane the ship prefers. The Slick magnetos also come in for their share of owner complaints.

Airworthiness Directives

The two big ADs on the Debonairs applied to the fuel tanks: one required prohibition of turning takeoffs or prolonged slipping in flight with less than half-full tanks, to prevent unporting and engine stoppage. The other called for inspection of the fuel cells for deterioration and leakage. A baffling kit is available to prevent unporting problems; buyers should see if this is installed, as a valuable safety factor.

Modifications

One-piece windshields are supplied by Great Lakes Aero Products at Flint, Minn., and Beryl D'Shannon Aviation Specialties, in Jordan, Minn. Clark three-light gear position indicators can be installed, through Harold M. Clark, Jr., Olympia, WA. Fiberglass tip tanks of 15-gallon capacity are supplied by Beryl D'Shannon.

A cabin and engine compartment fire suppression system is credited to Fike Metal Products in Blue Springs, MO.

Installation of an enlarged rear window and baggage compartment is done by Beryl D'Shannon.

A Sky-Ox oxygen system is provided by Rajay Industries in Long Beach, CA. Flap and aileron fairings and seals are part of an aerodynamic clean-up package from Smith Speed Conversions at Johnson, KS. The mod reportedly increases cruising speeds by up to 15 mph.

Associations

Debonair owners can rally to the flag of the American Bonanza Society located at Reading Municipal Airport, Box 3749, Reading, PA 19605.

Owner Comments

"Passengers who've never flown before feel comfortable, and my wife likes its 'face.' This is very important. She thinks it has a happy 'face' and looks ready to fly, even on the ground. If you have ever had a plane whose face your wife didn't like, you know what I mean.

"The 225 Continental seems an easily repairable engine. Using 100 LL, which is all I can get, having seen no 80 octane for a couple of years, the plugs load up fast. I have a six-cylinder EGT, but the setting always seems to work out on the flow gauge at about 12 gph, and that's what it clocks when I refuel. I change or clean plugs about every 20 hours: makes no difference if I've been on long trips flying high and lean or short trips flying low and dirty.

"Never had an inflight failure of anything except once a side of the exhaust manifold blew out (a hole about three inches across) on takeoff, and that was a rented Deb, not my own.

"With just a wing leveler (B-1) my present airplane will hold course and speed (given easy winds) even through moderate turbulence, it is so stable; and of course it has the famed Beech 'feel' in flying. I flew a new A-36 a few weeks ago and truly could not tell the difference except for extra climb-out power.

"You know that all Deb owners habitually overload their aircraft, especially those planes with large tanks (80 gals). You can get well over limits if you keep the weight forward and not lose trim capability. I don't advise it for others but I think the plane would fly full of bricks if it had to.

"Problems? The trim is too sensitive. The slightest shift in passenger position or no weight shift at all and the pilot is back at the trim wheel. However, this plane can be trimmed right into landing flare.

"Gas tank setting can be turned to off if you are not careful. My routine is *always* to look.

"Panel lighting poor, especially since VOR heads are mounted behind the throw-over wheel yoke. I am 6'2" and have to scrunch sometimes to see the dials and use a penlight at night to check on the dim things. I realize I could have better lighting installed. Point is, the factory could have.

"Fuel tanks: after six or eight years, they go. Replaced them on my first Deb; second one had new ones aboard."

"As an airline pilot with an extensive general aviation background, I believe the Beech Model 33 is the most satisfying single-engine X-country airplane that I have ever flown.

"The early Debonair provides an outstanding balance of economy and performance. The Continental IO-470 engine at 65 percent power will burn 11.5 gals/hr and at 10,000 feet MSL, will give an honest 150 knots TAS. I flight plan for one gallon every five minutes of flight time and can usually tell the line person how much fuel the tanks will hold within a half-gallon.

"The Debonair is a real four-place airplane. My full IFR airplane will *legally* carry four 170-pound adults, 100 pounds of baggage and full fuel (50 gallons). Standard fuel is enough for three hours flying plus an hour reserve. This is as long as I can sit in a light airplane without a stop anyway. VFR, I flight plan for 500-statute-mile legs. For IFR operation, I often would like to have more fuel.

"Factory-installed auxiliary tanks on early (1960-61) airplanes were of limited value. They only increased fuel capacity by 20 gallons and added quite a lot of weight. The Flight Extender tip tanks made by Beryl are a much better alternative.

"Cabin comfort improves with each model year up to about 1967. My aircraft has adequate cabin volume for four full-size adults plus lots of baggage. Ventilation is better than a Comanche but not nearly as good as a Cessna 210. Visibility is excellent. Noise level is average (high).

"My Debonair is the best-flying lightplane I have ever flown. Control forces are light at all speeds and control harmony is near perfect. Takeoffs feel 'solid' even at high altitude airports and good landings are easy. The Model 33 does have a tendency to yaw in turbulence, but does not Dutch-roll like the Model 35.

"The Model 33 is not a particularly good instrument airplane. The same qualities that make the Debonair such a pleasurable airplane to fly visually, make it a handful on instruments. It has almost 'neutral' stability and one must devote a great deal of attention to just controlling the aircraft. If any serious instrument flying is anticipated, a reliable autopilot should have high priority.

"Of the early Debonairs, the B-33 (1962-64) is the most airplane for the money. These models have a much improved instrument panel and a lot of standard equipment which was optional or not available on previous models.

"The Debonair is not a high maintenance airplane but *is* expensive to maintain. This is because very few standard aircraft parts are used on this airplane, and anything purchased from Beechcraft is outrageously expensive. I have found that most normally replaced parts are stocked by Beech service facilities and most other parts can be supplied by the factory in just a few days. Even obscure airframe parts for very old models can be supplied in a reasonable time. Service support has been excellent and I have even seen the factory take a part off their assembly line to get my aircraft back into the air.

"The quality of construction is extremely high and each part fits together like you would expect of a fine machine.

"The Continental engine on my airplane has proven extremely reliable with only routine maintenance."

"As an owner with a fair amount of mechanical ability, I do 95 percent plus of the maintenance myself. I find the bird relatively easy to maintain. If I have a complaint, it would be the price of Beech parts. They are quite high (approximately $120 for a throttle cable, $325 for an exhaust collector stack, $500 for a 40-gal. fuel cell, etc.) but factory service and support is quite good.

"From a safety point of view, the Debonair would be hard to beat. It has an enviable record in spite of us humans who fly it. Stalls give plenty of warning, and short-field performance is excellent—even when loaded to max gross. On instrument conditititions, it is quite stable, although it must have continuing attention from the pilot or from an autopilot in turbulent air."

"As you are aware, this model Beech with full fuel, four people and baggage, will exceed the aft c.g. limit, especially after some of the fuel has burned off. Therefore, the aircraft is very marginal with that type of load.

"One need only fly the other OEM's airplanes in order to appreciate the smooth, positive, quick response to control inputs this airplane has.

"To get this type of control response, though, Beech has eliminated the roll canceling capability some less responsive airplanes have. If a wing begins to drop, no matter how slowly, it will continue to drop until stopped and rolled level again. In addition, although this is a standard tail (I wouldn't fly in a V-tail, thanks to your expose), the aircraft still fish-tails, or yaws during turbulence (even light), even while at a high cruise speed.

"We realize we have a 12-year-old airplane, and very soon all that will be original on it will be the serial number; but maintenance costs are very high, if not exorbitant. We try to keep *everything* working, and that costs a lot. Over the last year, the plane has been deadlined for about 70 days due to maintenance. We recently installed a Teledyne Continental factory remanufactured zero-time engine and encountered nothing but trouble and costs for about seven weeks."

Twins

Piper Seneca

As heir apparent to the Twin Comanche, the Piper PA-34 Seneca has been an enormous marketing success since it burst upon the scene in 1972. But used-plane buyers should be aware that there's a difference of night and day between the models that were built before and after 1975.

The pre-1975 models had no turbocharging and possessed an absurdly low single-engine ceiling along with what many pilots regard as abominable handling characteristics both in the air and on the ground. Coupled with short range and a lackluster payload, these qualities made the airplane ripe for a wholesale redesign.

Piper came through with just that in the 1975 model, by replacing the four-cylinder Lycoming IO-360s with turbocharged six-cylinder Continental TSIO-360s. This provided the Seneca with a more than respectable single-engine ceiling, a significant increase in payload—and better aesthetics, to boot, since the new powerplants were housed in much better looking streamlined cowls.

On top of that, the aircraft's control system was modified to eliminate its awkward handling characteristics.

Nevertheless, the newer Continental powerplants have not been without their problems, and they have received "mixed reviews" from owners and maintenance and overhaul shops.

The Early Models
The 1972 Seneca first on the scene was an ill-suited adaptation of the Cherokee Six fuselage and wings to multi configuration. The nose gear steering was ponderously heavy, partly because the rudder was tied in with the aileron system, and every time the pilot kicked in left or right rudder, the ailerons responded as well, adding to the tug on the pedals.

This characteristic, engineered to satisfy the need to be able to raise a wing in flight with the rudders alone, gave the aircraft equally ponderous flight controls. The aircraft was at its worst in turbulent IFR work and in gusty crosswind landings, when the pilot could find himself banking left and right in great pendulum swings, as he attempted to keep the wings level.

Promoted as an ideal, simple stepup machine for single-engine pilots, the early Senecas were anything but that.

To make up for a serious deficiency in load-carrying ability, Piper in the 1973 model pulled a mostly paper-work exercise that boosted the gross and useful load by 200 pounds, but it did so at the sacrifice of an already low single-engine ceiling—which dropped from 5,200 feet to 3,650 feet.

A Rash of Fixes
The pre-75 models also were plagued with potentially expensive fixes that unleashed a series of service letters, bulletins and Airworthiness Directives. The main landing gear support structure was hit with such an AD in '73, and the outer wing spars in '74.

Piper came out with kits allowing installation of skin and rib reinforcement doublers in '74 after "wing skin irregularities" were found under the wings outboard of the main landing gear wells in some aircraft. They also brought out a reinforcement kit to buttress the aft wing assembly after cracks were found at the juncture of the main landing gear with the aft false spar.

An exhaust system that turned up serious cracking problems was replaced in '73 by a completely new, "vastly superior" (said Piper) exhaust system of longer life, that eliminated the repetitive inspections required on the earlier system. This was offered as a retrofit.

During the first year of operation, some Senecas also were found to have loose balance weight assemblies on the stabilator tips, and an AD was issued on this. There have since been at least two, and possibly three Seneca crashes due to stabilator failure. (Incidentally, Piper's first prototype Seneca crashed during testing when the stabilator fluttered.)

In 1975 the usable fuel dropped from 95 to 93 gallons, and it was found that possible rough finish on the landing gear oleo struts might have been causing the struts to bind, putting extra load on the wing in landing, and causing wing cracks.

Buyers looking at the older model Senecas should keep all these pointers in mind during their inspection of the aircraft.

The New II—A Whole New Ballgame
The 1975 Seneca II wrought major changes in the flying personality of the airplane. The turbocharged Continentals removed the onus of the low single-engine ceiling and shot it up to 13,400 feet. The powerful downspring that made the original Seneca awkward in the landing flare was replaced by a less potent one and a bobweight. Also, the rudder-aileron interconnect was removed, and a bungee smoothed out rudder steering during taxi. Furthermore, lateral control was improved by lengthening the ailerons.

Whereas the original Lycoming-powered model had seemed extremely noisy and vibration-prone, the new Continental pack-

The first Seneca *had normally aspirated Lycomings in blunt nacelles. Handling qualities were quite deficient.*

age quieted and smoothed things down significantly. The "poor-man's" automatic turbo control also made its debut on this airplane. Equipped with a simple bypass valve and an overboost relief valve, it eliminated the need for a sophisticated automatic wastegate. However, at the same time, it demanded more attention from the pilot on takeoff to prevent excess spoolup as the throttles were advanced. In addition, the manifold pressure was extremely sensitive to minor changes in rpm, airspeed and altitude; consequently, precise power management could be a real chore. This, of course, compounded the problems of pilots transitioning from singles, though the handling qualities of the aircraft were greatly improved.

Along with a jump in gross weight, the Seneca II offered an additional 186 pounds in useful load which the airplane desperately needed to take advantage of its truly commodious six-place cabin and 200-pound baggage capacity.

Pilots should be aware, however, that the Seneca II has a zero fuel weight limitation of 4,000 pounds. Therefore, anything above 4,000 pounds, up to the 4,570-pound gross weight must be in fuel only, not people or baggage.

A nice feature of the Seneca's baggage loading format is that half can be loaded in the nose compartment to ease weight and balance problems if need be. And everyone who talks about the airplane gives high marks to the both-sides, front-and-rear door configuration for loading and unloading of people and cargo. Also, club seating adds a little variety to the passenger format.

High Safety Marks

The National Transportation Safety Board's comparative accident figures show the Seneca to have the lowest fatal accident rate of seven popular classes of twins surveyed. Its total accident rate, however, placed it right in the middle of the pack.

If any one category of problem dominates the NTSB accident roster from 1971-1975, it is collapsing landing gear. Out of 57 reports, 15 dealt with this. Some of them were attributed to simple overload failures

The Continental TSIO-360: *Six cylinders and a "simplified" turbo system. Mechanics say: Nice running, but tough to work on.*

because of hard landings, or landing hot and attempting to turn off at too high a speed, but several were tracked to component failure.

The nose gear drag link bolt failed or was pulled from its fittings in two of these accidents.

The second largest problem area was related to engine failure or diminished power output from one or both engines—with 10 of these reported. On no less than four of these, dual instruction was involved, where the flight instructor yanked the mixture on one engine, and a problem developed on a go-around. In one case the wrong sparkplugs were used, and in another there was a problem relating to valves and plugs.

On the older Senecas two pilots were distracted enough by a cabin door opening in flight to crash. One occurred on an aborted takeoff; the other forgot to put the gear down before landing. The newer Senecas have improved door latches.

Powerplant Record

Since we had heard of a number of cases of Seneca engine failures, and several owners had registered complaints with us of oil loss and seepage problems, we asked for and received a five-year summary of the FAA's Service Difficulty Reports from Oklahoma City on the Continental TSIO-360 used in the Seneca II, the Cessna Turbo Skymaster and the Piper Turbo Arrow.

On the 135 Seneca engine problems listed in the FAA's tally (usually estimated to be

about 10 percent of the total number of problems actually experienced in the field), the largest portion (26) were related to electrical system failures—like condensers, capacitors, leads, coils, etc. The second largest group was attributed to cylinder failures and cracks (16). The third stemmed from turbo problems with scrolls, housings, brackets, etc. (9). And the fourth was directed at scarred or damaged pistons (6). Four broken crankshafts were reported, but in 1977 the Piper factory issued a service bulletin calling attention to the fact that there had been 12 engine stoppages due to "technically unexplained" crankshaft fractures.

There were only two reports of cracked crankcases on the Seneca IIs (out of a fleet of about 1,600 aircraft flying). This compares with 39 reports of cracked crankcases in the same basic engine, mounted in the rear of the push-pull Cessna Turbo Skymaster (out of a fleet of about 300 aircraft). By the same token, there were 33 reported cases of cylinder failures and cracks in the Skymaster engines.

Dipstick Mystery

One strange problem that surfaced in connection with the Seneca engines concerned oil dipstick calibration. Two Seneca II owners had notified us to complain that their dipsticks registered a quart and a half or so too little, which led service personnel to put in too much oil. Four reports of incorrect dipstick calibration were also listed

Model	Year Built	Number Built	Cruise Speed (mph)	Rate of Climb (fpm)	S.E. Service Ceiling (ft)	Useful Load (lbs)	Fuel (gals)	Engine	TBO (hrs)	Overhaul Cost	Average Retail Price
PA-34-200	1972	360	187	1,460	5,200	1,414	93	200-hp Lycoming	1,400	$5,800	$ 35,500
PA-34-200	1973	353	186	1,360	3,650	1,614	93	200-hp Lycoming	1,400	$5,800	$ 37,000
PA-34-200	1974	214	186	1,360	3,650	1,614	93	200-hp Lycoming	1,400	$5,800	$ 39,000
PA-34-200T	1975	327	204	1,340	13,400	1,800	93	200-hp Continental	1,400	$7,300	$ 63,000
PA-34-200T	1976	371	204	1,340	13,400	1,800	93	200-hp Continental	1,400	$7,300	$ 70,000
PA-34-200T	1977	433	204	1,340	13,400	1,800	93/123	200-hp Continental	1,400	$7,300	$ 82,000
PA-34-200T	1978	474	204	1,340	13,400	1,800	93/123	200-hp Continental	1,400	$7,300	$ 91,000
PA-34-200T	1979	530	204	1,340	13,400	1,800	93/123	200-hp continental	1,400	$7,300	$105,000

on the FAA's Service Difficulty rundown of Seneca IIs.

Each pilot who contacted us noted he had become involved with both Piper and Continental in a heated discussion of the problem, and that they were concerned about engine damage from overloading with oil because of the incorrectly registered dipsticks.

One engine maintenance expert we contacted, however, volunteered that the problem might stem from the fact that the Senecas have different dipsticks for the left and right powerplants. This is because the wings have such a pronounced dihedral; and since the dipstick is mounted on the left side on each engine, each has to measure a different oil level.

He speculated that the engines might occasionally come from the factory with the wrong dipsticks installed.

As for whether too much oil could damage the engine or would simply be thrown out of the breather harmlessly, our mechanic pointed out: "Too much oil is no good. Your crankshaft thrashes around in the oil, and bubbles and aerates it, so the oil pump picks up air and oil rather than pure oil. You can burn up an engine by putting in too much oil, since air is not a very good lubricant."

Mechanic's Nightmare
The judgment of other mechanics and overhaul shops was that the TSIO-360 powerplant was, in general, a nice, smooth running engine. One powerplant instructor at an air university though, insisted that the design posed a problem when things went wrong.

"It's a tough little engine to work on," he said. "It's cramped and nothing fits—it's just a mechanic's nightmare. It's good running and a dependable little engine, but if it starts giving you trouble, the repair bill looks like the gross national product."

He attributed the electrical accessory problems noted on the Service Difficulty list to the engine being "tightly cowled and tightly baffled, with a lot of heat built up inside."

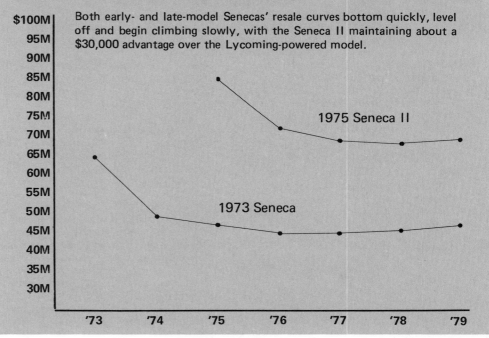

Aircraft Investment Value

Both early- and late-model Senecas' resale curves bottom quickly, level off and begin climbing slowly, with the Seneca II maintaining about a $30,000 advantage over the Lycoming-powered model.

1975 Seneca II

1973 Seneca

Some mechanics figured the cylinder and piston problems could be traced to pushing the engine too hard for prolonged periods under turbo boost. For that matter, fleet operators we talked to shared the opinion that the aircraft as a whole was not built ruggedly enough to be pushed too hard in commercial operations, though it seemed to stand up satisfactorily for personal use.

Among idiosyncrasies that turned up in our interviews was one complaint that the alternators put out too little power at low taxi rpms "to do the job," and the comment of one mechanic that it was necessary to reinforce the fiberglass area behind the spinner on the nose cowl because it seemed to have a tendency to crack.

Seneca II engines also are noted for cold-weather starting problems. To tackle this, Piper first issued special starting instructions for pilots, and then came out with an optional cold-weather priming kit for the aircraft.

Resale Value
As might be expected, the resale value curves for the pre- and post-75 Senecas are quite different. The average '73 Seneca, for example, dropped almost $16,000 the first year whereas a '75 Seneca II could be expected, on the average, to lose only around $13,000. On top of that, where the '73 model bottomed in four years, the '75 model started back up in resale value after only three years.

One used plane dealer we talked to suggested, however, that "blue book" prices for the older normally aspirated Senecas were, in his opinion "too high by as much as $5,000 to $6,000."

Modifications
There are just four mods of any significance on the Lycoming-powered Seneca: installation of cooling louvers on top of both nacelle accessory sections—by Advanced Aviation, Auburn, Wash.; turbocharging by Rajay; wingtip fuel tanks of 17 gallons each, by Robertson Aircraft Corp., Renton, Wash.; and a STOL/spoiler mod by Robertson that does wonders for the sluggish handling of the original Seneca.

(In 1976 optional fuel capacity up to 123 gallons usable was offered on the Seneca IIs by Piper, providing a much needed boost in range.)

And an STC by JB Systems, Inc. of Longmont, Colo. offered freon air conditioning to the Seneca II. The Robertson STOL kit i s also available for the Seneca II.

With its Cherokee Six fuselage, *the Seneca holds six with room—if not weight—to spare.*

Owner Comments

"We flew our Seneca 2,500 hours in three years with a total cost of $30,000 in maintenance costs. We lost six jugs; three were replaced under warranty, but we paid for the other three. At 1,400 hours, we lost the right engine. I examined it when it was torn down, and there had been detonation. Continental said those engines were overboosted. We ended up rebuilding both, at a cost by Reading Air Service of $14,511. After then our engine maintenance went to nil."

"We had problems with the dipsticks reading incorrectly. To get the dipstick to read 6¼ quarts, you had to put eight quarts in the engine. This could be a real hazard because if you put too much oil in, you can bend the rods."

"Lost nine jugs in 1,600 hours—average cost $600 per jug."

"Overall utility of my '77 Seneca II is superb. It handles well both on the ground and in the air. Control forces are quite well balanced. I like the way Seneca is off and running in short order, climbing at a solid 1,200 to 1,500 fpm. Landings require slightly more patience.

"The not-so-good news includes difficulty maintaining level pitch attitude in cruise configuration. This is especially annoying when accompanied by moderate to strong winds and thermal updrafts. Level pitch trim is particularly elusive at high altitudes. The only other substantial 'handling' complaint is a tendency to yaw in turbulence—a particularly nauseating event for the rear-most passengers.

"Also, zero-fuel weight limitation could be a problem for heavy haulers. Seating comfort is quite good with the exception of the rear-most seats (club configuration) which are much too 'low' (to allow for head room, I presume).

"Visibility in most directions (with the possible exception of rearward) is very satisfactory. All in all, I'm very pleased with this plane's capabilities.

"The bad news could be categorized under engine instrumentation and avionics interference, with the latter perhaps related to an alternator or voltage regulator. The most bothersome problem is the sensitivity and continuous discrepancy of engine instrument indications. Uneven surges in manifold pressure needles (even with slow, smooth power applications) and splits in fuel flow indicators are enough to drive even a seasoned pilot up a wall. Continuous engine adjustment and smooth power application seem to be an absolute must.

"An incessant 'buzzing' drone on the ADF audio and also the radios (test mode) is currently among the trouble-shooting list items, with alternators and/or voltage regulators as chief suspects. Other irritants include heater malfunction, generator popping off line, voltage spikes (suspect strobe package), faulty operation of optional fuel primer button (for start-up), a precessing DG (suspect bad bearings).

"Most of these items are being or have been 'diagnosed' by one or more fixed-base repair shops with limited corrective success. I've gotten fair to good cooperation from the factory on suggestions as to how to solve these glitches, but I'm becoming more impatient with each passing day.

"For a new aircraft (375 hours), I've had more than my share of headaches. Were it not for my appreciation of the overall utility of this bird, I'd be driven stark raving mad!"

"I feel compelled to pass along to prospective owners and pilots some little known facts about the Piper Seneca PA-34. This information was learned as a result of extensive investigation of a Seneca II accident at Benedum Airport, W. Va., 26 May 1977, in which my son was killed when the right engine crankshaft failed shortly after takeoff.

"First, Seneca II engines have been known to fail with little or no warning. In the case above, the engine failed with only 167 hours since new. Subsequently, Piper issued Service Bulletin No. 576 on 30 November 1977, indicating there had been 12 failures to that time. Teledyne-Continental has reportedly since changed crankshaft material and inspection procedures.

"Secondly, single-engine performance at low altitude is probably much less than the extrapolated performance curves presented in the pilot's handbook. The NTSB and others simulated the conditions of my son's accident at Vero Beach, Florida. It was found that when an engine was cut at less than 90 KIAS at 50 feet altitude, the Seneca was incapable of accelerating or climbing out of ground effect. Obsolete certification requirements (FAR Part 23, paragraph 67) allow Piper to demonstrate single-engine performance at 5,000 feet altitude. In the case of Seneca II's turbocharged engines, results are deceptively misleading with respect to lower altitude performance. This is because turbocharged engines operating at a fixed manifold pressure develop less power at low altitude than at higher altitudes up to their critical altitude.

"If you feel you can safely *live* with the above limitations, there are many other features of the Seneca II you will like very much. My son, an Embry-Riddle Air University graduate who was Part 135 qualified in the Seneca II, was a very strong proponent for the airplane."

Bill Moranville
528 S. Benita Blvd.
Vestal, N. Y. 13850

Editor's Note: The Michael H. Moranville Memorial Safe-Aero Research Foundation has been organized by the father for "the study and resolution of problems associated with engine failure at critical phases of flight. Recommendations continue to be available to Piper for correction of Seneca II limitations and avoidance of accidents similar to the one listed. These involve revision of emergency procedures, presentation of additional performance information, additional low-altitude performance tests, aerodynamic modifications to achieve better low-speed performance, and methods to attain higher engine reliability. Any progress made in achieving our safety goals will be reported. Pertinent information and support will be appreciated."

The Seneca II *received new turbo Continentals in handsomer nacelles, an extra little cabin window in the rear, and much improved handling characteristics. The engine nacelles, however, project up into the field of vision, restricting pilot vision in the pattern somewhat.*

Cessna Skymaster

Cessna's most ingenious aircraft, the 337 Skymaster, is one of aviation's greatest paradoxes. As a used-plane, it's both a great buy and a washout. Conceived as the safest twin flying, the 337 is probably one of the biggest used multi bargains to be found, since prices are quite low. But as an investment, the Skymaster is a flop. Values don't level off and eventually rise with inflation; they simply slide down a great toboggan run. And maintenance complaints are fairly high.

Although the recipient of some of Cessna's most intriguing technical innovation's—like centerline thrust and pressurization—the Skymaster somehow never made it as a smashing success, for reasons the company has often pondered. One popular theory is that so "safe" an airplane loses macho appeal to pilots.

Another theory is simply that the Skymaster doesn't go as fast as multiengine airplanes are supposed to. Since the 337 started life as a competitor to the Piper Twin Comanche with a mere 190-mph cruise as an economy twin, it has never been endowed with big enough engines to make it more of a demon speedster, and pull it out of the performance doldroms.

Aside from lackluster speed, the Skymaster suffers also from the lack of a genuine baggage compartment. The rear of the cabin can be devoted either to a fifth and sixth seat, or to baggage. A lower fuselage baggage pod can be added on at the cost of only a modicum of speed, but at the sacrifice of looks.

Centerline Thrust

The Skymaster's major rationale, of course, is elimination of the asymmetrical thrust problems of single-engine operation. Lose an engine on a Skymaster at climbout, and even at low speeds the aircraft won't twist irresistibly to one side or the other at high power settings. On one engine, however, the Skymaster at gross is no zephyr, even at sea level, since it will eke out a climb rate (on the normally aspirated model) of no greater than 235 to 300 fpm on the front engine, and slightly better on the rear one—provided the pilot feathers the right prop and cleans up the aircraft.

The shortage of muscle from just one engine to push the 337 around is impressed upon any pilot who puts the aircraft through its paces with one out, both in the air and on the ground. Lose a fan during taxi, especially on the grass, and it takes a surprising blast of power on the live engine to keep the Skymaster's bulk moving.

This is not to suggest the Skymaster is a cumbersome, awkward airplane under normal circumstances with both engines operating. Though it takes a ponderous heave to rotate on takeoff, once airborne the aircraft has more facile ailerons than most twins though it possesses the usual heavy Cessna pitch pressures. Most pilots also come to regard the aircraft as a kind of poor-man's STOL, and the airplane is no slouch at getting in and out of tight spaces. Visibility is surprisingly good for a twin, since the wing is set back quite far from the pilot, and there are no engine nacelles out on the wings to obscure an airport on downwind.

Safety

As, theoretically, the safest twin around, the Skymaster received lots of unfavorable publicity and lawsuits a few years back when it was found that pilots were occasionally losing an engine (the rear one, usually) on takeoff roll, and continuing the takeoff attempt with awkward results, not realizing they'd lost a fan, or perhaps not caring.

Early models had a warning light to tell pilots when an engine had failed, activated by torque changes. Proper takeoff technique is to advance the throttle for the rear engine first to make sure everything's working, and then feed in the front engine. A placard mandated by an AD warns pilots not to take off on one engine, if they didn't know. Another AD required raising the idle speed of the rear engine, so it would be less likely to poop out on takeoff, and pilots were told to taxi mainly by using the rear engine, to keep it warmed up and ready.

A 1979 National Transportation Safety Board study of light twin-engine aircraft accidents showed the Cessna Skymaster had the third worst fatal accident rate of 20 aircraft, after the Beech 18 and the Aero Commander 500, 520 and 560 series. In an attempt to isolate accident causes, we inspected a five-year rundown of accident briefs on the Skymaster from 1973 to 1977.

This examination showed that of the 29 fatal accidents reported during the period the greatest number—seven—were caused by weather related problems. One might reason that perhaps less-experienced pilots tend to migrate toward the Skymaster—supposedly a safe, easy stepup twin. The weather fatalities, however, suggest this is not so since most of the pilots involved had commercial tickets, were instrument rated and had lots of experience, but simply blundered into fog or ice they couldn't handle.

The next three accident categories that

Skymasters should be the safest twins flying, *but NTSB figures disclose a calamitous accident record. U.S. production of the aircraft has stopped, with Cessna's Reims plant in France alone building Skymasters.*

generated the highest frequency of fatal crashes did, however, involve the aircraft design. These were: engine failure on take-off, fuel exhaustion and stall/spins.

Three fatal accidents were caused by loss of power on takeoff and climbout. Two of those involved failure of the rear engine. On one, witnesses had noted the rear engine running during taxi, but it had stopped during the takeoff roll. The aircraft stalled in climbout and then caught fire after impact. The private pilot had 516 hours total, 212 in type.

In another fatal accident, the rear engine failed on takeoff because of a plugged rear fuel pump vapor ejector, the pilot failed to abort, and fire broke out after impact. The ATP pilot with 3,570 hours had three hours in type.

In the third fatal, both engines failed on takeoff, followed by a crash and fire. The private pilot had 1,800 hours, 94 in type.

There were two fatal accidents from engine failure because of fuel exhaustion, and two attributed to stall/spins. Most of the stall/spin or mush accidents appear unrelated to any particular aircraft deficiency. Of the two fatals, one occurred during a buzzing incident; the othr was attributed to pilot fatigue.

Two nonfatals were related to engine failure. One pilot actually attempted to take off with the rear engine out, and the prop not feathered. He hit the trees. Another pilot stalled after he lost one engine from fuel starvation.

In a surprising number of instances, pilots who lost just one engine were unable to bring the aircraft back to a safe landing, despite the fact that the centerline thrust spared them the usual multi-engine problems of asymmetrical thrust and the traditional stall/spin threat with an engine out.

Skymasters also were plagued with a high rate of nonfatal accidents. Here the greatest toll was taken by simple fuel exhaustion—just running completely out of fuel. This happened no less than 13 times. Though Cessna likes to stress the high accuracy of the fuel gauges in the Skymasters, thanks to the capacitance type of measuring system, the location of both fuel gauges on the right side of the instrument panel cannot make fuel monitoring any easier for the pilot in the left seat. The fact that there are only two gauges for four fuel tanks—two mains and two aux tanks, also adds to the complexity of the task, since while any one set of tanks is in use, the pilot cannot see at a glance how much fuel remains in the other tanks.

Skymaster pilots have to switch from main to aux tanks for each engine.

Second biggest cause of nonfatal accidents in Skymasters was hard landings. Eleven of these were called out during the five-year period studied. Most involved porpoising, and improper recovery from a bounced landing, often followed by a gear collapse.

Categories
There are four main classes of Skymasters. The aircraft was introduced in 1964 as a fixed-gear twin designated the 336. In 1967 the first turbocharged version was offered, followed in 1973 by the pressurized model. The clamshell door and smaller windows mandated by pressurization were carried over to the entire Skymaster line, except for bigger front-seat side windows for the non-pressurized models.

Note also that the pressurized version does not have a rear baggage door. Unlike most high-wing Cessnas, the Skymasters never had a left-side pilot's door. Entry is from the right front door.

With the pressurized model came a boost in horsepower from 210 each to 225 each. TBO for the more powerful engine and the turbo 210 is 1,400 hours, vs. 1,500 for the normally aspirated version.

Early models up through the '68 C version had TBOs of only 1,200 hours. This went to 1,500 hours with '69 models, thanks to the addition of nickel exhaust valves.

Gross weight on the Skymaster has risen from 4,200 pounds to 4,630 through the years, and to 4,700 pounds on the pressurized version.

Load Carrying
A 1972 model with a 4,630-pound gross and 1,935-pound useful load can handle a pretty good payload for a "light twin." With 150 pounds of optional equipment, the aircraft can heft full optional fuel of 131 gallons along with five adults and about 112 pounds of baggage. Range without reserve at 75 percent works out to about 1,060 sm, at 189 mph.

Model	Year Built	Number Built	Cruise Speed (mph)	Rate of Climb (fpm)	Useful Load (lbs)	Single-Engine Service Ceiling (ft)	Fuel Std/Opt (gals)	Engine	TBO (hrs)	Overhaul Cost	Average Retail Price
336	1964	195	173	1,300	1,580	8,200	93/131	210-hp Continental	1,200	$4,500	$ 16,500
337	1965	238	192	1,200	1,565	8,300	93/131	210-hp Continental	1,200	$4,600	$ 20,000
337 A	1966	284	192	1,200	1,585	8,200	93/131	210-hp Continental	1,200	$4,600	$ 21,750
337 B	1967	226	192	1,250	1,685	7,500	93/131	210-hp Continental	1,200	$4,600	$ 24,500
T-337 B	1967	226	225	1,250	1,515	20,000	93/131	210-hp Continental	1,400	$5,750	$ 29,250
337 C	1968	207	191	1,200	1,750	6,800	93/131	210-hp Continental	1,200	$4,600	$ 26,500
T-337 C	1968	207	224	1,155	1,705	18,600	93/131	210-hp Continental	1,400	$5,750	$ 30,500
337 D	1969	199	191	1,200	1,745	6,800	93/131	210-hp Continental	1,500	$4,600	$ 28,500
T-337 D	1969	199	224	1,185	1,485	16,200	93/131	210-hp Continental	1,400	$5,750	$ 32,500
337 E	1970	122	191	1,180	1,820	6,500	93/131	210-hp Continental	1,500	$4,600	$ 30,000
T-337 E	1970	122	223	1,105	1,780	14,400	93/131	210-hp Continental	1,400	$5,750	$ 35,000
337 F	1971-72	132	190	1,100	1,935	5,100	93/131	210-hp Continental	1,500	$4,600	$ 35,000
T-337 F	1971	132	223	1,105	1,780	14,400	93/131	210-hp Continental	1,400	$5,750	$ 37,500
337 G	1973-74	143	194	1,100	1,517	6,900	90/150	210-hp Continental	1,500	$4,600	$ 40,000
T-337 G-P	1973-74	194	235	1,250	1,533	18,700	151	210-hp Continental	1,400	$5,750	$ 60,000
337 G II	1975	64	194	1,100	1,517	6,900	90/150	210-hp Continental	1,500	$4,600	$ 50,000
T-337 G-P	1975	31	235	1,250	1,533	18,700	151	225-hp Continental	1,400	$5,750	$ 67,500
337 G II	1976	76	194	1,100	1,517	6,900	90/150	210-hp Continental	1,500	$4,600	$ 58,000
T-337 G-P	1976	31	235	1,250	1,533	18,700	151	225-hp Continental	1,400	$5,750	$ 80,000
337 G II	1977	66	194	1,100	1,517	6,900	90/150	210-hp Continental	1,500	$4,600	$ 67,500
T-337 G-P	1977	34	235	1,250	1,533	18,700	151	225-hp Continental	1,400	$5,750	$ 92,500
337 H II	1978	na	194	950	1,687	6,900	40/150	210-hp Continental	1,500	$5,900	$ 82,500
T-337 H II	1978	na	230	1,160	1,608	16,500	93/131	210-hp Continental	1,400	$7,300	$ 90,000
337 H II	1979	na	194	940	1,687	6,900	90/150	210-hp Continental	1,500	$5,900	$ 96,000
T-337 H II	1979	na	230	1,160	1,608	16,500	93/131	210-hp Continental	1,400	$7,300	$107,000
T-337 H-P	1978	na	235	1,120	1,533	18,700	150	225-hp Continental	1,400	$7,300	$107,000
T-337 H-P	1979	na	235	1,120	1,533	18,700	150	225-hp Continental	1,400	$7,300	$127,000

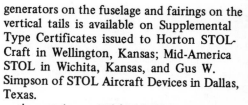

The first pressurized Skymaster *was this '73 model, with the distinctive small windows all around. Aircraft provides a 10,000-foot cabin altitude at the certified ceiling of 20,000 feet. Single-engine service ceiling is 18,700 feet, and either engine can maintain full pressurization.*

Maintenance

Skymaster owners report they have the most problems with the electrical system, the exhaust system and the brakes. And a nearly universal complaint is that they can't seem to eliminate excess coating of the rear cowl and belly and horizontal stabilizer with oil.

Another dominant gripe among Skymaster owners is that "you can't get parts."

Annual inspections cost an average of $987 among Skymaster owners reporting to us on our airframe and powerplant survey, though the tendency of shops was to quote a flat rate of around $510. Unscheduled airframe costs during the year came to about $600, while unplanned powerplant costs averaged $912, for a total of $1,512.

Average downtime during a year for these unscheduled repairs was only a week.

Airworthiness Directives

Aside from the aforementioned ADs requiring a placard to warn against taking off on one engine and raising rear engine idle speeds, among other noteworthy ADs there was an AD requiring inspection of aircraft with over 5,000 hours of service for wing front and rear spar lower cap cracks. And another required checking flap actuator jacks for proper lubrication to forestall inadvertent retraction of flaps. Another AD required installation of a cooling duct for the fuel gauges, to prevent overheating and smoking.

Modifications

There are several STOL mods available for Skymasters from a host of companies. The most elaborate is Robertson's, which installs drooped ailerons, recontoured wing leading edges, stall fences and flap actuated elevator trim springs. The Robertson mod also raises takeoff gross weight.

More modest STOL treatment, usually involving cuffing wing leading edges and modifying the wing tips and installation of vortex generators on the fuselage and fairings on the vertical tails is available on Supplemental Type Certificates issued to Horton STOL-Craft in Wellington, Kansas; Mid-America STOL in Wichita, Kansas, and Gus W. Simpson of STOL Aircraft Devices in Dallas, Texas.

A one-piece windshield STC is held by Beryl D'Shannon Aviation Specialties, Inc. in Leesburg, Fla., and an emergency exit door on top of the fuselage is STC'd by Floair, Inc. in Wichita, Kans.

An electrically driven freon air conditioning system STC is held by JB Systems, Inc. in Longmont, Colo., and DeVore Aviation in Roslyn Heights, N. Y. installs recognition lights on the trailing edge of Robertson wing tips. Also, a Fiquench fire extinguishing system is approved for the cabin and engine area by Fike Metal Products Corp., Blue Springs, Mo.

To accommodate wing-mounted weather radar, Renton Aviation in Renton, Wash. has an STC for installation of Bendix RDR 160 radar.

It should be noted that ownership of the above STCs, taken from the FAA's latest annual summary, may have changed hands in some cases.

Associations

At last word there was no association of Skymaster owners, though O. R. Whitaker (P.O. Box 1274, Liberal, Kans. 67901; tel. 316-624-2281) is attempting to organize one and has been contacting 337 owners with plans to issue a newsletter.

Owner Comments

"I have owned a 1973 model 337G for about 18 months and have flown it 300 hours. It is roomy and comfortable for two couples, with plenty of baggage space. My wife likes it because it is easy to board and because there is a good view from all seats. The manufacturer didn't cheat any more than normal on owner's manual performance figures, and it comes pretty close to delivering the claimed performance when it is 800 pounds under gross.

"I bought a Skymaster because flying terrifies me, and I think it is the safest airplane I possibly could be in—although its accident statistics do not bear this out. I got the opportunity to test its single-engine capabilities much earlier than desired. I had purchased the airplane in Kansas City, and 1:30 into the flight home, while IFR at 10,000 feet in VFR conditions above a solid undercast, I lost the front engine due to failure of the lube oil pump shaft. Flying to the nearest field and setting her down with only the rear engine running was no problem.

"The airframe and engines had 800 hours on them at that time and Continental made a fair and reasonable adjustment on a factory-remanufactured engine—one that would make me want to do business with them in the future.

"I could not be more pleased with the airplane itself. Unfortunately, the same is not true of the parts availability for the airframe or the Cessna avionics. Example: it recently took over eight weeks to get a replacement for the "ribbon assembly"—a wiring group which passes through the pilot's control column and connects to the autopilot disengage and electric trim switches on the yoke. Airframe parts availability hasn't been any better. Parts frequently must be reordered because orders are lost and never heard from and because wrong parts are shipped. It has been a real disappointment to find that a company like Cessna could do such an amateurish job of product support.

"If I were to replace the airplane now, it would be a difficult decision as to whether to buy another 337. There is no other airplane I would rather fly in this size and price category. But I don't know whether I would be willing to get back into the service hassle with another 337."

"Generally my 1968 Skymaster has met or exceeded book figures. We do have later style drooped wingtips, which may account for modest performance improvements.

"The only outstanding irritation is the rear engine's oil leaks—not a serious problem, but who likes a greasy rear engine cowl?

"Passenger cabin room is excellent. The noise level can largely be controlled if close attention is given to getting the props synchronized.

"Lack of baggage area is a pain, and the optional pod would seem to be a satisfactory solution at a nominal loss of speed. (Quoted as two or three mph.) Heater and cabin ventilation is good. Visibility is far superior to other twins.

"Parts and backup have given me no problem.

"I am currently spending about $40 per hour, which includes engine reserve, 100-hour engine inspection and radio maintenance. A fairly sizable amount is allocated for radios since they are older units. A noteworthy item is insurance cost. We received a better rate than most twins due to the centerline thrust safety factor.

"Had one experience where the complete electrical system kicked out due to high load. A complete electrical system shutdown is required to reset alternators. This happened on final, IFR at night, which was disconcerting. I was told, however, that it is not an unusual occurrence on Skymasters.

"Prior to the Skymaster I owned a Comanche 250, and had considered buying either a later Comanche or a 210. When I shopped the market, I discovered that Skymasters were a real bargain compared to the high-performance singles. The Skymaster offered good performance, safety and redundancy. It should be pointed out that redundancy goes well beyond just engines; i.e., alternators, voltage regulators, and vacuum systems. This is a tremendous consideration if anyone does much serious IFR flying. Fuel consumption is good for a twin. We usually get 18-19 gph at about 160 knots.

"Overall, I think it is a 'super' light twin that didn't make it big because of its unusual appearance and the ego problems of many individuals looking into this class of plane."

"My Skymaster is a 1965 model with 2,900 TT and low-time engines. I firmly believe the Skymaster to be one of the safest, most economical and best all-around twins for a pilot who only flies 100-200 hours annually.

"The biggest problem seems to be resale (for reasons unknown to me). I wanted to move up to a later model and found it very hard to get a reasonable price for mine. It was so bad, in fact, that I decided to completely redo this plane inside and out. This entails a new Collins radio package, new Alumigrip paint and new interior. For roughly $40,000 total investment, I have an IFR plane with up-to-date equipment.

"As for the normal complaints I usually hear about Skymasters, I have had no trouble with the rear engine overheating or problems with the gear.

"At 22 mp and 2400 rpm I indicate about 160 on 17-19 gph while flying, most of the time under 2,500 feet.

"My final comment is that a Skymaster is like an Edsel—owners like them, but don't try selling it since no one else does."

"We have owned a 336 for about five years. Over a two-year period, our total expense was $10,934, not including gas and oil. We flew the airplane for about 300 hours, for a hourly cost of $36.45. Gas and oil cost about $14 for a total of $50.45.

"Maintenance is our biggest item; it accounts for about $27 per hour, a substantial portion of which is for radios. As the airplane is 15 years old, there are a lot of replacement items—fuel and temperature gauges, bad ground, flap indicator (fixed eight times, never worked yet), leaks, new windshield, all that sort of thing. We cruise at 65 percent using 18 gph and true 136 knots. At about 70 percent we use about 20 gph and true 140 knots.

"It is noisy, funny-looking, very stable, and about the only twin in which you can take aerial pictures decently without a photo hole. We use it for business, and passengers like the two engines, once they get used to the airplane's looks.

"Since it would require doubling or tripling our investment to get anything that went much faster or farther, we will probably keep it until we are suddenly taken rich beyond the dreams of avarice, or Rutan's twin comes on the market. At which time we will sell the airplane for probably twice what we paid for it, albeit in inflated dollars."

"I own a 1973 pressurized 337 and have very much enjoyed flying the airplane. The operating expense in terms of fuel consumption and speed is not really bad compared to other airplanes. It has an excellent glide ratio, is very easy to fly, and the ease of entry and exit from the airplane is greater than many other twin-engine airplanes.

"I have had some problems with the air-

Clamshell door *is the only entrance to the pressurized 337s; there is no baggage door in the rear as in unpressurized models.*

plane. There is always oil on the belly and rear cowling of the airplane, and try as I might, I can't keep the oil off the plane. I had a generator problem caused by a bad diode, which was a 75-cent part that made the plane inoperable."

"I have a Robertson modified 1968 Turbo 337 with a cargo pod. It is easy to fly, but the Robertson mod makes it a bit heavy at low speeds.

"Maintenance has been high—lots of cracks in the exhaust system and the engines are very hard to work on. (One mechanic refused to touch them.)

"But the reason I would not get another Skymaster is that the Continental engines carry such a high price tag at overhaul time. Invariably, the cases are cracked, and this just about doubles the price to $9,000 each."

"In one of your issues, you state that a Skymaster with windmilling prop will not climb at all. My 1966 337 has a somewhat lower gross weight than later models and will climb at 360 fpm on one engine, with the dead prop feathered. This is 60 fpm more than the later heavier aircraft, and so with a windmilling prop, and lowered gear, I can get a climb rate of 20 fpm. Granted this is nothing to write home about, but it will give the pilot a bit of time to feather the prop, and so get a climb rate of 250 fpm. But it is important to leave the gear down, since the drag of the gear doors robs you of 130 fpm for the 10 seconds of the cycle."

"So far I've kept my maintenance costs down to about $400 per year by working with an independent mechanic (non-FBO) and doing a lot of work myself. By far the main complaint I have is that the exhaust system continually cracks, and needs constant repair."

"Only once in two and a half years have I had some maintenance done without finding something else wrong. I've had four mechanics and two avionics shops, but it seems that it doesn't make any difference who works on it. I have had only two flights where all the avionics were working. The radios are my biggest problem—ARC, of course. This is my first plane, and I am not sure if this isn't par for the course. Anyway, I love the bird, and wouldn't trade it for anything."

Skymaster pilots who lose an engine *on climbout are cautioned not to retract the gear until reaching a safe altitude because of the extra drag imposed by gear doors opening and closing.*

The recent appearance of "light-light twins" such as Beech's Model 76 and Grumman American's Cougar underlies the fact that the major manufacturers feel that there is sufficient potential in the owner-flown personal-transportation market to justify the hefty outlay of cash required to introduce and certificate a new model. Let us not forget, however, that there is one "light-light" twin that's available used and which was the first airplane of its class to be marketed: Piper's Twin Comanche, which was built from 1963 through 1972. During the nine-year lifetime of the model, some 2,150 of the aircraft were built.

When the original PA-30 was introduced in 1963, it filled the niche left in the Piper line by the discontinuation of the PA-23 Apache, which had metamorphosed into the PA-23-250 Aztec. Using the same thrifty 160-hp engines as the Apache, only fuel injected, the Twin Comanche offered better speed and range with almost equal room (at least for four) and racy styling, aided in this last by a pair of "tiger shark" engine nacelles with six-inch propeller extensions.

The new airplane was a success almost from the first, bought not only by individuals and businesses but by FBOs that wanted a relatively inexpensive and cheap-to-operate multi-engine trainer . . . and this was the beginning of the Twin Comanche's troubles with the infamous "stall/spin syndrome." Several fatal training accidents gave the Twin Comanche the reputation of a "hot" airplane, one that would be dangerous for training.

Stall/Spin
The actual problem was that the airplane, rather than not having sufficient control at low speeds, almost had too much. As originally placarded, the minimum control speed (V_{mc}) was very low due to the large rudder; in fact, it was only slightly above the airplane's stall speed. Moreover, these were the days when the FAA in its infinite wisdom recommended that demonstrations of V_{mc} be performed at as low an altitude as

possible, so as to maximize the asymmetric power. Thus, it was possible to get pretty close to the stall with full asymmetric power. If an inadvertent stall occurred—which was not too remote a possibility, since the Twin Comanche's high aspect-ratio wing tended to let go fairly briskly—asymmetric power could roll the airplane quite rapidly, resulting in a spin or similar departure. Obviously, this could be a real problem at low altitude.

Piper's initial fix was simple: increase the V_{mc} to 90 mph by placard. A further fix appeared in the form of a Piper stall-strip kit which was made available free to PA-30 operators; this stall strip, which later became standard on the counterrotating PA-39 versions, was *not* required by an AD note, as the speed placard was. Function of the strip was to provide a more predictable stall by ensuring initial flow separation over the inboard wing sections.

Price Range: $29,000-$56,000
The prospective Twin Comanche buyer will find a fairly wide range of models and prices, ranging from the 1963 PA-30 at around $29,000 to a loaded 1972 Turbo PA-39

somewhere around $56,000. Any model should give the owner a cruise speed in excess of 190 mph at a fuel consumption of about 16-17 gph; in other words, what you're getting is roughly Bonanza performance and operating costs, and roughly the same acquisition costs as Bonanzas of similar or slightly older vintage, with the added bonus of twin engines . . . which may not be a bonus come overhaul time. Let's take a look at the various models:

The basic Twin Comanche was built from 1963 through 1965. Like the single-engine Comanche of the same period, it had four-place seating (buckets in front, bench in back), with a roomy baggage area aft of the rear seat. Standard fuel is 90 gallons in four wing tanks, with tip tanks available to increase it to 120 gallons (224 usable).

The PA-30B was introduced in 1966 and featured the addition of a third rear window on each side and two additional seats in the erstwhile baggage area. The airplane can't honestly be called a six-place except for short flights, since there's no baggage space with all six seats in, and the useful load of 1,390 pounds leaves room for only half fuel (45-50 gallons) if all six seats are filled

The PA-39 *was an advanced version with counter-rotating props.*

and reasonably complete IFR radios are installed.

A major innovation for the PA-30B was the availability of factory-installed Rajay turbochargers. The tip tanks were standard on the Turbo versions, as was a gross weight increase of 125 pounds (to 3,725). Since the Rajay installation is used only for "normalizing"—i.e., restoration of sea-level manifold pressure, rather than increasing pressure beyond 30 inches Hg—the turbocharged airplanes are no more powerful than the normally-aspirated ones, and actually sacrifice a small amount of performance until altitudes are reached at which the normally-aspirated airplane can no longer maintain 75 percent power. Turbo versions cruise up to 220 mph at high altitude.

The Twin Comanche's turbocharger installation is a simple one; each turbo waste gate is controlled directly by a mechanical cockpit handle. This system, while cheap, simple, and usually reliable (although we have reader reports of the wastegate control cables burning out due to their proximity to exhaust heat), requires additional pilot workload, both because of the extra controls and because the lack of an automatic controller allows large fluctuations in manifold pressure due to airspeed changes, turbulence, temperature or mixture changes, etc. TBO on turbocharged engines is 1,800 hours, against 2,000 hours for the non-blower version.

The PA-30C was produced in 1969 and featured mainly detail improvements. The interior was spiffed up somewhat, most notably by a new instrument panel featuring an offset radio stack and flight instruments arranged in the standard "sacred six" pattern rather than Piper's earlier random-scatter arrangement; new "ram's horn" yokes replaced the earlier "square pretzel" ones.

Nineteen-seventy through 1972 saw the final model of the line, the PA-39 series. The type number was changed due to the incorporation of new counter-rotating engines, eliminating the problem of a critical engine. In fact, this marked the beginning of Piper's affair with counterrotating engines, which would later also appear on the Seneca and

Twin Comanche panel *is typical of its day: utilitarian and a bit jumbled.*

the Navajo C/R. It should be noted that earlier aircraft can be converted to the C/R configuration by the purchase of engines, props, and the appropriate kits from Piper ... although the value of such an expensive conversion is questionable unless the airplane is going to be used mainly for training. There is also some conjecture that parts for the right—or "backwards-turning"—engine may be somewhat more expensive than standard in some cases. Nineteen-seventy and 1971 airplanes were sold as six-place, while the final 1972 version was a four-place once again.

Useful options to look for on all models are the tip tanks if long flights are contemplated, prop de-ice (the airplane is *not* certificated for known icing conditions, but readers report that it carries ice fairly well), and avionics; many Twin Comanches left Lock Haven well equipped, including three-axis fully-coupled autopilots.

Handling is very similar to that of the single-engine Comanche; landings may be a bit easier, since one doesn't have to contend with the mass of the engine all the way out at the front. Most operators agree that it's rather reluctant to slow down, especially in ground effect, and it's best to have one's final approach speed pegged.

The AD situation is an interesting one; there are relatively few powerplant ADs, even in the turbocharged version. There are, however, a number of potentially expensive

structural notes, including replacement of the nose gear actuator tube, rebalancing of the stabilator, inspection/replacement of the stabilator torque tube bearings, and beefing-up of the aileron nose bulkheads. A late AD requires inspection of the aileron spar at 100-hour inspections. Piper kits are available for the various "beef-up" ADs, perhaps the most extensive being a fix for a cracking aft bulkhead which requires periodic tailcone pulls until the kit is installed.

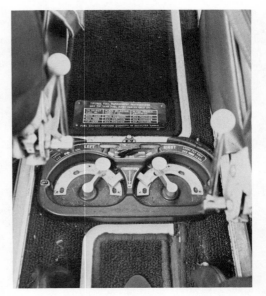

The fuel system *on tiptank-equipped aircraft is a complex one.*

Model	Year	Number Built	Average Retail Price	Cruise Speed (mph)	Rate of Climb (fpm)	Useful Load (lbs)	Fuel Std/Opt (gals)	Single-Engine Service Ceiling (ft)	Engine	TBO (hrs)	Overhaul Cost
PA-30	1963-65	901	$30,000	194	1,460	1,390	90/120	5,800	160-hp Lycoming	2,000	$5,200
PA-30B	1966-68	N/A	$36,500	194	1,460	1,350	90/120	5,800	160-hp Lycoming	2,000	$5,200
Turbo B	1966-68	N/A	$42,000	223	1,290	1,317	120	19,000	160-hp Lycoming	1,800	$5,200
PA-30C	1969	N/A	$42,000	198	1,460	1,330	90/120	7,100	160-hp Lycoming	2,000	$5,200
Turbo C	1969	N/A	$46,000	240	1,290	1,309	120	17,000	160-hp Lycoming	1,800	$5,200
PA-39 C/R	1970-71	N/A	$47,000	198	1,460	1,370	90/120	7,100	160-hp Lycoming	2,000	$5,200
Turbo C/R	1970-71	N/A	$52,500	221	1,290	1,309	120	12,600	160-hp Lycoming	1,800	$5,200
PA-39 C/R	1972	N/A	$50,000	198	1,460	1,370	90/120	7,100	160-hp Lycoming	2,000	$5,200
Turbo C/R	1972	N/A	$56,000	221	1,290	1,309	120	12,600	160-hp Lycoming	1,800	$5,200

Clubs and Mods

Prospective Twin Comanche buyers should get in touch with the International Comanche Society. (Their main concern is the single-engine line, but the folks know a lot about the twins, too. The airframes are virtually identical, don't forget.) Address: 1359 McClean Blvd., Wichita, Kansas 67203. According to the ICS, the best Twin Comanche shop in the country is Midwest Piper in Wichita, where chief mechanic John Dean is regarded as a Twin Comanche guru of sorts.

If you're looking for Twin Comanche modifications, look no further than J. W. Miller Aviation, Inc. at Horseshoe Bay Airport, Box 7757, Marble Falls, TX 78654; 512-598-2556. Miller offers a 200-hp Lycoming installation that turns the Twin-C into a fire-breather: 220 mph cruise, 1,900-fpm climb and 500 fpm single-engine climb. Cost is about $36,095, including a dorsal fin and new cowlings. If that isn't enough, there is Miller's Turbo 200 conversion, which for an extra $19,265, will give a 260-mph cruise at 20,000 feet. Miller also offers a sleek extended nose cone that holds seven cubic feet and 130 pounds of baggage ($3,450), nacelle baggage lockers that hold 75 pounds each ($3,845), integral aux tanks that increase fuel capacity by 38 gallons and gross weight by 180 pounds $6,950), plus de-ice equipment, one-piece windshields and other add-on doodads.

And, of course, there are the Robertson STOL mods, which Miller reports complement his nicely. A Robertson/Miller Turbo-STOL Comanche should certainly satisfy the macho-lust of just about anybody.

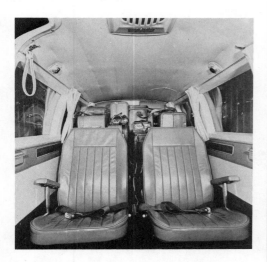

In 1966, Comanche twins and singles *were offered with optional fifth and sixth seats in lieu of baggage space, but with six passengers and no baggage, range was reduced to about 400 miles.*

Owner Comments

"The PA-30 has proven to be the best for my use in terms of comfort, speed, load, cost and utility. The airplane is stable and fast. One engine gets a little hairy, but it can be managed as long as there is no surprise element. I regularly obtain 160 knots block to block. Fuel consumption averages 17-18 gph, not the 15.5 many folks claim (both injectors were overhauled). Range is one thing I was looking for and now I have one stop from Detroit to Ft. Myers, Florida, with IFR reserves and a good cushion besides.

"A few words about landing qualities: the PA-30 is one of the easiest I've ever had in terms of approach and landing. The clue is twofold: first I fly "blue line" (105 indicated) through the entire approach, 90 over the fence and grease it on at 60 to 70 depending on gust and crosswind conditions. No amount of crosswind seems to be too much. Second is to keep CG in center of envelope or rearward. I use 100 pounds of ballast when flying alone or with light or no luggage. Without ballast it is slower and extremely difficult to land smoothly, with, it flares easily."

"We made the move to the PA-30s when gas prices drove us out of 310s. Are we ever glad we did. It is very hard to beat on fuel consumption—15 gph—and maintenance.

"The PA-30 is an excellent IFR platform, very simple systems, good resale market, great lines, and best of all, speed and economy.

"One and only possible minus. Landings can be an adventure.

"The Twin Comanche is in my way of thinking one of the most realistic twins ever built."

"We have a turbocharged model of the PA-30, and in our opinion, this is the best aircraft available today for economical, multi-engine, 4-place transportation.

We have a 1968 PA-30 with factory-installed Rajay turbochargers, oxygen, and tip tanks, bringing total fuel to 120 gallons (114 gallons usable). The tip tanks also permit the gross weight to increase from 3,600 to 3,725 pounds. The resultant useful load is 1,155 pounds (we do not carry the fifth and sixth seats) which would include four passengers, baggage, over four hours of fuel (77 gallons of the 114). Range would be over 800 miles at 200+ mph at 16-17 gallons per hour. We like to describe the price/performance as "Baron airspeeds with Comanche prices."

"Thus far, the Lycoming IO-320 C1A engines (as opposed to IO-320 B1A on the standard PA-30) have not shown any evidence of extra wear due to the turbos.

"The principal problem we have had with the turbos has been with burning out the cable linkage which closes the waste gate when the turbo is activated. Also, the hinges on the ram air shutoff box needed to be replaced. When using the turbos, we are careful to climb at higher airspeeds using a full rich mixture, cowl flaps open. Typical climb performance is 130 mph at 26 inches and 2400 rpm, yielding 800 feet-per-minute at most altitudes. Careful monitoring of cylinder-head temperatures is in order, especially in the summertime. The cable end burn-out problem was finally fixed with a new cable from Rajay, which was of a much heavier gauge than the original.

"My previous aircraft was a 1959 PA-24-250 which I flew for 1,000 hours in an eight-year period. Operating costs of the PA-30 (including inflation) are only slightly higher, although insurance costs are significantly higher due to the higher hull value ($1,500 for $36,000 hull vs. $600 for the PA-24)."

"My 1963 PA-30 has tip tanks and Rajay turbochargers. At 12,500 I get 205 mph on 16 gph at 65 percent power, with a full fuel load of 114 gallons, this is a seven-hour range. The airplane is only a three-place in this condition, however.

Takeoff and landing performance is good. I can operate in and out of an 1,800-foot grass strip without problems. Single-engine performance is good at altitude, but climb at gross is impossible. Landing difficulties and the hazards of stall/spins are much overrated. I have found bad landings no more common than in my previous Bonanza, an airplane praised for landing characteristics. Stalls are docile with straight ahead recovery as long as power is not assymetrical.

"Maintenance has been higher than anticipated but not unrelated to the condition of this airplane when purchased. The heater is inadequate and must by AD be overhauled every 500 hours. Engine maintenance has been low, however.

"In spite of turbocharging at an early age the engines have logged 1,750 hours and are running well. The most consistent problem is the plugging of fuel injector nozzles.

"I find the Twin Comanche no more expensive than a Bonanza of similar age, safer at night and in IFR, just as quiet and roomy, more stable in rough air and only slightly higher in fuel consumption (16 gph compared to 14 gph for my old 260-hp turbocharged Bonanza)."

"I have owned a 1965 Twin Comanche for four years, flying it approximately 550 hours in that time period.

"The airplane is used for both business and pleasure. Business use: flying from Seattle to points in the western United States, and occasionally as far east as New York and Boston. Pleasure: the plane is used into 2,000-foot mountain dirt strips, and into as short as 1,500 feet when the approaches are good.

"Generally speaking, the airplane's handling characteristics are excellent. I also do not have counterrotating engines, but in no sense feel these are essential to safe operation of the airplane. The airplane has good controllability about all three axis above 90 mph. Below that speed, it definitely tends to become sloppy, particularly if you are attempting final setups into a difficult approach mountain strip. The airplane does take a long time to settle out in longitudinal trim as it accelerates in cruise, but this certainly does not constitute a problem—just additional trimming.

"The airplane can consistently be landed smoothly—contrary to the many comments made about its landing characteristics—by using the technique on short final of full flaps and 90 until just prior to the threshold. When landing is assured, pull throttles and yoke. There is plenty of energy left for a good roundout. The airplane can be rotated for a nose-high landing on the mains every time with minimum bounce. I think many people have difficulty landing the Twin Comanche smoothly simply because they do not flare—get the yoke back far enough. If any power at all is carried the airplane will tend to float for quite a distance.

"The fuel system is simple and straightforward, allowing feed from either main or aux and crossfeed, and the fuel guages are relatively accurate.

"The airplane will operate easily in cruise between 7,000 and 15,000 feet (not turbo), and with very little difference in true airspeed performance. Fuel consumption, of course, drops appreciably at higher altitudes. I generally cruise at 8,000 to 11,000 feet. At 8,000, full throttle and 2300 rpm, the airplane will consistently run at 16½ gallons an hour, delivering approximately 198 mph. This is operating slightly below gross because I generally travel by myself or with one other person. With 90 gallons on board, it is possible to consistently flight plan 500 nautical miles with plenty of reserve.

"Cabin comfort is good, particularly with only two people. The traditional complaint about visibility out of a "tunnel" is overcome with time. My airplane still retains the original leather upholstery in outstanding condition, and that is a real pleasure.

"Crosswinds are not particularly difficult, but it is extremely important to either dump flaps immediately upon touchdown or land with little or no flaps in a strong crosswind. With full flaps, the airplane is very susceptible to being blown off the runway.

"Shortly after purchasing the airplane, I discovered that it was not possible to completely feather either propeller. Regardless of how much I slowed up the airplane, the propellers would still kick over. After removal for desludging, I discovered that during the Hartzell AD performed on most Twin Comanches, springs which should have been removed had been inadvertently left in—full feather is not possible without their removal. I recommend all Twin Comanche owners verify that they can, in fact, get a full feather on both engines.

"The heater is excellent, providing plenty of comfort down to -30 degrees C. Approximately once every 15 months, it is necessary to insert a .040 wire up the exhaust pipe and into an air-sensing tube, which is part of the safety control system. The end of this tube sometimes becomes clogged with carbon, causing the heater to shut down.

"I have had several ignition leads go bad just at the angle above the ¾-inch nut, where it can't been seen. I finally changed out the engine ignition harnesses entirely.

"The landing gear motor burned out on one occasion, apparently from age. This caused no difficulty, as the gear is easily uncoupled and locked in the down position with the Johnson bar. The airplane must be slowed up as recommended in the handbook, however, or air loads make it difficult to get the gear fully down.

"On one occasion, the left flap hung up on departure from a high-altitude field at gross. Flap retraction resulted in an almost uncontrollable roll to the right. Level flight was maintained with hard over left aileron. I pay more attention than usual now to the cleanliness of the flap rails. The cause of the hang-up was not determined, but I have tried to keep the rails clean and dry as recommended.

"The Northwest is ice country and it is almost impossible to fly hard IFR without occasionally encountering unexpected moderate to severe icing. The airplane will carry a fair amount of ice, although somewhat sluggishly. Clearly, no ice is recommended, but my point is that the airplane will not fall out of the sky even with a significant load of ice.

"Unquestionably, the Twin Comanche will fly, and fly well, on one engine. In all circumstances, except with gear and flaps, the airplane is eminently manageable. With fuel burnoff, I find the single engine service ceiling to be quite adequate even in high country, assuming the airplane is being operated at or above minimum enroute altitudes. At the very least, even in the roughest terrain, the airplane on one engine will either maintain altitude (depending on weight) or provide a drift-down angle which allows access to suitable lower terrain.

"Annuals seem to run in the neighborhood of $500-$600. The structure seems very solid, and you gain the impression that quite a load could be applied to the airframe without damage. The recent rash of structural ADs, while irritating, have not been show-stoppers such as is the case in the 210 "saddle."

"The basic airframe-engine-gross weight relationships in the Twin Comanche provide an extraordinarily cost-effective airplane in the general aviation environment. The best testimonial to this is the introduction of comparably set-up airplanes by both Grumman and Beech. While the Twin Comanche can be had, however, in good condition, in the $30,000 to $45,000 range, the newer vehicles will cost 3½ to 4 times that amount with no appreciable difference in performance. The Twin Comanche would be higher priced in the market place, but for the unjustified reputation it has for being difficult to fly.

"I think those who have had experience in the Twin Comanche rate it one of the great all-time contributions to general aviation—fun as well as efficient."

Beech Travel Air

The Beech Travel Air Model 95 is one of the best bargains among used economy light twins. Out of production for nearly a decade now and distinguished by its dowdy-looking vertical fin, this predecessor to the Baron line offers perhaps more airplane for the dollar than anything else in its class.

General Characteristics of the Series:

Speed—Owners report an honest 156 kts/180 mph with 65 percent cruise power and about 163 kts/188 mph with 70 percent at altitude. Few report pushing their airplanes to the 170-knot speed it is listed as capable of at 75 percent in brochure specs.

Economy—This is the Travel Air's forte, since the 180-hp Lycomings will oblige with a miserly 16-18 gph at cruise, which is almost as good as some of the big singles. The Twin Comanche, with 160-hp engines, gets better, but sacrifices 150 or so pounds of useful load.

Cabin Room—Standard Beech Bonanza-Baron cabin with gobs of headroom and footroom and plenty of beam width. The big windows lend to the feeling of spaciousness, and the sizable baggage space is a temptation toward overloading.

Load Carrying—With a useful load of around 1,500 pounds—or about 1,400 pounds equippped—figure on carrying full optional 112 gallons of fuel and maybe four adults, but probably no baggage. Count on a generous 800 to 900 nm range. Once again, owners warn about the tendency to overload because of the big, roomy cabin.

Cockpit Design—Standard Beech atypical power control, flap and gear arrangement with single, throw-over wheel, or optional dual-control bar.

Handling—Pleasant responsiveness and what one owner described as "tremendous aileron control." Some owners report a tendency to wallow around in turbulence, but good stability in smooth air. Like all low-powered twins, the Travel Air is regarded by many as a "bear" on one engine. But this usually translates into poor performance at low speeds—meaning at take-off and climbout—though the airplane will usually chug along decently with an engine out at cruise. The handicap, of course, is an embarrassingly low single-engine ceiling of 4,400 feet. Vmc is 70 kts/80 mph.

Visibility—Magnificent, thanks to typical Beech windows. Early models have two-piece windshields, though, with a center strut; later ones have one-piece windshields.

History

There are five categories of Travel Air models spanning the decade from 1958 to 1968:
1. Model 95; four seats, carbureted engines.
2. Model B95 with 100 pounds more gross weight, five seats.
3. Model B95A with longer cabin, up to six seats, another 100 pounds of gross weight and fuel injection engines.
4. Model D95A; beginning in 1966, new one-half-inch valves boost engine TBO from 1,200 to 2,000 hours.
5. Model E95 with bigger, more steeply slanted one-piece windshield.

Price figures are for aircraft equipped with dual navcom, VOR, marker beacon and glideslope with two-axis autopilot, oxygen and aux fuel tanks. Price assumes 600 hours on the engines, with good paint and interior and all ADs complied with.

The original Model 95 had four seats and a short, six-foot, 11-inch cabin, with a small rear window. The carbureted Lycoming O-360-A1A engines had a TBO of only 1,200 hours. By now, most of these probably have been updated with one-half-inch valves that raise the TBO to 2,000 hours. Conversion during overhaul to fuel injection configuration is considered a desirable move also, to avoid carburetor ice problems. Beech originally intended naming the aircraft the *Badger*, but

A 1964 D95A, *with enlarged rear window and full-length cabin.*

dropped the idea because that was the military code name for a Russian bomber.

The Model B95 earned a 100-pound increase in gross weight thanks to enlarged flaps, and added a fifth optional seat. Like all the other Travel Air models, it had Goodyear brakes that gained a reputation for bending and binding, and in fact doing everything but braking effectively. Some pilots report they can't run both engines at 2,200 rpm on the pre-takeoff check without the airplane creeping away, brakes on full. Cleveland brake replacements are recommended.

The Model B95A received the most significant changes in the history of the line. It was given fuel injected engines and an extended cabin—19 inches longer—along with a boost in gross weight. The tailplane was lengthened by 19 inches. Perhaps because of the change in the fuselage fineness ratio or the extra efficiency of the fuel injected engines, or both, the listed 75 percent cruise speed went up to 174 knots. We suspect it's still a bit optimistic. Structural baggage limit was 270 pounds in the rear and the same in the nose compartment.

with prices ranging between $30,000 to $35,000, this model appears to be

Stubby, unstylish vertical tail *is the aircraft's hallmark.*

the best buy of all the 95s.

The Model D95A received two significant changes: half-inch valves, bringing the engine up to a 2,000-hour TBO rating with the 1966 model and a lengthened nose. Also, a one-piece windshield was added, and in 1966 the upper air vent scoop was moved from the top of the fuselage into the dorsal fin. The rear baggage limit was raised to 400 pounds and the panel was redesigned to allow center-mounted radios.

Modifications
Travel Air owners interested in boosting the single-engine ceiling from 4,400 feet to 20,000 feet might consider the Rajay turbocharging system. Installation is estimated by the company at about 125 hours. It adds 45 pounds to the empty weight of the aircraft and brings the cruise at 20,000 feet to 217 knots. Rajay Industries, 2600 East Wardlow Rd., Long Beach Airport, Long Beach, Calif. 90801.

The E95 was the last of the Travel Airs. Reflecting the evolutionary changes of the Bonanza line fuselage, it received the enlarged, slanted windshield.

To change from two-piece to one-piece windshields, kits are available from several sources. One is Beryl D'Shannon Aviation specialties, which provides regular windshields and the newer, more steeply sloped windshields. Beryl is located at Rt. 2, Box 272, Jordan, Minn. 55352.

Beryl also sells pilot windows and door windows with vents.

Societies
We can find no association or society of Beech Travel Air owners, although the American Bonanza Society in Horseheads, N.Y., might be able to provide some moral support. Newsletter Editor Bill Guinther has had lots of experience with Travel Airs as a longtime Beech salesman and pilot. Their number is 607-739-5515.

Where To Go
A few dealers around the country seem to have more than average interest in handling Travel Airs. Some of those are: Grover Scruggs in Pine Bluff, Ark. 501-879-1341; Dan Futrell, Nashville, Ark. 501-624-2462; and Twin Center, Boulder, Colo. 303-444-1141.

The 180-hp Lycomings *with half-inch valves have good reliability, but the 4,400-foot single-engine ceiling is nothing to brag about.*

Model	Year	Number Built	Average Retail Price	Cruise Speed (mph)	Rate of Climb (fpm)	Useful Load (lbs)	Fuel Std/Opt (gals)	Single-Engine Service Ceiling (ft)	Engine	TBO (hrs)	Overhaul Cost
95, B95	1958-60	452	$30,000	169	1,250	1,465	80/112	4,400	180-hp Lycoming	2,000	$4,250
B95A	1961-63	99	$35,000	169	1,250	1,505	80/112	4,400	180-hp Lycoming	2,000	$6,250
D95A	1964-65	87	$42,000	169	1,250	1,645	80/112	4,400	180-hp Lycoming	2,000	$5,500
D95A	1966-67	66	$44,500	169	1,250	1,645	80/112	4,400	180-hp Lycoming	2,000	$5,500
E95	1968	13	$46,000	169	1,250	1,645	80/112	4,400	180-hp Lycoming	2,000	$5,500

Owner Comments

Maintenance and Operations
"We have found that maintenance and operations costs are high."

"The older models were really buggers on carburetor ice—I lost one once because of that . . . The Goodyear brakes were terrible.

"The engine cowlings are superior to the Aztec's, but not as good as the Baron's. They're troublesome to remove, and they develop cracks. The brakes are worth a lot of aggravation. I can't run up both engines at 2,200 rpm because the brakes won't hold."

"Make sure they check that the landing-gear gear box has oil in it every year on the annual. It's often overlooked."

Handling
"The flight controls are light and pleasant. The aircraft is forgiving, with plenty of warning before stalls. It is extremely easy to land smoothly even when the approach has not been set up properly. However, the rate of climb is poor. This is especially troublesome when attempting to climb at higher altitudes. The cruise speeds are disappointing. We have to use 150 knots for IFR planning."

"It takes a better than average pilot on one engine. If somebody asked me what should be the first twin they owned, I'd say it shouldn't be the Travel Air."

"It's a very nice-flying aircraft."

"I like the flying characteristics better than the Baron, where you have extra power and weight and heavier ailerons. But the airplane is marginal if you lose an engine."

Performance
"I get a good 156 knots on 65 percent power."

"Cruising at 7,500 feet, backing off on the power a tad below 70 percent, my Travel Air burns eight gph on each engine, and I'll be truing about 163 knots. With full fuel I carry four adults and damn little baggage. It's a good four-placer for about 1,000 nm, with no reserve."

General Impressions
"The aircraft appears to possess great structural strength. The airplane seems overly expensive for the total performance secured. It seems underpowered, but comfortable and strong, and it is a delight to land."

"Since I owned a Travel Air, I have spent about four years flying three different Twin Comanches. The latter is difficult to land and less spacious and comfortable inside. However, it seems clearly to outperform the Travel Air in climb, cruise and range despite having less horsepower. The useful load is about the same, but the Twin Comanche with tip tanks has a much

longer endurance and range potential. The Twin Comanche can be owned and operated for about the same cost as a Bonanza, but the Travel Air is a step up in expense."

"It's the Cadillac of the used light twin market."

"It's very easy to overload this airplane."

Rajay Turbo Modification
"I have a Rajayed 1965 D95A with which I am very happy. Parts are readily available, and sometimes from less expensive sources than Beech. There have been no serious ADs. The Lycoming 180 hp 360s are about as dependable an engine as I know of, and burn 18 gph normally aspirated and about 19 when turbocharging. I turn out 192-195 mph normally aspirated, and anywhere up to 220 mph at 20,000 feet.

"I've had the airplane over three years and, like all Beeches, it's a joy to fly. My only problem is that occasionally I would like to exceed the 600-pound limit on cabin load with full fuel, but with 112 gallons of fuel it's not much of a sacrifice to leave some fuel out, since I have very close to six hours' range with full fuel.

"Perhaps some other Travel Airs have higher useful loads than mine, but with my avionics I have 1,330 useful, and my fuel and oil weigh 688, leaving a cabin load of about 640.

"The Travel Air does not have the greatest single-engine ceiling, but it handles very well on one, and the Rajays push that single-engine ceiling over 15,000 feet." □

Rear cabin and nose baggage compartments *together can hold a whopping 670 pounds, structurally.*

Piper Aztec/Apache

Piper's PA-23 Aztec is one of general aviation's classic light twins. Over 4,000 Aztecs have been produced in a continuous production run that has lasted for 18 years and continues today. While other early light twins like the Cessna 310 and Beech Travel-Air have had their power and performance boosted considerably over the years, the Aztec has retained the same 250-hp Lycoming engines over its whole career.

The Aztec is known as a reliable, easy-to-fly aircraft with a spacious cabin and excellent short-field capabilities. In trade-off, the prospective Aztec purchaser must be prepared to accept low cruising speeds and fuel economy, more modest single-engine performance and ceilings.

History

The Aztec is a direct descendant of the Piper Apache, the first light twin, which first appeared in 1954. The Apache was pitifully underpowered with its 150-hp (later 160-hp) engines, however (listed single-engine climb rate was 180 fpm for the 160-hp model, but most Apache pilots report they are happy to maintain altitude on one engine).

The first Aztec—an Apache with 250-hp carbureted engines—was introduced in 1960. It had the same interior as the Apache, with two seats up front and a wide three-people bench rear seat. Gross weight was 4,800 pounds. In 1962, the B model appeared; it had a longer snout and standard six-place interior that made it easily distinguishable from the Apache. Fuel injection was optional in the B model, and there was also a nose baggage compartment. Gross weight of the B model remained the same, however.

In 1964, fuel injection became standard equipment, and a large rear cargo door was introduced as an option. These changes were considered major enough so that the airplane was given a new model number, the C. Gross weight of the C model jumped to 5,200 pounds, but naturally gross-weight climb performance degraded slightly, since power was unchanged. During the C model's third year, 1966, the Turbo Aztec was introduced, with AiResearch turbochargers that

increased service ceiling to 18,500 and cruise speed by 25 knots at altitude. The D model was virtually identical to the C, with only minor yearly detail changes until 1971.

In 1971, the E model Aztec appeared with an even longer snout, which provided more luggage space up front.

In 1976 Piper made a major effort to spruce up the airplane with the Aztec F. The F model has new wingtips and horizontal stabilizer for lighter control forces, plus a flap-trim interconnect that solved a pitch-up problem that had long been the bane of Aztec pilots. (More on that later.) In addition, long range tip tanks were made available that stretched range to well over 1,000 miles with IFR reserves. The F model is currently in production at Lock Haven, still selling at a healthy clip.

After a siege of problems with the new tail and its balance horns, Piper went back to the old stabilator with the 1980 model. On all pre-80 F models, check that Piper service instructions and improvements have been made.

Performance

Speed is not the Aztec's strong suit. Book cruise speeds for the older models were 205-210 mph (178-182 knots); the F model is listed at 202 mph (175 knots). Reader reports and *Aviation Consumer* flight evaluations have shown these figures to be

slightly high; under normal conditions, 190 mph (160-165 knots) seems to be about right for 75 percent cruise. At 65 percent power, speed drops to around 185 mph (155-160 knots).

One *Aviation Consumer* reader who's owned four Aztecs reports that the F model is noticeably slower than the D and E models. "I could get 160 knots at 65 percent with the old ones, but the F model I owned was five to 10 knots slower and used noticeably more fuel," he reports.

Fuel consumption of the Aztec is about 26-28 gph at intermediate cruise settings, which works out to a rather poor fuel economy of less than seven miles per gallon. This compares to almost nine mpg for the six-place Piper Seneca and Seneca II.

Weight-lifting, however, *is* the Aztec's strong point. Standard useful load in the straight Aztec and B models was 1,900 pounds; when gross was increased to 5,200, useful went up to 2,100-plus. Even with IFR equipment, this still leaves around 1,900 pounds useful for the C, D, E and F model (depending on equipment, of course) and 1,600-1,700 pounds for the early models.

With full fuel (144 gallons), this leaves well over 1,000 pounds for people and baggage—enough for six full-size adults and a smidgin of baggage, or five people and 200 pounds of gear. Aztecs have a zero-fuel

The Aztec is roomy, reliable and slow.

weight limit of 4,400 pounds, but at typical licensed empty weights of around 3,100 to 3,300 pounds, this still leaves 1,100 to 1,300 pounds for cabin payload in reduced-fuel situations.

Takeoff and landing performance of the Aztec is among the best of any light twin; obstacle takeoff distance is 1,250 feet for all models except the F. (The F is a bit more lackadaisical at 1,585.) This compares to 1,500-1,800 feet for various models of the 310 and 1,700-2,100 feet for the various Barons. Accelerate-stop distance is just 1,985 feet for the F model, and 2,200 for all pre-1976 Aztecs, which were notorious for inadequate brakes.

The Turbo Aztecs generally cruise 20-30 knots faster when at the optimum 24,000-foot altitudes, although most pilots prefer to fly them down at 12-15,000 feet, where speeds generally run around 180 knots on fuel flows of 34-36 gph.

Flight Characteristics

The airplane has one major handling quirk that has annoyed pilots for years and could be potentially dangerous for a pilot who's not very familiar with the airplane. This is the Aztec's notorious pitch-up with flap extension. Long-time owners learn to anticipate it, of course, but the tendency is still annoying and unnecessary. Piper finally got around to correcting the problem with the F model by adding a flap-trim interconnect that automatically retrims the stabilator when flaps are deployed or retracted. The F model also has lighter downspring forces which make flaring to

Some Aztecs are equipped with STCed three-bladed props. *Advantages: better ground clearance, less cabin noise.*

land a bit easier. Aileron response is also better in the F model due to recontoured wingtips.

On a single engine, the Aztec is docile and forgiving compared to many other light twins. Vmc is a low 80 mph (70 knots), at least 10 knots slower than the Baron and 310. Although single-engine rate of climb is rather poor (240 fpm for most models), it comes at a low single-engine climb speed of just 102 mph (91 knots)—again, substantially lower than the competition. This tends to soften the effect of the very low climb rate somewhat, but the Aztec still has the worst single-engine climb gradient of any normally aspirated light twin. Strangely enough, the Turbo Aztec fares better in comparison with the turbo competition, falling about in the middle in terms of single-engine climb gradient.

In compensation for the Aztec's poor single-engine climb, it offers docile handling with one feathered. "Things happen a lot slower in an Aztec than they do in other

twins," one Aztec pilot tells us. Another reports, "I know of no other light twin that can be dispatched on a flight with a low-time renter pilot and be expected to return safely, time after time."

The Aztec's pleasant handling and good short-field performance are the result of its big fat Clark Y airfoil wing, virtually the same airfoil as on the Piper Cub.

Modifications

Several mods have become popular with Aztec owners over the years. Before Piper introduced the Turbo Aztec in 1966, many standard Aztecs had been retrofitted with Rajay turbochargers, and these are quite common on the used-plane market today. Market price for an early Rajayed Aztec should be about $3,000 higher than the listed retail price. Performance of the Rajay mod is roughly comparable to the later Turbo Aztec, which used an AiResearch blower.

Another popular add-on feature of older

Model	Year	Number Built	Bluebook Retail	Engine	TBO (hrs)	Overhaul Cost	ADs	Cruise Speed (mph)	Standard Useful Load (lbs)	Rate of climb (fpm)	S.E. Rate of Climb (fpm)
PA-23	1960-61	500	$21,500-$23,000	250-hp Lycoming O-540-A1B5	1,200	6,000	15	206	1,900	1,650	365
PA-23B	1962-64	497	$27,000-$29,500	250-hp Lycoming O-540-A1D5	1,200	$6,000	13	205	1,900	1,650	365
PA-23C	1964-68	1,431	$32,000-$40,000	250-hp Lycoming IO-540-C4B5	1,200	$6,000	20	206	2,267	1,490	240
PA-23D	1969-70	638	$42,000-$47,000	250-hp Lycoming IO-540-C4B5	2,000	$6,000	18	210	2,158	1,490	240
PA-23E	1971-75	970	$52,000-$75,000	250-hp Lycoming IO-540-C4B5	2,000	$6,000	4-16	210	2,158	1,490	240
Aztec F	1976-79	426	$85,000-$137,000	250-hp Lycoming IO-540-C4B5	2,000	$6,000	13	202	2,151	1,400	235
TURBO AZTEC											
Turbo C	1966-68	811	$41,000-$46,000	250-hp Lycoming IO-540-J4A5	1,800	$6,500	18	236	2,170	1,490	1,490
Turbo D	1969-70	638	$48,000-$55,000	250-hp Lycoming IO-540-J4A5	1,800	$6,500	17	250	2,170	1,490	240
Turbo E	1971-75	970	$60,000-$82,000	250-hp Lycoming TIO-540-C1A	1,500	$6,500	4-14	226	1,980	1,530	265
Turbo F	1976-79	426	$92,000-$152,000	250-hp Lycoming TIO-540-C1A	1,800	$6,500	1-3	233	2,120	1,470	225

Aztecs is the Metcoair long-range tip tanks. These increase the fuel supply from 144 gallons to 192 gallons and stretch endurance to seven hours-plus. (Piper finally made long-range tanks available as an option on the F model.)

An annoying feature of older Aztecs was a problem that made it difficult for pilots to keep good prop synchronization. The airplanes reportedly came from the factory with remanufactured military surplus governors designed for Hamilton Standard propellers that had a much larger oil volume than the Aztec's Hartzells. As a result, they are difficult to control. Woodward governors are available, which are far superior, according to *Aviation Consumer* readers.

Many pilots fault the Aztec for its single hydraulic pump on the left engine. If that engine fails on takeoff, gear and flaps cannot be retracted, and it is virtually impossible to maintain altitude. (There is an emergency manual retraction handle but we defy any mortal to maintain control 100 feet off the ground while furiously pumping a lever on the floor.) Two companies have offered solutions for this problem. Dee Howard in Texas for a time offered an electric hydraulic pump that would operate normally in case of an engine failure, but this was discontinued. Robertson Aircraft currently offers a dual hydraulic pump that has been installed on many Aztecs. If you are seriously concerned about safety or fly out of short, tight fields this second hydraulic pump is almost a must.

Another common modification is Cleveland brakes. Older pre-F Aztecs had poor brakes that were a constant maintenance item and limited short-field landing capability. The Clevelands, adopted by Piper in 1976, have been retrofitted to many older Aztecs and are a definite plus when shopping for a used airplane.

Maintenance

By most reports, the Aztec is cheaper to maintain than most other light twins in the 250-300-hp class. The 250-hp Lycomings have an excellent record of reliability and a long 2,000-hour TBO. "They're the greatest engine ever made," one Aztec owner told us. "I overhauled mine at 2,100 hours, and the mechanic said they both could have gone another thousand hours." Overhaul cost for these engines is about $7,000, which works out to a very low overhaul reserve of $3.50 per hour per engine. (The Baron and 310, by comparison, run better than $4 per hour.) Up until 1967, the Aztec's TBO was only 1,200 hours, however, but those engines overhauled with updated valves and bearings are rated

the full 2,000 hours. This is a critical point to check when shopping for a used Aztec.

One large used plane broker tells us that some Aztecs which are not flown regularly may require a top overhaul after a thousand hours, but a well-cared-for airplane should easily run its full 2,000-hour TBO.

Turbo Aztecs have TBOs of either 1,500 or 1,800 hours, depending on the model. The 1966-69 and 1973-77 models have the 1,800-hour engines; '70-'72 Turbo Aztecs that have not been overhauled to later standards are rated at 1,500 hours.

Aztec airframe maintenance presents no special problems. Corrosion is not reported to be widespread, and the landing gear system is simple and robust. An annual inspection should cost from $1,200 to $1,500, assuming no major repair work is necessary. One *Aviation Consumer* subscriber reports he spends about $62 per hour to fly his Aztec 200 hours per year. Of that total, about $15 per hour is spent on maintenance. This corresponds to a $3/hour overhaul reserve per engine, plus annual expenditures of $1,800 for maintenance.

Aztecs have had a good number of ADs over the years, but all should have long since been complied with. The one major recent AD to check closely is the Hartzell propeller modification that has hit thousands of aircraft of a wide variety of types. The AD can be an expensive one, so make sure that it's been done on any Aztec you consider buying.

Turbo Aztecs present something more of a maintenance expense. TBO is slightly lower and it's not unusual for the turbocharger to wear out before the engine itself does. Turbocharger overhaul alone will cost

approximately $700 for 1970-77 models and $600 or so for '66-'69 Turbo Aztecs. Some turbochargers may need a de-coking of the main turbocharger bearing before overhaul, and the complex exhaust system will probably require more maintenance during its life than a standard Aztec's exhaust system.

Safety

The Aztec's safety record is not particularly good in comparison to other light twins, at least according to NTSB accident statistics. However, this does not take pilot experience into account. (Surprisingly, the number of Aztecs built over the years is virtually the same as the number of Cessna 310s and Beech Barons—all three number between 4,500 and 5,000—so the accident figures for the three types of aircraft can be compared directly.) During the period 1970-74, NTSB records list 323 Aztec accidents, 86 of them fatal. This compares to 325 for the 310 (71 fatal) and 251 for the Baron (68 fatal). (The Piper Twin Comanche has a population of only about half the other three twins, but if its accident statistics were adjusted to account for this, the Twin Comanche would register 460 total accidents (78 fatal). Thus the Aztec appears to have the highest incidence of fatal accidents among the four most popular light twins.

On the plus side, the Aztec had only six stall/spin accidents and 31 stall crashes during this period; both figures matched only by the 310. The Baron, by comparison, was credited with three times as many stall/spin accidents, which seems to bear out

The Aztec on floats *offers an unusual opportunity for pilots seeking multi-sea ratings. Note the unusual door on the pilot's side.*

pilot impressions of the Aztec's docile handling when an engine fails.

But the Aztec's sluggish single-engine climb seems to make up for the good handling—NTSB records show several cases of Aztec pilots who were unable to maintain altitude after an engine failure—including one crash during a single-engine go-around after the engine was purposely feathered for training purposes and then wouldn't restart.

The early straight Aztecs and B models with the carbureted engines suffered a very high incidence of carburetor ice accidents—astoundingly, the Aztec ranks behind only the Cessna 150, 172, Piper Cub/Super Cub and Cherokee in number of carb ice accidents and all of those aircraft are flying in far greater numbers than the Aztec. On an accident-per-aircraft basis, the Aztec has the highest incidence of carb ice accidents of any aircraft. For this reason we strongly recommend the injected versions of the Aztec B. (Incidentally, the early carbureted Aztecs can be retrofitted with fuel injection, an excellent option.)

Insurance rates don't necessarily reflect these accident statistics. We checked with several underwriters and found no significant differences in rates for these four types of aircraft.

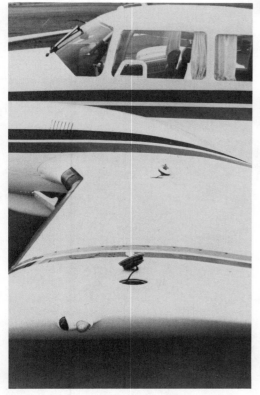

Piper's F model Aztec *was the first to receive wingtip tanks adding another 40 gallons of fuel for a total of 177.*

To what does the old-fashioned tubular-framed Piper Aztec owe its longevity as competing twins have reached for even higher horsepower, speed and load? Operators respect it for a kind of benign simplicity and reliability, and know the fuel and maintenance bills won't eat 'em alive. (Though we can recall getting charged

Apache 235, *immediate predecessor to the Aztec. It had a blunt nose and 235-hp Lycomings.*

Owner Comments

"I operate a Piper Aztec Model B, which I have owned since November 1973. From a performance and a handling point of view, I find the Aztec very dependable and satisfying. While the book indicates a 200 mile per hour true airspeed, I usually run a little over 190. I can account for the difference by age of engines, airplane de-icing equipment, etc., so that really doesn't disturb me. All of the other characteristics are as advertised—it's a very dependable machine. The Aztec has a comfortable cabin for four people.

"I think my maintenance costs have been a little high, but I bought a used airplane. Parts availability has been good. I keep elaborate records for tax purposes and find that, excluding cost of financing and depreciation, the Aztec costs about $62 an hour when I fly 200 hours a year. I would expect this to drop a bit lower

several hundred dollars on a 100-hour inspection just for unbuttoning and refastening all the panels on a turbo Aztec.)

Nevertheless, the Aztec is fairly forgiving to fly and will hold a sizable load of people and baggage, and we'd be surprised if even Piper's takeover of Aerostar will eclipse the old stalwart utility twin.

after the engines are rebuilt, since maintenance has been about $15 an hour of that total."

"I have flown the Piper Aztec for over 12 years. In the 500 horsepower class it is unchallenged. The electrical, fuel, hydraulic, heating and ice protection systems are predictable. The downspring added to the stabilator on the E models and later takes care of stability.

"Cruise is slower than the Cessna 310 or Beech Baron. The Aztec wasn't designed for speed—it's forte is utility. In training pilots for the multi-engine land rating the Aztec is excellent. The two luggage compartments are great for Air Taxi operations. In icing conditions, the Aztec fares better than the Cessna 310, and is equal to the Baron 58 that I have flown. The Robertson STOL modification almost makes the Aztec like a helicopter in a strong wind.

"In closing I know of no other light twin that can be dispatched on a flight with low time rental pilots, knowing it will return safely."

Cessna 310

With over two decades of nonstop production behind it, Cessna's 310 presents used-plane shoppers with plenty of performance for the money in the light-twin category, back through 19 model changes.

General characteristics of the series:

Speed
Count on a 75 percent cruise of up to 193 knots at altitude for the 260-hp models, but knock off seven or eight knots for a more comfortable 65 percent cruise figure.

Cabin Room
This is the airplane's strong suit, with a beamy, airy interior which allows passengers to wallow in comfort. Like most of its peers in the light-twin class, it's labeled a six-placer, but the last two seats are cramped for all but children, and with any kind of fuel and baggage, six will put the airplane over gross. Nevertheless, the four front seats are unrivaled for leg-, elbow- and head-room. The broad, sweeping windows on all but the earliest models provide superb airiness and visibility.

Baggage
The 310 will hold lots in a surprising number of compartments. Up until the advent of the long-nose R model in 1975 there was no forward baggage compartment, so pilots could dump baggage either in the fifth and sixth seat area (the seats pop out easily) or in the unique wing-locker compartments located in the aft section of the engine nacelles. With the R model, and addition of a nose compartment, baggage capacity rose from a hefty 600 pounds to an astonishing 950 pounds. Naturally, addition of a nose compartment facilitated balance considerations. The wing lockers are a nice touch since they permit loading along the top of the wing, presenting almost no shift in balance. Each will hold a couple of suitcases. Even if an extra fuel tank is located in the same nacelle, there's quite a bit of space left over for bags.

Some pilots like to keep a few standby quarts of oil and some paper tissues inside. At least one pilot has failed to secure the wing locker door and taxied off trailing a swirling cloud of tissues.

Preflight
But then, the pilot has lots to do before he's ready to button up, crank up and taxi away. The walkaround on the 310 is legendary since there can be as many as six fuel caps and eight sump drains. Line personnel must be closely monitored for proper refueling, since the number of aux tanks and their size varies from airplane to airplane. Also, oil dipsticks, inserted horizontally, must be carefully secured. If dislodged, oil may spill.

Systems
The fuel system on the 310 must be considered an abomination by any pilot who values straightforward fuel management. In addition to the two 50-gallon main tanks on the wingtips there can be two auxiliary tanks in the main wing (of either 20 gallons each or 31.5 gallons each), plus one or two optional wing locker tanks of 20 gallons each.

To add to the confusion, the pilot must not use the primary aux tanks until the mains have been used for an hour, with the small aux tanks, or an hour and a half with the larger ones. This is necessary to provide space in the main tanks for vapor and fuel returned from the engine-driven fuel pumps; otherwise, this fuel will simply be dumped overboard by the vent line. Since part of the fuel from the aux tanks is diverted back to the mains instead of being consumed by the engines, the aux tanks will run dry "sooner than may be anticipated," according to the pilot manual.

In 1977 the NTSB zeroed in on this idiosyncrasy as the cause of a fatal 310 crash at Rockford, Ill., where the pilot had lost all power from both engines on an instrument approach. The Safety Board's review of accidents involving fuel starvation for the years 1966 through '76 showed up 10 accidents in which "early" depletion of aux fuel was the most likely cause of the problem. As a result, the Board asked that an AD be issued requiring placards in the cockpit of Cessna 310s with aux fuel systems, cautioning pilots that only 30 minutes flight time may be available when using aux tanks.

The Board also recommended that pilot manuals be revised to specify the amount of fuel returned to another tank and the flight time available on the aux tanks. It said "the owner's manuals for the various models of the 310 series do not provide enough specific information for the pilot to determine the aux tanks' endurance, except through trial and error."

The NTSB mentioned also that earlier manuals generally contained more information than later ones, and the 310 J manual "was least descriptive of all."

The 1975 R Model *received bigger engines and a longer nose.*

Another complicating factor in the 310 is the use of wing locker fuel, whose transfer to the main tanks may necessitate crossfeed to maintain the proper fuel balance. To add to the mischief, some 310 pilots report chronic problems with the main fuel tank gauges, which may for no apparent reason simply register zero for long periods of time.

Handling

Difficult to land neatly, consistently. Comes down final approach with docility as long as power is retained, right on to touchdown. But pull off power and attempt to flare gracefully by applying judicious back pressure alone, and you are doomed to a rapid rate of sink, thanks to the aircraft's high wing loading.

A common trait of the bird on final is wallowing or Dutch roll, with the wing tending to continue a roll, once started. This makes the airplane less easily manageable on an instrument approach than, say, a Baron.

The first production 310s came out in 1955, with the so-called "tuna tanks" on the wingtips. The aircraft had a stubby nose with a long nose gear strut that actually was canted slightly forward.

In 1956 the A model introduced double rear windows. In 1958 the B model offered 30-gallon auxiliary wing tanks as an option for the first time, and the gross went up by 100 pounds. In 1959 the C model went from carbureted to fuel injected engines, and the gross went up once again. With the D model in 1960 the stubby vertical tail was abandoned in favor of a more dramatic-looking swept one.

The G model in 1962 saw the introduction of slanted tip tanks, which purported to ease some of the 310's stability prob-

Early model 310 *with straight tail and "tuna tanks."*

lems, since they acted like wing extenders with dihedral effect. Exotically styled, they also came with sharp points on both ends, which remain the nemesis of strolling passers-by.

With the H model in 1963 the cabin was enlarged, and the gross raised by 110 pounds. In the following year, the I model brought wing lockers to the world. The paired side windows were blended into one gorgeous big one and this was labeled "vista-view."

In '67 the L model was given optional aux tanks 10 gallons larger. And in '69 the first turbocharged model made its debut, along with the first optional wing locker tanks. The dark tunnel effect in the rear of the cabin was eliminated in dramatic fashion in '72 with the addition of a skylight in the

stern. Cessna called it "Omnivision."

And finally, in the most significant change of all, the 260-hp powerplants were dropped in favor of new 285-hp engines with the 1975 R model, the gross went up by 200 more pounds, and a nice, long nose compartment was added that provided extra baggage space.

Modifications

Robertson Aircraft Corporation in Renton, Washington, has an STC for modification of the nonturbo G and R models and the turbo P, Q and R.

The mod replaces the 310's split flap with a fowler flap. According to Robertson, this produces the best performance boost they've ever achieved on any airplane, after

Model	Year	Number Built	Average Retail Price	Cruise Speed (mph)	Rate of Climb (fpm)	Useful Load (lbs)	Fuel Std/Opt (gals)	Single-Engine Service Ceiling (ft)	Engine	TBO (hrs)	Overhaul Cost
310	1955-58	771	$ 17,500	215	1,600	1,740	102/133	8,000	240-hp Continental	1,500	$5,500
310	1959-61	543	$ 23,500	220	1,800	1,795	102/133	7,450	260-hp Continental	1,500	$5,750
310	1962-63	304	$ 27,500	220	1,690	2,037	102/133	7,450	260-hp Continental	1,500	$5,750
310	1964-65	400	$ 32,500	223	1,690	2,037	102/133	6,850	260-hp Continental	1,500	$5,750
310	1966-67	452	$ 37,500	222	1,540	2,075	102/143	6,850	260-hp Continental	1,500	$5,750
310	1968	198	$ 42,000	222	1,540	2,030	102/143	6,850	260-hp Continental	1,500	$5,750
310	1969-70	N/A	$ 49,500	221	1,540	2,086	102/184	6,850	260-hp Continental	1,500	$5,750
Turbo 310	1970	N/A	$ 63,000	256	1,962	1,802	102/184	18,100	285-hp Continental	1,400	$8,000
310	1971-72	N/A	$ 57,000	221	1,495	2,086	102/207	6,680	260-hp Continental	1,800	$5,750
Turbo 310	1971-72	N/A	$ 66,000	256	1,962	1,862	102/207	18,100	285-hp Continental	1,400	$8,000
310	1973-74	N/A	$ 66,000	221	1,495	2,086	102/207	7,400	260-hp Continental	1,800	$5,750
Turbo 310	1973-74	N/A	$ 77,000	256	1,962	1,962	102/207	18,100	285-hp Continental	1,400	$8,000
310	1975-76	N/A	$ 80,500	223	1,662	2,163	102/207	7,400	285-hp Continental	1,800	$6,750
Turbo 310	1975-76	N/A	$ 93,000	256	1,700	2,047	102/207	17,200	285-hp Continental	1,400	$8,000
310	1977	N/A	$ 95,000	223	1,662	2,163	102/207	7,400	285-hp Continental	1,800	$6,750
Turbo 310	1977	N/A	$110,000	256	1,700	2,047	102/207	17,200	285-hp Continental	1,400	$8,000
310	1978	N/A	$125,000	223	1,662	2,163	102/207	7,400	285-hp Continental	1,800	$6,750
Turbo 310	1978	N/A	$137,000	256	1,700	2,047	102/207	17,200	285-hp Continental	1,400	$8,000
310	1979	N/A	$145,000	223	1,662	2,163	102/207	7,400	285-hp Continental	1,800	$6,750
Turbo 310	1979	N/A	$160,000	286	1,700	2,047	102/207	17,200	285-hp Continental	1,400	$8,000

the Skymaster. For example, the power-off stall drops from 69 knots calibrated to 59 knots, and the approach speed from 94 knots down to 76 knots. Also, Vmc drops from 82 knots to 69 knots.

Cost of the modification on an owner's airplane will be $18,000, with about 15 working days required for the alteration.

For custom turbocharging of the early Cessna 310s, Rajay Industries in Long Beach, Calif., holds the STC. But business on this model has slackened off to such a great extent that the factory will make new kits only if it receives orders for four or more at a time.

Rajay's installation involves no changes to the innards of the engine such as valves, etc. Their warranty is for 12 months, parts and labor.

To our knowledge, two other major conversions are offered on the Cessna 310. One is Riley Aircraft Corp.'s Super 310, which replaces the turbocharged 285-hp engines on the T310-P and later models with -Js of 310 hp each. Cruise speed at 24,000 feet on this conversion is about 245 knots at 75 percent power.

Of course, Riley pioneered on Cessna 310 conversions with the Rockets back in the 1950s. They sported features like turbocharging, one-piece windshields and phenomenal speeds.

The other major conversion is offered by Colemill Enterprises in Nashville, Tenn. They have an Executive 600 modification that replaces the 260-hp engines with normally aspirated 300-hp Continental IO-520-E powerplants. This airplane gives an advertised 75 percent cruise of 198 knots.

Maintenance

Mechanics talk about corrosion on the rear auxiliary wing spars from exhaust gases on 310 models, on warping Goodyear brake discs and on "atrocious" cabin door leaks. Also, early models had heaters that were extremely hard to get at since access was only up through the nose wheel well. Later, an accessory door was added to simplify things. The older models also are known for a problem of nosewheel failures due to cracking in the bulkhead to which the gear is attached.

In addition, the early models had vibration and cracking problems with exhaust mufflers, and aux tank bladders may crack with age, especially if they inadvertently are left dry for long periods.

Buyers should also be aware of the history of crankcase cracking problems on the 285-hp Continental engines used in 1975 and later 310 models.

Owner Comments

"I have owned a 1966 'C' Baron and a 1969 'D' Aztec (with 'E' Model nose) and find my 1970 310 superior in the following areas:

"The noise level is lower than in the Baron or Aztec, and flight characteristics are much improved, especially in instrument conditions. There is a definite tendency to climb in a bank, due to the canted tip tanks; this eliminates the need for back pressure when banking.

"The fuel system is straightforward; crossfeed, uncomplicated and flexible; tank switching requires aux-pumps and fuel rich mixture, and 60 minutes of flight are required on mains before aux-tanks are selected, or fuel will be pumped overboard. This feature makes timing the aux-tanks difficult, if not impossible, since fuel is transferred back to the mains when in aux position. However, the gauges are very accurate and reflect the quantities in gallons and pounds

"I fly at full throttle above 8,000 feet and 2300 rpm for about 65 percent power, which returns a consistent 200 mph at about 24 gph with the EGT 50 degrees below peak on the rich side. With 140 gallons fuel a comfortable five hours' cruise is possible, and at lower power settings almost seven hours is available.

"Oil consumption seems higher than on my other planes (about one quart every three hours per engine), but the owner's manual recommends filling to 13 quarts for long flights, and not less than nine quarts for all conditions. This would indicate oil consumption of about that level.

"Baggage capacity and convenience are equal to the Baron's and less than the Aztec's with its cavernous rear compartment and nose storage. The rear space, with the enlarged door installed in the Cessna, is smaller and harder to use than the Aztec's but better than the Baron's, and the wing lockers are convenient for suit bags and slim suitcases. Useful load with the many, many options installed on this plane is 1,625 pounds, which allows full fuel and four people and 100 pounds of baggage, or full mains (100 gallons), six people, no baggage, etc.

"Takeoffs at gross seem unchanged from light loads, with liftoff above 90 mph, with definite rotation necessary. However, approaches near gross require more power, and normal approaches are made at 100 mph with about 15-17 inches mp. Abrupt throttle closing is to be discouraged since an immediate sink rate is established, and the manual advises approach with very little power or slow throttle closing with power.

"Crosswinds are not as easy to handle with the Cessna as with the Baron or Aztec, and my personal observation suggests 20-mph crosswinds as a limit for safe operation. Also, no more than half-flap in crosswind conditions is advisable.

"In summary, I like the large, roomy cabin, good noise level, flight characteristics, and especially the looks of the Cessna better than the Barons or Aztecs I have owned or flown. Approaches and landings are less comfortable than in Barons or Aztecs. Also of note, the takeoff ground run is about twice the ground roll on landing. This could get you into a short field and not let you out on a hot, humid day.

"All in all, the 310 is an excellent economical light twin at a modest price in today's market, and I rate it superior overall to its competition. It's the kind of plane that invites you to move up to the 400 series someday."

"Our company bought our Turbo 310Q brand-new in 1974. Total time to date is 2,380 hours. We average 700-800 hours per year flying, and the aircraft is maintained on a progressive inspection program at the local Cessna dealer. I am the only pilot who flies the aircraft and that's my sole duty. I have 6,000 hours total time with 2,500 in 310s.

"Our 310 is booted, with alcohol window, hot props, and has standard equipment for this type aircraft except for a King Silver Crown radio package and Bendix FCS 810 system. Useful load is 1,724 pounds.

"Our first set of engines went 1,258 hours, at which time a 1½-inch crack in the left engine case extended to 5½ inches, grounding the aircraft. The right case was cracked also, but held at one inch. During these hours we replaced a starter assembly housing, an ignition harness, a starter solenoid, and had a new paint job, all of which was paid for by Cessna. Most of the items that were not covered by warranty were small.

"At 900 hours a ring land cracked and we replaced the piston and ground an exhaust valve. The rest of the cylinders stayed good until the case went. Our second set of engines (remanufactured from Western Skyways) have gone 1,100 hours plus, and, aside from a hard-to-find oil leak at the beginning, have been good engines. Skyways completed our engine swap in 4½ days with a total cost of $23,000, firewall forward. Some mechanic's overtime was involved. We changed our exhaust system at this time because Cessna's seals were only lasting about 200 hours at $40 a seal and two hours worth of labor."

Beech's Baron is widely regarded as the "class" item among light twins—sort of a twin-engine Bonanza—with lots of performance, superb handling and a reputation for luxury and quality.

Nearly 5,000 Barons have been built over the past 20 years, ranging from the basic 260-hp 55 model to the pressurized 325-hp 58P. As an investment, the standard Baron has few peers, retaining a high proportion of its original value and, in most cases, appreciating steadily after a few years. For all its popularity and excellent reputation, however, some questions about safety and (in recent models at least) quality control deserve attention from the thoughtful used-Baron buyer.

History
The Baron was introduced in 1961 as an outgrowth of the Model 95 Travel Air series. That first Model 55 Baron had 260-hp Continental engines (up from 180 hp on the Travel Air) and a gross weight nearly 700 pounds higher than the Travel Air's. The 55 was Beech's answer to the very popular Cessna 310, which had been introduced six years previously.

The 1962 and 1963 Barons were called the A55, and offered a sixth seat as an option. The fuselage of the A55 was also 10 inches longer than the straight 55's. In 1964 it became the B55, a designation that is still current for the 1980 model of the 260-hp Baron. In 1966, the gross weight of the B55 was increased from 4,880 to 5,100 pounds (actually, the higher gross weight applied to the last 11 of the 1965 models as well). With the gross weight came another nose extension to accommodate a larger front baggage compartment.

In 1966, the 260-hp B55 was joined by the 285-hp C55, which offered blistering performance (242 mph top speed) and 200 pounds more gross weight. The 1966 and 1967 big-engine Barons were the C55s, evolving to the

D55 in 1968 and 1969, and finally to E55 in 1970. Since that time, the 260-hp B55 and the 285-hp E55 have remained virtually unchanged.

In 1967, the short-lived 56TC Baron was introduced. It was powered by monstrous turbocharged 380-hp Lycoming engines and a cruise speed of 284 mph was claimed. However, only 94 56TCs were sold over the next five years, and the airplane was discontinued after 1971. Apparently the lack of a large six-place cabin and pressurization doomed the airplane, and single-engine characteristics were reportedly, shall we say, challenging.

Taking up the slack from the unsuccessful 56TC in 1970 was the stretched 58 Baron, which at last provided a full six-seat interior instead of the four-plus-two arrangement of the standard-body Barons. It used the same 285-hp Continental engines as the big-engine 55 Barons, and had virtually the same performance as its short-bodied stablemate. The 58, with its wide double-door entry and club-car seating, has continued to be a strong seller.

In 1975, Beech introduced the

pressurized 58P, with 310-hp engines. These were upgraded to 325 hp in 1979. In addition to the pressurization and bigger engines, the 58P has 100 pounds extra gross weight and a cruise speed that is 22 mph higher than the standard 58 (by the book, at least). A "non-pressurized 58P" was introduced in 1976, called the 58TC. The TC has the same engines as the P model, and got the boost to 325 hp at the same time, in 1979.

Investment Value
Like the Bonanza, the Baron is a real blue-chip in resale value in most cases. A 10-year-old B55 is worth about 65 percent of its original value. (The comparable figure for a Cessna 310 is about 51 percent.) Put another way, a 1970 B55 originally cost $13,000 less than a 1970 310, but today is worth $5,000 more. The big-engine E55 also looks good; a 1975 E55 cost $146,000 new and is worth $105,000 today (72 percent). A 1975 310 returns 63 percent, and is worth a fat $20,000 less than the E55 on the used-plane market. The 58 series does even better; a 1975 long-

Top of the Baron line are the 58s, *here stacked up with the TC on top and the pressurized model on the bottom. The 58P has one rear left cabin door instead of double doors on the right side of the fuselage.*

body Baron is now worth 78 percent of its original value.

The pressurized Baron 58P, however, doesn't seem to match the rest of the family in resale value. "The P-Baron has taken a real hit on the used-plane market," one big broker told us. "Last year we picked up a '76 P model for $140,000. It listed for close to $300,000 when it was new." Based on Aircraft Price Digest "Bluebook" retail figures, a 1976 P-Baron is today worth 68 percent of its original price. For a straight 58 Baron, the figure is 79 percent. "For the same money that a used 58P costs, you can buy a 421 that's just one year older. And the 421 is full cabin class, a hell of a lot more airplane," explained the dealer.

Another resale loser among the Barons is the ill-fated 56TC. The net value of those big engines over the years has been just about zero; a used 56TC is worth almost exactly the same as an E55 of the same vintage, which had non-turbocharged engines of 100 less horsepower each.

Performance

Here is the Baron's strong suit. The big-engine Barons are faster than any light twin except the Aerostar, and the 260-hp 55, A55 and B55 aren't too far behind. Owners report real-world cruising speeds of about 220 mph for the B55 and 225-230 mph for the E55 and 58 models. The turbocharged versions—56TC, 58TC and 58P—are of course much faster at high altitude, with max cruise speeds ranging from about 240 mph for the 310-hp 58P and TC to well over 250 for the monster 56TC. The 325-hp 58TC and 58P, introduced in 1979, are listed by the books as about 10-15 mph faster than their 310-hp counterparts.

Standard fuel capacity in the small-body 55 Barons is normally 112 gallons (100 gallons usable), which gives a rather marginal endurance of less than four hours, with no reserve. Many 55s have optional tanks that raise capacity to a more reasonable 142 gallons (136 usable), good for over five hours at moderate cruise power. The 285-hp airplanes burn about five gph more than the 260s, so even the 142-gallon tanks are not exactly generous. The 1973 and later E55s, however, have an optional capacity of 166 gallons, which is satisfactory for most IFR flying.

All the 58 models have standard 166-gallon fuel tanks, and most have

optional tanks that raise capacity to 190 gallons. Obviously, a used Baron with long-range tanks is more desirable because of the greater flexibility for ultra-long-range flights with light passenger loads. (But extra tanks can be a mixed blessing from the maintenance standpoint. More on that later.)

Takeoff performance of the Baron is also excellent, particularly in the C, D and E55 models. Even at gross weight, an E55 needs little more than 1,000 feet to clear a 50-foot obstacle on takeoff (under standard conditions, of course). This requires some fairly extreme piloting technique that puts the airplane in the air below Vmc, however. With normal technique, takeoff distances under 2,000 feet are still possible at gross weight in the 55 Barons.

Throowver wheel, *reversed throttles and props, and aileron trim are standard on all the Barons. Only this 58P has the gear (left) and flap (right) levers in the standard position.*

Handling

A major reason for the Baron's popularity and owner loyalty is the aircraft's superb handling qualities. The Baron is responsive and well-harmonized, a delight to fly. "The Baron is a beautiful flying aircraft, and it is just plain fun to handle on the controls," is a typical owner comment. There are no handling idiosyncrasies (such as severe pitch-up with flap deployment, as in the Aztec) we're aware of. "Real aviators" like the fact that there are no downsprings or aileron-rudder interconnects in most models of the Baron.

The other side of the "responsive" coin is, of course, sensitivity in turbulent IFR conditions. The same light control forces that win oohs and ahs from pilots demand more attention in the clouds, and a good autopilot is

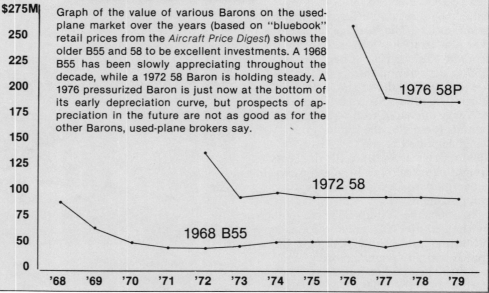

Investment Values

$275M

Graph of the value of various Barons on the used-plane market over the years (based on "bluebook" retail prices from the *Aircraft Price Digest*) shows the older B55 and 58 to be excellent investments. A 1968 B55 has been slowly appreciating throughout the decade, while a 1972 58 Baron is holding steady. A 1976 pressurized Baron is just now at the bottom of its early depreciation curve, but prospects of appreciation in the future are not as good as for the other Barons, used-plane brokers say.

1976 58P

1972 58

1968 B55

'68 '69 '70 '71 '72 '73 '74 '75 '76 '77 '78 '79

Model	Year	No. Built	Average Retail Price	Cruise Speed (mph)	Rate of Climb (fpm)	Useful Load (lbs)	S/E Ceiling (feet)	Fuel Std/opt (gals)	Engine	TBO (hours)	Overhaul Cost
56TC	1967-1969	83	$ 63,500	284	2,020	2,340	18,000	142/204	380-hp Lyc.	1,600	$12,000
A56TC	1970-1971	12	$ 73,000	284	2,020	2,390	18,600	142/204	380-hp Lyc.	1,600	$12,000
C55	1966-1967	451	$ 50,000	230	1,670	2,225	7,100	112/142	285-hp Cont.	1,500	$6,750
D55	1968-1969	315	$ 58,000	230	1,670	2,225	7,100	112/142	285-hp Cont.	1,500	$6,750
E55	1970-1971	82	$ 69,000	224	1,682	2,038	6,000	100/166	285-hp Cont.	1,500	$6,750
E55	1972-1973	95	$ 74,500	224	1,682	2,038	6,000	100/166	285-hp Cont.	1,500	$6,750
E55	1974	62	$ 90,000	224	1,682	2,038	6,000	100/166	285-hp Cont.	1,500	$6,750
E55	1975	62	$105,000	224	1,682	2,038	6,000	100/166	285-hp Cont.	1,500	$6,750
E55	1976	23	$120,000	224	1,682	2,038	6,000	100/166	285-hp Cont.	1,500	$6,750
E55	1977	29	$133,000	224	1,682	2,038	6,000	100/166	285-hp Cont.	1,500	$6,750
E55	1978	28	$145,000	224	1,682	2,038	6,000	100/166	285-hp Cont.	1,500	$6,750
E55	1979	N/A	$170,000	224	1,682	2,038	6,000	100/166	285-hp Cont.	1,500	$6,750

almost a necessity in a Baron flown IFR. One owner reports, "I have had several frightening moments because of its unstable flying characteristics in turbulence."

Like the Bonanza, the Baron is famed for its easy landings (except for the 58P), with a combination of pitch response and landing gear geometry that really boosts the egos of pilots. For many pilots, the way an airplane "feels" can overcome many performance shortcomings; the Baron's handling qualities have doubtless won over thousands of pilots who may have been on the verge of buying something else.

Accommodations

The Baron pilot sits high, wide and handsome, with a plush, roomy cockpit and a professional-looking panel thankfully devoid of the plastic found in most other airplanes. Headroom is particularly good.

The 55 Barons are labeled "six-seaters," but the two rear seats are cramped afterthoughts, suitable only for kids or midgets on long flights.

The 58 models have the famous "club car" seating, which puts the back four passengers face to face in the style of the Orient Express. Although lacking Orient-Express roominess, the rear compartment of the 58 is adequate by light aircraft standards, and the fifth and sixth seats at least qualify as small-sized adult repositories.

The 58 models also have a big, wide double-door entrance to the rear compartment, a very nice touch. The 55s have the standard single right-side pilot's door, which entails a certain amount of clambering for the hindmost travelers.

Baggage capacity is good, with front and rear compartments that allow reasonable balancing and good capacities in most models.

Up front, a couple of items on the panel are worth noting. First, the Baron's throttle quadrant is notorious for its reverse throttle and prop posi-tions: the prop lever is on the left, with the throttle in the middle. An airplane could not be certified that way today, but Beech keeps on building them that way for some reason. Also, the gear and flap levers are reversed from their normal position in other aircraft, which could lead to the sound of crunching metal when the pilot retracts the "flaps" during rollout after landing. (The 58P is an exception.) NTSB figures show many accidents of this type. The single throwover yoke is also an unusual feature, one that sometimes makes multi-engine instruction a tricky business (see "Safety" section for details).

The E55 Baron: *essentially a Bonanza fuselage with a Bonanza engine on each wing.*

Maintenance Checkpoints

The "curse of the cracking crankcase," has broken the bankbooks of more than a few 285-hp Baron owners. All 1976 and earlier IO-520-powered Barons had the crack-prone cases, and any potential buyer should, before he does anything else, find out whether the airplane has remanufactured engines with the "heavy case." (Any engine remanufactured after July 1976 should have the heavy case, but ask your mechanic to check it out anyway. Also, carefully check any 1977 Baron crankcase; some may still have the old-style "light case.") Any Baron with a light-case engine should be avoided altogether, or at least devalued by $5,000 to $10,000, depending on the remaining engine lifetime. In effect, a light-case Baron should be considered to have run-out engines that cannot be overhauled, and that must be replaced by remanufactured engines at a cost of about $5,000 to $10,000 each, depending on engine time. (In case of a crack, Continental will now pro-rate the $10,000 cost of a remanufactured engine over the full 1,500-hour TBO.)

Despite the epidemic of cracking crankcases, the Baron's owner loyalty is striking. One hyperenthusiastic 1974 Baron 58 owner wrote us, "Over a period of five years, my Baron operated flawlessly, with very minor problems, except the usual crankcase crack prob-

The small economy-sized *B55 Baron still has speed to burn.*

lems occurred at about 950 hours, necessitating the replacement of both engines at considerable expense ..."

The other big maintenance headache for Barons is the rubber bladder-type fuel cells. The lifetime of these cells can be as low as three or four years, and 10 years seems to be about the maximum. The tanks of any used Baron should be carefully checked for leakage, and a buyer would be wise to set aside a bladder replacement fund for the inevitable $3,500-plus wallop and accompanying downtime. Like the man in the cigar commercial says, "We're gonna get you..."

Some pre-1964 Barons may still have the so-called "light" cylinders, which proved troublesome and are subject to an AD requiring 20-hour inspections.

Other Baron problems to look out for: crazing windshields, unreliable Goodyear brakes, old B-series autopilots (very difficult to get service anymore), electric cowl flaps on pre-1974 models, 100-amp (Presto-Lite or Crittendon) alternators, and Airborne high-capacity vacuum pumps used for de-ice applications.

Safety

In terms of overall accidents, the Baron ranks about average among light twins, with 8.3 accidents per 100,000 flight hours, according to NTSB figures for the years 1972 to 1976. This is second only to the Aztec among the seven most popular light twins. However, the Baron's *fatal* accident rate is not so

Model	Year	No. Built	Average Retail Price	Cruise Speed (mph)	Rate of Climb (fpm)	Useful Load (lbs)	S/E Ceiling (feet)	Fuel Std/opt (gals)	Engine	TBO (hours)	Overhaul Cost
55	1961	190	$33,000	220	1,630	1,920	7,600	112	260-hp Cont.	1,500	$5,750
A55	1962-1963	309	$ 37,500	220	1,700	1,920	7,600	112	260-hp Cont.	1,500	5,750
B55	1964-1965	457	$ 43,250	225	1,670	2,025	7,600	112	260-hp Cont.	1,500	$5,750
B55	1966-1967	76	$ 48,500	225	1,670	2,025	7,600	112	260-hp Cont.	1,500	$5,750
B55	1968-1969	244	$ 54,500	225	1,670	2,025	7,600	112	260-hp Cont.	1,500	$5,750
B55	1970-1971	124	$ 60,000	225	1,670	2,025	7,600	112	260-hp Cont.	1,500	$5,750
B55	1972-1973	204	$ 71,500	225	1,693	2,025	7,600	100/136	260-hp Cont.	1,500	$5,750
B55	1974	173	$ 80,000	225	1,693	2,150	6,400	100/136	260-hp Cont.	1,500	$5,750
B55	1975	123	$ 88,500	225	1,693	2,150	6,400	100/136	260-hp Cont.	1,500	$5,750
B55	1976	96	$105,000	225	1,693	2,150	6,400	100/136	260-hp Cont.	1,500	$5,750
B55	1977	88	$120,000	225	1,693	2,150	6,400	100/136	260-hp Cont.	1,500	$5,750
B55	1978	88	$132,500	225	1,693	2,150	6,400	100/136	260-hp Cont.	1,500	$5,750
B55	1979	N/A	$150,000	225	1,693	2,150	6,400	100/136	260-hp Cont.	1,500	$5,750

Accident Rates	1972-1976	
Aircraft	Fatal Rate*	Total Rate*
1. Seneca	1.5	10.0
2. Twin Comanche	1.9	11.8
3. Cessna 310	2.2	9.8
4. Aztec	2.6	7.5
5. **Baron**	**2.8**	**8.3**
6. Cessna 337	3.1	10.4
7. Aero Commander 500 series	3.3	10.4
*Per 100,000 flight hours.		

good. Its 2.8 fatal rate puts it fifth out of the seven airplanes. (See chart above for details.)

There are several design-related characteristics of the Baron that have apparently led to accidents. Fuel unporting, stall/spins and icing are three subjects that potential used-Baron buyers should study carefully.

Pre-1970 Barons had fuel tanks that are susceptible to "unporting," which causes fuel starvation and engine failure. In extended slipping or skidding maneuvers, or turning-type take-offs, fuel can slosh away from the fuel line pickup if the tank is less than half

full. By 1971, the FAA had identified 16 accidents (in both Barons and Bonanzas, which had similar main tanks) apparently caused by unporting. Beech had issued a service letter as far back as 1961, stating that fuel unporting was a possibility in a turning takeoff, and that in such a case the air bubble in the fuel line would "reach the engine at about the same time the airplane becomes airborne, and could cause momentary power interruption." The letter went on to say "... this does not create a hazard." We think most Baron owners would take issue with that statement.

In 1969, an AD was issued, but it required no modification of the fuel system, merely a yellow arc on the fuel gauge and a warning not to take off or slip or skid if the fuel gauge was in the yellow arc. Beech modified the tanks in 1970 with baffles that eliminated the unporting problem. Retrofit tanks were offered for pre-1970 Barons, but very few were installed. If you're shopping for a pre-1970 airplane, find out whether the baffled tank was ever installed. If not, we strongly urge you to do it immediately after purchase.

The Baron has also come under fire for its stall/spin characteristics. According to an *Aviation Consumer* study, the Baron and Travel Air had nearly three times as many stall/spin accidents as any other light twin during the years 1970-74. Nearly seven percent of all Baron crashes during that period were fatal stall/spins, a proportion five times higher than the Cessna 310's and more than twice as high as any other light twin. The highly publicized Baron stall/spin accident that killed Missouri congressman Jerry Litton in 1976 didn't help the Baron's image much, and there are several lawsuits pending against Beech based on its allegedly dangerous stall/spin traits.

A 1974 Army test report on the single-engine stall characteristics of the T-42A, the military version of the Baron, sheds some light on the subject. (The special test came after a series of fatal stall/spin accidents during Army training flights.) The Army test pilot reported that the T-42A would enter a spin within one second after a single-engine stall unless immediate anti-spin action was taken. Even if stall recovery was initiated within one-quarter second

Model	Year	No. Built	Average Retail Price	Cruise Speed (mph)	Rate of Climb (fpm)	Useful Load (lbs)	S/E Ceiling (feet)	Fuel Std/opt (gals)	Engine	TBO (hours)	Overhaul Cost
58P	1976	85	$170,000	238	1,424	2,115	13,220	190	310-hp Cont.	1,400	$9,000
58P	1977	36	$197,500	248	1,529	2,115	14,400	166/190	310-hp Cont.	1,400	$9,000
58P	1978	45	$240,000	246	1,529	2,115	14,400	166/190	310-hp Cont.	1,400	$9,000
58P	1979	N/A	$300,000	267	1,481	2,200	13,490	166/190	325-hp Cont.	1,400	$10,000
58TC	1976	34	$165,000	246	1,461	2,320	14,400	166/190	310-hp Cont.	1,400	$9,000
58TC	1977	25	$177,500	246	1,461	2,320	14.400	166/190	310-hp Cont.	1,400	$9,000
58TC	1978	24	$200,000	246	1,461	2,320	14,400	166/190	310-hp Cont.	1,400	$9,000
58TC	1979	N/A	$225,000	267	1,418	2,412	13,450	166/190	325-hp Cont.	1,400	$10,000
58	1970-1971	174	$ 83,000	224	1,660	2,147	7,000	136/166	285-hp Cont.	1,800	$6,780
58	1972-1973	209	$ 88,500	224	1,660	2,147	7,000	166	285-hp Cont.	1,800	$6,780
58	1974	139	$105,000	224	1,660	2,147	7,000	166	285-hp Cont.	1,800	$6,780
58	1975	154	$120,000	224	1,660	2,147	7,000	166	285-hp Cont.	1,800	$6,780
58	1976	92	$140,000	224	1,660	2,147	7,000	166	285-hp Cont.	1,800	$6,780
58	1977	99	$162,500	224	1,660	2,147	7,000	136/194	285-hp Cont.	1,800	$6,780
58	1978	99	$177,500	224	1,660	2,147	7,000	136/194	285-hp Cont.	1,800	$6,780
58	1979	N/A	$200,000	224	1,660	2,147	7,000	136/194	285-hp Cont.	1,800	$6,780

The 58 Barons all have the club-seating option, *with cozy accomodations for the two rear passengers.*

after the stall break, said the Army report, a split-S and 1,000-foot altitude loss resulted. The author of the report also criticized the T-42A operator's manual for not warning of the serious consequences of a single-engine stall, and not explaining, for example, that single-engine stall speed was up to 20 knots higher than the listed stall speed under symmetric power conditions.

Later Baron manual revisions carry blunter warnings in the safety section, however.

A third safety-related criticism of the Baron has arisen recently over the airplane's icing characteristics. There is controversy over whether the "known-icing" version of the Baron was certified properly, and wind tunnel tests by an insurance company have suggested that tail stalls may occur under certain icing conditions. Beech con-

tends that the wind tunnel tests were improperly done and that their icing certification tests met all requirements. In any case, the NTSB is currently investigating the subject, and has uncovered nine fatal Baron accidents that it is checking to see if they may have been caused by tail stalls in icing conditions.

Warning yellow arc *at the bottom of the Baron fuel gauge tells when not to skid, slip, or take off.*

Modifications

We know of just one Baron engine conversion, the Colemill "President 600," which replaces the 260-hp engines of the 55, A55, or B55 with 300-hp Continentals. It is reportedly an outstanding performer, with no major problems except the possibility of cracked crankcases in pre-1977 conversions.

Smith Speed Conversions, of Johnson, Kansas, is now offering an aerodynamic cleanup modification that, it's claimed, increases cruise speed by approximately 15 mph. Cost is $13,900, depending on the precise configuration of each airplane.

Cosmetic mods, such as one-piece windshields and updated side windows are available from Beryl D'Shannon, Jordan, Minn.

We know of no owner's organization for the Baron, although the American Bonanza Society newsletter does occasionally publish material about the Baron. Also, the Barons and Bonanzas have enough in common that ABS membership might well benefit Baron owners.

Owner Comments

"Our company has owned three Barons in the past 12 years, and we hated to part with the first two. We purchased our present one, a 1974 B-55, when it was a young demonstrator with about 80 hours. We have flown it 1,100 hours now.

"Our '68 B-55 performed perfectly for 800 hours when we swapped it for a newer '73 E-55. A fine aircraft, but we had the usual problems with cracked cases on the 285 engines, noticeably more engine noise and about six more gallons per hour with only five knots or so more speed. A fine plane, but the B-55 is even better.

"Now take the B-55—responsive, economical (we use only 24 gallons per hour and cruise at 220 mph), very easy to handle in any type of crosswind, gentle in turbulent air, and the 260 Continentals are quiet. The B-55 sits good. You are over the panel with a perfect view. Perhaps the cabin is not as dramatic as the 58 model Baron, but most of our flying is with only one or two passengers or alone.

"The B-55 is primarily a VFR light twin or mild IFR with no heavy weather. We've had ice a few times and it doesn't carry it very well. The Century 3 autopilot guides the B-55 perfectly, and it is a fine night aircraft and good for normal

instrument operations—but *not* for rough weather."

"I took delivery of my new 1974 Beechcraft Baron 58 at the Beechcraft factory. I operated the aircraft for five years, and even though the aircraft was out of warranty, Beech continued to support certain items that they were not legally bound to support.

"When I ultimately sold the aircraft, the value had held remarkably strong, even against used pressurized aircraft such as the Cessna 340. My depreciation was a mere 10 percent over a five-year period.

"Over a period of five years, the Baron operated in a flawless manner with very minor problems, except the usual crankcase crack problems occurred at about 950 hours total time, necessitating the replacement of both engines at considerable expense. However, the airframe and component parts were all well within tolerances, except for the fuel gauges, which never were right. Total operation cost over the five-year period was approximately $20,000 per year, on the average.

"It is an extremely efficient form of transportation and consistently flies at 190 knots. Over the five-year period it averaged approximately 30 gallons-per-hour at altitudes 8,000 to 12,000 feet."

"I own a 1977 Beech Baron 55, which I purchased new in 1977. The aircraft now has 675 hours total time and has been piloted only by myself (4,000 hours) and a friend (1,000) who is also multi-engine and instrument rated.

"I have been involved in aviation a long time and I had always felt that owning a Beechcraft would be the ultimate in aircraft ownership, but if this aircraft is an example of current Beech quality and workmanship, I would not recommend a Beech Baron to any friends that are contemplating buying an airplane.

"In the first year of operation, I had literally scores of malfunctions, and spent more than $1,000 just to rent aircraft to ferry me back and forth to the maintenance base after dropping off the Baron for repairs.

"In addition, the following have happened to my Baron more recently.

1. 400 hrs—the right vacuum pump failed.
2. 450 hrs—the left magneto on the right engine failed.
3. 500 hrs—the heater motor required replacement.
4. 500 hrs—an oil seal in the right propeller hub failed.
5. 550 hrs—left engine failed in flight.
6. 575 hrs—new starter on remanufactured Continental engine failed.
7. 650 hrs—nose gear door control mechanism failed.
8. The hot props do not work, and the wiring is again protruding from behind the spinner.
9. The yaw damper does not work properly.

"The ease of handling in VFR flight makes the plane a delight to fly, but the same lightness of control can be hazardous in hard IFR. I have had several frightening moments because of its unstable flying characteristics in turbulence. I still feel that the Baron has the nicest landing characteristics, the best brakes, the best ground handling and the sleekest looks of any aircraft I have ever

All Barons have high gear-lowering speed *to facilitate rapid letdowns.*

flown."

"To me, the Baron is a beautiful-flying aircraft, and it is just plain fun to handle the controls. It flies well in rough air, and I have experienced only one occasion where I felt more comfortable with the gear down due to the rough air. I would say that the landing gear is superb. It is rugged, yet allows you to make consistent soft landings, and it handles crosswinds very nicely. The gear is very fast—about four seconds—but still rather easy to crank down if you have to.

"Stalls are normal, with plenty of warning. I also feel that single-engine handling is good.

"The Baron cabin is comfortable, with the seats high enough off the floor, as in the Bonanza. I have not yet been able to completely eliminate the air noise around the door, and the older-type pilot storm windows that open out seem to have whistles that are hard to eliminate. Heat is good and I haven't had undue problems with the gas heater. But I could use more capacity when the temperature is below about 15 degrees F. Fresh air is through a scoop on top of the cabin in the pre-1966 models and that creates noise. From 1966 on the scoop is in the tail and much quieter.

"I have also found a couple of problems purchasing a used Baron. *I am just about to replace my fourth gas tank and any older Baron with original tanks should be suspect.* My other big complaint is the inaccuracy of the fuel flow (pressure) gauges. On the 1964 B, I installed an Alcor (six-probe) EGT after I had the plane for a while and found that setting cruise mixture by the fuel flow gauge put me well below peak on the lean side. Sometime later I had to do a good bit of valve work on this engine. On my 1966 C, I also installed a six-probe Alcor and found that both engines were running on the lean side of peak when leaned by the fuel flow gauge, and I have since had to top both engines.

"I feel that Beech does a good job with their service notices, and I would recommend that a new owner get the service manual just to learn more about the plane.

"To me, there are two main differences between the B and C models. (The B has the IO-470 of 260 hp and the C has the IO-520 of 285 hp.) In my case, both IO-520s have had lower oil consumption than the IO-470. Second, the C (and I would have to assume the D and E) has a better weight and balance than the B. I assume this is due to the wider horizontal stabilizer.

"For example, the C will be in balance with full mains, 235 pounds in each front seat, 200 pounds in the other four seats and 180 pounds in the nose. The B would just be in balance with 190 pounds in each front seat, 180 pounds in the other four and 60 pounds in the nose baggage compartment.

"For anyone looking at a Baron with prop alcohol I would suggest checking the discharge from the small tube into the slinger ring. By turning the pump on and looking behind the spinner in the proper light you should be able to see the flow. I have had trouble each winter with one or both clogged.

"I have flown my 1966 C-Baron long enough in icing conditions to reduce the airspeed by about 30 knots, but noticed no other adverse flight factors. I know most of the ice came off the wing leading edge with the boots but can't say that I also looked at the tail. In the future I certainly will."

The pressurized Baron 58P *gives up the double door on the right side for a single hatchway on the left, opposite the pilot's entry door.*

Beech Baron

Aero Commander 500

The Aero Commander 500 series twin was the first successful multi-engine business airplane. The first model 520 was sold to the Chicago Tribune in 1952, two years before the appearance of the Piper Apache and three years ahead of the Cessna 310. The Aero Commander (later Rockwell Commander) 500 and 560 series of nonturbocharged twins was in continuous production for 28 years, until 1979.

The airplane was designed by Ted Smith (of Aerostar fame), and shares its general layout and several design aspects with the Aerostar (fuel system, hydraulic nosewheel steering, etc.), but from the pilot and passengers' point of view, the Commander is exactly the opposite of the Aerostar. The Shrike 500/560 series are generally sluggish performers whose strengths are stability and roominess. The Aerostar, on the other hand, is a hot performer that can be noisy and a bit cramped.

History of the Line
First of the 500 series was the 520, introduced in 1952. This airplane made headlines by flying at gross weight from Oklahoma to Washington, D.C. nonstop with one propeller removed and stowed in the baggage compartment. A total of 149 of the 520s were built, and they are rare birds indeed today. The 520 used the geared Lycoming GO-435 engines that put out 260 hp each—veritable powerhouses of their day (the Apache, don't forget, had only 150-hp engines in its early days; the 310 had 240-hp Continentals).

Performance of the 520 was excellent in its day, and, on paper at least, not much below that of a 1977 Rockwell Commander Shrike. A used 520 can be counted on today to carry three people and some baggage for about four hours at 150 knots or so.

The 560 Series
In 1954, Aero Commander souped up the engines (from the 260-hp GO-435 to the 270-hp GO-480) swept the tail and went to three-bladed props. The result was the 560, with a gross weight increase from 5,500 to 6,000 pounds. Because of the weight increase, however, performance actually declined. Listed rate of climb dropped from 1,700 fpm to 1,400, and speed remained the same by the book.

In 1955 came the first major airframe change in the 500/560 series. The fuselage was stretched 12 inches and the airplane renamed the 560A. Engine power was increased slightly. However, gross weight remained the same, and the 300 extra pounds of airframe weight came directly out of the useful load, which dropped to 1,500 pounds or so in the average airplane. That meant with full fuel, the 560-A was basically a three-passenger airplane, even though there were seven seats in the roomy cabin.

Aero Commander solved the limited load problem by introducing the 560E in 1957. The geared Lycoming was tweaked up to 295 hp, and the wingspan was increased by five feet. As a result, gross weight was increased 500 pounds to 6,500 pounds—by far the heaviest gross of any general aviation airplane at the time. (The Cessna 310 was still under 5,000 pounds at that point.) The hulking Aero Commander 560E loomed large over the business airplane field in terms of size and cost. During its four-year run from 1957 to 1960, the 560E cost nearly $100,000 equipped—a hefty price tag indeed in the days when a 310 cost $70,000 and an Aztec about $50,000. (Performance, however, was no better than the 310's—in fact, it was quite a bit slower.)

In 1958, after the 560E had been on the market for a year, Aero Commander realized it needed a low-priced twin to compete with the 310 and Aztec. The result was the model 500, which sold for $15,000 less than the 560E. The "economy" 500 had carbureted direct-drive 250-hp Lycoming engines instead of the complicated and expensive 295-hp GO-480s. Airframe and wing were identical to the 560E. Because of the lighter engine weight and clean engine nacelle, performance and load-carrying of the "economy" 500 were nearly the equal of the 560E. Range of the 500 suffered in comparison, however, because the smaller 250-hp Lycomings were dry-sump engines, and the FAA limited the fuel capacity to 156 gallons because it didn't like the idea of the engines running for eight or nine hours without oil replenishment.

In the early 60s, Aero Commander made engine changes on both the 560 and 500 series. To boost the 560's numbers up out of reach of the 500, the company brought out the 560F in 1961. The -F model had massive 350-hp injected IGO-540 engines (still geared, by the way) and a 1,000-

The 500S Shrike Commander *was the last of the 500 series. It was retired in 1978.*

pound increase in gross weight. The 500 also got an engine transplant in 1960 and became the 500A. The new engine was the 260-hp Continental IO-470, which supposedly put out 10 more horsepower than the 250 Lycoming, even though it had 70 fewer cubic inches. Unfortunately, however, the extra 10 horsepower proved illusory, and experienced Aero Commander pilots agree that the 500A is not nearly as sprightly in the air as the 500, despite book figures to the contrary.

Aero Commander continued to build the airplane with the Lycoming, however, by now injected and boosted to 290 hp. This model was known as the 500B.

The 500A died in 1963 after achieving a total sale that year of just five, but the 500B continued on. A year later, the top-of-the-line of the non-turbo Commanders, the 560F, was dropped when Aero Commander wisely decided that anybody who'd pay $150,000 for an airplane would probably want turbocharging and end up buying a 680. This left only the 500B to carry on among Rockwell's normally aspirated twins after 1965. The 500B became the 500U in 1966 and the 500S Shrike in 1968. By this time, the venerable design was facing stiff competition from the Cessna 310, Beech Baron and Piper Aztec, and sales began a slow decline. They reached their low point in 1972, when only four Shrikes were sold. About that time, Aero Commander became Rockwell and hired Bob Hoover to fly his famous aerobatic routine in a Shrike, and sales rebounded to more than 50 in 1973, but have been dipping steadily since then. The 1977 Shrike, in fact, was built on a special-order-only basis—a sad old age for a pioneering airplane. Production finally stopped in 1979.

Safety
In a special study by the NTSB on twin-engine aircraft accident rates, the Commander 500, 520 and 560 as a group was placed among the three worst models among 20 light twins studied. However, a five-year study by *The Aviation Consumer* of 500 series accident briefs showed no meaningful general trends suggesting specific design shortcomings. The greatest number of accidents, fatal and nonfatal, was attributed to weather problems and engine failures.

No consistent pattern of mechanical problems showed up among engine-failure related accidents in 500 models.

However, there were three in-flight structural breakups recorded during our five-year study period against Commander 500s, and a 1978 study by the FAA of structural failure accidents between 1966 and 1975 tagged the Aero Commander twins as having the second worst record among 11 classes of twins, second only after the Piper Twin Comanche.

Performance
The demise of the 500 and 560 series was inevitable because of the airplane's subdued performance and load-carrying abilities. Although the 500 towers over the competition on the flight line, it falls meekly behind in the air. A 1979 Shrike is nearly 20 knots slower than a 1979 310, for example—and costs a staggering $90,000 more when well equipped.

Book speeds of the 500 series run from about 170 knots for the oldest 520s and 560s to 200 knots for the 560F, but Aero Commander owners tell us that these figures are fairly optimistic. One owner of a late-model 500S reports he flight plans about 170 knots, a fairly typical real-world figure for most of the direct-drive 500 series. (Early 500 models are slower—about 160 knots.) Run-of-the-mill 560Es with the geared engines can be counted upon for perhaps 175 knots or so, with late-model 560Fs with their larger 350-hp engines good for perhaps 190 knots. If you're looking for blazing per-

Monster vertical tail *provides good engine-out controllability.*

formance or great economy of operation, the Aero Commander is not your airplane.

Flight Characteristics
One of the airplane's strong points is its solid, stable feeling in the air. The 500 and 560 are big airplanes—6,000 to 7,000 pounds gross weight—and they have a big-airplane aura about them that pilots and passengers like. Owners report excellent IFR characteristics. One owner writes, "In the air, the Shrike is a calm, forgiving bird with a knack for making the pilot appear to his passengers like 'airline pros.' Roll response is excellent and other controls respond without any adverse reaction. The Shrike's deck angle on climbout and descent is most comfortable for passengers; flaps are hydraulically operated and give no adverse pitch when used to maximum or minimum deflection."

A couple of other features have won praise from pilots: the fuel system is simple and safe, with all seven tanks (less than seven of them in some cases) tied together by one simple on-off selector valve. (The Aerostar has a somewhat similar system, but the Commander doesn't have the history of fuel system quirkiness of the Aerostar.)

Single-engine performance is adequate in

Model	Year Built	Number Built	Cruise Speed (mph)	Useful Load (lbs)	Rate of Climb (fpm)	Std/Opt Fuel (gals)	Engine	TBO (hrs)	Overhaul Cost	Average Retail Price
520	1952-54	149	197	1,700	1,700	150	260-hp Lyc GO-480	1,200	$10,000	$18-$20,000
560	1954-55	86	197	2,100	1,400	150	270-hp Lyc 60-480	1,400	$10,000	$22,000
560A	1955-56	220	212	1,750	1,510	156/223	275-hp Lyc GO-480	1,400	$10,000	$26,000
560E	1957-60	443	212	2,200	1,450	223	295-hp Lyc GO-480	1,400	$11,000	$35,000
560F	1961-64	545	230	2,820	1,587	223	350-hp Lyc IGO-540	1,200	$12,000	$47,000
500	1958-59	230	205	2,150	1,400	156	250-hp Lyc IO-540	1,200	$6,500	$33,000
500A	1960-63	401	218	1,995	1,400	156	260-hp Cont IO-470	1,200	$6,000	$42,000
500B	1960-65	734	218	2,400	1,700	156	290-hp Lyc IO-540	1,200	$7,500	$65,000
500U	1966-67	101	218	2,400	1,375	156	290-hp Lyc IO-540	1,200	$7,500	$72,000
500S Shrike	1968-9	115	203	2,115	1,340	156	290-hp Lyc IO-540	1,400	$7,500	$91,000
500S Shrike	1970-71	63	203	2,115	1,340	156	290-hp Lyc IO-540	1,400	$7,500	$100,000
500S Shrike	1972-73	58	203	2,115	1,340	156	290-hp Lyc IO-540	1,400	$7,500	$118,000
500S Shrike	1974-75	78	203	2,115	1,340	156	290-hp Lyc IO-540	1,400	$7,500	$140,000
500S Shrike	1976-77	36	203	2,115	1,340	156	290-hp Lyc IO-540	1,400	$7,500	$180,000
500S Shrike	1978	17	203	2,115	1,340	156	290-hp Lyc IO-540	1,400	$7,500	$225,000
500S Shrike	1979	N/A	203	2,115	1,340	156	290-hp Lyc IO-540	1,400	$7,500	$265,000

the more powerful models, but the 520, 500A and 560A tend to be fairly marginal. One advantage: the rudder trim is quick-acting and easy to reach, a definite plus in a single-engine emergency.

The 500/560 series' renowned rock-like stability has a catch, however. In its original configuration, the airplane was dangerously unstable when loaded near the aft c.g. limit. There are reported to have been 22 cases of in-flight structural failures caused by this extreme pitch sensitivity at aft c.g. The problem was corrected in 1975 by Air-worthiness Directive 75-12-9, which required installation of bob weights in the control system of all 500, -A, -B, -U, -S, 520, 560, -A, -E, and -F models, in addition to the turbocharged 680 models. Before purchas-ing any 500 series Commander, make abso-lutely sure this AD has been accomplished.

In ground handling, pilots used to steer-ing with the rudder pedals must learn a whole new technique that is disconcerting to some. To steer an airplane like the Shrike, the pilot holds the rudder pedals even, and presses lightly with one toe or the other to turn left or right. A light touch activates the hydraulics to turn the nosewheel; a hard squeeze activates the brake.

Creature Comforts
Here is where the 500 series reigns indubi-tably supreme. Its cabin is wider and higher than anything in its class, and the interior appointments of the special "Esquire" and "El Cid" versions that appeared in the early '70s are exceptional. The geared 560 models are noticeably quieter than the direct-drive 500s, because the propellers are only turning about 1700 rpm or so at cruise, instead of 2200-2400. Later models also have extra-thick glass, which reportedly reduces noise.

Although the cabin is roomy and can be sequestered away from the pilots' cockpit by curtains for a limousine-like privacy and luxury, the overhanging wing and underslung engine nacelles make for a dark tunnel effect that palls with some passengers. In fact, you

don't see much of the sky from the rear cabin of the Commander twins, though of course you have a grand view of the earth below.

Also, the baggage is stored in a monster compartment in the rear of the airplane, and you can't get at it in flight.

Maintenance
Because the airplane is so big and has rather complex systems—hydraulic flaps, gear, brakes and nosewheel steering, for example —the 500 series airplanes are rather expensive to maintain. One owner reports an average 100-hour inspection with no major dis-crepancies costs about $1,200 for his late-model 500S.

A shop specializing in twin Commander maintenance reports that a well-maintained 10-year-old 500 or 560 should cost about $1,500 for a 100-hour inspection. (Assuming no major discrepancies, of course.) That amounts to $15 per hour for routine main-tenance, a very healthy sum for an airplane in the light twin category.

"It's a hydraulic nightmare to a guy who doesn't know what he's looking for," one shop told us. "You've got to treat it like an old DC-3." (The bob-weight AD, we've been told, is another item to check carefully. In many cases it simply hasn't been done.)

The hydraulic system deserves a close look, mainly because there's so much of it. Older airplanes have rather antiquated sys-tems that should be carefully inspected— every single line, connection and fitting, along with the reservoir and accumulator. Most airplanes came with a single hydraulic pump from the factory, but many owners have installed a second pump. Don't under-estimate the complexity and cost of main-taining a creaky old hydraulic system.

Corrosion also seems to be a special prob-lem of older Commanders. "I looked at several airplanes that I rejected because of corrosion," one used Commander buyer told us. Wing spars especially should be care-fully checked. AD 65-6-1 also requires that

the front spar cap be reinforced; check for that on pre-1965 models.

Buyers of the 560 series will face an extra maintenance burden with the geared GO-480 engine and GO-540. Cost for overhauling both engines is about $20,000, and TBO is only 1,400 hours, for an overhaul cost of $13 per hour. Comparable figure for the straight 500 is about $8 per hour. The geared engines are also more sensitive to pilot mismanagement. If the previous owner habitually descends at very low power so that there is a negative torque on the engines from windmilling props, the used 560 buyer may end up replacing a very expensive gearbox. Carefully waggle the propellers to detect any play in the gearbox before buying a used 560.

Other tips for flying Commander twins: the 560 series airplanes with the geared engines have automatic mixture control. To avoid overleaning during climb, leave the throttle full open and reduce power with rpms. When the throttle is full open, the mixture stays in the full rich position, but once the throttle is retarded, the auto-matic leaning device takes over, which may cause the engines to overheat during climb. The aneroid sensors in the autolean system should be carefully checked, for the dia-phragms can dry out and crack with old age. This causes uneven leaning and erratic cylinder head temperatures. The consensus of mechanics we talked to was that the geared engines can go their full overhaul life, but only if they are flown carefully and properly. Try to find out how meticulous the previous owner of a used 560 was in his operation of the engines.

Conversions and Modifications
There are two major outfits in the Com-mander mod business. Mr. RPM, in Van Nuys offers a 400-hp Lycoming engine installation for 500S models that turns the lackluster Shrike into a screaming 240-mph machine—but at the staggering fuel flow rate of 40-45 gph. Cost of the 800 conversion is about $70,000. The company has for several years converted the 680 series with turbo-charged 400-hp engines, and the so-called Turbo 800 is renowned for its smoothness. The Shrike 800 conversion is brand new, however. Mr. RPM also will spruce up an old Commander with overhead windows, racy vertical fins, tail cones, auxiliary fuel tanks and reworked instrument panels. Mr. RPM, 7120 Havenhurst, Van Nuys, Calif. 91406. Tel.: 213-997-0117.

J.W. Miller Aviation in Marble Falls, TX, offers an extended nose cone for radar installation. Cost of the nose cone kit, uninstalled, is about $3,500. Mr. RPM, by the way, also installs the Miller nose cone.

Nestled under the wing *with underslung engine pods on either side, the passsenger cabin tends to be dark and cloistered. Later models have a pilot door in front.*

Owner Comments

"The 500 with 250-hp Lycoming engines is as economical to fly as an Aztec since it burns about the same amount of fuel; however, it can comfortably accommodate six passengers plus the pilot while providing an excellent instrument flight platform.

"Of the Aero Commanders, the 500A is nowhere near the aircraft that a straight 500 Aero Commander is because even though the 500A has IO-470 engines, rated at 10 more horsepower than a 500 with O-540 series engines, we find that the 500 has more *effective* horsepower because of the 70 cubic inch extra displacement."

"Performance of our Shrike as far as speed is concerned is lackluster, and we normally plan for 170 knots. We recognize that faster planes are available but have compromised speed for other attributes.

"Load-carrying ability is limited due to the way our Shrike is equipped, and we certainly could use about 200 pounds more useful load. After full fuel, we have a useful load of only 632 pounds.

"The advantages of the Shrike are obvious to anyone who has carefully compared the aircraft to its nearest competitors, such as the Baron 58 and the Aerostar 600, and have decided to effect a compromise on load and speed for all of the following reasons:

"It is truly a sturdy bird. One trip is a is a real convincer—fly it in turbulence for the clincher. It is probably the best instrument platform in its class. Neither the Baron nor the Aerostar we have flown compares. The length adds to its yaw stability, and the large rudder is powerful in all configurations, including single-engine performance.

"Economy of operation is sterling. We average 31 gph at 8,000-to-10,000 feet at 65 percent power. Oil consumption is nominal. (Fuel consumption includes climb to cruise altitude.)

"Cost of maintenance is also economical, averaging $1,200 per 100-hour inspection, including parts replacements. We have had some major parts replaced; however, we consider each replacement normal due to our operating policy.

"Availability of maintenance is improving as Rockwell recognizes the need to make repair stations more geographically accessible. Atlantic Aviation has recently come on board as an authorized service center. Their closest facility is Houston, Texas. We have been and will continue to service our aircraft at Downtown Park in Oklahoma City. Those people know the aircraft and have personnel that can diagnose and solve all of the Shrike's problems. Their parts supply is extensive and their proximity to the factory is helpful whether it be for advice or locating a part that might not be in their inventory.

"It is appropriate to digress for a moment to tell you of an occurrence involving a fuel injector line that broke. No one in the State of Florida had the line and we called everyone, including Hanger One, but to no avail. Then we called Ray Wilson at DTA. He located a line, and it was air expressed to us immediately. We left the next day thanks to Downtown Airpark.

"A special advantage of the Shrike which overcomes the nominal useful load is its lack of any loading problem. It is almost impossible to get the aircraft out of C.G. For pilots who do not watch their calculations as carefully as we do on each flight, this would be a distinct advantage.

"We love the way our Shrike handles both on the ground and in the air. The nosewheel power steering does take getting used to, but, once it is mastered we wonder how we did without it.

"Little airliner" look *is accentuated by the cockpit windows.*

"In the air the Shrike is a calm, forgiving bird with a knack of making pilots appear to their passengers as 'airline pros.' The roll response is excellent, and the other controls respond without any adverse reaction. The Shrike's angle of attack on climbout and descent is most comfortable for passengers. Flaps are hydraulically operated and give no adverse pitch when used to maximum or minimum delection.

"Passenger comfort and appointment are the best in almost any comparable class of plane. The interior is plush, with generous use of leathers and tasteful carpeting and curtains. The appointments and woodwork is quality, and the cabin reeks from the glorious cowhide aroma. We objectively compared finishing and size to the Aerostar and Baron. It is our contention that there is no contest, and the Shrike wins on all counts. Another feature for passenger comfort Rockwell generously heaps upon us is the double-thickness tinted glass. It keeps the sun and noise out of the cabin. After you achieve mastery of prop and manifold settings, the Shrike again leads its class in noise dampening. We came very close to buying a Baron 58, but fortunately my wife went along on a test hop and complained of a noisy back cabin. She commented that it was at least half again as noisy as our V-35A Bonanza. Not convinced, I rode in the rear forward-facing seat and came to the same conclusion. The salesman demonstrating the aircraft also acknowledged that noise was the most frequent criticism of the Baron 58.

"No in-depth study of the Shrike would be complete without commenting on those wonderful Lycoming IO-540 E1B5 engines. They start quickly even when hot, and run smoothly through all ranges of power. We now have 400 hours on both engines and we expect them to continue right to their TBO of 1,400 hours. It would be nice, however, to have them rated at 2,000 hours like the 600 Aerostar.

"Fuel management in the Shrike is simplicity itself, with single-point filling, gravity feed, no fuel selector, no tank switching—no more needs to be said."

Landing gear of the 500 *has a wide stance, and an emergency nitrogen-powered lowering device in case of hydraulic failure.*

Piper Aerostar

Few aircraft have gone through such dramatic highs and lows as the much-traveled Aerostar series. Yet few others have held onto such unyielding respect in the used-plane market.

As the brainchild of the late Ted Smith, the Aerostar was conceived as a kind of universal paradigm from which would spring all kinds of singles and twins, pistons and jets. Offered to and declined by the parent Rockwell company as a successor to the Aero Commanders (that, in turn, had been designed by Smith), the Aerostar project was then launched by the newly formed Ted Smith Aircraft Co., and the first Model 600 was certificated in 1967.

In one short year the aircraft was sold to, of all companies, American Cement. This relationship lasted a little less than two years before the aircraft was once again sold, this time to Butler Aviation. Shortly afterward, however, with the Aerostar name tainted by scandal and charges that the airframe was subject to corrosion because of improper manufacture, Ted Smith took over the airplane again to remove its scarlet letter and set it on a proper course.

This seemed a *fait accompli* when another uproar broke out in 1978 over the design of the Aerostar fuel system, and a number of double engine failures related to it.

Finally, Piper Aircraft Corp. took over the line and incorporated it as an avant-garde step-up from its aging, stalwart Aztec. This coup gave Piper the satisfaction of having acquired a trio of aircraft built on a common airframe, featuring a choice of normally aspirated, turbocharged and pressurized designs. It also presented Piper with the headache of coming up with a fuel system pilots could comprehend and live with.

Something else Piper did inherit, however, was possession of the undisputed speed demons of the light-twin fleet. Aerostars look fast; they fly fast. This

means an astonishing 218 knots/251 mph on a normally aspirated pair of 290-hp Lycomings or 240 knots/277 mph with turbos and pressurization at 24,000 feet. By comparison, the old Aero Commander Shrike with the same normally aspirated engines yields only about 176 knots.

Investment Value

The Aerostar models — all three of them—appear to represent an unusually fine investment value, judging from the figures we obtained from tracking three early models.

After a sharp plunge in resale value in just one year, rather than the three to five in normal patterns, the 1970 normally aspirated 600 and the turbocharged 601 leveled off and began ascending. In later years right up to the present both models kept climbing in value slowly.

The 1974 pressurized 601P we tracked never did take the initial plunge most aircraft betray, but instead bounced up and down to the present, pretty well maintaining its initial value, with perhaps a bit of a sag in the latest yearly dip.

Model Evolution

The design has undergone only two changes of any significance since its introduction in 1969. In 1973, with the 600A and 601A models, a new so-called "K" crankshaft was incorporated in the Lycoming IO-540 engines. This reduced vibration and boosted the TBO significantly from 1,400 to 2,000 hours on the normally aspirated 600As and from 1,400 to 1,800 hours on the turbocharged models. This came about with serial number 0144 and up.

The next big modification occurred in 1977 with the addition of 30 more inches in wingspan to the turbo model for better high-altitude performance. At the same time the gross weight was boosted by 300 pounds to 6,000 pounds. This began with serial number 213, designated the 601B, and in effect brought the turbocharged model up to the same configuration as the pressurized model. The normally aspirated model kept its lower 5,500-pound gross and shorter wing.

Another significant change affecting all three Aerostars in '77 was a hike in the zero-wing-fuel limitation from 5,400 to 5,900 pounds. This eliminated

With both engines humming along, *the Aerostars are the fastest aircraft in their class, even challenging the turboprops.*

what many felt was a serious payload shortcoming. Since it was a paperwork engineering exercise on the existing structure, it applied retroactively to the older Aerostars as well.

The year '77 was a good one for improvements in other areas as well. The flap extension speed was raised by 18 knots, making it easier to slow down the aircraft, and a positive down lock was incorporated into the landing gear handle to prevent inadvertent retraction of the nosegear on the ground. There is no squat switch on the gear itself, and in one instance the nosegear collapsed with the handle up and the engines running.

Pilots interested in the turbocharged Aerostars should note that several evolutionary changes were made. The first models had manual waste gate systems that worked off electric rocker switches. These were replaced on the B models with automatic systems. And in 1978 improved Piper waste gate systems were added, replacing the Rajays, giving much better high-altitude performance right up to 25,000 feet. It also boosted the critical altitude from 16,000 to 23,000 feet. Earlier models are described by pilots as going up to 25 grand when new, but then pooping out at lower altitudes after a few hundred hours' use. Dealers report a booming business on retrofitting these new waste gates to older model Aerostars at about $3,200 a set.

Handling Characteristics
Despite its image as a hot ship, the Aerostar is regarded affectionately by most pilots in terms of handling. Control response is quick and deft; an aileron-rudder link allows almost feet-on-the-floor maneuvering. Pilots rave about

White electric rocker switches *below the throttles are for pitch and rudder trim. Nose steering switch is just out of sight below them on the central quadrant. Mag switches are on either side of the quadrant.*

engine-out characteristics such as an unusually mild yaw reaction with an engine loss during cruise, and a stall speed set above minimum control speed (Vmc) for added protection. Ted Smith liked to boast that the aircraft really didn't need a minimum control speed, but the FAA required it.

Despite all this praise from pilots, however, there has recently been a surprising surge of fatal Aerostar engine-failure accidents in which the pilot was unable to maintain control after losing an engine.

The takeoff perhaps gives fliers the most cause for discussion. The aircraft, which rests on the ground with a negative angle of attack, tends to want to stay earthbound, and the heavy load on the nosewheel calls for a real heave of the control wheel to get the machine rotated and flying. Some advise a partial easing back on the wheel, at 40 to 50 knots, and holding it there to ease the transition to final rotation.

On final approach the aircraft benignly

tends to hold the airspeed determined by power setting, reacting hardly at all to variations in pitch.

In taxi operations, the pilot will have to become accustomed to steering not with the rudder pedals in conventional fashion, but by means of an electric rocker switch on the console beneath the throttle quadrant. It sounds eery, but works quite nicely and actually is great fun and allows unusually sharp maneuvering on the ramp.

One complaint that surfaces now and again about the Aerostars is vibration. Some blame it on the engines; some the props. One experienced Aerostar pilot has a theory he says he can prove every time. He maintains the problem is not related in any way to engines or props, but to an idiosyncracy stemming from the heavier than usual skin gauge used in the wings and fuselage.

According to this theory, the vibration is triggered when the aircraft flies through light turbulence, as when ascending or dropping through a haze layer. This sets

Model	Year	Number Built	Average Retail Price	Cruise Speed (kts)	Fuel Capacity (gals)	S-E Ceiling (feet)	Engine	TBO (hrs)	Overhaul Cost
600	1969-70	57	$ 83,000	224	174	6,150	Lycoming IO-540-G1B5	1,400	$7,400
600A	1973-75	87	$108,000	224	174	6,150	Lycoming IO-540-G1B5	2,000	$8,400
600A	176-78	273	$134,700	224	174	6,150	Lycoming IO-540-G1B5	2,000	$8,400
601	1969-70	70	$ 93,500	233	174	10,800	Lycoming IO-540-P1A5	1,400	$7,800
601A	1973-76	202	$125,000	233	174	10,800	Lycoming IO-540-P1A5	1,800	$7,800
601B	1977-78	223	$153,000	233	174	9,300	Lycoming IO-540-S1A5	1,800	$7,800
601P	1974-75	115	$156,000	230	174	9,300	Lycoming IO-540-S1A4	1,800	$7,800
601P	1976-77	189	$174,000	230	174	9,300	Lycoming IO-540-S1A5	1,800	$7,800
601P	1978	102	$202,000	230	174	9,300	Lycoming IO-540-S1A5	1,800	$7,800

up a resonant, tuning fork-like vibration in the structure of the airplane that passes when the disturbance layer is passed.

The high wing loading of the aircraft typically handles normal chop with greater than usual aplomb and no abnormal vibration.

The designer's fondness for electric controls has given rise to the Aerostar moniker as an "electric aircraft." Indeed, the center console is home to a raft of unobtrusive electric switches— not only for steering, but for pitch and rudder trim—and even for turbocharging. A pair of rocker switches on the pre-B models allowed the pilot to close and open the waste gate by electric motor with little nudges of the switches. At least this eliminated the need for another pair of power levers on the throttle quadrant.

Cabin Comfort
With the constant-section fuselage, none of the up to six riders on the Aerostar can boast of more, or complain of less space, which is quite plentiful, with a small aisle between the seats. Though no conventional club-seating is available, there is a fold-out table arrangement for five seats.

Thanks to the big cabin windows, everybody has lots of light. Thanks to the mid-wing arrangement, though, only the pilots really have a great view of anything except the sky and the wing and engine nacelles. Pilot visibility naturally is fantastic.

The greatest discomfort burden Aerostars have imposed through the years is one of terrible cockpit din, thanks to the droning of the props right outside the window. Pilots report the

anguish diminished in stages with later models—especially the pressurized ones—as more and more soundproofing measures were taken.

Baggage
The Aerostars will carry a healthy amount of baggage—up to 240 pounds—but it must be heaved into a chest-high compartment accessible only from the outside rear fuselage.

Systems Engineering
Aside from the lack of a nose-gear squat switch previously mentioned, which may result in inadvertent, unwanted retraction, the Aerostar lacks another feature in standard configuration that might result in failure to retract when it is most desired—on takeoff with failure of the right engine, housing the single hydraulic pump. An electric hydraulic pump is offered as an important option, however.

The shortcoming on which the most attention has been cast, of course, involves the fuel system. The Aerostars have a 44-gallon fuselage tank and wet wing tanks, each of which holds 66.5 gallons. Though everything is supposed to work automatically, with no need to switch tanks, it is critical always to have fuel in the fuselage tank. Otherwise, inadvertent unporting of the supply line from either of the wing tanks to its respective engine, in a climb or dive, can result in engine stoppage. Line crews must always be advised to fill the center tank first.

However, in some situations, the fuselage tank does not feed evenly along with both wing tanks, as it should, and depletion of the center tank can trigger a single or a double engine stoppage.

Pilots like not having to fiddle with cowl flaps *on the Aerostar, which has none. The turbo model's 9,300-foot single-engine ceiling is way below that of most other turbocharged twins in its class.*

Adding to the confusion was a fuel-monitoring setup that allowed the pilot to read either total fuel in all three tanks or fuel in the left or right wing separately. But he must calculate the amount of fuel in the fuselage tank. The fact that the fuel quantity gauge is located on the very right extreme corner of the instrument panel way out of the pilot's normal scan certainly does not improve the situation.

The first fix to prevent inadvertent depletion of the center tank was an Airworthiness Directive mandating a low-fuel warning light for the center tank. Later, a sweeping AD required installation by Dec. 31, 1979 of a new triple fuel gauge showing fuel levels simultaneously in all three tanks. Or owners might install a single gauge showing a continuous readout of the center tank, with provision for switching to readouts on left or right wing tanks separately.

The AD also required a series of checks to insure a good seal of fuel filler caps and reduced the max usable fuel from 174.5 to 165.5 gallons (41.5 gals. in the fuselage tank and 62 gals. in each wing tank). In addition, an overpressure relief valve was ordered installed in the wing tanks.

The reason for the fuel cap checks was to prevent negative pressures from developing in the wing tanks, restricting fuel flow and causing premature depletion of the fuselage tank.

FAA tests made in connection with the AD also showed that it is rarely possible to fill the wing tanks to their full capacity unless the aircraft is dead level on the ramp and special fueling procedures are used. With normal fueling techniques, discrepancies up to nine gallons were noted. This is because of the configuration of the wing tanks — long and thin and tapering toward the tip.

Split clamshell doors *require the pilot to enter last. Waving of arms out the top section when the engines are running is not advised.*

Safety Record

A four-year printout by the National Transportation Safety Board of Aerostar accidents from 1971 through 1975 showed the fuel starvation/exhaustion/mismanagement bugaboo to have contributed to the largest number of accidents—four—along with weather problems. Another 12 accidents related to the fuel system—three of them fatal—have occurred since 1974. The other accidents disclosed no particular pattern that would point to specific design deficiencies. In fact, the aircraft appeared less prey to the hard-landing, overshoot/undershoot syndrome of some heavy, "hot" aircraft.

Also, we noted no stall/spin accidents.

Other ADs

Other significant ADs included several in 1970 and '71 involving: installing a kit to prevent failure of the wing flap tracks and jamming the ailerons; inspection of fuel pressure indicators for ruptured diaphragms to prevent fuel discharge into the engine compartment and possible fire; inspection of the cabin door lock pins to prevent possible separation of the door; replacing the main landing gear side brace assemblies to prevent collapse of the gear.

Maintenance

Owners who reported to us seemed on the whole satisfied with their maintenance experience with the aircraft, and characterized it as average. They described factory backup with the Ted

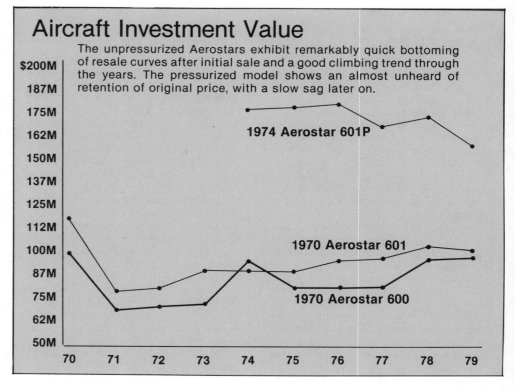

Aircraft Investment Value

The unpressurized Aerostars exhibit remarkably quick bottoming of resale curves after initial sale and a good climbing trend through the years. The pressurized model shows an almost unheard of retention of original price, with a slow sag later on.

1974 Aerostar 601P

1970 Aerostar 601

1970 Aerostar 600

Smith organization as fair to good, but had not had sufficient experience to rate the new Piper management. However, one owner reported that he had misgivings. "My only reservations stem from the Piper takeover...and their distribution and service policies," he said. "One of my reasons for purchase of the Aerostar from Ted Smith was to avoid the problems with which I was plagued during my ownership of four different Piper aircraft."

No significant patterns of maintenance difficulty showed in owner comments, except we received a couple complaining about wing fuel tank leakage around the rivets.

The average cost of an annual inspection reported to us was $1,165.

As for parts availability, more owners rated it good or average than terrible, under Ted Smith's aegis, at least.

The brouhaha in 1970 over Aerostar corrosion problems was triggered when Butler Aviation International brought suit against American Cement Corp. in seeking to rescind its acquisition of the Aerostar line. The FAA, however, never grounded any Aerostars after inspecting more than 100 of the 130 or so built at that time. The agency said many of the aircraft showed no evidence of corrosion, though others had some, but none serious enough to ground the aircraft.

Summary

In all, then, the Aerostars might well be regarded as the cream of the owner-flown twins in terms of speed, looks and handling. They get much more performance out of 580 or so horsepower than any other airplane in their class.

Up till now the Achilles heel has been the fuel system. The new FAA-mandated checks and gauges, however, should make the whole works more manageable and safer, provided the pilot knows the aircraft's idiosyncracies and how to cope with them.

Wing tanks should be filled when absolutely level *to ensure they're up to capacity. A low oleo strut can foil this exercise. Centering the nosewheel on takeoff while manipulating electric steering, throttles, brakes and control wheel takes some learning.*

Owner Comments

"I selected my Model 601P Aerostar after owning a Piper Arrow 180D, an Aztec D and E and a Turbo B-Navajo.

"After 350 hours' operating time, I cannot express sufficiently the satisfaction I have received from my Aerostar. No fuel problems have been apparent, and outside of minor waste gate controller adjustment, the aircraft has been free of any problems normally associated with a new aircraft and so evident in the ownership of my previous Piper aircraft.

"My total maintenance, other than the normal oil filters and grease, has been as follows: brake shoes replacement at 275 hours; main landing gear tires at 275 hours; two ADs on fuselage drain and landing gear scissors; one hydraulic pump failure (warranty).

"The interior appointments are outstanding, and the exterior paint has been subjected to severe weather involving heavy rain, snow, ice and hail, but remains in excellent condition.

"When comparing all my previously owned aircraft, I find the Aerostar in a class by itself. The workmanship of the aircraft, as well as its performance, put it more in the class of heavy commercial aircraft. The heated windshield installation in the near future will complete my needs for this outstanding aircraft.

"The performance data as outlined on the specification sheets has been, in each case, easily achieved or exceeded.

"My only reservations stems from the Piper takeover in May of 1978 and their distribution and service policies. One of my big reasons for purchase of the Aerostar from Ted Smith was to avoid the problem with which I was plagued during my ownership of four different Piper Aircraft."

"Main assets are speed, comfort and ease of entry. Excellent air handling. Main disadvantage of my '76 model 600A: Noise. What would "Q" tips do?

"The much maligned fuel system has been no problem. If the fuselage tank is always filled, the system does what Ted Smith designed. I do not like electric fuel switches, though. It would be possible to be on crossfeed, have electrical failure and not be able to get back to normal! The original gauge is really Mickey Mouse for such a 'class' airplane. The new gauges will be fine.

"Linemen are not aware of the "Belly First" filling schedule, nor do they pay attention to a "low wing" problem. With the long, flat wing tanks, a few degrees downslope will prevent proper filling, resulting in a bad weight imbalance and much less range than the pilot expected after a "fill all tanks" fuel order. Even on a level ramp, the difficulty of maintaining even balance of the oleo pressure on the main struts makes monitoring of fueling super critical before long flights.

"Some problems: persistent wing tank leaks at certain rivets, difficult main strut pressure balance, main tires wear on inside, one alternator failed, two voltage regulators failed, sheared shaft in hydraulic pump, right main gear hydraulic line split. Trim actuator motor ($600). This motor can be burned out from conflict between manual switch and autopilot inputs.

"Parts are not readily available even from the factory, and the prices are exorbitant (e.g., trim motor). It remains to be seen whether new Piper ownership will improve this situation.

"The Lycoming engines have been super. In over 800 hours, not a skip or stumble (tough to start when hot), normal oil consumption, and highly predictable fuel flow. The absence of cowl flaps is great. After fooling with them on other makes, particularly the turbo models, it's a pleasure to eliminate another chore. I've never seen the heat needles in the red.

"Personal preferences: 'Normal' rudder pedal ground steering would be better."

Original fuel gauge *was way on the right side of the instrument panel and would show either right wing, left wing or total fuel, but not fuselage fuel.*

You need three hands to taxi and begin a takeoff run.

"It's an electric airplane: fuel switches, all trim controls, nose steering, air conditioning, heater, no manual backups.

"Hydraulic pumps should be standard on both engines. Overhead windows are fine for view, but hot on the front seat passengers."

"We have owned two 600As and have found both to be fantastic airplanes when compared to their competition.

"They are truly the 'sportscars' of the recip aircraft—agile, responsive and fast on less fuel than an Aztec, Turbo 310 or C model Baron. The 600A has a range and performance ahead of any of these.

"Like all aircraft, it has drawbacks, such as more than its share of AD notes. It's a little noisier than most of the competition, but a big plus is parts availability. We have bought both while they were damaged, and parts availability is unsurpassed in the industry.

"We ordered and received all the parts and repaired the aircraft in less time than it took us to receive a left-hand gas tank for a V35 Beech Bonanza—AOG (three months and two days)."

"We purchased a 1974 600A Aerostar new, early in 1975 and have flown it for 1,100 hours. I am extremely pleased with the Aerostar.

"We have been lucky (I am told) with maintenance. Our largest annual was $634. We have experienced only two delays for mechanical reasons. One was for magneto problems (cracked magneto block), $99 repair, and one starter failure at a private grass airport and repair including transportation for A&P and starter was $379.

"We have experienced no problem with parts, since we have required few. The plane is a joy to fly. With our normal light loads we always get a true 210 knots from 10-12,000 feet and an average fuel burn of 28 gph. Our complaints are only two: noise level and vibration.

"When all is said and done, I believe it is a great plane, and we would again buy the Aerostar today."

Interim move to prevent premature use of fuel *in the critical center tank was a low-fuel warning light, here on the annunciator panel. Later a triple fuel gauge, showing fuel for all tanks simultaneously, was installed.*

Cessna 421

Cessna's 421 is the ultimate refinement of the piston-engined lightplane. It has become a favorite of corporations and air taxis mainly because of its carrying capacity (up to 10 people) and its spacious, quiet, pressurized cabin. But to get its almost-turboprop capabilities, the 421 has to wring every last ounce of power out of the GTSIO-520 Continental engines—and therein lies the rub. Even under the best of conditions, 421 engines are good for a TBO of only 1,200 hours—and many 421 owners get a lot less than that. At up to $20,000 *per engine* for overhaul, that works out to about $30 per hour for overhaul reserve—nearly double that of the Cessna 414, which is virtually identical except for its smaller engines.

Buying a used 421 is complicated by the fact that the airplane's reliability is extremely sensitive to pilot technique. Overboosting on takeoff (especially during the first takeoff of the day, when the oil isn't warm) or a too-rapid descent can drastically shorten engine life—and if you're looking at a 10-year-old airplane that's had three or four owners, you have no way of knowing how it's been flown and maintained. More than one used-421 buyer has been wiped out by astronomical maintenance costs. That's one reason why old 421s are available for as little as $80,000—a bargain-basement price for a six-passenger pressurized airplane.

History

The 421 first appeared in 1968, the same year as the Beech Duke. (The pressurized Navajo wasn't introduced until 1970.) The 421 was a big airplane for its day, with a roomy cabin, 375-hp geared Continentals and a gross weight of 6,800 pounds. It was an immediate hit, racking up 200 sales its first year. (The Duke managed only 16.) In 1969 came the first major design changes and a new model number: the 421A. The first A model had a longer snout (it now contained a baggage locker), and a foot added to each wing. This allowed the gross weight to be increased 410 pounds to 7,250;

useful load, cruise speed and service ceiling all increased.

The 421B was built from 1970 until 1975. Major changes included an increase in the pressure differential (from 4.2 to 4.4), a 150-pound boost in standard useful load and new flaps, all in 1973. In its last year, 1975, the 421B got a new pressurization system (differential went up to 5.0) and was offered for the first time with the "known icing option" package.

In 1976 came the big change to the 421C. The dramatic swept-up tip tanks were eliminated in favor of a wet wing, which boosted maximum fuel capacity from 255 to 270 gallons. Tail and rudder size were increased, and the mechanical gear was changed to hydraulic. In addition, air conditioner capacity was increased by 25 percent, and the fuel selector was simplified. The 1977 and later 421C remained basically unchanged from the 1976 model.

Performance

The early 421 and 421As had a book cruise speed of about 230 knots under ideal conditions, but owners tell us that 210 knots is more like it. At this speed, fuel consumption is

about 40-45 gallons per hour. The 421B is a bit faster; count on perhaps 220 knots at the same fuel consumption. The 421C, with its higher aspect ratio, clean bonded wing, and more powerful turbocharger, is listed at 240 knots at 20,000 feet under optimum conditions. Most operators, however, like to baby their engines (a good idea, as we'll see later), and the normal cruising speeds of most 421s in the real world is around 200-220 knots at reduced power settings.

But all the 421s must go very high to get decent performance. At 10,000 feet, for example, even a new 421C will manage barely 200 knots at 75 percent power, and well under that at the normal 65 percent power setting. Considering the fact that light twins like the Baron, 310 and the Aerostar 601 can almost match that figure, it's clear that one doesn't purchase a 421 for speed alone.

To go with its very spacious cabin, the 421 has good load-carrying abilities. Early models have a useful load of around 2,000-2,200 pounds when well-equipped—enough for 202 gallons of fuel and four to five people. Starting with the 421B in 1970, useful load climbed by about 300 pounds, which made it practical to use full optional fuel

All pre-'76 models Cessna 421s *sported the big tiptanks. Buyers should check effectiveness of factory-built radomes, which sometimes woefully fail to meet radar needs.*

(255 gallons) with a reasonable passenger load. Optional fuel was increased to 270 gallons in 1976 with the 421C.

Resale Market

The 421 holds its value very poorly on the used-plane market. A 1968 model, for example, is today worth only about 40 percent of its original list price. Taking into account inflation, which has halved the value of the dollar in the past 10 years, a 1968 421 has lost *80 percent* of its real value. This is an extraordinarily high rate of depreciation.

By comparison, a 1968 Bonanza is today worth its original price, for a real depreciation of only about 50 percent.

Later model 421s seem little better. We talked to one used-plane dealer who in 1979 unloaded a superbly equipped 1977 421C with 500 hours on it for $240,000—a full $200,000 depreciation in a little over a year. "I was happy to get rid of it at that price," he told us. Another dealer confirmed, "Yes, the '76, '77 and '78 models are terribly depreciated. I have trouble selling them."

Actually, the depreciation sounds higher than it really is, because no new 421 is ever sold at anywhere near list price. Cessna dealers get a 20-percent markup on the 421, but most are happy to sell for five to ten percent above their cost—and there have been cases of dealers selling brand-new 421s for a $500 profit (that's about $80,000 below list price). Although Cessna Chairman Russ Meyer has personally implored dealers to stop such heavy discounting of Cessna's top-of-the-line piston airplane, the practice continues to be widespread. So, if a brand-new zero-time 421 has already depreciated 15 percent from list price before it's even sold, it's no surprise that a two-year-old 421 has depreciated by 30 percent.

From a depreciation standpoint, a 1974-76 model is the best choice, for they have already suffered the early sharp dropoff in value, and are now depreciating only slight-

Main trouble spots *on the 421 panel have been the ARC avionics, particularly the 400 series autopilots.*

ly. (Most aircraft "bottom out" after about four years and then begin to climb in value because of inflation.)

The depreciation of 1976-79 model 421s has been heightened by the introduction of the Chancellor and the Conquest, which bracket the 421 above and below. The Chancellor is very similar to the 421, except for the less powerful (but more reliable) engines and slightly inferior performance, yet its price is $100,000 less. At the other end of the scale, the Conquest is skimming off the top of the 421 market. All this tends to depress new 421 prices, and the chain-reaction continues on down the line to at least the '76 models.

Unfortunately, the pre-1976 421s suffer a couple of major liabilities. First, they have the old-fashioned tip tanks rather than the wet wings introduced in the 1976 421C, and therefore have less performance. Also, pre-1976 421s had the crack-prone crankcases (as did the '76 models, for that matter).

Handling

The 421 is a big, heavy aircraft, and is generally praised by pilots for its straightforward manners in the air. There are some noticeable differences among the various models, however. The stretched nose of the 421B makes it a bit easier to land than the straight 421s and 421As. The big switch to the wet-wing in 1976 eliminated the massive tip tanks. Roll control improved in gusty conditions because the pilot no longer had to fight the inertia of a heavy fuel-laden tank at the end of the wing. The C-model also had an extended fuselage, larger fin and rudder, which gives better control during engine-out situations.

Passenger Comfort

The 421 is undisputed comfort champion of piston-engine aircraft. Its cabin is 55 inches wide, wider even than the small King Airs. The 421 is also perhaps the quietest piston plane flying, with its slow-turning geared-

Model	Year Built	Number Built	Cruise Speed (mph)	Rate of Climb (fpm)	Useful Load (lbs)	Single-Engine Service Ceiling (ft)	Fuel (gals)	Engine	TBO (hrs)	Overhaul Cost	Average Retail Price
421	1968	200	255	1,700	2,563	13,340	255	375-hp Continental	1,200	$13,500	$ 80,000
421A	1969	158	261	1,700	2,563	13,340	255	375-hp Continental	1,200	$13,500	$ 85,000
421B	1970	56	261	1,700	2,588	13,340	255	375-hp Continental	1,200	$14,000	$125,000
421B	1971	147	270	1,850	3,024	13,000	255	375-hp Continental	1,200	$14,000	$130,500
421B	1972	175	270	1,850	3,024	13,000	255	375-hp Continental	1,200	$14,000	$135,000
421B	1973	186	270	1,850	3,024	13,000	255	375-hp Continental	1,200	$14,000	$145,500
421B	1974	165	270	1,850	3,024	13,000	255	375-hp Continental	1,200	$14,000	$157,500
421B	1975	170	270	1,850	3,024	13,000	255	375-hp Continental	1,200	$14,000	$177,500
421C	1976	171	279	1,940	2,878	14,900	270	375-hp Continental	1,200	$16,500	$222,000
421C	1977	150	279	1,940	2,878	14,900	270	375-hp Continental	1,200	$16,500	$260,000
421C	1978	124	279	1,940	2,878	14,900	270	375-hp Continental	1,200	$16,500	$295,000
421C	1979	100	279	1,940	2,878	14,900	270	375-hp Continental	1,200	$16,500	$340,000

down propellers and turbo-muffled exhaust. The 421's large cabin is a major reason for the airplane's popularity among corporate operators. (It also allows up to 10 seats in later models, which suits air taxi and small commuter operators just fine.)

Engines

The 421 has used the six-cylinder Continental GTSIO-520 engines since its introduction, and the marriage has been a stormy one. The "Gitso" engine (all those heiroglyphics stand for Geared Turbo Supercharged Injected Opposed) churns out 375 hp at 3400 rpm—better than 60 hp per cylinder. The almost inevitable result: The TBO of 1,200 hours is the shortest of any piston engine now in production. At an overhaul cost of up to $20,000 per side, we are looking at an engine reserve cost of $30 per hour. By comparison, the 380-hp Lycoming TIO-541 in the Duke costs about the same to replace, but has a 1,600-hour TBO for an overhaul cost-per-hour 33 percent less.

The GTSIO-520 is well-known for being sensitive to temperature changes and overboosting. As a result, the reliability of the engines may depend to a large degree on how they are flown. Careful piloting technique is required to prevent overcooling during letdown and overheating on the ground in the summer. Either can result in cylinder problems—and any cylinder problem, decrees Continental, must be cured by replacement, not repair. Cost of a new cylinder is about $1,500, installed.

The other chronic pilot-technique problem is overboosting—although the pilot isn't always the only culprit. The overboost relief "popoff" valve was inadequate in early models, according to one old 421 hand we talked to. Overboosting most often occurs during takeoff when the engine is not fully warmed up. The 421 turbo controller is supposedly automatic, but unless the oil is thoroughly heated up, the controller cannot respond quickly. As a result, pilots must

Roomy cabin is 421's major appeal. This arrangement seats five, plus pilot, copilot and bar.

very carefully and gradually open the throttle for takeoff and constantly monitor manifold pressure during the ground roll.

Unfortunately, even superb piloting technique can't guarantee reliability in the 421's engines. We're told of one 421 owner who flew absolutely by the book,—and even limited his manifold pressure to two inches less than the recommended figure for takeoff, climb and cruise. His reward was an unending stream of engine maintenance bills that finally forced him to sell the airplane. On the other hand, a mechanic at a prestigious overhaul shop swears that one of his customers flew a GTSIO-520 in a 421 4,000 hours before overhauling it! There seems to be no clear pattern of engine reliability. Some 421 owners are driven into bankruptcy by their engines; others seem happy as clams.

The 1968 and 1969 models with the -D engines may be more prone to engine problems. One dealer who's sold scores of used 421s told us, "I've never seen an old one that made it to TBO. The later ones seem to be okay."

The lesson in all this for the used 421 buyer is clear: study the engine logs with fanatical care. If you're looking at an older 421 with 1,500 hours on the airframe and 800 since overhaul, there must be a reason the engines only went 700 hours the first time. Avoid like the plague engines with troublesome histories.

If possible, scrutinize the pilot of the 421 you're looking at. Is he a superprofessional by-the-book type? Ask him what special technique he uses to avoid overcooling or overboosting. If you get a blank look in response, run the other way.

The ideal used 421 is a corporate airplane flown exclusively by professional pilots with no history of engine problems. We'd hesitate to settle for anything less.

Other things to look for in the engine compartment:

• One used-plane dealer tells us that early 1976 models—the first 421Cs with the -L engine, had "terrible engine problems." If you're looking at one of these, check the engine and logs with extra care.

• The 421, along with most other Cessna 400 series twins, has a long history of exhaust system problems, and there were several fatal in-flight fires. A whole string of ADs was issued to combat the leaks; make sure these have been complied with to the letter. The 1977 and later models have improved stainless steel in the exhaust system, so they should not present as much as a problem. In any case, have your mechanic inspect a prospective 421's exhaust system with a fine-tooth comb. Replacement can run as high as $10,000, and regular exhaust

system maintenance will be very high.

• The 421, like many other Continental-powered airplanes, suffers "The Curse of the Cracking Crankcase." The problem was finally solved by a fourth-generation "heavy" case in mid-'76, but any 421 built before then (and not overhauled since) should be viewed with a jaundiced eye. Make sure that you're getting the right "heavy" cases; several beef-ups were made over the years, but only the last one worked.

Airframe Maintenance

The 421 is an exceedingly complex airplane, and any aircraft of this category—Duke, pressurized Navajo, or whatever—will cost a bundle in airframe maintenance. The 421 has some particular trouble spots, however. Here are some of the potentially expensive ones:

• The 421C model (1976-79) had redesigned landing gear legs. Unfortunately, they seem to be crooked. As a result, tire wear on the C models is excessive, and there's not much anyone seems to be able to do about it. A new tire for a 421C costs $75.

• Cessna's air conditioning system is universally acclaimed as lousy. For example, the fan and motor that cool the radiator on the ground are designed to freewheel in flight. Not surprisingly, the motors wear out with astonishing speed. Cost to replace: $500-plus. Many 421s have been retrofitted with air conditioners built by JB Systems in Longmont, Colorado. JB air can also be fitted to 421s with nacelle tanks, which cannot accept the Cessna factory air conditioning system.

• Alternators are a major problem in 421s. The Presto-Lite ALV 9400 100-amp alternators have suffered chronic bearing failure for years, and even 1979 421s have the same problem. FAA records suggest that about 10 percent of these alternator failures result in accessory case damage and metal contamination of the oil system. If this occurs, the only alternative is a new engine ($20,000).

• The 1968, '69 and '70 models reportedly had poorly designed pressure controller valves. The replacement parts are difficult to get, we're told, and cost about $4,000.

• Extra corrosion proofing has been available as a factory option on 421s, and it's a good thing to look for on used 421s.

• Like many other older aircraft, the 421 suffers from leaky rubber fuel cells. Check them closely for leaks. Replacement cost for a full set is close to $10,000.

FAA service difficulty reports confirm reader and mechanic reports of continuing problems with alternators, air conditioners, exhaust systems, crankcases, cylinders, and, in 421 and 421A models, leaking fuel cells. The reports also reveal the following additional trouble spots with the 421:

•Rudder and rudder trim system damage is quite common with all 421 models, the result of that huge control surface flapping around in the wind.

•The Weldon boost pumps in the 421C have a very poor record. (One *Aviation Consumer* reader tells us he's replaced five pumps in less than two years.)

•Windshields have a tendency to crack around the heating elements on the 421B. (AD 77-9-2 addresses this matter; check compliance carefully.)

•The ARC/Cessna 400 autopilot system has a very poor reliability record, with many reports of abrupt and violent maneuvers due to sudden malfunctions.

Operating Costs

Astronomical, to say the least. Actual costs vary widely from operator to operator, but if you plan for $220 per hour, you won't be far wrong. Fuel is about $70 per hour, overhaul reserve $35; figure about $25 per hour for routine maintenance and "minor" unscheduled problems fixed during 100-hour inspections. Insurance, tiedown and depreciation all vary greatly according to usage.

Most charter outfits charge about $1.50 per mile for 421 flights, which works out to about $300 per hour on a block-to-block basis. Subtracting crew costs and profit brings the probable actual costs in commercial operation down to about the $220 figure.

Several charter outfits tell us that on a per-mile basis, the 421 is as expensive to operate as a turboprop such as the MU-2—or even Citation jet. Another operator reports that until the price of jet fuel jumped in 1974, he charged the same per-mile rate for both his 421 and his Learjet. Now the Lear costs about 20 percent more to run.

Used 421 vs. Used Turboprop

As for purchase price, 1968-72 421s cost less than any turboprop on the used-plane market. But for the price of a 1973 or 1974 421, it's possible to buy a Mitsubishi MU-2 turboprop, and an old King Air is not much more expensive. Considering the generally better reliability of turboprops, anyone considering a late-model 421 should at least think about the propjet alternative.

Fuel efficiency has always been one of the 421's big selling points against turboprop aircraft, but unexpected engine expenses often more than make up the difference for many operators. Engine overhaul costs are similar; turboprops cost two or three times as much to replace but last two or three times as long.

One Man's Problems with a 1977 421C

"Boy, did I get a lemon!" That is the essential message of dozens of letters received every month at *The Aviation Consumer*. One recent letter from the owner of a 1977 Cessna 421C recounts a long string of breakdowns and malfunctions over a 19-month period. As an example of the kind of maintenance headaches that can befall a 421 owner, we offer the following summary of one man's airframe and avionics problems with his 421. (This summary does *not* include engine problems.)

EGT—Seven squawks, four on left engine gauge, three on right. One gauge replaced, one probe replaced.

ENGINE-DRIVEN FUEL PUMP—Left pump failed and replaced three times, right pump failed and replaced twice.

ELECTRIC FUEL PUMP—Right pump failed and replaced once, left pump failed and replaced twice.

LANDING GEAR—Ten squawks, mostly due to poor adjustment, causing extremely rapid, uneven tire wear. Owner was told no further adjustments could be made and that the problem was insoluble.

FUEL DRAINS—Right forward drain was replaced five times because of leaks. Better news on the right side, however—that drain only had to be fixed twice.

TACHOMETER—Three squawks, instrument replaced once.

COMPASS—Had to be recalibrated three times.

STATIC SYSTEM—Had to be blown out three times, although cover always in place on the ground.

ALTERNATORS—Right alternator failed three times (two replacements, one repair). Left alternator failed twice.

AVIONICS COOLING FAN—Two failures.

HSI—Twelve separate failures. Instrument was replaced five times.

AUTOPILOT—Twenty-two squawks. Sample: "In heading mode, sharp left turns, in Nav mode, violent rolls to right . . . Autopilot in any mode tends to invert aircraft . . . Violent yoke displacements . . ."

ALTITUDE ALERT—Eight squawks.

VORS AND COMMS—Ten Squawks.

DME—Five failures. Two repairs, two replacements, still inop on low frequencies.

RMI—Three failures. "Card 45-60 degrees off heading . . ."

TRANSPONDER—Two failures. "Continuous ident . . ."

The owner reports that the airplane spent 164 days on the ground for maintenance in those 19 months. (That's more than one day in four.) Total maintenance invoices for the period totaled nearly $25,000 (not counting work done under warranty by Cessna). He listed 19 revenue flights canceled because of mechanical failures, resulting in $13,000 of lost revenue. The failures included one engine failure on takeoff, plus an emergency single-engine landing when the fire warning light went on. (The light, it turned out, was malfunctioning.)

Obviously, not everyone has this sort of trouble with the 421. But with an airplane as complex as this one, when you get a lemon, the taste is sour indeed. The need for careful inspection of the airplane itself and its maintenance records cannot be overemphasized.

Piper Navajo

Piper's Navajo is beloved by charter and corporate operators. It has a reputation as a reliable airplane with straightforward flying characteristics and good load-carrying abilities—sort of a cabin-class Aztec. A major plus is the Lycoming IO-540 series engines used in all Navajos except the pressurized model. The basic Navajo has 300 horsepower and a TBO of 2,000 hours, and even the 350-hp Chieftain has a 1,600-hour TBO. (Compare that to the 1,200- to 1,400-hour TBOs of the Continental-powered Cessna 400 series cabin twins, the Navajo's chief rival in the marketplace.) The Chieftain is currently one of the hottest planes on the used-plane market, mostly because of the resurgence of the air-taxi business.

The first Navajo appeared in 1967, in two versions: a nonturbo 300-hp model and a turbocharged 310-hp variant. (The turbochargers were very unreliable for the first three years, however; make sure that any 1967-69 Turbo Navajo has been retrofitted with the improved turbos, which were first used on the 1970 models.) Once the reliable turbochargers were added, Piper dropped the normally-aspirated 300-hp version.

The year 1970 also saw the introduction of the Pressurized Navajo. The airframe was virtually identical, but completely new 425-hp engines were added. (More on the P-Navajo's checkered career later.)

In 1972, the Navajo B was introduced, but there was no real difference between the B and earlier 310-hp versions. (The only significant change was the addition of wing-locker baggage compartments.) In 1973, the Navajo Chieftain was added to the line. The Chieftain featured a stretched fuselage, two more seats and 350-hp engines in place of the 310s. Performance of the Chieftain was much better than the B, and useful load was 250 pounds higher. The Chieftain was an immediate hit (it outsold the B and the P-Navajos by a wide margin) and is still the most popular version of the airplane.

In 1975, the Navajo C/R was introduced, with counter-rotating 325-hp engines, which supposedly eliminate "torque effect" on takeoff and improve single-engine safety by eliminating the "critical" engine. However, the appeal of the C/R is strictly psychological, according to veteran Navajo pilots, and probably not worth the $10,000-$12,000 premium the C/R commands on the used-plane market. In fact, the C/R may be a *less* desirable airplane because of its slightly lower useful load, higher fuel consumption and lower engine TBO (1,600 hours vs. the 1,800 of the standard 310-hp Navajo).

The same year the C/R was introduced, the standard B model was renamed the C, but again there were no major changes. In fact, the Navajo is unusual because of the continuity of its design. Except for interior furnishings and the instrument panel, the standard 310-hp Navajo has remained virtually unchanged throughout its lifespan. Piper apparently realizes it has a good airplane, and so far has not fiddled with its success formula.

In 1977 the pressurized model was dropped after sales declined almost to zero—mostly because of the bad reputation of the engines. The current model lineup includes the 310-hp Navajo C, the 325-hp Navajo C/R and the stretched 350-hp Chieftain.

Performance and Handling

The Navajos are praised by pilots for their straightforward flying characteristics. Performance is not exactly spectacular, but it is on par with other cabin-class twins such as the Cessna 402. Cruise speeds are listed at 190-200 knots (220-230 mph) at max cruise and optimum conditions, but real-world speeds are usually a tad less. Useful loads of well-equipped Navajos run around 2,000 pounds and 2,300 for the Chieftain. (All standard-fuselage Navajos have a 6,500-pound gross weight, while the Chieftain's is 7,000.) With a full load of fuel (most Navajos have 192-gallon tanks), about 800-900 pounds is left for payload.

The Navajo's one performance shortcoming is single-engine rate of climb. None climbs better than a sickly 270 fpm on one engine, and the Chieftain can manage only 230 fpm.

Maintenance

The prime reason for the Navajo's dominance over its Cessna rivals is its reputation

The big Chieftain *in the foreground can be identified by the extra window. It seats up to 10. The C/R in the rear is two feet shorter, and has 50 less horsepower.*

as a low-maintenance airplane. The 310-hp TIO-540-A engines are superbly reliable. "They are without peer among high-horse-power turbocharged engines," one over-hauler confirmed. "They go 1,800 hours easy, and I've had plenty in here with over 2,000 hours." The 325-hp -F and 350-hp -J versions on the C/R and Chieftain are not quite so reliable (their TBOs are 1,600 hours) and have a higher incidence of crack-ing crankcases. (Lycoming designed a beefed-up case for the -F and -J models in late 1978, and it's not known whether the new ones will have the same problem.)

The Navajo has had a bundle of AD notes, but most are minor and inexpensive. Recent ADs have targeted the landing gear and flap systems; make sure these have been com-plied with.

One glaring maintenance flaw has never been corrected. The Navajo has rather limited nosewheel steering limits. As a result nosewheel struts are regularly snapped and broken when turned too far by ground per-sonnel. One owner reports he's replaced five nose struts. Check the nosewheel strut care-fully for cracks or a "quickie" welding fix.

Resale Market

Navajos are always in demand, particularly the Chieftains. A 1974 Navajo is worth $138,000 retail; by comparison, a Cessna 402B of the same vintage (with an identical new list price) is today valued at only $115,000. The market for Chieftains is very strong right now because of the boom in the commuter airline business. "Last year I could get a nice '73 or '74 Chieftain for $115,000-$120,000 wholesale," one used-plane broker told us. "Now I've got to pay $135,000-$140,000." Retail for a '74 Chief-tain is $160,000.

The non-turbocharged 300-hp Navajos, built from 1967-69, are extremely rare these days (many have been converted to the turbo 310 engines) but they are highly prized by air taxi outfits. With no turbos to maintain and 2,000-hour TBOs, they are perfect for low-altitude short hops.

Desirable features to look for on a used Navajo are three-bladed props, de-ice equip-ment (virtually all Navajos have hot props, but not all have boots; a hot windshield is preferable to an alcohol windshield), wing lockers and the Altimatic 5 autopilot with flight director.

The Chieftain has optional crew and cargo doors. These are highly desired options and will raise the value of the airplane by about $5,000.

Wing lockers *and a separate over-wing win-dow-door for the pilot characterize the Chieftain.*

It's been rumored that some of the 1972 Navajos now flying are "flood" airplanes that were slightly damaged when the Susque-hanna overflowed its banks in June, 1972, and inundated the Piper plant in Lock Haven. (Navajo production was subsequent-ly moved to Lakeland, Fla.) The FAA says that no Navajos damaged on the production line ever were licensed, but that it's possible that a few finished airworthy airplanes may have been repaired and returned to action. If you are shopping for a 1972 model, it might be worthwhile to trace the serial num-ber and find out just exactly when and where it rolled off the production line.

Model	Year Built	Number Built	Cruise Speed (mph)	Rate of Climb (fpm)	S-E Rate of Climb (ft)	S-E Service Ceiling (ft)	Useful Load (lbs)	Engine	TBO (hrs)	Overhaul Cost	Average Retail Price*
PA-31-300	1968-69	n.a.	210	1,440	270	5,750	2,600	300-hp Lycoming IO-540-M	2,000	$ 8,400	$ 77,500-$82,000
PA-31-310	1967-70	680	247	1,395	245	15,800	2,650	310-hp Lycoming TIO-540-A1A	1,800	$10,800	$ 85,000-$110,000
PA-31-310	1971-72	166	247	1,395	245	15,800	2,650	310-hp Lycoming TIO-540-A2C	1,800	$10,800	$117,000-$122,000
PA-31-310	1973-75	458	233	1,445	245	15,200	2,500	310-hp Lycoming TIO-540-A2C	1,800	$10,800	$130,000-$145,000
PA-31-310	1976-78	232	233	1,445	245	15,200	2,500	310-hp Lycoming TIO-540-A2C	1,800	$10,800	$155,500-$185,500
PA-31P	1970-72	104	253	1,740	240	12,100	2,800	425-hp Lycoming TIGO-540-E1A	1,200	$15,000	$115,000-$130,000
PA-31P	1973-75	146	253	1,740	240	12,100	2,800	425-hp Lycoming TIGO-540-E1A	1,200	$15,000	$140,000-$170,000
PA-31P	1976-77	31	253	1,740	240	12,100	2,800	425-hp Lycoming TIGO-540-E1A	1,200	$15,000	$190,000-$210,000
PA-31-350 Chieftain	1973-75	628	250	1,390	230	13,700	2,800	350-hp Lycoming TIO-540-J2BA	1,600	$10,800	$150,000-$170,000
PA-31-350 Chieftain	1976-78	559	250	1,390	230	13,700	2,800	350-hp Lycoming TIO-540-J2BA	1,600	$10,800	$180,000-$230,000
PA-31-325 CR	1975-76	n.a.	225	1,500	255	15,300	2,400	325-hp Lycoming TIO-540-F2BA	1,600	$10,800	$155,000-$170,000
PA-31-325 CR	1977-78	n.a.	225	1,500	255	15,300	2,400	325-hp Lycoming TIO-540-F2BA	1,600	$10,800	$180,000-$200,000
PA-31-310 C	1979	n.a.	225	1,500	255	15,300	2,400	325-hp Lycoming TIO-540-F2BA	1,800	$10,800	$225,000
PA-71-325 CR	1979	n.a.	225	1,500	255	15,300	2,400	325-hp Lycoming TIO-540-F2BA	1,600	$10,800	$235,000

*Prices listed are for aircraft with mid-time engines, no damage history, all ADs complied with and the following equipment: dual Navcom and VOR, ILS, transponder, encoding altimeter, ADF, DME, autopilot, radar, prop and boot de-ice. Options such as RNAV, radio altimeter, RMI, air conditioning, cargo door, etc., will add to the listed value. Prices listed are retail; dealer wholesale prices are approximately 10-15 percent below retail.

The Aviation Consumer Used Aircraft Guide

P-Navajo Problems

The Pressurized Navajo (PA-31P) is the black sheep of the Navajo family. Introduced in 1970, it was immediately plagued with severe engine problems and was finally discontinued in 1977 after only 12 airplanes were sold that year. (Total production from 1970-77 was 288.) The Lycoming 425-hp geared TIGO-541 engine was a radical departure from the well-proven TIO-540s used in previous Navajos. To boost horsepower from 310 to 425, rpm was increased to 3200. (Since 3200 rpm is an unacceptably high propeller speed, reduction gearing had to be added for the prop.) Unfortunately, the engine in its original form was a disaster in the field, and user reports indicate that even with all the modifications that were eventually made, the average life expectancy of the engine is not much more than 800 hours. (Nominal TBO is 1,200 hours.) One owner of a 1976 P-Navajo with "up-to-date" engines reports that one engine had to be overhauled at 450 hours, and both had to be overhauled at 750 hours—at a cost of $18,000 per engine. That's a total cost of $54,000 for 750 hours of flying—$70 per hour for overhaul reserve.

Cylinders were redesigned in 1976 to combat cracking problems, and thrust bearings were modified in 1973 after leakage problems. Another major trouble-spot was oil leakage in the push rod seals. There were also serious problems in the first couple of years with the engine accessories. Lycoming says it now has the major problems of the TIGO-541 ironed out, and emphasizes the need for good piloting technique. (Continental gives the same litany in defense of its similarly trouble-prone GTSIO-520 engine in the Cessna 421.)

The P-Navajo does have its staunch de-

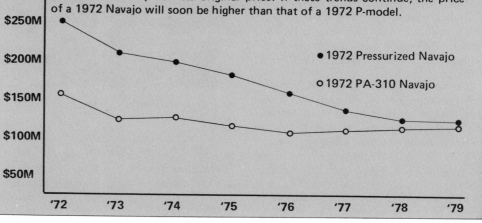

Aircraft Investment Value

The graph starkly displays the contrast between the standard Navajo and its pressurized stablemate in terms of resale value. A 1972 Navajo B, with an original list price of $158,000 never depreciated to less than $120,000—76 percent of the original price—and is now appreciating steadily. The P-Navajo, on the other hand, has declined in value for seven consecutive years and is now worth barely half its original price. If these trends continue, the price of a 1972 Navajo will soon be higher than that of a 1972 P-model.

● 1972 Pressurized Navajo

○ 1972 PA-310 Navajo

fenders, all of whom blame the engine problems on poor piloting technique. Unfortunately, not even Piper was fully aware of the ultra-sensitivity of the P-Navajo engines in the beginning. "Even the people who taught Piper's ground school on the P-Navajo didn't know what the hell they were talking about the first few years," says Gene Lock, who was a factory P-Navajo demo pilot for many years. Lock lists several cardinal sins of P-Navajo pilots that he believes inevitably lead to engine problems:

●Descending too fast with reduced power, which cools the engines too quickly and causes cylinder and valve problems. Gear and flaps should be used if necessary so that engine power can be maintained during descent. Lock says he has popped out the gear at altitudes as high as 22,000 feet.

●Revving the engine after a cold start. Since the TIGO engine is geared down 2:1 and the tach reads propeller rpm, pilots accustomed to direct-drive engines tend to idle the engines too fast—up to 2000 rpm, which of course registers on the tachometer as only 1000. Lock says indicated rpm should not exceed 700 after a cold start.

●Taking off with low oil temperature. A temp of 140 is the absolute minimum for takeoff.

●Running full rich during cruise climb. Lycoming and the P-Navajo manual called for full-rich cruise climb in the early days, but Lock insists this damages the engine.

●Rapid rpm changes at altitude. "You should never make a fast move with any control at any time with this engine," says Lock.

●Shutting down the engine without allowing a spooldown time for the turbocharger. Navajos have clumsy ground handling, and pilots often will use a burst of power for ground maneuvering after landing. At least five minutes of low-idle running should be allowed after even the briefest burst of power from the engine.

Whether the responsibility for the P-Navajo's engine problems lie with Lycoming or the pilots who fly the airplane is not clear. But the fact remains that serious problems have occurred, and the condition of the engines should be the prime concern

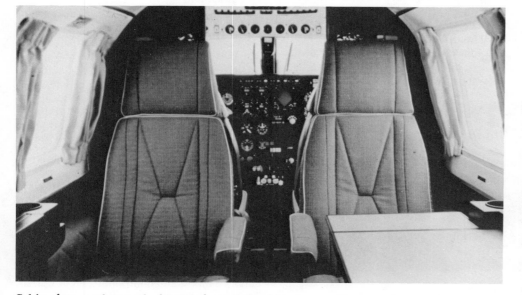

Cabin class, *with superb, big windows, lots of headroom. Note overhead pilot console.*

of anyone who purchases a Pressurized Navajo.

The pressurization system was also a source of trouble during the first couple of years. (The big problem was a leaking accumulator can for the door seals.) This was fixed in 1972, however, and the pressurization system has reportedly given few problems since then.

The exhaust system has also been a problem, particularly the shock mounts for the brackets that support the system. AD 76-6-9 requires frequent inspections in 1970-76 models.

The poor reputation of the P-Navajo engines has depressed its value on the used-plane market considerably, at least compared to the other Navajo models. A 1975 P-Navajo, for example, has a retail "bluebook" price of $197,500—only 57 percent of its original list price. A 1975 Navajo Chieftain, on the other hand, has retained 81 percent of its value, while a 1975 Navajo C is worth 82 percent of its original cost. (It should be noted that the P-Navajo's chief competitors, the Cessna 421 and Beech Duke, also have very low resale values. The 1975 models of those two aircraft are worth only about 60 percent of their original prices.)

Used aircraft dealers confirm the low demand for the P-Navajo. "They're a real pain to sell. I've lost a fortune on them," one told us. "The market is very depressed." On the other hand, Texas Jet, Inc., the country's largest specialist in used Navajos, insists that the market for P-Navajos is good, although they don't dispute the fact that pressurized models are worth proportionally far less (compared to their original list prices) than the other Navajos.

Despite its high power, performance of the P-Navajo is virtually the same as the Chieftain. Cruise speed is only three mph faster, and single-engine rate of climb is still rather sickly—240 fpm. Gross weight is 800 pounds higher, but so is the empty weight; useful load of the P-Navajo is almost the same as the Chieftain's. (Considering the

The Colemill Panther *conversion installs bigger Chieftain engines in smaller Navajo airframes. Bent-tip props are intentional.*

425-hp engines' bigger appetite for fuel, payload for a long trip is actually less.) Take-off performance is slightly better than the Chieftain's but landing distance is 50 percent longer. And of course, the pressurized model has a smaller cabin and two fewer seats. For three years (1970-72), the P-Navajo was the only high-performance Navajo available, but when the Chieftain was introduced in 1973, with reliable engines, a bigger cabin, similar performance, and a price tag nearly $70,000 lower, it was the beginning of the end for the pressurized model.

The P-Navajo's max cruise speed by the book is 253 mph. But in the real world, P-Navajo pilots report that they count on 200 knots (230 mph) at 22,000 feet, with a fuel burn of 35 gph. (Block-to-block fuel burn is said to be about 50 gph.) Cruise-climb rate is about 1,000 fpm.

Purchasers of used Pressurized Navajos should use extreme caution. Compliance with all Lycoming service bulletins is an absolute must. Check carefully the engine maintenance history. If the airframe has 2,000 hours and is on its fourth set of engines, beware. Frequent changes of ownership and pilot are a bad sign, for they increase the chances of pilot mismanagement

that can aggravate engine problems. The ideal P-Navajo would be a one-owner, one-pilot airplane with a long and flawless engine history. We're not sure we'd settle for anything else unless the price is absurdly low.

Safety
The Navajo's safety record is good. Its accident rate is lower than all cabin twins except the Queen Air, and significantly better than the Cessna 400 series airplanes. A look at NTSB accident reports for the Navajo shows a huge number of gear-up landings and gear collapses—nearly 50 in all. Check any Navajo for evidence of gear repair. There has also been a significant number of engine failures and fuel mismanagement accidents.

The Navajo is generally praised by pilots for its straightforward flying characteristics, and apparently these subjective feelings are backed up by accident statistics.

Modifications
The only engine modification available for the Navajo is the Colemill "Panther" conversion, which replaces the 310- or 325-hp engines of the standard short-body Navajo with the 350-hp TIO-540-J of the Chieftain. (The mod also incorporates the new Hartzell "Q-tip" prop.) Performance is reportedly eye-opening, although there is a slight reduction in useful load. About 30 Navajos have already been converted. Cost is $70,000 exchange. Colemill Enterprises, P.O. Box 60627, Nashville, TN; 615-226-4256.

Cypress Aviation in Lakeland, Florida (the same city in which new Navajos are now built) does a booming business in cargo door conversions for Chieftains that don't already have that feature. Cost is $4,785. Cypress also offers a raft of other Navajo modifications, including crew doors, aux fuel tanks, interior mods, air conditioning, etc. Cypress Aviation, 813-644-3003/1550.

Though there's plenty of room *for full dual instrumentation and radar on the Navajo panel, even more controls are relegated to an overhead console, not showed here.*

Owner Comments

"I was co-owner of a 1976 PA-31P Navajo. This aircraft was used for charter work and was flown only by experienced commercial pilots.

"The major problem was the engines. These are Lycoming 425-hp geared engines At about 450 hours, one engine had to be rebuilt. At 720 hours, both engines were found to have an excessive amount of metal particles in the oil filters and had to be rebuilt. There was a lot of general wear, plus some cracked rings and connecting rods. The propellers were also excessively worn and had to be rebuilt as well. The cost was about $18,000 per side. The aircraft was out of service for two months due to parts unavailability from Lycoming, according to the overhaul facility.

"Subsequent to the aircraft going in for the overhaul, I was told by mechanics at other facilities that it is rare for those particular engines to get to their 1,200-hour TBO, with the average engine life probably being about 800 hours."

"We presently own a 1969 PA-31 nonpressurized Piper Navajo and have been most impressed with the comfort and maintenance record of this aircraft. One complaint is that at gross weights the single-engine performance is marginal; however, we are presently putting a Panther conversion on our Navajo, and I'm sure this will more than correct that aspect.

"We certainly feel that the Navajo is probably one of the few truly great airplanes that Piper has ever built and are very happy with the maintenance record and backup of parts. Performance on two engines is good, but a little marginal on single-engine performance."

"We purchased our 1976 Navajo Chieftain new. It now has 1,450 total hours. I must say that this airplane, in conjunction with the King Silver Crown Radio package, has been the most reliable airplane I have ever flown.

"My only real complaint is the very limited nosewheel steering limits. This limited steering makes the airplane extremely vulnerable to damage to the nose gear strut when being towed by a tractor. To date, we have replaced five struts. In my opinion, this is a most inexcusable design by Piper.

"Overall a very high rating for the Chieftain."

"Our airplane (1976 Navajo C/R) flies an average of 93 hours per month. Airframe parts availability is the biggest problem. Very rarely does the distributor have what we need in stock. The engines had leaky valves and required top overhauls at 800 hours; otherwise, they have been trouble-free. The dry air pumps are the biggest source of failures. The ADs have been a source of extra cost, particularly the propellers. Overall, however, we have had no problems keeping our schedule due to unexpected maintenance.

"We changed engines at 1,400 hours due to a crack in the crankcase of the left engine. We also have an elevator trim problem that Piper so far has not been able to resolve—we run out of nose-down trim during cruise and descent."

"Our 1968 Navajo has been a maintenance hog. Parts costs are out of sight, and reliability of new parts right out of the box is zero. I have yet to replace a faulty component with a new one that worked the first time. Once it gets out of the shop, however, the Navajo is a truly superior flying machine."

"I bought my '71 aircraft new and put 500 hours on it in two years. It was completely

trouble-free, and our only problem in that time was a one-hour delay for a faulty oil temperature gauge. One design weakness is the brakes, which wear out very quickly. It helps to baby them."

"I own a 1976 Piper Navajo C/R PA-31-325.

"Performance: Lives up to book figures. Typically 185 knots at 12,000 feet and 6,500 pounds gross weight.

"Handling: comfortable for control and stability, nice to fly. On ground in close quarters, one will build up thigh muscles on the nosewheel steering.

"Maintenance: fairly low, average 100-hour or annual inspection, $1,500.

"Comfort: I am 6'4" and 220 pounds Once I get into the left seat, it's comfortable, except for rear seat by the door in the winter. The heater doesn't quite reach that far back.

"Parts availability: good if your parts man is good. Reading Aviation is excellent.

"Cost of Operation: fuel consumption @ 65 percent power is 38 gph the first hour and 32 gph each additional hour. If your flights are less than one hour duration, always use 38 gph.

"Idiosyncrasies: always wait four minutes from the time engines are at idle after you land to cool the turbocharger main bearing before shutdown. Keep main landing gear uplock lubricated to prevent the main landing gear from falling out at cruise. Change heater combustion motor brushes and igniter every 500 hours of heater operation.

"One reason I have experienced such good service from this airplane is due to one-pilot, one-shop, one-owner corporate operation."

Pilots rate flight characteristics *of the Navajos highly, but tend to be more critical of ground handling.*

Beech Duke

Beech's Duke pressurized twin is billed as the ultimate personal airplane, and it would be hard to argue its hairy-chested macho appeal. The Duke is sleek, well-built and carries perhaps the most prestigious status symbol of them all—a monumental price tag. A new one can cost nearly $500,000, and you'll have to get a pretty ratty old one if you want to spend less than $100,000. For this kind of money, you absolutely must know the ins and outs of the used Duke market, for some models have had some serious problems that, if uncorrected, could cause astronomical maintenance costs.

History

The Duke was first introduced in 1968 and was then known as the model 60. Since then the airplane has undergone steady refinement, but no major changes in configuration. The A60 model was introduced in 1971, and had a modest increase in gross weight, up 50 pounds from 6,725 to 6,775 (useful load actually went down a bit, however) and modest decreases in performance because of the extra weight. (According to the book figures, short-field performance of the straight 60 is much better than the A60, but Duke owners tell us the early figures were very optimistic, and that the A60 is only slightly poorer in takeoff and landing performance than its predecessor.)

The B60 was introduced in 1974, and featured a slightly larger cabin, more fuel capacity, with small degradations in speed and useful load; otherwise there have been no major configuration changes since.

Engines on all Dukes are 380-hp Lycoming TIO-541s. Early models of this engine were troublesome nightmares with 1,200-hour TBOs, but the engine has been improved over the years with various modifications; TBO is now 1,600 hours, and we've talked to several Duke owners who have gone well past that figure. We'll go into detail about the various engine modifications and what to look for later in the article.

Performance

The Duke is a movin' machine, but it does slurp up the petroleum. Owners report a maximum cruise speed of about 220 knots (250 mph) at 68-70 percent power at 24,000 feet. This is a bit better than other pressurized twins, with the exception of the fleet Aerostar 601P, which can fly 10-15 knots faster on about 25 percent less fuel. The Duke's fuel flow at 220 knots is about 40 gph. Fuel consumption can be reduced to about 30 gph at 55 percent power, but speed drops down to 185 knots or so—and you might as well be flying a 310. One owner tells us he flightplans at 195 to 200 knots with 65 percent power, burning 40 gph, however.

For a pressurized aircraft designed to cruise above 20,000 feet, climb performance is critical, and the Duke again makes a good showing in this department. One corporate operator reports about 28 minutes to 24,000 feet—at full gross and on a warm day. Other owners confirm that the airplane climbs well at high altitudes, reportedly 700 to 1,000 fpm depending on weight. Climb performance of the Duke is generally considered superior to any other owner-flown pressurized twin—except, again, for the pressurized Aerostar.

With a standard fuel capacity of 142 gallons, range is rather limited, but virtually all Dukes have optional long-range fuel tanks with capacities ranging from 202 to 232 gallons, depending on the model. With optional tanks full, a four-hour trip can be made with IFR reserves at a good cruising speed. That translates into a full-fuel maximum range of about 900 nm; at reduced power, range may be stretched well over 1,000 nm. This is about average for this class of aircraft.

The Duke is definitely not a STOL airplane, however; most operators consider a 3,000-foot runway the absolute minimum. Motorcycle daredevil Evel Knievel once ordered the pilot of his Duke to land on a drag strip. He didn't make it, and the plane ended up with its nose poked through the truck trailer that Knievel uses as a mobile dressing room. Owners also report that initial climb after takeoff is rather poor. "It doesn't really seem to start climbing well until it's got 500 feet under it," one corporate pilot told us.

According to the book, single-engine performance is about average for this class of airplane—that is to say barely adequate under ideal conditions. Single-engine ceiling is 15,100 feet.

Beechcraft Duke *is widely known for sleek good looks, snob appeal and astronomical maintenance bills in early models.*

Weight and Loading

Here's where the Duke shines. Useful load of late-model Dukes generally runs better than 2,000 pounds, even when loaded with equipment. Earlier model Dukes weigh several hundred pounds less empty and tend to have less equipment; some straight 60 and A60 models have useful loads approaching 2,300 pounds. These numbers are markedly superior to anything else in the Duke's class, and the equal of even the cabin-class Cessna 421. Since the Duke has only six seats to fill (the 421 has seven), there's plenty left for baggage and fuel.

Unfortunately, the Duke's healthy appetite for fuel cuts into payload somewhat; other small pressurized twins will use a couple hundred fewer pounds of fuel over a long trip. Nevertheless, the Duke is still a full-fuel-plus-two-to-four-people airplane. One corporate operator reports he routinely flies six people and 136 gallons of fuel (enough for a three-hour, 600-mile trip) in a lavishly equipped Duke. However, another private owner is at gross with full optional fuel, two people and 100 pounds of baggage.

Unlike some other Beech airplanes, the Duke is not sensitive to balance. "You can hardly get it out of c.g." reports one owner. The plane has ample baggage capacity, since the huge nose compartment holds 500 pounds. There is no rear compartment. "I wore out three calculators running payload-range numbers on all the pressurized twins, and the Duke came out on top for the operation we have," claims a Duke pilot.

Passenger Comfort

For an aircraft that is often used as a corporate aircraft to haul around executives, passenger comfort is an important, if not critical, factor. One company pilot, in fact, reports that his company chose the Duke partly because the company president was

This custom-designed panel *has RCA color radar as a centerpiece, with King Gold Crown radios disguised on either side, Foster Airdata RNAVs below.*

rather elderly and feeble, and didn't like to negotiate the airstair doors of other pressurized airplanes.

Frankly, though, it's difficult to imagine he found the single retractable step of the Duke much of an improvement.

Although users rate the Duke high in overall passenger comfort, it must be noted the airplane has a typical Beech cabin, tapering at the rear like the Barons and Bonanzas. This means that two men would find things cramped sitting together in the rearmost seats. The B60 model introduced in 1974 did offer a bit more lateral cabin room by reworking the side panels and ducting, and recent models are supposed to have gained a couple of inches in apparent aisle space thanks simply to reengineered seats.

The Duke has a cabin pressure differential of 4.7, which is higher than any other six-place pressurized piston aircraft. It allows a cabin altitude of 10,000 feet at maximum cruising altitude of 24,000 feet.

Flight Characteristics

Pilots praise the Duke's manners in the air. It is a rock-solid instrument platform (as one might expect from the heaviest of all the six-passenger airplanes). Pitch changes with flap and gear extension are minimal and pilots tell us the Duke trims up well and holds its airspeed—all big plusses for instrument flying. "It flies beautifully in the 19,000-20,000-foot range and gives you a nice, secure feeling," comments one owner.

Looked at in another way, however, stability translates as heaviness on the controls. The airplane indeed demands rather ponderous inputs on ailerons and elevators, and at least one owner said he'd like to see a bit more alacrity and responsiveness in the bird. We'd frankly rate it about on a par with the likes of a Cessna 340, however.

Cockpit Engineering

Praise be, that on the Duke, Beech has placed the power controls in the standard order, along with the gear and flap levers. (In the Barons, they are all "reversed.") The flap system is beautifully simple; the lever has three positions: up, approach and landing, with little lights for transition, APH and LDG. And there are even two separate control wheels as standard (not throwover).

Cowl flap operation is electric. Glance out the window to see if they are extended or not.

The gear whirrs down in a zippy four seconds flat, and can be lowered for drag at the typically phenomenal Beech airspeed of 175 knots.

Visibility out the front of the Duke is what we'd call barely adequate, and to see over the glareshield, an average-height pilot who pulls the seat forward (and up, automatically) may find his head nestled against the headliner.

Incidentally, thanks to the narrow open-

The massive 380-hp Lycomings *had major problems up till 1976.*

ing to the front cockpit, getting to and from the pilot seats takes a bit of elasticity.

Once snugly seated, however, the Duke pilot can be assured of a beautifully smooth, quiet ride rarely matched in a piston twin.

Safety Record

The Duke doesn't have a bad fatal accident record, but NTSB statistics show a surprising number of gear collapse accidents, which usually don't hurt anybody but can be painfully expensive.

Of the 500 or so Dukes built, seven have had fatal crashes. Three of these were IFR approach accidents caused by pilot error. A fourth occurred when the airplane accumulated ice and was unable to maintain altitude over the Utah mountains.

Three of the fatal crashes were not weather-related. In one Duke accident, which killed noted air race and sport pilot Leroy Penhall, a propeller overspeeded. Penhall was unable to maintain control of the airplane while attempting to return to the airport. Investigators believe Penhall failed to exercise the props before takeoff (it was a very cold day) and congealed oil caused the overspeed. Two other fatal Duke crashes were a result of mid-air structural breakups—one likely caused by severe turbulence, the other under unknown circumstances.

There have been no reported Duke accidents due to fuel unporting, which has caused several Baron and Bonanza crashes. (The three airplanes share a similar wing and main fuel tank.)

Among NTSB's listing of non-fatal Duke accidents, landing gear collapses and inadvertent gear retractions lead the way. At least two gear retractions on rollout were laid to Beech's inconsistency in the placement of gear and flap levers of its different-model twins. In one case, a pilot who'd been flying Queen Airs inadvertently hit the Duke gear lever instead of the flaps during rollout.

The positions of the levers in the Duke, it turns out, are the reverse of their locations in the Queen Air.

The substantial number of gear collapse accidents is no doubt a reflection of the Duke's heaviness (nearly 7,000 pounds) and high touchdown speeds. Also, the plane has a tendency to wheelbarrow during braking, which can result in blown tires and/or collapsed gear. Anyone shopping for a used Duke should snoop carefully through the logbooks for evidence of any landing gear damage.

Operating Costs

Any pressurized twin-engine airplane costs a small fortune to maintain, of course, but the Duke seems to stand out even in this posh company. Beechcrafts, of course, are considered the Cadillacs of the industry, and the owner pays accordingly. Two Duke owners we queried for this report used virtually the same phrase when they described the high charges they've been socked with for parts and maintenance: "Anytime you take a

Duke to get fixed, man, they see you coming a mile away." (See the "Other Service Problems" sections for specific examples of some of the extraordinarily high repair costs incurred by Duke owners.)

One Duke operator gave us this breakdown of direct operating expenses:

    Fuel $50/hr
    Oil $1
    Overhaul reserve $20
    Maintenance $23

This works out to a total of $94 per hour to keep the plane flying. Tiedown, insurance and depreciation are of course extra.

An owner gave this sampling of the cost of parts for his Duke: Battery $1,000, generator $2,800, tires $90, $240 for a small cowl flap motor, new engines installed were $35,000. He reported maintenance costs of $72 per hour. Another owner reported a grand total operating cost (including depreciation) of $166/hr based on 300 hrs/yr, and $127/yr based on 500 hrs/yr. One Duke owner who found he couldn't afford the airplane's upkeep reports, "We

Rear cabin *is long on elegance, short on shoulder room for rear-seat passengers.*

Model	Year	Number Built	Cruise Speed (mph)	Useful Load (lbs)	Fuel Std/Opt (gals)	Rate of Climb (fpm)	S.E. Service Ceiling	Engine	TBO (hrs)	Overhaul Cost	Average Retail Price
Duke 60	1968	16	271	2,625	142/204	1,615	15,700	380-hp Lycoming	1,200	$24,000	$102,000
	1969	107	271	2,625	142/204	1,615	15,700	380-hp Lycoming	1,200	$24,000	$105,000
Duke A60	1970	22	272	2,600	142/202	1,601	15,100	380-hp Lycoming	1,200	$24,000	$120,000
	1971	30	272	2,600	142/202	1,601	15,100	380-hp Lycoming	1,200	$24,000	$128,000
	1972	21	272	2,600	142/202	1,601	15,100	380-hp Lycoming	1,200	$24,000	$135,500
	1973	43	272	2,600	142/202	1,601	15,100	380-hp Lycoming	1,200	$24,000	$145,000
Duke B60	1974	60	268	2,395	142/232	1,601	15,100	380-hp Lycoming	1,600	$24,000	$162,000
	1975	56	268	2,395	142/232	1,601	15,100	380-hp Lycoming	1,600	$24,000	$175,000
	1976	53	268	2,395	142/232	1,601	15,100	380-hp Lycoming	1,600	$24,000	$202,500
	1977	43	268	2,395	142/232	1,601	15,100	380-hp Lycoming	1,600	$24,000	$223,500
	1978	40	268	2,395	142/232	1,601	15,100	380-hp Lycoming	1,600	$24,000	$227,000
	1979	33	268	2,395	142/232	1,601	15,100	380-hp Lycoming	1,600	$24,000	$325,000

almost cried when we had to give it up for something more economical." It seems typical of Duke owners that they wince when paying the bills, but still feel deep affection and fierce loyalty for the airplane. Many wouldn't fly anything else.

Engine Troubles

Pre-1976 Dukes had some major engine problems, and any buyer of a used Duke should make it his number one priority to determine if the engines have had the fixes for those problems. At $24,000 a pair, the 380-hp Lycoming TIO-541s can be expensive nightmares if something goes wrong. The engine problems of the Dukes fall into three main categories:

• Turbochargers. Model 60, A60 and the 1974 B60 models had cast-iron turbo housings, and they had a tendency to crack from the heat. (A turbocharger failure in a pressurized airplane, don't forget, can be critical, since partial or total cabin depressurization will result.) In 1974, stainless steel blowers were fitted, and the cracking problems stopped. Almost all cast-iron turbo housings have been replaced with the stainless steel ones by now, but a few of the old ones remain. Be absolutely positive you're not getting one of them, or at least get a price reduction to cover the cost of replacement.

• Crankcases. Continental isn't the only company to have crankcase cracking problems. Dukes up through 1977 had a high incidence of cracks. The problem was solved when Lycoming beefed up the cases, effective with engine serial number 781.

• Cylinders and pistons. TBO of the TIO-541 was only 1,200 hours until 1974, mostly because of cylinder problems. Engines built or overhauled with improved pistons and cylinders since then have a TBO of 1,600 hours. The original problem (crack-

Fuel selector is conventional; *on, off and cross-feed positions, with no switching required for auxiliary tanks.*

Latest version *of the Duke is the B60, which has a slightly roomier cabin.*

ing around the exhaust ports) was exacerbated by less-than-perfect pilot technique during letdown. If power was reduced too much, the engines cooled too quickly, resulting in cylinder distress. Dukes built in 1976 and later (engine serial number 804 and up) have the completely "up-to-date" engines with 1,600-hour TBO, and owners report getting 1,800 and even 2,000 hours out of them.

Other Service Problems

In keeping with its big-ticket image, the Duke was equipped with a jet-style nickel cadmium (ni-cad) battery. This has proven to be a persistent and expensive nuisance for Duke owners. The battery is improperly cooled, and a slight misadjustment of the voltage regulator can ruin it. Average life of a Duke battery is two years or less. Now this doesn't seem so bad, except for the fact that a new battery costs $1,400! Current production Dukes now have lead-acid batteries; and Beech is also offering lead-acid conversion kits for older Dukes ($800). Summing up, look for a Duke with a lead-acid system.

Mixture control cables also have a troublesome history. Again, this doesn't sound like a big deal, but the bill for replacing them both is $2,500. Be sure to determine whether this modification has been performed.

Turbocharger controllers are also notoriously unreliable, and it's a good idea to check for manifold pressure drift during demonstration ride. One large used-plane dealer told us that only three or four of the last 25 Dukes he'd flown had properly working controllers.

Which Model?

During the first six or seven years of its life, the Duke had a rather poor reliability record,

and proved very expensive to maintain. But starting with the 1976 models, Beech seems to have gotten most of the problems under control, and later Dukes, we feel, are no more expensive to maintain than other high-horsepower piston twins like the Cessna 421 and the new Rockwell 700 (although the Duke's has much less room than either of those airplanes).

Therefore, a buyer shopping for a Duke who can't afford the $200,000 to $300,000 for a late model should use extreme caution when shopping for a straight 60 or A60 model in the $100,000-$175,000 range. It's a Catch-22 situation—if you can't afford to consider a late-model airplane, you're less likely to be able to afford the higher maintenance of the older models. The solution to the dilemma: careful study of the airplane. If all service bulletins have been complied with, and the engines have been updated to the latest standards, and the airplane has been flown competently by a professional pilot, there's no reason an older Duke can't be reasonable to maintain. But beware of the marginal older airplane that's had less than top-flight service and lots of different owners. If you buy a Duke and get a lemon, the taste will be sour indeed.

If you're looking for raw performance, the Aerostar 601P is a better bet, but for style the Duke is still pretty much unsurpassed among light airplanes. There are only about 450 Dukes flying, and this exclusivity adds to the airplane's appeal for many people. It also means a rather unstable used market. "The Duke market goes up and down," one big used-plane dealer told us. "For a few months there'll be a glut of them for sale, but all of a sudden the supply dries up and you can't find one anywhere." This fact makes it even more important to shop around in various parts of the country.

Owner Comments

"For looks, handling, and comfort, rate the Duke tops. But for that kind of horsepower (760) one would hope that you could slip through the sky a little faster and carry another 100 or 200 pounds. Our Baron had as much full-fuel useful load.

"Our Duke was a high maintenance aircraft. Most parts and labor were higher than on a smaller or less sophisticated airplane. It gave you the feeling that they saw you and your Duke coming.

"A nicad battery was $1,000, generator $2,800, tires $90, $240 for a small cowl flap motor, special brake pads $100 a set; new engines installed were $35,000. The annuals were about $1,000. Parts usually had to come from a district Beechcraft center or from the factory.

"Fuel and oil ran through at $50 per hour, and our maintenance was up around $72 per hour over a two-year period.

"It was a "mean machine" but proved expensive. We almost cried when we had to give up pressurization for something more economical."

"I cannot say enough good things regarding the performance, handling, maintenance and comfort of the Duke. It will take on weather as well as sunshine. I have had no problem with parts availability. (However, I happen to be hangared next door to a Beechcraft dealer, and we have an excellent supply line to Wichita.)

"It is an expensive monster, but I don't feel that the Duke has any equal in the twins available today. The Lycoming engines are extremely reliable, as is the entire airplane."

"For my money, it is the best owner-flown twin available, and we have been very pleased with it. The Duke is an honest airplane and an excellent instrument platform. The Lycoming TIO-541 engine has to be the easiest starting engine, hot or cold, I have ever flown with. Our first engines had 1,200-hour TBOs, but we ran them 1,385 hours. The new engines have 1,600-hour TBOs, and we expect 1,800 hours before we touch them. Our first set of engines had a tendency to leak oil, but the new ones run bone dry.

"In the past, people had some trouble with the earlier engines but I attribute this as much to rapid throttle jockeying by inexperienced second-owner pilots as to anything else. So far as I am concerned, anyone who purchases a Duke and does not go through the Beech Duke school is making a great mistake.

"The Duke, we find, burns about 43 gallons per hour on a less than three-hour flight; 40 gallons per hour on a flight of over three hours. Our speed is about three mph less than the book shows, but ours has every available option, including King Gold Crown and the heavy H-14 autopilot. The load carrying capacity is four people, plus luggage, plus full-fuel (202 gallons).

"The negative features of the airplane include the fact it is certainly not a short-field aircraft; our minimum field length is 3,000 feet. The Models 60 and A60 had shorter exhaust stacks, which tend to cause corrosion on the flaps. At engine change time, we installed the new B60 type pipes, which eliminated the problem.

"Perhaps the best way to describe our feelings is to say that our next new airplane will be a Duke."

"The Duke is a fast aircraft, but the published specifications are overstated. My airplane runs consistently about 10 knots less than book performance. Unlike with other airplanes I've owned, the performance specifications are figured on 600 pounds less than certified gross. The Duke handles very well, slows up for landing easier than comparable aircraft because of the high gear and flap speed, and in my opinion, it is easier to land than a 300 series Cessna. It is a quiet airplane and very comfortable, although the pilot and co-pilot need some practice to get in and out of their seats easily.

"As far as maintenance is concerned, I have not owned the airplane long enough to be able to assess what my costs are going to be on the long haul. My plane is currently going through an annual, and the left flap has to be replaced as a result of corrosion from the exhaust stack, which I understand has been a problem in several other Dukes.

"Several of the earlier Dukes do not have a prop synchronizer and the props will simply not stay in synch no matter how hard you try. A prop synch is a must for this airplane, and I had to have one retrofitted. I have had a lot of problems with the heater when I first bought the airplane but I feel that most of these were a function of the maintenance of the prior owners.

"The Duke has been criticized as being a fuel hog. My Duke burns between 40 and 42 gallons per hour in cruise at approximately 68 percent power and 67 to 70 gallons per hour in climbout. I have installed a Fueltron in my Duke to monitor the fuel more closely.

"In summary, I am satisfied with my Duke and look forward to flying it many more hours."

"I purchased a 1973 Duke; selling price was $165,000. It was equipped with King avionics, RCA 47 radar, air conditioning, all deicing equipment, club seating and other standard items. Total time was 68 hours on both the airframe and engines.

"I have been extremely pleased with its performance and flight characteristics. Average annual inspections are about $2,500. It is a little difficult to get into pilot and co-pilot seats, but once there, things are very comfortable. Workmanship is of the highest quality. It flies and feels like a solid, safe aircraft.

"There are roomier aircraft available, but none as sporty looking. The 400 Series Cessnas are big, but either underpowered or powered with the 520 geared engine, making them hard to maintain.

"I do not see anything on the market that comes close to the Duke's looks, power and handling characteristics. It is the Mercedes-Benz of the light twin market."

This '78 model *has most of the bugs worked out of it—but watch the earlier models!*

Mitsubishi MU-2

Pilots browsing through the light turboprops as a natural stepup from a piston twin might be drawn to the Mitsubishi MU-2s by the lure of dazzling speed, unbeatable short-field work and a less-than-shocking purchase price. Judging from the comments of pilots, however, they would be less likely to base their choice on ease of transition into the left front seat.

A glance at the roster of new cabin-class piston twins shows that aircraft like the Cessna 421 are going for around $495,000 new, with the Beech Duke not far behind at $468,000 and the Piper Navajo and Aerostar coming in at nearly $300,000 equipped. This makes a used '68-'71 Mitsubishi MU-2F, for example, a rather attractive alternative at around $330,000. Try to break into the turbine market with something else like a used King Air, even of the same vintage, and the ante goes up to around $500,000.

Naturally, there's a catch in the step-up to turbines; in fact, there are two. One is greatly increased cost of operation per hour; the other is aircraft handling and ease of pilot transition.

Though the MU-2s were among the earliest turboprops to appear on the market, they have always had what many would describe as avant-garde design features—such as a small-area, high-speed wing that sprouts nearly full-span flaps for landing and takeoff, and that uses spoilers instead of ailerons for roll control.

The MU-2s are the result of a true international amalgam. The airframe is built in Japan by Mitsubishi and shipped to the United States for assembly and addition of AiResearch engines along with avionics and other systems. After an initial marketing relationship with Mooney Aircraft in 1965, Mitsubishi set up a wholly-owned subsidiary for assembly and sales in '69 (when Mooney went bankrupt).

Since the debut of the first MU-2B model, Mitsubishi has brought out nearly a dozen upgraded models, representing one major fuselage enlargement, two boosts in engine power and four jumps in gross weight.

Model Changes
The MU-2D followed the -2B, offering integral wet-wing tanks instead of bladder tanks, higher weights, higher pressurization and the four-position flaps.

The F model received engines of 665 shp, up from 575, and extra fuel.

The G was the first stretched version, with a cabin about five feet longer, with pods added to both sides of the fuselage to take the landing gear and allow the cabin to be enlarged.

In the J model the interior was redesigned slightly to provide another 11 inches of cabin room. Also, extra soundproofing was added to the later Js.

The L received bigger 715 shp engines, increased gross weight and pressurization.

The M boosted gross, pressurization, and certified altitude.

The N and the P offered the engine slowdown and four-bladed props for sound reduction.

The Solitaire and Marquise with -10 engines boosted altitudes and speeds.

Investment Value
Plotting the investment value of the Mitsubishi MU-2s discloses that the short-bodied model (we tracked the 1968 F model) yields a surprisingly shallow curve, dipping below $300,000 only once and then starting back up to a '79 figure of around $312,000. The longer model (we followed the '70 G model) actually starts higher and ends up lower than its stablemate, suggesting a drop in popularity.

For comparison we tracked the 1968 Beech King Air B90 model and the '70 King Air 100, which might be considered comparable to the F and G Mitsubishis. The results showed the Beechcraft to represent an even better investment value. This year, in fact, the larger Beech King Air 100 is almost back up to its original cost (in underinflated 1970 dollars, of course).

One broker we talked to said they tried to avoid the Mitsubishi Bs and Ds, though there was a "very warm market" for the F models.

The short F model was the first to receive the 151A engine with 90 extra shaft horsepower. In the long-bodied series, the L with its higher power rating would be preferred over the Gs and Js that preceded it.

The long model MU-2s *have bulbous wheel fairings on the lower fuselage and slightly lower cruise speed than the short version. An L (foreground) and an M model are shown here.*

Cabin Sound Levels

Perhaps the most significant improvement came only a couple of years ago, with the '77 P and N models, when a major effort was made to combat the aircraft's reputation for annoying cabin noise levels. A big change was made at that time by slowing down the engine rpm, adding a fourth prop blade and enlarging the prop diameters.

Owners say this hushes the cabin sound levels dramatically, by 10 dbA or so, though ironically the greatest din is still experienced during taxi, since the AiResearch Garrett TPE 331 engines are spooling up at around 65 percent rpm, unlike the P&W PT-6 turboprop engines, which idle in a more subdued, conventional fashion.

In fact, if there were one main complaint aired by MU-2 pilots, especially about the earlier models, it was the inescapable noise—and vibration—of the Mitsubishi aircraft.

One pilot for a 1975 M model said his company had taken sound level readings in the aircraft that showed extremely high decibel ratings in front, becoming progressively lower toward the back of the cabin. They recorded levels of from 95 to 102 dbA in the pilot and copilot seats, down to 87 to 90 dbA in the middle seats and 80 to 85 dbA in the rear seats—cruising at an altitude of 22,000 feet. He figured that later models with the engine slowdown dropped an average of 10 dbA across the board inside the cabin.

Cabin Room

Despite the apparent small cabin size when viewed from the outside, owners describe the interior as quite roomy and comfortable. The short models seat six in an executive configuration, the long ones eight, though more can be crammed in for air taxi hauling by eliminating facing seats and tables. The long models even come with private toilets and cabin-size baggage areas. The short ones have three separate baggage bays in back of the cabin, with the front one pressurized.

Two areas in which pilots were universally complimentary was riding comfort in turbulence and structural integrity. Thanks to the high wing loading on the MU-2s, the aircraft sails through chop with small discomfort. And everyone raved about the Sherman tank "structural integrity" of the Mitsubishi aircraft.

Payload

Payload appears quite good, especially on later models with higher-output engines not power limited by temperatures on warm days. The chief pilot of an organization that operated a short '75 MU-2 M model said he could fill the fuel tanks, allow 250 pounds for himself and his Jepps, etc., and still load on board five passengers and 214 pounds of baggage. His payload was 1,376 pounds.

When it comes to out-and-out speed, the Mitsubishis lead the pack and always have. The later models can be expected to yield over 300 knots (short models) and the long models only a whisker under that. Only the Swearingen IIIB comes close at 300 knots, and the Cessna Conquest at 293 knots. The small Beech King Air C90 trails way back at 222 knots and even the King Air 100 only makes it to 248 knots. The Piper Cheyenne I checks in at about 249 knots and the II at 283 kts.

A typical seats-full range on the later MU-2s works out at a bit over 1,000 nm, which is average for this class of aircraft, though it's overshadowed by some like the Conquest (1,232 nm) and Swearingen IIIB (1,393 nm).

The earlier model MU-2s (Bs, Ds and Fs from '67 through '71) had cruise speeds that were lower by 35 to 65 knots, and commensurately lower range.

Handling

When it comes to handling, there is common agreement that the MU-2s are more demanding for the stepup pilot than other turboprops like the Beech King Air and the Piper Cheyenne. The feel of the aircraft is different because of the spoilers. And many confess that the other side of the coin relating to the MU-2's outstanding short-field performance is that the airplane can be a bear to land with finesse.

Pilots talk about descent rates on final as high as 2,000 fpm, if called for, with the props back in flight idle and 40 degrees of flaps hanging from nearly the full length of the MU-2 wing. The flare calls for a skilled touch to prevent slamming the aircraft on the runway. And even when the mains are on, the nosewheel is sure to fall like an axed tree no matter how the pilot tries to hold it off with elevator.

One owner complained that he was forever experiencing flight director failures which, correctly or not, he attributed to the pounding they took each time the nose slammed down on landing. And a professional pilot for a charter service is said to have frightened away customers from repeat business because of his tendency to hit down hard on every landing.

It is generally agreed that the short models are the worst in this regard.

Model	Year	Average Retail Price	Normal Cruise (kts)	Normal Altitude (ft)	Gross Weight (lbs)	Certified Ceiling (ft)	Engine	Shaft Horsepower	TBO (hrs)	Overhaul Cost
SHORT CABIN										
MU-2B	1967	$ 175,000	240	15,000	8,930	25,000	TPE-331/25AA	575	2,000	$44,000
MU-2D	1968	$ 190,000	250	15,000	9,350	25,000	25AA	575	2,000	$44,000
MU-2F	1968-71	$ 330,000	270	18,000	9,920	25,000	151A	665	3,100	$46,000
MU-2K	1972-74	$ 437,000	300	21,000	9,920	25,000	251M	665	3,000	$46,000
MU-2M	1975-76	$ 535,000	295	21,000	10,470	28,000	251M	665	3,000	$49,000
MU-2P	1977-78	$ 700,000	290	19,000	10,470	28,000	252M	665	3,000	$49,000
Solitaire	1979	$ 925,000	295	25,000	10,470	31,000	-10	665	3,000	$52,000
LONG CABIN										
MU-2G	1970-71	$ 332,000	240	16,000	10,800	25,000	151A	665	3,100	$47,000
MU-2J	1972-74	$ 475,000	280	19,000	10,800	25,000	251M	665	3,600	$47,000
MU-2L	1975-76	$ 572,000	280	19,000	11,575	25,000	251M	715	3,600	$49,000
MU-2N	1978	$ 815,000	275	19,000	11,575	25,000	252M	715	3,600	$49,000
Marquise	1979	$1,095,000	295	23,000	11,575	31,000	-10	715	3,000	$52,000

One MU-2 flier offered this parallel: "If you can fly a Rockwell Shrike or a single-engine Mooney, you can fly and comfortably land a Mitsubishi. It wants to float down the runway, so you want to get it right down there on the flare. You don't want a 30-foot initiation of flare; you want it at three feet. And you want to keep the power on till touchdown.

"People transitioning into this aircraft tend to slow it up in the flare and get back to flight idle, trying to hold the nose off. It doesn't work. This airplane has to be flown onto the runway. Once you've got the mains on, the nosegear is going to plant itself. It seems abrupt to the pilot."

But this pilot said the aircraft could take the punishment. "That nosegear is tough," he said. "I don't know of any damage to the MU-2 nosewheels because of this characteristic."

Safety Record

Nevertheless, the number two accident problem with the MU-2 models in a 13-year accident rundown (1965 through 1978) provided by the National Transportation Safety Board for *The Aviation Consumer* turned out to be hard landings. The number three problem area was undershoots—as might be expected in an aircraft that can be set up for a high sink rate on final, with the possibility of getting behind the power curve.

Of the nine pilots involved in hard landings or undershoots, only two might be considered to have low time in the MU-2. Pilot time-in-type for hard landing accidents turned out to be: 1,790 hours, 3,160, 51, 500 and 195. For undershoots, the pilot experience level in type went like this:

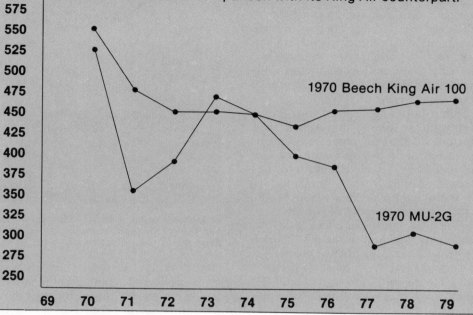

Aircraft Investment Value

MU-2G, the first stretched model, and King Air 100 start out pretty close in value, but after a spurt in 1973, the Mitsubishi plummets steeply. The short MU-2F model, not plotted here, does much better in comparison with its King Air counterpart.

1970 Beech King Air 100

1970 MU-2G

2,869 hours, 598, 37 and 435.

The leading probable cause for accidents in the MU-2 was engine failure. This also was blamed for the greatest number of fatal accidents in the MU-2—three. On all three of these fatals, only one engine failed, but the pilot was unable to make a safe return with the remaining powerplant. One occurred on takeoff and climbout with snow, low ceilings and visibility; the others occurred in the landing pattern, and on final approach. A stall/spin was blamed in each case, with the pilots accused of "diverting attention" from flying the aircraft.

Similarly, on all four nonfatal engine failure accidents (or incidents), only one powerplant was lost; nevertheless, only one of these pilots managed to bring the aircraft back to an uneventful landing on an airport on the remaining engine.

A look at pilot experience in engine-out problems shows that all the fliers had thousands of hours of flying time, and most had at least a couple thousand in the MU-2. The lowest time in type, in fact, was 169 hours.

This might suggest that the loss of an engine, especially on takeoff and climbout and in the landing pattern, can be a serious cause for concern in the MU-2 aircraft. In fact, the only safe return with an engine out was made when the failure occurred during normal cruise and the pilot apparently had the time to sort things out and make it to an airport.

In another fatal MU-2 crash, the pilot had shut down one engine because of loss of oil pressure and apparently decided to abort an emergency landing and execute a missed approach, when he went in.

It should be noted that the six engine failure accidents (and one incident) were all evidently the result of some sort of malfunction. Another four

Dominant features of the MU-2: *nearly full-span flaps and spoilers for lateral control.*

engine failures occurred because of fuel exhaustion, caused, in turn, by pilot mismanagement; and three other fuel exhaustion accidents were the result of mechanical failures.

Though there are three main sets of fuel tanks in the MU-2, the monitoring system would not appear to be inordinately demanding. There is one main (segmented) tank in the central wing section into which outer wing tanks feed by electrical fuel pump and into which the tip tanks feed by pressurization from engine bleed air.

Since both engines feed from the center tanks, there is not even a need for crossfeed arrangement, and all the pilot has to do is monitor the transfer of fuel from the outer tanks into the center ones.

We noted no accidents from landings with asymmetrical tip loadings.

The last significant cause of MU-2 accidents disclosed in the NTSB briefs is gear-up landings. In the years surveyed there were seven of these altogether—and in four of these the pilot simply forgot to lower the gear.

Service Difficulties

Examination of the FAA's Oklahoma City Service Difficulty program on the MU-2 for 1974 through 1979 reveals several evident recurring problem areas. These involved thermal battery runaway (one of these caused a fatal accident), climate control system malfunctions, cracks and loose rivets in wing and stabilizer skins and in flap wells, and cracked landing gear wheels.

One complaint aired by pilots we talked to involves the Bendix fuel control system introduced on the 251 series engine with the MU-2 K (short) and J (long) models. The Woodward fuel

Instrument panel of an MU-2G model. *Each flap position is prominently marked with lights to the right of the throttle quadrant. Left and right engine annunciator lights are located at top of glare shield. Gear-lowering speed: 170 knots.*

controller used on earlier models was much preferred. One operator said they had experienced "lots of downtime" as a result of Bendix breakdowns, though both Bendix and AiResearch picked up most of the repair tab, if not the fuel bills to fly back and forth for frequent repairs.

This operator converted its M model to the Woodward governor and has operated trouble free since then. An STC covers the conversion.

Another complaint centered on the climate control system after an "absolutely trouble free" AiResearch system was replaced with a new Hamilton Standard one that had a greater capacity, apparently, for both air output and temperature control problems.

How well does the MU-2 stand up to day-to-day use in commercial fleets, and what kind of backup support can owners expect? We encountered two vigorous complaints about what were described as aircraft chronic malfunctions and poor factory support. But by far the majority of the pilots and operators we were able to interview described the aircraft as reasonable to maintain and characterized backup support as good to excellent. Typical comments on maintenance went: "Not out of line," "pretty good," "routine," "virtually no squawks," "we're pleased."

One subscriber, however, said that his MU-2 (a '79 P model) was

"chronically defective" and a lemon that no one could seem to keep repaired. He complained of problems "with all systems," and 25 days of downtime in three months with 100 hours of flying time. And he claimed further that 15-20 hours were devoted to ferry time and maintenance flights.

The other protester finally "got rid of it" after he encountered what he said were terrible maintenance problems. "There were no spare parts for anything." He reported chronic problems with O-rings on brakes, leaky fuel tanks, serious prop vibration and cracked wing skins. He finally went to a Beech King Air, which he described as a much more satisfactory aircraft.

Naturally, operators of large piston twins must brace for the quantum cost jump when they make the move to turboprops, but there are those who maintain that the fantastic speed of the MU-2 series will actually deliver a better cost per seat mile than the piston machines.

Nevertheless, an MU-2 operator can expect to lay out anywhere from $2,500 to $3,500 on the average for a 100-hour inspection. One chief pilot estimated the cost per hour, including everything fixed and variable from fuel to insurance and salaries worked out to $241 (based on 1,020 hours of flying time a year).

Another pilot estimated direct operating costs at $40 per hour plus fuel costs (of $70 to $110/hr.).

MU-2 Accidents from 1965-78	
Probable Cause	Accidents
Engine Failure	7
Hard Landings	5
Undershoots	4
Gear-up Landings (Pilot forgot to lower gear)	4
Fuel Exhaustion (Pilot mismanagement)	4
Fuel Exhaustion (Mechanical problem)	3
Gear-up Landing (Mechanical problem)	3
Weather	3
Stall	2
Ground Loop/Swerve	2
Flight Control System Failure	1
Mid-air Collision	1

The short-fuselage Mitsubishis, *like this MU-2M, take skill and finesse for smooth landings.*

check of elevator trim tabs to prevent failure.

The most significant ADs on the AiResearch engines in the MU-2s involved checking engine oil filters for metal particles relating to problems with high-speed pinion gear shaft assemblies.

STCs

Among the more interesting Supplemental Type Certificates issued to MU-2s were: several battery temperature warning and monitoring systems, offered by AiResearch, Mitsubishi and KS Avionics, at Castro Valley, Calif. Also, auxiliary fuel tank installations in the main landing gear fairings, by AiResearch; addition of a baggage compartment in the main landing gear wheel pods, by Mitsubishi; plus portable jump seats by Ward International Aircraft in Fort worth, Tex., installation of electrically heated glass windshield on the pilot's side by AiResearch; and installation of a right-side fuselage window by AiResearch.

Airworthiness Directives

The brunt of the burden of Airworthiness Directives appears to have fallen on the first, or B model MU-2. Perhaps the most critical AD called for checking wing flap actuator jack screws for cracks to prevent fatigue failure. Also, the nose gear actuating system had to be modified to prevent failure, and front windshields checked for cracks and optical distortion from discharge of unusually hot defogging air caused by an air conditioning system failure.

Other ADs on the B models called for inspection of control levers on prop pitch control units, and installation of heatproof insulation to prevent possible fire in the baggage compartment from engine bleed air tubing, along with a

Owner Comments

"The airplane is one of the hardest to fly I know of. It's almost impossible to make a good, soft landing, probably because of the high wing loading. You can't keep the nose off, either; it just comes down with a bang. On the rollout after landing, especially with full tip tanks, the plane sets up a rolling motion from side to side, and it's disconcerting because nothing seems to stop it—you can feed in opposite controls or even try to aggravate it and there's no difference.

"On takeoff, you have to horse the nose off, and then when it does come off, it pops up. You might lift off at 100 knots and still have 30 or 40 knots to go before single-engine climb speed, which is kind of a long wait. If you lose an engine, do not try to keep the airplane going straight ahead. If you do that, you will not be able to accelerate to single-engine climb. Instead, center the ball—that's the most important thing— but allow the plane to make a gentle turn, and then she'll accelerate. Once you get the speed, she'll climb fine on one engine.

"It takes a strong man to fly the MU-2, and if you lose an engine, you'd better be mighty strong or quick with the trim. Funny thing, though—I've never heard a single complaint from the customers. Everybody riding in back thinks it's a wonderful airplane."

"We've been very pleased with the low maintenance on our G model. In the last two years the factory support has been outstanding. Historically, lacking a conventional distribution system, they did have some problems. Prior to '76 there may have been some delivery problems with parts, but I think Mitsubishi has identified that area today.

"When we bought our airplane, they sent a man to handle all the service warranty matters. He carried with him all the materials, all the AOG (aircraft on ground) 24-hour service numbers, etc. Recently we lost a starter-generator on a Friday afternoon. They put one on Emery to us Friday evening, which we received Saturday morning. And that's a rather uncommon $7,500 part.

"If the part is available through a Mitsubishi service center, they prefer you contact them. If the service center can't ship immediately, the factory will. Are there enough service centers—at 38? There are not!

"The transition to a Mitsubishi would take a professional about five hours and a non-pro about 25 hours. If a doctor or attorney, to pick on the poor chaps, or a company executive were to buy the aircraft to fly single pilot, all-weather, he would be well advised, one, to always fly with a safety pilot for the first 100 hours

and, two, not to operate the aircraft unless he's flying it 10 hours a month."

"The MU-2 is a beautiful bird once it's in the air and flying, but after 100 hours it won't fly. You simply cannot get spare parts, and that's why I got rid of it and got a King Air. I kept losing O-rings on the brakes, and had leaking fuel tanks they couldn't fix. We went through three flight directors because of the way the nose drops when you land the aircraft. We flew the short P model, and it's impossible to hold the nosewheel off after you touch down. It's very tricky to land, and I've had pro pilots in it who wouldn't go up again.

"On top of that we had prop vibration that you wouldn't believe and cracked skin under the wing.

"The sales people are nice and they try hard, but there's no backup for the company. I'm very happy with my King Air."

"The strong point on the airplane is the airframe; it's built like a Sherman tank. The Garrett engines have been excellent, and we've found the maintenance to be not out of line."

"We got an MU-2 because we wanted the fastest aircraft for the money. With our short model we get 300 mph at 75 gph vs. 230 mph in a King Air for the same fuel consumption."

Cessna Citation

For any pilot keen on taking that last step to the Olympian heights of the pure jet from a big piston twin or turboprop, the Cessna Citation is the most logical choice. Though not the cheapest available on the used-plane marketplace in initial price—the old Lear 23 is—it would be the least wicked for transition and the least likely to break the bank in upkeep and fuel costs.

Furthermore, the Citation would provide a golden investment opportunity with a resale value that never seems to stop climbing—especially the SP (single-pilot) model.

Judging from our research among owners and operators, pilots and maintenance chiefs, the Cessna Citation has become something of minor legend among bizjets. The Learjet may be the rocketship and the Gulfstream II the Rolls-Royce, but the Citation is old-faithful, reliable, relatively cheap to fly and the least offensive to people who live around airports. For short-range hops it can't be beat.

As for price, the first '72 model Citation 500s are going for around $715,000, which makes them quite competitive with many of the used turboprops on the market.

Turboprop Challenger?
The argument presumably will rage forever as to the Citation's ability to challenge the turboprops in economy of operation and ability to get in and out of short fields. Let it suffice to say that the Citation is the only pure jet we know of that comes close enough to make the choice a real teaser.

And for the flier who has the wherewithal and the inclination to fly a jet solo when conditions permit, the Citation SP version is the only business jet to date that will allow this indulgence. It would be frosting on the cake if such a pilot could cull through the older Citations on the market and snatch one away for a bargain price and fly it solo. But, alas, this cannot be, since a specific certification granted

to particular models, beginning in 1977, allows the single-pilot mode. Therefore, older birds without SP certification cannot simply be equipped to match the SP versions and legally flown without a copilot.

Investment Value
And judging from the resale value curve, the SP versions are in great demand. The price of a single-pilot Citation takes off without so much as a dip as soon as the first sale transaction is finished.

The standard model—take the '72 Model 500—displays the more modest resale pattern of most popular aircraft. It slowly sheds about $100,000 worth over the first four years and then begins climbing back up. Today it is worth more, in paper money, than it was when it rolled off the assembly line.

Said one Citation operator in 1980, "It's a tremendous investment value. They're going up at the rate of 30 to 35 percent a year. Two years ago we bought one for $400,000. Today we could get $800,000 for it."

Easy to Fly
Ease of handling is one of the Citation's graces. Newcomers don't have to worry

about wobbling on climbout with the wings wagging mercilessly the first time, as is possible in the Learjets. And Vref speed (1.3 Vso, or 1.3 times the approach configuration stall speed) on final approach can be as low as 89 knots with a low landing weight, and need be no higher than about 110 knots in calm conditions heavily loaded (in the Model 500, for example).

The stall reaction is of the Cherokee genre—a good buffet, lots of warning, easy recovery. By comparison, they won't even let you stall a Learjet—the stick shaker serves as a wrist slap, instead, on the approach to a stall. The Citation is the only jet we know of certificated without the need for an artificial stall warner.

Of course, the tradeoff is that Citation performance, by normal jet standards, is rather tepid. One Model 500 I operator we talked to said they figured on a 300-*mph* (it sounds better than 261-knot) block speed and a touchdown in four hours. They counted on a true airspeed at 37,000 feet of only 330 knots/389 mph, and said it would take 39 minutes to climb to that cruise altitude. The standard quip about Citation cruise speed is the one about bird strikes up the tail pipe.

If the Citation doesn't fly very fast,

Cessna's Citation: *far from supersonic, but in the eyes of economy-minded operators, still quite super.*

it doesn't burn much fuel either, by comparison with other jets. One west coast operator said their affection for the Citations was rising along with the price of jet fuel. Where the fuel cost per hour in the Learjet has zoomed, they said, from $216 to $332, in the Citation it has gone from $115 to $175.

Another much-touted virtue of the Citations is their ability to get safely in and out of shorter fields than other biz-jets. Three thousand feet is the round figure most often tossed out as a fair bottom end limit in runway length, allowing for balanced field performance. We know one corporate operator, though, that has 4,000 feet written into its operating manual as the minimum. On the other hand, we heard one story about the corporate executive who was picked up at Block Island—runway 2,500 feet—and rushed to a board meeting after his sailboat became becalmed. Naturally, the crew carefully calculated the trip with a light load, and they made it without incident.

Single-Pilot Mode

The single-pilot certification is a matter of no little dispute among Citation pilots. Some regard it as a shameful safety compromise; others a sensible move that extends the usefulness of the aircraft. Obviously, pilots will have to decide for themselves where they have to draw the line on carrying a copilot, depending on ATC workload in the

So simple that one pilot can fly it legally, *in the SP version. Vertical engine gauges are not known for their long lifespans.*

area where they are operating and pilot currency and proficiency and ability to cope with the higher speeds.

The aircraft certainly can be no more of a handful than most turboprops or even big piston twins, and some might argue forcefully that the jet is even simpler to operate—for the pilot who is well checked out in the bird. Naturally, a type rating is necessary at least for the pilot in command.

Although pilots rated the Citation high in handling ease, many had

discouraging words for cockpit comfort in the summer. "Roasted," "baked," and "parboiled" is what Citation pilots become behind those big windows in front. "The heat is brutal," said one. "If the crew is comfortable in front, the passengers are not." One pilot noted that the lack of cross ventilation—thanks to only one openable storm window, on the left—contributed to the problem. The freon air conditioner available as an STC might offer some recourse.

Model	Year	No. Built	Average Retail Price	Cruise Speed (mph)	Rate of Climb (fpm)	Fuel Capacity (lbs)	Useful Load (pounds)	Certificated Ceiling (feet)	Engine	TBO (hours)	Overhaul Cost (1 engine)
Citation 500	1972	64	$ 715,000	400	2,900	3,618	5,046	35,000	P&W JT-15D1	2,400	$50-80,000
Citation 500	1973	54	$ 740,000	404	2,900	3,780	5,046	41,000	P&W JT-15D1	2,400	$50-80,000
Citation 500	1974	90	$ 785,000	404	2,900	3,780	5,166	41,000	P&W JT-15D1	2,400	$50-80,000
Citation 500	1975	91	$ 850,000	404	2,900	3780	5,166	41,000	P&W JT-15D1	2,400	$50-80,000
Citation 500	1976	46	$ 975,000	404	2,900	3780	5,166	41,000	P&W JT-15D1	2,400	$50-80,000
Citation I 500	1977	23	$1,125,000	405	3,250	3,807	5,034	41,000	P&W JT-15D1	3,000	$50-80,000
Citation I 501 SP	1977	53	$1,175,000	405	3,250	3,807	5,034	41,000	P&W JT-15D1	3,000	$50-80,000
Citation I 500	1978	8	$1,200,000	405	3,250	3,807	5,034	41,000	P&W JT-15D1	3,000	$50-80,000
Citation I 501 SP	1978	36	$1,250,000	405	3,250	3,807	5,034	41,000	P&W JT-15D1	3,000	$50-80,000
Citation I 500	1979	69	$1,450,000	405	3,250	3,807	5,034	41,000	P&W JT-15D1	3,000	$50-80,000
Citation I 501 SP	1979	18	$1,450,000	405	3,250	3,807	5,034	41,000	P&W JT-15D1	3,000	$50-80,000
Citation II	1978	46	$1,850,000	414	3,250	4,784	6,097	41,000	P&W JT-15D-4	2,400	$50-80,000

Safety Record

The Cessna Citation has a rather remarkable safety record. It is so remarkable, in fact, that there is only one fatal crash recorded in this country—that of baseball star Thurman Munson in 1979. At least one other fatal Citation crash is rumored to have happened overseas somewhere, but details are hard to come by.

Safety Board evidence suggests that Munson's crash was due in large part to his botching the last of a series of touch-and-go landings with poor speed control on final approach and forgetting to lower the flaps and landing gear. The lack of a qualified copilot obviously also raised the cockpit workload.

Aside from this crash, there was only a handful of accidents—five, to be exact—in Citations over the entire eight-year period surveyed by the National Transportation Safety Board for *The Aviation Consumer* from 1970 through 1977.

Two of them were overshoots and the other three followed engine failures.

Since one of the special qualities of the Citation is its ability to get in and out of fields considered too short for most business jets, it's interesting that there were not more overshoots. Pilots say, however, that the Citation will float and float like any Mooney if the flier is trying for a greaser touchdown to impress passengers in back.

In the process, a thousand or more feet of runway can be lost. To get decently short touchdown runs, therefore, the pilot has to come down final at Vref and *place* it emphatically on the runway. Some pilots even pop the spoilers low in the flare before touchdown when every inch of runway is important.

In one of the two overshoots reported, the pilot (a 10,000-hour ATP with 366 hours in type) simply misjudged distance and speed. In the other overshoot the pilot slid the aircraft on an icy runway and groundlooped into a snow bank to keep from going off the runway. He had been told the braking was fair.

In only one of the engine failures was there some unexplained powerplant malfunction. In another there was seagull ingestion on takeoff, and in the third the pilot simply ran out of fuel because contamination of the fuel probes by glycerol gave misleadingly high fuel gauge readings.

In the aborted takeoff caused by seagull ingestion, one other factor contributed to difficulty in coming to a safe stop on the runway: the tires were hydroplaning on the wet runway.

Citation pilots say the aircraft is quite subject to hydroplaning, and there are only three effective (optional) antidotes: thrust reversers, anti-skid brakes and a drag chute.

The standard toe-shaker anti-skid warning device on the airplane is described as a joke by pilots we talked to. "When you get the warning," one flier told us, "it has announced to you that you have just blown a tire."

Maintenance

Although most operators seem to characterize the Citation as average or better than average in its maintenance demands, a few common gripes are generally aired. Cockpit instruments seemed to cause the most trouble. Number one culprit in the eyes of many users is the vertical engine gauge setup in the Citation. These break down with alarming frequency, according to operators we interviewed. "Atrocious," was the characterization of one jet school operator, John Dunning of Danbury Airways, of both the early Simmonds Precision gauges and the Amotek gauges that replaced them later. "They fail continuously," he said. "On our aircraft the expected life on these is 200 to 250 hours."

Other pilot gripes concern the vertical gyros on the Bendix flight director and the light emitting diodes on the RCA radios. The LEDs burn out in

Optional thrust reversers *add a modicum of weight and a lot of security on short, wet runways.*

hot climates, as a problem. Replacements go about $1,000 each, he said. segments with "great regularity," said one operator.

One operator also mentioned delamination of cabin windows, especially in

An operator of several Citations said his organization did its earnest best when buying replacement equipment to try to avoid going through Cessna and paying its higher prices, going instead directly to suppliers wherever possible. He mentioned significant savings in everything from master brake cylinders to standby horizons and even drag chutes.

This operator noted with some chagrin that a Cessna modification allowing a boost in gross weight of 350 pounds cost around $250 for parts in the form of new wheel halves—and a whopping $5,000 in paperwork—meaning certification rights.

On the whole though, people we interviewed expressed considerable

There's gold in them thar Citations—*appreciating at a healthy rate each year.*

satisfaction with the Citation's general maintenance record. "Outstanding," "superlative," were some of the characterizations, with one corporate maintenance chief saying it was the one aircraft in their mixed fleet that was always out flying, rarely in the hangar for maintenance.

Even the maintenance manual for the Citation was described as unusually complete. "It's about five or six times thicker than the Gates manual (for the Learjet)," said Mike Bonnell, executive vice-president for Flight Proficiency Service in Texas, a jet school. "It's very, very thorough."

Service Difficulties

A computer run of Service Difficulty Reports by the FAA's Flight Standards Service at Oklahoma City for *The Aviation Consumer* showed the Citation has experienced a surprising number of worn and frayed control cables. We counted 77 reports. The greatest number, 28, involved aileron cables. Next highest: 18 on flap control cables. Elevator and rudder trim cable problems were also reported by users.

The Citation landing gear system appears to have its share of problems, too, judging from the 45 reports on malfunctions by operators. The wheels themselves came in for a significant number of Service Difficulty Reports: 24 in all, most involving cracked or broken wheels.

A fairly large number of reports centered on engine difficulties, with no less than 18 engine

Figure on being able to carry up to 350 pounds *in the nose baggage compartment.*

failures—many involving broken turbine blades.

In addition, nine operators reported speed brake malfunctions, often due to switch failures; and eight reported that moisture inside the rudder trim rod had frozen and cracked the metal.

Airworthiness Directives

The Citations have enjoyed a very modest AD history, with only two of any significance through the years since the first Citation made its appearance in late 1971. The first, back in 1973, called for inspection to detect cracks that might have formed in the left and right side windows of the cockpit.

The second is potentially much more significant, and calls for inspection of upper and lower spar cap stems at wing station 37 to check for cracks.

This applies to aircraft with 600 or more hours. If cracks 0.3 inch or longer are found, the wing must be repaired or modified.

Cessna is providing a kit for $1,575. An estimated 120 man-hours is needed for installation for a total cost of approximately $7,000. Cessna is not offering to pay anything toward the cost of the repair, unless the airplane is in the three-year warranty.

Modifications

There is a raft of mods on the Citation, many of them involving different seating configurations—adding couches, lounge seats or toilets or a beverage service buffet (in the baggage compartment).

There are Supplemental Type Certificates also for installation of a stretcher, cargo liner and retention system and even a tail cone ski rack.

Cessna itself has an STC for a side-looking camera hatch. And Keith Products Inc. of Richardson, Texas, has one for a freon air conditioning system.

One of the largest holders of Citation STCs, Branson Aircraft Corp., Denver, Colorado, also offers one with an extended range fuel tank and relocation of the aft pressure bulkhead.

The most ambitious modification is done by Advanced Systems Technology in Washington state. They modify the wing to thicken it near the root and add on 18-inch tip extensions. The finished result has a raised gross weight and increased fuel capacity. A better climb rate and cruise speed is claimed for the aircraft, called the Eagle. Owners can have their Citation 500 or 501 modified for $225,000 in about six weeks or can buy an Eagle outright from the Aircraft Sales and Leasing Div., IASCO, in Burlingame, Calif.

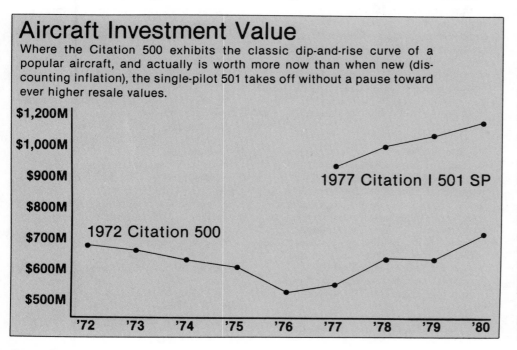

Aircraft Investment Value

Where the Citation 500 exhibits the classic dip-and-rise curve of a popular aircraft, and actually is worth more now than when new (discounting inflation), the single-pilot 501 takes off without a pause toward ever higher resale values.

1977 Citation I 501 SP

1972 Citation 500

$1,200M								
$1,000M								
$900M								
$800M								
$700M								
$600M								
$500M								
'72	'73	'74	'75	'76	'77	'78	'79	'80

Big cockpit windows *and poor cooling capacity can roast pilots in summer. Only the left side has a storm window; so no cross ventilation.*

Model History

After introduction of the '72 model in late '71, the gross weight (ramp) was raised in '73 by 650 pounds to 11,650 starting with number 71. A retrofit kit was available for up to $10,000.

In '75, starting with serial number 214, the maximum operating altitude was raised from 35,000 feet to 41,000. A new pressurization system increased the pressure differential from 7.6 psi to 8.5, and fuel capacity went up by 135 pounds to 3,807 pounds. A retrofit kit was available for the increased usable fuel and fuselage structural changes needed.

In '75 with serial number 275 the gross weight went up again by 350 pounds to 12,000 and a new Sperry/Collins avionics package replaced the Bendix/RCA one.

In '76 thrust reversers became available as an option. They were retrofittable.

The Citation 1 introduced in '77 offered a longer wing and upgraded JT15D-1A engines. The Citation II in 1978 offered a four-foot-longer cabin, five inches more aisle height and new engines putting out 2,500 pounds thrust each (up from 2,200 pounds.)

The engine TBO has been going up gradually through the years. At last word it stood at 3,000 hours and was expected to go to 3,300 hours next.

Owner Comments

"The book performance schedules have checked out very accurate. Handling is very similar to conventional multi-engine flying. Single-engine operation at gross weight, as in any ME aircraft, requires strict attention to the manufacturer's recommended procedures. The use of Cesscom maintenance schedules simplifies all the required inspection and is well worth the cost.

"Since new, our aircraft has been given TLC by the factory maintenance facilities at Sacramento, Calif., although I am told our aircraft has been especially bug-free compared to some; we've always been able to fly away at our promised time. Only once in over two years has a flight been rescheduled for a mechanical delay. A hot-start required a new fuel control unit which was replaced in less than 24 hours by the crew from the Sacramento maintenance base. This was accomplished on a ramp some 70 miles from Sacramento. That without a doubt is about the best factory support you can get!

"One area where I might contribute some personal experience is single-pilot operation. Our company has been an SP operation for over two years and, as I look back, no major problems have been encountered. The Sperry A/P FD system (required for SP ops), is every pilot's dream in operational simplicity and reliability. Even with the outstanding equipment package offer by Cessna, I would strongly recommend anyone considering SP operation ask themselves the following:

"Do you fly over 300 hours a year? How much time will be weather flying? International ops (typically two pilots are required)? Same routes? Duty time per day? High-density airport operation? Company insurance policy may dictate two pilots.

"The added expense of two-pilot operations would really be a small point in considering which way to go.

"All-in-all, Cessna has done a hell of a job in producing this thoroughbred, and it will prove to be the Citation of aircraft for many years to come."

"I think it's an outstanding airplane. I really like it. We've had very, very few problems at all. As a matter of fact, I'd say the reliability is outstanding. It flies like a big Cessna 150. You have to keep in mind the fact that the airplane wasn't built to compete with the Lear or the Sabreliner. It was built to compete with turboprops. And it does an outstanding job at that."

"Operationally, it does exactly what the book says. Figure on 750 miles. It just isn't a long-range airplane. The only complaint I have about the airplane is that it's so bloody hot in the summertime with all that plexiglass up front. You just cook to death. I understand the new Citation III has two air cycle machines, and that gives you better cockpit comfort. It got so hot sometimes that I figured it was a hazard to flight.

"But other than that, it's a nice little airplane—fun to fly."

"I would say the Citation is a really good airplane from a maintenance standpoint—less trouble than a Lear. We sold it after a year because it was too small and too slow. It was taking seagulls up the tail pipe."

"The aircraft is acknowledged as one of the most stable jets built. The handling characteristics are really good. Of course, it's a low-performance airplane. The Citation is easy to land, though it's hard to land in one place. It's got quite a bit of residual thrust at idle and a relatively low wing loading for a jet airplane.

"It doesn't slow down very quickly if you're at or above Vref. We have a single-pilot version, but you'd never operate that way with the chairman of the board in back. But I think it's easier to fly than a King Air, and that's legal single-pilot.

"Our Citations have held up pretty well considering the hard training use they're put to. Matching up the Lear and the Citation, though, I think the former may be just a bit more rugged from a maintenance standpoint. The Citation has a very simple instrument panel, for example, and to do that takes a lot of machinery behind the panel to make those automated systems work. The Lear-jet systems are less automated, which means you have a slightly higher cockpit workload. From a maintenance trouble-shooting standpoint, the Lears are much more straightforward.

"Cessna has been pretty good in backup support. They went through a time when they were having some trouble because they sold so many airplanes. But they always tried to get what we needed, even when they had to take it off an assembly line airplane."

Helicopters

Helicopters

The siren song appeal of the helicopter must be weighed against a few crass realities. These may not be immediately apparent to the fixed-wing pilot who is moved to add a rotary-wing rating to his ticket.

The motive in this departure from the general format of the *Used Aircraft Guide* is to present some thoughts and guidelines to moving into the used helicopter arena. Later on, we have printed an unusual "white paper" on the caveats of buying a used helicopter by someone who should know—Michael K. Hynes, president of Brantly-Hynes Helicopter, Inc.

Naturally, there can be tremendous benefits to operating a helicopter, from literally flying from door to door rather than going through the bother of driving to and from airports. Often the slower helicopter can beat its faster fixed-wing competitor door-to-door over surprising distances—especially in urban areas.

The other side of the convenience coin is the unhappy fact that some cities and states prohibit helicopters from making unannounced arrivals and departures from their turf, disturbing their sanctity with the typical rotary-wing din and whirlwind. In these cases it may be necessary to operate in and out of the airport like the fixed-wing crowd, or to go through the rigamarole of officially establishing a heliport at your house or office or plant.

Probably the biggest millstone of the helicopter is its cost. Helicopters are generally more expensive than fixed-wing aircraft to buy (pound for pound, horsepower for horsepower, seat for seat), operate, maintain, insure and learn to fly.

Flight Instruction Costs

Take flight instruction. Around the country the dual charge for helicopter instruction is $125 to $140 an hour in a piston-engine Bell 47G ($250 an hour in a turbine-powered 206 Jet Ranger). Figure on about 35 hours to transition to helicopters, and that comes to around $4,655 for starts.

The list price for a new piston-powered helicopter can be rather steep, also. The two-place Robinson R22, for example, at $48,850, is the least expensive available. A three-place Enstrom F-28 C-2 goes for about $103,000, while the three-place Hughes 300 sells for around $86,000.

Direct operating costs for piston choppers range from $30 to $60 an hour. One of the reasons for the high cost is the reserve needed to cover shorter TBOs for helicopters. The lifetime of various components also may run less than the engine TBO. For example, the tail rotor lifetime for some of the older Bell 47s may be only 600 hours (and cost about $600); the transmission is also 600 hours (about $2,500 for overhaul). On top of that, the entire helicopter will come in for an overhaul, including engine, at 1,200 hours for around $9,000. The Hiller 12Es are slated for overhaul at only 1,000 hours.

What's Available?

How do the various piston-powered helicopters stack up on the used market? Perhaps in greatest demand are the various Bell 47 models which, although out of production, seem to be considered the Cadillacs of the industry. The price of used Bells may be inflated because of their use as ag machines.

Although they are not very fast, the Bells are nice-flying ships with forgiving handling characteristics (easy recovery should rotor rpm decay a bit) and decent autorotation qualities. Bell still provides good parts support, also, according to operators.

The Brantly B2 and B2B, along with the big five-place 305, now has the factory support of Brantly-Hynes Helicopters in Frederick, Okla. This company is concerning itself to a large extent with backing up the used Brantly fleet, while at the same time carrying on a reconditioning program and, to a lesser degree, building new Brantlys.

One of the main advantages of the Hughes 300 series (and older 269s) is that they have the support of the giant parent company behind them. The 300 has long been used as a training ship, and all-around utility craft.

Brantly Inducement

As an inducement to get into helicopters, the company is offering "free" flight training programs at the factory for purchasers, giving up to 50 hours of chopper time. We assume the cost of the training comes out of the price of the helicopter, naturally. Nevertheless, with a reconditioned B2 going for

Hughes 300: *no frills, but an industry staple, with the backing of the Hughes empire, in a sometimes sickly piston helicopter industry.*

Helicopters

Probably the biggest piston helicopter around, *the Brantly 305 carries five and boasts surprising cruise speeds in the 120-mph range.*

from $17,000 to $25,000, this might represent a pretty good deal.

The B2 Brantlys are among the most sensitive and quick-responding helicopters (twitchy and squirrelly, some might characterize them), and are renowned for their spectacular autorotations and minimal blade inertia for full power-out touchdowns. But it's generally felt that once you master a Brantly, everything else you transition into later on will be duck soup, by comparison.

One of the *Aviation Consumer* editors who got his rotary-wing rating in a Brantly some years ago hedged a bit on the duck soup metaphor, but corroborated the general concept that exposure to the Brantly equips you to tackle just about anything else with a minimum of travail.

Powered by the reliable 180-hp Lycoming carbureted engine, the Brantly B2s also are quite fast for the power—figure on a 90-mph cruise, with about 10 gph fuel consumption.

The Brantly company quotes a "realistic" operating cost for an average B2 owner as about $35 an hour, and $10 less for dealers and commercial operators. A typical annual inspection for a well-cared for B2 should run about $960, according to Brantly-Hynes.

Enstrom

The Enstroms take the prize for good looks and comfort and boast cruise speeds of over 100 mph—a rarity in piston choppers. But operators and mechanics we talked to say parts support has been quite bad, with delays of sometimes months in getting items from the factory.

Enstrom Helicopter Corp. virtually shut down production in October, 1979, but the company was bought by Bravo Investment Corp., a Saudi Arabian group, and it plans a resumption of production.

Mechanics we interviewed also described the Enstroms as difficult to maintain. As for flying qualities, the Enstrom has a relatively massive rotor system that provides good inertia for autorotations, but at the other end of the scale may be a bit less forgiving in recovering a loss of blade speed than, say, a Bell 47. And while its rather stiff cyclic control might be considered a boon in long cruise and patrol flights, this characteristic is felt to be a handicap in hovering work and described as "unnatural" for flight training by some flight instructors.

Going Shopping?

Where might one shop for a used helicopter? Aside from *Trade-A-Plane* and the Brantly-Hynes company, Air Associates in Chicago is one of the big used-chopper dealers and brokers. Ed Eckard, executive vice-president, pledges to give helicopter shoppers the straight scoop on what might be the most sensible buy for their needs—with no axe to grind and no pushing the higher-cost models. But he warns: "There are no super, great deals in this business."

The implication is that one should be careful to check out the history of those "marvelous steals." Naturally, a long session with the logbooks of any used helicopter by an experienced helicopter pilot or mechanic is a necessity to avoid unpleasant surprises.

Anyone who expects to buy and operate a helicopter also would be wise to check the

proximity of trained rotary-wing maintenance personnel, since these are even fewer and farther between than good fixed-wing mechanics.

The industry also has been plagued by the availability of "bogus parts," not made by or approved by the manufacturers. Since it often is difficult to ascertain which parts are suspect, buyers are advised to carefully check the reputation of their sources of parts supply.

And since the art of helicopter piloting is so demanding and the variables so numerous, experienced chopper pros advise cautious, slow exposure to helicopter flight experiences with an instructor—even if he just comes along for the ride. One we talked to suggested this go on for as many as 500 to 750 hours.

We think this is quite conservative, however, and suggest that no one be deterred by these ominous forewarnings until giving the choppers a fair try (and maintaining composure and optimism through the first tough hours). There's nothing in aviation quite so challenging—and satisfying.

Michael K. Hynes, president of Brantly-Hynes, Inc., has some strong feelings about new buyers of used helcipopters being inadvertently led down the primrose path into the "wonderful world of rotorcraft." He offers this candid viewpoint for prospective helicopter owners.

With the strong increase in the use of helicopters we are seeing many new rotocraft owners each year. One of the primary concerns of the helicopter industry should be the education of these new owners in the proper maintenance requirements of their newly acquired helicopters. This is important to the industry both from a safety standpoint and from an economic one.

Usually when the subject of helicopter maintenance comes up, the general reaction of any helicopter owner is that maintenance costs are too high. If you took a survey of *ex*-helicopter owners you would find that the number one reason they sold their helicopters was the maintenance cost.

Were maintenance costs really too high? Or were costs normal, but the anticipated maintenance budget originally set too low by these new owners?

All manufacturers publish estimated operating costs, but more than once I have read owners' comments that you should take the factory estimates and double them to be close to the true operating cost. Are the manufacturers that far off or are they deliberately misleading the general public when it comes to maintenance cost budgets?

Why the Difference?

Reviewing some past data and talking with many owners who feel they were misled by the manufacturers into thinking their costs would be much lower than they actually were, we find several areas where the projections and the facts seem to disagree.

The first area of disagreement is the age of the helicopter being operated; the second is the annual utilization of the machine, and the third is inflation.

The records show that today some 92 percent of our heliopters in service are *used* helicopters.

If we check the production and registration records still further, we will find that about 54 percent of the helicopter fleet is over four years old and 25 percent of the fleet is now over 10 years old. Some 1,000 helicopters change ownership each year. Most often these units are purchased by someone who is entering "the wonderful world of helicopters" for the first time.

If you check the typical price guide for used helicopters you can see where quite a few makes and models of helicopters are available at reasonable prices. As a result of advertising and other publicity helicopters are now receiving, many people are attracted to the industry and are making decisions to purchase their first helicopter.

Last year the average price for a new helicopter was over $250,000, a figure that most of the newcomers to the industry find hard to believe. This kind of price tag stops them cold at first, but then they discover that they can buy a good used helicopter for less than 20 percent of that. The average price of a used helicopter is often much less than $40,000. This is lower than for many

Slickest of all the piston choppers *is the Enstrom Model 280C Shark. But parts availability has been a sour note.*

fixed-wing airplanes and certainly within reach of most potential helicopter buyers.

Unfortunately, in the helicopter business, just like any other, you generally get what you pay for (or perhaps a little less). To the first-time helicopter buyer, low price can mean the beginning of maintenance problems.

Low Price No Bargain!

More than once, we have seen a buyer put all his money into the helicopter and leave nothing as a maintenance reserve. With bank interest rates high and hull insurance costs even higher, many first-time owners prefer to pay cash for the helicopter. They do this because the lending agency will require hull insurance if there is a loan on the helicopter. To avoid this so-called double cost, all available funds go into the purchase price.

The operating costs for any complex equipment usually runs from five to 10 percent of the cost of the equipment. The catch

to this rule of thumb that most new owners of used helicopters don't often realize is that the five to 10 percent figure is based on the current selling price of *new* similar helicopters. Too often the buyer is budgeting only on the purchase price, not the replacement price. For example, a good used helicopter sells for $35,000; the new model of the same helicopter sells for $85,000. The annual maintenance budget needs to be $5,000 to $9,000, not $1,500 to $3,500 as some owners think.

Every day we come across owners who are shocked at the cost of their first annual inspection. The older the helicopter, often the worse will be its condition and its records. With the accident rate not getting any better and with product liability insurance getting harder to buy, the better maintenance shops will no longer just sign off maintenance records. Where the past history of certain parts has been ignored or obvious mistakes in the records have been overlooked, today both the FAA and individual mechanics with their reputation at stake are refusing to sign for work that they can't prove was done correctly.

Annual Use a Factor

The second area overlooked by buyers of used helicopters is annual utilization. I doubt you would buy an electric typewriter and put it out in your backyard for a few years and then expect to put it into service without some major repair work. Well, a helicopter that has been sitting in some open field for a few years isn't ready to be put to use either.

Lack of use can cause great harm to a helicopter. A typical example of this relates to engine overhaul life. Take the IVO-360-A1A Lycoming engine, which is more or less a typical helicopter powerplant. Its overhaul life is 900 hours in the manufacturer's guidelines. Our experience shows that this engine goes to 1,000 or more hours when flown on

One of Bell's "unsinkable" 47G models, *which have won an excellent reputation in the used-helicopter market.*

a regular basis. However in the average helicopter, it seldom goes to 500 hours before the first overhaul. Very often we see where it is given a top overhaul in 350 to 450 hours.

A buyer who looks at a helicopter with only 200 hours on the engine may think he has 700 hours of trouble free flying ahead of him. If this overhaul was done three or four years ago, I doubt the engine will last 100 hours before needing major maintenance, unless the helicopter was properly stored and carefully inspected before being put back into service. If this same owner has been planning on a three or four dollar per hour engine cost, he's about $4,000 short in his maintenance reserve before he even starts to use his machine.

This same storage problem holds true for other major items such as transmissions, gearboxes and bearings. The typical helicopter has over 100 bearings that all need to be greased on a regular basis, even if the helicopter isn't being flown! Dust, dirt and rainwater getting into these bearings will cut their useful life down to just several hours, not the several hundred hours they should last.

Manufacturers' estimated operating costs literature is usually advertising material and is used to demonstrate the good features of their helicopters. The projected costs are laid out to sell the helicopter, certainly not to discourage a potential new buyer. The manufacturer is an expert in maintaining a helicopter and uses only the best operating conditions to come up with his cost projections. From a realistic viewpoint, there is no other way he can estimate the operating costs except by using a first-class, factory recommended maintenance system as the standard. Unfortunately very few helicopters see this type of maintenance throughout their lives.

The first buyer of a brand-new helicopter

usually has a maintenance facility to back up the helicopter. However, over the years, as the ownership of the helicopter changes hands (very often each time to a less educated buyer), the likelihood of its getting proper maintenance becomes less and less. A word of caution to new buyers of older helicopters should then be to pay close attention to where and by whom the helicopter has received its maintenance, in addition to what has been done.

There are no Bargains!
There are no bargains in buying used helicopters. I feel the worst decision a first-time helicopter buyer could make is to purchase a helicopter that has been in storage for several years. My experience over the last five years is that such a machine takes from

Sample prices of used helicopters

Model	Years	Price
Brantly B2, A, B	1959-67	$17,000-$23,000
Brantly B2B	1975-77	$36,000-$38,000
Enstrom F28, A	1966-75	$22,000-$35,000
Hiller 12E	1959-65	$35,000-$42,000
Hughes 269A	1961-66	$21,000-$22,000
Hughes 300	1969-71	$31,000-$40,000
Hughes 300	1972-75	$41,000-$48,000
Bell 47G2, A	1959-63	$27,000-$36,000
Bell G3B2	1968-73	$46,000-$53,000
Bell 47J2A	1964-66	$40,000-$42,000
Bell 47G5	1966-73	$41,000-$58,000

$3,500 to $5,000 to get back into first-class condition, as well as needing about 100 flight hours before all the bugs are discovered and fixed. Unless you have the facilities, the skilled manpower and the money, buying such a helicopter will be very disappointing.

Inflation
The third maintenance cost consideration that is difficult to get helicopters owners to understand is related to inflation. Though

Robinson R-22 *is still a newcomer to the helicopter scene; it's only been on the market since early 1980.*

manufacturers publish cost estimates, even they can't project inflation very accurately. Looking back through old sales literature covering the last 10 years or so, one notes the amazing way prices have gone up.

When someone buys a turbine helicopter for about $80,000 and through some bad luck has to pull the engine, he is surprised to find out that the overhaul will cost $30,000 to $40,000.

More than one helicopter is sitting parked somewhere because the owner can't afford the parts to fix it. It's especially sad where the owner hasn't the money for repairs but he still has a big mortgage. How does he explain to his local banker that he needs to borrow several thousand dollars more to fix up his helicopter? The bank may have already loaned to the maximum limit on the helicopter, and if you tell him it's now broken and can't fly, he may want you to pay off the loan! To add to the financial problem, the insurance costs continue while this hard-pressed owner tries to figure a way out of his maintenance and financial problems.

To help promote growth in the helicopter industry, the manufacturers should pay more attention to the used helicopter market and take some steps to assist the first-time owners of older helicopters. The automobile industry has for years advertised the "OK Used Car." I have never seen any manufacturer, except ourselves, advertise "An OK Used Helicopter"!

Used helicopters often provide the first-time entrance to our industry. If we want to keep these people as helicopter owners, we need to take care of them even if they didn't buy the helicopter new from the factory. Industry wide, some 85 percent of new unit sales are made to present owners of helicopters.

With this thought in mind, new owners with old helicopters could use a little guidance and tender loving care from the industry as a whole.

Michael Hynes and one of his earlier model Brantlys. *His company is reconditioning used Brantlys, building new ones and offering free flight training, to boot.*

Index